Health, Illness, and Medicine

Health, Illness, and Medicine

A Reader In Medical Sociology

Edited by

Gary L. Albrecht, NORTHWESTERN UNIVERSITY
Paul C. Higgins, UNIVERSITY OF SOUTH CAROLINA

Rand McNally
College Publishing Company
Chicago

Sponsoring Editor	Geoffrey Huck
Project Editor	Theresa M. Ludwig
Designer	Kristin Nelson
Cover	Jerry Hutchins

79 80 81 10 9 8 7 6 5 4 3 2

To our parents

Contents

Preface

1 Social Aspects of Medical Care:
Conceptual Approaches to the Field   1

Gary L. Albrecht

PART I

**Social and Cultural Dimensions of
Medical Behavior**   15

2 Sex, Illness, and Medical Care:
A Review of Data, Theory, and Method   16

Constance A. Nathanson

3 Culture and Symptoms—An Analysis
of Patients' Presenting Complaints   41

Irving Kenneth Zola

4 The Delivery of Medical Care in China   63

Victor W. Sidel and Ruth Sidel

PART II

Demography of Health and Illness   79

Section1
An Overview

5 Changing Patterns of Health and
Disease During the Process of National
Development   81

Abdel R. Omran, M.D., Dr. P.H.

6 On the Science and Technology
of Medicine   94

Lewis Thomas, M.D.

Section 2
Demography of Acute and Chronic Illness

7 Occupational Stress and Coronary Heart Disease:
A Review and Theoretical Integration   108

James S. House

8 Class, Family, and Schizophrenia:
A Reformulation   129

Melvin L. Kohn

PART III

**Social Psychology of Illness
and Its Management**   145

Section 1
Sick Role

9 The Sick Role Revisited   146

Miriam Siegler and Humphrey Osmond

Section 2
The Labeling of Illness:
The Case of Mental Illness

10 On Being Sane in Insane Places   167

D. L. Rosenhan

11 Individual Resources and Mental Hospitalization:
A Comparison and Evaluation of the Societal
Reaction and Psychiatric Perspectives   186

Walter R. Gove and Patrick Howell

Section 3
Chronic Illness

12 Time for a Change:
From Micro- to Macro-Sociological
Concepts in Disability Research   206

Herbert Bynder and Peter Kong-Ming New

13 Deviants as Active Participants in the Labeling Process:
The Visibly Handicapped   217

Teresa E. Levitin

Section 4
Utilization of Health Services

14 Pathways to the Doctor—From Person to Patient   228

Irving Kenneth Zola

Section 5
Doctor-Patient Communication

15 Physician-Patient Communication and Patient Conformity
with Medical Advice   243

Bonnie L. Svarstad

16 The Negotiated Diagnosis and Treatment
of Occlusal Problems   260

Gary L. Albrecht

Section 6
Moral Evaluation of the Patient

17 Some Contingencies of the Moral Evaluation and
Control of Clientele: The Case of the Hospital
Emergency Service   274

Julius A. Roth

PART IV

Medical Personnel: Conflicting Perspectives   291

18 Conflicting Perspectives in the Hospital   292
Eliot Freidson

19 Advisory and Coercive Functions in Psychiatry   297
Arlene Kaplan Daniels

20 Decision Rules, Types of Errors and Their
Consequences in Medical Diagnosis   312
Thomas J. Scheff

21 Women in Health Care   327
Vicente Navarro

PART V

Organization and Delivery of Health Care   339

x

Section 1
Organization of Medicine

22 The U.S. Health Care System   341
Beaufort B. Longest, Jr.

23 Everyday Work Settings of the Professional   370
Eliot Freidson

Section 2
Delivery of Health Services

24 Equal Treatment and Unequal Benefits:
    The Medicare Program   384
Karen Davis

Section 3
The Politics of Health Care

25 The Necessity and Control of Hospitalization   416
Julius A. Roth

26 Medical Malpractice   442
David S. Rubsamen

27 Health and the Corporate Society   456
Vicente Navarro

PART VI

The Future of Medicine   468

28 The Future of Health and Medicine:
    The Issues We Face   469
Paul C. Higgins

Name Index   481

Subject Index   494

Preface

Medical sociology is developing at a rapid pace during a period when health care delivery is a major national and international concern. There is a growing consensus among professionals, politicians, and the public that health is not simply a commodity to be delivered by doctors in a health care institution; good health is a value that involves the entire community. Most individuals view good health as a key component in the quality of life. At the same time, people express dissatisfaction with the cost, quality, and access to health care. Health is a societal goal that many people feel has not been attained and there is some question whether or not it can be attained.

Researchers, planners, practitioners, and consumers are focusing their attention on different aspects of the health care issue. No simple solution has yet emerged. The complexity of the problem has become apparent. Scholars and concerned citizens are realizing that health care and health status cannot be understood simply from a medical or social perspective. The integration of various perspectives is necessary to understand the interrelationships of health, illness, and medicine. Medical sociology is an integral element in this study.

Medical sociology, put somewhat simply, is concerned with the beliefs and practices surrounding health and illness, and society's response to these issues. It encompasses a wide range of substantive areas: definitions of health and illness; epidemiology and demography of health and illness; the etiology of morbidity and mortality; the social and cultural dimensions of health and illness; the social psychology of health and illness; medical personnel and their behavior; and the organization, delivery, and politics of health care services. *Health, Illness, and Medicine* examines these essential topics.

To understand health, illness, and medicine in one's own society, alternatives, either to the present state of affairs in one's own society or to those that exist in different societies, must be studied and basic assumptions must be reexamined.

To understand what is, one must be able to imagine what could be. We suggest that medical behavior is an eminently social, cultural, and historical phenomenon, which must be studied within the context of differing perspectives, values, and cultures. This reader includes articles that examine health, illness, and medicine in the United States as well as in other cultures.

Because the field of health care is growing so rapidly and is multidisciplinary by nature, students of health and medical care delivery systems frequently get lost in a maze of complex details and do not work within a disciplinary focus or theoretical framework. *Health, Illness, and Medicine* provides a definite sociological framework. The text can be used in a variety of courses at the graduate or undergraduate level in sociology, medicine, hospital administration, nursing, public health and community health, and allied health professions.

The objectives of this reader are: (1) To serve as an introduction to the field of medical sociology by defining the field and raising critical issues, theories, and concepts through current research articles and original contributions to the reader; (2) To provide a sociological perspective to the study of health; (3) To present theories and conceptual frameworks that are used to integrate a wide variety of medical material; and (4) To provide selected in-depth material not found in textbooks.

The book is organized around three general sociological themes: (1) The ways in which medical problems are caused, distributed, diagnosed, treated, and interpreted; (2) The continuing fight for control of medical work by the medical profession; and (3) The physical, social, political, and economic influences that shape medical practice. These themes provide the book with a sociological perspective without sacrificing detail or comprehensiveness.

The text contains an introduction, five parts, and a conclusion. The introduction discusses health, illness, and medicine as social phenomena. In this introductory section the discipline of medical sociology is defined, the distinction between *sociology of medicine* and *sociology in medicine* is drawn, and the major themes of the text are presented.

In Part I, *Social and Cultural Dimensions of Medical Behavior,* we suggest that medical behavior must be viewed as an outgrowth of the social and cultural milieu in which the behavior is observed. Our goal in this section is to encourage students to view medical behavior in a wider, less ethnocentric perspective. By suggesting that medical behavior cannot be understood solely from the "rational-scientific" perspective, we lay the groundwork for students to be receptive to alternatives to and critical discussions of the present situation.

In Part II, *Demography of Health and Illness,* we present an overview of the epidemiology and demography of health and illness. The historical transition in health and illness is related to the socioeconomic development of society. By focusing on specific cases of medical demography—coronary heart disease, diabetes, venereal disease, and schizophrenia—we suggest the importance of a sociological perspective in understanding the etiology of illness. The social psychology of illness is examined in Part III, *Social Psychology of Illness and Its Management.* Utilization of services, doctor-patient interaction, chronic, acute, and mental illness, and the relation between life change and illness are discussed in this part. Our goal is to explore the attitudes, beliefs, practices, and relations among participants that influence illness and its management.

In Part IV, *Medical Personnel: Conflicting Perspectives,* we survey health personnel, their behavior and perspectives from the "lowly" attendant to the "exalted" doctor. We suggest that the relations among health personnel affect medical care. In this and the following section, we emphasize that health care cannot be understood solely as the outcome of the lone practitioner but must be viewed as the result of conflicting perspectives, differing interests, and variable work settings and organizations.

In Part V, *Organization and Delivery of Health Care,* we raise issues concerning the organization of health care and the delivery of services—HMOs, PSRO, Medicare, and others. We stress that health care must be viewed within the political-economic structure of society. Alternatives to our present health care system are suggested.

In Part VI, *The Future of Medicine,* we provide a discussion of some of the issues that must be faced in deciding the future of medicine: societal values, expectations, allocation of resources, responsibility for care, ethical decisions of transplants, control of medicine, and the morality of medicine.

Health, Illness, and Medicine presents the reader with a myriad of complex issues and with a perspective to approach and deal with these vital issues.

G. L. A.
P. C. H.

Social Aspects of Medical Care: Conceptual Approaches to the Field

GARY L. ALBRECHT

Overview

Health is a major worldwide social issue. People of every nation and social group are demanding an increasingly higher quality of life in which good health is viewed as an inalienable human right. In this broad context health is measured by mortality and morbidity indices and also is extended to include absence of pain and suffering and the presence of general wellbeing. There is an effective social marketing taking place around the world that expands health definitions to include the quality of life. Good health is a value that is used to sell jogging equipment, natural foods, deodorants, and winter vacations.

Expansion of the definition of health beyond levels of health status and physical and social functioning has produced a growing consumer demand. In an enlarged effort to meet this demand, 139 billion dollars, 8.6 percent of the gross national product, was spent directly on health in the United States in 1976 (Gibson and Mueller, 1977); yet consumers still were not satisfied. For these reasons, the production, delivery, and consumption of health care is a pressing political issue. Because of the saliency of the issue, the numbers of consumers, and the dollars involved, many interest groups are involved in these problems and are fighting over strategies and results. These complex problems are unlikely to disappear quickly because financial and political stakes are large.

These circumstances provide the opportunity for sociologists to make lasting contributions to health care delivery problems and to their own discipline; yet the results have been less than impressive. This mixed review of sociological work in medicine is due to the difficulty of the problems, the limited strength of sociological tools, the physician's traditional lack of enthusiasm for social science research, and the undisciplined way in which many sociologists have worked on health problems.

Health, Illness, and Medicine is organized with these factors in mind. This chapter provides a conceptual focus to medical sociology and outlines the major themes that organize the book. The contributions of sociology to medicine and health care delivery problems are contingent on the degree to which sociologists understand complex medical environments and the quality of their analytical tools. The relationship between sociology and medicine need not be parasitic, as viewed by some physicians, or prostituting, as charged by some sociologists. In fact, history demonstrates that mutual collaboration on interdisciplinary problems is a most effective strategy in achieving specific solutions and developing theory. The practice of medicine and the delivery of health care occur in social contexts and require a social perspective to be efficacious. On the other hand, sociology as a discipline must test theory in a content area. The medical arena is an ideal location to develop theories and empirically test their applications because of the magnitude, richness, and complexity of health care problems. Therefore, sociology and medicine have much to gain by collaboration based on mutual respect. However, effective mutual collaboration must be based on a clear understanding of differences in disciplinary perspectives. This chapter addresses the distinctions between sociology *of* medicine and sociology *in* medicine and sets forth the sociological themes that integrate the book: social interpretations of medical phenomena, the continuing fight for control of medical work by the medical profession, and environmental influences on medical practice. Here environment refers to the physical, social, political, and economic contexts in which medicine is practiced.

Conceptualization of the Field

Much effort has been exerted to justify the existence of medical sociology as a legitimate, professional subspecialty within the disciplines of sociology and medicine. This concern with self-definition and legitimation is typical of professionals who seek to establish an area of interest as a specialty. To achieve this purpose, authors of sociological texts have underscored the longstanding interests of sociologists such as Durkheim, Ogburn, Spencer, Robert and Helen Lynd, Parsons, Hollingshead, Strauss, Becker, Scheff, Freidson, and Mechanic (Freeman, Levine, and Reeder, 1972; Twaddle and Hessler, 1977; Cockerham, 1978). Certainly the study of medicine is neither new nor tangential to the field of sociology. There is a longstanding tradition of social research in the health arena dating back to the first modern study of a population's health conducted in Hagerstown,

Maryland from 1921 to 1924. The United States Public Health Service has been carrying out national health surveys with considerable sophistication since 1935, providing information on the demography of health and illness. Furthermore, medical professionals have been interested in social factors in health for centuries. Social epidemiology was well established in the 19th century (Graham and Reeder, 1972).

While the sociological study of medicine, health, and illness is longstanding (Rosen, 1974), the growth of the subdiscipline, medical sociology, is rather recent. The section on Medical Sociology of the American Sociological Association was established in 1960. It is now one of the largest and most rapidly growing sections in the Association. The growth of this subspecialty was accelerated in 1966 when the *Journal of Health and Social Behavior* became an official publication of the American Sociological Association. Medical sociologists have become one of the most active groups in the International Sociological Association. The growth of such journals as *Social Science and Medicine, Medical Care, International Journal of Health Services, Health Services Research,* and *Milbank Memorial Fund Quarterly*, and the number of medical sociology articles in general sociological literature attest to the dynamism of the field. The rapid growth of medical sociology as a subspecialty is due, in part, to recent acceptance of sociologists by physicians. The expansion of the National Institute of Health and foundation of the National Institute of Mental Health in the late 1940s released research and training funds designed to encourage collaboration between medical and social scientists. It is now difficult to find medical schools, nursing schools, and schools of public health without sociologists and departments of behavioral science. Until recently physicians exercised tight control over medical practice, research, and training by keeping social scientists out of these work areas (Stevens, 1971).

Many sociologists and other social scientists are actively involved in the study of health and illness. Consequently it is important to distinguish the disciplinary contributions of medical sociologists from those of other social scientists and to clarify the distinction between the sociology *of* medicine and sociology *in* medicine.

The study of medicine has attracted historians, economists, political scientists, geographers, and anthropologists, as well as sociologists. Each of these groups is distinguished by the type of questions asked, the conceptual tools used, and the methodologies employed to address a problem.

Medical historians document the development of medical practice in a society. They ask the question, "How has history influenced the type and form of medical practice seen today?" Historians use records and documents to acquire a thorough knowledge of the past. They use historical knowledge to explain present medical practices and predict the future course of medical practice. Two notable examples of historical analysis and application are George Rosen's *From Medical Police to Social Medicine* (1974) and Rosemary Stevens' *American Medicine and the Public Interest* (1971).

Medical economists are concerned with the demand, production, supply, manpower, and cost dimensions of medical care delivery. At present, the major interest of economists concerns the issue of controlling the cost of medical care (Mechanic, 1978). The apparent facts are that medical care costs are rising more rapidly than the cost of living and that they account for an increasing portion of the GNP. Consumers and employers are bearing the burden of these costs. Politicians, under pressure from their constituents, have turned to economists for methods to control and reduce these costs. As Mechanic (1978) has pointed out, costs can be reduced by decreasing demand or improving the cost-effectiveness of services. Economists use models to manipulate cost, demand, and treatment variables and to determine optimal solutions given the constraints of the problem. The proposed solutions advocate a variety of approaches: increased regulation; free market dynamics; decrease demand by making the consumers bear more of the direct health costs; and, delivering services through paraprofessionals. All of these recommended solutions have considerable political consequences.

Political scientists are interested in the manner in which vested interest groups exercise their power to affect policies, programs, and laws. While other groups are concerned with the equitable delivery of medical products, political scientists are aware that health care solutions, to be lasting and effective, must be worked out within the political environment. Political scientists study the power of different interest groups as expressed through lobbies and votes in determining specific forms of medical care delivery. For instance, the political scientist might be quick to point out that national health insurance will be accepted only if it takes a form acceptable to physicians, hospitals, insurance companies, pharmaceutical groups, health product suppliers, the government, and consumer interest groups. Such a solution may not be the most cost-efficient but it will be a pragmatic solution.

Medical geography is a relatively new field that encompasses ideas and research scattered across various medical specialties—epidemiology, parasitology, physical anthropology, demography, etc. Medical geography provides a unifying conceptual framework (May, 1977) that facilitates the examination of relationships among disease, pathological factors, and geographical factors such as climate, soils, population distribution, and vegetable life. The geographer recognizes that disease is a complex phenomenon that appears only if causal factors occur simultaneously in space and time. Disease, then, is a function of the physical environment. For instance, contraction of malaria is dependent on being bitten by a malarial mosquito. This event is in turn dependent upon proximity to mosquito breeding grounds, blood type, wind, climate, and time of year.

Medical anthropologists have had some difficulty distinguishing their work from that of medical sociologists (Foster, 1974). Both sociologists and anthropologists are interested in how social and cultural phenomena influence health status. The differences between the two disciplinary approaches are in perspective and method. The differences are perhaps sharpest "in the more wholistic view of medical anthropology, its constant awareness of cultural context as a point of reference for everything that comes under its scrutiny, and for the participant-observer technique of the anthropologist as contrasted with the more particularistic, less personal, less intimate, and generally more formalized techniques of the sociological investigator" (Landy, 1977). While this statement is generally true, the distinctions are somewhat cloudy because anthropologists are increasingly using sociological concepts and survey methods and sociologists are attending to cultural differences (Zola, 1966) and using qualitative methods (Becker et al., 1961). Regardless of difficulties in distinction, the reader should be aware that anthropology has made some unique contributions to the study of medicine. Anthropologists ask how culture influences medical care and how medical care affects culture. Responses to these fundamental questions have spanned the work of physical, social, and cultural anthropologists and have resulted in the development of cultural ecology and ethnomedicine as subfields. Anthropologists conceptualize disease as a cultural product. As such, cultural changes have an enormous impact on health and medical care delivery. Malinowski raised many of these issues in his classic work *Magic, Science and Religion* (1948).

Scientific work does not take place in a vacuum; sociologists are influenced by and influence anthropologists, geographers, political scientists, economists, historians, and physicians. Professionals who study medical care are influenced by their disciplinary training and the work of other professionals in the same content area. A tension develops when professionals are expected to retain their disciplinary identity *and* to merge their contributions with those of other professionals. The finest scholars seem to thrive on the tension between professional self-identity and interdisciplinary collaboration.

The medical sociologist is concerned with the ways in which social groups influence and are influenced by illness and medical care. The sociological perspective focuses on the *social* aspects of medicine with particular emphasis on the position of medicine in the structure of society. Given a specific social structure, the sociologist is interested in the social processes that define relationships between groups within that structure. The study of medical care and the treatment of illness in a society is a concern of the sociologist because the practice of medicine affects every aspect of complex societies. In fact, health appears consistently as a primary positive social value that permeates the fabric of most societies.

Because health is valued so highly in American society, medical sociologists historically have been reluctant to criticize the American health care delivery system or medical professionals. In many senses they had accepted the axiom "the doctor knows best." This attitude was reinforced by the writings of many sociologists who came from families of health professionals. There was a built-in positive bias toward those people and institutions dedicated to alleviating human suffering. Only recently have medical sociologists and the American public begun to question seriously the goals and performance of medical professionals and institutions. The work of Freidson (1970), Krause (1976), Navarro (1976), Thomas (1976), and Illich (1976) has given support to public concerns that something is wrong with the American health care system. Sociologists have directed their criticisms toward the social structure and process dimensions of medical practice.

Sociology of Medicine

While the sociological approach to the study of medicine differs from that of other disciplines, the outlook of individual sociologists is influenced by the intellectual and organizational contexts in which they work. Robert Strauss (1957) made a distinction between sociology *of* medicine and sociology *in* medicine to indicate these differences.

The sociology *of* medicine refers to sociologists standing back and analyzing medical practice from their theoretical perspective. Sociology *in* medicine refers usually to sociologists who are more "on the firing line" and involved in settings where medical care is being delivered. This distinction, while useful, is somewhat artificial. Good researchers and scholars must combine intense observation *and* first hand experience with an intellectual detachment that allows them to see the whole picture clearly. Some observers point out that scholars working in the sociology of medicine do more basic and theoretical work than those working in *sociology in medicine*. The *sociology in medicine* group is supposed to be more applied and pragmatic, but this distinction is difficult to maintain.

A more useful view of medical sociology is to examine the institutional affiliations of the scholars, the type of questions that they ask, and the work they do. Medical sociologists in sociology departments, management schools, schools of public health, medical schools, health foundations, and government are doing theoretical and applied health research. They apply their conceptual skills to the study of medical practice. The major theoretical problems of social organization, stratification, social and geographical mobility, social control, deviance, sociology of knowledge, mass communication, demography, and social change are examined within the medical context.

The theoretical perspective of sociologists has guided an impressive body of research. The contributions and growth of knowledge have been reciprocal between sociology and medicine. While the sociological perspective has detailed the complexity of medical care delivery in a highly developed country, identified problems, and suggested solutions, research in the sociology of medicine has advanced sociological theory and concepts. Researchers need to develop and test theory in a content area; the practice of medicine provides such a testing ground. Research in the field of medical sociology has produced the sick role concept, labeling theory, stress theories, models of the professions and professionalization, theories of social control, access and utilization models of human services, organizational theory, theories of innovation diffusion, and new knowledge about stratification and mobility. Research in the sociology of medicine affords the scholar the opportunity to develop theories and produce useful knowledge in an important area in society.

Sociology in Medicine

Sociology *in* medicine often has been characterized as atheoretical, applied, and dominated by physicians' views of the world. While this criticism is not without foundation, this work has produced a number of significant theories and applications useful for improving medical care.

A classic research tradition in the sociology in medicine area has been social epidemiology. Interest in disease identification and calculation of risk has been expanded recently in programs of community medicine and public health. Social epidemiologists are interested in understanding the etiological chain of events that produces disease and the corresponding risks associated with the causal factors. Once the causes of the disease have been identified and the natural history of the disease has been described, techniques can be developed for breaking the etiological chain of events and controlling the impact of the disease on a population. Epidemiologists have demonstrated that most diseases are influenced by both social and biological factors. This is particularly true in the case of chronic diseases, which characterize the majority of health problems in industrial countries (Glazier, 1973). Chronic diseases are, in large part, a function of lifestyle. Smoking is related to lung cancer and heart disease, drinking alcoholic beverages to cirrhosis of the liver, and animal fat diet and stress to coronary heart disease. As a result of these data, epidemiological researchers have been forced to develop biosocial causative models that have added a new dimension to sociological theory and generated a new subspecialty. On the applied level, knowledge of these causal chains has led schools of public health and departments of community medicine to develop intervention strategies aimed at controlling the incidence and prevalence of specific diseases. These schools and departments have been established to train professionals to implement prevention and intervention strategies.

While social epidemiology has had a marked impact on world medicine, in the United States major attention is being given to the tradeoffs between the cost of, quality of, and access to medical care. The medical sociologist traditionally has carried out the research on access and utilization, the economist has been concerned with costs, and the physician with quality of care. Given finite resources and a huge demand, difficult decisions must be made between cost, quality, and access. The concern with controlling costs by decreasing demand for health services and improving the effectiveness of treatment has given rise to the fields of health services research and health care delivery. The health care delivery field is oriented toward improving treatment in hospitals and outpatient clinics. The model used for research in this area examines the "relationship between the setting in which physicians work (structure), physician performance (process) and the outcome of medical care (result) " (Donabedian, 1977). This approach draws heavily on sociological theory and research and operations research.

Health services research is a term sometimes used synonymously with health care delivery. The field draws heavily on sociology, economics, and operations research. It differs from medical care delivery work by not confining its focus to hospitals and outpatient clinics. Health services research is concerned with the efficiency and outcome of all forms of medical care. The University of Munich Study Group on Health Systems Research surveyed the literature in this area during 1977 and 1978 and found the most research studies cataloged under the topics health services research, systems analysis of health care institutions, operations research in health care, cost-effectiveness, cost-benefit analysis, and health indicators. These *key words* are suggestive of the research being done.

Hospital administrators and managers of health care institutions are trained typically in schools of business or public health. These individuals are interested in the optimal management of health care institutions. The research conducted by these managers is similar in content to health services research but emphasizes the effect of management decisions on the outcome. Much of this work leans heavily on sociological theory and research while emphasizing cost-efficient solutions to problems.

Integrating Themes

This book takes a definite approach to the study of medical care. While other disciplinary views bring fresh insights to the study of medical care delivery, the sociology of medicine uniquely situates medical care delivery in a social context. The sociology of medicine approach foresakes an eclectic, applied perspective for the unifying theories and concepts of one discipline. This book does not discuss every topic in the field. Instead, the book is unified around three central themes: interpretations of medical phenomena; the continuing fight for control of medical work by the medical profession; and environmental influences on medical practice. These three themes embody many of the major theories and concepts in the sociology of medicine and focus on current problems in health care delivery.

Interpretations of Medical Phenomena

The longstanding tradition in medicine is to discover what ails the patient before interpreting the findings in light of some paradigm or theory. Treatment is contingent on what is discovered and what interpretation makes sense to the interested parties. Because of the complexity and importance of evaluations and interpretations of medical phenomena, experts were trained to fill these roles. These experts became professionals when society recognized their role and sanctioned their work. Thus, professionals are those whose assessment and interpretation of medical phenomena are legitimate and authoritative.

While there is considerable agreement about the processes of identification and interpretation of medical phenomena, controversies have raged over who should do the identification and interpretation, what methods should be used, what treatments are acceptable, and how outcome is to be assessed. The sociologist is excited about these issues because they indicate that in many ways the practice of medicine is a social process.

Social interpretation of medical phenomena has a longstanding historical precedent. The Greeks viewed health as a state of equilibrium in the physical and social environment. A citizen of sound body and sound mind was the Platonic ideal. The Romans also valued this balance of man and his environment. The Greek and Roman conceptual model of mind and body in balance with the physical and social environment was replaced in Western society by the Christian emphasis on the mind and the spirit. Christians valued the mind more than the body. The priest as a legitimate representative of the church was responsible for the mind and spirit. The doctor was responsible for the body. The priest emphasized spiritual health and the hereafter whereas physicians stressed physical health on earth. There is no doubt that the Christian view of health was dominant for centuries. This dualistic model of health was questioned seriously with the rapid development of physical and social sciences after the Renaissance. Although physicians now control the body, and psychiatrists, psychologists, and religious authorities control the spirit, there is considerable attention being given to treating the "whole person" within the environment. This brief synopsis points out that the practice of medicine has been, and continues to be, influenced dramatically by conceptual models based on social and cultural values.

To understand the practice of medicine, the different competing models used to identify and interpret medical phenomena must be appreciated. Malinowski points this out brilliantly in *Magic, Science and Religion* (1948). When an individual experiences pain in the elbow, there may be observable physiological signs, perceptions of stress, or religious feelings of guilt antecedent to the pain symptom. A faith healer, physician, or religious figure may intervene. The pain may diminish, increase, or remain stable. What is responsible for the phenomena and who should be credited with the results? The situation is complicated further when the person experiencing the pain has many antecedent conditions that presumably could explain the pain and turns to numerous professionals for help. How is causality to be attributed under these circumstances? Malinowski suggests that causality is determined in terms of specific explanatory models. These models are based on strong cultural values and applied within a social context.

This discussion explains why there is considerable controversy about which conceptual model should be used to evaluate, interpret, and treat medical phenomena. There is disagreement about what medical care systems can and should deliver. Health, as defined by the World Health Organization, is impossible to deliver. To say that "health is a state of complete physical, mental, and social wellbeing and not merely the absence of disease or infirmity" is to say nothing because the definition is so inclusive (Callahan, 1973). There is no profession that could deliver this product even if it was economically feasible. Personal happiness is impossible to deliver. For these reasons, the medical profession prefers to concentrate its energies on organically based pathologies, generally referred to as sickness or illness.

A number of conceptual models are used to describe and explain how medical professionals deal with illness. The most popular is the medical model. Although it is presented in different forms it generally assumes that illness is involuntary, organically based, falls below a socially defined, minimal standard of acceptability, and is to be treated by physicians (Veatch, 1973). This model, employed by medical professionals, is the theoretical basis of the sick role concept, which assumes that sick persons are not responsible for their illness, are exempted from normal role responsibilities, are expected to get well, and are expected to seek professional medical help usually from a physician (Parsons, 1951). The medical model best expresses the values and ideology of the medical profession. The sick role concept sets forth the corresponding set of expectations for the patient. The basic assumption is that diagnosis, interpretation, and treatment of illness are the responsibility of the physician; the patient's role is to cooperate and obey the doctor's orders. American people have been taught and now generally accept these values.

Because the medical model is accepted by most physicians and patients, it is acknowledged as the acceptable way of conceptualizing the treatment of illness. In recent years, however, this view has come under attack. Illich (1975) has argued persuasively that medical intervention often causes as much harm as it does good and that medicine should not be a monopoly that promises more than it can deliver.

The labeling theory is an alternative to the medical model. Proponents of labeling theory argue that much of what is known as sickness is a result of societal reaction to labeled deviance. When individuals are labeled sick, based on some symptoms, the societal reaction to this label reinforces the sick symptoms and behavior. This theory reinforces the fact that symptoms are interpreted in a social context.

In addition to the medical model and the labeling theory, there are many other models that explain sick behavior. The psychoanalytic model locates sickness in the psyche; the moral model conceptualizes the sick person as bad; the impaired model views the disabled as having conditions not amenable to treatment; and the social model portrays the sick person as a victim (Siegler and Osmond, 1973:42-43). Recent sociobiological theories and Moss' (1973) model of biosocial resonation bring us back to the Greek ideal of a sound body and a sound mind in balance with the physical and social environment. All of these models underscore the point that to understand medical practice one must appreciate the different conceptual perspectives and the way in which medical phenomena are interpreted in a social context.

The Continuing Fight for Control of Medical Work by the Medical Profession

Physicians in the United States constitute a unique profession; they have enjoyed many of the characteristics of a self-regulated monopoly. Doctors have considerable control over their work. This professional autonomy has been the result of historical developments over the last 200 years (Stevens, 1971). Physicians control their own selection, educational certification, and quality control processes. They have substantial control over their fee structures and working conditions. During recent years this autonomous control over medical work has been challenged seriously from within and without the medical profession.

Navarro (1976) and Krause (1977) have argued that the particular form of medical care dominant in the United States will not be determined by some abstract model of what is best for all of the nation's people, but by the interest groups that wield the most political power. The corporate and upper-middle class have a disproportionately strong influence on the means of production and service delivery in the United States. The medical profession has capitalized on this situation by practicing medicine in a manner that rewards the corporate and upper-middle classes. This strategy worked well until recently. Consumer expectations have risen well beyond what can be delivered reasonably and costs have escalated beyond control.

Since the medical profession does not seem to be able to meet consumer expectations at a reasonable price, federal, state, and local governments, insurance companies, employers, consumers, and hospitals are proposing mechanisms for regulating the work of physicians. These regulatory threats are being taken very seriously and are being fought on a variety of fronts. Doctors do not want to lose any of the control they presently enjoy. The American Medical Association and other organized groups of doctors have developed strategies for regulation and control that insure the physicians' role as regulators. The AMA supported national health insurance plans embody these strategies. Compromise will invariably be required and, professional autonomy will be one of the last concessions.

The extensive external pressures on physicians to relinquish some control over their work are matched by similar internal forces. Less than 50 percent of the physicians in the United States belong to the American Medical Association. Many younger doctors question the effects of a self-regulated profession on the delivery of services. Some doctors argue that the quality and cost of medical care are best controlled in a more open competitive environment. This approach might reduce physicians' fees, give health administrators more control, and place greater emphasis on prevention rather than on expensive technological intervention. Another internal threat is posed by the physicians' assistants, nurses, physical therapists, and midwives who argue that they can competently do much of the traditional work of a physician and at a lower cost. The established medical profession has been fighting these forces of change that threaten to diminish physicians' control over their work. The sociologist is interested in the organizational dynamics and the adaptation of the profession in a complex social environment. The theoretical issues expressed here are representative of all other professions and the practical consequences have considerable economic and social impact.

Environmental Influences on Medical Practice

The practice of medicine takes place in a physical, social, and cultural environment. These environments shape medical practice by providing a unique set of contingencies that must be addressed. The physical and social environments of medical care in the United States are ones in which chronic diseases have replaced communicable and infectious diseases as the major causes of morbidity and mortality. Environments and lifestyle have a major impact on these diseases. Meaningful intervention in this situation depends on changing living patterns and lifestyles, not surgery and drugs.

The technical environment of current medical practice is very sophisticated. Microelectronics, computers, and molecular biology have entered the hospital and revolutionized medical practice. Technical capabilities such as computerized axial tomography (CAT) scanners, organ transplants, dialysis, miniaturized surgery, and cloning have expanded the horizon of future advances and have escalated the costs of health care. Agreement on "ordinary means," criteria of death, and ethical procedures are not so easy to determine. Questions of access and payment for extraordinary procedures also are difficult to resolve.

The organizational environment of medical care is one of highly specialized, multiple hospital systems. There is a growing emphasis on outpatient clinics, preventive medicine, and health maintenance organizations. Concern over regulation of the providers of medical care and cost containment of services pervade the organizational environment.

The larger social environment is characterized not only by technical and organizational complexity but also by a set of social and political realities. Health is becoming a political commodity; it is a resource that has an independent value in society. Citizens are more willing to sacrifice material possessions and allocate more of their disposable income to medical care than they were years ago. Developing countries are increasingly demanding medical care to help them control morbidity and extend life spans.

Medical care is one of the largest industries in the Western world. Many components of this industry, such as hospitals, pharmaceutical groups, construction businesses, and hospital supply companies, exert strong pressures on government to insure the *growth status* of health care. The study of medical care is myopic if it does not attend to the influence of these interest groups on the health care delivery system. The practice of medicine is contingent on the ways in which systems are organized and interrelate with the environments in which the systems operate. The sociologist is interested in these relationships. Such studies lead to refined theories of organizations and adaptive strategies that maximize organizational effectiveness.

References

Becker, H. S., Geer, B., Hughes, E. C., & Strauss, A. L. *Boys in white: Student culture in medical school.* Chicago: University of Chicago Press, 1961.

Callahan, D. The WHO definition of health. *The Hastings Center Studies 1 (3)* 1973, 77–88.

Cockerham, W. C. *Medical sociology*. Englewood Cliffs, N. J.: Prentice-Hall, 1978.

Donabedian, A. Measuring the quality of medical care. In L. Corey, M. F. Epstein, & S. E. Saltman (Eds.) *Medicine in a changing society*. St. Louis: Mosby, 1977, pp. 151–74.

Foster, G. Medical anthropology: Some contrasts with medical sociology. *Medical Anthropology Newsletter 6 (1)* 1974, 1–6.

Freeman, H. E., Levine, S., & Reeder, L. G. Present status of medical sociology. In H. E. Freeman, S. Levine, & L. G. Reeder (Eds.) *Handbook of medical sociology,* (2nd Ed.) Englewood Cliffs, N.J.: Prentice-Hall, 1972, pp. 501–22.

Freidson, E. *The profession of medicine*. New York: Dodd, Mead, 1970.

Gibson, R. M., & Mueller, M. S. National health expenditures. *Social Security Bulletin 40* (April) 1977, 3–23.

Glazier, W. H. The task of medicine. *Scientific American 228* 1973, 13–17.

Graham, S., & Reeder, L. G. Social factors in the chronic diseases. In H. E. Freeman, S. Levine, & L. G. Reeder (Eds.) *Handbook of medical sociology,* (2nd Ed.) Englewood Cliffs, N.J.: Prentice-Hall, 1972, pp. 63–107.

Hughes, E. F. X., Baron, D. P., Dittman, D. A., Friedman, S., Longest, B. B., Pauly, M. V., Smith, K. R. *Hospital cost containment programs: A policy analysis*. Cambridge, Mass.: Ballinger, 1978.

Illich, I. *The medical nemesis*. New York: Pantheon, 1976.

Krause, E. *Power and illness: The political sociology of health and medical care*. New York: Elsevier, 1977.

Landy, D. (Ed.) *Culture, disease and healing: Studies in medical anthropology*. New York: Macmillan, 1977.

Malinowski, B. *Magic, science and religion*. New York: Free Press, 1948.

May, J. M. Medical geography: Its methods and objectives. *Social Science and Medicine 11* (November) 1977, 715–30.

Mechanic, D. Approaches to controlling the costs of medical care: Short range and long range alternatives. *New England Journal of Medicine 298* (February 2) 1978, 249–54.

Moss, G. E. *Illness, immunity and social interaction: The dynamics of biosocial resonation*. New York: Wiley, 1973.

Navarro, V. *Medicine under capitalism*. New York: PRODIST, 1976.

Parson, T. *The social system*. Glencoe, Ill.: Free Press, 1951.

Rosen, G. *From medical police to social medicine*. New York: Science History Publications, 1974.

Siegler, M., & Osmond, H. The sick role revisited. *The Hastings Center Studies 1(3)* 1973, 41–58.

Stevens, R. *American medicine and the public interest*. New Haven: Yale University Press, 1971.

Strauss, R. The nature and status of medical sociology. *American Sociological Review 22* 1957; 200–204.

Thomas, L. Rx for Illich. *New York Review of Books* (September) 1976: 3–4.

Twaddle, A. C., & Hessler, R. M. *A sociology of health*. St. Louis: Mosby, 1977.

Veatch, R. M. The medical model: Its nature and problems. *The Hastings Center Studies 1(3)* 1973: 56–76.

Zola, I. K. Culture and symptoms: An analysis of patients' presenting complaints. *American Sociological Review 31* (October) 1966: 615–30.

PART I

Social and Cultural Dimensions of Medical Behavior

Health, illness, and medical practice are cultural and social products. A strictly medical or physiological perspective of health will not capture the full complexity of medical behavior. As we will see in this part, the definition of illness and society's response to illness are influenced by the prevailing culture of the community, the ways of thinking about, perceiving, or evaluating an object or situation. The values and beliefs of a community shape what its members recognize as illness and how they deal with it.

Social factors, which express the ongoing relationships among people and the institutions and organizations that they create, also influence health, illness, and medicine. Sex, race, and social class are convenient but oversimplified indicators of some of those relationships. For example, does the relationship between men and women in this society affect health, illness, and medicine? Many researchers say it does. All of the following selections indicate the necessity of understanding health, illness, and medicine *within* the cultural and social contexts in which they are located.

Nathanson points out marked sex, age, and marital differences in mortality, morbidity, and medical care in the United States and Great Britain. She then reviews theories on biological differences, social and psychological stress, lifestyle, and institutionalized sex roles that are used to explain these differences. Zola shows how individuals from different cultural backgrounds locate and describe symptoms of the same diagnosed illness in different ways. In the final selection, Sidel and Sidel conclude by describing medical care in China and by showing how it can be, at least partially, the result of planned political change.

Sex, Illness, and Medical Care: **2**
A Review of Data, Theory, and Method

CONSTANCE A. NATHANSON

Introduction

"In all societies certain things are selected as reference points for the ascription of status. . . . *The simplest and most universally used of these reference points is sex*" [1, 115–16]. There can be few more convincing demonstrations of this statement than to review the world's literature on mortality, morbidity, and medical care. Data collected by national and international administrative bodies, as well as by individual investigators, are almost universally tabulated by sex. As a consequence of this uniform practice, there exists an enormous wealth of statistical material on sex differences in almost every dimension of health, ranging from crude death rates to the frequency of home visits by a physician. The bulk of these data, however, have been collected with the aim of describing mortality and morbidity in selected populations. While sex has been used as a primary basis of more detailed classification, there has been relatively little sustained attention to the broad range of sex differences across a variety of health indices. The purpose of this paper is to focus the attention of social scientists on these sex differences in illness and medical care and on the problems of understanding and interpretation that they present.

In carrying out this purpose, the paper is limited both by considerations of space and by the nature of the available data. While there are significant sex dif-

From *Social Science and Medicine* 11 (1977) © 1977, Pergamon Press, Ltd. Reprinted with permission.

ferences in patterns of mental illness, these differences have received somewhat more attention than have differences associated with physical disease [2, 7]. Consequently, this paper will focus on physical rather than mental illness. Secondly, although reasonably reliable data on mortality are available from *developed* countries for much of the 20th century, comparable morbidity data have only recently begun to be collected. Since one aim of this paper is, wherever possible, to be international in scope, it will focus primarily on the *contemporary* picture of sex differences in health indices, although changes in mortality will be briefly considered. Furthermore, while mortality data are published for most countries of the world, indices of morbidity and the utilization of health services are not readily available, even for the majority of developed countries. This paper relies heavily on certain indices which have been employed in more than one country, but the overall description of sex differences in morbidity and mortality is strongly weighted with the United States experience. The limitations of this approach are recognized and highlight the need for data collection on a more international basis. Finally, this paper is limited by the very nature of its subject matter. "Sex," "illness," and "medical care" are not coherent conceptual categories, but only indices to a bewildering variety of underlying biological, psychological, and social processes. No single theory or set of hypotheses will possibly encompass this variety. Consequently, while this paper has a certain descriptive unity of focus, it is conceptually and theoretically eclectic. In this sense, it reflects the state of the literature on sex differences in illness and medical care, in which *ad hoc* speculation concerning cause and effect relationships is the rule rather than the exception. One function of the present paper will be to define and order the alternative directions that speculation may take, with the hope that future investigation in the area of sex differences will be more precisely directed to the examination of specific alternatives.

The body of the paper is divided into four sections. The first section is entirely descriptive, and will summarize the current state of knowledge with respect to sex differences in mortality, morbidity, and medical care. The following two sections will consider, respectively, the methodological and the theoretical issues that arise in evaluating and interpreting these data. Finally, the last section will indicate some directions for future research into sex differences in health status.

Sex Differences in Illness and Medical Care

In a relatively short paper it is possible to do no more than call attention to the most salient and consistently reported sex differences in indices of health and medical care. Five topics will be covered in this section: first, the sources of data employed in this paper; secondly, overall sex differences in mortality, morbidity, and the use of health services; third, principle causes of differential mortality and morbidity; and finally, variations in the pattern of sex differences by age and by marital status.

Sources of Data

Mortality data both as to the cause of death and demographic characteristics of the deceased are based on information recorded on the death certificate and classified as to cause by the International Classification of Diseases. Death registration is considered to be virtually complete in all the economically developed countries [8]. These data are compiled annually by the United Nations and by the World Health Organization, and are widely reported in a variety of secondary sources.

The morbidity data presented in this paper come from two principle sources, the United States Health Interview Survey and the British General Household Survey. The Health Interview Survey (HIS) is a continuing weekly household sample survey, conducted in the United States since July, 1957. In this survey, data are collected to describe the distribution in the population of chronic and acute illness, associated disability, and the use of health services. The General Household Survey (GHS) was inaugurated in 1971. Data are obtained, also from a national household sample, covering a wide variety of topics including current health status. While differences in question wording limit the direct comparability of health *levels* between the U.S. and British surveys, they are sufficiently similar in the types of data collected to warrant the comparison of sex ratios for a variety of health indices. The World Health Organization reports *morbidity statistics* for a number of countries based on hospital inpatient data, but morbidity is here *completely* confounded with utilization of services, a problem inherent to some degree in almost all measures of morbidity that are currently employed.

The two most widely used indices of medical care are hospital discharge or separation rates and physician visit rates. Hospital inpatient data are compiled by WHO as indicated, and are also available from several other sources. Data for the present paper were obtained from the Hospital Discharge Survey conducted annually by the U.S. National Center for Health Statistics, *Hospital Morbidity*, published by Statistics Canada, the British GHS, and several *ad hoc* research investigations carried out in the United States. (These investigations, as well as the other sources described will be cited specifically as the data are presented.) Both the HIS and the GHS report physician visits, and these data are also available from special research studies carried out in several other Western and Eastern European countries and in Israel. Data on more detailed aspects of medical care including preventive care, health expenditures, and the like, are limited almost entirely to the United States.

Overall Sex Differences

In all developed countries and for all ages the death rate for females is appreciably below that for males, and has been so at least since the beginning of the 20th century [8–10]. Sex ratios based on age-adjusted death rates for 18 countries of *low mortality* are presented in Table 2-1. In addition to the uniformly favorable mortality experience of women, two further points concerning sex differences in mortality should be noted. First, the variability of death rates among the countries listed in Table 2-1 is considerably greater for males than females.

(The standard deviation of male rates is about 1½ times that of female rates, and this difference is constant from 1930 to 1960.) Secondly, the difference between male and female death rates has increased markedly during the 20th century, due primarily to excess mortality in men [10–13].

The apparent contrast between male excess mortality and female excess morbidity—women get sick and men die—was observed in England as early as 1927 [14] and has been exciting sporadic comment since that time [2, 15–18].

Table 2-1   Sex Ratios
(Female/Male) of
Age-Adjusted Death
Rates for Selected
Countries of Low
Mortality

Country		Ratio
U.S., white		0.61
England and Wales		0.63
Scotland		0.68
Australia*		0.63
New Zealand+		0.67
Canada		0.67
Ireland		0.77
Netherlands		0.74
Belgium		0.65
France		0.60
Switzerland		0.69
West Germany		0.70
Denmark		0.78
Norway		0.73
Sweden		0.76
Finland		0.63
Portugal		0.74
Italy		0.71
Average	1960	0.68
	1950	0.77
About	1930	0.85

Source: This table is adapted from Table 3–4 in Spiegleman, M., & Erhardt, C. L. International comparisons of mortality and longevity. In C. L. Erhardt, & J. E. Berlin (Eds.) *Mortality and Morbidity in the United States.* Cambridge, Mass.: Harvard University Press, 1974, pp. 39-64.
Note: The statistical measures for 1950 and about 1930 were taken from Spiegelman, M. *An international comparison of mortality rates at the older ages.* Proceedings of the World Population Conference, Rome, 1, 289. New York: United Nations Department of Economic and Social Affairs, 1955.
Age-adjusted on the bases of the age-distribution of the total population of the United States Census of April 1960.
*Excludes full-blooded Aborigines.
+Excludes Maoris.

Table 2-2 Sex Ratios (Female/Male) for
Selected Morbidity Indices,
United States and Great Britain,
1971

Index	United States	Great Britain
Acute conditions	1.19	1.15
Chronic conditions	0.89	1.08
Days of restricted activity	1.28	1.14
Days of bed disability	1.34	1.17
Days lost from work	1.20	0.88

Ratios calculated by the author from data presented in U.S. Department of Health, Education, and Welfare, *Current estimates from the health interview survey, United States, 1971*. Vital and Health Statistics, Series 10, No. 79, and Office of Population Censuses and Surveys, Social Survey Division. *The General Household Survey: Introductory Report*. London: H.M.S.O., 1973. Ratios shown are for adults 17 and over in the United States, 15 and over in Great Britain. Pregnancy associated illness and disability have been excluded from these data.

Sex differences in several indices of morbidity, as reported to household interviewers in Great Britain [19] and the United States [20] are shown in Table 2-2. Data are presented for adults (15 and above in Great Britain, 17 and above in the United States), and exclude illness and disability associated with pregnancy and its aftermath. Rates for each index were calculated on somewhat different bases in the two countries and are not shown. However, the direction of the sex ratios is remarkably consistent. When morbidity is measured, as it is in these surveys, by behavioral indices (restriction or limitation of activity, medical consultation, going to bed, staying away from work) adult women almost invariably report more *acute* illness and associated disability than adult men. Unfortunately, it has not been possible to obtain comparable *morbidity* data for other countries.

With scattered exceptions, adult women also make more physician visits than adult men, and they do so in all countries where the relevant data have been obtained. Comparable data on physician visits were collected in seven countries as part of an international collaborative study of medical care [21]. Sex ratios based on two-week physician visit rates as reported in this study are presented in Table 2-3. Age groups are those used in the published table from which these data were taken, with the omission of the age group 15-44. About 10-15 percent of physician visits by women in this age group are accounted for by pre- and postnatal care, and these were not excluded from the reported rates. Of the 24 sex ratios shown for age groups above 44, only seven reflect a higher rate of physician visits by men than by women. (Discussion of the differences in these ratios by age is reserved for a later section.) Surveys conducted in Israel and Finland [22, 23] have obtained identical results, and these differences persist in the United States, at least, when obstetrical visits *are* excluded [2, 15]. The obverse of these findings is obtained in studies focused on low utilizers of physi-

Table 2–3   Sex Ratio (Female/Male) for Physician
Visits, Ages 0–14, 45–64, 65 and
Above—Selected Countries

Country	0–14	45–64	65+
Canada			
Grande Prairie	0.94	1.72	2.14
Saskatchewan	0.60	0.56	0.97
Fraser	1.18	0.89	1.06
Jersey	0.83	1.67	1.03
United States			
Northwestern Vermont	0.67	1.31	0.83
Baltimore, Maryland	0.73	1.08	1.25
Argentina			
Buenos Aires	0.84	1.14	1.17
United Kingdom			
Liverpool	0.80	1.11	1.18
Finland			
Helsinki	0.83	1.82	1.18
Poland			
Lódź	0.63	1.32	1.85
Yugoslavia			
Banat	0.98	0.80	0.83
Rijeka	0.86	1.75	0.54

Source: Ratios calculated by the author from data presented in White,
K. L., et al. Ecologic results. In D. L. Rabin (Ed.) International Comparisons of Medical Care. *Milbank Memorial Fund Quarterly 50* (1) 1972:
31–44.

cians' services [24, 25]. This population of "non-attenders" is predominantly
male.

Data describing more detailed aspects of ambulatory medical care are limited to the United States. Women are more likely than men to report a regular
source of care [26, 27] and are much more likely to obtain various types of preventive care [15, 28, 29]. Evidence regarding a more basic dimension of preventive health care is reported by Andersen and Anderson [27]. Among men, they
observe, the most prevalent reason for having a physical examination is that it is
required for work or insurance purposes, while women are likely to be examined
voluntarily, in response to symptoms or as a preventive measure. In perhaps
related findings, women are reported to be generally better informed about disease than are men [30, 31].

Total rates of hospitalization are higher for women than for men, even when
these rates are age-standardized and exclude obstetrical conditions [15, 19, 27,
32–34]. More detailed analyses of hospital data from Canadian [35] and United
States [15, 36] sources report surgical procedure rates for women 1½ times the
comparable rates for men. Sex differences in average length of hospital stay are
less consistent in direction, although the majority of sources report longer hospital stays among men [19, 27, 32–35, 37].

In the United States the total cost of medical care is higher for women than for men [27, 38], hardly a surprising finding in view of women's greater use of medical services. Furthermore, this difference persists well beyond the child-bearing ages. Women are larger consumers of medicines than men both in Great Britain [39] and in the United States [40]. This difference is reflected in drug expenditure data from the United States both for prescribed and for nonpre-scribed medications [41].

This section has rapidly reviewed what are perhaps, by now, familiar statis-tics to most students of health and medical care. In all European countries and in North America, male mortality rates are higher than those of females. However, for all countries where the necessary data are available, women report more acute illness than men and make substantially greater use of health services. In the following pages, these differences will be examined in more detail, by specific cause, and by age and marital status.

Causes of Death and Disease

Excessive mortality among adult males in recent decades, resulting in an increasing divergence of male and female death rates, has been attributed to three principal causes of death, cardiovascular disease, cancer, and bronchitis [13]. Of these, cardiovascular disease makes by far the largest contribution to mortality [10, 12, 13]. Other leading causes of death among adults in Europe and North America are diabetes, tuberculosis, influenza, pneumonia, cirrhosis of the liver, suicide, and accidents [8]. Diabetes is the only condition among these major killers for which higher death rates are reported for women than for men. Particularly large differences in the sex ratio have been observed for those condi-tions (cirrhosis, suicide, accidents) which may be wholly or partially attributed to overt acts of the individual [9, 12, 18, 42].

In a recent paper, Verbrugge [18] has suggested that the apparent contrast between male mortality and female morbidity is due, in part, to the fact that women, while having more illness than men, have it in milder forms. This hypoth-esis is consistent with data on sex differences in morbidity rates for specific con-ditions. Women have higher rates than men for acute conditions and for the disability associated with these conditions, but they have lower rates of chronic conditions in almost all age groups. The specific acute conditions reported more frequently by females both in Great Britain and the United States are upper respi-ratory infections and influenza [19, 20] and, in the United States, genitourinary disorders. Injuries are the only large group of acute conditions for which males have consistently higher rates; the same pattern is found in hospital morbidity data for all countries where this information is reported by sex [33, 34, 43–45]. While no data are available to compare case-fatality rates for these acute condi-tions, it is at least plausible that injury is more frequently associated with mortality than are the acute conditions predominant among females. Males have slightly higher chronic condition rates than females, and this difference is primarily accounted for by disease groups (heart disease, cerebrovascular disease, bron-chitis) that are also frequent causes of mortality. In contrast to this pattern, women report fewer chronic conditions than men, and the specific conditions for

Table 2–4 Hospital Discharge Rates by Sex and Condition, Canada, 1971, and United States, 1968

Discharge Rates per 1000 Population	Canada*		United States+	
	Male	Female	Male	Female
Total discharge rate	1367.3	1950.3	1191.9	1658.2
Discharge rate excluding obstetrical conditions	1367.3	1477.2	1191.9	1245.4
Discharge rate excluding *all* sex specific conditions	1285.5	1289.3	1139.3	1084.6

*Rates calculated by the author from data presented in Statistics Canada, *Hospital Morbidity.* Ottawa, 1971.
+Rates drawn directly from U.S. Department of Health, Education, and Welfare. *Inpatient utilization of short-stay hospitals by diagnosis, United States, 1968.* Vital and Health Statistics, Series 13, No. 12, 1973: 4–7.

which they do show an excess (principally arthritis and rheumatism) are relatively nonlethal [18–20].

Additional light on specific conditions which contribute substantially to morbidity among women is provided by detailed analyses of hospital morbidity statistics from Canada and the United States. This analysis, presented in Table 2–4, compares total hospital discharge rates for men and women, and then successively refines these rates, first, by excluding obstetrical conditions and secondly, by excluding *all* conditions associated with the reproductive organs and therefore specific to one sex or the other. This procedure entirely eliminates the difference in hospital discharge rates between the two sexes. Among the total group of conditions specific to women, slightly over 70 percent (in both countries) represent obstetrical conditions, and this is not unexpected. However, almost 30 percent (accounting for 10 percent of all hospital discharges among women) are nonobstetrical "diseases of the female genital organs." Approximately 40 percent of these diseases fall into the two categories of disorders of menstruation and prolapsed uterus, lending some slight weight, perhaps, to the 19th century physician's view of woman as the "product and prisoner of her reproductive system" [46: 335]. However, 5 percent of all hospital episodes among men are similarly caused by conditions of the reproductive organs.

Variations by Age

From the standpoint of developing explanatory hypotheses, a description of overall sex differences in mortality, morbidity, and medical care does little more than whet the appetite. Not only is an examination of variations in sex ratios among different population subgroups more likely to be fruitful in *generating* hypotheses, but any hypotheses that are advanced must be consistent with these variations. An analysis based on published data is limited, however, by the population characteristics that *other* analysts have thought important. The most frequently reported of these characteristics, in addition to sex, are age and marital status.

Figure 2-1   Sex Ratios (Female/Male) for Mortality and Acute Illness by Age,
Great Britain and the United States, 1971

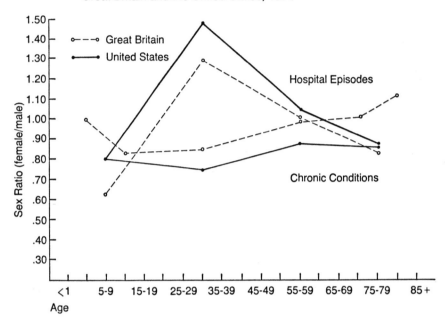

Source: Sex ratios calcuated by the author from the following sources:
Mortality
   World Health Organization, *World Health Statistics Annual, 1971.* Volume 1, Vital Statistics and Causes of Death. Geneva, 1974; U.S. Department of Health, Education, and Welfare. *Vital Statistics of the United States, 1971.* Volume II, Mortality. Rockville, Md., 1975.
Acute Illness
   Office of Population Censuses and Surveys (19).
   U.S. Department of Health, Education, and Welfare (20).
   Available data did not permit the calculation of mortality and acute illness sex ratios for exactly corresponding age groups.

Changes in the pattern of sex differences over the life span are shown in Figures 2-1 and 2-2 for Great Britain and the United States. Sex ratios (female/male) for mortality and acute illness rates are presented in Figure 2-1 and for chronic conditions and hospital episodes in Figure 2-2. Ratios of less than 1.00 reflect higher male rates, while ratios above 1.00 mean that rates are higher among females. Several points are dramatically illustrated by these figures. First, the patterns of change in sex differences by age are remarkably parallel in the two countries. Not only is this true of mortality as would be predicted from overall similarities in social and economic development, but it is also true for the much softer health indices based largely on household survey data. Differences between the United States and Great Britain in population composition and medical care organization, not to speak of differences in survey methods, make this parallelism all the more striking. The second point to note about these figures is the convergences of all sex ratios toward equality between the sexes both at the beginning and at the end of life. It is during the broad span of middle

Figure 2–2   Sex Ratios (Female/Male) for Chronic Conditions and Hospital
Episodes by Age, Great Britain and the United States, 1970–1971

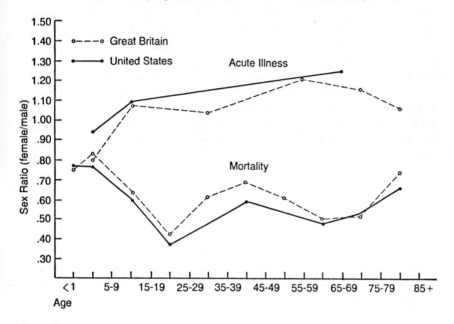

Source: Sex ratios calculated by the author from the following sources:
Chronic conditions
    Office of Population Censuses and Surveys (19).
    U.S. Department of Health, Education, and Welfare, *Utilization of Short-stay Hospitals, Summary of
Nonmedical Statistics, United States 1970.* Vital Health and Statistics, Series 13, No. 14, 1973.
    Data did not permit calculation of all ratios for exactly corresponding age groups.

life, ranging from school entrance to retirement, that differences in the illness
experience of the two sexes are most marked. Finally, these figures demonstrate
graphically a point that has already been made verbally—over the age span during which sex differences are most profound, males have greater mortality and
higher rates of chronic conditions, while females report more acute illness and
make greater use of health services. Indices of illness *behavior*—activity restriction, days in bed, sickness absence from work—show the same general age specific pattern as acute illness, while the pattern for physician visits resembles that
of hospital episodes.

A number of more detailed aspects of the variation in sex differences by age
are illustrated by these figures, and confirmed by other sources. By *all* indices of
health status, pre-school age boys are less well off than girls in this age group.
Infant mortality among males is about one-half to one-third above that of females
in all developed countries [9]. Commenting on the evidence of sex differences in
illness during early childhood, the authors of the GHS remark that "small boys
are not only more liable to acute sickness than small girls, but also . . . the nature
of their sickness is more serious, or more seriously regarded" [19: 299]. Following the pre-school years, however, divergent trends in patterns of sex differences

are quickly established. A marked increase in male relative to female mortality rates occurs in the age group 15-24. This increase has been widely noted [9, 12] and is attributed primarily to deaths from accidents among young men. Comparing Sweden and the United States, Fuchs [9] has commented that while infant mortality sex ratios in the two countries are very similar, the gap between male and female death rates in early adulthood is much larger in the United States. This difference is attributed to different lifestyles of Swedish and American youth.

It is during the prime of adult life that men and women differ most radically in their illness experience, as has already been observed. Women in the reproductive age-groups utilize both physician and hospital services at almost one-and one-half times the rate of men in this age-group, exclusive of utilization associated with pregnancy. Men, on the other hand, show a second marked increase in their relative mortality, extending from ages 45–64, but there is no corresponding change in other health indices. The size of this increase in relative mortality varies both among countries, and between regions within the same country [9], and is due primarily to male mortality from heart disease [9, 12].

Beginning at about age 65, there are further changes in the illness experience of the two sexes. Chronic illness rates among women begin to approach or exceed those of men, although men in this, as in younger age groups, are more likely to be rendered "unable to carry on" their major activity by chronic illness [47]. Finally, while women over 65 are less likely than men in this age group to be hospitalized, when they do enter a hospital their length of stay is longer [17, 19, 33, 48].

This brief review has documented wide variation over the life cycle in the pattern of sex differences in health indices. However, although sex ratios for mortality, morbidity, and use of health services are inconsistent among themselves, they vary in parallel fashion among several countries of Europe and North America. These observations suggest that variations in sex ratios are produced by common underlying processes and, furthermore, that these processes are probably social rather than biological in nature. Speculation as to the precise nature of these processes is reserved to a later section of this paper.

Variations by Marital Status

In all developed countries, the unmarried have significantly higher death rates than the married, and this differential is much greater for males than for females [9, 10]. A middle-aged unmarried man living in the United States has a probability of death about five times that of a married woman in the same age range, and similar, although somewhat less marked, differences are observed for other countries in Europe and North America. Based on a detailed analysis of sex mortality differentials by marital status, Gove [42] remarks that the differences between married and unmarried (single, divorced, separated, widowed) men are particularly large for those causes of death where "one's psychological state would appear to affect one's life chances" (suicide, homicide, accidents, cirrhosis of the liver, and several other conditions of less obvious social-psychological etiology).

While sex *mortality* differentials by marital status are reasonably well established, this is much less true of differences in reported illness and in the use of health services. Data are not always cross-classified by marital status, marital status categories are not uniform among different sources of data, and the apparent effects of marital status, when this information is given, are not always in the same direction. Consequently, generalizations made in this paper concerning the influence of marital status on patterns of sex differences in illness and medical care are highly tentative and subject to amendment or disproof by subsequent investigation.

The married of both sexes fare better than the unmarried in most studies of morbidity based on data collected in household surveys [19, 49–51]. It has been suggested, however, that, from the standpoint of health status, the married state is less advantageous to women than to men [3, 52, 53]. The relative protection that marriage affords to each sex may be examined by dividing morbidity rates of the unmarried by those of the married [42, 54]. If the ratios formed by this procedure are greater than 1.00, then married persons are better off. Furthermore, if marriage is, indeed, less advantageous to women, then their ratios should be consistently lower than the corresponding ratios for men.

Morbidity rates by marital status, age, and sex are published in the report of the General Household Survey [19], and these data have been used to calculate the ratios presented in Table 2–5. This table illustrates two points. First, of the 32

Table 2-5   Ratios Produced by Dividing Morbidity Rates of the Unmarried by the Rates of the Married, Great Britain, 1971

Morbidity Index and Unmarried Category (Ratio)		Age			Average Ratio
		15–44	45–65	65+	
Limiting long-standing illness					
Single:	Male	0.97	1.13	—	1.05
	Female	0.95	1.36	0.95	1.09
Widowed, divorced, separated:	Male	1.30	1.22	1.07	1.20
	Female	1.66	1.42	1.14	1.41
Presence of restricted activity					
Single:	Male	1.03	0.83	1.16	1.01
	Female	1.09	1.10	1.21	1.13
Widowed, divorced, separated:	Male	—	1.16	1.43	1.30
	Female	1.01	1.15	1.15	1.10
Number of restricted days					
Single:	Male	0.87	0.84	—	0.86
	Female	0.97	1.37	1.17	1.17
Widowed, divorced, separated:	Male	—	1.17	1.66	1.42
	Female	1.41	1.22	1.03	1.22

Source: Ratios calculated by the author from morbidity rates presented in the *General Household Survey: Introductory Report.* London: H.M.S.O., 1973.

ratios shown in this table, 26 are greater than 1.00, again confirming that married people of both sexes report less illness and associated disability than the unmarried. The only exceptions to this generalization occur in comparing married with single persons, and these exceptions are equally frequent among men and women. Secondly, there is no basis in the data presented *here* for concluding that marriage affords more protection against morbidity to men than to women. On the contrary, in 10 of the 14 comparisons between the sexes made possible by this table, unmarried women report *more* morbidity relative to the married than do unmarried men. The reader should be cautioned, however, that these are data from a single source and that both age and marital status are reported in very broad categories. The question of how marital status affects sex differentials in morbidity is an area much in need of further study.

In order to look at the influence of marital status on use of health services, the same procedure as described above, division of unmarried utilization rates by those of the married, has been employed. In this case a ratio greater than 1.00 means that these services are being used at a higher rate by unmarried as compared to married persons, while greater use by the married will result in a ratio of less than 1.00. While the general direction of marital status effects on morbidity was the same for both sexes, this is not true of comparable effects on medical care. Unmarried/married ratios of hospital discharge rates by age and sex are presented in Table 2–6. These ratios are based on rates calculated from hospital discharges reported to the U.S. National Center for Health Statistics in 1970 [33]. In all but two of 15 possible comparisons, male ratios are larger than female ratios, indicating that unmarried men use more hospital services relative to their married counterparts than do unmarried women. There is, furthermore, an absolute reversal between the two sexes. Two-thirds of the ratios presented for men are greater than 1.00, reflecting higher utilization by *unmarried* as compared to married men, while two-thirds of the female ratios are less than 1.00, indicating higher utilization by *married* than by unmarried women. These data on hospitalization by marital status are consistent with information from at least one additional source [15]. Physician visits by marital status follow the same pattern (based on calculations by the author from HIS data [55]).

The data reported in this section of the paper may be summarized very briefly. By *all* criteria of health status, unmarried men are less favorably situated than married men. They have higher mortality rates, report more morbidity, and make more use of physicians and hospitals. The picture with respect to women is less consistent, however. While unmarried women also experience less favorable mortality rates than married women, the difference is considerably narrower than among men. In the data presented in this paper, unmarried women report *more* morbidity than women who are married, but make *less* use of hospital services. Finally, although the protection against mortality afforded by marriage is clearly more substantial for men than for women, there is no consistent evidence in these data for a parallel effect on *morbidity*. The reader is again reminded that generalizations concerning patterns of morbidity and medical care are based on scattered evidence and should be regarded with appropriate caution.

Table 2-6   Ratios Produced by Dividing Hospital Discharge Rates of the
Unmarried by Those of the Married, United States, 1970

Unmarried category (ratio)		15–24	25–44	Age 45–64	65+	Average Ratio
Single:	Male	0.96	1.19	1.07	0.89	1.03
	Female	0.56	0.91	0.92	0.93	0.83
Separated:	Male	1.61	1.52	1.11	0.86	1.28
	Female	1.04	1.12	0.84	0.71	0.93
Divorced:	Male	0.91	1.27	1.06	0.69	0.98
	Female	1.24	1.18	0.92	0.60	0.99
Widowed:	Male		1.19	1.28	1.31	1.26
	Female		0.93	1.03	1.21	1.06

Source: Rates and ratios calculated by the author from U.S. Bureau of the Census, Census of Population: 1970, Volume 1. Characteristics of the Population—Part 1. United States Summary. Section 2. U.S. Government Printing Office, Washington, D.C. 1973, Table 203; and U.S. Department of Health, Education, and Welfare. *Utilization of Short-Stay Hospitals: Summary of Non-Medical Statistics*, United States, 1970. Vital and Health Statistics, Series 13, No. 14, 1973, Table 17.

Issues of Method

In evaluating the data that have been presented one of the first questions that arises concerns their validity. That is, how accurately do they represent the true character of sex differences in mortality, morbidity, and medical care. Two issues of methodology that bear particularly on the question of validity are, first, the selection of health indices and, secondly, the procedures that are employed for collection of data.

Selection of Health Indices

As indicated earlier, mortality data are based on information recorded at the time of death and coded using a system of classification common to all developed countries. Experts in mortality statistics agree, however, as to the existence of differences in recording procedures both between countries and even among physicians within the same country [8, 45]. "What goes on the death certificate will be influenced by the health habits of the population, the stage of illness at which medical care is sought, the system of medical care and the training of its personnel, and even the legal structure" [8: 51]. The opportunity for the sex of the deceased to affect recording procedures clearly exists, although the author is unaware of any data bearing directly on this point. There is some evidence, however, that the patient's sex is a factor both in the diagnosis of disease and in its treatment [6, 46, 56–64] and, consequently, might also be expected to influence the assignment of cause of death. Insofar as this influence is present, reported sex differences in mortality from specific causes will imperfectly reflect the true nature of these differences.

If mortality data may be affected by individuals' health behavior and by local systems of medical care, how much more will this be true of data purporting to measure morbidity. Almost all of the information available to us concerning the distribution of disease in populations is based not on clinically observable disease, but on the *behavior* of individuals, either as afflicted persons or as representatives of the health care system. Insofar as this behavior varies with the sex of the subject independently of the actual presence or absence of disease, then the data used to measure sex differences in disease will be measuring these behavioral differences instead. This problem is illustrated by the health indices employed in the British General Household Survey and the U.S. Health Interview Survey.

Both of these national surveys define chronic as well as acute illness on the basis of activity restriction, either restriction of the individual's *usual* activity or restriction of activity "compared with most people of your own age." The HIS also accepts medical attention as a criteria for the presence of acute illness. Sex differences in willingness, or ability, to restrict activities are commonly assumed to exist [65–68], although there is little concrete data to support this assumption. Ample evidence of sex differences in medical attention has been presented earlier in this paper. However, even if it is accepted that sexual status does influence morbidity reports based on behavioral indices, the direction of this influence is far from clear. In a study carried out by the U.S. National Center for Health Statistics [69] in which interview reports of chronic illness were matched with medical records, the *total* amount of overreporting of illness was found to be slightly higher among females than among males. However, among persons over 65, the "accuracy and completeness of reporting" was substantially greater among women than among men.

These brief comments have done little more than call attention to the fact that sexual status *may* independently influence reports of death and disease. More detailed description and analysis of this influence must wait upon further investigation.

Procedures of Data Collection

The procedures that are employed in data collection are of particular concern in the evaluation of health survey data, although "interviewer bias" may be present in any situation where information is obtained through personal interaction (e.g., between physician and patient). Biases in health survey data arising out of the relationship between interviewer and respondent have been documented by the U.S. National Center for Health Statistics [70]. However, little consideration has been given to bias specifically caused by the respective sexual statuses of these two parties to the health survey.

Employment as an interviewer for the HIS is limited to women because "the typical respondent, a housewife, is generally thought to be more willing to reveal health information to another woman than to a man" [71: 4]. Furthermore, HIS procedures allow interviewers to obtain information from a "related adult" if the intended respondent is not at home and, indeed, 80 percent of HIS respondents are women. Consequently, the bulk of HIS information concerning *male* illness and use of health services is obtained by *women* from *women*! Proxy interviews generally understate the morbidity of the absent person, but this may be only one of many effects of these data collection procedures on the value of HIS data for comparing sex differences in health status.

Interviewers for the GHS are apparently also predominantly female. However, GHS procedures are much more strict with respect to the acceptance of proxy interviews and only 9 percent of GHS interviews were completed by proxy. The fact that a higher proportion of health information referring to men was obtained directly from male respondents may partially account for the lower male/female sex ratios found for most morbidity indices reported in GHS as compared with HIS data.

The methodological issues raised in this section of the paper create some uncertainty as to the exact meaning of various indices of health status that are commonly used. This uncertainty also gives rise to different causal interpretations of the myriad sex differences in mortality, morbidity, and medical care reported earlier in the paper. In the next section, four major classes of interpretation will be briefly considered.

Issues of Interpretation

In the introduction to this paper, it was pointed out that no single explanatory framework would be able to account for the variety of processes grouped together under the general heading of "sex differences in illness and medical care." The first problem that arises is to decide *what* is the dependent variable to be explained, for any particular set of observed sex differences may be the outcome of: (1) a real disease process; (2) behavior of the individual in response to real or perceived illness; (3) diagnostic and treatment practices of health care providers. In an empirical situation, of course, all three of these processes may be at work simultaneously, so that selection of a particular theoretical focus becomes partly a matter of the interests and orientation of the observer. Depending on this theoretical focus, one of four major explanatory frameworks may be employed to account for observed sex differences in health status. These differences have been attributed to: (1) biological differences between males and females; (2) differences in the social and/or psychological stress levels to which men and women are exposed; (3) differences in the characteristic behavior patterns or lifestyles of men and women; (4) institutionalized sex roles, leading to differential treatment of men and women by representatives of the health care system. It is seldom that all four alternatives are explicitly considered in any single piece of work. A single framework may be used to generate hypotheses, as, for example, in Gove's work on mortality differentials by marital status [42], or, more frequently, bits and pieces of one or more frameworks are employed in *ad hoc* fashion to account for isolated findings.

The Biological Framework

The crucial biological differences between males and females are genetic in origin. The female possesses two large X chromosomes, the male one X and a very much smaller Y. The X chromosome carries many genes in addition to those responsible for sex determination, giving the female "options for variability not open to the male" [72: 905]. This genetic difference has been held responsible for sex differences in infant mortality [72] as well as for greater male susceptibility to disease generally [73–77]. A genetic hypothesis appears to be consistent with the data on sex differences in mortality and morbidity among preschool age children, but the divergent paths assumed by these differences in older age groups suggest that other factors come quickly into play.

In addition to genetic makeup, males and females also differ in their hormonal balance and, among women, this balance changes markedly with age. Hormonal factors have been postulated to explain both low rates of coronary heart disease among women prior to the menopause [78] and low susceptibility to certain cancers following the menopause [79]. Neither of these hypotheses has been confirmed, and, indeed, Moriyama, Krueger, and Stamler state that the coronary heart disease hypothesis "finds no specific support in mortality data" [78: 116]. Arguing in more general terms, several recently published analyses of sex differences in mortality have concluded that the sharp increases in these differences observed in recent decades cannot be explained by biological factors [10, 12, 13].

In the past, and today in many less developed countries, the biological process of reproduction played a major role in mortality among women of childbearing age. While this is no longer true in the developed countries, women in this age group, and particularly married women, remain high users of health services. Furthermore, much of this excess use appears to be accounted for by disorders of the reproductive system. To what extent these findings can be explained by biological processes, and to what extent by women's unique social roles, or even by the behavior of their medical advisors, is by no means clear.

The Stress Framework

The concept of stress, here defined as the exposure of the individual to conflicting or ambiguous expectations for his behavior, has been explored in some depth with the aim of identifying its role in the etiology of disease [80, 81]. Differences in levels of conflict and ambiguity associated with male, as compared with female sex role expectations, have been hypothesized and advanced as possible explanations of certain sex *differences* in disease rates [3, 13, 82, 83]. Or, in other studies lacking an explicit comparative framework, the peculiar vulnerability of one sex has been attributed to stress generated by problems in the fulfillment of sex role expectations [84–86]. There is no consensus among the investigators whose work has been cited as to *which* sex experiences the greatest stress, and, indeed, the answer to this question will undoubtedly vary depending on other dimensions of the social situation. For this reason, the stress framework is unlikely to prove fruitful as a *general* explanation for patterns of sex differences in death and disease.

Recent work [10, 13] employing a variety of arguments, has rejected the differential stress explanation for increases in male mortality during the last century and has strongly suggested that sex differences in cigarette smoking are *the* major explanatory variable. The potentially lethal consequences of many sex-linked patterns of behavior, including cigarette smoking, are highlighted by data on sex differences in mortality from specific causes reviewed earlier in this paper. While sociologists have devoted considerable attention to the role of stress in disease, these sex-linked behavior patterns have been relatively neglected. It is to a consideration of these patterns that we turn next.

The Lifestyle Framework

Not only is sex universally employed as a basis for the ascription of social status, but "all societies prescribe different attitudes and activities to men and to women" [1: 116]. One rarely considered dimension of these attitudes and activities is the degree to which they protect the individual against insults to his biological or psychological integrity, on the one hand, or threaten this integrity, on the other. There is some evidence for sex differences along this dimension, however [42, 87], and these differences constitute a third framework for the interpretation of variation among males and females in mortality, morbidity, and use of health services. This framework may be summarized in the form of two very general hypotheses: (1) Attitudes and activities prescribed for men in the countries of Europe and North America *both* expose them to high risk of mortality and morbidity *and* restrain them from "giving in" to illness by restricting their activities or making use of health services; (2) Attitudes and activities prescribed for women in these same countries *both* expose them to less risk directly *and* permit or encourage them to be more responsive to perceived illness.

Focusing on the problem of sex differences in mortality, Gove [42: 47] has listed three behavioral factors "creating different life chances for men and women." These are:

1. Social norms regulating appropriate behavior for men and women—it is socially more appropriate for men to smoke and drink;
2. Lifestyle differences, creating different risks of exposure to death and disease;
3. Modal personality differences—men are more aggressive and willing to take risks.

Gove's concern, of course, is to explain *mortality* among men. Excess morbidity and use of health services among women have also been attributed to sex differences in characteristic behavior patterns [2: 59]:

1. Women *report* more illness than men because it is culturally more acceptable for them to be ill—"the ethic of health is masculine";
2. The sick role is relatively compatible with women's other role responsibilities and incompatible with those of men.

In all of these five statements contrasting sex-linked patterns of behavior, the attitudes and activities ascribed to men are less self-protective than those ascribed to women.

Men do have higher mortality from conditions where risk-taking is an important factor, and women do make more use of both preventive and curative health services. Furthermore, these differences are most pronounced during that portion of the life cycle when sex differences in expected behavior are also likely to be most profound. However, much more work is needed to develop this framework and, particularly, to find measures of the "protective" dimension of behavior that are independent of the sex differences in health status this dimension purports to explain.

The Institutionalized Sex Role Framework

Sex differences in illness, in diagnosis, and in medical treatment have been attributed to variations in the behavior and attitudes of medical practitioners toward their male and female patients [6, 46, 56–64]. Much of this literature appears to have been stimulated by feminist concern for the exploitation of women by physicians and, consequently, tends to focus on women's health problems rather than on sex differences directly.

Based on analysis of historical materials, primarily from 19th century American sources, several authors have suggested that physicians' diagnostic and treatment practices have the aim of reinforcing traditional sex role definitions and particularly of establishing masculine control over the female sex [46, 59, 60, 62]. In the 19th century, this effort took the form of attributing a large proportion of illness in women to disorders of the reproductive system and treating the patient accordingly. Contemporary physicians are similarly accused of arbitrarily defining women's complaints as psychosomatic [61, 64] and using mood-modifying drugs, as they earlier used gynecological surgery, to calm their unruly patients [58, 59, 88].

It is a plausible hypothesis that observed sex differences in morbidity and use of health services are influenced by physician as well as by patient behavior. Physicians prescribe drugs, recommend surgery, and hospitalize their patients—and all of these actions are directed more frequently toward women than toward men. However, there are no well-designed studies in which the relative influence of physician and patient on diagnostic and treatment outcomes is directly compared and related to variations in sex role expectations. Furthermore, the attention of investigators using the institutionalized sex roles framework has been directed toward women, as noted earlier. There has been no comparable effort to determine how sex role expectations may affect the definition and treatment of complaints presented by men, so it is difficult to evaluate the extent to which women's experience is unique. Thus, while the hypothesis of medical practitioner influence on reported sex differences in health status is both intriguing and important, it has so far received very little systematic support.

Summary and Directions for Future Research

The purpose of this paper has been to summarize current knowledge concerning sex differences in mortality, morbidity, and use of health services and to indicate a few of the methodological and interpretive problems that are presented by these data. The limitations of this review both in scope and in breadth of focus have already been noted. In trying to cover the most important points, many interesting, but isolated, findings have not been reported. Furthermore, the data are not as international in scope as the author would have preferred.

With these limitations in mind, the principal points of the review may be briefly recapitulated. In all developed countries, male mortality rates are higher than the rates of females, but in all countries for which data are available, women report more acute illness than men and make greater use of health services. Within the framework set by this broad pattern, there are systematic variations in the direction and magnitude of sex differences by cause of death and disease, by age, and by marital status. These variations suggest that the social and psychological concomitants of gender identity play a major role in accounting for observed sex differences in health status. Several alternative interpretations of this role have been advanced and are outlined in this review.

Between the wealth of statistical data on sex differences in disease and the limited, often casual efforts at interpretation of these data, there is a profound gap of both theory and method. This gap is due partly to the relative inaccessibility to social scientists of data frequently buried in administrative reports and partly to a lack of sustained and self-conscious attention to these data from a sociological perspective. Consequently, although the broad pattern of sex differences is reasonably clear, there have been very few detailed analyses, either of this pattern itself or of the underlying processes by which it is generated. Currently, the most important tasks of investigators interested in sex differences in disease and medical treatment are, first, to focus on the answering of specific questions defined so that the answers are relevant to an underlying theoretical framework, and secondly, to encourage the collection of strictly comparable morbidity and utilization data in a variety of countries, using the same health indices. While the collection of statistics and their tabulation by sex will doubtless continue, this effort needs to be supplemented and informed by more careful attention to the meaning of these statistics. The choice of specific questions to which future research attention might be directed is partly a matter of personal preference. However, certain issues appear to the author to have particular importance, and it is to these issues that the following remarks are addressed.

There is, in the first place, a clear need for further refinement and clarification of the health indices that are currently employed. In the absence of information concerning the relative contribution of biological, psychological, and social processes to reported disease rates, it is difficult to know whether research in the area of sex differences should focus primarily on illness itself, on illness behavior, or on the behavior of medical practitioners. Secondly, in order to move beyond the description of sex differences to the explanation of these differences, the focus of research should be on the study of deliberately selected variations both in sex-linked behavior patterns and in illness and utilization patterns. For example, while it is clear that marital status is associated with substantial variation in patterns of illness and illness behavior among both men and women, the basis or bases of these variations have not been determined. Further clarification of this issue requires, as a first step, isolation of the specific social and/or biological variables for which marital status is an index and, secondly, examination of the consequences of differences in these underlying variables for mortality, morbidity, and use of health services.

Variation by marital status is only one of several types of variation in the overall pattern of sex differences that are highlighted by this review. Understanding of the overall pattern will be most rapidly advanced by research that is focused on specific variations, selected either on a theoretical basis, in order to test the value of one or more interpretive frameworks, or because they present a particular empirical problem that demands solution.

References

1. Linton, R. *The study of man.* New York: Appleton-Century, 1936.
2. Nathanson, C. A. Illness and the feminine role: A theoretical review. *9 (57)* 1975.
3. Gove, W. R., & Tudor, J. Adult sex roles and mental illness. *American Journal of Sociology 78 (812)* 1973.
4. Philips, D. L., & Segal, B. E. Sexual status and psychiatric symptoms. *American Sociological Review 34 (58)* 1969.
5. Broverman, I. K., et al. Sex role stereotypes and clinical judgements of mental health. *Journal of Consulting Clinical Psychology 34 (1)* 1970.
6. Cheek, F. E. A serendipitous finding: Sex roles and schizophrenia. *Journal of Abnormal Social Psychology 69 (392)* 1964.
7. Dohrenwend, B. P., & Dohrenwend, B. S. *Social status and psychological disorder: A casual inquiry.* New York: Wiley, 1969.
8. Spiegelman, M., & Erhardt, C. L. International comparisons of mortality and longevity. In C. L. Erhardt & J. E. Berlin (Eds.) *Mortality and morbidity in the United States.* Cambridge, Mass.: Harvard University Press, 1974, pp. 39–64.
9. Fuchs, V. R. *Who shall live? Health, economics, and social choice.* New York: Basic Books, 1975.
10. Retherford, R. D. *The changing sex differential in mortality.* International Population and Urban Research, University of California, Berkeley. Studies in Population and Urban Demography No. 1. Westport, Conn.: Greenwood Press, 1975.
11. Madigan, F. C. Are sex mortality differentials biologically caused? *Milbank Memorial Fund Quarterly 21 (202)* 1957.

12. Enterline, P. E. Causes of death responsible for recent increases in sex mortality differentials in the United States. *Milbank Memorial Fund Quarterly 38 (313)* 1961.
13. Preston, S. H. An international comparison of excessive adult mortality. *Population Studies 24 (5)* 1970.
14. Fairfield, L. Health of professional women. *The Medical Woman's Journal 34* (95) 1927.
15. Avnet, H. H. *Physician service patterns and illness rates.* Group Health Insurance, Inc., 1967.
16. Anderson, O. W., & Andersen, R. Patterns of use of health services. In H. E. Freeman, et al. (Eds.) *Handbook of medical sociology.* Englewood Cliffs, N.J.: Prentice-Hall, 1972, pp. 386–406.
17. Cole, P. Morbidity in the United States. In C. L. Erhardt & J. E. Berlin (Eds.) *Mortality and morbidity in the United States. Cambridge, Mass.: Harvard University Press, 1974, pp. 65*–104.
18. Verbrugge, L. M. Morbidity and mortality in the United States. Unpublished paper. Department of Social Relations and Center for Metropolitan Planning and Research, Johns Hopkins University, Baltimore, 1975.
19. Office of Population Censuses and Surveys, Social Survey Division. *The General Household Survey: Introductory report.* London: H.M.S.O., 1973.
20. U.S. Department of Health, Education, and Welfare. *Current estimates from the health interview survey, United States, 1971.* Vital and Health Statistics, Series 10, No. 79.
21. White, K. L., et al. Ecologic results. In D. L. Rabin (Ed.) International Comparisons of Medical Care. *Milbank Memorial Fund Quarterly 50 (1)* 1972: 31–44.
22. Shuval, J. T., et al. *Social functions of medical practice.* San Francisco: Jossey-Bass, 1970.
23. Nyman, K., & Kalimo, E. National sickness insurance and the use of physicians' services in Finland. *Social Science and Medicine 7 (541)* 1973.
24. Densen, P. M., et al. Concerning high and low utilizers of services on a medical care plan and the persistence of utilization levels over a three-year period. *Milbank Memorial Fund Quarterly 37 (217)* 1959.
25. Kessel, N., & Shepard, M. The health and attitudes of people who seldom consult a doctor. *Medical Care 3 (6)* 1965.
26. Solon, J. Patterns of medical care: Sociocultural variations among a hospital's outpatients. *American Journal of Public Health 55 (884)* 1966.
27. Andersen, R., & Anderson, O. W. *A decade of health services.* Chicago: University of Chicago Press, 1967.
28. U.S. Public Health Service. Population characteristics and participation in the poliomyelitis vaccination program. *PHS* No. 723. Washington, D.C.: U.S. Government Printing Office, 1969.
29. Foster, A., et al. Use of health services in relation to the physical home environment of an Indian population. *Public Health Reports 88 (715)* 1973.
30. Suchman, E. Social patterns of illness and medical care. *Journal of health and human behavior 6 (2)* 1965.
31. Feldman, J. J. *The dissemination of health information.* Chicago: Aldine, 1966.
32. Lerner, M. *Hospital use by diagnosis.* Research Series No. 19, Center for Health Administration Studies, University of Chicago, 1961.

33. U.S. Department of Health, Education, and Welfare. *Inpatient utilization of short-stay hospitals by diagnosis, United States 1968.* Vital and Health Statistics, Series 13, No. 12, 1973.
34. Statistics Canada. *Hospital morbidity.* Ottawa, 1971.
35. Boucher, L. *Canadian women: Their vital and health statistics.* Health Division, Statistics Canada, Ottawa, 1975.
36. U.S. Department of Health, Education, and Welfare. *Surgical operations in short-stay hospitals, United States, 1968.* Vital and Health Statistics, Series 13, No. 11, 1973.
37. U.S. Department of Health, Education, and Welfare. *Average length of stay in short-stay hospitals: Demographic factors, United States, 1968.* Vital and Health Statistics, Series 13, No. 13, 1973.
38. Feldstein, P. J. Research on the demand for health services. *Milbank Memorial Fund Quarterly 44 (128)* 1966.
39. Dunnell, K., & Cartwright, A. *Medicine takers, prescribers, and hoarders.* London: Routledge & Kegan Paul, 1972.
40. Levine, J. The nature and extent of psychotropic drug usage in the United States. Washington, D.C.: Statement before the Subcommittee on Monopoly of the Selected Committee on Small Business. 9 1969.
41. U.S. Department of Health, Education, and Welfare. *Prescribed and nonprescribed medicines. Type and use of medicines, United States, July 1964–June 1965.* Vital and Health Statistics, Series 10, No. 39, 1967.
42. Gove, W. R. Sex, marital status, and mortality. *American Journal of Sociology 79 (45)* 1973.
43. World Health Organization. II. Special subject. Morbidity statistics: Hospital in-patients, 1964. *World Health Statistics Report 21* 1968.
44. World Health Organization. II. Special subject. Morbidity statistics: Hospital in-patients, 1964. *World Health Statistics Report 24* 1971.
45. World Health Organization. II. Special subject. Children of school age and their mortality and hospital morbidity throughout the world. *World Health Statistics 28* 1975.
46. Smith-Rosenberg, C., & Rosenberg, C. The female animal: Medical and biological views of woman and her role in nineteenth century America. *Journal of American History 60 (332)* 1973.
47. U.S. Department of Health, Education, and Welfare. *Limitation of activity due to chronic conditions, United States, 1969 and 1970.* Vital and Health Statistics, Series 10, No. 80, 1973.
48. Passman, M. J. Hospital utilization by Blue Cross members in 1964 according to selected demographic and enrollment characteristics. *Inquiry 3 (82)* 1966.
49. Berkman, P. L. Spouseless motherhood, psychological stress, and physical morbidity. *Journal of Health and Social Behavior 10 (323)* 1969.
50. Rivkin, M. O. Contextual effects of families on female responses to illness. Unpublished Ph.D. dissertation. Johns Hopkins University, Baltimore, 1972.
51. Ortmeyer, C. E. Variations in mortality, morbidity, and health care by marital status. In C. L. Erhardt & J. E. Berlin (Eds.) *Mortality and morbidity in the United States.* Cambridge, Mass.: Harvard University Press, 1974, pp. 159–88.
52. Renne, K. S. Health and marital experience in an urban population. *Journal of Marriage and the Family 33 (337)* 1971.

53. Gove, W. R. The relationship between sex roles, marital status, and mental illness. *Social Forces 51 (34)* 1972.
54. Durkheim, E. *Suicide.* Glencoe, Ill.: Free Press, 1951.
55. U.S. Department of Health, Education, and Welfare. *Physician visits, volume, and interval since last visit—United States, 1971.* Vital and Health Statistics, Series 10, No. 97, 1975.
56. Gross, H. S., et al. The effect of race and sex on the variation of diagnosis and disposition in a psychiatric emergency room. *Journal of Nervous Mental Disorders 148 (638)* 1969.
57. Singer, B. S., & Osborn, R. W. Social class and sex differences in admission patterns of the mentally retarded. *American Journal of Mental Deficiency 75 (160)* 1970.
58. Cooperstock, R. Sex differences in the use of mood-modifying drugs: An explanatory model. *Journal of Health and Social Behavior 12 (238)*1971.
59. Barker-Benfield, B. The spermatic economy: A nineteenth century view of sexuality. *Feminist Studies 1 (45)* 1972.
60. Smith-Rosenberg, C. The hysterical woman: Sex roles and role conflict in nineteenth century America. *Social Research 38 (652)* 1972.
61. Lennane, K. J., & Lennane, R. J. Alleged psychogenic disorders in women—A possible manifestation of sexual prejudice. *New England Journal of Medicine 288 (288)* 1973.
62. Wood, A. D. The fashionable diseases: Women's complaints and their treatment in nineteenth century America. *Journal of Interdisciplinary History 4 (25)* 1973.
63. Ehrenreich, B., & English, D. Complaints and disorders: The sexual politics of sickness. *Glass Mountain Pamphlet 2.* Old Westbury, N.Y.: The Feminist Press, 1973.
64. Ehrenreich, B. Gender and objectivity in medicine. *International Journal of Health Services 4 (617)* 1974.
65. Barker, R. G., et al. *Adjustment to physical handicap and illness.* New York: Social Science Research Council, 1953.
66. Mechanic, D. Perception of parental responses to illness: A research note. *Journal of Health and Human Behavior 6 (253)* 1965.
67. Glaser, W. A. *Social settings and medical organization.* New York: Atherton, 1970.
68. Parsons, T., & Fox, R. Illness, therapy, and the modern urban American family. *Journal of Social Issues 8 (31)* 1952.
69. U.S. Department of Health, Education, and Welfare. *Net differences in interview data on chronic conditions and information derived from medical records.* Vital and Health Statistics, Series 2, No. 57, 1973.
70. U.S. Department of Health, Education, and Welfare. *The influence of interviewer and respondent psychological and behavioral variables on the reporting in household interviews.* Vital and Health Statistics, Series 2, No. 26, 1968.
71. U.S. Department of Health, Education, and Welfare. *Quality control and measurement of nonsampling error in the health interview survey.* Vital and Health Statistics, Series 2, No. 54, 1973.
72. Naeye, R. L., et al. Neonatal mortality, the male disadvantage. *Pediatrics 48 (902)* 1971.

73. Hamburg, D. A., & Lunde, D. T. Sex hormones in the development of sex differences in human behavior. In E. E. Maccoby (Ed.) *The development of sex differences.* Stanford, Ca.: Stanford University Press, 1966, pp. 1–24.
74. Davidson, R. G. The Lyon hypothesis. *Journal of Pediatrics 65 (765)* 1964.
75. Washburn, T., Medearis, D., & Childs, B. Sex differences in susceptibility to infection. *Pediatrics 35 (37)* 1965.
76. Childs, B. Genetic origin of some sex differences among human beings. *Pediatrics 35 (57)* 1965.
77. Michaels, R. H., & Rogers, K. D. A sex difference in immunologic responsiveness. *Pediatrics 47 (120)* 1971.
78. Moriyama, I. M., Krueger, D. E., & Stamler, J. *Cardiovascular diseases in the United States.* Cambridge, Mass.: Harvard University Press, 1971.
79. Lilienfeld, A. M., Levin, M. L., & Kessler, I. I. *Cancer in the United States.* Cambridge, Mass.: Harvard University Press, 1972.
80. Cassell, J. Physical illness in response to stress. In S. Levine & N. A. Scotch (Eds.) *Social stress.* Chicago: Aldine, 1970.
81. Dodge, D. L., & Martin, W. T. *Social stress and chronic illness.* Notre Dame: University of Notre Dame Press, 1970.
82. Hinkle, L. E., Jr., & Wolff, H. G. Health and the social environment: Experimental investigations. In A. H. Leighton, et al. (Eds.) *Explorations in social psychiatry.* New York: Basic Books, 1957, pp. 105–37.
83. Nathanson, C. A., Rhyne, M. B. Social and cultural factors associated with asthmatic symptoms in children. *Social Science and Medicine 4 (293)* 1970.
84. Scotch, N. A. Sociocultural factors in the epidemiology of Zulu hypertension. *American Journal of Public Health 53 (1206)* 1963.
85. Wardwell, W. I., Bahnson, C. B., & Caron, H. S. Social and psychological factors in coronary heart disease. *Journal of Health and Human Behavior 4 (154)* 1963.
86. Wardwell, W. I., Hyman, M., & Bahnson, C. B. Stress and coronary heart disease in three field studies. *Journal of Chronic Disabilities 17 (73)* 1964.
87. Suchman, E. A. Accidents and deviance. *Journal of Health and Social Behavior 11 (4)* 1970.
88. Fidell, L., & Prather, J. Mood-modifying drug use in middle class women. Paper presented at the Western Psychological Association Meeting, Sacramento, Calif., April 25, 1975.

Culture and Symptoms—An Analysis of Patients' Presenting Complaints

IRVING KENNETH ZOLA

The Conception of Disease

In most epidemiological studies, the definition of disease is taken for granted. Yet today's chronic disorders do not lend themselves to such easy conceptualization and measurement as did the contagious disorders of yesteryear. That we have long assumed that what constitutes disease *is* a settled matter is due to the tremendous medical and surgical advances of the past half-century. After the current battles against cancer, heart disease, cystic fibrosis, and the like have been won, Utopia, a world without disease, would seem right around the next corner. Yet after each battle a new enemy seems to emerge. So often has this been the pattern that some have wondered whether life without disease is attainable.[1]

Usually the issue of life without disease has been dismissed as a philosophical problem—a dismissal made considerably easier by our general assumptions about the statistical distribution of disorder. For though there is a grudging recognition that each of us must go sometime, illness is generally assumed to be a relatively infrequent, unusual, or abnormal phenomenon. Moreover, the general kinds of statistics used to describe illness support such an assumption. Specifically diagnosed conditions, days out of work, and doctor visits do occur for each

---

From *American Sociological Review 31* 1966:615–30, Copyright 1966, American Sociological Association. Reprinted with permission.

1. Rene Dubos, *Mirage of Health,* Garden city, N. Y.: Anchor, 1961. On more philosophical grounds, W.A. White, in *The Meaning of Disease,* Baltimore: Williams and Wilkins, 1926, arrives at a similar conclusion.

of us relatively infrequently. Though such statistics represent only treated illness, we rarely question whether such data give a true picture. Implicit is the further notion that people who do not consult doctors and other medical agencies (and thus do not appear in the "illness" statistics) may be regarded as healthy.

Yet studies have increasingly appeared which note the large number of disorders escaping detection. Whether based on physicians' estimates[2] or on the recall of lay populations,[3] the proportion of untreated disorders amounts to two-thirds or three-fourths of all existing conditions.[4] The most reliable data, however, come from periodic health examinations and community "health" surveys.[5] At least two such studies have noted that as much as 90 percent of their apparently healthy sample had some physical aberration or clinical disorder.[6] Moreover, neither the type of disorder, nor the seriousness by objective medical standards, differentiated those who felt sick from those who did not. In one of the above studies, even of those who felt sick, only 40 percent were under medical care.[7] It seems that the more intensive the investigation, the higher the prevalence of clinically serious but previously undiagnosed and untreated disorders.

Such data as these give an unexpected statistical picture of illness. Instead

---

    2. R. J. F. H. Pinsett, *Morbidity Statistics from General Practice.* Studies of Medical Population, No. 14, London, H.M.S.O., 1962; P. Stocks, *Sickness in the Population of England and Wales, 1944–1947.* Studies of Medical Populations, No. 2, London, H.M.S.O., 1944; John Horder and Elizabeth Horder, "Illness in General Practice," *Practitioner 173* (August) 1954, pp. 177–85.

    3. Charles R. Hoffer and Edgar A. Schuler, Measurement of Health Needs and Health Care. *American Sociological Review 13* (December) 1948, pp. 719–24; Political and Economic Planning, *Family Needs and the Social Services.* George Allen and Unwin, Ltd., London, 1961; Leonard S. Rosenfeld, Jacob Katz and Avedis Donabedian, *Medical Care Needs and Services in the Boston Metropolitan Area.* Boston: Medical Care Evaluation Studies, Health, Hospitals, and Medical Care Division, United Community Services of Metropolitan Boston, 1957.

    4. That these high figures of disorder include a great many minor problems is largely irrelevant. The latter are nevertheless disorders, clinical entities, and may even be the precursors of more medically serious difficulties.

    5. See for example, Commission on Chronic Illness, *Chronic Illness in a Large City,* Cambridge: Harvard University Press, 1957; Kendall A. Elsom, Stanley Schor, Thomas W. Clark, Katherine O. Elsom, and John P. Hubbard, Periodic Health Examination—Nature and Distribution of Newly Discovered Disease in Executives. *Journal of the American Medical Association, 172* (January) 1960: 55–61; John W. Runyan, Jr., Periodic Health Maintenance Examination—I. Business Executives. *New York State Journal of Medicine 59* March 1959: 770–74; Robert E. Sandroni, Periodic Health Maintenance Examination—III. Industrial Employees, *New York State Journal of Medicine* 59 (March) 1959: 778–81; C. J. Tupper and M. B. Becket, Faculty Health Appraisal, University of Michigan. *Industrial Medicine and Surgery 27* (July) 1958: 328–32; Leo Wade, John Thorpe, Thomas Elias, and George Bock, Are Periodic Health Examinations Worth-While? *Annals of Internal Medicine 56* (January) 1962: 81–93. For questionnaire studies, see Paul B. Cornerly and Stanley K. Bigman, *Cultural Considerations in Changing Health Attitudes,* Department of Preventive Medicine and Public Health, College of Medicine, Howard University, Washington, D.C., 1961; and for more general summaries, J. Wister Meigs, Occupational Medicine. *New England Journal of Medicine 264* (April) 1961: 861–67; George S. Siegel, *Periodic Health Examinations—Abstracts from the Literature.* Public Health Service Publication No. 1010, Washington, D.C.: U.S. Government Printing Office, 1963.

    6. See Innes H. Pearse and Lucy H. Crocker, *The Peckham Experiment.* London: George Allen and Unwin, Ltd., 1949; *Biologists in Search of Material.* Interim Reports of the Work of the Pioneer Health Center, Peckham, London: Faber and Faber, 1938; Joseph E. Schenthal, Multiphasic Screening of the Well Patient. *Journal of the American Medical Association 172* (January) 1960: 51–64.

    7. See Innes H. Pearse and Lucy H. Crocker, *The Peckham Experiment.* London: George Allen and Unwin, Ltd., 1949; *Biologists in Search of Material.* Interim reports of the work of the Pioneer Health Center, Peckham, London: Faber and Faber, 1938; Joseph E. Schenthal, Multiphasic Screening of the Well Patient. *Journal of the American Medical Association 172* (January) 1970: 51–64.

of it being a relatively infrequent or abnormal phenomenon, the empirical reality may be that illness, defined as the presence of clinically serious symptoms, is the statistical *norm*.[8] What is particularly striking about this line of reasoning is that the statistical notions underlying many "social" pathologies are similarly being questioned. A number of social scientists have noted that the basic acts or deviations, such as law-breaking, addictive behaviors, sexual "perversions," or mental illness, occur so frequently in the population[9] that were one to tabulate all the deviations that people possess or engage in, virtually no one could escape the label of "deviant."

Why are so relatively few potential "deviants" labelled such or, more accurately, why do so few come to the attention of official agencies? Perhaps the focus on how or why a particular deviation arose in the first place might be misplaced; an equally important issue for research might be the individual and societal reaction to the deviation once it occurs.[10] Might it then be the differential response to deviation rather than the prevalence of the deviation which accounts for many reported group and subgroup differences? A similar set of questions can be asked in regard to physical illness. Given that the prevalence of clinical abnormalities is so high and the rate of acknowledgment so low, how representative are "the treated" of all those with a particular condition? Given further that what *is* treated seems unrelated to what would usually be thought the objective situation, i.e., seriousness, disability, and subjective discomfort, is it possible that some selective process is operating in what gets counted or tabulated as illness?

---

8. Consider the following computation of Hinkle et al. They noted that the average lower middle-class male between the ages of 20 and 45 experiences over a 20-year period approximately one life-endangering illness, 20 disabling illnesses, 200 nondisabling illnesses and 1,000 symptomatic episodes. These total 1,221 episodes over 7,305 days or one new episode every six days. And this figure takes no account of the duration of a particular condition, nor does it consider any disorder of which the respondent may be unaware. In short, even among a supposedly 'healthy' population scarcely a day goes by wherein they would not be able to report a symptomatic experience. Lawrence E. Hinkle, Jr., Ruth Redmont, Norman Plummer, and Harold G. Wolff, An Examination of the Relation between Symptoms, Disability, and Serious Illness in Two Homogeneous Groups of Men and Women. *American Journal of Public Health 50* (September) 1960: 1327–36.

9. See Fred J. Murphy, Mary M. Shirley, and Helen L. Witmer, The Incidence of Hidden Delinquency. *American Journal of Orthopsychiatry 16* (October) 1946: 686–96; Austin L. Porterfield, *Youth in Trouble*. Fort Worth: Leo Potishman Foundation, 1949; James F. Short and F. Ivan Nye, Extent of Unrecorded Delinquency, *Journal of Criminal Law, Criminology, and Police Science 49* (December) 1958: 296–302; James S. Wallerstein and Clement J. Wyle, Our Law-abiding Lawbreakers. *Probation 25* (April) 1947: 107–12; Alfred C. Kinsey, Wardell B. Pomeroy, and Clyde C. Martin, *Sexual Behavior in the Human Male*. Philadelphia: W. B. Saunders, 1953; Stanton Wheeler, Sex Offenses: A Sociological Critique. *Law and Contemporary Problems 25* (Spring) 1960: 258–78; Leo Srole, Thomas S. Langer, Stanley T. Michael, Marvin K. Opler, and Thomas A. C. Rennie, *Mental Health in the Metropolis*. New York: McGraw-Hill, 1962; Dorothea C. Leighton, John S. Harding, David B. Macklin, Allister M. MacMillan and Alexander H. Leighton, *The Character of Danger*. New York: Basic Books, Inc., 1963.

10. As seen in the work of: Howard S. Becker, *Outsiders*. Glencoe, Ill.: Free Press, 1963; Kai T. Erikson, Notes on the Sociology of Deviance. *Social Problems 9* (Spring) 1962: 307–14; Erving Goffman, *Stigma–Notes on the Management of Spoiled Identity*. Englewood Cliffs, N. J.: Prentice-Hall, 1963; Wendell Johnson, *Stuttering*. Minneapolis: University of Minnesota Press, 1961; John I. Kitsuse, Societal Reaction to Deviant Behavior: Problems of Theory and Method. In Howard S. Becker (Ed.) *The Other Side*. Glencoe, Ill.: Free Press, 1964, pp. 87–102; Edwin M. Lemert, *Social Pathology*. New York: McGraw-Hill, 1951; Thomas J. Scheff, The Societal Reaction to Deviance: Ascriptive Elements in the Psychiatric Screening of Mental Patients in a Midwestern State. *Social Problems 11* (Spring) 1964: 401–13.

44 Irving Kenneth Zola

The Interplay of Culture and "Symptoms"

Holding in abeyance the idea that many epidemiological differences may in fact be due to as yet undiscovered etiological forces, we may speculate on how such differences come to exist or how a selective process of attention may operate. Upon surveying many cross-cultural comparisons of morbidity, we concluded that there are at least two ways in which signs ordinarily defined as indicating problems in one population may be ignored in others.[11] The first is related to the actual prevalence of the sign, and the second to its congruence with dominant or major value-orientations.

In the first instance, when the aberration is fairly widespread, this, in itself, might constitute a reason for its not being considered "symptomatic" or unusual. Among many Mexican-Americans in the Southwestern United States, diarrhea, sweating, and coughing are everyday experiences,[12] while among certain groups of Greeks trachoma is almost universal.[13] Even within our own society, Koos has noted that, although lower back pain is a quite common condition among lower-class women, it is not considered symptomatic of any disease or disorder but part of their expected everyday existence.[14] For the population where the particular condition is ubiquitous, the condition is perceived as the normal state.[15] This does not mean that it is considered "good" (although instances have been noted where not having the endemic condition was considered abnormal)[16] but rather that it is natural and inevitable and thus to be ignored as being of no consequence. Because the "symptom" or condition is omnipresent (it always was and always will be), there simply exists for such populations or cultures no frame of reference according to which it could be considered a deviation.[17]

In the second process, it is the "fit" of certain signs with a society's major

11. Here we are dealing solely with factors influencing the perception of certain conditions as symptoms. A host of other factors influence a second stage in this process, i.e., once perceived as a symptom, what, if anything, is done. See, for example, Edward S. Suchman, Stages of Illness and Medical Care. *Journal of Health and Human Behavior* 6 (Fall) 1965: 114–28. Such mechanisms, by determining whether or not certain conditions are treated, would also affect their over- or under-representation in medical statistics.

12. Margaret Clark, *Health in the Mexican-American Culture*. Berkeley: University of California Press, 1958.

13. Richard H. Blum, *The Management of the Doctor-Patient Relationship*. New York: McGraw-Hill, 1960, p. 11.

14. Earl L. Koos, *The Health of Regionsville*. New York: Columbia University Press, 1954.

15. Erwin W. Ackerknecht, The Role of Medical History in Medical Education. *Bulletin of History of Medicine* 21 (March-April) 1947: 135–45; Allan B. Raper, The Incidence of Peptic Ulceration in Some African Tribal Groups. *Transactions of the Royal Society of Tropical Medicine and Hygiene* 152 (November) 1958: 535–46.

16. For example, Ackerknecht, op. cit. noted that pinto (dichromic spirochetosis), a skin disease, was so common among some South American tribes that the few single men who were not suffering from it were regarded as pathological to the degree of being excluded from marriage.

17. It is no doubt partly for this reason that many public health programs flounder when transported *in toto* to a foreign culture. In such a situation, when an outside authority comes in and labels a particularly highly prevalent condition a disease, and, as such, both abnormal and preventable, he is postulating an external standard of evaluation which, for the most part, is incomprehensible to the receiving culture. To them it simply has no cognitive reality.

values which accounts for the degree of attention they receive. For example, in some nonliterate societies there is anxiety-free acceptance of and willingness to describe hallucinatory experiences. Wallace noted that in such societies the fact of hallucination *per se* is seldom disturbing; its content is the focus of interest. In Western society, however, with its emphasis on rationality and control, the very admission of hallucinations is commonly taken to be a grave sign and, in some literature, regarded as the essential feature of psychosis.[18] In such instances it is not the sign itself or its frequency which is significant but the social context within which it occurs and within which it is perceived and understood. Even more explicit workings of this process can be seen in the interplay of "symptoms" and social roles. Tiredness, for example, is a physical sign which is not only ubiquitous but a correlate of a vast number of disorders. Yet amongst a group of the author's students who kept a calendar noting all bodily states and conditions, tiredness, though often recorded, was rarely cited as a cause for concern. Attending school and being among peers who stressed the importance of hard work and achievement, almost as an end in itself, tiredness, rather than being an indication of something being wrong, was instead positive proof that they were doing right. If they were tired, it must be because they had been working hard. In such a setting tiredness would rarely, in itself, be either a cause for concern, a symptom, or a reason for action or seeking medical aid.[19] On the other hand, where arduous work is not gratifying in and of itself, tiredness would more likely be a matter for concern and perhaps medical attention.[20]

Also illustrative of this process are the divergent perceptions of those bodily complaints often referred to as "female troubles."[21] Nausea is a common and treatable concomitant of pregnancy, yet Margaret Mead records no morning sickness among the Arapesh; her data suggest that this may be related to the almost complete denial that a child exists, until shortly before birth.[22] In a Christian setting, where the existence of life is dated from conception, nausea becomes the external sign, hope, and proof that one is pregnant. Thus in the United States, this symptom is not only quite widespread but is also an expected and almost welcome part of pregnancy. A quite similar phenomenon is the recognition of dysmenorrhea. While Arapesh women reported no pain during menstruation,

---

18. Anthony F. C. Wallace, Cultural Determinants of Response to Hallucinatory Experience. *Archives of General Psychiatry 1* (July) 1959: 58–69. With the increased use of LSD, psychodelics, and so forth, within our own culture such a statement might have to be qualified.

19. For the specific delineation of this process, I am grateful to Barbara L. Carter, Non-Physiological Dimensions of Health and Illness. Brandeis University, Waltham, 1965.

20. Dr. John D. Stoeckle, in a personal communication, has noted that such a problem is often the presenting complaint of the "trapped housewife" syndrome. For detail on the latter see Betty Friedan, *The Feminine Mystique.* New York: Dell, 1963; and Richard E. Gordon, Katherine K. Gordon, and Max Gunther, *The Split-Level Trap.* New York: Dell, 1962. We realize, of course, that tiredness here might be more related to depression than any degree of physical exertion. But this does not alter how it is perceived and reacted to once it occurs.

21. This section on 'female troubles' was suggested by the following readings: Simone de Beauvoir, *The Second Sex.* New York: Knopf, 1957; Helene Deutsch, *The Psychology of Women.* New York: Grune and Stratton, 1944; and Margaret Mead, *Male and Female,* New York: Morrow, 1949.

22. Margaret Mead, *Sex and Temperament in Three Primitive Societies.* New York: Mentor, 1950.

quite the contrary is reported in the United States.[23] Interestingly enough the only consistent factor related to its manifestation among American women was a learning one—those that manifested it reported having observed it in other women during their childhood.[24]

From such examples as these, it seems likely that the degree of recognition and treatment of certain gynecological problems may be traced to the prevailing definition of what constitutes "the necessary part of the business of being a woman."[25] That such divergent definitions are still operative is shown by two recent studies. In the first, 78 mothers of lower socioeconomic status were required to keep health calendars over a four-week period. Despite the instruction to report *all* bodily states and dysfunctions, only 14 noted even the occurrence of menses or its accompaniments.[26] A second study, done on a higher socioeconomic group, yielded a different expression of the same phenomenon. Over a period of several years the author collected four-week health calendars from students. The women in the sample had at least a college education and virtually all were committed to careers in the behavioral sciences. Within this group there was little failure to report menses; very often medication was taken for the discomforts of dysmenorrhea. Moreover, this group was so psychologically sophisticated or self-conscious that they interpreted or questioned most physical signs or symptoms as attributable to some psychosocial stress. There was only one exception—dysmenorrhea. Thus even in this "culturally advantaged" group, this seemed a sign of a bodily condition so ingrained in what one psychiatrist has called "the masochistic character of her sex" that the woman does not ordinarily subject it to analysis.

In the opening section of this paper, we presented evidence that a selective process might well be operating in what symptoms are brought to the doctor. We also noted that it might be this selective process and not an etiological one which accounts for the many unexplained or overexplained epidemiological differences

---

23. Mead, *Sex and Temperment in Three Primitive Societies.* New York: Mentor, 1950. As far as the Arapesh are concerned, Mead does note that this lack of perception may be related to the considerable self-induced discomfort prescribed for women during menstruation.

24. Reported in Mead, ibid. The fact that one has to learn that something is painful or unpleasant has been noted elsewhere. Mead reports that in causalgia a given individual suffers and reports pain because she is *aware* of uterine contractions and not because of the occurrence of these contractions. Becker, op. cit., 1963, and others studying addictive behaviors have noted not only that an individual has to learn that the experience is pleasurable but also that a key factor in becoming addicted is the recognition of the association of withdrawal symptoms with the lack of drugs. Among medical patients who had been heavily dosed and then withdrawn, even though they experience symptoms as a result of withdrawal, they may attribute them to their general convalescent aches and pains. Stanley Schacter and Jerome Singer, Cognitive, Social, and Physiological Determinants of Emotional State. *Psychological Review 69* (September) 1962: 379–87, have recently reported a series of experiments where epinephrine-injected subjects defined their mood as euphoria or anger depending on whether they spent time with a euphoric or angry stooge. Subjects without injections reported no such change in mood responding to these same social situations. This led them to the contention that the diversity of human emotional experiences stems from differential labelling of similar physical sensations.

25. A term used by Drs. R. Green and K. Dalton, as quoted in Hans Selye, *The Stress of Life.* New York: McGraw-Hill, 1956, p. 177.

26. John Kosa, Joel Alpert, M. Ruth Pickering, and Robert J. Haggerty, Crisis and Family Life: A Re-Examination of Concepts. *The Wisconsin Sociologist 4* (Summer) 1965: 11–19.

observed between and within societies.[27] (There may even be no "real" differences in the prevalence rates of many deviations.[28]) Such selective processes are probably present at all the stages through which an individual and his condition must pass before he ultimately gets counted as "ill." In this section we have focused on one of these stages, the perception of a particular bodily state as a symptom, and have delineated two possible ways in which the culture or social setting might influence the awareness of something as abnormal and thus its eventual tabulation in medical statistics.

Sample Selection and Methodology

The investigation to be reported here is not an attempt to prove that the foregoing body of reasoning is correct but rather to demonstrate the fruitfulness of the orientation in understanding the problems of health and illness. This study reports the existence of a selective process in what the patient "brings" to a doctor. The selectiveness is analyzed not in terms of differences in diseases but rather in terms of differences in responses to essentially similar disease entities.

Specifically, this paper is a documentation of the influence of "culture" (in this case ethnic—group membership) on "symptoms" (the complaints a patient presents to his physician). The measure of "culture" was fairly straightforward. The importance of ethnic groups in Boston, where the study was done, has been repeatedly documented;[29] ethnicity seemed a reasonable urban counterpart of the cultures so often referred to in the previous pages. The sample was drawn from the outpatient clinics of the Massachusetts General Hospital and the Massachusetts Eye and Ear Infirmary; it was limited to those new patients of both sexes between 18 and 50 who were white, able to converse in English, and of

---

27. For example, Saxon Graham, Ethnic Background and Illness in a Pennsylvania County. *Social Problems 4* (July) 1956: 76–81, noted a significantly higher incidence of hernia among men whose backgrounds were Southern European (Italy or Greece) as compared with Eastern European (Austria, Czechoslovakia, Russia or Poland). Analysis of the occupations engaged in by these groups revealed no evidence that the Southern Europeans in the sample were more engaged in strenuous physical labor than the Eastern Europeans. From what is known of tolerance to hernia, we suggest that, for large segments of the population, there may be no differences in the actual incidence and prevalence of hernia but that in different groups different perceptions of the same physical signs may lead to dissimilar ways of handling them. Thus the Southern Europeans in Graham's sample may have been more concerned with problems in this area of the body, and have sought aid more readily (and therefore appear more frequently in the morbidity statistics). Perhaps the Southern Europeans are acting quite rationally and consistently while the other groups are so threatened or ashamed that they tend to deny or mask such symptoms and thus keep themselves out of the morbidity statistics.

28. In studying the rates of peptic ulcer among African tribal groups Raper, op. cit., first confirmed the stereotype that it was relatively infrequent among such groups and therefore that it was associated (as many had claimed) with the stresses and strains of modern living. Yet when he relied not on reported diagnosis but on autopsy data, he found that the scars of peptic ulcer were no less common than in Britain. He concluded: "There is no need to assume that in backward communities peptic ulcer does not develop; it is only more likely to go undetected because the conditions that might bring it to notice do not exist."

29. Oscar Handlin, *Race and Nationality in American Life.* New York: Garden City, Doubleday, 1957; Oscar Handlin, *Boston's Immigrants.* Cambridge: Harvard University Press, 1959.

either Irish Catholic, Italian Catholic, or Anglo-Saxon Protestant background.[30] These were the most numerous ethnic groups in the clinics; together they constituted approximately 50 percent of all patients. The actual interviewing took place at the three clinics to which these patients were most frequently assigned (the three largest outpatient clinics): the Eye Clinic, the Ear, Nose and Throat Clinic, and the Medical Clinic.

In previous research the specific method of measuring and studying symptoms has varied among case record analysis, symptom checklists, and interviews. The data have been either retrospective or projective, that is, requesting the subject either to recall symptoms experienced during a specific time period or to choose symptoms which would bother him sufficiently to seek medical aid.[31] Such procedures do not provide data on the complaints which people actually bring to a doctor, a fact of particular importance in light of the many investigations pointing to the lack of, and distortions in, recall of sickness episodes.[32] An equally serious problem is the effect of what the doctor, medicineman, or health expert may tell the patient on the latter's subsequent perceptions of and recall about his ailment.[33] We resolved these problems by restricting the sample to new patients on their first medical visit to the clinics and by interviewing them during the waiting period *before* they were seen by a physician.[34]

The primary method of data collection was a focused open-ended interview dealing with the patient's own or family's responses to his presenting complaints. Interspersed throughout the interview were a number of more objective measures of the patient's responses—checklists, forced-choice comparisons, attitudinal items, and scales. Other information included a demographic background ques-

---

30. Ethnicity was ascertained by the responses to several questions: what the patients considered their nationality to be; the birthplaces of themselves, their parents, their maternal and paternal grandparents; and, if the answers to all of these were American, they were also asked whence their ancestors originated. For details, see Irving Kenneth Zola, *Sociocultural Factors in the Seeking of Medical Aid.* Unpublished doctoral dissertation, Harvard University, Department of Social Relations, 1962.

31. The range of methods includes: case research analysis—Berta Fantl and Joseph Schiro, Cultural Variables in the Behavior Patterns and Symptom Formation of 15 Irish and 15 Italian Female Schizophrenics. *International Journal of Social Psychiatry 4* (Spring) 1959: 245–53; check lists—Cornerly and Bigman, op. cit.; standardized questionnaires—Sydney H. Croog, Ethnic Origins and Responses to Health Questionnaires. *Human Organization 20* (Summer) 1961: 65–69; commitment papers—John B. Enright and Walter R. Jaeckle, Psychiatric Symptoms and Diagnosis in Two Subcultures. *International Journal of Social Psychiatry 9* (Winter) 1963: 12–17; interview and questionnaire—Graham, op. cit.; Mark Zborowski, Cultural Components in Response to Pain. *Journal of Social Issues 8* (Fall) 1952: 16–30; interview and psychological tests—Marvin K. Opler and Jerome L. Singer, Ethnic Differences in Behavior and Psychopathology: Italian and Irish. *International Journal of Social Psychiatry 2* (Summer) 1956: 11–12; observation—Clark, op. cit.; and Lyle Saunders, op. cit.

32. See Jacob J. Feldman, The Household Interview Survey as a Technique for the Collection of Morbidity Data. *Journal of Chronic Diseases 11* (May) 1960: 535–57; Theodore D. Woolsey, The Health Survey. Presented at the session, "The Contributions of Research in the Field of Health," 1959 AAPOR Conference, May, 1959, Lake George, New York.

33. Charles Kadushin, The Meaning of Presenting Problems: A Sociology of Defenses. Paper read at the 1962 annual meeting of the American Sociological Association.

34. This particular methodological choice was also determined by the nature of the larger study, that is, how patients decided to seek medical aid, where the above mentioned problems loom even larger. While only new admissions were studied, a number of patients had been referred by another medical person. Subsequent statistical analysis revealed no important differences between this group and those for whom the Massachusetts General Hospital or the Massachusetts Eye and Ear Infirmary were the initial source of help.

tionnaire, a review of the medical record, and a series of ratings by each patient's examining physician as to the primary diagnosis, the secondary diagnosis, the potential seriousness, and the degree of clinical urgency (i.e., the necessity that the patient be seen immediately) of the patient's presenting complaint.

The Patient and His Illness

The data are based on a comparison between 63 Italians (34 female, 29 male) and 81 Irish (42 female, 39 male), who were new admissions to the Eye, Ear, Nose, and Throat Clinic, and the Medical Clinics of the Massachusetts General Hospital and the Massachusetts Eye and Ear Infirmary, seen between July, 1960, and February 1961.[35] The mean age of each ethnic group (male and female computed separately) was approximately 33. While most patients were married, there was, in the sample, a higher proportion of single Irish men—a finding of other studies involving the Irish[36] and not unexpected from our knowledge of Irish family structure.[37] Most respondents had between 10 and 12 years of schooling, but only about 30 percent of the males claimed to have graduated from high school as compared with nearly 60 percent of the females. There were no significant differences on standard measures of social class, though in education, social class, occupation of the breadwinner in the patient's family, and occupation of the patient's father, the Irish ranked slightly higher.[38] The Italians were overwhelmingly American-born children of foreign parents: about 80 percent were second generation while 20 percent were third. Among the Irish about 40 percent were second generation, 30 percent third, and 30 percent fourth.

With regard to general medical coverage, there were no apparent differences between the ethnic groups. Approximately 62 percent of the sample had health insurance, a figure similar to the comparable economic group in the Rosenfeld survey of metropolitan Boston.[39] 60 percent had physicians whom they would call family doctors. The Irish tended more than the Italians to perceive themselves as having poor health, claiming more often they had been seriously ill in the past. This was consistent with their reporting of the most recent visit to a doctor: nine of the Irish but none of the Italians claimed to have had a recent major operation (e.g., appendectomy) or illness (e.g., pneumonia). Although

---

35. Forty-three Anglo-Saxons were also interviewed but are not considered in this analysis. They were dropped from this report because they differed from the Irish and Italians in various respects other than ethnicity: they included more students, more divorced and separated, more people living away from home, and more downwardly mobile; they were of higher socioeconomic and educational level, and a majority were fourth generation and beyond.

36. Opler and Singer, op. cit.

37. Conrad M. Arensberg and Solon T. Kimball, *Family and Community in Ireland*. Cambridge: Harvard University Press, 1948.

38. In Warner's terms (W. Lloyd Warner, *Social Class in America*. Chicago: Science Research Associates, 1949), the greatest number of patients was in Class V. Only a small proportion of new Irish and Italian patients were what might be traditionally labelled as charity cases, although by some criteria they were perhaps "medically indigent."

39. Rosenfeld, op. cit.

there were no differences in the actual seriousness of their present disorders (according to the doctor's ratings), there was a tendency for the examining physician to consider the Irish as being in more urgent need of treatment. It was apparent that the patients were not in the throes of an acute illness, although they may have been experiencing an acute episode. There was a slight tendency for the Irish, as a group, to have had their complaints longer. More significantly, the women of both groups claimed to have borne their symptoms for a longer time than the men.

In confining the study to three clinics, we were trying not only to economize but also to limit the range of illnesses. The latter was necessary for investigating differential responses to essentially similar conditions.[40] Yet at best this is only an approximate control. To resolve this difficulty, after all initial comparisons were made between the ethnic groups as a whole, the data were examined for a selected subsample with a specific control for diagnosis. This subsample consisted of matched pairs of one Irish and one Italian of the same sex who had the same primary diagnosis and whose disorder was of approximately the same duration and was rated by the examining physician as similar in degree of "seriousness." Where numbers made it feasible, there was a further matching on age, marital status, and education. In all, 37 diagnostically matched pairs (18 female and 19 male) were created; these constituted the final test of any finding of the differential response to illness.[41]

Table 3–1   Distribution of Irish and Italian
Clinic Admissions by Location
of Chief Complaint

Location of Complaint	Italian	Irish*
Eye, ear, nose, or throat	34	61
Other parts of the body	29	17
Total	63	78

Note: $\chi^2 = 9.31$, p <.01.
*Since three Irish patients (two women, one man) claimed to be asymptomatic, no location could be determined from their viewpoint.

40. This is similar to Zborowski's method, in his study of pain reactions, of confining his investigation to patients on certain specified wards. Op. cit.

41. These pairs included some 18 distinct diagnoses: conjunctivitis; eyelid disease (e.g., blepharitis); myopia; hyperopia; vitreous opacities; impacted cerumen; external otitis; otitis media; otosclerosis; deviated septum; sinusitis; nasopharyngitis; allergy; thyroid; obesity; functional complaints; no pathology; psychological problems.
   To give some indication of the statistical significance of these comparisons, a sign test was used. For the sign test, a "tie" occurs when it is not possible to discriminate between a matched pair on the variable under study, or when the two scores earned by any pair are equal. All tied cases were dropped from the analysis, and the probabilities were computed only on the total N's excluding ties. In our study there were many ties. In the nature of our hypotheses, as will appear subsequently, a tie means that at least one member of the pair was in the predicted direction. Despite this problem, the idea of a diagnostically-matched pair was retained because it seemed to convey the best available test of our data. Because there were specific predictions as to the direction of differences, the probabilities were computed on the basis of a one-tailed sign test. This was used to retest the findings of Tables 1–6. See Sidney Siegel, *Non-Parametric Statistics for the Behavioral Sciences.* New York: McGraw-Hill, 1956, pp. 68–75.

Location and Quality of Presenting Complaints

In the folklore of medical practice the supposed opening question is "Where does it hurt?" This query provides the starting point of our analysis—the perceived location of the patient's troubles. Our first finding is that more Irish than Italians tended to locate their chief problem in either the eye, the ear, the nose, or the throat (and more so for females than for males). The same tendency was evident when all patients were asked what they considered to be the most important part of their body and the one with which they would be most concerned if something went wrong. Here, too, significantly more Irish emphasized difficulties of the eye, the ear, the nose, or the throat. That this reflected merely a difference in the conditions for which they were seeking aid is doubtful since the two other parts of the body most frequently referred to were heart and "mind" locations, and these represent only 3 percent of the primary diagnoses of the entire sample. In the retesting of these findings on diagnostically matched pairs, while there were a great many ties, the general directions were still consistent.[42] Thus even when Italians had a diagnosed eye or ear disorder, they did not locate their chief complaints there, nor did they focus their future concern on these locations.

Table 3–2   Distribution of Irish and
Italian Clinic Admissions by
Part of the Body
Considered Most Important

Most Important Part of the Body	Italian	Irish
Eye, ear, nose, or throat	6	26
Other parts of the body	57	55
Total	63	81

Note: $\chi^2 = 10.50$, $p<.01$.

Pain, the commonest accompaniment of illness, was the dimension of patients' symptoms to which we next turned. Pain is an especially interesting phenomenon since there is considerable evidence that its tolerance and perception are not purely physiological responses and do not necessarily reflect the degree of objective discomfort induced by a particular disorder or experimental procedure.[43] In our study not only did the Irish more often than the Italians deny that pain was a feature of their illness but this difference held even for those

---

42. For the prediction that the Irish would locate their chief complaint in eye, ear, nose, or throat, and the Italians in some other part, 8 matched diagnostic pairs were in favor of the hypothesis, 1 against, 28 ties (p = .02); for the same with respect to most important part of the body there were 12 in favor of the hypothesis, 2 against, 23 ties (p = .006).

43. William P. Chapman and Chester M. Jones, Variations in Cutaneous and Visceral Pain Sensitivity in Normal Subjects, *Journal of Clinical Investigation 23* (January) 1944: 81–91; James D. Hardy, Harold G. Wolff, and Helen Goodell, *Pain Sensations and Reactions*. Baltimore: Williams and Wilkins, 1952; Ronald Melzack, The Perception of Pain. *Scientific American 204* (February) 1961: 41–49; Harry S. Olin and Thomas P. Hackett, The Denial of Chest Pain in 32 Patients with Acute Myocardial Infection. *Journal of the American Medical Association 190* (December) 1964: 977–81; Zborowski, op. cit.

patients with the same disorder.[44] When the Irish were asked directly about the presence of pain, some hedged their replies with qualifications. ("It was more a throbbing than a pain . . . not really pain, it feels more like sand in my eye.") Such comments indicated that the patients were reflecting something more than an objective reaction to their physical conditions.

Table 3-3   Distribution of Irish and Italian Clinic Admissions by Presence of Pain in Their Current Illness

Presence of Pain	Italian	Irish
No	27	54
Yes	36	27
Total	**63**	**81**

Note: $\chi^2 = 10.26$, p<.01.

While there were no marked differences in the length, frequency, or noticeability of their symptoms, a difference did emerge in the ways in which they described the quality of the physical difficulty embodied in their chief complaint. Two types of difficulty were distinguished: one was of a more limited nature and emphasized a circumscribed and specific dysfunctioning; the second emphasized a difficulty of a grosser and more diffuse quality.[45] When the patients' complaints were analyzed according to these two types, proportionately more Irish described their chief problem in terms of specific dysfunction while proportionately more Italians spoke of a diffuse difficulty. Once again, the findings for diagnostically matched pairs were in the predicted direction.[46]

Diffuse Versus Specific Reactions

What seems to emerge from the above is a picture of the Irish limiting and understating their difficulties and the Italians spreading and generalizing theirs. Two other pieces of information were consistent with this interpretation: first, an enumeration of the symptoms an individual presented—a phenomenon which might

---

44. For the prediction that Italians would admit the presence of pain and the Irish would deny it, 16 matched diagnostic pairs were in favor of the hypothesis, 0 against, 21 ties (p = .001).

45. Complaints of the first type emphasized a somewhat limited difficulty and dysfunction best exemplified by something specific, e.g., an organ having gone wrong in a particular way. The second type seemed to involve a more attenuated kind of problem whose location and scope were less determinate, and whose description was finally more qualitative and less measurable.

46. For the prediction that the Italians would emphasize a diffuse difficulty and the Irish a specific one; there were 10 diagnostically-matched pairs in favor, 0 against, 27 ties, (p = .001).

reflect how diffusely the complaint was perceived; second, the degree to which each patient felt his illness affected aspects of life other than purely physical behavior.

The first measure of this specific-diffuse dimension—number of distinguishable symptoms[47]—was examined in three ways: (1) the total number presented by each patient; (2) the total number of different bodily areas in which the patient indicated he had complaints, e.g., back, stomach, legs; (3) the total number of different qualities of physical difficulty embodied in the patient's presenting complaints.[48] The ethnic differences were consistent with the previous findings. Compared to the Irish, the Italians presented significantly more symptoms, had symptoms in significantly more bodily locations, and noted significantly more types of bodily dysfunction.[49]

Table 3–4 Distribution of Irish and Italian Clinic Admissions by Quality of Physical Difficulty Embodied in Chief Complaint

Quality of Physical Difficulty	Italian	Irish*
Problems of a diffuse nature	43	33
Problems of a specific nature	20	45
Total	63	78

Note: $\chi^2 = 9.44$, $p<.01$.
*Since three Irish patients (two women, one man) claimed to be asymptomatic, no rating of the quality of physical difficulty could be determined from their viewpoint.

The second analysis, the degree to which a patient felt his illness affected his more general well-being, was derived from replies to three questions: (1) Do you think your symptoms affected how you got along with your family? (2) Did you become more irritable? (3) What would you say has bothered you most

---

47. This number could be zero, as in a situation where the patient denied the presence of *any* difficulty, but others around him disagreed and so made the appointment for him or "forced" him to see a doctor.

48. Qualities of physical difficulty were categorized under nine headings.

49. The distributions for these two tables closely resemble those of Table 5 ($p = .018$ for bodily locations; $p = .003$ for types of bodily dysfunctions).

about your symptoms?[50] An admission of irritability scale was created by classifying an affirmative response to any of the three questions as an admission that the symptoms affected extra-physical performance. As seen in Table 3–6, the Irish were more likely than the Italians to state that their disorders had not affected them in this manner. Here again the asides by the Irish suggested that their larger number of negative responses by the Irish reflected considerable denial rather than a straightforward appraisal of their situation.

Table 3–5 Distribution of Irish and Italian Clinic Admissions by Number of Presenting Complaints

Number of Presenting Complaints	Italian	Irish
Zero	0	3
One	5	21
Two	15	22
Three	14	16
Four	10	7
Five	9	7
Six or more	10	5
Total	**63**	**81**

Note: $p < .001$.
The Mann-Whitney U-test was used. Probabilities were computed for one-tailed tests. They are, however, slightly "conservative"; with a correction for ties, the probabilities or levels of significance would have been even lower. See Siegel, Nonparametric Statistics for the Behavioral Sciences. New York: McGraw-Hill, 1956.

To examine these conclusions in a more rigorous manner, we turned to our subsample of matched diagnostic pairs. In general, the pattern and direction of the hypotheses were upheld.[51] Thus, even for the same diagnosis, the Italians expressed and complained of more symptoms, more bodily areas affected, and more kinds of dysfunctions than did the Irish, and more often felt that their symptoms affected their interpersonal behavior.

---

50. For the latter question, the patient was presented with a card on which were listed eight aspects of illness and/or symptoms which might bother him. One of these statements was, "That it made you irritable and difficult to get along with."

51. For the prediction that the Italians would have more symptoms in all instances there were: for total number, 24 matched diagnostic pairs in favor of hypothesis, 7 against, 6 ties ($p = .005$); for number of different locations, 16 in favor, 5 against, 16 ties ($p = .013$); for number of different qualities of physical difficulties, 22 in favor, 9 against, 6 ties, ($p = .025$). For the prediction that Italians would admit irritability and Irish would deny it, there were 17 in favor, 6 against, 14 ties ($p = .017$).

Table 3–6   Distribution of Irish and Italian
Clinic Admissions by
Responses to Three Questions
Concerning Admission of
Irritability and Effect of
Symptoms on Interpersonal
Behavior

Response Pattern	Italian	Irish
No on all three questions	22	47
Yes on at least one question	41	34
Total	**63**	**81**

Note: $\chi^2 = 7.62$, p< .01.

The following composite offers a final illustration of how differently these patients reacted to and perceived their illnesses. Each set of responses was given by an Italian and an Irish patient of similar age and sex with a disorder of approximately the same duration and with the same primary and secondary diagnosis (if there was one). In the first two cases, the Irish patient focused on a specific malfunctioning as the main concern while the Italian did not even mention this aspect of the problem but went on to mention more diffuse qualities of his condition. The last four responses contrast the Italian and Irish response to questions of pain and interpersonal relations.

Sociocultural Communication

What has so far been demonstrated is the systematic variability with which bodily conditions may be perceived and communicated. Until now the empirical findings have been presented without interpretation. Most of the data are quite consistent with those reported by other observers.[52] Although no data were collected in our investigation on the specific mechanics of the interplay between being a member of a specific subculture and the communication of "symptoms," some speculation on this seems warranted.

In theorizing about the interplay of culture and symptoms, particular empha-

---

52. The whole specific-diffuse pattern and the generalizing-withholding illness behavior dovetails neatly with the empirical findings of Opler and Singer, op. cit., Fantl and Schiro, op. cit., and Paul Barrabee and Otto von Mering, Ethnic Variations in Mental Stress in Families with Psychotic Children. *Social Problems 1* (October) 1953: 48–53. The specific emphasis on expressiveness has been detailed especially by Zborowski, op. cit. and the several studies of Italian mental patients done by Anne Parsons, Some Comparative Observations on Ward Social Structure: Southern Italy, England, and the United States. *Tipografia dell'Ospedale Psichiatrico.* Napoli, April, 1959; Family Dynamics in Southern Italian Schizophrenics. *Archives of General Psychiatry 3* (November) 1960: 507–18; Patriarchal and Matriarchal Authority in the Neapolitan Slum. *Psychiatry 24* (May) 1961: 109–21. The contrast on number of symptoms has been noted by Croog, op. cit., and Graham, op. cit.

Diagnosis	Question of Interviewer	Irish Patient	Italian Patient
1. Presbyopia and hyperopia	What seems to be the trouble?	I can't see to thread a needle or read a paper.	I have a constant headache and my eyes seem to get all red and burny.
	Anything else?	No, I can't recall any.	No, just that it lasts all day long and I even wake up with it sometimes.
2. Myopia	What seems to be the trouble?	I can't see across the street.	My eyes seem very burny, especially the right eye . . . Two or three months ago I woke up with my eyes swollen. I bathed it and it did go away but there was still the burny sensation.
	Anything else?	I had been experiencing headaches, but it may be that I'm in early menopause.	Yes, there always seems to be a red spot beneath this eye.
	Anything else?	No.	Well, my eyes feel very heavy . . . at night they bother me most.
3. Otitis externa A.D.	Is there any pain?	There's a congestion . . . but it's a pressure not really a pain.	Yes . . . if I rub it, it disappears. . . I had a pain from my shoulder up to my neck and thought it might be a cold.
4. Pharyngitis	Is there any pain?	No, maybe a slight headache but nothing that lasts.	Yes, I have had a headache a few days. Oh, yes, every time I swallow it's annoying.
5. Presbyopia and hyperopia	Do you think the symptoms affected how you got along with your family? Your friends?	No, I have had loads of trouble. I can't imagine this bothering me.	Yes, when I have a headache, I'm very irritable, very tense, very short-tempered.
6. Deafness, hearing loss	Did you become more irritable?	No, not me . . . maybe everybody else but not me.	Oh, yes . . . the least little thing aggravates me . . . and I take it out on the children.

sis was given to the "fit" of certain bodily states with dominant value orientations. The empirical examples for the latter were drawn primarily from data on social roles. Of course, values are evident on even more general levels, such as formal and informal societal sanctions and the culture's orientation to life's basic problems. With an orientation to problems usually goes a preferred solution or way of handling them.[53] Thus a society's values may also be reflected in such preferred solutions. One behavioral manifestation of this is defense mechanisms—a part of the everyday way individuals have of dealing with their everyday stresses and strains.[54] We contend that illness and its treatment (from taking medicine to seeing a physician) is one of these everyday stresses and strains, an anxiety-laden situation which calls forth coping or defense mechanisms.[55] From this general reasoning, we would thus speculate that Italian and Irish ways of communicating illness may reflect major values and preferred ways of handling problems within the culture itself.[56]

For the Italians, the large number of symptoms and the spread of the complaints, not only throughout the body but into other aspects of life, may be understood in terms of their expressiveness and expansiveness so often in sociological, historical, and fictional writing.[57] And yet their illness behavior seems to reflect something more than lack of inhibition and valuation of spontaneity. There is something more than real in their behavior, a "well-seasoned, dramatic emphasis to their lives." In fact, clinicians have noted that this openness is deceptive. It only goes so far and then. . . Thus this Italian overstatement of "symptoms" is not merely an expressive quality but perhaps a more general mechanism, their special way of handling problems—a defense mechanism we call dramatization. Dynamic dramatization is one way to cope with anxiety by

---

53. Florence R. Kluckhohn, Dominant and Variant Value Orientations. In *Personality in Nature, Society and Culture.* Clyde Kluckhohn, Henry A. Murray and David M. Schneider (Eds.) New York: Knopf, 2nd. ed., 1956, pp. 342–57; Florence R. Kluckhohn and Fred L. Strodtbeck, *Variations in Value Orientation.* Evanston, Ill.: Row Peterson, 1961; John Spiegel, Some Cultural Aspects of Transference and Counter-Transference. In *Individual and Family Dynamics.* Jules H. Masserman (Ed.), New York: Greene and Stratton, 1959, pp. 160–82; John P. Spiegel, Conflicting Formal and Informal Roles in Newly Acculturated Families. In *Disorders of Communication* Vol. XLII, Research Publications, Association for Research in Nervous and Mental Disease, 1964, 307–316; John P. Spiegel and Florence R. Kluckhohn, The Influence of the Family and Cultural Values on the Mental Health and Illness of the Individual, Unpublished Progress Report of Grant M-971, U. S. Public Health Service.

54. Anna Freud, *The Ego and the Mechanisms of Defense.* London: Hogarth, 1954.

55. That illness is almost an everyday problem is shown by the data in our opening section on the prevalence of illness. That illness and its concomitants are anxiety-laden is suggested by the findings of many studies on patient delay. Barbara Blackwell, The Literature of Delay in Seeking Medical Care for Chronic Illnesses. *Health Education Monographs 16,* 1963: 3–32; Bernard Kutner, Henry B. Malcover and Abraham Oppenheim, Delay in the Diagnosis and Treatment of Cancer. *Journal of Chronic Diseases.* 7 (January) 1958: 95–120; *Journal of Health and Human Behavior 2* (Fall) 1961: 171–78.

56. Speculation as to why the Italians and the Irish, with similar problems of hardship and poverty, should develop dissimilar ways of handling such problems, is beyond the scope of this paper.

57. In addition to the references cited in footnotes 52 and 53, we have drawn our picture from many sociological, literary, and historical works. A complete bibliography is available on request. For the compilation and annotation of many of these references, I am particularly indebted to Mrs. Marlene Hindley.

repeatedly overexpressing it and thereby dissipating it. Anne Parsons delineates this process in a case study of a schizophrenic woman. Through a process of repetition and exaggeration she was able to isolate and defend herself from the destructive consequences of her own psychotic breakdown. Thus Anne Parsons concludes:

> rather than appearing as evidence for the greater acceptance of id impulses the greater dramatic expression of Southern Italian culture might be given a particular place among the ego mechanisms, different from but in this respect fulfilling the same function as the emphasis on rational mastery of the objective or subjective world which characterizes our own culture (U.S.A.)[58]

While other social historians have noted the Italian flair for show and spectacle, Barzini has most explicitly related this phenomenon to the covering up of omnipresent tragedy and poverty, a way of making their daily lives bearable, the satisfactory *ersatz* for the many things they lack.

> The most easily identifiable reasons why the Italians love their own show. . . First of all they do it to tame and prettify savage nature, to make life bearable, dignified, significant and pleasant for others, and themselves. They do it then for their own private ends; a good show makes a man *simpatico* to powerful people, helps him get on in the world and obtain what he wants, solves many problems, lubricates the wheels of society, protects him from the envy of his enemies and the arrogance of the mighty—they do it to avenge themselves on unjust fate.[59]

Through many works on the Southern Italian there seems to run a thread—a valued and preferred way of handling problems shown in the tendency toward dramatization. The experience of illness provides but another stage.

But if the Italian view of life is expressed through its fiestas, for the Irish it is expressed through its fasts.[60] Their life has been depicted as one of long periods of plodding routine followed by episodes of wild adventure, of lengthy postponement of gratification of sex and marriage, interspersed with brief immediate satisfactions like fighting and carousing. Perhaps in recognition of the expected and limited nature of such outbursts that the most common Irish outlet, alcoholism, is often referred to as "a good man's weakness." Life was black and long-suffering, and the less said the better.[61]

It is the last statement which best reflects the Irish handling of illness. While

---

58. Anne Parsons, *Psychiatry*, op. cit., p. 26.

59. Luigi Barzini, *The Italians,* New York: Bantam, 1965, p. 104.

60. In addition to the papers in footnote 52, Arensberg and Kimball, op. cit. remains the classic reference work.

61. The ubiquitous comic spirit, humor, and wit for which the Irish are famous can be regarded in part as a functional equivalent of the dramatization by Italians. It is a cover, a way of isolating life's hardships, and at the same time a preventive of deeper examination and probing. See Sigmund fat, Yard & Co., 1916. Also, while their daily life was endowed with great restrictions, their fantasy life was replete with great richness (tales of the "wee folk").

in other contexts the ignoring of bodily complaints is merely descriptive of what is going on, in Irish culture it seems to be the culturally prescribed and supported defense mechanism—singularly most appropriate for their psychological and physical survival.[62] When speaking of the discomfort caused by her illness, one stated, "I ignore it like I do most things." In terms of presenting complaints this understatement and restraint was even more evident. It could thus be seen in their seeming reluctance to admit they have any symptoms at all, in their limiting their symptoms to the specific location in which they arose and finally in their contention that their physical problems affected nothing of their life but the most mitention that their physical problems affected nothing of their life but the most minute physical functioning. The consistency of the Irish illness behavior with their self-fulfilling prophecy. Thus their way of communicating complaints, while doing little to make treatment easy, did assure some degree of continual suffering and thus further proof that life is painful and hard (that is, "full of fasts").[63] Secondly, their illness behavior can be linked to the sin and guilt ideology which seems to pervade so much of Irish society. For, in a culture where restraint is the *modus operandi,* temptation is ever present and must be guarded against. Since the flesh is weak, there is a concomitant expectation that sin is likely. Thus, when unexpected or unpleasant events take place, there is a search for what they did or must have done wrong. Perhaps their three most favored locations of symptoms (the eyes, ears, and throat) might be understood as symbolic reflections of the more immediate source of their sin and guilt—what they should not have seen; what they should not have heard; and what they should not have said.

In these few paragraphs, we have tried to provide a theoretical link between membership in a cultural group and the communication of bodily complaints. The illness behavior of the Irish and the Italians has been explained in terms of two of the more generally prescribed defense mechanisms of their respective cultures— with the Irish handling their troubles by denial and the Italians theirs by dramatization.[64]

Qualifications and Implications

The very fact that we speak of trends and statistical significance indicates the tentativeness of this study. In particular, the nature of sample selection affected

---

62. Spiegel and Kluckhohn, op. cit., state that the Irishman's major avenue of relief from his oppressive sense of guilt lies in his almost unlimited capacity for denial. This capacity they claim is fostered by the perception in the rural Irish of a harmonic blending between man and nature. Such harmonizing of man and nature is further interpreted as blurring the elements of casuality, thus allowing for continually shifting the responsibility for events from one person to another and even from a person to animistically conceived forces. Thus denial becomes not only a preferred avenue of relief but also one supported and perhaps elicited by their perception of their environment.

63. Their "fantasying" and their "fasting" might be reflected in the serious illness they claim to have had in the past and the dire consequences they forecast for their future. We do not know for a fact that the Irish *had* more serious illnesses than the Italians, but merely that they claimed to. The Italians might well have had similar conditions but did not necessarily consider them serious.

64. The Anglo-Saxons complete the circle with an emphasis on neutralizing their anxiety.

the analysis of certain demographic variables since the lack of significant differences in some cases may be due to the small range available for comparison. Thus, there were no Italians beyond the third generation and few in the total sample who had gone to college. When comparisons were made within this small range (for example, only within the second generation or only within the high school group) there were, with but one exception, no significant differences from previously reported findings.[65] Despite the limitations cited, it can be stated with some confidence that, of the variables capable of analysis, sociocultural ones were the most significant. When a correlational analysis (and within this, a cluster analysis) was performed on all the codable and quantifiable material (including the demographic data, the health behaviors and attitude scales) the variable which consistently correlated most highly with the "illness behaviors" reported in this study was ethnic group membership.

There is one final remark about our sample selection which has ramifications, not for our data analysis, but rather for our interpretation. We are dealing here with a population who had decided to seek or was referred for medical aid at three clinics. Thus we can make no claim that in a random selection of Irish, they will be suffering primarily from eye, ear, nose, and throat disorders or even locate their chief symptoms there. What we are claiming is that there are significant differences in the way people present and react to their complaints, not that the specific complaints and mechanisms we have cited are necessarily the most common ones. (We would, of course, be surprised if the pattern reported here did not constitute one of the major ones.) Another difficulty in dealing with this population is the duration of the patients' disorders. Since the majority of these patients have had their conditions for some time, one may wonder if similar differences in perception would exist for more acute episodes, or whether the very length of time which the people have borne their problems has allowed for coloration by sociocultural factors. As a result of this we can only raise the issues as to whether the differences reported here between members of a cultural group exist only at a particular stage of their illness or reflect more underlying and enduring cultural concerns and values.[66]

While there has long been recognition of the subjectivity and variability of a patient's reporting of his symptoms, there has been little attention to the fact that this reporting may be influenced by systematic social factors like ethnicity.

---

65. The previously reported ethnic differences with respect to presenting complaints did begin to blur. The Italian and the Irish males tended to 'move' toward the 'middle position' of the Anglo-Saxon Protestant group. In many of the major comparisons of this study, the Anglo-Saxon group occupied a position midway between the responses of the two other ethnic groups, though generally closer to the Irish. For example, when asked about the presence of pain some 70 percent of the Irish males denied it, as compared to almost 60 percent of the Anglo-Saxon males, and 40 percent of the Italian males.

66. Such a problem was explicitly stated and investigated by Ellen Silver, The Influence of Culture on Personality: A Comparison of the Irish and Italians with Emphasis on Fantasy Behavior. Mimeographed, Harvard University, 1958, in her attempted replication of the Opler and Singer work, op. cit., and was emphasized by the somewhat ambiguous findings of Rena S. Grossman, "Ethnic Differences in the Apperception of Pain," unpublished undergraduate honors thesis, Department of Social Relations, Radcliffe College, 1964, in her replication of Zborowski's findings, op. cit., on a non-hospitalized population.

Awareness of the influence of this and similar factors can be of considerable aid in the practical problems of diagnosis and treatment of many diseases, particularly where the diagnosis is dependent to a large extent on what the patient is able and willing, or thinks important enough, to tell the doctor.[67] The physician who is unaware of how the patient's background may lead him to respond in certain ways, by not probing sufficiently, may miss important diagnostic cues or respond inappropriately to others.[68]

The documentation of sociocultural differences in the perception of and concern with certain types of symptoms has further implications for work in preventive medicine and public health. It has been found in mental health research that there is an enormous gulf between lay and professional opinion as to when mental illness is present, as well as when and what kind of help is needed.[69] If our theorizing is correct, such differences reflect not merely something inadequately learned (that is, wrong medical knowledge) but also a solidly embedded value system.[70] Such different frames of reference would certainly shed light on the failures of many symptom-based health campaigns. Often these campaigns seem based on the assumption that a symptom or sign is fairly objective and recognizable and that it evokes similar levels of awareness and reaction. Our study adds

---

67. Several examples are more fully delineated in Irving Kenneth Zola, Illness Behavior of the Working Class: Implications and Recommendations. In Arthur B. Shostak and William Gomberg, (Eds.) *Blue Collar World*. Englewood Cliffs, N. J.: Prentice-Hall, 1964, pp. 350–61.

68. This may be done to such an extreme that it is the physician's response which creates epidemiological differences. Such a potential situation was noted using data from the present study and is detailed in Irving Kenneth Zola, Problems of Communication, Diagnosis, and Patient Care: The Interplay of Patient, Physician, and Clinic Organization. *Journal of Medical Education 38* (October) 1963: 829–38.

69. The explanations for such differences have, however, more often emphasized negative aspects of the respondents' background—their lower education, lower socioeconomic status, lesser psychological sophistication, and greater resistance and antipathy—by virtue of their membership in certain racial and cultural minorities. See Bernard Bergen, Social Class, Symptoms, and Sensitivity to Descriptions of Mental Illness—Implications for Programs of Preventive Psychiatry. Unpublished doctoral dissertation, Harvard University, 1962; Elaine Cumming and John Cumming, *Closed Ranks: An Experiment in Mental Health Education*. Cambridge: Harvard University Press, 1957; Howard E. Freeman and Gene G. Kassebaum, Relationship of Education and Knowledge to Opinions about Mental Illness. *Mental Hygiene 44* (January) 1960: 43–47; Gerald Gurin, Joseph Veroff, and Sheila Feld, *Americans View Their Mental Health*. New York: Basic Books, 1960; Jum C. Nunnally, *Popular Conceptions of Mental Health*. New York: Holt, Rinehart & Winston, 1961; Glenn V. Ramsey and Melita Seipp, Attitudes and Opinions Concerning Mental Illness. *Psychiatric Quarterly 22* (July) 1949: 1–17; Elmo Roper and Associates, *People's Attitudes Concerning Mental Health*. New York: Private Publication, 1950; Shirley Star, The Public's Ideas about Mental Illness. Paper presented to the Annual Meeting of the National Association for Mental Health, Indianapolis, 1955; Shirley Star, The Place of Psychiatry in Popular Thinking. Paper presented at the annual meeting of the American Association for Public Opinion Research, Washington, D.C., 1957; Julian L. Woodward, Changing Ideas on Mental Illness and Its Treatment. *American Sociological Review 16* (August) 1951: 443–54.

70. This approach is evident in such works as Stanley King, op. cit.; Clyde Kluckhohn Culture and Behavior. In Gardner Lindzey, *Handbook of Social Psychology*. Cambridge: Addison-Wesley, 1954; Vol. 2, pp. 921–76; Walter B. Miller, Lower Class Culture as a Generating Milieu of Gang Delinquency. *Journal of Social Issues 14* (July) 1958: 5–19; Marvin K. Opler, *Culture, Psychiatry and Human Values*. Springfield, Ill.: Charles C. Thomas, 1956; Marvin K. Opler, *Culture and Mental Health*. New York: MacMillan, 1959; Benjamin D. Paul, *Health, Culture, and Community—Case Studies of Public Reactions to Health Programs*. New York: Sage, 1955; Lyle Saunders, *Cultural Differences and Medical Care*. New York: Sage, 1954; Henry J. Wegroski, A Critique of Cultural and Statistical Concepts of Abnormality. In Clyde Kluckhohn, Henry A. Murray, and David M. Schneider, *Personality in Nature, Society, and Culture*. New York: Knopf, revised edition, 1956, 691–701.

to the mounting evidence which contradicts this position by indicating, for example, the systematic variability in response to even the most minor aches and pains.

The discerning of reactions to minor problems harks back to a point mentioned in the early pages of this report. For, while sociologists, anthropologists, and mental health workers have usually considered sociocultural factors to be etiological factors in the creation of specific problems, the interpretative emphasis in this study has been on how sociocultural background may lead to different definitions and responses to essentially the same experience. The strongest evidence in support of this argument is the different ethnic perceptions for essentially the same disease. While it is obvious that not all people react similarly to the same disease process, it is striking that the pattern of response can vary with the ethnic background of the patient. There is little known physiological difference between ethnic groups which would account for the differing reactions. In fact, the comparison of the matched diagnostic groups led us to believe that, should diagnosis be more precisely controlled, the differences would be even more striking.

The present report has attempted to demonstrate the fruitfulness of an approach which does not take the definition of abnormality for granted. Despite its limitations, our data seem sufficiently striking to provide further reason for re-examining our traditional and often rigid conceptions of health and illness, of normality and abnormality, of conformity and deviance. Symptoms, or physical aberrations, are so widespread that perhaps relatively few, and a biased selection at best, come to the attention of official treatment agencies like doctors, hospitals and public health agencies. There may even be a sense in which they are part and parcel of the human condition. We have thus tried to present evidence showing that the very labelling and definition of a bodily state as a symptom or as a problem is, in itself, part of a social process. If there is a selection and definitional process, then focusing solely on reasons for deviation (the study of etiology) and ignoring what constitutes a deviation in the eyes of the individual and his society may obscure important aspects of our understanding and eventually our philosophies of treatment and control of illness.[71]

---

71. This is spelled out from various points of view in such works as: Samuel Butler, *Erewhon.* New York: Signet, 1961; René Dubos, op. cit.; Josephine D. Lohman, (participant) Juvenile Delinquency: Its Dimensions, Its Conditions, Techniques of Control, Proposals for Action. Subcommittee on Juvenile Delinquency of the Senate Committee on Labor and Public Welfare, 86th Congress, S. 765, S. 1090, S. 1314, Spring, 1959, p. 268; Talcott Parsons, Social Change and Medical Organization in the United States: A Sociological Perspective. *Annals of the American Academy of Political and Social Science* 346 (March) 1963: 21–34; Edwin M. Schur, *Crimes Without Victims—Deviant Behavior and Public Policy.* Englewood, New Jersey: Prentice-Hall, 1965; Thomas Szasz, *The Myth of Mental Illness.* New York: Hoeber-Harper, 1961; Thomas Szasz, *Law, Liberty, and Psychiatry.* New York: MacMillan, 1963; Irving Kenneth Zola, Problems for Research—Some Effects of Assumptions Underlying Socio-Medical Investigations. In Gerald Gordon (Ed.) *Proceedings, Conference on Medical Sociology and Disease Control,* National Tuberculosis Association, 1966: 9–17.

The Delivery of Medical Care in China   4

VICTOR W. SIDEL
RUTH SIDEL

The health of the Chinese people has changed greatly over the past few decades. The change is apparent in many ways, some that are reflected in the anecdotes that returning visitors tell and others that are evident in the few available statistics. In the second category perhaps the most dramatic is the reported change in the principal causes of death. In China during the 1930s and 1940s the leading causes of death were on the one hand infectious and parasitic diseases and on the other complications of malnutrition (in many cases a euphemism for starvation). Today it appears that the leading causes of death, at least in a large city such as Shanghai, are the same as those in the developed nations of the West: cancer, stroke, and heart disease.

On the surface this change might seem merely to substitute one termination of life for another. Its significance, however, is inescapable: it is evidence that the people of China are dying at progressively higher ages. Other statistics point to the same conclusion. For example, in the 1930s the life expectancy of a newborn child in Shanghai was some 40 years. Data compiled by the city's Bureau of Public Health in 1972 suggest that today the life expectancy is more than 70 years. The data are all the more remarkable when one considers that they are from what is one of the poorer and technologically less developed nations in the world.

In some ways the anecdotal evidence is even more convincing than the statistical, much of which is fragmentary and unconfirmed. Almost all visitors from abroad who travel the urban lanes and country paths they knew 25 years or more ago comment on the change in appearances. Where sick children and ailing adults were once a commonplace sight, today they are rarely seen; both children and adults appear to be in excellent health.

How have the Chinese, with their limited technical resources, managed to do this? The answer is that their revolution of 25 years ago gave rise to many changes in the Chinese way of life, including changes in the methods of delivering health care. To understand the nature of these changes and to see today's pattern of Chinese medical and social services in context, it is necessary to know something about former conditions.

In 1949 the population of China was estimated to be 540 million, some 85 percent of which was rural. With respect to the practice of what the Chinese call "Western medicine," there were then in China 40,000 Western-style physicians at most and perhaps 90,000 beds in Western-style hospitals. If these medical resources had been evenly distributed, the ratio of physicians to potential patients would have been one to every 13,000 and of beds per patient one to every 6,000. Instead, of course, most of the resources were concentrated in a few cities, and even there most of the population depended on practitioners of traditional Chinese medicine for such care as they received.

Beginning in 1949 China's new government confronted this deficiency in health resources by initiating a dual program. Some of the strategies adopted by the new Ministry of Health were unique to China; others were the same strategies that have been adopted by many other technologically underdeveloped nations. In the first category were innovative efforts to involve the bulk of the population in "mass movements." These were aimed primarily at improving public health and sanitation. A further innovation was an attempt to enlist the practitioners of traditional medicine in overall health programs.

In the second category were programs that emphasized the training of large numbers of new health workers. The principal efforts to increase the numbers of health personnel were directed on the one hand toward the training of "middle level" health workers and on the other toward the establishment of "centers of excellence." These centers were urban training facilities that were expected to pioneer new medical techniques and also to provide a flow of skilled personnel to areas of special need.

Following Russian models, the Ministry of Health set up a number of "middle medical schools." Students who had reached the intermediate level of the secondary school system were sent to middle medical schools for a three-year course that prepared them to work as "assistant doctors." This is a category comparable to the Russian *feldsher,* a physician's assistant who is expected to act as a physician when necessary. At the same time the middle medical schools trained other personnel as nurses, midwives, technicians, and pharmacists.

The Ministry of Health also expanded the existing program of "higher" medical education. Some medical schools were moved from the coastal cities to the interior and some new schools were founded. Here again Russian models were followed. Separate faculties were responsible for pediatrics, for general medicine, for stomatology (dentistry and other treatment of diseases of the mouth), and for public health. The period of study at the higher medical schools was five or six years; the students were recruited from those who had completed the senior level of secondary school. At the pinnacle of this higher-educational system was the China Medical College in Peking. Here an eight-year curriculum was offered, its objective being to train teachers and research personnel.

By 1965 the ambitious program had produced more than 100,000 new physicians and some 170,000 assistant doctors. In the same period, however, China's population had grown from 540 million to about 725 million. Even though the physician-to-patient ratio of one to 5,000 was substantially better than it had been in 1949, it was still far from the ratio of one to 1,000 or better that is typical of richer nations. The progress of the Health Ministry's innovative programs also had been good but large gaps remained. Even though some traditional methods had been adopted, practitioners of traditional medicine were still looked on as second-class physicians. By the same token the mass-movement programs had successfully attacked a number of public-health problems, but professional or, as the Chinese say, "expert" health workers continued to dominate Chinese medicine. Perhaps most important of all, the center of gravity of medical care remained in China's urban areas. The inadequate level of health care delivered to the rural Chinese, who are the vast majority of the nation's population, led to criticism of the Ministry of Health. This was climaxed in 1965 by an action that proved to be a forerunner of the "Cultural Revolution" of 1966–1969: publication of what is now known as "Chairman Mao's June 26 Directive." "In medical and health work," the directive ordered, "put the stress on the rural areas."

Both of us work in the field of medical and social services in the U.S. and have studied the delivery of these services in a number of other countries. We thus felt ourselves fortunate to be among the first Americans to be invited to visit China by the Chinese Medical Association soon after the "Ping-Pong breakthrough" of 1971. By then the Cultural Revolution had wound down and we were eager to see what its effects had been. We were able to observe several aspects of contemporary Chinese medicine, including the delivery of medical care, in September and October of 1971 and then again in greater depth in September and October of 1972. We traveled with representatives of the Chinese Medical Association to the nation's two largest cities, Peking and Shanghai, to a number of provincial cities and towns, and to rural areas in both the densely populated coastal regions and the less crowded interior.

A foreigner thinks of Shanghai and Peking as being purely urban areas. In reality, of the almost 11 million Chinese who live in the "independent municipality" of Shanghai five million inhabit the 10 rural counties that surround the city proper. The rural five million are the population of some 200 "communes": self-governing political and economic units that are each divided into between 10 and 30 "production brigades." The production brigades are subdivided into "production teams," each several hundred strong. In all, the rural population of Shanghai incorporates some 2,700 production brigades and nearly 28,000 production teams.

One example of rural health care that we saw in 1971 was provided by the

Ma Chiao commune outside Shanghai proper. We visited one brigade of the commune, the Sing Sing brigade, with a total population of 1,850 subdivided into 12 production teams. The brigade health station, where we interviewed the staff, was served by four "barefoot doctors" and a midwife. Each production team in the brigade, we learned, had one to three additional health aides.

It is worth mentioning here that the term *barefoot doctor* is a literal translation of the Chinese appellation *(chijiao yisheng)* that has been given these health workers. We never met a barefoot doctor who was barefoot. Moreover, these workers are not addressed as "doctor" *(yisheng* or, more honorifically, *dafu)* by their patients but are called "comrade" *(tongzhi).* The barefoot doctors, who generally receive three to six months' initial training, followed by continuing on-the-job education, evidently think of themselves not as "expert" health workers but as peasants who do some medical work.

The eldest of the four barefoot doctors at the brigade health station, Ho Shichang, was 30. Before his medical training his education had consisted of six years of primary school, completed at age 13. Between then and the start of his medical training in 1964 Ho worked as a farmer; in 1971 he still spent about half of his working time farming. The year before Mao's June 26 Directive was issued Ho had been one of 274 students who spent three months at the county hospital receiving basic training from the 13 health workers on the hospital staff. He later spent three additional months at the commune hospital for practical training; he still spends one day a week there as part of his continuing practical education.

Like his colleagues, Ho is responsible for treating the "light diseases" of his fellow brigade members: minor injuries, gastrointestinal illness, colds, and bronchitis. He also administers immunization against diphtheria, tetanus, whooping cough, measles, smallpox, poliomyelitis, Japanese B encephalitis, and meningococcal meningitis. Another of his public health duties is to supervise the collection, treatment, and storage of human excreta for utilization as fertilizer. The actual work may be overseen by the production-team health aides, but the responsibility is his, as are continuing campaigns against pests such as flies, fleas, cockroaches, and snails (the last is the intermediate host of the organism that causes schistosomiasis).

The contents of Ho's medical bag provide a good measure of his capacity to treat various diseases (see Table 4–1). In the U.S. 39 of these medications are in use; only nine of them can be obtained without a physician's prescription. When Ho encounters a problem beyond his scope, he refers the patient to the commune hospital. (The 200 or so commune hospitals in rural Shanghai have an average of 30 beds each.) If the matter is more serious, the patient is referred to the county hospital.

Ho and his colleagues divide their time about equally between farmwork and duty at the brigade health station. As members of the commune they share in the produce the commune raises. They also share in the commune's cash income, which is divided among the commune's members on the basis of the "work points" each earns. They receive no extra income for their work as barefoot doc-

Medications

*Adona (cardiac stimulant) ampules
Adrenalin ampules
Aminophyllin tablets and ampules
Ammonium chloride tablets and solution
*Analgin tablets and ampules
Aspirin-phenacetin-caffeine tablets
Atropine tablets
Belladonna extract tablets
*Berberine tablets
Brown's mixture tablets and liquid
Caffeine sodium benzoate ampules
Chloromycetin ampules and capsules
Chlorpheniramine maleate tablets
Chlorpromazine tablets and ampules
*Chlothamine tablets
*DCT tablets
Demerol
*DPP in tablets
Ephedrine
*Furazolidone tablets
Lactobacillus tablets
*Lobodura tablets
Luminal tablets
Nikethamide ampules
Nitrofurantoin tablets
Penicilin, crystalline
Penicillin, procaine
Phenolax tablets
*8-p-phenylbenzylatropinium bromide
tablets
Phenylbutazone tablets
Piperazine citrate tablets
Promethazine tablets
Probanthine tablets
Reserpine tablets
Sodium bicarbonate tablets
Sulfadiazine tablets and ampules
Sulfaguanidine tablets
Sulfamethazine tablets

Sulfamethoxpyridazine tablets
Sulfathiazole tablets
*Syntomycin capsules
Terramycin tablets
Tetracycline tablets
Valium tablets
Vitamin B1 tablets
Vitamin B2 tablets
Vitamin C tablets
Vitamin K tablets
*Vitamin U tablets
Yeast tablets

Topical agents
Alcohol
Boric acid ointment
Eye drops
Gentian violet
Iodine tincture
Mercurochrome
Nose drops
Sulfa ointment

Equipment
Acupuncture needles
Adhesive tape
Bandages and gauze
Cotton sponges and swabs
Drinking cups
Forceps
Fountain pen
Hypodermic needles
Notebook for records
Paper bag
Rubber tubing
Scissors
Sphygmomanometer
Syringes (2 cc. and 5 cc.)
Thermometers (oral and rectal)

Medical supplies at the disposal of barefoot doctors include 50 medications and 8 topical agents. The names are the most familiar ones; some are proprietary and some generic. Of the 39 medications used in U.S. practice, 30 (bold) are available only by prescription. The items marked with an asterisk are not generally available in the U.S.

tors, but their health-station service earns them work points, so that they lose no income either.

At the time of our visit in 1971 Ho was one of 7,700 barefoot doctors working in the communes of rural Shanghai. This represented a new high in the level of health care. In the late 1950s, as part of the initial effort to train health auxiliaries, health teams from the city proper had trained some 3,900 rural residents in health care. During the retrenchment of 1961–1965, however, training was largely discontinued and many rural health aides returned to full-time farmwork.

The program that has produced most of the barefoot doctors in China today began only after Mao's June 26 Directive of 1965. By 1968 in the Shanghai area some 4,500 barefoot doctors had been trained, and the new trainees had themselves trained an additional 29,000 health aides to provide part-time health care at the production-team level.

Like Shanghai, Peking has a substantial rural population. The city's nine urban districts have four million residents, but three million more live in the nine counties outside the city proper. During our 1971 visit we found that the delivery of medical care in this rural area differed very little in pattern from the system in rural Shanghai. The commune we visited, the Shuang Chiao commune, had a population of 38,000, subdivided into six production brigades and 77 production teams. The commune hospital had a clinical laboratory and X-ray facilities but had no beds and served outpatients only; any patient requiring hospitalization was referred to the county hospital. At this commune we visited the aid station of one production team, the Shuang Pei team, which was staffed by a single barefoot doctor. Liu Yu-cheng, age 23, had completed the lower level of secondary school. When Mao's June 26 Directive was issued, the other members of the Shuang Pei team nominated Liu for medical training. His basic training had come from a mobile team of physicians who normally worked in Peking proper but were then assigned to the Shuang Chiao commune hospital; the instruction period lasted for three months. Since that time Liu has been given short leaves of absence for further study. Not long before our visit he had spent three months in the city studying traditional Chinese medicine.

During our visit in 1972 we saw one of the commune hospitals in the rural area outside Peking. The hospital had opened in May, 1971. It has 30 beds, and its staff of 48 serves a commune with a total population of 46,000. Seven of the staff members are physicians; five are Western-trained and two are traditional practitioners. All seven are on loan from the staff of a hospital in Peking proper. The balance of the staff consists of 15 nurses, 25 health auxiliaries, 11 technicians and administrators and one cook. In the 17 months between opening day and our visit in October, 1972, some 8,000 members of the commune had received care as outpatients (an average of 500 per month) and 500 more had entered the hospital for treatment (an average of one patient per bed per month).

Medical care in urban China follows the same pattern of decentralization that we observed in the rural areas. In Peking proper, for example, each of the nine urban districts has an average population of about 400,000. The city's municipal medical services include four specialized research hospitals and 23 general hospitals; ten of the general hospitals have more than 500 beds.

Each of the nine districts is subdivided into "neighborhoods." In the West District of Peking, which we visited, there were nine such neighborhoods; the one that was our host, the Fengsheng Neighborhood, has a population of 53,000. One municipal hospital in the West District, the People's Hospital, is where any Fengsheng Neighborhood patients are sent if care at one of the specialized hospitals is not required. Within the neighborhood itself the only hospital-like facility is exclusively for outpatient care. Its staff of 90, however, provides the nucleus of the neighborhood health-care apparatus. The staff includes seven Western-trained physicians and 20 practitioners of traditional medicine, 31 nurses and technicians, 18 administrative and other personnel and 14 trainees. The public-health department is responsible for supervising the urban equivalent of the rural production-team aid stations: a total of 25 health stations operated by Lane Committees.

The Fengsheng Neighborhood has 132 lanes in all, so that each of the 25 Lane Committees represents the residents of five or six lanes, or some 400 families. Each Lane Committee health station is staffed morning and afternoon by local housewives who have the title Red Medical Worker. The daily hours are from 8:00 to 11:00 A.M. and from 1:00 to 5:30 P.M.

The health station we visited was maintained by the Wu Ting Lane Committee. Its plain single room was furnished with an examination couch, a cabinet for medical supplies, and a table and chairs. Three Red Medical Workers were present; we talked at some length to one of the women, Yang Hsio-hua. Yang was 38 years old and had worked at the health station for two years. Married some 20 years ago, she has three children, 19, 15, and 11. She had become a Red Medical Worker by volunteering for a month's basic training at the Fengsheng Neighborhood medical facility. During that time she learned how to take a medical history and how to conduct simple physical examinations, including such routines as measuring blood pressure. She was instructed in the uses of a number of drugs, both Western and traditional, and she had learned the techniques of acupuncture and intramuscular and subcutaneous injection.

A physician from the neighborhood medical facility visited the Wu Ting health station as often as three times a week. Yang and her fellow medical workers visited the neighborhood facility when they had questions. She observed that seven to ten patients visited the health station during morning hours and that four or five more might come in the afternoon.

At the health station much of the emphasis is on preventive medicine, in particular immunization against infectious diseases. Most immunization of local children is accomplished at the station. If necessary, one of the medical workers will call for a child at home or even administer an inoculation there. For example, one Lane Committee health-station immunization chart we saw showed that of 160-odd children eligible for immunization against measles in 1971, a total of 154 had received inoculations by the time of our visit. Other charts showed the comparative incidence of infectious diseases from 1958 on. Measles has evidently become uncommon since immunization first began in 1965 [see figure 4–2].

Neighborhood factory workers seldom use the Lane Committee health stations because their own factory medical facility is more convenient. Their dependents, however, do use the Lane Committee stations, and the factory will reimburse half the cost of treatment. The charge is never more than ten fen and is usually smaller. (One hundred fen make one yüan and one yüan is equal to about 40 U.S. cents.) Nonetheless, the income from the fees, together with a subsidy that each Lane Committee health station receives from its Neighborhood Committee, allows the Red Medical Workers to receive a monthly stipend of

Figure 4–1

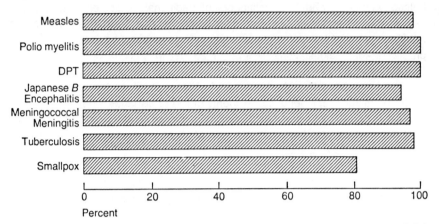

Immunization of children against nine infectious diseases is routine. Bars show the percentage of eligible children immunized in 1971 at one Lane Committee health station.

Figure 4–2

Incidence of measles in one Peking neighborhood has fallen sharply since 1965, the year routine inoculation of children against measles was begun. All immunization is free.

Figure 4–3

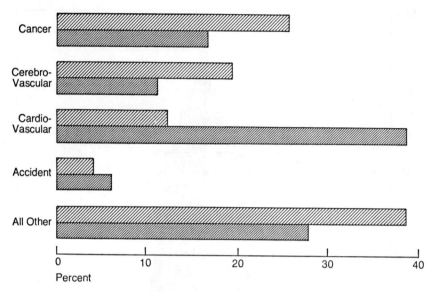

Leading causes of death in Shanghai during the first six months of 1972 *(dark)* are contrasted with those in the U.S. *(darker)* as a whole during 1968. In both instances cancer, stroke, and heart disease were responsible for more than 55 percent of all deaths; the parallel indicates that the Chinese are living longer and more of them are dying from diseases of old age.

about 15 *yüan*, roughly a third of the wage that a beginning factory worker would be paid.

China has by no means solved its medical problems. For example, both tuberculosis and trachoma are far more prevalent than they are in richer nations. What we have seen of the delivery of medical care in both rural and urban areas, however, convinces us that public health and medical care in China are better than they are in other nations handicapped to a similar degree by technological underdevelopment. One striking instance of this is the success of the Chinese campaign for birth control.

Health workers both in the countryside and in the cities have as one of their main responsibilities a program to make contraception popular. The urban Red Medical Workers make a point of explaining to their patients how a lower birth rate will benefit not only their neighborhood and their city but all China. At the same time the medical workers stress the part that birth control plays in the "liberation" of women, a concept that is substantially more radical in tradition-bound China than in Western countries. An example of the effectiveness of the urban effort is provided by the records of one Lane Committee health station in the city of Hangchow. The data represent only a small sample: 369 married couples with wives of childbearing age. Within this group 24 percent of the women and 3 percent of the men had been permanently sterilized. Another 27 percent of

Figure 4-4

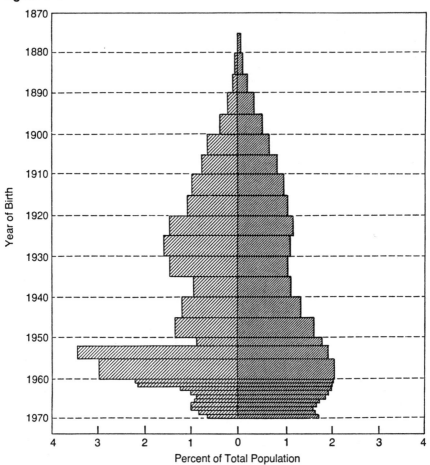

Population profile of the 478,000 inhabitants of the Luwan district of Shanghai in 1971 *(left)* is compared with that of the U.S. as a whole in 1970 *(right)*. The "rectangular" U.S. profile is characteristic of the age distribution found in more developed countries. The "bulge" in the number of Chinese births between 1952 and 1960 may partly reflect the absence of official support for birth control during this period. The "pinch" in Chinese births in the 1963–1970 period, with an eight year total that is scarcely half the U.S. total in the same period, probably reflects a greater use of birth control methods by the urban Chinese.

the women and 19 percent of the men regularly used contraceptives. Of the 98 wives who reportedly did not use contraceptives, ten were pregnant, seven were newly married, and 16 were still nursing (a period when, it is mistakenly believed by some, a woman cannot conceive). The crude annual birth rate for the population served by the Lane Committee health station is at the remarkably low level of eight per 1,000.

Birth statistics for Shanghai in 1972 are equally remarkable. The reported rate for the city proper is 6.4 per 1,000 and for the entire independent municipality 10.6 per 1,000. By way of comparison, in 1972 the lowest rate in any of the 50

Figure 4–5

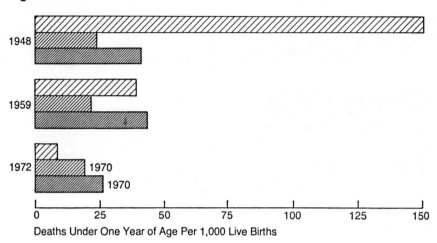

Deaths Under One Year of Age Per 1,000 Live Births

Infant deaths in the first year in urban Shanghai *(light)* are compared with the deaths of white *(dark)* and nonwhite *(darker)* infants in New York City in 1948, in 1959, and in 1972. (The comparable New York figures are for 1970, the latest year for which they are available.) The data for Shanghai are from the Chinese Medical Association; the 1972 rate, less than 1 percent of all live births, is so low that it has met with some skepticism.

states in the U.S. was 12.6 per 1,000 (in Maryland). In this connection the 1972 crude death rate for Shanghai proper is reported as being 5.6 per 1,000. Assuming that both figures are correct, this means that the city's natural growth rate is less than a tenth of 1 percent (0.8 per 1,000). This is one of the lowest natural growth rates in any urban area in the world.

Birth-control statistics from rural areas are substantially different. For example, one commune in the rural counties outside Peking, with a total population of 46,000, has compiled contraception statistics for 5,777 married couples where the wife is of childbearing age. Only 8 percent of the wives and 2 percent of the husbands have been permanently sterilized. Another 41 percent of the wives use contraceptives, the "pill" being favored over intrauterine devices by 23 percent to 18 percent. Among the husbands 9 percent use the condom, bringing the total of contraceptive users to 50 percent. During 1971 there were 1,181 births in the commune, so that the crude birth rate was slightly less than 24 per 1,000. The 1971 statistics for the 450,000 inhabitants of Shunyi County, a rural district outside Peking, are quite similar. There the married couples where the wife is of childbearing age number 49,297, and 59 percent of them practice contraception. The number of births in the county in 1971 was 9,504, which means a crude birth rate slightly above 21 per 1,000.

The birth rates in both of these rural samples seem high compared with the rates in the urban areas we have cited. Chinese health officials hope to see the national rate eventually fall to about 15 per 1,000. Nonetheless, even the rural rate is substantially below the former national rate, which is estimated to have

Figure 4–6

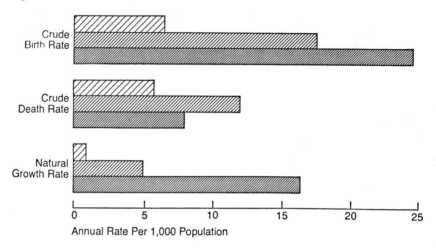

Natural growth rate, the excess of births over deaths is shown for urban Shanghai *(light)* and for the white *(dark)* and nonwhite *(darker)* population of New York City. The New York data are for 1970; Shanghai data for 1972 suggest a notably low rate.

been 45 per 1,000 or higher. (For purposes of comparison the current crude birth rate for Southeast Asia is estimated to be 43 per 1,000.)

One still unresolved medical issue is how to achieve an effective union of Western and traditional medical practices. It will probably never be known exactly how many practitioners of traditional medicine there were in 1949, but they were estimated to number in the hundreds of thousands, and they provided at least some degree of health care to a large and faithful clientele, particularly in the rural areas. Nonetheless, then as now certain difficulties stood in the way of integrating the traditional and the Western-style practitioners.

Traditional Chinese medicine is much more than a collection of empirical remedies. It is based on a large body of theory, accumulated over some 3,000 years, that includes, for example, the concept of a "natural" balance between yin and yang. One declared objective of the People's Republic of China, however, is to lead the population away from the "superstitions of feudalism" and toward the practice of "scientific methods."

With eminent practicality Mao dismissed this theoretical conflict early in the 1950s by declaring that traditional Chinese medicine was a "great treasure-house" and urging that traditional and Western practices be merged. Some progress in this direction was made in the 1950s and early 1960s, but it is only since the Cultural Revolution that emphasis on unifying the two streams has increased significantly. For example, students in the Western-style medical schools now receive more than casual instruction in traditional medicine, and those who study traditional medicine are also taught Western practices. At the same time the years since 1949 have seen the general adoption of certain traditional tech-

Figure 4–7

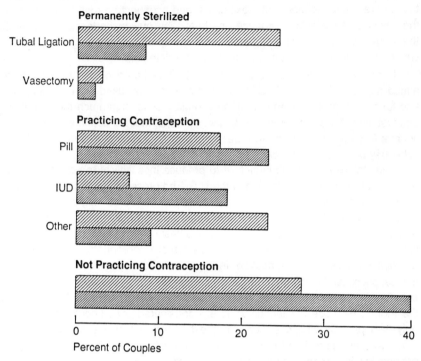

Contraceptive practices in an urban area *(light)* and in a rural area *(dark)* are compared; the urban sample is from a commune outside Peking. Sterilization is nearly three times greater in the urban than in the rural sample and substantially fewer rural males use contraceptives. The bias seems to be reflected in the difference between urban and rural birth rates: below 10 per 1,000 in some urban areas and above 20 per 1,000 in some rural ones.

niques: the use of herbal preparations, of gymnastic and respiratory exercises, and of two related treatments, moxibustion and acupuncture.

Traditional Chinese pharmacology emphasizes herbal remedies, usually in the form of a broth or tea that the patient drinks. In the countryside today health workers not only gather and prepare wild herbs but also cultivate a number of them. Moreover, the medicine cabinets in rural and urban health stations are stocked with herbal remedies as well as with Western ones. Some herbal remedies are even available as sterile preparations for injection. Medical investigators in China suspect that, just as one traditional herbal remedy, *ma huang*, has been found to contain ephedrine as its active principle, others may prove to contain similar specific pharmacological compounds. A substantial part of current pharmacological research is concerned with examining this possibility.

One tenet of Chinese traditional medicine is that the internal organs of the body are connected to points on the skin by way of channels called *ching lo* that run throughout the body close to the skin. Stimulation of a point along a channel is supposed to affect the internal organ attached to that channel. Although the existence of such channels has never been demonstrated anatomically, it is on this theoretical foundation that moxibustion and acupuncture rest. In moxibustion the stimulus to the skin is produced by heat. The pulverized leaves of an herb, the mugwort, are wrapped in a paper cone, the tip of the cone is ignited, and the smoldering herb is placed on or near the appropriate point.

In acupuncture the stimulus is applied by inserting a needle to a predetermined depth in the patient's skin. Acupuncture can be used both for diagnosis and for treatment. It is even taught in secondary schools in much the same way that first aid is taught in some U.S. school systems. Indeed, health workers whom we met in both rural and urban areas said that as a routine treatment for headache they preferred acupuncture to aspirin.

The Chinese use of acupuncture to produce insensitivity to pain during surgery has attracted much attention in the U.S. The procedure is actually less common in China than widely circulated American accounts might lead one to believe. It is usually called acupuncture anesthesia in English (and in English language publications of Chinese origin). "Anesthesia," of course, implies a general loss of sensation by the patient. It would be more appropriate to use the term analgesia, a loss of pain sensation. In any event the Chinese say that the effect is most successful when the surgical procedure is "above the waist," so that acupuncture for this purpose is largely confined to surgery of the head, the neck, and the thorax. Because the technique is still considered experimental it is applied only with patients who specifically request it and, within this group, only with those who are considered to be "not too anxious" about surgery. Most surgical patients in China receive conventional anesthetics.

With respect to "mass movements" in Chinese health care, the first nationwide "Patriotic Health Campaigns" were launched in the 1950s. The targets were "four pests": flies, mosquitoes, rats, and the "grain-thieving" sparrow. (The ecologically unjust charge against sparrows was later withdrawn and bedbugs were substituted.)

Similar mass movements continue today, expanded and redirected to include other public-health problems, such as the handling of human excreta, the purity of the water in local wells and streams, methods of food preparation and even the disposal of trash. In the countryside the departments of health in commune and brigade hospitals supervise the campaigns; in the cities district and neighborhood hospital personnel have the same responsibility. In both rural and urban areas the ultimate responsibility rests with the local health workers and the aides they have trained. For example, in Hangchow the Red Medical Workers at one Lane Committee health station set aside three days a month for "cleanup work" with the assistance of their fellow residents. The time is spent removing trash and inspecting potential pest breeding places. Full-scale sessions, however, usually coincide with major festival days and with the state celebrations on May 1 and October 1.

The mass-movement approach has apparently helped the Chinese to dispose of such "social" illnesses as drug addiction and venereal disease. For example, early in the 1950s checklists of the symptoms of syphilis were posted in every community center. A slogan ("We don't want to take syphilis into Communism") was promulgated, mass surveys were conducted, and social pressure was brought to bear on suspect individuals who failed to seek medical attention. Elimination of prostitutes as carriers of venereal disease was accomplished by giving them the opportunity to engage in "socially constructive" work. As with the birth-control campaign, the Chinese effort to control "social" illnesses seems to have met with greater success than similar efforts in comparably poor nations and even in some technologically advanced ones.

A summary of China's achievements in transforming the delivery of medical care since 1949 shows an interweaving of three main threads: decentralization, demystification, and continuity with the past. Following a pattern that many students of community medicine would be happy to see more widely emulated in Western countries, the delivery of medical care in China begins at the lowest possible level in both the city and the countryside. Initial medical attention is in the hands of health aides who are part of the community they serve. From this initial point of contact a clearly organized system of referral leads level by level up to a plateau of sophisticated medical specialization. (It is worth noting that in some technical areas, such as the treatment of severe burns and the replantation of limbs, Chinese medicine may be ahead of Western medicine.) The patient with a problem that cannot be handled at one level of this decentralized structure moves on to the level above. The system is an efficient, low-cost one. Moreover, it has the advantage of building social cohesion and local self-reliance by emphasizing neighborliness and service for others from the lowest level up.

From the Chinese point of view demystification runs parallel to decentralization. The front-line medical workers are men and women with little in the way of formal education. They work part time and receive their instruction in health care through brief programs that emphasize the practical. They urge participation on the part of the people they look after. For example, each individual is expected, as a patient, to look out for his own health and, as a citizen, to look out for the health of the community. Under these circumstances it is no wonder that much of the mystery medicine so often holds for the layman has been effectively dispelled. Demystification has also been furthered by shortening the term of formal medical education and by assigning urban physicians to periodic tours of duty in the countryside. The two steps express with respect to medicine the determination of Mao and others to eliminate "elitism" in general.

As for continuity with the past, we have already noted the pragmatic adoption of certain traditional Chinese medical practices. What is less commonly appreciated is that the social structure involved in the decentralization process (for example, the pyramidal succession that leads from courtyard to lane, from lane to neighborhood, and from neighborhood to district) preserves, albeit with differences in method and purpose, much of the traditional Chinese social organization. Thus the past is interwoven with the present in many ways. Indeed, in assessing the applicability of Chinese medical methods abroad it is often difficult to judge which methods might be used successfully in other societies and which are so culture-linked as to be uniquely Chinese.

For ourselves, with a concern for the improvement of medical and social services in the U.S., the lessons from China may be more general than specific. Certainly they transcend medical technology and enter the spheres of politics and economics. It seems to us that the Chinese have managed to overcome severe problems, to improve their system of medical care, and to enhance the health of their population only by making medical change an integral part of a change in Chinese society as a whole. We in the U.S. face social and medical problems that, although they are quite different from China's in many ways, are equally difficult. It remains to be seen whether or not we shall meet them in as determined and comprehensive a way as the Chinese have met theirs.

PART II
Demography of Health and Illness

Demography is the study of human population, its characteristics, and the interrelationships among those characteristics. Demographers of health and illness investigate the incidence and prevalence of disease and changes in these rates over time. Incidence indicates the number of new cases of a disease or illness that develop during a specific time frame. Prevalence refers to how many people are afflicted with a certain illness at a specific time.

Demographers are interested in how incidence and prevalence of disease and illness are related to social characteristics such as sex, race, and social class. For example, those from the lower class have a higher risk of infant mortality than those from the upper class. Intervention to improve health status is dependent on an understanding of the causes of these relationships. Often the relationships of social characteristics to health status are only fully understood when they are examined in a societal context.

Omran makes this point clearly when he outlines three different models of change in health, disease, and mortality. He emphasizes that in the epidemiological transition, there is a shift from problems of communicable and infectious diseases to man-made and degenerative disease as a country moves from a developing to an industrial society. Thomas discusses the effects of technological advances in health care since 1950 on disease patterns and disability in the United States. House presents a stress model for understanding the impact of lifestyle on coronary heart disease. Kohn analyzes how social class may be related to schizophrenia.

Changing Patterns of Health and Disease During the Process of National Development

5

ABDEL R. OMRAN, M.D., Dr.P.H.

Several changes occur in patterns of health and disease during the process of national development—a process made up of a complex network of social, economic, cultural, environmental, and health components. The pace, type, and extent of these changes as well as their determinants and consequences are best described in terms of the theory of the epidemiologic transition. The epidemiologic transition accompanies the economic change from low per capita income to high per capita income; it is the transition from high mortality (with famine and infectious diseases as the major causes of death) and high fertility to low mortality (with man-made and degenerative diseases as the principal causes of death) and low fertility. The theory of epidemiologic transition focuses on the complex changes in patterns of health and disease over time and on the interactions between these patterns and their economic, demographic, and sociologic determinants. There can be little doubt that such a transition has taken place in the developed countries of the world and that a transition is still under way in less developed societies.

Phases in the Changing Patterns of Health and Disease

Changes in patterns of disease and death that occur during the transition can be characterized as moving through three distinct phases: the Age of Pestilence and

Famine, the Age of Receding Pandemics, and the Age of Degenerative and Man-Made Diseases.

Age of Pestilence and Famine

During the first phase of the epidemiologic transition, the health picture is dominated by the high prevalence of endemic diseases and chronic undernutrition accentuated by frequent severe epidemics of infectious diseases and famines. Under such conditions, mortality is high, and in the face of such high mortality, fertility is sustained at equally high levels and population growth is usually stationary or cyclic. This pattern characterizes premodern and pre-industrial societies, in which communities are traditionbound, economically underdeveloped (usually with very low per capita income), and predominantly agrarian (with primitive or manual agricultural techniques); in addition, women are of low status, the extended family is common, illiteracy rates are high, and medical care is inadequate or completely lacking. These are the cultural, demographic, physical, and biological prerequisites for the epidemic prevalence of infection and human starvation.

Age of Receding Pandemics

During the second phase of the epidemiologic transition, pandemics begin to recede and famines become less frequent. With concurrent changes in endemic diseases and undernutrition, mortality starts to decline. Fertility during most of this stage continues to be high, resulting in a rising rate of natural population increase as mortality declines—hence the population "explosion." Toward the end of this phase of the transition, fertility begins to decline, lowering somewhat the rate of population growth. It must be added that while pandemics of infection and malnutrition are receding, certain other diseases either increase in incidence and/or increase in their relative contribution to mortality. Examples include emerging industrial diseases, malignancies, cardiovascular diseases, and stroke.

Almost all the developed countries have passed through the Age of Receding Pandemics; almost all the less developed countries are still within this stage. In Western countries, pandemics of infection and widespread chronic malnutrition receded during the 18th and 19th centuries in response to the agricultural and industrial revolutions, which brought about many societal and environmental changes such as improvement in nutrition and standards of living, increased urbanization, modernization, better education, and improved status for women. Sanitary and medical improvements were few and came too gradually and too late in this stage in most countries to be responsible for the changes in health and disease patterns. In the less developed countries, this stage of the transition has come late, for the most part after World War II, and has been triggered by the use of insecticides, antibiotics, chemotherapy, environmental sanitation, and other measures borrowed from or introduced by Western or international organizations.

Age of Degenerative and Man-Made Diseases

Further improvements in social, economic, and environmental conditions—coupled with great strides in science and technology—occur along with economic modernization and increased per capita income during the last stage of the transition. Degenerative and man-made diseases, especially cardiovascular disease, stroke, cancer, radiation injury, occupational hazards, drug addiction, mental illness, and geriatric disease are dominant. Infectious, epidemic, and deficiency diseases recede further; thus degenerative and man-made diseases are responsible for a large proportion of the low general mortality. Fertility also declines, and population growth slows; an exception is the baby boom that followed World War II in many countries now in this last stage of the transition.

Models of the Changing Patterns of Health and Disease

Depending on the pace of change and the particulars of the transition in the modern era, three models of the epidemiologic transition can be delineated: the classical model, an accelerated model, and the delayed model.

Classical Model of Transition

The transition as it occurred in Western societies represents the classical model, in which the transition from high mortality and fertility and low per capita income to low mortality and fertility and high per capita income was slow, taking 100 to 200 years. The classical model of the transition was triggered primarily by the social and economic changes generally known as the Industrial Revolution.

Accelerated Model of Transition

The transition as it occurred in Japan represents the accelerated model, in which the transition was rapid (taking only a few decades in the 20th century) and occurred in response to intensified industrialization. Japan depended predominantly on induced abortion to lower the birth rate.

Delayed Model of Transition

The transition occurring in most of the developing countries of the world can be classified as the delayed model. In these countries, the recession of mortality occurs more in response to medical than to social determinants, and fertility is still high in most such countries, having started to decline in only a few.

Some Details of the Changed Patterns of Health and Disease in Developed Countries

The following brief account of specific disease patterns, mortality profiles, and population changes—as they have occurred in the classical epidemiologic transition—will serve as a framework within which to examine these changes as they are occurring or will occur in the developing countries. For the sake of simplicity, the following epidemiologic, social, and demographic profiles of the classical transition are given in Tables 1–4:

Table 5–1: Population Profile
Table 5–2: Social and Economic Profiles
Table 5–3: Mortality and Disease Profiles
Table 5–4: Community Health Profile

For descriptive purposes, the following periods in the history of the developed countries of the West can be said to have coincided with these specific stages of the transition:

1. The Age of Pestilence and Famine characterized the premodern and early modern (that is, the pre-industrial) period up to about the middle of the 18th century.
2. The Age of Receding Pandemics coincided with the period that included the latter half of the 18th century and virtually all of the 19th.
3. The Age of Degenerative and Man-Made Diseases characterizes the 20th century, the modern epoch. (See Figure 5–1, p. 93)

The description of each of these profiles for each stage of the classical model of the epidemiologic transition not only shows the progressive changes in patterns of health and disease but also helps to illuminate some of the determinants and consequences of these changes.

The demographic transition—that is, the change in the population profile over time—seems to be dominated by the disease and mortality patterns of a society. In the Age of Pestilence and Famine, mortality is very high and fluctuating, with high peaks in the years of epidemics and famines. Fertility is also high, but the resulting population growth is very small, if population grows at all.

During this period the economy is essentially that of a subsistence level; per capita income is very low; and social and living standards are very low. Medical services and education are grossly inadequate, if available at all. Poor nutrition compounds the problems of poor sanitary environments and crowded living conditions to contribute to the high prevalence of infectious diseases. Life expectancy is low—about 20 years of age—and child mortality is very high, as is mortality among women of reproductive age.

During the transition from the Age of Pestilence and Famine through the Age of Receding Pandemics, children and women benefit the most from the dramatic changes in patterns of health and disease. When pandemics begin to recede in response to improving standards of living, social welfare measures, early improvements in nutrition, and early sanitary measures, childhood survival is significantly improved. As women are better nourished and as public health measures become more widely available, they survive through the reproductive span and their fertility is improved. Thus, there are subsequent waves of youth moving

Table 5-1 Population Profile of the Classical (Western) Model of the Epidemiologic Transition

Age of Pestilence and Famine	*Age of Receding Pandemics*	*Age of Degenerative and Man-Made Diseases*
The pattern of growth until about 1650 is cyclic, with minute net increments; mortality dominates, with crude death rates of from 30 to more than 50 per 1,000 population and with frequent higher peaks. Fertility is sustained at a high level of 40 or more per 1,000 population. The population is predominantly young, with very large young and very small old dependency ratios and a slight excess of males (100+ M/100F). Residence is mainly rural, with a few crowded, unsanitary, war-famine-epidemic ridden cities of small to medium size.	*Population Growth* Mortality continues high (30-50 per 1,000), but peaks are less frequent and the general level begins to decline to about 30 per 1,000. Fertility remains high (40+ per 1,000), but several decades after mortality declines, fertility also starts to decline. Population growth is explosive for most of this period. *Population Composition* The population is still young, although the proportion of older people begins to increase. The male/female ratio is near unity (100M/100F), but improved female survival tends toward an excess of females. Residence is still primarily rural, but with a progressive exodus from farm to factory. Selective migration to new colonies relieves population pressure somewhat in homo countries but upsets the age-sex composition.	Mortality declines rapidly to below 20 per 1,000; then the rate of decline slows. Fertility declines to below 20 per 1,000 (with occasional rises, e.g., the post-World War II baby boom) and becomes the chief pacemaker of population growth; fluctuation is by design more than by chance. Population growth is small but persistent. There is a progressive aging of the population as fertility continues to decline and more people, especially females, survive to middle and old age. The male/female ratio continues to decrease. There is a high and increasing old dependency ratio, especially for women. Residence is increasingly urban, with excessive growth of cities (megalopolitanism) and alarming formation of slums, environmental pollution, and unwieldy social and political problems.

up the population pyramid as more and more of them survive and as women live long enough to produce more children.

During the transition from infectious- to degenerative-disease predominance, women usually move from a level of mortality consistently higher than that of men to one lower. A similar peculiarity also becomes manifest in urban-rural mortality patterns; during the early phase of the transition, morbidity and mortality are higher in the urban areas; but during the later phases of the transition, urban rates fall below rural rates.

The epidemiologic transition affects demographic patterns in complex ways. In a fairly stable population with high levels of vital rates and low levels of food supply, a small increase in food availability due to agricultural or transportation improvements, coupled with improvements in personal habits and better sanita-

Table 5-2   Social and Economic Profiles of the Classical (Western) Model of the Epidemiologic Transition

Age of Pestilence and Famine	Age of Pestilence and Famine	Age of Receding Pandemics
Society is traditional, with a fatalistic orientation sustained by rigid, hierarchical sociopolitical structures. Clan or extended family structures with large family size, multiple-generation households, and home-centered lifestyles are dominant. Women are cast strictly in the mother role with virtually no rights or responsibilities outside the home.	Standards are very low; grossly unsanitary conditions prevail at both the public and private levels, and comforts and luxuries are limited to a few elites. Food available to the masses is of poor quality with chronic and occasionally acute shortages. Children and women in the fertile years are most adversely affected. Subsistence economies characterize predominantly agrarian societies which depend on manual, labor-intensive production methods. Occasional breakthroughs and sporadic rises in wages are largely undermined by low incentives and cosmic catastrophes, while labor efficiency is marred by debilitative and enervative diseases.	*Society* A traditional/provincial outlook persists among the lower classes, while the upper and emerging middle classes of businessmen adopt "faith in reason." An era of rising expectations touches nearly all segments of society. *Family and Women* Extended family systems and large family size still prevail, especially in rural areas; nuclear families prevail increasingly in urban centers. The maternal role begins to allow a little involvement in activities outside the home.

tion, can lower general mortality rates from infectious and deficiency diseases. This general lowering of mortality and morbidity can, in turn, increase the effectiveness of the labor force and may also bring a slight increase in survival through the reproductive span as well as in fertility performance. Recent evidence indicates that childhood nutritional levels can also influence later mental effectiveness.

The improved childhood survival experience presumably removes many of the complex social, emotional, and economic rationales for high birth rates and may indeed provoke serious strains within families that are adapted to an expectation of having few children survive to adulthood. The improvements in survival came slowly in the classical epidemiologic transition, thus allowing for gradual adaptation of fertility control practices as they became desirable. Childhood mortality is declining more rapidly in developing countries, however, and it becomes more important than ever to elucidate further the exact processes linking mortality and fertility declines.

Table 5–2 (Continued)

Age of Receding Pandemics	Age of Degenerative and Man-Made Diseases	Age of Degenerative and Man-Made Diseases
Living Standards Standards are still quite low, but hygiene and sanitation improve gradually except in city slums, where bad conditions grow worse.	Rational-purposive lifestyles prevail; bureaucracy and depersonalization foster anomic groups.	Progressive rises in living conditions are enjoyed by large segments of the population.
Nutrition Early improvements in agriculture and crop rotation gradually bring better availability and quality of food, although women and children are still at a nutritional disadvantage.	Nuclear families and small family size norms become institutionalized. Women are increasingly emancipated from traditional roles and become better educated and more career-oriented.	People become extremely conscious of nutrition, especially that of children and mothers. There is, however, a tendency to over nutrition, including consumption of rich and high-fat foods.
Economic Profile Preconditions for economic "take-off" appear. Improvements in agriculture and land-use, coupled with modest development of transportation-communication networks, encourage industrialization; leading sectors of production, e.g., textiles and lumber, emerge.		Scientific expertise and applied technology covering the gamut of economic activities produce spiraling growth initially. Then a stage of high mass consumption brings tapered growth as production shifts from producer to consumer goods and services; public welfare and leisure spending increase.

Examples of specific changes in disease patterns between the Age of Pestilence and Famine and the Age of Degenerative and Man-Made Diseases are given in Table 5–1.

Japan's Accelerated Transition and Prospects for Developing Countries

Japan's epidemiologic transition was similar to the classical transition experienced by Western countries except that it took a little over one-quarter of a century as compared to more than a century in the West. Japan started to industrialize after World War I, and by World War II it was already an industrial power with a base from which to become a highly developed country very rapidly after the war. With industrialization and modernization, there occurred a demographic transition from high birth and death rates in the 1920s to low birth and death rates in the 1950s. An epidemiologic transition took place as well, with degenerative and man-made diseases very rapidly replacing infectious diseases as the leading causes of morbidity and mortality.

It is clear that almost all the developing countries have entered the transition with an Age of Pestilence and Famine characterizing their histories until the first half of the 20th century. Although some countries—for example, Chile—showed a mortality decline (that is, entered the Age of Receding Pandemics) in the interwar period, most of the less developed countries entered this stage after World War II. With only a few exceptions, the less developed countries are still in the Age of Receding Pandemics, experiencing rapidly declining mortality but sustaining high fertility levels. As a result, population growth in most of the developing countries is explosive. It should be noted that the recession of epidemics in these

Table 5–3   Mortality and Disease Profiles of the Classical (Western) Model of the Epidemiologic Transition

Age of Pestilence and Famine	Changing Epidemiology of Selected Diseases	Age of Receding Pandemics

Life expectancy fluctuates around 20, and childhood mortality is very high: A third of all deaths occur in children from 0 to 5; 200-300 infant deaths occur per 1,000 births, and the neonatal to post-neonatal death ratio is small. Proportionate mortality for 50+ ages is low since few reach that age. Females in the adolescent and reproductive years are at a higher risk of dying than males, but at a lower risk at older ages. Mortality is somewhat higher in urban than in rural areas.
 	
Leading causes of death and disease are the epidemic scourges, such as plague, smallpox, cholera and typhus, endemic, parasitic and deficiency diseases, the pneumonia-diarrhea-
  malnutrition
complex in children, and the tuberculosis-puerperal-
  malnutrition
complex in females. Manifest famines occur, and severe malnutrition underlies disease and death from most other causes.
	Tuberculosis is more virulent in young females, especially in their fertile years.
	  Smallpox is typically a childhood disease.
	  Heart disease rates are low, with high rheumatic to arteriosclerotic ratio.
	  Deficiency disease symptomatology is typical and highly prevalent.
		Mortality Pattern
		There is considerable change in mortality level and pattern with the recession of pandemics. Life expectancy increases to 30 to 40+. Mortality declines favor children under 15 and women in the fertile years. Infant mortality drops below 150 per 1,000 births, and the neonatal to post-neonatal ratio increases progressively. Proportionate mortality of the 50+ ages increases to close to 50 percent.
		
		Leading Causes of Death
		Although some epidemic diseases start to recede, the leading causes of death and disease are endemic, parasitic and deficiency diseases, epidemic scourges, and childhood and maternal complexes. Cholera sweeps Europe in successive waves before disappearing. Industrial and other noninfectious diseases increase. Undernutrition, although somewhat ameliorated, continues to be important.

Table 5–3   (Continued)

Age of Receding Pandemics	Age of Degenerative and Man-Made Diseases	Age of Degenerative and Man-Made Diseases
Tuberculosis mortality peaks with industrialization; it is still more virulent in young females. Smallpox starts to occur less in children and more in adults due to vaccination of children. Heart disease increases, and there is a decrease in the rheumatic to arteriosclerotic ratio. Death from starvation becomes rare and many deficiency diseases such as scurvy start to disappear.	Life expectancy reaches an unprecedented high of 70+ and is about three or more years higher for women than for men. Risks for females of all ages decrease, and maternal mortality declines to a minimum. The age profile shows reductions in childhood mortality, which accounts for less than 10 percent of the total deaths, while deaths at 50+ years increase to 70 percent or more of the total. Infant mortality is less than 25 per 1,000, and the ratio of neonatal to post-neonatal deaths is large and still increasing. Heart diseases, cancer, and stroke replace infection as prime killers. Pneumonia, bronchitis, influenza, and some viral diseases remain problems. Polio rises, then tapers off. Scarlet fever begins to disappear.	Tuberculosis is low but persists in slum populations and in older disadvantaged individuals, especially males. Smallpox is rare; when it does occur, it is a disease of adults. Heart disease is high, with a very low rheumatic to arteriosclerotic ratio. Starvation is rare; pellagra disappears; rickets drops off.

countries has been the result more of medical change than of social change. The introduction of insecticides and the widespread use of immunization, chemotherapy, and antibiotics have been the major determinants in the control of epidemics and of endemic diseases. Improved nutrition and sanitation control programs have also had an impact on mortality levels.

A few developing countries have begun to show a decline in both fertility and mortality. These include Ceylon, Taiwan, Korea, and Guatemala, which are attempting to emerge from the critical phase of Receding Pandemics to the more favorable phase of Degenerative and Man-Made Diseases. However, although heart disease, stroke, and cancer have begun to move into the leading causes of death in these countries, infectious diseases still predominate. To illustrate this point, Table 5–5 gives the ten leading causes of death for the following countries: (1) the United States, as an example of a developed country which has been in the Age of Degenerative and Man-Made Diseases since early in the century, (2) Japan, as an example of a country which has achieved an accelerated transition, (1) the United States, as an example of a developed country which has been in the Age of Degenerative and Man-Made Diseases since early in the century, (2)

Japan, as an example of a country which has achieved an accelerated transition, (3) Chile, as an example of a less developed country still trapped in the Age of Receding Pandemics, and (4) Ceylon, as an example of a less developed country about to emerge from the Age of Receding Pandemics into the Age of Degenerative and Man-Made Diseases.

Since the problems associated with population pressure in developing coun-

Table 5 — 4   Community Health Profile of the Classical (Western) Model of the Epidemiologiic Transition.

Age of Pestilence and Famine	Health Systems and Services	Age of Degenerative and Man-Made Diseases
1. Epidemics are frequent and devastating; famines are frequent in certain areas.	*Leading Community Health Problems and Programs*	1. Morbidity comes to overshadow mortality as an index of health as degenerative, man-made, and chronic disease problems (such as mental illness, drug addiction, radiation hazards, and pollution) Increase.
2. Endemic infections and parasitic diseases are prevalent.	1. Epidemics and famines continue to be major problems, but their magnitude progressively declines. Heart disease and cancer increase but are still overshadowed by infection.	
3. Chronic malnutrition and manifest deficiency diseases are widespread.	2. Endemic infection and parasitism also recede to some extent toward the end of the period.	2. Endemic infection and parasitism almost disappear except in certain pockets among underprivileged minority or racial groups.
4. Maternal and child health problems are severe.	3. Occupational health problems arise in industrializing areas.	3. Maternal and child health problems are brought under control, but geriatric problems become more serious.
5. Environmental problems are appalling; these include contaminated water supplies, human waste problems, prevalence of insects and rodents, reservoirs of infection, poor food sanitation, and poor housing.	4. Maternal and child health continues to be problematic, especially at beginning of this period.	4. Humanitarian workmen's legislation controls many occupational hazards, but new procedures and materials in industry create new hazards, e.g., electrical, chemical, and radiation hazards.
6. Health problems are prevalent in both rural and urban areas.	5. Sanitary environmental hazards start to show signs of receding toward the end of this period.	5. Environmental sanitation problems are ameliorated, but pollution due to industrialization and urbanization grows larger.
7. Accidents occur mostly in the home.	6. Urban health problems increase as a result of in-migration and crowding under unsanitary conditions. Later, urban areas begin to benefit from sanitation.	6. The rising cost of medical care becomes a serious problem in many countries.
	7. Accidents occur in both home and factory.	7. Traffic and transportation accidents prevail.

Table 5–4   (Continued)

Age of Pestilence and Famine	Age of Receding Pandemics	Age of Degenerative and Man-Made Diseases
1. The only health care systems are indigenous systems which often rely on witchcraft and poor practices in the care of the sick. 2. No decisive therapies are available. 3. Immunization is not available. 4. There is no environmental sanitation. 5. The only effective measures for epidemic control are isolation and quarantine.	1. The recession of epidemics and relief of famines are triggered by improvement of nutrition and rising standards of living. 2. The beginnings of the sanitary revolution accelerate the recession of epidemics toward the end of the period. Refuse removal begins in London in 1848 and a network of sewers in 1865. Private wells were the main source of water until the introduction of some waterworks in the 18th and 19th centuries (without purification until the 19th century). Personal hygiene improved as soap and washable undergarments came into widespread use. 3. Isolation and quarantine measures for control of epidemics were more stringently enforced. 4. Medical advances, such as the development of antiseptics by Lister in 1865, made surgery safer. Immunization against smallpox was introduced by Jenner in 1798. 5. Organized health services were started in some countries and progressed in quality and quantity.	1. Modern nationwide organized health programs develop with comprehensive, integrated systems of curative and preventive health, intensive research, and advances in medical and surgical care. 2. Special categorical health programs are developed, for example, for maternal and child care, venereal disease control, and tuberculosis control. 3. Rigorous sanitary measures become more widespread, including adequate water purification with the introduction of chlorination, sewage treatment, refuse disposal, insect and rodent control, better housing, and town planning. 4. Case finding and mass screening for some diseases become widespread. 5. Insecticides, chemotherapy, and antibiotics further accelerate the recession of epidemics. 6. Health systems are advanced by prosperous societies drawing on adequate health manpower and an enlightened public.

tries are becoming more intense, the need to understand the processes of the epidemiologic and demographic transitions therefore becomes more urgent. Whether or not the developing countries of today can undergo an accelerated transition in a way similar to Japan remains an important question and depends upon the many complex determinants of morbidity and mortality and the reaction of fertility practices to changes in mortality.

Table 5–5   Leading Causes of Death (For Selected Countries)

United States (1967)	Percent of Total Deaths	Japan (1968)	Percent of Total Deaths
Heart disease	33.8	Cerebrovascular disease	25.5
Cancer	16.8	Cancer	16.8
Vascular lesions	10.9	Heart disease	11.1
Accidents	6.1	Accidents	5.9
Childhood diseases	3.5	Pneumonia	3.7
Hypertension	3.3	Hypertensive disease	2.6
Pneumonia	3.0	Tuberculosis	2.5
Diabetes	1.9	Bronchitis, etc.	2.2
Cirrhosis of the liver	1.5	Suicide	2.1
Suicide	1.3	Childhood diseases	2.0
Birth rate/1,000 population	17.8	Birth rate/1,000 population	18.5
Death rate/1,000 population	9.4	Death rate/1,000 population	6.8
Rate of natural increase	0.84%	Rate of natural increase	1.17%

Chile (1966)	Percent of Total Deaths	Ceylon (1966)	Percent of Total Deaths
Pneumonia	14.7	Childhood diseases	12.2
Heart disease	11.3	Gastritis, diarrhea, etc.	6.4
Cancer	11.3	Heart disease	6.4
Childhood diseases	6.8	Pneumonia	5.8
Cerebrovascular disease	6.2	Accidents	3.6
Gastroenteritis	5.4	Cancer	3.2
Accidents	4.8	Anemias	2.5
Cirrhosis of the liver	4.2	Tuberculosis	1.8
Tuberculosis	3.5	Suicide	1.7
Influenza	2.8	Vascular lesions	1.5
Birth rate/1,000 population	30.1	Birth rate/1,000 population	32.3
Death rate/1,000 population	10.2	Death rate/1,000 population	8.3
Rate of natural increase	1.99%	Rate of natural increase	2.40%

Source: Official Records of the World Health Organization, *Fourth Report on the World Health Situation, 1965–68. 192,* Geneva: World Health Organization, 1971.

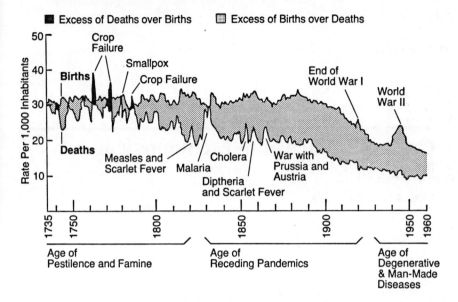

Figure 5–1   The Epidemiologic Transition in Denmark: 1735–1960

Source: "A New Science Emerges," *Population Bulletin 10* 1954, p. 60. Reprinted by permission of the Population Reference Bureau.

References

Omran, A. R. The epidemiologic transition: A theory of the epidemology of population change. *Milbank Memorial Fund Quarterly 49* 1971: 509–38.

On the Science and Technology of   6
Medicine

LEWIS THOMAS, M.D.

The common theme running through almost all the criticisms leveled at the American health-care system these days is the charge of inadequacy or insufficiency. There are not enough doctors and nurses, and those around lack sufficient interest and compassion; there are not enough clinics, and those around lack sufficient time to see everyone; there are too few medical schools, medical centers, and specialized hospitals, with inequities in their distribution around the country; most of all, there is not enough money, not enough commitment.

And yet, the system has been expanding with explosive force in the last quarter-century. It has been nothing short of a boom. In 1950, the total national expenditure in health care was estimated at $10 billion. By 1972, it had risen to over $70 billion. In 1974, it was $110 billion. This year it will at least exceed $130 billion, and it will be still larger if a national health-insurance program emerges. According to some more or less official estimates it could exceed $250 billion by the 1980s.

Whatever the defects, it cannot be claimed that the nation has been failing to react. Any enterprise that amplifies itself over a 25-year period in this exuberant fashion is surely making a try. It is, whatever else, a massive effort to improve.

The question is: What are we improving? What, in fact, have we been trying to accomplish with these vast sums?

An alien historian would think, from a look just at the dollar figures for each of those years, that some sort of tremendous event must have been occurring since 1950. Either (1) the health of the nation had suddenly disintegrated, requir-

From *Daedalus,* the Journal of the American Academy of Arts and Sciences, Boston, Mass., (Winter, 1977). *Doing Better and Feeling Worse: Health in the United States.* Reprinted with permission.

ing the laying on of new resources to meet the crisis, or (2) the technology for handling health problems had undergone a major transformation, necessitating the installation of new effective resources to do things that could not be done before, or (3), another possibility, perhaps we had somehow been caught up in the momentum of a huge, collective, ponderous set of errors. If any of these explanations is the right one, we ought at least to become aware of it, since whatever we are improving will involve, in the near future, an even more immense new bureaucracy, an even larger commitment of public funds, regulations that will intervene in every aspect of the citizen's life, and, inevitably, still more expansion. This paper will deal with the arguments around each of these three possible explanations.

The Health of the Nation, 1950–1975

There is, to begin with, no real evidence that health has deteriorated in this country, certainly not to the extent indicated by the new dollars spent each year for health care. On the contrary, we seem to have gotten along reasonably well.

There is perhaps more heart disease, but this is to be expected in a generally older population living beyond the life expectancy of 50 years ago. Heart disease is, after all, one of the ways of dying, and death certificates do not usually distinguish between heart failure as the result of time having run out and other forms of heart disease, except by noting age. The total numbers have increased somewhat, and perhaps there are also somewhat more cases of coronary occlusion in middle-aged men, but we have not suddenly been plagued, just since 1950, by new heart disease in anything like frightening numbers.

Cancer, stroke, kidney disease, arthritis, schizophrenia, cirrhosis, multiple sclerosis, senility, asthma, pulmonary fibrosis, and a few other major diseases are still with us, but the change in incidence per capita is not sufficient to account for the move from a $10 billion enterprise to a $130 billion one.

Aging is not in itself a health problem, although a larger number of surviving old people obviously means proportionately more people with the disabling illnesses characteristic of the aged. However, the increased number of such patients since 1950 is not great enough to account for much of the increased investment.

Meanwhile, there has been a general improvement in the public health with respect to certain infectious diseases which were major problems in the 25-year period prior to 1950. Lobar pneumonia, scarlet fever, crysipelas, rheumatic fever, subacute bacterial endocarditis, typhoid fever, poliomyelitis, diphtheria, pertussis, meningococcal meningitis, staphylococcal septicemia, all of which filled the wards of municipal and county hospitals in the earlier period, have become rarities. To be sure, new sorts of bacterial infection have appeared in hospital communities, as complications of other therapy in most instances, but the total number of these is a small figure alongside the infectious diseases of the pre-antibiotic, pre-immunization period.

On balance, then, no case can be made for a wave of new illnesses afflicting
our population in the years since 1950. If anything, we are probably a somewhat
healthier people because of the sharp decrease in severe infectious disease.

But this is not the general view of things: the public perception of the public
health, in 1975, appears to be quite different. There is now a much more acute
awareness of the risk of disease than in earlier periods, associated with a greater
apprehension that a minor illness may turn suddenly into a killing disease. There
is certainly a higher expectation that all kinds of disease can be treated effectively. Finally, personal maladjustments of all varieties—unhappiness, discontent,
fear, anxiety, despair, marital discord, even educational problems—have come to
be regarded as medical problems, requiring medical attention, imposing new,
heavy demands for care. In addition, there are probably many more people in this
country requiring specialized rehabilitation services for disabilities resulting from
physical trauma (Korea and Vietnam veterans, automobile- and industrial-acci-
dent victims, etc.).

Health-Care Technology, 1950–1975

Has the effective technology for medical care changed in the past 25 years to a
degree sufficient to explain the increased cost? Is there in fact a new high technology of medicine?

Despite the widespread public impression that this is the case, there is little
evidence for it. The most spectacular technological change has occurred in the
management of infectious disease, but its essential features had been solidly
established and put to use well before 1950. The sulfonamides came to medicine
in the late 1930s, penicillin and streptomycin a few years later, and the major
advances in the control and cure of infectious disease occurred during the 1940s.
There has been no quantum leap in anti-infectious technology since 1950. Several new virus vaccines have been developed. The antibiotics have come into
more widespread use (probably with considerable overuse and waste); a multi-
plicity of new variants of antibiotics and chemotherapeutic agents has appeared
on the market, but one would not expect that the rational use of this technology,
even allowing for the high cost of development and marketing, would have
proven to be anything like the previous cost of hospital care in the absence of
such a technology. A typical case of lobar pneumonia, pre-antibiotic, involved
three or four weeks of hospitalization; typhoid was a 12- to 16-week illness; meningitis often required several months of care through convalescence; these and
other common infectious diseases can now be aborted promptly, within just a few
days. The net result of the anti-infection technology ought to have been a very
large decrease in the cost of care.

There have been a few other examples of technology improvement, comparable in decisive effectiveness, since 1950, but the best of these have been for
relatively uncommon illnesses. Childhood leukemia and certain solid tumors in
children, for example, can now be cured by chemotherapy in a substantial pro-

portion of cases, but there are only a few thousand of these per year in the country. Endocrine-replacement therapy has become highly effective and relatively inexpensive ("relative" considering the cost of caring for untreated endocrine abnormalities) for a variety of disorders involving the adrenals, pituitary, parathyroid, ovary, and thyroid; in particular, the biochemical treatment of thyroid dysfunction has improved markedly. Hematology has offered new and effective replacement treatment for certain anemias. Immunologic prophylaxis now prevents most cases of hemolytic disease of the newborn. Progress in anesthesia, electrolyte physiology, and cardiopulmonary physiology has greatly advanced the field of surgery, so that reparative and other procedures can now be done which formerly were technically impossible.

But the list of decisive new accomplishments is not much longer than the contents of the above paragraph.

We are left with approximately the same roster of common major diseases which confronted the country in 1950, and, although we have accumulated a formidable body of information about some of them in the intervening time, the accumulation is not yet sufficient to permit either the prevention or the outright cure of any of them. This is not to suggest that progress has not been made, or has been made more slowly than should reasonably have been expected. On the contrary, the research activity since 1950 has provided the beginnings of insight into the underlying processes in several of our most important diseases, and there is every reason for optimism regarding the future. But it is the present that is the problem. We are, in a sense, partway along, maybe halfway along. At the same time, medicine is expected to do something for each of these illnesses, to do whatever can be done in the light of today's knowledge. Because of this obligation, we have evolved "halfway" technologies, representing the best available treatment, and the development and proliferation of these are partly responsible for the escalating costs of health care in recent years. Associated with this expansion, the diagnostic laboratories have become much more elaborate and complex in their technologies; there is no question that clinical diagnosis has become much more powerful and precise, but at a very high cost and with considerable waste resulting from overuse.

This way of looking at contemporary medicine runs against the currently general public view that the discipline has by this time come almost its full distance, that we have had a long succession of "breakthroughs" and "major advances," and that now we should go beyond our persistent concern with research on what is called "curative" medicine and give more attention to the social aspects of illness and to preventive medicine.

It does not, in fact, look much like the record of a completed job, or even of a job more than half begun, when you run through the list, one by one, of the diseases in this country which everyone will agree are the most important ones. A handy index for this sort of exercise is the annual *United States Vital Statistics Report,* in which are tabulated the ten leading causes of death, as well as the commonest non-fatal illnesses requiring attention from the health-care system.

The questions to be asked are the following: For how many of these ill-

nesses do we now possess a decisively effective technology for cure or prevention, directed at a central disease agent or mechanism, comparable to the
treatment, say, of pneumococcal lobar pneumonia with penicillin? Are we failing
to employ effective measures because of deficiencies in the health-care system?
To what extent do present mortality and morbidity rates simply reflect the
absence of any known technology that works?

In the following section, these questions are explored. It should be emphasized here that we will not be discussing the availability of medical treatment in
general. Obviously, there is a great deal that can be done for patients with the
diseases considered below in the way of supportive care, the amelioration of
symptoms, and sometimes the extension of life. In some conditions, this amounts
to what might be called partial control of the disease, but this is not the question
at hand. What we are examining here is the capacity of medicine to cure outright
or to prevent completely—in situations analogous to lobar pneumonia or
poliomyelitis.

Listed below are the ten leading causes of death from disease in the United
States in 1974:

Cardiovascular disease (39 percent of total deaths in 1974): In general, cardiovascular disease lacks any decisive, conclusive technology with the power to
turn off, reverse, or prevent disease. There are two possible exceptions: rheumatic heart disease is known to be preventable when the antecedent streptococcal infection can be quickly terminated by early antibiotic treatment or prevented
by prophylaxis; some forms of congenital heart disease can be completely cor-
rected by surgery. Except for these, the other therapies now available are
directed at secondary results of already established disease: coronary-care units
and specialized ambulances, designed primarily for coping with cardiac standstill
and arrythmias, anticoagulant treatment to prevent extension and recurrence
(largely given up in recent years), digitalis and diuretics for myocardial failure,
drug therapyto inhibit arrythmias, and surgical replacement of already damaged
coronary arteries or valves.

As to coronary disease, it is believed in some quarters that dietary lipids are
an ecologic factor. It is also proposed that lack of exercise, excessive emotional
stress, and various usually unstipulated environmental influences are somehow
implicated in pathogenesis. The evidence for these beliefs is still inconclusive. In
any event, intervention to correct them would involve grand-scale, societal
reforms of living habits. Meanwhile, the actual pathologic events which cause the
coronary lesions remain unknown. Until these are elucidated in some detail, a
direct approach to coronary disease must await the future.

Hypertension is a separate disease state, frequently associated with cardiac
disease. This will be considered below.

Cancer (19 percent of total deaths in 1974): Up to now, the technologies
available for the treatment of cancer are all in the "halfway" category, in the
sense that they deal with the already established disease and represent efforts to
destroy, by one means or another (surgery, radiation, chemotherapy, immuno-

therapy), existing cancer cells. There are no methods for reversing the neoplastic process in cells or for preventing their emergence from normal cells. Prevention would be possible for a few types, if exposure to the known environmental carcinogens, e.g., cigarettes, asbestos, and certain industrial chemicals, could be eliminated. But prevention in the sense of eliminating the biological steps involved in the transformation of cells is not yet feasible.

Cerebrovascular diseases (11 percent of total deaths in 1974): Stroke results from disease of the arteries of the brain, usually associated with atherosclerosis or hypertension. Since no therapy exists for preventing or reversing atherosclerosis, this class of strokes is neither preventable nor reversible. Hypertension is considered below.

Once stroke occurs, therapy is limited to efforts at minimizing the extent of disability, largely a matter of retraining, rehabilitation, and speech therapy. No treatment exists for preventing the recurrence of stroke. Anticoagulant therapy, once attempted on a large scale, is no longer in general use.

Kidney disease (10.4 percent of total deaths in 1974): The major forms of kidney disease responsible for most cases of renal failure and death are chronic glomerulonephritis and pyelonephritis.

At the present time, no effective treatment exists for chronic glomerulonephritis, beyond measures aimed at compensating for the loss of renal function, e.g., electrolyte adjustment, chronic dialysis and, in a relatively few cases, kidney transplantation. Some cases are perhaps prevented by early treatment of antecedent streptococcal infection, but the initial cause in most instances is unknown. The essential lesion is a deposit of an antigen-antibody complex within the walls of glomerular capillaries, followed by injury to the vessels probably mediated by leucocytic lysosomes and complement. A direct therapeutic approach to these vents cannot be conceived until more detailed scientific information becomes available.

Chronic pyelonephritis can probably be prevented in some instances by early treatment of the acute infection, but in most cases the kidney lesions develop gradually and unobtrusively, and once established they are not reversible. It is believed by some that bacterial protoplasts are involved in etiology, perhaps also with an associated immunologic injury to the tissues, even if this is so, currently available anti-microbial therapy is not effective.

Pulmonary disease (approximately 4.5 percent of total deaths in 1974): Included under this heading, in the *Vital Statistics Report,* are influenza and pneumonia, bronchitis, emphysema and chronic obstructive lung disease.

Almost all cases of primary bacterial and mycoplasmal pneumonia are treatable and curable by use of the appropriate antibiotic.

Influenza can be prevented in some cases by immunization, provided the antigenic strain is recognized early enough in an outbreak to prepare vaccine. Once it has occurred, there is no therapy for the influenza viral infection itself. Bacterial superinfections, when they occur, are reversible except in the occasional cases of sudden, overwhelming infection to which pregnant women and debilitated elderly people are most prone. Antibiotic treatment of uncomplicated influenza is ineffective and probably hazardous.

Bronchitis, emphysema, and chronic pulmonary obstructive disease are still unsolved etiologic problems. Cigarette smoking and air pollution are suspected as causes, but the actual mechanisms underlying the injury to lung tissue remain unknown. Although technologies exist for the improvement of aeration by the damaged lungs, and thus for some prolongation of life, there are no measures available for stopping or reversing the progress of disease.

Diabetes mellitus (1.9 percent of total deaths in 1974): Although the discovery of insulin fifty years ago made possible the survival of most diabetics who would otherwise have died in diabetic coma, the blood-vessel disorder which is a major aspect of the disease is unaffected by insulin and remains a mystery. Hence, the disabilities and deaths of diabetics, mostly in middle-age and later, are now due to chronic kidney disease and the occlusion of arteries in one or another part of the body. Virtually nothing is known about the cause of vascular lesions, and there is no therapy to stop or reverse the process.

Cirrhosis of the liver (1.8 percent of total deaths in 1974): The chief cause of cirrhosis is unquestionably alcohol taken in excess and over a long period of time. If alcoholism could be prevented, cirrhosis would become a relatively rare affliction. The hepatic lesions are to some extent reversible, and the disease can sometimes be stopped and even reversed in its early stages by simple abstention.

This, however, represents about the total of today's effective therapy. The mechanism of hepatic cell injury by alcohol is not understood, nor is the process by which the liver becomes progressively atrophic and fibrosed. Nutritional deprivation, believed a few years back to play a central role, is no longer thought to be centrally involved. Once the disease is firmly established, there is no known method for turning it around. Surgical measures have been developed for reducing ascites (that is, fluid accumulation in the abdomen) and the back pressure of portal blood, whith some ameliorative effort on the symptoms of cirrhosis, but the injury to the liver itself is unalterable.

Perinatal disease (1.5 percent of total deaths in 1974): Much of the infant mortality in the earliest days of life is associated with prematurity, and obstructive disease of the lungs accounts for much of this. At the present time, there is no effective therapy for this pulmonary disease, caused by hyaline, membranous deposits which occlude the alveolar walls. The mechanisms leading to these deposits are unknown.

Bacterial and viral infections account for a majority of other neonatal deaths. The bacterial infections are treatable with antibiotics, but often occur abruptly in overwhelming form. The viral infections are untreatable.

Hemolytic disease of the newborn, formerly a common cause of death, is now preventable by immunologic treatment during pregnancy; some cases can be cured by total blood replacement and transfusions.

Congenital malformations and deficiencies (0.7 percent of total deaths in

1974): Although surgical measures are available for the correction of some types of congenital malformation, such as cardiac and intestinal anomalies, most of them are untreatable. A few of the highly disabling and fatal enzyme deficiencies can be recognized during early pregnancy and thus prevented by abortion. The biochemical and genetic nature of these rare disorders is currently under investigation in many laboratories, and there is some optimism that methods for reversing the defects will eventually be found.

Peptic ulcer: Few human ailments have been subjected to as great a variety of medcal and surgical treatments over the years as peptic ulcer, often with enthusiastic predictions of success, but always replaced by new and different therapies. The main problem hampering decisive progress is that the mechanism that produces peptic ulcers is not understood, and therefore there is no basis for devising a genuinely rational method of treatment or prevention. This is not to say that it is not a treatable condition, of course. There are many ways in which the symptoms and the progress of the disease can be alleviated. Nevertheless, it must be ranked as an essentially unexplained disorder.

The foregoing list accounts for approximately 80 percent of all deaths in this country. It does not, of course, account for the major part of the work of physicians, nor the greatest element of cost for the health-care system. We are afflicted, obviously, by a great (but it must be said, finite) array of non-fatal illnesses varying in severity and duration, and it is here that the greatest demands for technology are made. For the purposes of this paper, some of the commonest of these self-limited or non-fatal diseases are listed below:

Acute respiratory infections: These and the acute gastroenteric infections and intoxications (see below) make up the great majority of transiently disabling illnesses with which people are afflicted in a year's turning.

The common cold and the array of other respiratory viral infections including influenza (sometimes called "grippe") are essentially untreatable. The measures employed for alleviating discomfort—bed rest, aspirin, a good book—are no different today from what one's grandmother would have prescribed. There is, in short, no medical technology for such illnesses. The administration of antibiotics, antihistamines, vitamin C, and various other "cold remedies" probably have no effect other than reassurance. There is a general apprehension that such illnesses may lead to other, more severe, respiratory infections, such as pneumonia, if not monitored by a physician, but there is in fact no evidence for this. By and large, people with these illnesses get better by themselves, usually within a day or two. The most frequent complications are the result of untoward reactions to unnecessary therapy, most often the antibiotics used in the hope of preventing complications.

Gastrointestinal infections: The general run of acute gastrointestinal illnesses, usually caused by a virus or salmonella infection or by staphylococcal toxin, are common, self-limited, and entirely without hazard. Intervention by medicine would be desirable, since these are unpleasant experiences for the afflicted, and there are in fact several symptomatic measures for partial relief, but the illnesses are usually so short in duration that no therapy is necessary. As in the case of acute respiratory infections, grandmother's advice is as good as any, maybe better.

Arthritis: Both rheumatoid arthritis and osteoarthritis, which account for more than 5 million illnesses each year, are unexplained, mystifying diseases for which no therapy beyond analgesic drugs is available. Rheumatoid arthritis is currently believed by a consensus of clinical investigators to be caused by an unknown infectious agent, probably with a still unidentified immunopathologic component. The partial relief provided by salicylates and related drugs, and by gold salts, are still unexplainable. In approximately 35 percent of all cases the disease subsides spontaneously and vanishes. Prolonged, chronically disabling forms of arthritis can be partially benefited by surgical removal of inflamed synovial (joint) tissues. Prolonged hospitalization and various forms of rehabilitative care are required in some cases. In the absence of information concerning etiology, it is probable that treatment will remain at a symptomatic, empirical level not very different from the measures of 50 years ago.

Osteoarthritis remains totally unexplained. Surgical treatment is useful in some (notably hip) cases; otherwise therapy is limited to analgesic drugs.

The neuroses: It is frequently said that at least 75 percent of the patients seeking help in doctors' offices or clinics have complaints for which there is no "organic" explanation. Some of these patients are not really ill, but simply in need of reassurance that they do not have one or another disease which they are worried about. Others are beset by family, economic, or various other social problems which seem temporarily insoluble, and for which they seek advice. Still others, an unknown number, are disabled by classical psychoneuroses.

The possible therapeutic approaches to such problems have not changed significantly in the past quarter-century. Counseling, comforting, and what is called psychotherapy are essentially the same procedures as in earlier times, without any real elements of technology, nor is there any statistical evidence for their effectiveness. An immense store of so-called "tranquilizer" drugs has been provided by pharmaceutical research in recent years, but there is little information as to the efficacy of its contents. They may provide transient symptomatic relief, but it is unlikely that they alter the underlying processes of these illnesses. In short, there is no real technology available for the treatment of "functional" illness, psychoneurosis, or the various forms of social maladaptation. It seems safe to say that nothing much has happened since 1950 to alter the situation one way or the other.

The psychoses: Schizophrenia and the manic-depressive psychoses account for the greatest part of mental illness requiring hospitalization and prolonged ambulatory care. Drug therapy evolved since 1950 has greatly improved the "manageability" of schizophrenia, but it has not much changed the disease itself. The manic-depressive psychoses are improved in some instances by pharmacologic treatment, including lithium, and also in some by electric shock. All forms of psychosis remain unexplained, however, in terms of identifiable mechanisms attributable to dysfunction in the central nervous system, and therapy directed at underlying processes has not advanced beyond what was available before 1950.

Parkinsonism: The introduction of L-Dopa as therapy for Parkinsonism in the mid-1960s by Cotzias and his associates represents a milestone in neurological medicine. Although not all patients are uniformly benefited, and some become refractory or display untoward reactions to the drug, many do well and have their lives transformed.

Essential hypertension: In some respects, hypertension is a paradigm illustrating a central dilemma in today's health-care system. Drugs are now available with the capacity to reduce blood-pressure levels to normal. At the same time, however, the actual mechanisms of the disease remain without explanation, and it is not yet known whether the reduction of blood pressure has any effect on the underlying vascular disturbance. There is now some evidence, still incomplete, that prolonged treatment with anti-hypertensive drug decreases the incidence of stroke as a complication of hypertension. There may also be an effect on the incidence of coronary occlusion, although the evidence for this is less conclusive. There appears to be no doubt that drug treatment can prolong survival in patients with malignant hypertension.

On the basis of these observations, it has been proposed that large-scale screening programs be set up, so that all of the ten million or more young, potentially vulnerable people with hypertension in this country can be identified and treated. This means that great numbers of patients with essential hypertension will be placed on lifelong treatment with complex pharmacologic agents, necessarily persuaded to stay under treatment because of the threat of a fatal outcome. At the same time it is a certainty that many patients with essential hypertension, if not treated, would nevertheless be able to look forward to the statistical probability of a normal life span. Indeed, there are reasons to believe that essential hypertension is a normal state of affairs for some people. The difficulty is that there is no way to predict which patients will eventually have cardiac, cerebral, or renal complications associated with hypertension; in the absence of such knowledge, all hypertensives must be treated. Meanwhile, the disease itself remains an enigma. If a mass screening and therapy program is launched it will be done in the hope that treating a symptom of disease will have long-range beneficial effects. Moreover, it will involve drug therapy, with certain predictable side effects, and perhaps still others unpredicted thus far, aimed at the protection of a minority of the patients to be treated.

The Cost of Worry in the Health-Care System

Nothing has changed so much in the health-care system over the past 25 years as the public's perception of its own health. The change amounts to a loss of confidence in the human form. The general belief these days seems to be that the body is fundamentally flawed, subject to disintegration at any moment, always on the verge of mortal disease, always in need of continual monitoring and support by health-care professionals. This is a new phenomenon in our society.

It can be seen most clearly in the content of television programs and, especially, television commercials, where the preponderance of material deals with the need for shoring up one's personal health. The same drift is evident in the contents of the most popular magazines and in the health columns of daily newspapers. There is a public preoccupation with disease that is assuming the dimension of a national obsession.

To some extent, the propaganda which feeds the obsession is a result of the well intentioned efforts by particular disease agencies to obtain public money for the support of research and care in their special fields. Every mail brings word of the imminent perils posed by multiple sclerosis, kidney disease, cancer, heart disease, cystic fibrosis, asthma, muscular dystrophy, and the rest.

There is, regrettably, no discernible counter-propaganda. No agencies exist for the celebration of the plain fact that most people are, in real life, abundantly healthy. No one takes public note of the truth of the matter, which is that most people in this country have a clear, unimpeded run at a longer lifetime than could have been foreseen by any earlier generation. Even the proponents of good hygiene, who argue publicly in favor of regular exercise, thinness, and abstinence from cigarettes and alcohol, base their arguments on the presumed intrinsic fallibility of human health. Left alone, unadvised by professionals, the tendency of the human body is perceived as prone to steady failure.

Underlying this pessimistic view of health is a profound dissatisfaction with the fact of death. Dying is regarded as the ultimate failure, something that could always be avoided or averted if only the health-care system functioned more efficiently. Death has been made to seem unnatural, an outrage; when people die — at whatever age—we speak of them as having been "struck down," "felled." It is as though in a better world we would all go on forever.

It is not surprising that all this propaganda has imposed heavy, unsupportable demands on the health-care system. If people are educated to believe that they may at any moment be afflicted with one or another mortal disease and that this fate can be forestalled by access to medicine, especially "preventive" medicine, it is no wonder that clinics and doctors' offices are filled with waiting clients.

In the year 1974, 1,933,000 people died in the United States, a death rate of 9.1 per 1,000, or just under 1 percent of the whole population, substantially lower than the birth rate for the same year. The life expectation for the whole population rose to 72 years, the highest expectancy ever attained in this country. With figures like these, it is hard to see health as a crisis, or the health-care system, apart from its huge size and high cost, as a matter needing emergency action. We really are a quite healthy society, and we should be spending more time and energy in acknowledging this, and perhaps trying to understand more clearly why it is so. We are in some danger of becoming a nation of healthy hypochondriacs.

For all its obvious defects and shortcomings, the actual technology of health care is not likely to be changed drastically in the direction of saving money—not in the short haul. Nor is it likely that changes for the better, in the sense of greater effectiveness and efficiency, can be brought about by any means other than more scientific research. The latter course, although sure, is undeniably slow and unpredictable. While it is a certainty, in my view, that rheumatoid arthritis, atherosclerosis, cancer, and senile dementia will eventually be demystified and can then become preventable disorders, there is no way of forecasting when this will happen; it could be a few years away for one or the other, or decades.

Meanwhile, we will be compelled to live with the system as we have it, changing only the parts that are in fact changeable. It is not likely that money problems can induce anyone—the professionals or the public at large, or even the third-party payers—to give up the halfway technologies that work only partially when this would mean leaving no therapeutic effort at all in place. For as long as there is a prospect of saving the lives of 50 percent, or even only 33 percent, of patients with cancer by today's methods for destroying cancer cells, these methods must obviously be held onto and made available to as many patients as possible. If coronary bypass surgery remains the only technical measure for relieving untractable angina in a relatively small proportion of cases, it will be continued, and very likely extended to larger numbers of cases, until something better turns up. People with incapacitating mental illness cannot simply be left to wander the streets, and we will continue to need expanding clinics and specialized hospital facilities, even though caring for the mentally ill does not mean anything like curing them. We are, in a sense, stuck with today's technology, and we will stay stuck until we have more scientific knowledge to work with.

But what we might do, if we could muster the energy and judgment for it, is to identify the areas of health care in which the spending of money represents outright waste, and then eliminate these. There are discrete examples all over the place, but what they are depends on who is responsible for citing them, and there will be bitter arguments over each one before they can be edited out of the system, one by one.

The biggest source of waste results from the general public conviction that contemporary medicine is able to accomplish a great deal more than is in fact possible. This attitude is in part the outcome of overstated claims on the part of medicine itself in recent decades, plus medicine's passive acquiescence while even more exaggerated claims were made by the media. The notion of preventive medicine as a whole new discipline in medical care is an example of this. There is an arguably solid base for the prevention of certain diseases, but it has not changed all that much since the 1950s. A few valuable measures have been added, most notably the avoidance of cigarette smoking for the prevention of lung cancer; if we had figured out a way of acting on this single bit of information, we might have achieved a spectacular triumph in the prevention of deaths from cancer, but regrettably we didn't. The same despairing thing can be said for the preventability of death from alcohol.

But there is not much more than this in the field of preventive medicine. The truth is that medicine has not become very skilled at disease prevention—not, as is sometimes claimed, because it doesn't want to or isn't interested, but because the needed information is still lacking.

Most conspicuous and costly of all are the benefits presumed to derive from "seeing the doctor." The regular complete checkup, once a year or more often, has become a cultural habit, and it is only recently that some investigators have suggested, cautiously, that it probably doesn't do much good. There are very few diseases in which early detection can lead to a significant alteration of the outcome: glaucoma, cervical cancer, and possibly breast cancer are the usually cited examples, but in any event these do not require the full, expensive array of the complete periodic checkup, EKG and all. Nevertheless, the habit has become fixed in our society, and it is a significant item in the total bill for health care.

"Seeing the doctor" also includes an overwhelming demand for reassurance. Transient upper-respiratory infections and episodes of gastroenteritis account for most of the calls on a doctor because of illness, and an even greater number of calls are made by people who have nothing at all the matter with them. It is often claimed that these are mostly unhappy individuals, suffering from psychoneuroses, in need of compassionate listening on the part of the physician, but a large number of patients who find themselves in doctors' offices or hospital clinics will acknowledge themselves to be in entirely good health; they are there because of a previous appointment in connection with an earlier illness, for a "checkup," or for a laboratory test, or simply for reassurance that they are not coming down with something serious—cancer, or heart disease, or whatever. OR they may have come to the doctor for advice about living: what should their diet be? should they take a vacation? what about a tranquilizer for everyone's inevitable moments of agitation and despair? I know a professor of pediatrics who has received visits from intelligent, well-educated parents who only want to know if their child should start Sunday school.

The system is being overused, swamped by expectant overdemands for services that are frequently trivial or unproductive. The public is not sufficiently informed of the facts about things that medicine can and cannot accomplish. Medicine is surely not in possession of special wisdom about how to live a life.

It needs to be said more often that human beings are fundamentally tough, resilient animals, marvelously made, most of the time capable of getting along quite well on their own. The health-care system should be designed for use when it is really needed and when it has something of genuine value to offer. If designed, or redesigned, in this way, the system would function far more effectively, and would probably cost very much less.

Conclusion

If our society wishes to be rid of the diseases, fatal and non-fatal, that plague us the most, there is really little prospect of doing so by mounting a still larger health-care system at still greater cost for delivering essentially today's kind of technology on a larger scale. We will not do so by carrying out broader programs of surveillance and screening. The truth is that we do not yet know enough. But there is also another truth of great importance: we are learning fast. The harvest of new information from the biological revolution of the past quarter-century is just now coming in, and we can probably begin now to figure out the mechanisms of major diseases which were black mysteries a few years back as accurately and profitably as was done for the infectious diseases earlier in this century. This can be said with considerable confidence, and without risk of overpromising or raising false hopes, provided we do not set time schedules or offer dates of delivery. Sooner or later it will go this way, since clearly it can go this way. It is simply a question at this stage of events of how much we wish to invest, for the health-care system of the future, in science.

Occupational Stress and Coronary Heart Disease: A Review and Theoretical Integration

7

JAMES S. HOUSE

The role of social and psychological factors in the etiology of chronic diseases, especially coronary heart disease, has received increasing attention from medical and social scientists in the last decade (e.g., Epstein, 1965; Graham and Reeder, 1972; Jenkins, 1971; Syme and Reeder, 1967). Notions of social and psychological "stress" have been central in much research and theory on the causes of coronary heart disease; yet the stress and heart disease literature remains fragmentary, scattered, and theoretically unintegrated, due both to the disciplinary diversity of researchers on stress and coronary disease and the nebulous status of stress as a concept or theoretical framework. Research on social factors in heart disease is done within medicine, public health, psychology, and sociology, but the communication and cooperation level among workers in various disciplines remains rather low. Even more importantly, only recently have social scientists engaged in more basic research on "stress" begun to articulate what constitutes the study of stress in relation to heart disease or anything else.

The purposes of this paper are: (1) briefly to present a paradigm for stress research derived from convergences in the thinking of a variety of basic

This paper is based in part on a report prepared for the Secretary's Committee on Work in America, Department of Health, Education, and Welfare. I am grateful for the helpful comments and suggestions of the following people on earlier drafts of this paper: Sidney Cobb, John R. P. French, Jr., Elizabeth Bates Harkins, Wendy F. House, Berton Kaplan, George Maddox, Erdman Palmore, and Thomas Regan. Work on this paper has also been supported in part by a Biomedical Sciences Support Grant (5SO5RRO770-07) from the National Institutes of Health and by Public Health Service Research Grant (HD0068) from NICHD.
From *Journal of Health and Social Behavior,* 15, (March 1974): 12–27. Copyright 1974, American Sociological Association. Reprinted with permission.

researchers in the area of stress; (2) to review and integrate via this framework available evidence on the relationship of one type of stress—occupational stress—to coronary heart disease; and (3) to derive from the first two steps some conclusions as to what we know and what we need to know about the role of occupational stress in the etiology of heart disease. This general approach should also interest those seeking to integrate and evaluate the evidence on the relationship of any form of social stress to a wide variety of outcomes (e.g., physiological disease, psychological disorders, behavioral "pathologies").

A Paradigm for "Stress Research"

Recent reviews of the concepts of social or psychological "stress" have found it virtually impossible to define what is meant by "stress" in any but the most general terms (cf. Appley and Trumbull, 1967; Lazarus, 1966; Levine and Scotch, 1970; Syme and Reeder, 1967). Most see stress as occurring when an individual confronts a situation where his usual modes of behaving are insufficient and the consequences of not adapting are serious. This is usually a situation where the demands made exceed existing abilities or where clear obstacles exist to fulfilling strong needs or values (e.g., McGrath, 1970; French et al., 1974). Thus job dissatisfaction, high level or work load or responsibility, role conflict, and unemployment or job termination can all be considered forms of occupational stress and will be so considered here. McGrath (1970, 11) suggests that it may be more fruitful to talk about "stress research" as a paradigm rather than "stress" as a concept, and others basically concur (Levine and Scotch, 1970, 279–90; Jenkins, 1971).

A variety of authors (McGrath, 1970, 15–17; Levine and Scotch, 1970, 280–81; French et al., 1974) see five classes of variables as necessary in any comprehensive paradigm of stress research: (1) objective social conditions conducive to stress; (2) individual perceptions of stress; (3) individual responses (physiological, affective, and behavioral) to perceived stress; (4) more enduring outcomes of perceived stress and responses thereto; and (5) individual and situational conditioning variables that specify the relationships among the first four sets of factors. Figure 7–1 presents a model relating these five classes of variables. The arrows between boxes indicate hypothesized causal relationships, while the arrows coming down from the box labelled "conditioning variables" indicate that social and individual variables condition or specify the nature of these relationships (as explained below).

Generally, sociological and epidemiological research has sought to ascertain the relationship between objective social conditions and outcome variables such as physical disease, mental disorder, or behavioral "pathology." Illustrative of this approach are investigations relating standard demographic variables (occupation, education, religion, ethnicity, place of residence, etc.) of combinations thereof (as in the concepts of social and geographic mobility or status inconsistency) to these outcomes. Such efforts are a major first step in stress research, but neither

Figure 7-1   A Paradigm of Stress Research

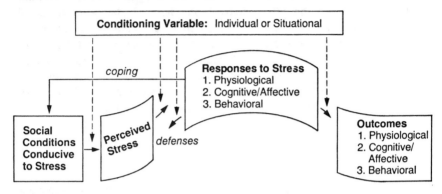

Note: Solid arrows between boxes indicate presumed causal relationships among variables. Dotted arrows, indicating an interaction between the conditioning variables and the variables in the box at the beginning of the solid arrow in predicting variables in the box at the head of the solid arrow.

positive nor negative results of such studies are definitive, and very often the results are negative or contradictory across studies. For example, Marks's (1967) comprehensive review of the relationship of demographic variables to heart disease finds few strong and consistent results.

The reason for this is that whether or not an objective social condition is stressful depends upon the perceptions of individuals subjected to it. Even if we find a relationship between a given social condition and a relevant outcome, we can only infer how and why this condition is stressful. If we find no relationship, we may only have failed to specify adequately the conditions under which the relationship holds. Thus, we must be attuned to when and why potentially stressful situations are, or are not, perceived as stressful by the persons involved. As we will see below, some evidence suggests that men in more "difficult or demanding" jobs do experience more heart disease, but not all men in such jobs do so. For example, people of differing abilities and training react differently to the same levels of work load and responsibility—some finding it a pleasant challenge, others experiencing it as more than they can handle, i.e., stressful. Likewise, differences in needs of values may make some feel dissatisfied or frustrated in a given job while others are quite happy.

Thus, as Figure 7-1 indicates, the experience of stress is a subjective response resulting from the interaction of particular objective social conditions and particular personal characteristics (e.g., abilities, needs, and values). Characteristics of social situations (e.g., highly competitive vs. cooperative relationships with co-workers) may also condition the degree to which a potentially stressful condition (e.g., a heavy work load) actually results in perceived stress. In short, this paradigm says (1) that the relationship between social conditions and outcomes like heart disease is mediated through the individual's perception of the situation, and (2) that the perceived meaning of objective conditions depends on both the nature of the person and the nature of the social situation.

But there are still further contingencies. Even if a number of persons experience the same degree of subjective stress in a situation, seldom do they all manifest the same type or degree of outcomes such as physical illness of mental disorders. How the person responds (or adapts) to the situation is crucial. Responses to perceived stress may be physiological, psychological (cognitive/affective), and/or behavioral in nature (as indicated in Figure 7–1).

The importance of man's capacity to respond actively to stressful situations in determining their outcomes has only recently been fully recognized (cf. Coelho et al., in press; Lazarus, 1966; Mechanic, 1962; 1970). Since responses to stress involve complex interdependencies among variables at different levels (physiological, psychological, behavioral) and over time, they raise difficult analytical issues. Hence our empirical knowledge about this area of the stress paradigm is scant. A few theoretical and intuitive insights can only serve to emphasize the need for more solid empirical work.

In most discussions a major dichotomy is drawn between (1) responses (generally psychological in nature) serving primarily to alter the perception of the situation, and (2) responses (generally behavioral) seeking to alter the objective nature of the situation (cf. Lazarus, 1966; Mechanic, 1962; French et al., 1974). Following psychoanalytic terminology, French et al. (in press) call the former defenses and the latter coping—the terminology used in Figure 7–1. By definition, coping is potentially more successful in relieving stress, since only coping can eliminate the objective sources of perceived stress. But Mechanic (1962) makes the important point that where coping is impossible (e.g., in the face of incurable diseases) or is hindered by high levels of anxiety, defenses may constitute the only adaptive strategy, or at least a part of it.

To be more concrete, one person faced with extreme work load may reorganize his schedule and activities, gain new skills, or call on others for assistance in meeting the demands made on him (all forms of coping). Another may try to deny or repress his stressful perceptions (defenses). Still another may be immobilized and do nothing (a possible response in any situation). Successful coping attempts alleviate objective sources of stress; unsuccessful attempts may lead to prolonged exertion culminating in a heart attack, an ulcer, or a nervous breakdown. Defenses may temporarily relieve anxiety but, since they involve perceptual distortions, they are likely to create attendant neurotic problems and/or to bring on further stresses (as the person becomes less in touch with reality). The typical physiological responses associated with different psychological and behavioral acts are presently unclear as, for the most part, are the personal and situational factors determining choice of response modes.

A final contingency is noted in the model of Figure 7–1. That is, even if we know the objective conditions, the level of perceived stress, and the response to it, the outcome may still depend on other characteristics of the person. For example, genetic predispositions to heart disease seem to exist and may be present for other diseases as well. Thus the same responses to the same perceived stress may yield different outcomes as a function of genetic (or other physiological) characteristics of the person.

In sum, the present model of "stress research" is presented as a heuristic device for clarifying and integrating existing research and suggesting critical areas for further research. Its utility lies in the scope of material it can encompass and in the breadth of questions it suggests. As Mechanic (1970, 106) has put it:

> Stress theory does not really help the experimenter design a better experiment from either a theoretical or methodological standpoint. But in studying more complex situations than the typical experiment or field study usually encompasses, it does help the investigator to ask more meaningful questions and to consider variables he might not have looked at had he used a more limited and conventional perspective.

Direct theoretical and methodological gains, while general in nature, also accrue from using this model.

Specifying Outcomes: General Health Versus Specific Diseases

It is important (1) to note that stress may be a generic cause of many diseases, rather than a specific cause of only one, and (2) to justify briefly the focal place of heart disease in the study of stress and physical health.

Most research on stress and disease has concentrated on identifying social and psychological precursors of specific chronic diseases. Implicit in such a research strategy is a "specificity hypothesis," which presumes a somewhat unique pattern of social and psychological factors is implicated in each type of disease. However, it should be recognized that a number of researchers view stress in work or elsewhere as having relatively non-specific effects.

This perspective is embodied in Selye's (1956) seminal work on stress. He saw a wide variety of environmental events or "stressors" as all producing a single specific pattern of bodily reaction. There is an initial lowering of bodily resistance during which a variety of infectious diseases (e.g., tuberculosis) may develop, that under normal circumstances would be successfully resisted. There follows an activation of bodily defense mechanisms characterized by arousal of the autonomic nervous system; adrenaline discharge; increased heart rate, blood pressure, and muscle tone; and increased digestive secretion coupled with lowered levels of resistance to inflammation in the stomach (and other bodily tissues). If this bodily state is prolonged, it results in a wide range of what Selye termed "diseases of adaptation" (e.g., cardiovascular-renal diseases, rheumatism and arthritis, ulcers, inflammatory, and allergic diseases, etc.)—that is, diseases caused by the body's own attempts to adapt to stress rather than by any external agent directly.

A small but growing body of research suggests that certain occupational and life stresses relate to a wide variety both of physical conditions and of psychological disorders so that, as Syme (1967, 178) has said, "perhaps researchers ought to be thinking about the forces in the social environment which lead to breakdown of health in general" rather than just to specific diseases. One example of such research is Hinkle's (1961) report that one-fourth of his study population had over one-half of the diseases, both physical and mental. Similarly, Holmes and Rahe (e.g., 1967) have shown that change in a person's life situation from whatever cause (marriage, occupational and geographic mobility, deaths of friends and relatives, etc.) is associated with increased incidence of a wide variety of diseases, both physical and mental. Cobb (1972) finds an excess of "every psychosomatic disease that could be studied" in men in a "high stress" occupation (air traffic controllers) compared to a control group.

On the other hand, this belief in a very general decline of health in the face of stress is probably an oversimplification. Existing epidemiological evidence clearly shows notable differences in the rates of morbidity and mortality from different causes in different demographic groups. Graham and Reeder (1972) document that such differentials appear even for specific types of diseases within a general category such as cancer or ulcers. Data reported below show that more specific types of stress (e.g., job dissatisfaction) are related to some diseases but not others. Thus, there is also good evidence that the effects of various types of occupational stress are relatively specific, relating only to certain diseases or clusters of disease entities.

It would be useful, then, to have future research on social stress in relation to any chronic disease include, whenever possible, a variety of indices of physical and mental disorder. Only then can we learn more clearly the extent to which: (1) specific forms of stress relate to specific diseases, (2) different diseases result from the same kind of stress depending on other individual or situational characteristics, or (3) a general increase in all forms of disease occurs in the face of occupational or other social stress.

Heart Disease as a Focus

Given that most evidence does, and probably will continue to, focus on specific disease entities, criteria are needed for selecting diseases that should receive priority in planning future research and social policy. For those concerned with the effects of occupational stress on health, primary emphasis must go to diseases that are the greatest sources of mortality and disability, especially in the population of working age (under 65 years). In regard to both mortality and disability, cardiovascular diseases, especially coronary heart disease (e.g., heart attacks), dwarf all others in the United States and most developed countries (cf. Felton and Cole, 1963; Graham and Reeder, 1972; Moriyama et al., 1971).

Among the cardiovascular diseases, coronary heart disease (CHD) or "heart attack" is by far the most serious problem—accounting for one-third of all deaths (and three-fifths of those due to cardiovascular diseases). The problem is particularly serious among younger males: CHD is the leading cause of death among males, 35+ years of age. The second leading cause of mortality from cardiovascular disease is cerebrovascular disease or "stroke," accounting for 11 percent of all deaths and 20 percent of all cardiovascular mortality. In general, there are many similarities in the physiological and behavioral factors (e.g., high blood pressure, cholesterol, and smoking) that predispose people to both CHD and "stroke," and the problem of stroke is less acute at younger ages. While stroke will not be considered separately here, this should not suggest that there may not be important differences in the etiology of stroke versus heart disease in terms of the relevant types of social stress. The most prevalent form of cardiovascular disease is hypertension or high blood pressure, but its importance derives largely from its role as a precursor of CHD and stroke (Moriyama et al., 1971).

Empirical Evidence

Two kinds of evidence point to an important role for occupational stress in the etiology of heart disease. First, there are standard epidemiological studies comparing morbidity or mortality rates for different demographic categories such as race, sex, age, occupation, education, ethnicity, region, or place of residence. While an observed difference between demographic categories in incidence of disease is ambiguous with respect to the causal mechanisms that produce it, such data are useful in suggesting hypotheses about the impact of occupational stress on heart disease. Stress is only one of the possible causal mechanisms, and well-designed research should assess relevant competing causes, such as diet, exercise, smoking, or family history. But a second type of research is needed to establish adequately a relationship between occupational stress and heart disease: it must relate specific types of stress to heart disease and show that the differential distribution of stress across demographic categories accounts, at least in part, for observed differences in mortality or morbidity between groups.

This literature review considers both broad demographic comparisons and more focused studies of specific types of occupational stress in relation to heart disease. The more focused studies present the major evidence relating specific objective work conditions and/or subjective perceptions of stress to heart disease. The process by which individual and social situational characteristics condition relationships of objective work conditions and/or subjective perceptions thereof to heart disease is also considered briefly. Unfortunately, no good empirical evidence is available on the influence of response modes upon the relationship between occupational stress and heart disease. This is a problem needing future research.

Demographic Comparisons
Aside from its increase with age, perhaps the most striking fact about the distribution of coronary heart disease (CHD) in the American population of working age is the degree to which it afflicts young and middle-aged males and spares young and middle-aged white females. Throughout the period of peak occupational endeavor (ages 25 to 64 years), the mortality rate from CHD among white males is from 2.75 to 6.50 times greater than the white female rate, while non-white males die from CHD at a rate only 1.35 to 1.91 times greater than the non-white female rate. Among females, those who are black or of lower social status run a

significantly greater risk of death from CHD, but there are no sizeable or consistent race of status differences among males (see mortality data for 1959–61 in Moriyama et al., 1971, 58–64; also see Antonovsky, 1968; Marks, 1967).

Interestingly, few have speculated about the potential role of occupational stress in producing these sex differences. Moriyama et al. (1971) discount the possibility that the unique female hormonal make-up prior to menopause can account for the difference, since no noticeable increase in female death rates follows the age of menopause. But these same authors then suggest only that we look to differences in diet, physical activity, and smoking as explanations; they do not mention occupational or other social stress. If occupational stress contributes to the sex differences in CHD mortality, there should be evidence of a declining sex difference as female employment and equality increase. And, in fact, Moriyama et al. (1971) report that, between 1940 and the late 1950s, male CHD death rates steadily increased, while white female rates steadily declined; but since then the male rate seems to have levelled off, while the female rate (for ages 35 to 54 years) is rising.

The sizeable occupational differences in CHD morbidity and mortality also suggest the potential etiological importance of occupational stress (Guralnick, 1963). In a number of studies cited here, men in occupations involving "greater stress" showed higher susceptibility to heart disease. Yet, such occupational comparisons have generally produced few interpretable results since little effort has been made to specify types of stresses which might explain occupational differences. As Suchman (1967), Jenkins (1971), and others have suggested, identification of specific stresses and their differential distribution across occupations is *sine qua non* for establishing work-related stress as an explanation of occupational differences in heart disease. Demographic comparisons can suggest the potential relevance of occupational stress to CHD, but more focused studies must demonstrate that relevance.

Focused Studies

Studies of social psychological aspects of work in relation to CHD constitute the largest and most productive body of research relating occupational stress to chronic diseases. The studies to be reviewed here use essentially two measures of health: (1) actual disease entities such as heart attacks; and (2) behavioral and physiological factors known to increase the risk of such disease (high levels of cigarette smoking, obesity, blood sugar, blood pressure, cholesterol, etc.). Studies using actual disease as the dependent variable are of two types—retrospective and prospective. In a retrospective study persons with heart disease are compared on measures of occupational stress with a control group of persons without this disease. A major methodological flaw here is that differences between the heart disease and control groups may be a result rather than a cause of heart disease. In a prospective design asymptomatic persons are interviewed about their lives and work and then followed until some develop heart disease. Here the evidence is more convincing that the social psychological characteristics differentiating those who do and do not incur the disease are, in fact, causes of the disease.

Studies utilizing "risk factors" of heart disease as dependent variables are usually cross-sectional, and occasionally prospective. In a cross-sectional study, occupational stress and risk factors are measured at about the same time and their associations determined. Although correlations cannot establish causality, it is usually more plausible to assume, for example, that job satisfaction affected blood pressure rather than vice versa. A number of longitudinal and/or experimental studies clearly demonstrate that changes in work-related variables cause changes in risk factors. Despite the flaws in any single study, a rather convincing pattern of results emerges from the studies considered below.

Job Satisfaction and Self-Esteem

A number of retrospective studies in the United States and other countries found that persons with coronary disease were significantly more dissatisfied with their overall jobs or aspects thereof (e.g., tedious details, lack of recognition, poor relations with co-workers, poor working conditions), and/or had more work "problems" and difficulties (Jenkins, 1971). Three different smaples of occupations (N's = 16, 12, and 36, respectively) studied by Sales and House (1971) produced consistently negative and generally very significant correlations across occupations between average levels of job satisfaction and heart disease mortality rates. The relationships were strongest for intrinsic job satisfaction measures and in white collar, as opposed to blue collar, occupations. Relationships between average levels of job dissatisfaction and mortality from a variety of other causes (tuberculosis, cancer, diabetes, influenza, pneumonia, and accidents) were nonexistent. Controlling for occupational status via partial correlation did not seriously diminish the relationship between satisfaction and CHD.

House (1972) reported correlations between a three item index of job satisfaction and a variety of heart disease risk factors (e.g., smoking, obesity, cholesterol, blood pressure, and blood sugar) for a sample of 288 men representing the full range of occupations in a total community (the Tecumseh Community Health Study of the University of Michigan). Correlations across the total sample were near zero. However, further analyses revealed rather different correlations in specific age and occupational subgroups. As in the Sales and House study, correlations were in the expected negative direction more often among white-collar than among blue-collar workers. Interestingly, the expected relationships generally emerged for men 45 or more years of age, but a positive relationship was found for younger men. Among older men (i.e., 45+ years of age), correlations between satisfaction and a CHD risk summary measure were significantly negative for professionals and salaried managers (r = −.31) and for industrial foremen and workers (r = −.25).

These results highlight a persisting problem in the occupational stress and heart disease literature. The subject population for most studies is restricted to white-collar workers and/or specific organizations. Results from such homogeneous samples often do not replicate across the full range of more heterogeneous populations. The dangers in generalizing from quite limited samples to all employed males (much less females) cannot be overemphasized.

Self-esteem in work is closely related to job satisfaction. House (1972) found occupational self-esteem in work to be even more strongly and negatively associated with heart disease risk than was job satisfaction, again especially among middle-aged and older white-collar workers. However, Kasl et al. (1968) and Kasl and Cobb (1970) longitudinally compared male blue-collar workers terminated by factory closings with a steadily employed control group. Self-esteem declined with job loss and rose with reemployment. Significant negative correlations between self-esteem and CHD risk factors emerged both at any given point in time and over time.

In an earlier study, Kasl and French (1962) found that men whose occupational self-esteem was low frequented their company dispensaries much more often than those with higher self-esteem. Perhaps low work self-esteem predisposes men to a wider variety of illnesses than just heart disease. Men who felt their jobs were dull and boring also make more dispensary visits. In contrast, Caplan (1971) and French et al. (1965) found no clear relationships between self-esteem and heart disease risk among professional workers. Nevertheless, evidence is mounting to support a contention that low satisfaction and self-esteem in work predispose men to heart disease, and perhaps to other diseases as well.

Job Pressures

The layman's conception of occupational "stress" is reflected best in studies about effects of high levels of work load, responsibility, and role conflict or ambiguity—what will here be termed job "pressures." A series of studies by French and his colleagues have found associations between feelings of work overload and elevated heart disease risk in a variety of populations. Work overload refers to feelings that job demands exceed one's capacities, given one's available time, resources, and abilities. Deadlines are a frequent source of overload. Among 104 university professors, men who felt overloaded had significantly higher cholesterol and significantly lower self-esteem (French et al., 1965). An unpublished study of 22 white-collar employees of the National Aeronautics and Space Administration (NASA) related feelings of overload to higher levels of heart rate and cholesterol (Caplan and French, 1968), but a later study of a large NASA sample failed to replicate that finding (Caplan, 1971). These studies also found significant positive correlations between subjective reports of work overload and more objective measures (ranging from wives' reports of the number of hours their husbands worked to direct observational measures of the demands made on men by others in the organization). These objective measures were also associated with elevated heart disease risk, but the results suggest that the effects of objective job conditions are mediated through the person's subjective experience of overload or "stress" (as is assumed in the framework developed above).

These data are in line with earlier studies relating work load and job pressures to changes in heart disease risk factors. A seminal investigation found marked increases in serum cholesterol in tax accountants as the April 15 dead-line for filing federal income tax returns approached (Friedman et al., 1957). A number of studies have found significantly higher levels of cholesterol in medical students on the day before examinations as compared with times when they were not facing tests (see review by Sales, 1969b). It is plausible that these changes are attributable to increased work load under tax deadline or examina-tion pressures. They also highlight what it is about work overload, as opposed to sheer work load, that makes it stressful—the feeling that one does not have enough time or ability and hence may fail (Pepitone, 1967).

Responsibility for the work of others has recently been implicated as a corre-late of selected heart disease risk factors and possibly other illnesses. Caplan (1971) found the NASA managers, scientists, and engineers who spent a higher percentage of their time on such responsibilities smoked more cigarettes and had higher diastolic blood pressure. Studies showing high levels of CHD risk factors among executives (e.g., Montoye et al., 1967) might also support this responsibil-ity hypothesis, although consistently positive relationships have not been found between managerial status and actual CHD (Hinkle et al., 1968).

House's (1972) total community study produced further support for the role of job pressures in heart disease risk. A composite measure of job pressures (including work overload, responsibility, and role conflict) was associated with significantly greater heart disease risk in virtually the whole range of occupations. As with the findings on job satisfaction and self-esteem in this study, occupational stress effects were much more pronounced among men 45 to 65 years of age.

Several studies have also documented a relationship between occupational pressure or stress and actual coronary heart disease. Russek (1962) asked a number of practicing professionals to rank several categories of practice within the fields of medicine, dentistry, and law by the amount of "occupational stress" involved in each specialty. Regardless of the specific profession involved, individ-uals in the "high stress" categories reported higher incidences of coronary dis-ease. A second Russek (1965) study compared 100 young coronary patients and 100 controls. Here Russek (1965, 189) found that "prolonged emotional strain associated with job responsibility" preceded the heart attacks of 91 percent of the patients, while such strain was evident in only 20 percent of the control group. Further, this between-group difference exceeded those for family history of heart disease, diet, obesity, smoking, and physical exercise. In a similar study (Miles et al., 1954), 50 percent of heart disease patients, but only 12 percent of a control group, reported working long hours with few vacations prior to disease onset. Weiss et al. (1957) and Pearson and Joseph (1963) report similar conclusions.

Thus, there is rather consistent evidence that job pressures (measured both objectively and subjectively), such as work overload, responsibility, and role con-flict, significantly increase heart disease risk and actual coronary heart disease. Of all findings reviewed here, these have been replicated in the largest number of studies and across the widest range of populations. Further corroboration of these results appears in the data on personality and social situational factors influencing these relationships.

Incongruity and Change

A final set of factors seems increasingly important as sources of occupational stress leading to heart disease, though their exact social psychological meaning is unclear. A variety of evidence is accumulating that a life history of occupational mobility or rapid change in occupational environment predisposes men to heart disease. Caplan (1971), following Terreberry (1968), speaks of "complexification of occupational environments (or rate at which things change of become increasingly complex) as a form of work overload taxing one's ability to adapt to new demands. Both occupationally or geographically mobile persons who expose themselves to change, complexity, and new demands and those whose environment changes rapidly seem to experience greater heart disease (cf. review by Smith, 1967) and perhaps greater illness of all kinds (e.g., Holmes and Rahe, 1967). The accumulating evidence that persons whose status is incongruent on two dimensions (e.g., men with low education in high status jobs) are more prone to heart disease may reflect effects of work overload (the job demands exceed their capacity) or prior occupational mobility rather than "status incongruity" per se (cf. reviews by Smith, 1967; Jenkins, 1971; see also Hinkle et al., 1968). The evidence on the relationship of status consistency to heart disease, however, must be subjected to rigorous methodological scrutiny that has recently been applied to this concept in sociology (see Hodge and Siegel, 1970). Attention must also be paid to the specification of intervening or conditioning variables as indicated in the model of Figure 7–1 (cf. House and Harkins, 1973).

Conditioning Variables

Conditioning Personal Characteristics

Thus far, direct relationships between objective aspects of work situations or subjective perceptions thereof and heart disease have been considered. Where the evidence is based on subjective reports of dissatisfaction or job pressures, these subjective reports are presumably the outcome of interactions between objective situational characteristics (role demands or expectations, the nature of the job, and its rewards) and individual characteristics (motives, needs, abilities, etc.). However, attempts to document this empirically are just beginning with at least modest success (e.g., Blood and Hulin, 1967; Caplan, 1971; French et al., in press; Turner and Lawrence, 1965).

More importantly, a large and growing body of literature indicates that men with a certain type of "behavior pattern" are more prone to coronary heart disease. This behavior pattern has been most extensively investigated by Friedman, Rosenman, and Jenkins, who labelled it the "Type A behavior-pattern," characterized by:

> excessive drive, aggressiveness, ambition, involvement in competitive activities, frequent vocational deadlines, (and) an enhanced sense of time urgency. . . . The converse . . . pattern, called Type B is characterized by the

relative absence of this *interplay of psychological traits and situational pressures"* (Jenkins et al, 1967, 371, emphasis added).

In a long series of studies (including an ongoing prospective study of 3,400 men now followed for over eight years) the Type A (relative to Type B) has been shown to be significantly higher on known heart disease risk factors and significantly more likely (by a factor of 1.4 to 6.5 in different analyses) to have an actual "heart attack" (see Jenkins, 1971; and Sales, 1969a, 1969b, for thorough reviews of these studies). The risk of recurrent and fatal heart attacks has also been shown to be higher for the Type A. Other investigators have found similar results, and in several studies, the Type A variable has been shown to have significant predictive power even when levels of a whole range of standard physiological risk factors are statistically controlled (Jenkins, 1971). The meaning of these results remains unclear, however, since the Type A pattern reflects "an interplay of psychological traits and situational pressures." To some extent these results may further demonstrate the importance of work overload and other "job pressures" reviewed above.

What role is played by psychological traits? Sales (1969a) suggested that the Type A person possesses personality traits (e.g., impatience, ambition, competitiveness, aggressiveness) causing self-selection into jobs involving greater "stress" (e.g., "time urgency," "frequent vocational deadlines," etc.), but no direct empirical test of this proposition has yet been made. Similarly, House (1972) suggested that a central psychological trait of the Type A is his "desire for social achievement" (reflected in ambition, competitiveness, aggressiveness, etc.), a trait apparently analogous to what others term "status-seeking" or extrinsic motivation for working (i.e., desire for money, status, recognition) as opposed to intrinsic motivation (i.e., desire for interesting, self-satisfying work). House predicted that persons with extrinsic motivations for working were more likely to choose jobs involving greater occupational stress and, hence, to experience heart disease, while intrinsically motivated persons would avoid highly stressful work and, hence, heart disease. Partial support for these hypotheses were found among white-collar workers, but, among lower blue-collar factory workers, intrinsic motivation was positively related to occupational stress and heart disease risk. These and other findings from that sutyd indicate the difficulty of generalizing from the limited samples usually studied in this field (i.e., white collar, and often professional, workers) to all employed men.

Another approach to the meaning of the Type A behavior pattern asserts that under potentially stressful objective conditions Type A persons are more prone to perceive stress and manifest increases in heart disease or its risk factors. Caplan (1971) found support for this contention in research on NASA professionals. He proposes that the dramatic and consistent results derived from the Friedman et al. program of research may be due to the fact that the classification of a man as Type A indicates that he both possesses certain personality traits and experiences greater situational pressures. The role of personality in leading men into situations of stress and/or in accentuating the effects of such situations deserves further research.

Conditioning Social Characteristics

Just as personality factors may determine whether a person experiences stress and how he reacts to it, so may other characteristics of the work situation. As already noted, social and organizational change are likely to increase the stresses felt by individuals. Existing evidence indicates that individuals in positions involving great contact with external environments (and hence more varied and perhaps changing inputs) suffer greater emotional strain (Kahn et al., 1964) and heart disease risk (Caplan, 1971). Alternatively, the surrounding social environment may provide resources mitigating stress effects on individuals. Prescriptive theories of work organizations suggest that social support from peers, superiors, and subordinates improves the ability of men to cope with job stresses and, therefore, should enhance physical and mental health (e.g., Likert, 1967).

Caplan (1971) found little relationship between perceived occupational stress and heart disease risk among NASA professionals reporting high levels of social support from co-workers; for those reporting low social support levels, occupational stress was significantly and positively correlated with heart disease risk. Seashore (1954) reported similar results in industrial work groups with measures of mental health as the relevant outcome, and other research on coronary disease is at least consistent with Caplan's results. Matsumoto (1970) hypothesized that Japan's low rate of heart disease, as compared with the United States, is not due so much to the presence of lesser occupational or social stress, but to the nature of Japanese work and other institutional structures which provide greater social support.

As populations studied in research on heart disease increase in variety, evidence is emerging that stresses which relate to heart disease or its risk factors in some groups may not do so in others. We have already noted differences between age and occupational groups in these regards. These results suggest differences between the groups in personality or environment that are the more proximate causes of differential susceptibility to disease. Further research is greatly needed to specify precise personality and social environmental variables conditioning relationships between objective or subjective indicators of stress and heart disease.

Occupational Stress and Longevity

Given the accumulating evidence relating occupational stress to coronary heart disease and the significance of heart disease as a cause of death, occupational stress should also be a potent predictor of general mortality and, conversely, longevity. Evidence from demographic comparisons and from at least one focused study suggests that this is so.

Demographic Comparisons

In general, women, whites, and persons of higher educational or social status live longer and have lower age-adjusted mortality rates from many, though not all, diseases (cf Palmore and Jeffers, 1971; Kitigawa and Hauser, 1968). Social status differentials are greater among women than men, and larger for communicable diseases than for such major chronic diseases as ulcer, stroke, arthritis, cancer, or heart disease (Kitigawa and Hauser, 1968; Lerner, 1969). Thus, social status and color differentials in general mortality probably stem more from poor living conditions and inadequate medical care or from social stress outside of work than from occupational stresses per se. There are, of course, occupational differences in most disease incidences, but in many cases the reasons for them remain unclear. However, the sex difference in longevity, just as that in heart disease mortality discussed above, again suggests a central role of work in the genesis of disease (cf. discussion in Palmore and Jeffers, 1971, 284 ff).

Focused Studies

The best evidence that "stress" in life and work determines mortality and longevity comes from the Duke Longitudinal Study of Aging (Palmore, 1969a, 1969b; Palmore and Jeffers, 1971). This panel study has been carried out on 268 volunteers, ages 60 to 94 years (median age 70), at the time of their initial interview and physical examination. Although not a random sample, the distribution of the volunteers by sex, race, and occupation approximated that of the area from which they were drawn. The dependent variable was a Longevity Quotient—the number of years a person actually lived divided by the actuarially expected number of years remaining at the time of the initial examination.

For the total sample, *work satisfaction* was the strongest predictor of the Longevity Quotient ($r = .26$). It remained one of the three strongest predictors for all subgroups of the sample except for blacks, and was strongest ($r = .38$) among those (males, age 60 to 69 years) most likely to be working full-time. The second best longevity predictor ($r = .26$) in the total sample was the interviewing social worker's rating of the respondent's overall "happiness." These two social psychological measures (1) predicted longevity more accurately than either an overall physical functioning rating by the examining physician ($r = .21$) or a measure of the use of tobacco ($r = .21$); and (2) remained a strong predictor even when the aforementioned physical variables were controlled via multiple regression.

Conclusions

Traditional sociological and epidemiological research on social factors in heart disease has most often involved comparing disease rates across categories of standard demographic variables such as occupation, sex, race, or ethnicity. "Stress" is often presumed to be a mediating variale in such research, but the nature of the stress seldom is specified carefully and almost never measured independently. As noted above, such research can at best yield suggestive results. Only when all variables that mediate and/or condition the relationship between objective social conditions and health outcomes are explicitly conceptualized and measured can we have an adequate understanding of the effect of social stress on heart disease.

This paper outlines a framework specifying types of variables necessary to complete understanding of the nature and effects of social stress. A review in terms of this framework, both of traditional research involving demographic comparisons and of focused studies that have attempted to relate specific forms of occupational stress to longevity and heart disease, leads to a number of conclusions. There is considerable evidence that occupational stress plays a significant role in the etiology of coronary heart disease and probably other chronic diseases as well. Particularly noteworthy is the accumulation of studies documenting a relationship between stress and heart disease even when a variety of more medically recognized variables (e.g., heredity, diet, exercise, etc.) are controlled. However, we are just beginning to understand the complexities in the relationship between occupational stress and heart disease.

First, work is needed to specify the physiological processes through which occupational stress operates. In many ways the evidence linking stress to heart disease is like that linking cigarette smoking to CHD—in neither case do we know exactly how (in a physiological sense) these factors produce disease. This is important knowledge to have from a practical, as well as theoretical, viewpoint. There are clear ways in which our knowledge of occupational stress could be utilized in preventive medicine (e.g., changing the nature of jobs, more careful personnel selection and training, etc.), and work organizations provide a lever for instituting large-scale changes, something which is lacking for other forms of stress (e.g., family or urban stress) and most traditional biomedical risk factors (e.g., diet or smoking). However, if we cannot reduce people's exposures to stress, smoking, or certain foods, we need to know what bodily processes are affected by these variables so that individuals at risk can receive compensatory treatment. The evidence reviewed above suggests that occupational stress affects known risk factors such as cholesterol and blood pressure, but may also increase the incidence of disease through other unspecified mechanisms (perhaps, for example, by decreasing clotting time in the blood). Combined efforts of biomedical and social scientists are needed in this further research.

Second, much research derives from studies of workers in selected organizations or segments thereof. Most typically, the populations involved have been white males in professional and managerial occupations. Research on more representative populations often indicates that results from such limited populations do not generalize to all segments of the total population. This has been especially evident in the failure of some findings to generalize across color (whites versus blacks), occupational (e.g., white collar versus blue collar), and age (younger versus older) lines. Almost nothing is known about how results from studies of working males relate to the experience of working females. To increase the generalizability or "external validity" of our knowledge, populations studied should be as representative of the total population as feasible. Evidence that a result does not generalize across major demographic groups suggests that there are important individual (physiological or psychological) or social environmental variables mediating the relationships in question. Further work, of course, is needed to specify the precise nature of these variables. Multiple disease outcomes should be included in such studies wherever feasible in order to evaluate the degree to which occupational stresses and specific forms thereof produce a "general decline in health" or only relate to certain specific diseases.

Finally, research that is more limited in terms both of the populations studied and the disease outcomes considered remains the most feasible and useful vehicle for increasing the internal validity of our knowledge about the nature of occupational stress and its effects on individuals. The complex interplay between the person and his environment, including processes of coping with stress, especially deserve attention. The theoretical framework developed at the beginning of this paper in conjunction with the findings reviewed here, suggests clear foci for future research.

Future studies should seek to deal with at least two of the classes of social psychological variables listed above in addition to some outcome (e.g., heart disease). Simultaneous assessment of objective conditions of work, subjective perceptions of stress, and individual and/or social situational characteristics can produce answers to the following kinds of questions:

1. Are certain kinds of individuals (e.g., Type A or extrinsically motivated persons) more likely to seek out objective conditions conducive to stress; and/or are these persons more likely to perceive a given situation as stressful?
2. Are given objective conditions (e.g., levels of work load, responsibility) more likely to be perceived as stressful under some situational conditions (e.g., competition, non-supportive relationships with coworkers, inequalities of power or status) than others (cooperation, supportive relations with co-workers, more equal power and status)?

Simultaneous consideration of individual responses to stress (coping processes) in conjunction with measures of other individual or social situational characteristics, objective conditions of work, and subjective perceptions thereof can produce answers to the following kinds of questions:

1. What kinds of coping or adaptation responses mitigate the effects of stress on health, and which exacerbate these effects?
2. Are certain kinds of coping responses effective only for certain kinds of stresses? For certain types of persons? In certain situations?
3. What individual (physiological or psychological) and social situational characteristics determine the kind of strategy a person chooses for coping with given stresses?
4. Do certain strategies, if unsuccessful, make one kind of disease outcome more likely than another?

Ultimately, we need rigorous empirical research aimed at testing specific hypotheses—research of the type exemplified in the "focused studies" reviewed above. The review of evidence presented here suggests a vast fund of such hypotheses worthy of test. Nevertheless, this review exhausts neither the kinds of stresses that may have important effects on physical health, nor the kinds of individual and/or social characteristics that may condition relationships between stress and health. More traditional epidemiological studies are still of use in suggesting additional relevant factors and hypotheses (e.g., the trends in sex differences reviewed above). Likewise, in an area as uncharted as the relationship of occupational stress to heart disease, careful observational and clinical methods will continue to be necessary in suggesting further new variables and hypotheses for more rigorous study in the future. Two of the most impressive programs of research on social and psychological factors in heart disease have consistently used a combination of clinical and more rigorous statistical methods (i.e., Friedman and Rosenman's work on Type A, French's work on overload). Finally, the framework utilized here sees "stress" as a complex process of interaction between individuals and their situations. There is a need for longitudinal and/or experimental field studies that can establish more firmly the causal role of forms of occupational stress in the etiology of chronic disease and can provide the kinds of time sequence data necessary to understand the coping process. The existing evidence suggests the utility of, and need for, actual field experimentation where possible.

In sum, the study of the relationship of occupational stress and other forms of social stress to heart disease has advanced greatly in the last ten to fifteen years. Further research will have a dual import: for social science, it offers opportunities to learn more about stress as a generic phenomenon that has implications for a wide range of outcomes (e.g., mental disorders, suicide, delinquency, social movements, and collective behavior) beside heart disease and other chronic diseases; for medicine and society, it shows promise of significantly increasing our ability to predict and, hence, control the current "epidemic" of heart disease.

References

Antonovsky, A. Social class and the major cardiovascular diseases. *Journal of Chronic Diseases 21* (May) 1968: 65–108.

Appley, M. H., & Trumbull, R. (Eds.) *Psychological stress.* New York: Appleton-Century-Crofts, 1967.

Blood, M. R., & Hulin, C. L. Alienation, environmental characteristics, and worker responses. *Journal of Applied Psychology 51* (June) 1967: 284–90.

Caplan, R. Organizational stress and individual strain: A social-psychological study of risk factors in coronary heart disease among administrators, engineers, and scientists. Unpublished Ph.D. thesis. University of Michigan, Ann Arbor, 1971.

Caplan, R., & French, R. P., Jr. Final report to NASA. Unpublished manuscript. University of Michigan, Ann Arbor, 1968.

Cobb, S. A report on the health of air traffic controllers based on aeromedical examination data. Unpublished report to the Federal Aviation Agency. University of Michigan, Ann Arbor, 1972.

Coelho, G. V., Hamburg, D. A., & Adams, J. E. (Eds.) *Coping and adaptation: Interdisciplinary perspectives.* New York: Basic Books, 1974.

Epstein, F. H. The epidemiology of coronary heart disease: A review. *Journal of Chronic Diseases 18* (August) 1965: 735–74.

Felton, J. S., & Cole, S. The high cost of heart disease. *Circulation 27* (May) 1963: 957–62.

French, J. R. P., Jr., Tupper, C. J., & Mueller, E. Workload of university professors. Cooperative Research Project No 2171, U.S. Office of Education. University of Michigan, Ann Arbor, 1965.

French, J. P. R., Jr., Rodgers, W., & Cobb, S. Adjustment as person-environment fit. In G. V. Coelho, D. A. Hamburg, & J. E. Adams (Eds.) *Coping and adaptation: Interdisciplinary perspectives.* New York: Basic Books, 1974.

Friedman, M., Roseman, R. H., & Carroll, V. Changes in the serum cholesterol and blood clotting time of men subject to cyclic variation of occupational stress. *Circulation 17* (May) 1957: 852–961.

Graham, S., & Reeder, L. G. Social factors in the chronic illness. In H. E. Freeman, et al. (Eds.) *Handbook of medical sociology.* Englewood Cliffs, N.J.: Prentice-Hall, 1972, pp. 63–107.

Guralnick, L. Mortality by occupation and cause of death among men 20 to 64. National Center for Health Statistics. *Vital Statistics Special Reports 53 (3)* 1963.

Hinkle, L. E., Jr. Ecological observations on the relation of physical illness, mental illness, and the social environment. *Psychosomatic Medicine 23* (July-August) 1961: 289–97.

Hinkle, L. E., Jr., Whitney, L. H., Hehman, E. W., Dunn, J., Benjamin, B., King, R., Platum, A., & Flehinger, B. Occupation education, and coronary heart disease. *Science 161* (July) 1968: 238–46.

Hodge, R. W., & Siegel, P. M. Nonvertical dimensions of social stratification. In E. O. Laumann, P. M. Siegel, & R. W. Hodge (Eds.) *The logic of social hierarchies.* Chicago: Markham, 1970, pp. 512–20.

Holmes, T. H., & Rahe, R. H. The social readjustment rating scale. *Journal of Psychosomatic Research 11* (August) 1967: 213–25.

House, J. S. The relationship of intrinsic and extrinsic work motivations to occupational stress and coronary heart disease risk. Unpublished Ph.D. thesis. University of Michigan, Ann Arbor, 1972.

House, J. S., & Harkins, E. B. Why and when is status inconsistency stressful? Unpublished manuscript. Duke University, Durham, N.C., 1973.

Jenkins, C. D. Psycologie and social precursors of coronary heart disease. *New England Journal of Medicine 284* (February) 1971: 244–55, 307–17.

Jenkins, C. D., Rosenman, R. H., & Friedman, M. Development of an objective psychological test for the determination of the coronary-prone behavior pattern. *Journal of Chronic Diseases 20* (June) 1967: 371–79.

Kahn, R. L., Wolfe, D. M., Quinn, R. P., Snock, J. D., & Rosenthal, R. A. *Organizational stress: Studies in role conflict and ambiguity.* New York: Wiley, 1964.

Kasl, S. V., & French, J. R. P., Jr. The effects of occupational status on physical and mental health. *Journal of Social Issues 18* (July) 1962: 67–89.

Kasl, S. V., Cobb, S., & Brooks, G. Changes in serum uric acid and cholesterol levels in men undergoing job loss. *Journal of the American Medical Association 206* (November) 1968: 1500–07.

Kasl, S. V., & Cobb, S. Blood pressure changes in men undergoing job loss: A preliminary report. *Psychosomatic Medicine 32* (January-February) 1970: 19–38.

Kitigawa, E. M., & Hauser, P. M. Education differentials in mortality by cause of death: United States, 1960. *Demography 5* (February) 1968: 318–53.

Lazarus, R. S. *Psychological stress and the coping process.* New York: McGraw-Hill, 1966.

Lerner, M. Social differences in physical health. In J. Kosa, A. Antonovsky, & I. K. Zola (Eds.) *Poverty and health: A sociological analysis.* Cambridge, Mass.: Harvard University Press, 1969, pp. 69–112.

Levine, S., & Scotch, N. *Social stress.* Chicago: Aldine, 1970.

Likert, R. *The human organization: Its management and value.* New York: McGraw-Hill, 1967.

Marks, R. Factors involving social and demographic characteristics: A review of empirical findings. In S. L. Syme, & L. G. Reeder (Eds.) Social Stress and Cardiovascular Disease. *Milbank Memorial Fund Quarterly 45* (April) 1967 *II*: 51–108.

Matsumoto, Y. S. Social stress and coronary heart disease in Japan: A hypothesis. *Milbank Memorial Fund Quarterly 48* (January) 1970: 9–13.

McGrath, J. E. (Ed.) *Social and psychological factors in stress.* New York: Holt, Rinehart, 1970.

Mechanic, D. *Students under stress.* New York: Free Press, 1962.

Mechanic, D. Some problems in developing a social psychology of adaptation to stress. In J. McGrath (Ed.) *Social and psychological factors in stress.* New York: Holt, Rinehart, 1970, pp. 101–23.

Miles, H. H. W., Waldfogel, S., Barrabee, E., & Cobb, S. Psychosomatic study of 46 young men with coronary artery disease. *Psychosomatic Medicine 16* (November-December) 1954: 455–77.

Montoye, H. J., Faulkner, J. A., Dodge, H. J., Mikkelson, W. M., Willis, R. W. III, & Block, W. D. Serum uric acid concentration among business executives with observations on other coronary heart disease risk factors. *Annals of Internal Medicine 66* (May) 1967: 838–50.

Moriyama, L. M., Krueger, D. E., & Stamler, J. *Cardiovascular diseases in the United States.* Cambridge, Mass.: Harvard University Press, 1971.

Palmore, E. B. Physical, mental, and social factors in predicting longevity. *Gerontologist 9* (Summer) 1969 a: 103–08.

Palmore, E. B. Predicting longevity: A follow-up controlling for age. *Gerontologist 9* (Winter) 1969 b: 247–50.

Palmore, E. B., & Jeffers, F. (Eds.) *Prediction of life span.* Boston: Heath, 1971.

Pearson, H. E. S., & Joseph, J. Stress and occlusive coronary-artery disease. *The Lancet 1* (February) 1963: 415–18.

Pepitone, A. Self, social environment, and stress. In M. H. Appley & R. Trumbull (Eds.) *Psychological stress.* New York: Appleton-Century-Crofts, 1967, pp. 182–99.

Russek, H. I. Emotional stress and coronary heart disease in American physicians, dentists, and lawyers. *American Journal of Medical Science 243* (June) 1962: 716–25.

Russek, H. I. Stress, tobacco, and coronary heart disease in North American professional groups. *Journal of the American Medical Association 192* (April) 1965: 189–94.

Sales, S. M. Differences among individuals in affective, behavioral, biochemical, and physiological responses to variations in work load. Unpublished Ph.D. thesis. University of Michigan, Ann Arbor, 1969 *a*.

Sales, S. M. Organizational roles as a risk factor in coronary heart disease. Administrative Science Quarterly *14* (September) 1969 *b*: 225–26.

Sales, S. M., & House, J. Job dissatisfaction as a possible risk factor in coronary heart disease. *Journal of Chronic Diseases 23* (May) 1971: 861–73.

Seashore, S. Group cohesiveness in the industrial work group. Institute for Social Research. University of Michigan, Ann Arbor, 1954.

Selye, H. *The stress of life.* New York: McGraw-Hill, 1956.

Smith, T. Sociocultural incongruity and change: A review of empirical finding. In S. L. Syme & L. G. Reeder (Eds.) Social Stress and Cardiovascular Disease. *Milbank Memorial Fund Quarterly 45* (April) 1967 *II*: 17–46.

Suchman, E. A. Factors involving social and demographic characteristics: Appraisal and implications for theoretical development. In S. L. Syme & L. G. Reeder (Eds.) Social stress and cardiovascular disease. *Milbank Memorial Fund Quarterly 45* (April) 1967 *II*: 109–16.

Syme, S. L. Implications and future prospects. In S. L. Syme & L. G. Reeder (Eds.) Social stress and cardiovascular disease. *Milbank Memorial Fund Quarterly 45* (April) 1967 *II*: 175–81.

Syme, S. L. & Reeder, L. G. Social stress and cardiovascular disease. *Milbank Memorial Fund Quarterly 45* (April) 1967 *II*.

Terreberry, S. The organization of environments. Unpublished Ph.D. thesis. University of Michigan, Ann Arbor, 1968.

Turner, A. N., & Lawrence, P. R. Industrial jobs and the worker: An investigation of response to talk attributes. Harvard University Graduate School of Business Administration, Division of Research. Harvard University, Cambridge, Mass., 1965.

Weiss, E., Dlin, B., Rollin, H. R., Fischer, H. K., & Bepler, C. R. Emotional factors in coronary occlusion. *Archives of Internal Medicine 99* (April) 1957: 628–41.

Class, Family, and Schizophrenia: A Reformulation

8

MELVIN L. KOHN

A multitude of studies carried out in several countries consistently suggests that schizophrenia[1] occurs most frequently at the lowest social-class levels of urban society. Reviews and assessments of this research literature by the Dohren- wends (1969), Kohn (1968), Mishler and Scotch (1963), and Roman and Trice (1967), all come to the same conclusion: despite serious shortcomings in the research, the weight of evidence clearly points to an especially high rate of schi- zophrenia at the bottom of the social-class hierarchy.[2] What is not clear is *why* class is related to schizophrenia.

Revised version of a paper presented at the Seventh World Congress of Sociology, Varna, Bulgaria, September 1970.

1. The classic definition of schizophrenia (Bleuler 1950, 14) considers it to be a group of dis- orders whose "fundamental symptoms consist of disturbances of association and affectivity, the predi- lection for fantasy as against reality, and the inclination to divorce oneself from reality." In common with most American investigators, I use the term broadly, to refer to those severe functional disorders marked by disturbances in reality relationships and concept formation (cf. Rosenbaum 1970, 3 –16). Unfortunately, available research evidence does not enable me to differentiate clinical subtypes of schi- zophrenia or to make such important distinctions as that between "process" and "reactive" forms of disturbance (cf. Garmezy, 1965).

2. The cited works provide references to virtually all studies of class and schizophrenia pub- lished through 1968. The evidence comes from research conducted in Canada, Denmark, Finland, Great Britain, Norway, Sweden, Taiwan, and the United States—an unusually large number of countries and cultures for establishing the generality of any relationship in social science. Moreover, the excep- tions are few and partial: they occur in small cities and rural areas or in special subpopulations of larger cities; none contradicts the larger generalization of an especially high rate of schizophrenia at the lowest social-class levels of urban populations.

Judging from data about patients newly admitted to psychiatric treatment (e.g., Hollingshead and Redlich, 1958,236), the incidence of schizophrenia is approximately three or four times as great at the bottom of the class hierarchy as at the top.

One unresolved issue is whether the relationship of class to schizophrenia is linear or is disconti- nuous, with an especially high rate in the lowest social class but little variation above that level (cf. Kohn, 1968, 157; Rushing, 1969). I have attempted to make my formulation consistent with either possibility.

Discussions of the class—schizophrenia relationship have generally focused on interpretations that, in effect, explain away its theoretical significance. Some argue that the statistical relationship between social class and rates of schizophrenia is only artifactual, the result of methodological error.[3] Others accept the statistical relationship as real, but assert that schizophrenics are found disproportionately in lower social classes (or in declining occupations or in central city areas) because of the impairment they have suffered or because of some characterological defect of non-social origin.[4] The social statuses of schizophrenics, from this point of view, tell us something about how schizophrenics fare in society but little or nothing about what produces schizophrenia.

Other interpretations emphasize the processes by which people come to be perceived as mentally disordered and what happens to them after they are so perceived. One such interpretation asserts that psychiatric and other authorities are especially prone to stigmatize and hospitalize lower-class people: they victimize the powerless.[5] Similar, though more subtle explanations focus on the processes by which families, employers, police, and others come to label some deviant behaviors as mentally disordered, thereby setting in motion complex changes in social expectation and self-conception that sometimes eventuate in hospitalization.[6] From this point of view, social position matters not because of its role in producing the initially deviant behavior but because it affects other people's perceptions of and reactions to that behavior. The class—schizophrenia relationship documents the discriminatory readiness of many people to see signs of mental disorder in lower-class behavior.

Even those interpretations that accord a primary causal significance to social-structural conditions have deemphasized the importance of class, per se,

---

3. The principal issues are the adequacy of indices, the completeness of the search procedures used, and the relative merits and defects of incidence and prevalence as statistical measures. I (1968) have discussed these issues in an earlier paper.

4. Most germane, and prototypic of all such interpretations, is the well-known drift hypothesis, which asserts that schizophrenics have "drifted" into lower social classes (or into poorer neighborhoods) as a consequence of their disorder. In recent years, the drift hypothesis has been much amended, to include the possibility that schizophrenics may not actually have declined in class position, but may simply not have achieved the class positions ordinarily reached by people of their class origins or educational attainments.

The most important studies are those by Dunham (1965), Goldberg and Morrison (1963), Turner (1968), and Turner and Wagenfeld (1967). Other references are given in Dohrenwend and Dohrenwend, (1969, 45–48) and in Kohn (1968). After a detailed review of the evidence (Kohn, 1968, 158–160), I concluded that downward social mobility does not provide a sufficient explanation of the class–schizophrenia relationship. A point of view contrary to mine is argued forcefully by Dunham (1965) and by Ødegaard (1956).

5. This interpretation is a logical outgrowth of Goffman's (1959) analysis of the "moral career of the mental patient," which sees hospitalization as the end-product of a "funnel of betrayal," with the psychiatrist as a major culprit. Goffman deals only in passing with the possibility of class differences in the likelihood of victimization, but some of his followers argue that psychiatrists are especially prone to hospitalize lower-class people and to diagnose them as schizophrenic; middle-class people are spared, if not hospitalization, at least the stigma of being called schizophrenic.

6. Scheff (1966) presents a cogent formulation of the labeling theory approach as applied to mental disorder. But Gove (1970) marshals evidence that this approach is based on assumptions that are inconsistent with what is known: principally, that people strongly resist seeing deviant behavior as mentally disordered; the pressures, instead, are to interpret even grotesque behavior as somehow normal and situationally explainable.

emphasizing instead such related processes as social isolation, social integration, discrepancies between aspirations and achievements, and minority position in the community—to name but a few of the most prominently suggested.[7] These interpretations are, for the most part, consistent with existing data and must be acknowledged to be plausible. But they largely neglect the most straightforward possibility of all—that social class is related to schizophrenia primarily because the conditions of life built into lower social-class position are conducive to that disorder.

I think it is time to devote a larger portion of our efforts to devising and testing formulations about how and why lower-class conditions of life might contribute to schizophrenia. The purpose of this paper is to offer one such formulation. It is necessarily tentative, for it is based on seriously incomplete information; at critical places, there is no directly pertinent evidence and I can only speculate.

Genetics and stress

Any interpretation of the role of social class in the development of schizophrenia must take into account two other clusters of variables—genetics and stress.[8]

Genetics

Recent studies of monozygotic twins and of adopted children demonstrate that although genetics alone cannot provide a sufficient explanation of schizophrenia, some genetic mechanism must be involved.[9] Geneticists do not agree on what is inherited—whether it be a vulnerability specifically to schizophrenia, a vulnerability to mental disorder more generally, or even a type of personality structure. Nor is it certain whether the mode of genetic transmission is monogenic or polygenic. Important as these questions may be, they can for my immediate purposes be passed over; all that need be accepted is that genetics plays some substantial part in schizophrenia.

One could argue, in fact, that genetics explains why *class* is related to schizophrenia. If there is a heritable component in schizophrenia, there must have been higher than usual rates of the disorder among the parents and grand-

---

7. Although some of these interpretations have been addressed to mental illness in general, they are equally applicable to schizophrenia. On social isolation, cf. Hare (1956), Jaco (1954), Kohn and Clausen (1955). On social integration, cf. Leighton et al., (1963). On discrepancies between aspirations and achievements, cf. Kleiner and Parker (1963), Myers and Roberts (1959), Parker and Kleiner (1966). On occupying a minority position in the community, cf. Schwartz and Mintz (1963), Wechsler and Pugh (1967).

8. It is widely believed that there must also be a biochemical abnormality in schizophrenia. I omit that possibility from this discussion because of Kety's (1960; 1969) conclusion, based on his critical reviews of the research literature, that positive biochemical findings have thus far failed to stand the test of replication. There is of course no necessary incompatibility between biochemical and social-psychological interpretations of schizophrenia, provided that neither claims to be exclusive.

9. For a comprehensive assessment of the genetic evidence, cf. Rosenthal (1970). Other valuable discussions are to be found in Kringlen (1966, 1967), Rosenthal (1962, 1968), Shields (1968), Slater (1968). For discussions of the mode of genetic transmission, cf. Gottesman and Shields (1967), Heston (1970), Rosenthal (1970).

parents of schizophrenics. Moreover, since schizophrenia is debilitating, there would have been downward social mobility in earlier generations. Thus, schizophrenics could come disproportionately from lower-class families, not because the conditions of life experienced by lower-class people have pernicious effects, but because there is a concentration of genetically susceptible people in the lower social classes.

These processes of multigenerational mobility may well contribute to the increased propability of schizophrenia for people of lower-class position. The question, though, is whether there could have been *enough* downward mobility attributable to the genetically induced disabilities of earlier generations to account for the heightened incidence of schizophrenia found today in the lower social classes.

Since there are no data about the mobility rates of parents and grandparents of schizophrenics, one can only extrapolate from existing data about the rates of intergenerational occupational mobility of (male) schizophrenics. Turner and Wagenfeld (1967, 110) show that the absolute amount of downward mobility has been almost nil: 36 percent of the schizophrenics in their sample have fallen and 35 percent have risen from their fathers' occupational levels, for a net decline of less than one-tenth of a step on a seven-point occupational scale. In the general population, though, there has been a net rise of nearly one-half step on the same seven-point scale. Thus, schizophrenics have lagged behind the general population in not rising about their fathers' occupational levels.

The effect of this failure of upward mobility could be an increase from one generation to the next in genetic susceptibility to schizophrenia at lower-class levels. But such an increase would probably not be great, even over several generations, for three main reasons. First, it can reasonably be assumed that the schizophrenics' parents and grandparents were, on the average, less disturbed and therefore less likely to lag in mobility than were the schizophrenics themselves. Second, we need not assume that the entire lag in intergenerational mobility is genetically induced or has genetic consequences. Finally, it would take a large amount of downward mobility, not just a moderate lag in upward mobility, to increase the genetic susceptibility of the lower social classes appreciably. These considerations make it seem improbable that class differences in the incidence of schizophrenia result entirely, or even largely, from genetically induced, intergenerational social mobility.

Stress

Investigators of the role of stress in shcizophrenia face a perplexing problem in defining and indexing stress (cf. Dohrenwend and Dohrenwend, 1969; Lazarus, 1966; Scott and Howard, 1970). A narrow conception would have that term apply only to externally induced events that can be assumed to be psychically painful to virtually everyone who experiences them. Such a conception achieves rigor at the price of excluding from its purview those traumas that may have been self-induced, as well as all those traumas that are painful for some people but not for everyone. It also excludes such real if self-defined misfortunes as failure to attain a longed-for goal. In fact, the only experiences that can be assumed to be externally induced and to be painful for everyone are such crises as serious illness, death of close relatives, hunger, and loss of one's job; and even these misfortunes may not be equally painful to all who experience them. But broader conceptions of stress are also problematic. At the extreme, if any event that produces subjectively experienced pain in some individual is considered to be stressful, formulations that attribute to stress a causal role in schizophrenia become tautological.

Research workers have for the most part dealt with this dilemma by (explicitly or implicitly) defining as stressful those events that usually are externally induced and that can be expected to be painful to most people who experience them. Such events occur with greater frequency at lower social-class levels: people at the bottom of the class hierarchy experience great economic insecurity and far more than their share of serious ill health, degradation, and the afflictions attendant on inadequate, overcrowded housing, often in over-populated, under-serviced areas.

Is stress conducive to schizophrenia? A definitive study would require direct, rather than inferential, measurement of stress; a research design that takes social class explicitly into account; and, of course, an adequate index of schizophrenia. Not surprisingly, no study meets all these criteria. Therefore, one can make only a tentative overall appraisal, recognizing that some pertinent studies do not index stress as well as we should like, others do not explicitly control social class, and some are addressed to mental disorder in general rather than specifically to schizophrenia.

My appraisal of the research evidence is based primarily on the studies by Birley and Brown (1970), Brown and Birley (1968), Eitinger (1964), Langner and Michael (1963), and Rogler and Hollingshead (1965). These studies do indicate that stress is associated with the occurrence of schizophrenia. Moreover, Rogler and Hollingshead (1965, 409–411) show that the relationship between stress and schizophrenia does not simply reflect the high levels of stress prevalent in the lower social classes. From their investigation of schizophrenics and matched controls in the lowest social class of San Juan, Puerto Rico, they report that during the year before the onset of symptoms, the schizophrenics experienced notably greater stress than did the controls.[10] Even when judged by the harsh

---

10. A cautionary note: the Rogler–Hollingshead study is based on schizophrenics who are married or living in stable consensual unions. One would assume then to be predominantly "reactive" schizophrenics—precisely the group whom clinical studies describe as having had normal childhood social experiences, good social adjustment, and extreme precipitating circumstances. So these findings may apply only to reactive schizophrenia, not to process schizophrenia. It may also be that some of the stress experienced by the schizophrenics resulted from their already disordered behavior. Still, Rogler and Hollingshead present a strong case that externally induced stress is important for some types of schizophrenia.

standards of life of the San Juan slums, the stresses that preceded the onset of schizophrenia were unusually severe.

As with genetics, one must reverse the question and ask whether stress can explain the relationship of class to schizophrenia. The Rogler–Hollingshead study cannot help us here, for it is limited to one social class. Unfortunately for our purposes, the only study that does provide data for all levels of social class, that by Langner and Michael (1963), is addressed to mental disorder in general rather than to schizophrenia in particular. This study is nevertheless germane, for it provides a powerful argument against stress explaining why social class is related to mental disorder. At any given level of stress, people of lower social-class position are more likely to become mentally disturbed than are people of higher social-class position. In fact, the more sources of stress, the greater the class difference in the proportion of people who manifest psychotic symptoms. The implication is that the relationship of class to mental disorder (hence, if we may extrapolate, to schizophrenia) is not attributable to the amount of stress that people endure. There must be important class differences in how effectively people deal with stress.

Part of the explanation for lower-class people dealing less effectively with stress may be that the stress-producing situations they face are less alterable by individual action than are those encountered by people of higher social-class position. Many of their stresses arise from economic circumstances over which few individuals have much control, lower-class individuals least of all. Moreover, lower-class people have little money or power to employ in coping with the consequences of stress. It also appears (cf. Dohrenwend and Dohrenwend, 1969, 137–139) that fewer institutional resources are available to them, either for escaping stressful situations or for mitigating the consequences of stress.

Still, important as class differences in the modifiability of stress-producing situations and in the availability of external resources may be, they do not provide a complete explanation of lower-class people's greater difficulty in dealing with stress. There is one more element that need be taken into account: lower-class conditions of life also limit people's *internal* resources (cf. Dohrenwend and Dohrenwend, 1969, 140–143).[11] Understanding how lower-class conditions of life may impair people's internal resources for dealing with stress is, I believe, crucial to understanding how class contributes to schizophrenia. It is therefore the heart of my formulation.

I would add that class position affects people's ability to deal, not only with situations that by my limited definition are stressful, but also with many other dilemmas and uncertainties in a rapidly changing, complex society. From this perspective, interpreting the role of social class in the genesis of schizophrenia requires an explanation of how lower-class conditions of life adversely affect people's ability to deal with stress, with complexity, and with change.

---

11. Pertinent, too, are the discussions by Brewster Smith (1968) of "the competent self," by Foote and Cottrell (1955) of "interpersonal competence," and by Phillips (1968) of "social competence."

Class, Family, and Schizophrenia

If internal resources for dealing with complex and stressful situations are at issue, then that primary socializing institution, the family, is probably somehow involved. The many studies of the role of the family in the development of schizophrenia are pertinent here, even though most of them have been addressed to a question quite different from ours. The purpose of these investigations has generally been to find some pattern of interpersonal relationship unique to the families of schizophrenics. To the best of my knowledge, though, no well-controlled study has shown a substantial difference between the patterns of parent–child relationship characteristic of families that produce schizophrenic offspring and those characteristic of ordinary lower- and working-class families.[12] From a traditional, single-factor perspective, two interpretations of this negative finding are possible.

One would be that the family plays no important part in the genesis of schizophrenia. This interpretation holds that the patterns of parent—child relationship typical of schizophrenia-producing families merely reflect those of the lower social classes from which schizophrenics disproportionately come,[13] without having been instrumental in the disorder.

The alternative interpretation would assert that the family does play a critically differentiating role in schizophrenia, but that the statistical evidence is not yet in. From this point of view, most well-controlled studies have been too limited in focus. They have dealt with such relatively concrete aspects of family life as the overall pattern of role-allocation, parental bestowal of warmth and affection, and disciplinary practices, but have missed more subtle interpersonal processes that recent clinical investigations have emphasized.[14] Future studies may show clear and convincing evidence of important differences between schizophrenia-producing families and ordinary families of lower social-class position.

There is, however, a third possible interpretation. Instead of looking to the family for a total explanation of schizophrenia, this interpretation attempts only to explain how lower-class families may contribute to the disorder in genetically vulnerable people who are subject to great stress. From this perspective, the family is important for schizophrenia, not because the family experiences of schizophrenics have differed in some presently undisclosed manner from those of

---

12. This sweeping conclusion is based on my inability, and that of others who have reviewed the research literature, to find a single study that finds important differences in patterns of parent–child relationship between schizophrenics and ordinary persons of lower social-class background. Several well-controlled studies find an absence of difference (cf. Kohn and Clausen, 1956; Mishler and Waxler, 1968; Rogler and Hollingshead, 1965).

For a comprehensive, if now dated, review of research on family and schizophrenia, cf. Sanua (1961); see also the introduction to, and references included in, Kohn and Clausen (1956), the discussion and references in Mishler and Waxler (1965), and Rosenbaum (1970, 140 –163).

13. For an incisive review of research on class and family, cf. Bronfenbrenner (1958). For references to studies completed since Bronfenbrenner's review, and to studies done outside the United States, cf. Kohn (1969, 4).

14. In support of this position are indications that lower-class families with schizophrenic offspring, although no different from other lower-class families in role-patterning, may manifest disturbed, even pathological, patterns of communication (cf. Behrens et al, 1968; Rosenthal et al, 1968).

other people of lower social-class background, but precisely because they have been similar. If this be the case, there is no reason to restrict our interest to processes that are unique to the family, such as its particular patterns of role allocation. We should expand our focus to include, even to emphasize, processes that the family shares with other institutions—notably, those processes that affect people's ability to perceive, to assess, and to deal with complexity and stress.[15]

The family, I suggest, is important principally because of its strategic role in transmitting to its offspring conceptions of social reality that parents have learned from their own experience. In particular, many lower-class families transmit to their offspring an orientational system[16] too limited and too rigid for dealing effectively with complex, changing, or stressful situations. This point of view is, I believe, consonant with recent psychiatric thinking about the family and schizophrenia, which emphasizes those communicational and cognitive processes in schizophrenia-producing families that contribute to the schizophrenic's difficulties in interpreting social reality.[17] What is new is the assertion that these conceptions of reality, far from being unique to families whose offspring become schizophrenic, are widely held in the lower social classes, in fact arise out of the very conditions of life experienced by people in these segments of society.

Social Class and Conceptions of Reality

Although admittedly speculative, this formulation is a direct extrapolation from what is known about the relationship between social class and conceptions of reality (cf. the review by Rossi and Blum, 1968). My (1969, Chaps. 4 and 5) own research indicates that the lower a man's social-class position, the more likely he is to value conformity to external authority and to believe that such conformity is all that his own capacities and the exigencies of the world allow; in particular, the lower a man's social-class position, the more likely is his orientational system to be marked by a rigidly conservative view of man and his social institutions, fearfulness and distrust, and a fatalistic belief that one is at the mercy of forces and people beyond one's control, often, beyond one's understanding.

Lee Rainwater (1968, 241), reviewing more intensive studies of lower-class population groups, arrives at essentially the same conclusion:

> All investigators who have studied lower-class groups seem to come up with compatible findings to the general effect that the lower-class world view involves conceptions of the world as a hostile and relatively chaotic place in

15. One implication is that it is not only the social class of one's parental family, but also one's adult social-class position, that matters for schizophrenia. This point is often overlooked, particularly in discussions of the drift hypothesis.

16. By orientation (or orientational system), I mean conceptions of the external world and of self that serve to define men's stance toward reality.

17. Especially relevant here is the work of Lyman Wynne and his associates (cf. Singer and Wynne 1965; Wynne 1967; Wynne and Singer, 1963). See also Bateson et al., (1956), Mishler and Waxler (1965), Schunam (1967).

which you have to be always on guard, a place in which one must be careful about trusting others, in which the reward for effort expended is always problematic, in which good intentions net very little.

One need not argue that this orientational system is held by all lower-class people, or that lower-class people hold these beliefs and values to the exclusion of others, more characteristic of higher social classes (cf. Miller, 1964; Rodman, 1963). It does seem to be well established, though, that these conceptions of social reality are most prevalent at the bottom of the social hierarchy.

The existence of class differences in beliefs and values is hardly accidental, nor even cultural in the sense employed by "culture of poverty" theorists who see lower-class orientations as something handed down from generation to generation independently of current social conditions.[18] On the contrary, social class embodies such basic differences in conditions of life that subjective reality is necessarily different for people differentially situated in the social hierarchy. Lower-class conditions of life allow little freedom of action, give little reason to feel in control of fate. To be lower class is to be insufficiently educated, to work at a job of little substantive complexity, under conditions of close supervision, and with little leeway to vary a routine flow of work. These are precisely the conditions that narrow one's conception of social reality and reduce one's sense of personal efficacy (cf. Kohn, 1969, chaps. 9 and 10).

The characteristically lower-class orientational system, molded as it is by actual conditions, may often be useful. It is, for example, attuned to the occupational demands that lower-class people must meet; a self-directed stance would probably bring few rewards and might easily lead to trouble. Moreover, participant-observation studies of lower-class life (cf. Liebow, 1966; Whyte, 1943) make it vividly apparent that, in an environment where one may be subject to diverse and often unpredictable risks of exploitation and victimization, this perspective may serve other protective functions as well. It is a way of keeping one's guard up. It provides a defensive strategy for people who really are vulnerable to forces they cannot control.

But there are times when a defensive posture invites attack, and there are times when the assumption that one is at the mercy of forces beyond one's control—even though justified—leaves one all the more at their mercy. An orientational system predicted on conforming to the dictates of authority sees social reality too simply and too fearfully to permit taking advantage of options that might otherwise be open. It is too inflexible for precisely those problematic and stressful circumstances that most require subtlety, flexibility, and a perceptive

---

18. For a systematic statement of the culture of poverty thesis, cf. Lewis (1965,xlii–lii). For critiques of this and related concepts, cf. Roach and Gusslin (1967), Rossi and Blum (1968), Valentine, (1968). The principal issue, as I see it, is not whether there are class differences in values, orientation, and cognitive style—there certainly are—but whether the lower-class orientational systems, once transmitted from parents to children, are amenable to change. My data show that if there is a discrepancy between early family experience and later educational and occupational conditions, the latter are likely to prevail (Kohn, 1969, 135–137). The practical implications of this finding are as important as they are obvious: the most efficacious way to alleviate the burdens of lower social-class position is not by therapy, resocialization, or other efforts to teach middle-class values and orientation, but by changing the social conditions to which lower-class people are subject.

understanding of larger social complexities. So limited an orientational system is an an impediment for anyone subjected to stressful or problematic circumstances, a catastrophe for those so unfortunate as to be genetically vulnerable to schizophrenia.

It is likely, too, that this orientational system helps shape the distinctively inflexible schizophrenic response to threat. One reason for the disproportionately high incidence of schizophrenia at lower social-class levels may be that schizophrenic disorders build on conceptions of reality firmly grounded on the experiences of these social classes.

Conclusions

To try to explain the relationship of class to schizophrenia without considering genetics and stress would be extremely difficult. One would be hard pressed to resolve the apparent contradiction that, although lower-class conditions of life appear to be conducive to schizophrenia, the absolute incidence of schizophrenia in even the lowest social class is small. When, however, one brings genetics and stress into consideration, the task becomes more manageable. It is no longer necessary to find in class itself an explanation of schizophrenia. Instead, the interpretive task is to explain how social class fits into an equation that includes genetics, probably stress, and undoubtedly other, as yet unrecognized, factors.

My formulation suggests that the constricted conditions of life experienced by people of lower social-class position foster conceptions of social reality so limited and so rigid as to impair people's ability to deal resourcefully with the problematic and the stressful. Such impairment would be unfortunate for all who suffer it, but would not in itself result in schizophrenia. In conjunction with a genetic vulnerability to schizophrenia and the experience of great stress, though, such impairment could well be disabling. Since both genetic vulnerability and stress appear to occur disproportionately at lower social-class levels, people in these segments of society may be at triple jeopardy.[19]

References

Bateson, G., Jackson, D. D., Haley, J., & Weakland, J. Toward a theory of schizophrenia. *Behavioral Science 1* (October) 1956: 251–64.

Behrens, M. I., Rosenthal, A. J., & Chodoff, P. Communication in lower-class families of schizophrenics: II Observations and findings. *Archives of General Psychiatry 18* (June) 1968: 689–96.

Birley, J. L. T., Brown, G. W. Crises and life changes preceding the onset or relapse of acute schizophrenia: Clinical aspects. *British Journal of Psychiatry 116* (March) 1970: 327–33.

---

19. In trying to make my point forcefully, I may have exaggerated statistical tendencies, making it seem as if class differences in orientational systems were differences in kind rather than in degree. I hope it is clear from the general argument, though, that all the relevant variables—genetics, stress, conceptions of reality—must be seen as probabilistic; the formulation depends on the joint occurrence of these necessary conditions.

Bleuler, E. *Dementia praicox or the group of schizophrenias.* New York: International Universities Press, 1950.

Bronfenbrenner, U. Socialization and social class through time space. In E. E. Maccoby, T. M. Newcomb, & E. L. Hartley (Eds.) *Readings in social psychology.* New York: Holt, Rinehart, 1958.

Brown, G. W., & Birley, J. L. T. Crises and life changes and the onset on schizophrenia. *Journal of Health and Social Behavior 9* (September) 1968: 203–14.

Dohrenwend, B. P., & Dohrenwend, S. B. *Social status and psychological disorder: A causal inquiry.* New York: Wiley, 1969.

Dunham, H. W. *Community and schizophrenia: An epidemological analysis.* Detroit: Wayne State University Press, 1965.

Eitinger, L. *Concentration camp survivors in Norway and Israel.* Oslo: Universitetsforlaget, 1964.

Foote, N. N., & Cottrell, L. S. *Identity and interpersonal competence: A new direction in family research.* Chicago: University of Chicago Press, 1955.

Garmezy, N. Process and reactive schizophrenia: Some conceptions and issues. In M. M. Katz, J. O. Cole, & W. E. Barton (Eds.) *The role and methodology of classification in psychiatry and psychopathology.* PHS Publication No. 1584. Washington, D.C.: Government Printing Office, 1965.

Goffman, E. The moral career of the mental patient. *Psychiatry 22* (May) 1959: 123–42.

Goldberg, E. M., & Morrison, S. L. Schizophrenia and social class. *British Journal of Psychiatry 109* (November) 1963, 785–802.

Gottesman, I. I., & Shields, J. A polygenic theory of schizophrenia. *Proceedings of the National Academy of Sciences 58* (July) 1967: 199–205.

Gove, W. R. Societal reaction as an explanation of mental illness: An evaluation. *American Sociological Review 35* (October) 1970: 873–84.

Hare, E. H. Mental illness and social conditions in Bristol. *Journal of Mental Science 102* (April) 1956: 349–57.

Heston, L. L. The genetics of schizophrenic and schizoid disease. *Science 167* (January 16) 1970: 249–56.

Hollingshead, A. B., & Redlich, F. C. *Social class and mental illness: A community study.* New York: Wiley, 1958.

Jaco, E. G. The social isolation hypothesis and schizophrenia. *American Sociological Review 19* (October) 1954: 567–77.

Kety, S. S. Recent biochemical theories of schizophrenia. In D. D. Jackson (Ed.) *The etiology of schizophrenia.* New York: Basic Books, 1960, pp. 120–45.

Kety, S. S. Biochemical hypotheses and studies. In L. Bellak & L. Loeb (Eds.) *The schizophrenic syndrome.* New York: Grune & Stratton, 1969, pp. 155–71.

Kleiner, R. J., & Parker, S. Goal-striving, social status, and mental disorder: A research review. *American Sociological Review 28* (April) 1963: 189–203.

Kohn, M. L. Social class and schizophrenia: A critical review. In D. D. Rosenthal & S. S. Kety (Eds.) *The transmission of schizophrenia.* Oxford: Pergammon, 1968, pp. 155–73. (Reprinted in Rosenbaum, 1970, pp. 164–88; In Wechsler, et al., 1970, pp. 113–28).

Kohn, M. L. *Class and conformity: A study in values.* Homewood, Ill.: Dorsey, 1969.

Kohn, M. L., & Clausen, J. A. Social isolation and schizophrenia. *American Sociological Review 20* (June) 1955: 265–73.

Kohn, M. L., & Clausen, J. A. Parental authority behavior and schizophrenia. *American Journal of Orthopsychiatry 26* (April) 1956: 297–313.

Kringlen, E. Schizophrenia in twins: An epidemological-clinical study. *Psychiatry 29* (May) 1966: 172–84.

Kringlen, E. *Heredity and environment in the functional psychoses: An epidemological-clinical twin study.* Oslo: Universitetsforlaget, 1967.

Langner, T. S., & Michael, S. T. *Life stress and mental health.* New York: Free Press, 1963.

Lazarus, R. S. *Psychological stress and the coping process.* New York: McGraw-Hill, 1966.

Leighton, D. C., Harding, J. S., Macklin, D. B., MacMillan, A. M., & Leighton, A. H. *The character of danger: Psychiatric symptoms in selected communities.* New York: Basic Books, 1963.

Lewis, O. *La vida: A Puerto Rican family in the culture of poverty—San Juan and New York.* New York: Random House, 1965.

Liebow, E. *Tally's corner: A study of negro street-corner men.* Boston: Little, Brown, 1966.

Miller, S. M. The American lower classes: A typological approach. In F. Riessman, J. Cohen, & A. Pearl (Eds.) *Mental health of the poor.* New York: Free Press, 1964.

Mishler, E. G., & Scotch, N. A. Sociocultural factors in the epidemology of schizophrenia: A Review. *Psychiatry 26* (November) 1963: 315–51.

Mishler, E. G., & Walker, N. E. Family interaction processes and schizophrenia: A review of current theories. *Merrill-Palmer Quarterly of Behavior and Development 11* (October) 1965: 269–315.

Mishler, E. G. & Walker, N. E. *Interaction in families: An experimental study of family processes and schizophrenia.* New York: Wiley, 1968.

Myers, J. K., & Roberts, B. H. *Family and class dynamics in mental illness.* New York: Wiley, 1959.

Ødegaard, O. The incidence of psychoses in various occupations. *International Journal of Social Psychiatry 2* (Autumn) 1956: 85–104.

Parker, S., & Kleiner, R. J. *Mental illness in the urban Negro community.* New York: Free Press, 1966.

Phillips, L. *Human adaptation and its failures.* New York: Academic Press, 1968.

Rainwater, L. The problem of lower-class culture and poverty-war strategy. In D. P. Moynihan (Ed.) *On understanding poverty: Perspectives from the social sciences.* New York: Basic Books, 1968, pp. 229–59.

Roach, J. L., & Gursslin, O. R. An evaluation of the concept 'culture of poverty.' *Social Forces 45* (March) 1967: 383–92.

Rodman, H. The lower-class value stretch. *Social Forces 42* (December) 1963: 205–15.

Rosenbaum, C. P. *The meaning of madness: Symptomatology, sociology, biology, and therapy of the schizophrenias.* New York: Science House, 1970.

Rosenthal, A. J., Behrens, M. I., & Chodoff, P. Communication in lower class families of schizophrenics: I Methodological problems. *Archives of General Psychiatry 18* (April) 1968: 464–70.

Rosenthal, D. Problems of sampling and diagnosis in the major twin studies of schizophrenia. *Journal of Psychiatric Research 1* (September) 1962, 116–34.

Rosenthal, D. The heredity-environment issue in schizophrenia. In D. Rosenthal & S. S. Kety (Eds.) *The transmission of schizophrenia.* Oxford: Pergammon, 1968, pp. 413–27.

Rosenthal, D. *Genetic theory and abnormal behavior.* New York: McGraw-Hill, 1970.

Rossi, P. H., & Blum, Z. D. Class, status, and poverty. In D. P. Moynihan (Ed.) *On understanding poverty: Perspectives from the social sciences.* New York: Basic Books, 1968, pp. 36–63.

Rushing, W. A. Two patterns in the relationship between social class and mental hospitalization. *American Sociological Review 34* (August) 1969: 533–41.

Sanua, V. D. Sociocultural factors in families of schizophrenics: A review of the literature. *Psychiatry 24* (August) 1961: 246–65.

Scheff, T. J. *Being mentally ill: A sociological theory.* Chicago: Aldine, 1966.

Schuh^m, A. I. The double-bind hypothesis a decade later. *Psychological Bulletin 68* (December) 1967: 409–16.

Schwartz, D. T., & Mintz, N. L. Ecology and psychosis among Italians in 27 Boston communities. *Social Problems 10* (Spring) 1963: 371–74.

Scott, R., & Howard, A. Models of stress. In S. Levine & N. A. Scotch (Eds.) *Social stress.* Chicago: Aldine, 1970.

Shields, J. Summary of the genetic evidence. In D. Rosenthal & S. S. Kety (Eds.) *The transmission of schizophrenia.* Oxford: Pergammon, 1968.

Singer, M. T., & Wynne, L. C. Thought disorder and family relations of schizophrenics: Methodology using projective techniques; results and implications. *Archives of General Psychiatry 12* (February) 1965: 187–212.

Slater, E. A review of earlier evidence on genetic factors in schizophrenia. In D. Rosenthal & S. S. Kety (Eds.) *The Transmission of Schizophrenia.* Oxford: Pergammon, 1968, pp. 15–26.

Smith, M. B. Competence and socialization. In J. A. Clausen (Ed.) *Socialization and society.* Boston: Little, Brown, 1968, pp. 270–320.

Turner, R. J. Social mobility and schizophrenia. *Journal of Health and Social Behavior 9* (September) 1968: 194–203.

Turner, R. J., & Wagenfield, M. O. Occupational mobility and schizophrenia: An assessment of the social causation and social selection hypotheses. *American Sociological Review 32* (February) 1967: 104–13.

Valentine, C. A. *Culture and Poverty: Critique and counter-proposals.* Chicago: University of Chicago Press, 1968.

Wechsler, H., & Pugh, T. F. Fit of individual and community characteristics and rates of psychiatric hospitalization. *American Journal of Sociology 73* (November) 1967: 331–338.

Wechsler, H., Solomon, L., & Kramer, B. M. (Eds.) *Social psychology and mental health.* New York: Holt, Rinehart, 1970.

Whyte, W. F. *Street corner society: The social structure of an Italian slum.* Chicago: University of Chicago Press, 1943.

Wynne, L. C. Family transactions and schizophrenia: Conceptual considerations for a research strategy. In J. Romano (Ed.) *The origins of schizophrenia.* Amsterdam: Excerpta Medica International Congress Series No. 151, 1967.

Wynne, L. C., & Singer, M. T. Thought disorder and family relations of schizophrenics: A classification of forms of thinking. *Archives of General Psychiatry* 9 (September) 1963: 191–206.

PART III
Social Psychology of Illness and Its Management

Social psychologists examine interpersonal behavior, the relationships among people which often occurs in face-to-face encounters. People's attitudes and the impressions they form of what is happening influence their interaction with others. Interaction among people is always set within the cultural values and institutions of society.

The social psychology of illness and its management is concerned with how the interaction among people who often have conflicting interests and beliefs shapes illness and society's response to it. Illness and its management is a complex phenomenon which involves assumptions of when one is sick and how a sick person should behave; interaction between putatively sick people and those in their environment such as family, friends and later (though not always) medical personnel; and evaluations that the people involved make of one another. Encounters between people, between the sick and those who heal for example, are stressed in understanding the social psychology of illness and its management.

Siegler and Osmond discuss Parson's famous concept of the "sick role" and how rarely that role is achieved. Rosenhan argues that mental illness is not necessarily due to a physiological condition but may be the result of other people's reactions to the labeled individual. Gove and Howell criticize the labeling or societal reaction perspective by arguing that mental hospitals are in fact filled with behaviorally incompetent people. Levitin, Bynder, and New outline the varied problems that the disabled person faces today. Zola presents a theoretical statement of how people come to see themselves as in need of going to a doctor.

Svarstad and Albrecht analyze interaction between the doctor and patient. Svarstad examines how patient conformity with doctor's advice is influenced by the doctor's efforts to instruct and motivate the patient, the patient's expectations and attitudes and the feedback a patient gives to the doctor. Within cultural and social conditions, Albrecht emphasizes negotiation between the dentist and patient in the diagnosis and treatment of occlusal problems.

In the concluding chapter, Roth demonstrates how the management of illness is *not* a morally neutral activity. The medical profession evaluates people as more or less worth treating or curing.

The 'Sick Role' Revisited   9

MIRIAM SIEGLER
HUMPHREY OSMOND

In a series of papers from 1951 to 1958, Talcott Parsons developed his concept of the sick role.[1] Since that time, medical sociologists have found this a useful formulation, and a fairly extensive literature has grown up around it.[2] However, the fact that it is an ideal concept has given rise to a problem which Freidson has noted: when one goes to examine actual cases of occupancy of the sick role, they rarely correspond with this ideal.[3] This tends to cast doubt on the usefulness of the concept. It is our view, however, that by mapping out the different kinds of deviance from the sick role, one may come to have a clearer understanding of its

From *Hastings Center Studies*, 1 1973, 41–58. Copyright 1973, The Hastings Center. Reprinted with permission.

   1. Talcott Parsons, *The social system*. Glencoe, Ill.: Free Press, 1951, pp. 428–79; The mental hospital as a type of organization. In M. Greenblatt, D. J. Levinson, & R. H. Williams (Eds.) *The patient and the mental hospital*. Glencoe, Il.: Free Press, 1957, pp. 108–29; Definitions of health and illness in the light of american values and social structure. In E. G. Jaco (Ed.) *Patients, Physicians and Illness*. Glencoe, Ill.: Free Press, 1958, pp. 165–87; Illness and the role of the physician: A sociological perspective. In C. Kluckholm, H. A. Murray, & D. M. Schneider (Eds.) *Personality in Nature, Society, and Culture*. New York: Knopf, 1961, pp. 452–60. Illness, therapy and the modern urban american family. In E. G. Jaco (Ed.) *Patients, Physicians and Illness*. Glencoe, Ill.: Free Press, 1958, pp. 235–45. Written with Renee C. Fox.
   2. S. W. Bloom, *The doctor and his patient*. New York: Sage, 1963; J. G. Bruhn, An operational approach to the sick-role concept. *British Journal of Medical Psychology 35* 1962: 289–92; R. L. Coser, A home away from home. In D. Apple (Ed.) *Sociological Studies of Health and Sickness*. New York: McGraw-Hill, 1960, pp. 154–72; K. T. Erikson, Patient role and social uncertainty—A dilemma of the mentally ill. *Psychiatry 20* 1957: 263–74; Eliot Friedson, *Patients' views of medical practice*. New York: Sage. 1961; G. Gordon, *Role theory and illness: A sociological perspective*. New Haven: College and University Press, 1966; S. V. Kasl & S. Cobb, Health behavior. *Archives of Environmental Health 12* 1966: 246–66, 531–41; G. G. Kasselbaum & B. Baumann, Dimensions of the sick role in chronic illness. *Journal of Health and Human behavior 6* 1965: 16–27; Stanley H. King, Social psychological factors in illness. In H. E. Freeman, S. Levine, & L. G. Reeder (Eds.) *Handbook of Medical Sociology*. Englewood Cliffs, N.J.: Prentice-Hall, 1963, pp. 397–419; also S. Polgar, Health action in cross-cultural perspective, and R. N. Wilson, Patient-practitioner relationships, both in the *Handbook of Medical Sociology;* David Mechanic and E. H. Volkart, Stress, illness behavior and the sick role. *American Sociological Review 26* 1961: 51–58.
   3. Eliot Freidson, *Patients' views of medical practice*. New York: Sage, 1961.

value and meaning, just as one may deduce much of an organ's actual function by studying its pathology.

Parsons describes four essential aspects of the sick role. First, depending on the nature and severity of the illness, the sick person is exempted from some or all of his normal social role responsibilities. Second, the sick person cannot help being ill, and cannot get well by an act of decision or will. Third, the sick person is expected to want to get well as soon as possible. Fourth, he is expected to seek appropriate help, usually that of a physician, and cooperate with that help toward the end of getting well.

What, then, would be an ideal experience of Parsons's sick role? We believe it would go something like this. An ailing person would notice that he had unusual symptoms of some sort, or he would find that he was unable to carry out his normal responsibilities. He would consider the possibility of illness, and go to a doctor. He would tell the doctor the history of the illness and the symptoms. The doctor would examine him, then tell him the diagnosis, the prognosis, and the appropriate treatment. The patient would not blame himself or anyone else for the illness. He would follow the doctor's orders, take his medicine, modify his usual activities as directed, and report changes in his condition. If the illness proved to be a fatal one, he would make his exit as gracefully as possible. If the illness proved amenable to treatment, the doctor would monitor the patient's progress with the aid of objective measurements, and would tell him when it was safe to discontinue the treatment and take up his usual occupation. The patient would then leave the sick role (having paid his bill and thanked the doctor) and resume his normal life. Alas, this ideal sequence of events almost never occurs. At every point along the way, there is the possibility, indeed the likelihood, that the patient may leave the sick role for one of a number of other roles.

What is the source of the alternate roles to the sick role? It seems that illness can only be perceived in a few ways, and these limited possibilities, each with many variations, recur again and again over the centuries, sometimes couched in different terminology but quite recognizably the same. Thus we read in the *Malleus Malificarum,* published in 1486, that a person who is bewitched should visit his exorcist three times a week, and if he fails to improve, it is because of his sins or because those who brought him lack sufficient faith.[4] Here we see a protopsychoanalytic model of illness, with its concomitant role of the bewitched person.

In a series of previous papers, we have constructed eight basic models of illness derived from these recurrent views.[5] We have used as our examples three highly controversial illnesses—schizophrenia, alcoholism, and narcotics addic-

---

4. H. Kramer and J. Sprenger, *Malleus malificarum.* Translated by the Rev. M. Summers. London: Pushkin Press, 1948.

5. Miriam Siegler, F. E. Cheek, & Humphrey Osmond, Attitudes toward naming the illness. *Mental Hygiene 52* 1968: 266–38; Miriam Siegler & Humphrey Osmond, Models of madness. *British Journal of Psychiatry 112* 1966: 1193–1203; Models of drug addiction. *International Journal of Addictions 3* 1968: 3–24; The impaired model of schizophrenia. *Schizophrenia 1* 1969: 192–202; Miriam Siegler, Humphrey Osmond & H. Mann, Laing's models of madness. *British Journal of Psychiatry 115* 1969: 947–58; Miriam Siegler, Humphrey Osmond, & S. Newell. Models of alcoholism. *Quarterly Journal of Studies on Alcohol 29* 1968: 571–81.

tion—in which disputes about these different viewpoints have been especially sharp. The models we have constructed so far are: medical, moral, psychoanalytic, social, psychedelic, impaired, family interaction, and conspiratorial. Of these, we shall be giving examples of all but the last two.

Each model yields a role for the ill person, that is, a set of rights and duties. In the medical model, in which it is assumed that illnesses have natural causes, the role of the sufferer is called the sick role. In the psychoanalytic model, in which the psyche is located as the source of the illness, the resultant role is called by the rather unsatisfactory term, analysis and in the moral model, the sick person is seen as "bad" rather than "sick," or else it is said that he became sick because he was bad. A "good" role is also possible in this model, in which the person tries to be "good" so that he will no longer be "sick." In any case, the moral model assumes a willful component of illness. The assumption of the impaired model is that the sufferer's state (blind, crippled, retarded, and so forth) is fixed once and for all and will not respond to further intervention. A person in the impaired role is typically expected to accept a lower status than a normal person since he is visibly damaged and cannot fully occupy a normal role. The impaired role is unique among these roles, since it was discovered empirically by Gordon, in a study designed to validate the sick role. The social model yields the role of social victim, and the psychedelic model, the role of the enlightened one.

Denying the Sick Role

In this paper, we shall describe a number of failures to achieve or sustain the sick role. In each of our cases we can show which of Parsons's four postulates were violated by the patient, and so we will present our cases in the order in which they deviate from these basic conditions of the sick role. Our examples are drawn from two main sources, the literature of medical sociology, and the greatest fictional work on the sick role, Thomas Mann's *The Magic Mountain.* Mann's novel might be subtitled "One Hundred Ways to Deviate from the Sick Role," for few of the patients at the International Sanitorium Berghof resemble in any way our description of an ideal tenant of the sick role. Hans Castorp, the hero of *The Magic Mountain,* occupies each of the alternate roles in succession.

Very often, the first step toward occupying the sick role is the acknowledgement that one must curtail or abandon one's normal social role. For some patients, this presents a stumbling block. An extreme case is reported by Lederer:

> A physician, in middle age, sustained an acute coronary heart attack. His professional colleagues, who diagnosed his illness, advised immediate and absolute bed rest, quiet, and heavy sedation, all of which the patient stoutly refused on the grounds of his heavy schedule of work with his own patients. He persisted in his medical work and died suddenly in his office twenty hours later.[6]

6. H. D. Lederer, How the sick view their world. *Journal of Social Issues 8* 1952: 4–15.

Although few sick people reject the sick role so completely, many cannot make peace with their altered status. One class of people for whom the sick role is particularly onerous consists of those for whom life is primarily verbal rather than physical. Such individuals ignore their own bodily processes as much as possible and sometimes develop a style of locomotion which implies that if they were only able to move quickly enough, they would be able to abandon their bodies altogether. Such a one is Herr Settembrini, the Italian humanist whom Hans Castorp meets on the Magic Mountain. Settembrini regards disease as a degradation and sees no possibility of dignity in the sick role. When Hans first meets him, he pours out a stream of malicious gossip and slander about the Berghof. He implies that the Berghof is really Hell, and refers to the two physicians as "the judges of our infernal regions." He credits Dr. Behrens with having invented "the summer season," i.e., persuaded patients to stay on throughout the year, whereas previously it was thought that the climate of the Berghof was especially salutary only in the colder months. "One must give the devil his due," he says. He tells Hans that he must not suppose that their rooms are unheated for medical purposes—it is only to save the management money. At the fortnightly concerts, Settembrini stays for only half an hour, to give himself the illusion of being a guest. He does not like music doled out for the good of his health, reeking of the prescription counter. Settembrini reserves his greatest contempt for the other patients, who use the excuse of their illness to indulge in a life of idleness and flirtation. He tells Hans:

> I would urge it upon you: hold yourself upright, preserve your self-respect, do not give ground to the unknown. Flee from this sink of iniquity, this island of Circe, whereon you are not Odysseus enough to dwell in safety. You will be going on all fours—already you are inclining toward your forward extremities, and presently you will begin to grunt—have a care!

Hans and his cousin Joachim, who are trying, each in his own way, to be good patients, find Settembrini's mocking attitude seditious and distasteful. It makes them uneasy to talk with someone who is so lacking in medical piety. But, on one occasion, Settembrini goes too far and is revealed as a crypto-patient. He sets out to reduce their faith in the accuracy of the X-rays. Are they aware, he wants to know, that some patients have no spots on their X-ray plates, but die of tuberculosis anyway? And with others, who have spots on their plates, it is found at the autopsy that they really had some other disease. Hans says:

> "Can you see spots on your plate, Herr Settembrini?"
> "Yes, it shows some spots."
> "And you really are ill too?"
> "Yes, I am unfortunately rather ill," replied Settembrini, and his head drooped. There was a pause, in which he gave a little cough. Hans Castorp, from his bed, regarded his guest, whom he had reduced to silence. It seemed to him that with his two simple inquiries he had refuted Settembrini's whole position, even the republic and the *bello stile*.

Settembrini is the Coriolanus of the sick role. The Roman general refused to show his battle wounds to the populace, although that was the time-honored way of establishing his right to rule them. Settembrini refuses to give the others visible evidence that he is a tuberculosis patient like themselves, although there could be no other explanation for his residence at the Berghof. In both cases, the reason is the same: the unwillingness to give the body its due. But Settembrini, for all his mocking, is no fool; he occupies the sick role no less than the others, for he knows that his life is at stake, and his beautiful philosophy must be housed, however unwillingly, in a fragile and mortal human body.

It is one of the privileges of the sick role to be exempted, to varying degrees, from one's normal social responsibilities. But this exemption is conditional on taking up the responsibilities inherent in the sick role—trying to get well, seeking help, accepting treatment, and so forth. In many illnesses, the duties of the sick role are sufficiently dreadful that no one is likely to prefer them to those of normal life. But in some slowly developing illness, such as tuberculosis, it is possible to claim the privileges of the sick role without being over-taxed by one's duties as a patient. If the space released by the abandonment of one's usual duties is not entirely taken up by the duties of the sick role, a moral vacuum occurs. The person may now be both "sick" and "bad."

We see this possibility illustrated in Frau Chauchat, a resident at the Berghof. Traveling across Europe from one tuberculosis sanitorium to another, Frau Chauchat uses her illness to justify a footloose existence to which she is suited by temperament, but otherwise not entitled. Although married, she spends little time in Russia with her husband and wears no wedding-band. At the Berghof, she slams doors, comes late to meals, bites her fingernails, rolls her bread into little pellets, and gazes at the male patients in a direct and shameless way. Hans Castorp soon joins the band of her lovesick admirers. The patients at the Berghof are fascinated by her, because she does what many would like to do but dare not: she openly uses her illness as an excuse for badness. In fact, her sickness and badness are so thoroughly intertwined that her occupancy of the sick role becomes a disputed issue among the other patients:

> If she was ill—and that she was, probably incurably, since she had been up here so often and so long—her illness was in good part, if not entirely, a moral one: as Settembrini had said, neither the ground nor the consequences of her "slackness," but precisely one and the same thing.

It is because of this possible abuse of the sick role that most people are reluctant to grant it to another if there is any suspicion that it may be used in this way. Davis, in his study of polio victims, found three families in which this was an issue:

> In three other families, the parents questioned the legitimacy of the child's complaints in the belief that he might be feigning illness so as to win attention and indulgence. According to Mrs. Baker, for example, when her son Gerald complained of a stiff neck, "I thought he was just playing because sometimes when he's sick he loves to be pampered, you know. And he likes his meals brought up to bed to him." None of these families

entertained this particular misconstruction of the child's onset illness for long. In effect they tested the possibility that the child was malingering (as, apparently, all three children in question were known to have done before), found this hypothesis inadequate, and then quickly dropped it in favor of some other explanation.[7]

The parents abandoned the malingering hypothesis because their children became rapidly sicker, and while no one wishes to give the sick role to someone who is "bad," it is even worse to give the "bad" role to someone who is sick. Any real or supposed failure to recognize that a child is seriously ill is almost certain to make the parents guilty. It is not just that treatment may be delayed, although this can occur, but rather that our expectations of other people's moral responsibility hinge on their being *capable* of doing the "right" thing. A sick person may not be *unwilling,* but *unable* to do what is expected of him. It is significant that in our most protective and ethically sensitive relationship, that toward children, we incur the greatest guilt if we do not confer the sick role as soon as it is needed. To deny a sick child the sick role is a particularly inhumane act.

Blamelessness and the Will

One of the conditions of the sick role is that the patient is not to blame for being sick. He cannot help having the illness, nor can he get well by an act of will. In the medical model, illness is seen as deriving from natural causes, rather than from any human action or intention. The most common alternative view of illness is the moral one in which the illness is precisely the patient's fault: it is the punishment for immoral behavior. These two views always seem to be present, even in illnesses where one would expect the medical model to hold clear title. Davis reports the presence of the moral model in his account of polio patients:

> The tendency to attribute volitional elements to the illness was strikingly revealed in interviews with the polio children themselves, particularly the younger ones, shortly after their admission to the receiving hospital. Not knowing yet that they had polio—or, if they did, not knowing quite what this meant—they frequently gave as the cause of their paralysis "running around too much," "playing when my mother said I shouldn't" or "falling down when I played too rough." In other words, the paralysis was seen as a kind of punishment for a behavioral transgression.[8]

These children, although very ill, were not yet in the sick role, and would not be until they had been convinced that the source of the illness lay outside of themselves. It would clearly be dysfunctional for them to blame themselves for the illness; however much guilt might be mobilized in this way, it would not alter

---

7. F. Davis, *Passage through crisis: Polio victims and their families.* New York: Bobbs-Merrill, 1963, p. 21.

8. F. Davis, *Passage through crisis: Polio victims and their families.* New York: Bobbs-Merrill, 1963, p. 21.

the course of the illness. They needed to see the illness itself as the enemy against which they must pit all their resources of courage, energy and patience. It would be pointless as well as inhumane to allow them to sustain this inept moral view.

If the patient himself is not to blame because the illness has natural causes, it follows that the patient's family are equally blameless. But, just as the children were prone to blame themselves, so were their parents. One of the fathers, Mr. Baker, put it:

> What made me come here? . . . Here's where Gerry got sick . . . Is that my fault? I was calling the tricks . . . I played the wrong card. I got caught. It was my fault. That's what goes through your mind. That's what you think. Your better judgment says, we can't control these things. We know we can't. But it's still there. It's still something to think about.[9]

Davis reports that there were two sources of absolution for the parents. First, the doctor told them that they could not have prevented the illness, or in any way lessened its severity. The other source of comfort was the reaction of the community in which the parents lived. Neighbors expressed concern and compassion, sent cards and presents to the sick child, helped the stricken family with their practical problems, said special prayers for the child in church, and so forth. As Davis points out, these were not the reactions that "guilty" parents would have elicited from the community. There seems to have been a high degree of consensus that no one was to blame for the illness. The stricken child and his family were moved quickly and efficiently into the sick role.

Some illnesses seem to command the sick role more readily than others. Leprosy is a prime example of an illness which for centuries conferred on its sufferers the bad role rather than the sick role. Alcoholism is an example of an illness which is still in a transitional phase. It was only in 1956 that the American Medical Association officially recognized alcoholism as an illness. It was the alcoholics themselves who discovered that they could not manage without the sick role. Typically, alcoholics adopt a moral model when they first find that they are in difficulty. They believe themselves to be bad and attempt to control their drinking directly by will power. This does not seem to work well. The position taken by Alcoholics Anonymous is that the alcoholic, unlike a normal person, is powerless over alcohol. The third member of A.A., Bill D., tells of his introduction to this view by the first two members, Bill W. and Dr. Bob:

> One of the fellows, I think it was Doc, said, "Well, you want to quit?" I said, "Yes, Doc, I would like to quit, at least for five, six, or eight months until I get things straightened up, and begin to get the respect of my wife and some other people back, and get my finances fixed up and so on." And they both laughed very heartily, and said, "That's better than you've been doing, isn't it?" Which of course was true. They said, "We've got some bad news

---

9. F. Davis, *Passage through crisis: Polio victims and their families.* New York: Bobbs-Merrill, 1963, p. 21.

for you. It was bad news for us, and it will probably be bad news for you. Whether you quit six days, months, or years, if you go out and take a drink or two, you'll end up in this hospital tied down, just like you have been in these past six months. You are an alcoholic." As far as I know that was the first time I had ever paid any attention to that word. I figured I was just a drunk. As they said, "No, you have a disease, and it doesn't make any difference how long you do without it, after a drink or two you'll end up just like you are now." That certainly was real disheartening news, at the time.[10]

According to Alcoholics Anonymous, the alcoholic is not to blame for having a physiologically peculiar reaction to alcohol. Nor can he by any act of will rid himself of this addictive response. His will power is mobilized, instead, for the task of refusing the first drink, for if he can do that, he will not set off the uncontrollable chain of events which alcohol produces in him. By accepting the fact that the illness lies outside his control, the alcoholic paradoxically becomes more responsible for himself. He is now being asked to do something which does lie within his control, living within the limitations of his illness, which requires him to refuse the first drink. The function of the sick role for alcoholics is all the more impressive in that there is as yet no satisfactory treatment for the illness. All that the occupancy of the sick role can do for alcoholics at the present time is remove blame; yet that is frequently enough to tip the balance in their favor.

Vincent Tracy provides an interesting example of an alcoholic who was not able to utilize Alcoholics Anonymous because he rejected the sick role. Tracy is evidently a charismatic man who did not appreciate sharing an illness with several million others. Most members of Alcoholics Anonymous find it comforting to hear the stories of other alcoholics at meetings, and to know that they are not alone in their struggle. But for Tracy, it had the opposite effect; it depressed and embarrassed him, and he was not able to stay sober through this program. But later, while on the Bowery, he had an experience of revelation, after which he was able to stop drinking. He then set out to help other alcoholics by inspiring them with his vision of a new life. In order to do this, he opened "Tracy Farms," a guest house in a rural setting. Each day, he gives inspiring lectures to his guests based on his own moral view of alcoholism. He tells them that they are bad, not sick:

> Some people claim it helps a lush to tell him he is sick. I don't see how. It might be comfortable to lay it to the adrenal glands, as is being done now. Anyone would rather look upon excessive drinking as a glandular deficiency instead of a moral deficiency. Is it easier for a man to rid himself of a personal vice than to cure himself of a disease for which there is no dependable medical treatment, and no known specific remedy?
>
> Sure, it was welcome to have a cause outside yourself, the suggestion that what troubled you was a disease and not a vice. This made it a physical deficiency rather than a moral deficiency. Anything was welcome by which

---

10. *Alcoholics Anonymous.* New York: Alcoholics Anonymous World Services, 1955, pp. 187–88.

the blame could be placed outside of yourself and not on yourself, where it belonged.[11]

Tracy is evidently afraid that the sick role is the easy way out for alcoholics. He sees it as consisting only of rights and not duties. If this were true, it would indeed be unworkable. But the duties of alcoholics in the sick role at the present time are heavy ones; members of A.A. are sober in more than one sense. They have found that they must adopt a complicated regimen called "the A.A. way of life" in order to have the strength to stay away from alcohol.

Bewitched and Bewildered

In addition to the bad role, there is another common alternative to the sick role. It is the role a person has when his illness is attributed to a breakdown or failure in his relationships with others. As Dr. Krowkowski, the psychoanalyst of the Berghof, put it: "Symptoms of disease are nothing but a disguised manifestation of the power of love: and all disease is only love transformed." In one version of this role, the sick person is someone who is bewitched; a spell has been put on him by another person, and the role of the therapist is to exorcise the spell. This may or may not involve finding out who cast the spell. Another version of this role is that of the analysand. The psychoanalyst inquires into the most vital relationships of the analysand, in an effort to find out what is making him ill. With the aid of various techniques, such as free association and dream interpretation, the analysand comes to experience these relationships in a new way. This change in the analysand's psychic economy will, it is hoped, be reflected in a remission of the symptoms which brought him to the analyst.

The bewitched or analysand role is very different from the sick role. Far from reassuring the family that they could not possibly have caused the illness, the therapist often locates the source of the illness in the family's failure to love the analysand. The analysand is often encouraged to separate himself from his family, whereas the medical patient may find that he will now be more dependent on his family than he was before he became ill. The medical patient is told that the illness is an ego-alien force which lies outside of his control, whereas the analysand is encouraged to see his illness as an integral part of his personality. In the sick role, diagnosis is important, for treatment, prognosis follows from it, and the patient cannot be expected to cooperate unless he knows something about the illness; in the analysand role, diagnosis is unimportant, because the etiology of every case is unique and the treatment is always the same.

In some illnesses, there is a tendency for the ill person to oscillate between the sick role and the role of the bewitched person or analysand. Today, schizophrenia is such an illness; in the nineteenth century, as Vaillant has pointed out,

11. Beth Day, *No hiding place*. New York: Henry Hold, 1957, pp. 243–244.

tuberculosis was seen in this light.[12] Our example here is provided by the fatal illness of the poet, John Keats. Some time during the year 1818, Keats came to believe that he had only a thousand days—three years—to live. At the end of this year he nursed his younger brother, Tom, through the final stages of tuberculosis. Judging from the regimen he then adopted, it now seems clear that he believed that he might be developing the illness himself. A few months later, Keats coughed up blood for the first time. He showed the blood on his bed sheet to his friend, Brown. He said: "This is unfortunate. I know the colour of that blood. It's arterial blood. There's no mistaking that colour . . . That blood is my death-warrant. I must die." With his medical training and his personal experience of nursing his mother and his brother through fatal illnesses, he was clear about his own fate.

Having confirmed for himself his worst doubts and fears, Keats then had a short period of serenity. He was, for the moment, safely ensconced in the sick role. Ward writes:

> Like most invalids in the first days of recovery, he saw everything around him shining in a new light. "How astonishingly does the chance of leaving the world impress a sense of its natural beauties on us," he wrote to Rice. . . Rice had written Keats to warn him against the "haunting and deformed thoughts and feelings" that often assailed him after one of his own relapses. Yet, to Keats, his illness seemed to have the opposite effect. "As far as I can judge in so short a time," he wrote, "it has relieved my mind of a load of deceptive thoughts and images and makes me perceive things in a truer light." There can be no doubt that he was thinking of Fanny Brawne. The brooding jealousies of the previous months had lifted like a mist.[13]

Soon, however, he became worse, and a specialist was called in to see him. After examining Keats, he said that there was "no pulmonary affection and no organic defect whatever." He told Keats that his illness was "all on his mind," and recommended fresh air and exercise. Following this prescription, Keats made a trip to town to dine with a friend and came back much worse. He wrote to his sister, "The Doctor assures me that there is nothing the matter with me except nervous irritability and a general weakness of the whole system which has proceeded from my anxiety of mind of late years and the too great excitement of poetry." The doctor, having used his medical authority to assure Keats that there was nothing wrong with him, successfully evicted him from the sick role. Keats soon began to share his doctor's view that the illness was "all on his mind," and he began to hate the reviewers who had been unfavorable to his poems and who had ruined his chance of success. Deprived of the blame-free sick role, he had to cast about for some other explanation for his illness.

When Keats' health began to deteriorate further, his friends decided to send him to Italy, a standard course of action for English consumptives. His physician

---

12. G. Vallant, Tuberculosis: An historical analogy to schizophrenia. *Psychosomatic Medicine 24* 1962: 225–33.

13. E. Ward, *John Keats: The making of a poet.* New York: Viking Press, 1963, p. 349.

in Rome, Dr. James Clark, also believed that the cause of the illness was "mental exertions"; his prescription was fresh air, moderate exercise, and avoidance of worry. By Christmas, Keats was extremely bitter, for he felt that the voyage to Italy was to no purpose, and that he was cut off from Fanny Brawne and his friends. Then he passed into another stage of his illness. Ward writes:

> A new calm succeeded the black despair of the weeks before. Severn sensed that Keats at last had given up not only the thought but even the desire for recovery. Yet it seemed that this quietude relieved him as no medicine had done.[14]

Keats died in February, 1821. His autopsy showed that his lungs were entirely destroyed. Then began a series of disgraceful quarrels among those who had loved him, each accusing the other of having caused his death. Brown wrote Severn that Keats' disease was "all on the mind" and that it was the result of the cruelty of his brother George. "I sit planning schemes of vengeance on his head," he wrote, "—that canting, selfish, heartless swindler—who will have to answer for the death of his brother." Haydon wrote that Keats died because of "want of nerve to bear abuse." Shelley believed that Keats' final hemorrhage had been brought on by an unfavorable article in the *Quarterly*. Byron's contribution was:

> John Keats, who was killed off by one critique
> Just as he promised something great
> If not intelligible, with Greek
> Contrived to talk about the gods of late
> Much as they might have been supposed to speak.
> Poor fellow! His was an untoward fate;
> 'Tis strange, the mind, that fiery particle
> Should let itself be snuffed out by an article.

Fanny Brawne, Keats' beloved, was not spared in this free-for-all; it was said that Keats had been killed by her cruelty, and that she was not fit to have been his wife.

Describing this series of events in terms of the sick role, it falls into four stages. First, Keats was relieved when the doubts and fears which had been gnawing at him were swept away by the certainty that he had tuberculosis, and he had a period of calm, although he now knew that he had a fatal illness. Second, his physician's insistence that it was "all on the mind" sabotaged his occupancy of the sick role and caused him to look for the source of his illness in his personal relationships. This was a miserable period for Keats, although medically he was not worse off than he had been at the time of his first hemorrhage. Third, when he knew that he was ill beyond any hope of recovery, he re-entered the sick role and put aside his preoccupations with the state of his relationships. Fourth, after his death, he was retroactively removed from the sick role by his friends, who took to quarreling amongst themselves as to which of them was to

---

14. E. Ward, *John Keats: The making of a poet.* New York; Viking Press, 1963, p. 394.

blame for his death. Even if nothing further could have been done for him medically, the firm insistence that the illness was due to natural causes, rather than inadequacy and malice, could have prevented enormous suffering, both on the part of Keats himself, and later on the part of his friends and relatives. Unfortunately, tuberculosis was not at that point sufficiently well organized as an illness to command the sick role for its sufferers in an unequivocal way. Today it would be unthinkable for the friends and relatives of someone who had died of tuberculosis to behave in this fashion.

It is interesting to contrast the reactions of Keats's friends to his death with the reactions produced by the death of 17-year-old Johnny Gunther, who died of a brain tumor after an illness of 15 months. Letters poured in to the Gunthers, describing Johnny as a gallant and heroic soul. Dr. Wilder Penfield, the famous neuro-surgeon, who had been a consultant on Johnny's case, wrote to his parents: "You two, by your restless effort, kept him alive a year longer than should be expected. You could have done no more. It was worth while."[15]

Undershooting and Overshooting

The sick role cannot be maintained where there are outright accusations of blame on the part of the patient and those close to him. But there is also a subtle form of blame which undermines the sick role, although less obviously: self-pity. One might suppose that self-pity would be allowable in the sick role, but this is not so. A patient who indulges in self-pity implies that he is suffering needlessly and unfairly, which in turn implies that someone, somewhere, is to blame for the illness. The very fact that no accusations are levelled at particular people makes it difficult to deal with, as there is nothing to refute. Those who care for the sick person will soon show signs of uneasiness and even hostility if the patient persists in expressing self-pity.

Betty MacDonald, after learning that she had tuberculosis, described her reaction upon her return home that evening:

> There was a fire in the fireplace. There was fresh hot coffee. There was infinite love and abundant sympathy. There may have been too much sympathy because after a while I became almost overcome with my own bravery, selflessness and power of mind over body. To think that for the whole past year I had been going my way, working, playing, and laughing, while all this time I was seriously, perhaps fatally, ill. I wallowed in self-pity. Instead of admitting to myself that it was a great relief to know what was wrong with me and that I was really sick instead of ambitionless and indolent, I dripped tears on Mother's blue down quilt as I created doleful mental pictures of little Anne and Joan putting flowers on "Mommy's" fresh grave. I was a big, non-sense-of-humor saddo. I coughed all night and enjoyed doing it.[16]

---

15. John Gunther, *Death be not proud*. New York: Harper and Brothers, 1949, p. 145.
16. Betty MacDonald, *The plague and I*. Philadelphia: Lippincott, 1948, p. 36.

Having tried for a year to explain her symptoms away and maintain her normal social role, Mrs. MacDonald now aimed for the sick role, but in her enthusiasm she overshot the mark and landed in a bog of self-pity. Fortunately, this was only a temporary reaction; by the next morning she had given up self-pity as a means of coping with her illness.

The sick role requires of its occupants that they try to get well as soon as possible and that, to this end, they cooperate with whatever treatment has been prescribed for them. In other words, they must be "good" patients. But unfortunately, there is no guarantee that one will be rewarded for this goodness by improving health. Yet the patient who has serious illness is sorely tempted to make this equation, for being a good patient may be the only thing that he can do to exert control over his situation. John Gunther describes this response in his adolescent son, Johnny, who was fatally ill with a brain tumor:

> Hoping with such vehemence to recover, yearning with such desperation to be all right again, refusing stalwartly to admit that his left hand, too, was showing a little weakness now, he became heartbreakingly dutiful about everything the doctors asked. He was still limited as to fluids; drop by drop, he would measure the exact amount of water he was permitted. All he wanted was to obey, to obey, and so get back to school.[17]

Roth describes this phenomenon among tuberculosis patients in a sanitorium:

> Patients sometimes use what might be called a moral basis for categorizing each other. There are differences between patients in the degree to which they follow the treatment regimen that is recommended by the physicians, especially that part of it that deals with rest and the restriction of activities. Quite often, those who follow the doctor's recommendations most strictly feel that they should thereby get well more quickly and be discharged from the hospital more quickly in comparison with those who frequently disregard the physician's recommendations. . . The "good" patient believes, so to speak, that he should get time off for good behavior.[18]

These patients are open to severe disappointment if those around them who are not so "good" improve more quickly, or if their own progress pursues a course unrelated to their compliant behavior. Roth says, "Some of the patients who were apparently so conforming and cooperative in the early part of their stay even end by leaving the hospital against advice."

Joachim, Hans Castorp's cousin, is just this sort of patient. At first, he is very reluctant to take up the sick role because he is eager to begin his career as an army officer. But, having agreed to stay at the Berghof until he is pronounced cured, he tries to be an exemplary patient. He absorbs much technical information about his illness and impresses his cousin with his expertise. He carefully

---

17. John Gunther, *Death be not proud.* New York: Harper and Brothers, 1949, p. 45.

18. J. A. Roth, *Timetables: Structuring the passage of time in hospital treatment and other careers.* New York: Bobbs-Merrill, 1963, p. 38.

obeys all the rules of the treatment regimen and refrains from using his position in the sick role for other purposes. Unlike the other patients who use their enforced idleness to indulge in endless flirtations, Joachim devotes himself entirely to his cure, so that he may get well as quickly as possible. He appears to be an ideal occupant of the sick role, but Dr. Behrens, with his experienced eye for these things, recognizes that this is not so and tells Joachim that he has no talent for being sick. Behrens proves to be correct, for Joachim cannot tolerate the unpredictable fluctuations in his illness; he is implicitly expecting to be "promoted" step by step, as he would in the army. Joachim finally tells Dr. Behrens: "I'm going home if it kills me." He leaves against medical advice, tastes his new career with his regiment briefly, and then gets sicker and returns to the Berghof to die. At the end, when it is courage that is required, rather than submission to the fickleness of the illness, Joachim comes through with flying colors; he dies like a soldier.

In contrast to those patients who believe that by being "good" they will be rewarded with rapid recovery, there are other patients who come to abandon the idea of recovery altogether. They are willing to give up their normal responsibilities, they do not blame themselves or anyone else for the illness, and they cooperate with the treatment; their difficulty is with the third requirement of the sick role, the duty to try to get well as soon as possible. In a tuberculosis sanitorium described by Roth, such patients were in the minority:

> Patients who openly admit to their fellow patients that they are in no hurry to get out of the hospital and are willing to stay just as long as the doctors want them to are sarcastically chided about "having found a home" in the hospital, and it is hinted among other patients that such patients are not quite normal mentally.[19]

But in the Berghof, half a century earlier, most of the patients fell into this category. Settembrini tells the cousins the story of a man who was allowed to go home, provisionally, as much improved. He took no interest in anything except his temperature, and felt that his wife and mother did not understand him. His mother finally told him to leave, and so he went back "home" to the Berghof. His wife realized that he would probably find himself a mate among the other patients.

It would be a mistake to see these patients as wanting to stay in the sick role, which has as one of its conditions the desire to get well as soon as possible. These patients have rather abandoned the sick role for the impaired role, in which no further change is expected. The impaired role has a lower status than the sick role, but life at the Berghof is so luxurious for these wealthy patients that they do not care. It is true that no one takes them seriously, and their life is ordered for them by the resident physicians, but in return for this child-like status, they are allowed to spend their days as children do, playing card games, taking

---

19. J. A. Roth, *Timetable: Structuring the passage of time in hospital treatment and other careers.* New York: Bobbs-Merrill, 1963, p. 44.

up hobbies, having meals served to them, "playing" with each other, or, most often, doing nothing at all. In order to enjoy this particular variant of the impaired role, one must have a docile temperament, a great deal of money, and an illness, like tuberculosis in its early stages, which lends itself to such a life.

Cooperation and Information

In the sick role, the patient has the duty to try to cooperate with the treatment. In many illnesses, this is not much of a problem, either because the illness lasts only a short time or because the nature of the treatment is such that not much is required of the patient. But in some illnesses which last a long time and have a complicated regimen, the patient must know a great deal about the illness in order to cooperate.

Betty MacDonald noted the lack of cooperation among the patients at The Pines, the tuberculosis sanitorium where she spent a year as a patient:

> The staff at The Pines had but one motivating factor—to get the patients well. This motivating factor, like a policeman's nightstick, was twirled over our heads twenty-four hours a day. And by necessity, too, because a tuberculosis sanitorium is a paradox. It should be a place where the patients are striving to get well, aided by doctors and nurses, but is actually a place where the patients are trying to kill themselves, but are prevented, in many cases, by the doctors and nurses.[20]

Mrs. MacDonald does not offer any explanation for this perverse behavior, but the reason is not far to seek: the patients do not have sufficient information about the illness to cooperate. She describes her thoughts as she lay on her bed early in her stay:

> I made up my mind that before that day ended I was going to have a talk with the charge nurse. I was going to ask her if keeping the patients half frozen was part of the cure; what the term "taking the cure" meant; what tuberculosis was; what the germ looked like, what its effect on the lung was; what rest had to do with the cure; if t.b. was actually curable; why some people, like the man in my office, could have t.b. for twenty years and live normal lives while others, like me, in less than one year became completely incapacitated; why I couldn't rest during rest hours; why I was so nervous; if, as time went on, I would become more restless or more well-adjusted. There were hundreds more questions I could ask but these would do for a start and would give me something to go on. Give me a basic understanding of the disease, The Pines and the cure. I was sure I could be more intelligently cooperative if I knew what I was doing.[21]

Some information about the illness was gradually forthcoming in the form of printed lessons. But the critical information for maintaining the sick role is the

---

20. Betty MacDonald, *The plague and I*. Philadelphia: Lippincott, 1948, p. 60.
21. Betty MacDonald, *The plague and I*. Philadelphia: Lippincott, 1948, p. 77.

progress of the patient's own illness, and this was completely lacking. Mrs. Mac-Donald says: "Of this progress we were told nothing. The only way we could tell if we were getting well or dying was by the privileges we were granted."[22]

In the tuberculosis sanitoria described by Roth, all the patients were preoccupied with the system of privileges that prevailed in their particular hospital. Where the hospital did not provide such a system, the patients noticed the regularities themselves, and then if they did not get privileges at what they believed to be the proper times, they felt that they had been cheated. Roth says:

> Physicians are frequently annoyed because patients are always thinking in terms of the class they are in or the privileges they have rather than about the improvement that has taken place in their lungs ... The patients are interested in recognizable steps toward discharge such as are provided in a classification system or in an ordered series of privileges. The physician with experience in reading X-rays and in interpreting other diagnostic indices can also keep in mind a rough series of steps toward discharge and thus provide himself with another basis for categorizing patients and making decisions concerning their treatment. The patients, however, do not know enough about the finer points of interpreting the diagnostic tests to enable them to do so, and the staff does not supply them with the information needed to make such interpretations even if they did know how. They therefore stick to those clues that are more readily understandable to them, namely, the privileges and the classification system. Physicians will probably be successful in getting patients to focus on their clinical improvement only if they are able to reduce such improvement to a series of ratings or classifications similar to those now in use in many hospitals for designating the patient's permitted level of activity.[23]

Interestingly enough, patients found it quite reasonable to be "held back" if they had a cough, weakness or a fever. But it should be noted that while a cough and weakness are directly observable, it is only the use of the thermometer that makes fever observable. An instrument which measures how sick the patient is at a particular time is the best possible aid for keeping him in the sick role. It will be remembered that the point at which Hans Castorp challenged Settembrini's mockery was the point at which the latter cast doubt on the accuracy of the X-rays. This was a serious blow to aim at the sick role, for the X-rays were one of the few means of objectifying and quantifying the illness. As we have seen with John Keats, it is difficult to sustain the sick role in the absence of measurement.

If there is an ideal course of a patient through the sick role, then Hans Castorp is an example of the very opposite of that ideal, for, in his seven year stay at the Berghof, he makes detours from the sick role at almost every point and into every available alternate role. When he first comes to the Berghof to visit his cousin, he appears to be on a temporary leave from his usual social role, that of shipbuilding engineer. But, although he does not know it yet, his work has little

---

22. Betty MacDonald, *The plague and I*. Philadelphia: Lippincott, 1948, p. 142.

23. J. A. Roth, *Timetables: Structuring the passage of time in hospital treatment and other careers*. New York: Harper and Brothers, 1949, pp. 37–38.

real appeal for him; he is all too ready to abandon his responsibilities in the "flat-land." The author implies that just as Hans is sick and does not know it, so the society in which Hans is about to make a place is sick but does not know it. The invisible corruptness of that society, soon to burst forth in World War I, is now manifest in the subtle demoralization of the young. Thus, the first role in which we see Hans is that of social victim, his illness a personal response to his society's failings. Before long, he finds that he has tuberculosis, and takes up the sick role, giving promise of being an ideal patient. After awhile, however, in imitation of Frau Chauchat, he begins to experiment with the "bad" role: "He tried, for instance, how it would feel to sit at table with his back all relaxed, and discovered that it afforded sensible relief to the pelvic muscles. Again, one day, instead of punctiliously closing a door behind him, he let it slam; and this too he found both fitting and agreeable."

Next, he and his cousin go through a period of paying visits to the moribund patients. They gradually acquire the name Good Samaritans and Brothers of Charity. Hans says: "I visit the ones who aren't here for the fun of the thing, lead-ing a disorderly life—the ones who are busy dying."

He is deeply offended by the gay life of those of his fellow patients who have adopted the impaired role. This phase passes also, however, and then he begins to pay regular visits to Dr. Krokowski, the psychoanalyst. He has now taken up the role of the analysand.

When Joachim tells Dr. Behrens that he intends to leave the Berghof, Behrens tells Hans that he may leave too. But Hans does not want to go, for he has embarked on yet another role:

> It would be the abandonment of certain comprehensive responsibilities which had grown up out of his contemplation of the image called *Homo Dei;* it would be the betrayal of that appointed task of "stock-taking," that hard and harassing task, which was really beyond the powers native to him, but yet afforded his spirit such nameless and adventurous joys; that it was his duty to perform, here in his chair, and up there in his blue-blossomed retreat.

Hans has now taken up nothing less than the task of enlightenment. One day, on his skies, lost in a snowstorm on the top of a mountain, he has a vision in which he understands at last his own preoccupation with sickness and death:

> The recklessness of death is in life, it would not be life without it . . . I will let death have no mastery over my thoughts. For therein lies goodness and love of humankind, and in nothing else. Death is a great power. One takes off one's hat before him, and goes weavingly on tiptoe . . . Love stands opposed to death. It is love, not reason, that is stronger than death . . . *For the sake of goodness and love, man shall let death have no sovereignty over his thoughts.* And with this—I awake.

But by that very evening, Hans' vision is already fading from his mind. By this time, Hans has lived so long at the Berghof that without even noticing it, he slips into the impaired role. He begins to play solitaire, like the others, although he had previously found this diversion beneath his contempt. The doctors, recognizing what is happening, announce that they have at last found the source of his mysterious fevers. They succeed in interesting him briefly in a new treatment, but this project dies a natural death, and he returns to his card playing. By this time, he has abandoned all contact with the flat-land; he sends no mail and receives none. He no longer orders his favorite cigars from Hamburg, but buys a local brand that he likes as well. His watch falls from his night-table and breaks, but he does not get it fixed. He remains in the impaired role until he is blasted out of it by the beginning of World War I.

Imparting and Sustaining

As we have seen, the sick role appears to be a highly unstable social role. Far from being adhesive, as some people fear, it is very difficult to keep people in the sick role even when the illness in question falls undisputedly within the province of medicine. The sick role is like a narrow, slippery path that one must traverse from the inception of an illness until its conclusion. At every point one may lose one's footing and slide into some other role. The consequences of these sudden departures from the sick role are often serious and sometimes fatal. They are of three general kinds. First, the failure to occupy the sick role may result in a prolongation of the illness or even in death. If a person fails to give up his normal social role when necessary, if he tries to get well too fast or not fast enough, if he does not cooperate with the treatment, he may jeopardize his life. Oddly enough, we do not have a term for people who do this, although we call those who demand the sick role when they are not sick "malingerers." When Joachim is on his death-bed as a result of his failure to comply with the demands of the sick role, Dr. Behrens calls him "crazy."

Second, the failure to occupy the sick role may result in the deterioration or destruction of one's most vital relationships. Those who blame themselves or those around them for their illness cut themselves off from the practical and emotional support that they need until they are well. Blame of any kind has a corrosive effect on the relationships of the patient and his family, and good morale in the sick room cannot be maintained in the face of accusations and counter-accusations.

Third, a person who fails to maintain the sick role may find himself in the impaired role. Unlike the sick role, the impaired role is easy to maintain and difficult to leave, since it is meant to be permanent. But it carries with it a loss of full human status. It is true that the impaired role does not require the exertions of cooperating with medical treatment and trying to regain one's health, but the price for this idleness is a kind of second-class citizenship.

Death or prolonged illness, destruction of vital relationships, loss of full human status: these are the costs of not having the sick role when it is needed. Put in its positive form, we can now begin to see what it is that the sick role does for its occupants. The function of the sick role is to have the life, maintain the vital relationships, and insure the full human status of the sick person until he gets well or dies.

Dr. Samuel Johnson said that "a man, sir, should keep his friendships in constant repair." So it is with the sick role. It must be given and accepted explicitly. It must be sustained and repaired explicitly. It must be terminated explicitly. The question, then, is how is this to be done? And perhaps even more important, how does one ensure that during their long apprenticeship physicians acquire this ability and learn how to transmit these skills to their juniors and students? We can only speculate about these matters, for little seems to be known about them at present. Young doctors learn the art of inducting patients into the sick role by osmosis, as it were. It is held to be a "natural thing for doctors to do."

In some medical schools, academic teachers, especially those with a scientific bent, are liable to sneer at the bedside manner and the mumbo jumbo which goes with it. It seems to these "science" doctors that the great advances of our day have rendered these social niceties unnecessary, old fashioned, and even fraudulent. Patients, it is said, ought to flourish on medical science alone. Patients themselves, and this includes doctors who have become patients, are not always convinced that this austere diet of moral support is sufficient. The reminiscences of a well-known physician, Dr. Hugh Barber, reflects a fairly general attitude not confined to surgeons:

> There is a story told of Mr. Lloyd Roberts of Manchester, when saying goodbye to a class of students who had qualified to practice, how he would remark: "All you fellows can succeed in practice, if you have a mind to. There are two ways of making a reputation—either you can be clever or you can be kind." And then turning to a particular man, he would say, "Well, there you are, Brown, you can always be kind."[24]

It is understandable, if inadmirable, that those with prestigious academic positions, scientific doctors and medical administrators, might be incurious about the essential encounter between patient and doctor which occurs at the bedside, in the office or in the out-patient department. Few prizes or academic distinctions are awarded for adding to our knowledge of this ancient ritualistic art form. It seems less excusable that clinicians themselves are so little concerned with these matters and with improving one of medicine's most potent weapons in the battle against illness. An ailing person who does not accept the sick role when necessary, who does not remain within its protecting confines for an appropriate time, and who fails to relinquish it in a fitting manner when allowed to do so, may endanger his life so that trivial disease becomes fatal.

One wonders why so little has been done to examine a skill which must be acquired if one is to practice clinical medicine, and which may not be unteachable, as has been suggested, but rather seldom, if ever, taught. It sometimes seems that the ability to impart the sick role and sustain patients in it is perceived as enfolding the young doctor at graduation or at least during internship. In a pro-

---

24. Hugh Barber, *The occasion fleeting.* London: H. K. Lewis, 1947, p. 91.

fane profession, it appears to be presumptuous, unlucky, or even sacrilegious to discuss such mysterious and obscure matters. Since those who teach medicine and surgery are certainly clinicians, as are some of those who teach its derivative (often incorrectly named basic) sciences, it may seem a waste of time to deal with such obvious matters when there is so much to be learned. This supposedly unimportant task has sometimes been assigned to or acquired by psychiatrists, largely by default. Their explanation of the doctor-patient relationship as a kind of transference is less impressive when one learns that the transference itself was invented by Freud to account for this same doctor-patient relationship.

Perhaps, just as young husbands do not always relish being told how to improve their amatory skills, so young doctors (and older doctors, too) tend to be impatient with discussions of the doctor-patient relationship. It is something which "everyone knows." Yet it sometimes happens that what everyone knows, no one knows. In clinical medicine and surgery, most patients accept, are maintained in and relinquish the sick role almost automatically. Provided that the cross-cultural differences between doctor and patient are not very large (and due to the universal nature of the sick role, they must be very large to be noticed), that no extreme personal antipathies exist between patient and doctor, that the patient's perceptions and judgments are not much impaired, and so long as the doctor himself is not grossly aberrant, somehow or other the doctor-patient relationship will be sustained. While this might not be ideal, it will suffice to carry patients through illness without damage to patient or doctor, and without scandal, recrimination or litigation. Resolution may be by recovery, impairment, or death, but one way or another the patient accepts and relinquishes the sick role. This cannot be the best that medicine could or should do, but one can get by in this modest way—just.

It is in psychiatry, where the judgment of patients is sometimes impaired and where differences in values may come to be considered as signs of illness, that there has been more uncertainty regarding these matters than in the rest of medicine. During the last 30 years or so, this uncertainty seems to have been increasing steadily, because psychiatrists, largely unknown to themselves and unaware of the consequences for their patients, have neglected to employ the medical model and so have failed to maintain their patients in the sick role. It is perhaps this neglect which made psychiatry so suitable for our own initial studies employing conceptual models, for no other branch of clinical medicine shows any signs of following the psychiatric example.[25]

Clinical medicine today, as always throughout its long history, is greatly influenced by a variety of sciences and their derivative technologies. Some of these sciences have been oddly termed "basic," although a modest reading of history shows that they, and indeed the majority of sciences, sprang from medicine itself. The skillful application of these new developments, in the form of better treatment and care, has changed patients' expectations. Illnesses once considered to be fatal or at best crippling are now seen as recoverable, prevent-

25. See the first three items, in particular, listed in footnote 5.

able, or even trivial. These changes would have astonished our forebears and are still surprising to those who started medicine twenty-five years or more ago; yet although their scientific, technical, social, and political implications have received much attention, neither the profession nor the public seem to have been concerned with their effects on the doctor-patient relationship, the acquisition of the sick role and the exercise of "Aesculapian Authority."[26] This vitally important body of knowledge is transmitted from generation to generation of doctors in a haphazard fashion. Yet without this knowledge, the physician or surgeon will fail to acquire his patient's confidence, however great his technical skill, while the greatest booby or even an impostor who possesses it will be accepted and even revered by patients. It is surprising that things are not worse, but most moral people, and therefore most patients, respond automatically with behavior appropriate to the sick role when they feel ill, and thus maintain their doctors in an appropriate relationship, provided only that they are able to learn by implication, and it seems that most, but not all, are.

The questions which we have raised here cannot be answered in a brief article. We do not presume to tell those who teach and those who learn that combination of craft, art, and many sciences, which together constitute clinical medicine, what should be done. However, we believe that unless such questions are faced, the distinguishing features of clinical medicine can easily be distorted or even lost altogether among those "more pressing issues" which the myriad specialists involved in medicine today consider have a prior call upon the time of student and teacher alike.

If we are correct, there is nothing of greater importance in clinical medicine than maintaining the relationship between doctor and patient. This relationship is very old, and upon it (to paraphrase a naval prayer) the safety of medicine depends. Nothing should be done wittingly or unwittingly which might harm those who are served by and those who serve this ancient enterprise of clinical medicine, which for millenia has eased the sufferings and can now increase the good health of our species.

---

26. T. T. Paterson, Notes on Aesculpian authority. Unpublished manuscript; and Miriam Siegler & Humphrey Osmond, Aesculpian Authority. *Hastings Center Studies 1 (2)* 1973: 41–52.

The Labeling of Illness: The Case of Mental Illness

On Being Sane in Insane Places

10

D. L. ROSENHAN

If sanity and insanity exist, how shall we know them?

The question is neither capricious nor itself insane. However much we may be personally convinced that we can tell the normal from the abnormal, the evidence is simply not compelling. It is commonplace, for example, to read about murder trials wherein eminent psychiatrists for the defense are contradicted by equally eminent psychiatrists for the prosecution on the matter of the defendant's sanity. More generally, there are a great deal of conflicting data on the reliability, utility, and meaning of such terms as "sanity," insanity," "mental illness," and "schizophrenia".[1] Finally, as early as 1934, Benedict suggested that normality and abnormality are not universal.[2] What is viewed as normal in one culture may be seen as quite aberrant in another. Thus, notions of normality and abnormality may not be quite as accurate as people believe they are.

To raise questions regarding normality and abnormality is in no way to question the fact that some behaviors are deviant or odd. Murder is deviant. So, too,

The author is professor of psychology and law at Stanford University, Stanford, California, 94305. Portions of these data were presented to colloqiums of the psychology departments at the University of California at Berkeley and at Santa Barbara; University of Arizona, Tucson; and Harvard University, Cambridge, Massachusetts.

From *Science,* 179 (January, 1973): 250–258. Copyright 1973 by the American Association for the Advancement of Science. Reprinted with permission.

1. P. Ash, *Journal of Abnormal Social Psychology 44 (272)* 1949; A. T. Beck, *American Journal of Psychiatry 119 (210)* 1962; A. T. Boisen, *Psychiatry 2 (233)* 1938; N. Kreitman, *Journal of Mental Science 107 (876)* 1961; N. Kreitman, P. Sainsbury, J. Morrisey, J. Towers, & J. Scrivener, *Journal of Mental Science 107 (876)* 1961, 887; H. O. Schmitt, & C. P. Fonda, *Journal of Abnormal Social Psychology 52 (262)* 1956; W. Seeman, *Journal of Nervous Mental Disorders 118 (541)* 1953; For an analysis of these artifacts and summaries of the disputes, see J. Zubin, *Annual Review of Psychology 13 (373)* 1967; L. Phillips, & J. G. Draguns, *Annual Review of Psychology 22 (447)* 1971.

2. R. Benedict, *Journal of General Psychology 10 (59)* 1934.

are hallucinations. Nor does raising such questions deny the existence of the personal anguish that is often associated with "mental illness." Anxiety and depression exist. Psychological suffering exists. But normality and abnormality, sanity and insanity, and the diagnoses that flow from them may be less substantive than many believe them to be.

At its heart, the question of whether the sane can be distinguished from the insane (and whether degrees of insanity can be distinguished from each other) is a simple matter: do the salient characteristics that lead to diagnoses reside in the patients themselves or in the environments and contexts in which observers find them? From Bleuler, through Kretchmer, through the formulators of the recently revised *Diagnostic and Statistical Manual* of the American Psychiatric Association, the belief has been strong that patients present symptoms, that those symptoms can be categorized, and, implicitly, that the sane are distinguishable from the insane. More recently, however, this belief has been questioned. Based in part on theoretical and anthropological considerations, but also on philosophical, legal, and therapeutic ones, the view has grown that psychological categorization of mental illness is useless at best and downright harmful, misleading, and pejorative at worst. Psychiatric diagnoses, in this view, are in the minds of the observers and are not valid summaries of characteristics displayed by the observed.[3-5]

Gains can be made in deciding which of these is more nearly accurate by getting normal people (that is, people who do not have, and have never suffered, symptoms of serious psychiatric disorders) admitted to psychiatric hospitals and then determining whether they were discovered to be sane and, if so, how. If the sanity of such pseudopatients were always detected, there would be *prima facie* evidence that a sane individual can be distinguished from the insane context in which he is found. Normality (and presumably abnormality) is distinct enough that it can be recognized wherever it occurs, for it is carried within the person. If, on the other hand, the sanity of the pseudopatients were never discovered, serious difficulties would arise for those who support traditional modes of psychiatric diagnosis. Given that the hospital staff was not incompetent, that the pseudopatient had been behaving as sanely as he had been outside of the hospital, and that it had never been previously suggested that he belonged in a psychiatric hospital, such an unlikely outcome would support the view that psychiatric diag-

3. See in this regard H. Becker, *Outsiders: Studies in the sociology of deviance.* New York: Free Press, 1963; B. M. Braginsky, D. D. Bragnisky, & K. Ring, *Methods of madness: The mental hospital as a last resort.* New York: Holt, Rinehart, 1969; G. M. Crocetti, & P. V. Lemkau, *American Sociological Review 30 (577)* 1965; E. Goffman, *Behavior in public places.* New York: Free Press, 1964; R. D. Laing, *The divided self: A study of sanity and madness.* Chicago: Quadrangle, 1960; D. L. Phillips, *American Sociological Review 28 (963)* 1963; T. R. Sarbin, *Psychology Today 6 (18)* 1972; E. Schur, *American Journal of Sociology 75 (309)* 1969; T. Szasz, *Law, liberty, and psychiatry.* New York: Macmillan, 1963; T. Szasz, *The myth of mental illness: Foundations of a theory of mental illness.* New York: Hoeber-Harper, 1963; For a critique of some of these views see W. R. Gove, *American Sociological Review 35 (873)* 1970.
4. E. Goffman, *Asylums.* Garden City, N.J.: Doubleday, 1961.
5. T. J. Scheff, *Being mentally ill: A sociological theory.* Chicago: Aldine, 1966.

nosis betrays little about the patient but much about the environment in which an observer finds him.

This article describes such an experiment. Eight sane people gained secret admission to 12 different hospitals.[6] Their diagnostic experiences constitute the data of the first part of this article; the remainder is devoted to a description of their experiences in psychiatric institutions. Too few psychiatrists and psychologists, even those who have worked in such hospitals, know what the experience is like. They rarely talk about it with former patients, perhaps because they distrust information coming from the previously insane. Those who have worked in psychiatric hospitals are likely to have adapted so thoroughly to the settings that they are insensitive to the impact of that experience. And while there have been occasional reports of researchers who submitted themselves to psychiatric hospitalization[7] these researchers have commonly remained in the hospitals for short periods of time, often with the knowledge of the hospital staff. It is difficult to know the extent to which they were treated like patients or like research colleagues. Nevertheless, their reports about the inside of the psychiatric hospital have been valuable. This article extends those efforts.

Pseudopatients and Their Settings

The eight pseudopatients were a varied group. One was a psychology graduate student in his 20s. The remaining seven were older and "established." Among them were three psychologists, a pediatrician, a psychiatrist, a painter, and a housewife. Three pseudopatients were women, five were men. All of them employed pseudonyms, lest their alleged diagnoses embarrass them later. Those who were in mental health professions alleged another occupation in order to avoid the special attentions that might be accorded by staff, as a matter of courtesy or caution, to ailing colleagues.[8] With the exception of myself (I was the first pseudopatient and my presence was known to the hospital administrator and chief psychologist and, so far as I can tell, to them alone), the presence of pseu-

---

6. Data from a ninth pseudopatient are not incorporated in this report because, although his sanity went undetected, he falsified aspects of his personal history, including his marital status and parental relationships. His experimental behaviors therefore were not identical to those of the other pseudopatients.

7. A. Barry, *Bellevue is a state of mind.* New York: Harcourt Brace Jovanovich, 1971; I. Belknap, *Human problems of a state mental hospital.* New York: McGraw-Hill, 1956; W. Caudill, F. C. Redlich, H. R. Gilmore, & E. B. Brody, *American Journal of Orthopsychiatry 22 (314)* 1952; A. R. Goldman, R. H. Bohr, & T. A. Steinberg, *Professional Psychologist 1 (427)* 1970; *Roche Report 1* (13) 8 1971.

8. Beyond the personal difficulties that the pseudopatient is likely to experience in the hospital, there are legal and social ones that, combined, require considerable attention before entry. For example, once admitted to a psychiatric institution, it is difficult, if not impossible, to be discharged on short notice, state law to the contrary notwithstanding. I was not sensitive to these difficulties at the outset of the project, nor to the personal and situational emergencies that can arise, but later a writ of habeas corpus was prepared for each of the entering pseudopatients and an attorney was kept "on call" during every hospitalization. I am grateful to John Kaplan and Robert Bartels for legal advice and assistance in these matters.

dopatients and the nature of the research program was not known to the hospital staffs.[9]

The settings were similarly varied. In order to generalize the findings, admission into a variety of hospitals was sought. The 12 hospitals in the sample were located in five different states on the East and West coasts. Some were old and shabby, some were quite new. Some were research-oriented, others not. Some had good staff-patient ratios, others were quite understaffed. Only one was a strictly private hospital. All of the others were supported by state or federal funds or, in one instance, by university funds.

After calling the hospital for an appointment, the pseudopatient arrived at the admissions office complaining that he had been hearing voices. Asked what the voices said, he replied that they were often unclear, but as far as he could tell they said "empty," "hollow," and "thud." The voices were unfamiliar and were of the same sex as the pseudopatient. The choice of these symptoms was occasioned by their apparent similarity to existential symptoms. Such symptoms are alleged to arise from painful concerns about the perceived meaninglessness of one's life. It is as if the hallucinating person were saying, "My life is empty and hollow." The choice of these symptoms was also determined by the *absence* of a single report of existential psychoses in the literature.

Beyond alleging the symptoms and falsifying name, vocation, and employment, no further alterations of person, history, or circumstances were made. The significant events of the pseudopatient's life history were presented as they had actually occurred. Relationships with parents and siblings, with spouse and children, with people at work and in school, consistent with the aforementioned exceptions, were described as they were or had been. Frustrations and upsets were described along with joys and satisfactions. These facts are important to remember. If anything, they strongly biased the subsequent results in favor of detecting sanity, since none of their histories or current behaviors were seriously pathological in any way.

Immediately upon admission to the psychiatric ward, the pseudopatient ceased simulating *any* symptoms of abnormality. In some cases, there was a brief period of mild nervousness and anxiety, since none of the pseudopatients really believed that they would be admitted so easily. Indeed, their shared fear was that they would be immediately exposed as frauds and greatly embarrassed. Moreover, many of them had never visited a psychiatric ward; even those who had, nevertheless had some genuine fears about what might happen to them. Their nervousness, then, was quite appropriate to the novelty of the hospital setting, and it abated rapidly.

---

9. However distasteful such concealment is, it was a necessary first step to examining these questions. Without concealment, there would have been no way to know how valid these experiences were; nor was there any way of knowing whether whatever detections occurred were a tribute to the diagnostic acumen of the staff or to the hospital's rumor network. Obviously, since my concerns are general ones that cut across individual hospitals and staffs, I have respected their anonymity and have eliminated clues that might lead to their identification.

Apart from that short-lived nervousness, the pseudopatient behaved on the ward as he "normally" behaved. The pseudopatient spoke to patients and staff as he might ordinarily. Because there is uncommonly little to do on a psychiatric ward, he attempted to engage others in conversation. When asked by staff how he was feeling, he indicated that he was fine, that he no longer experienced symptoms. He responded to instructions from attendants, to calls for medication (which was not swallowed), and to dining-hall instructions. Beyond such activities as were available to him on the admissions ward, he spent his time writing down his observations about the ward, its patients, and the staff. Initially these notes were written "secretly," but as it soon became clear that no one much cared, they were subsequently written on standard tablets of paper in such public places as the dayroom. No secret was made of these activities.

The pseudopatient, very much as a true psychiatric patient, entered a hospital with no foreknowledge of when he would be discharged. Each was told that he would have to get out by his own devices, essentially by convincing the staff that he was sane. The psychological stresses associated with hospitalization were considerable, and all but one of the pseudopatients desired to be discharged almost immediately after being admitted. They were, therefore, motivated not only to behave sanely, but to be paragons of cooperation. That their behavior was in no way disruptive is confirmed by nursing reports, which have been obtained on most of the patients. These reports uniformly indicate that the patients were "friendly," "cooperative," and "exhibited no abnormal indications."

The Normal Are Not Detectably Sane

Despite their public "show" of sanity, the pseudopatients were never detected. Admitted, except in one case, with a diagnosis of schizophrenia,[10] each was discharged with a diagnosis of schizophrenia "in remission." The label "in remission" should in no way be dismissed as a formality, for at no time during any hospitalization had any question been raised about any pseudopatient's simulation. Nor are there any indications in the hospital records that the pseudopatient's status was suspect. Rather, the evidence is strong that, once labeled schizophrenic, the pseudopatient was stuck with that label. If the pseudopatient was to be discharged, he must naturally be "in remission"; but he was not sane, nor, in the institution's view, had he ever been sane.

The uniform failure to recognize sanity cannot be attributed to the quality of the hospitals, for, although there were considerable variations among them, several are considered excellent. Nor can it be alleged that there was simply not

---

10. Interestingly, of the 12 admissions, 11 were diagnosed as schizophrenic and 1, with the identical symptomatology, as manic-depressive psychosis. This diagnosis has a more favorable prognosis, and it was given by the only private hospital in our sample. On the relations between social class and psychiatric diagnosis, see A. B. Hollingshead, & F. C. Redlich, *Social class and mental illness: A community study.* New York: Wiley, 1958.

enough time to observe the pseudopatients. Length of hospitalization ranged from 7 to 52 days, with an average of 19 days. The pseudopatients were not, in fact, carefully observed, but this failure clearly speaks more to traditions within psychiatric hospitals than to lack of opportunity.

Finally, it cannot be said that the failure to recognize the pseudopatients' sanity was due to the fact that they were not behaving sanely. While there was clearly some tension present in all of them, their daily visitors could detect no serious behavioral consequences—nor, indeed, could other patients. It was quite common for the patients to "detect" the pseudopatients' sanity. During the first three hospitalizations, when accurate counts were kept, 35 of a total of 118 patients on the admissions ward voiced their suspicions, some vigorously. "You're not crazy. You're a journalist, or a professor [referring to the continual note taking]. You're checking up on the hospital." While most of the patients were reassured by the pseudopatient's insistence that he had been sick before he came in but was fine now, some continued to believe that the pseudopatient was sane throughout his hospitalization.[11] The fact that the patients often recognized normality when staff did not raises important questions.

Failure to detect sanity during the course of hospitalization may be due to the fact that physicians operate with a strong bias toward what statisticians call the type 2 error (5). This is to say that physicians are more inclined to call a healthy person sick (a false positive, type 2) than a sick person healthy (a false negative, type 1). The reasons for this are not hard to find: it is clearly more dangerous to misdiagnose illness than health. Better to err on the side of caution, to suspect illness even among the healthy.

But what holds for medicine does not hold equally well for psychiatry. Medical illnesses, while unfortunate, are not commonly pejorative. Psychiatric diagnoses, on the contrary, carry with them personal, legal, and social stigmas.[12] It was therefore important to see whether the tendency toward diagnosing the sane insane could be reversed. The following experiment was arranged at a research and teaching hospital whose staff had heard these findings but doubted that such an error could occur in their hospital. The staff was informed that at some time during the following three months, one or more pseudopatients would attempt to be admitted into the psychiatric hospital. Each staff member was asked to rate each patient who presented himself at admissions or on the ward according to the likelihood that the patient was a pseudopatient. A ten-point scale was used, with a one and two reflecting high confidence that the patient was a pseudopatient.

---

11. It is quite possible, of course, that patients have quite broad latitudes in diagnosis and therefore are inclined to call many people sane, even those whose behavior is patently aberrant. However, although we have no hard data on this matter, it was our distinct impression that this was not the case. In many instances, patients not only singled us out for attention, but came to imitate our behaviors and styles.

12. J. Cumming, & E. Cumming, *Community Mental Health 1 (135)* 1965; A. Farina, & K. Ring, *Journal of Abnormal Psychology 70 (47)* 1965; H. E. Freeman, & O. G. Simmons, *The mental patient comes home.* New York: Wiley, 1963; W. J. Johanssen, *Mental Hygiene 53 (218)* 1969; A. S. Linsky, *Social Psychiatry 5 (166)* 1970.

Judgments were obtained on 193 patients who were admitted for psychiatric treatment. All staff who had had sustained contact with or primary responsibility for the patient—attendants, nurses, psychiatrists, physicians, and psychologists—were asked to make judgments. Forty-one patients were alleged, with high confidence, to be pseudopatients by at least one member of the staff. Twenty-three were considered suspect by at least one psychiatrist. Nineteen were suspected by one psychiatrist *and* one other staff member. Actually, no genuine pseudopatient (at least from my group) presented himself during this period.

The experiment is instructive. It indicates that the tendency to designate sane people as insane can be reversed when the stakes (in this case, prestige and diagnostic acumen) are high. But what can be said of the 19 people who were suspected of being "sane" by one psychiatrist and another staff member? Were these people truly "sane," or was it rather the case that in the course of avoiding the type 2 error the staff tended to make more errors of the first sort—calling the crazy "sane"? There is no way of knowing. But one thing is certain: any diagnostic process that lends itself so readily to massive errors of this sort cannot be a very reliable one.

The Stickiness of Psychodiagnostic Labels

Beyond the tendency to call the healthy sick—a tendency that accounts better for diagnostic behavior on admission than it does for such behavior after a lengthy period of exposure—the data speak to the massive role of labeling in psychiatric assessment. Having once been labeled schizophrenic, there is nothing the pseudopatient can do to overcome the tag. The tag profoundly colors others' perceptions of him and his behavior.

From one viewpoint, these data are hardly surprising, for it has long been known that elements are given meaning by the context in which they occur. Gestalt psychology made this point vigorously, and Asch[13] demonstrated that there are "central" personality traits (such as "warm" versus "cold") which are so powerful that they markedly color the meaning of other information in forming an impression of a given personality.[14] "Insane," "schizophrenic," "manic-depressive," and "crazy" are probably among the most powerful of such central traits. Once a person is designated abnormal, all of his other behaviors and characteristics are colored by that label. Indeed, that label is so powerful that many of the pseudopatients' normal behaviors were overlooked entirely or profoundly misinterpreted. Some examples may clarify this issue.

---

13. S. E. Asch, *Journal of Abnormal Social Psychology 41 (258)* 1946; S. E. Asch, *Social Psychology.* New York: Prentice-Hall, 1952.

14. See also I. N. Mensh, & J. Wishner, *Journal of Personality 16 (188)* 1947; J. Wishner, *Psychological Review 67 (96)* 1960; J. S. Bruner, & R. Tagiuri, In G. Lindzey (Ed.) *Handbook of social psychology.* Cambridge, Mass.: Addison-Wesley, 1954, pp. 634–54; J. S. Bruner, D. Shapiro, & R. Tagiuri, In R. Tagiuri & L. Petrullo (Eds.) *Person Perception and Interpersonal Behavior.* Stanford, Calif.: Stanford University Press, 1958, pp. 277–88.

Earlier I indicated that there were no changes in the pseudopatient's personal history and current status beyond those of name, employment, and, where necessary, vocation. Otherwise, a veridical description of personal history and circumstances was offered. Those circumstances were not psychotic. How were they made consonant with the diagnosis of psychosis? Or were those diagnoses modified in such a way as to bring them into accord with the circumstances of the pseudopatient's life, as described by him?

As far as I can determine, diagnoses were in no way affected by the relative health of the circumstances of a pseudopatient's life. Rather, the reverse occurred: the perception of his circumstances was shaped entirely by the diagnosis. A clear example of such translation is found in the case of a pseudopatient who had had a close relationship with his mother but was rather remote from his father during his early childhood. During adolescence and beyond, however, his father became a close friend, while his relationship with his mother cooled. His present relationship with his wife was characteristically close and warm. Apart from occasional angry exchanges, friction was minimal. The children had rarely been spanked. Surely there is nothing especially pathological about such a history. Indeed, many readers may see a similar pattern in their own experiences, with no markedly deleterious consequences. Observe, however, how such a history was translated in the psychopathological context, this from the case summary prepared after the patient was discharged.

> This white 39-year-old male . . . manifests a long history of considerable ambivalence in close relationships, which begins in early childhood. A warm relationship with his mother cools during his adolescence. A distant relationship to his father is described as becoming very intense. Affective stability is absent. His attempts to control emotionality with his wife and children are punctuated by angry outbursts and, in the case of the children, spankings. And while he says that he has several good friends, one senses considerable ambivalence embedded in those relationships also .

The facts of the case were unintentionally distorted by the staff to achieve consistency with a popular theory of the dynamics of a schizophrenic reaction.[15] Nothing of an ambivalent nature had been described in relations with parents, spouse, or friends. To the extent that ambivalence could be inferred, it was probably not greater than is found in all human relationships. It is true the pseudopatient's relationships with his parents changed over time, but in the ordinary context that would hardly be remarkable — indeed, it might very well be expected. Clearly, the meaning ascribed to his verbalizations (that is, ambivalence, affective instability) was determined by the diagnosis: schizophrenia. An entirely different meaning would have been ascribed if it were known that the man was "normal."

---

15. For an example of a similar self-fulfilling prophecy, in this instance dealing with the "central" trait of intelligence, see R. Rosenthal, & L. Jacobsen, *Pygmalion in the classroom.* New York: Holt, Rinehart, 1968.

All pseudopatients took extensive notes publicly. Under ordinary circumstances, such behavior would have raised questions in the minds of observers, as, in fact, it did among patients. Indeed, it seemed so certain that the notes would elicit suspicion that elaborate precautions were taken to remove them from the ward each day. But the precautions proved needless. The closest any staff member came to questioning these notes occurred when one pseudopatient asked his physician what kind of medication he was receiving and began to write down the response. "You needn't write it," he was told gently. "If you have trouble remembering, just ask me again."

If no questions were asked of the pseudopatients, how was their writing interpreted? Nursing records for three patients indicate that the writing was seen as an aspect of their pathological behavior. "Patient engages in writing behavior" was the daily nursing comment on one of the pseudopatients who was never questioned about his writing. Given that the patient is in the hospital, he must be psychologically disturbed. And given that he is disturbed, continuous writing must be a behavioral manifestation of that disturbance, perhaps a subset of the compulsive behaviors that are sometimes correlated with schizophrenia.

One tacit characteristic of psychiatric diagnosis is that it locates the sources of aberration within the individual and only rarely within the complex of stimuli that surrounds him. Consequently, behaviors that are stimulated by the environment are commonly misattributed to the patient's disorder. For example, one kindly nurse found a pseudopatient pacing the long hospital corridors. "Nervous, Mr. X?" she asked. "No, bored," he said.

The notes kept by pseudopatients are full of patient behaviors that were misinterpreted by well-intentioned staff. Often enough, a patient would go "berserk" because he had, wittingly or unwittingly, been mistreated by, say, an attendant. A nurse coming upon the scene would rarely inquire even cursorily into the environmental stimuli of the patient's behavior. Rather, she assumed that his upset derived from his pathology, not from his present interactions with other staff members. Occasionally, the staff might assume that the patient's family (especially when they had recently visited) or other patients had stimulated the outburst. But never were the staff found to assume that one of themselves or the structure of the hospital had anything to do with a patient's behavior. One psychiatrist pointed to a group of patients who were sitting outside the cafeteria entrance half an hour before lunchtime. To a group of young residents he indicated that such behavior was characteristic of the oral-acquisitive nature of the syndrome. It seemed not to occur to him that there were very few things to anticipate in a psychiatric hospital besides eating.

A psychiatric label has a life and an influence of its own. Once the impression has been formed that the patient is schizophrenic, the expectation is that he will continue to be schizophrenic. When a sufficient amount of time has passed, during which the patient has done nothing bizarre, he is considered to be in remission and available for discharge. But the label endures beyond discharge, with the unconfirmed expectation that he will behave as a schizophrenic again.

Such labels, conferred by mental health professionals, are as influential on the patient as they are on his relatives and friends, and it should not surprise anyone that the diagnosis acts on all of them as a self-fulfilling prophecy. Eventually, the patient himself accepts the diagnosis, with all of its surplus meanings and expectations, and behaves accordingly (5).

The inferences to be made from these matters are quite simple. Much as Zigler and Phillips have demonstrated that there is enormous overlap in the symptoms presented by patients who have been variously diagnosed,[16] so there is enormous overlap in the behaviors of the sane and the insane. The sane are not "sane" all of the time. We lose our tempers "for no good reason." We are occasionally depressed or anxious, again for no good reason. And we may find it difficult to get along with one or another person—again for no reason that we can specify. Similarly, the insane are not always insane. Indeed, it was the impression of the pseudopatients while living with them that they were sane for long periods of time—that the bizarre behaviors upon which their diagnoses were allegedly predicated constituted only a small fraction of their total behavior. If it makes no sense to label ourselves permanently depressed on the basis of an occasional depression, then it takes better evidence than is presently available to label all patients insane or schizophrenic on the basis of bizarre behaviors or cognitions. It seems more useful, as Mischel[17] has pointed out, to limit our discussions to *behaviors,* the stimuli that provoke them, and their correlates.

It is not known why powerful impressions of personality traits, such as "crazy" or "insane," arise. Conceivably, when the origins of and stimuli that give rise to a behavior are remote or unknown, or when the behavior strikes us as immutable, trait labels regarding the *behavior* arise. When, on the other hand, the origins and stimuli are known and available, discourse is limited to the behavior itself. Thus, I may hallucinate because I am sleeping, or I may hallucinate because I have ingested a peculiar drug. These are termed sleep-induced hallucinations, or dreams, and drug-induced hallucinations, respectively. But when the stimuli to my hallucinations are unknown, that is called craziness, or schizophrenia—as if that inference were somehow as illuminating as the others.

The Experience of Psychiatric Hospitalization

The term "mental illness" is of recent origin. It was coined by people who were humane in their inclinations and who wanted very much to raise the station of (and the public's sympathies toward) the psychologically disturbed from that of witches and "crazies" to one that was akin to the physically ill. And they were at least partially successful, for the treatment of the mentally ill *has* improved considerably over the years. But while treatment has improved, it is doubtful that

---

16. E. Zigler, & L. Phillips, *Journal of Abnormal Social Psychology 63 (69)* 1961. See also R. K. Freudenberg, & J. P. Robertson, *Archives of Neurological Psychiatry 76 (14)* 1956.

17. W. Mischel, *Personality and assessment.* New York: Wiley, 1968.

people really regard the mentally ill in the same way that they view the physically ill. A broken leg is something one recovers from, but mental illness allegedly endures forever.[18] A broken leg does not threaten the observer, but a crazy schizophrenic? There is by now a host of evidence that attitudes toward the mentally ill are characterized by fear, hostility, aloofness, suspicion, and dread.[19] The mentally ill are society's lepers.

That such attitudes infect the general population is perhaps not surprising, only upsetting. But that they affect the professionals—attendants, nurses, physicians, psychologists, and social workers—who treat and deal with the mentally ill is more disconcerting, both because such attitudes are self-evidently pernicious and because they are unwitting. Most mental health professionals would insist that they are sympathetic toward the mentally ill, that they are neither avoidant nor hostile. But it is more likely that an exquisite ambivalence characterizes their relations with psychiatric patients, such that their avowed impulses are only part of their entire attitude. Negative attitudes are there too and can easily be detected. Such attitudes should not surprise us. They are the natural offspring of the labels patients wear and the places in which they are found.

Consider the structure of the typical psychiatric hospital. Staff and patients are strictly segregated. Staff have their own living space, including their dining facilities, bathrooms, and assembly places. The glassed quarters that contain the professional staff, which the pseudopatients came to call "the cage," sit out on every dayroom. The staff emerge primarily for caretaking purposes—to give medication, to conduct a therapy or group meeting, to instruct or reprimand a patient. Otherwise, staff keep to themselves, almost as if the disorder that afflicts their charges is somehow catching.

So much is patient-staff segregation the rule that, for four public hospitals in which an attempt was made to measure the degree to which staff and patients mingle, it was necessary to use "time out of the staff cage" as the operational measure. While it was not the case that all time spent out of the cage was spent mingling with patients (attendants, for example, would occasionally emerge to watch television in the dayroom), it was the only way in which one could gather reliable data on time for measuring.

The average amount of time spent by attendants outside of the cage was 11.3 percent (range, 3 to 52 percent). This figure does not represent only time spent mingling with patients, but also includes time spent on such chores as folding laundry, supervising patients while they shave, directing ward cleanup, and sending patients to off-ward activities. It was the relatively rare attendant who spent time talking with patients or playing games with them. It proved impossible to obtain a "percent mingling time" for nurses, since the amount of time they spent out of the cage was too brief. Rather, we counted instances of emergence

---

18.   The most recent and unfortunate instance of this tenet is that of Senator Thomas Eagleton.

19.   T. R. Sarbin, & J. C. Mancuso, *Journal of Clinical Consulting Psychology 35 (159)* 1970; T. R. Sarbin, *Journal of Clinical Consulting Psychology 31 (447)* 1967; J. C. Nunnally, Jr., *Popular conceptions of mental health.* New York: Holt, Rinehart, 1961.

from the cage. On the average, daytime nurses emerged from the cage 11.5 times per shift, including instances when they left the ward entirely (range, 4 to 39 times). Late afternoon and night nurses were even less available, emerging on the average 9.4 times per shift (range, 4 to 41 times). Data on early morning nurses, who arrived usually after midnight and departed at 8 a.m., are not available because patients were asleep during most of this period.

Physicians, especially psychiatrists, were even less available. They were rarely seen on the wards. Quite commonly, they would be seen only when they arrived and departed, with the remaining time being spent in their offices or in the cage. On the average, physicians emerged on the ward 6.7 times per day (range, 1 to 17 times). It proved difficult to make an accurate estimate in this regard, since physicians often maintained hours that allowed them to come and go at different times.

The hierarchical organization of the psychiatric hospital has been commented on before,[20] but the latent meaning of that kind of organization is worth noting again. Those with the most power have least to do with patients, and those with the least power are most involved with them. Recall, however, that the acquisition of role-appropriate behaviors occurs mainly through the observation of others, with the most powerful having the most influence. Consequently, it is understandable that attendants not only spend more time with patients than do any other members of the staff—that is required by their station in the hierarchy—but also, insofar as they learn from their superiors' behavior, spend as little time with patients as they can. Attendants are seen mainly in the cage, which is where the models, the action, and the power are.

I turn now to a different set of studies, these dealing with staff response to patient-initiated contact. It has long been known that the amount of time a person spends with you can be an index of your significance to him. If he initiates and maintains eye contact, there is reason to believe that he is considering your requests and needs. If he pauses to chat or actually stops and talks, there is added reason to infer that he is individuating you. In four hospitals, the pseudo-patient approached the staff member with a request which took the following form: "Pardon me, Mr. [or Dr. or Mrs.] X, could you tell me when I will be eligible for grounds privileges?" (or "when I will be presented at the staff meeting?" or "when am I likely to be discharged?"). While the content of the question varied according to the appropriateness of the target and the pseudopatient's (apparrent) current needs the form was always a courteous and relevant request for information. Care was taken never to approach a particular member of the staff more than once a day, lest the staff member become suspicious or irritated. In examining these data, remember that the behavior of the pseudopatients was neither bizarre nor disruptive. One could indeed engage in good conversation with them.

20. A. H. Stanton, & M. S. Schwartz, *The mental hospital: A study of institutional participation in psychiatric illness and treatment.* New York: Basic Books, 1954.

The data for these experiments are shown in Table 10–1, separately for physicians (column 1) and for nurses and attendants (column 2). Minor differences between these four institutions were overwhelmed by the degree to which staff avoided continuing contacts that patients had initiated. By far, their most common response consisted of either a brief response to the question, offered while they were "on the move" and with head averted, or no response at all.

The encounter frequently took the following bizarre form: (pseudopatient) "Pardon me, Dr. X. Could you tell me when I am eligible for grounds privileges?" (physician) "Good morning, Dave. How are you today?" (Moves off without waiting for a response.)

It is instructive to compare these data with data recently obtained at Stanford University. It has been alleged that large and eminent universities are characterized by faculty who are so busy that they have no time for students. For this comparison, a young lady approached individual faculty members who seemed to be walking purposefully to some meeting or teaching engagement and asked them the following six questions.

1. "Pardon me, could you direct me to Encina Hall?" (at the medical school: " . . . to the Clinical Research Center?").
2. "Do you know where Fish Annex is?" (there is no Fish Annex at Stanford).
3. "Do you teach here?"
4. "How does one apply for admission to the college?" (at the medical school: " . . . to the medical school?").
5. "Is it difficult to get in?"
6. "Is there financial aid?"

Without exception, as can be seen in Table 10–1 (column 3), all of the questions were answered. No matter how rushed they were, all respondents not only maintained eye contact, but stopped to talk. Indeed, many of the respondents went out of their way to direct or take the questioner to the office she was seeking, to try to locate "Fish Annex," or to discuss with her the possibilities of being admitted to the university.

Similar data, also shown in Table 10–1 (columns 4, 5, and 6), were obtained in the hospital. Here too, the young lady came prepared with six questions. After the first question, however, she remarked to 18 of her respondents (column 4), "I'm looking for a psychiatrist," and to 15 others (column 5), "I'm looking for an internist." Ten other respondents received no inserted comment (column 6). The general degree of cooperative responses is considerably higher for these university groups than it was for pseudopatients in psychiatric hospitals. Even so, differences are apparent within the medical school setting. Once having indicated that she was looking for a psychiatrist, the degree of cooperation elicited was less than when she sought an internist.

Table 10–1 Self-Initiated Contact by Pseudopatients with Psychiatrists and Nurses and Attendants, Compared to Contact with Other Groups

Contact	Psychiatric hospitals		University campus (nonmedical)	University medical center Physicians		
	(1) Psychiatrists	(2) Nurses and attendants	(3) Faculty	(4) "Looking for a psychiatrist"	(5) "Looking for an internist"	(6) No additional comment
Responses						
Moves on, head averted (%)	71.0	88.0	0.0	0.0	0.0	0.0
Makes eye contact (%)	23.0	10.0	0.0	11.0	0.0	0.0
Pauses and chats (%)	2.0	2.0	0.0	11.0	0.0	10.0
Stops and talks (%)	4.0	0.5	100.0	78.0	100.0	90.0
Mean number of questions answered (out of 6)	*	*	6.0	3.8	4.8	4.5
Respondents (No.)	13.0	47.0	14.0	18.0	15.0	10.0
Attempts (No.)	185.0	1283.0	14.0	18.0	15.0	10.0

*Not applicable.

Powerlessness and Depersonalization

Eye contact and verbal contact reflect concern and individuation; their absence, avoidance, and depersonalization. The data I have presented do not do justice to the rich daily encounters that grew up around matters of depersonalization and avoidance. I have records of patients who were beaten by staff for the sin of having initiated verbal contact. During my own experience, for example, one patient was beaten in the presence of other patients for having approached an attendant and told him, "I like you." Occasionally, punishment meted out to patients for misdemeanors seemed so excessive that it could not be justified by the most radical interpretations of psychiatric canon. Nevertheless, they appeared to go unquestioned. Tempers were often short. A patient who had not heard a call for medication would be roundly excoriated, and the morning attendants would often wake patients with, "Come on, you m—f—s, out of bed!"

Neither anecdotal nor "hard" data can convey the overwhelming sense of powerlessness which invade the individual as he is continually exposed to the depersonalization of the psychiatric hospital. It hardly matters *which* psychiatric hospital — the excellent public ones and the very plush private hospital were better than the rural and shabby ones in this regard, but, again, the features that psychiatric hospitals had in common overwhelmed by far their apparent differences.

Powerlessness was evident everywhere. The patient is deprived of many of his legal rights by dint of his psychiatric commitment.[21] He is shorn of credibility by virtue of his psychiatric label. His freedom of movement is restricted. He cannot initiate contact with the staff, but may only respond to such overtures as they make. Personal privacy is minimal. Patient quarters and possessions can be entered and examined by any staff member, for whatever reason. His personal history and anguish is available to any staff member (often including the "grey lady" and "candy striper" volunteer) who chooses to read his folder, regardless of their therapeutic relationship to him. His personal hygiene and waste evacuation are often monitored. The water closets may have no doors.

At times, depersonalization reached such proportions that pseudopatients had the sense that they were invisible, or at least unworthy of account. Upon being admitted, I and other pseudopatients took the initial physical examinations in a semipublic room where staff members went about their own business as if we were not there.

On the ward, attendants delivered verbal and occasionally serious physical abuse to patients in the presence of other observing patients, some of whom (the pseudopatients) were writing it all down. Abusive behavior, on the other hand, terminated quite abruptly when other staff members were known to be coming. Staff are credible witnesses. Patients are not.

A nurse unbuttoned her uniform to adjust her brassiere in the presence of an

---

21.   D. B. Wexler, & S. E. Scoville, *Arizona Law Review 13 (1)* 1971.

entire ward of viewing men. One did not have the sense that she was being seductive. Rather, she didn't notice us. A group of staff persons might point to a patient in the dayroom and discuss him animatedly, as if he were not there.

One illuminating instance of depersonalization and invisibility occurred with regard to medications. All told, the pseudopatients were administered nearly 2100 pills, including Elavil, Stelazine, Compazine, and Thorazine, to name but a few. (That such a variety of medications should have been administered to patients presenting identical symptoms is itself worthy of note.) Only two were swallowed. The rest were either pocketed or deposited in the toilet. The pseudopatients were not alone in this. Although I have no precise records on how many patients rejected their medications, the pseudopatients frequently found the medications of other patients in the toilet before they deposited their own. As long as they were cooperative, their behavior and the pseudopatients' own in this matter, as in other important matters, went unnoticed throughout.

Reactions to such depersonalization among pseudopatients were intense. Although they had come to the hospital as participant observers and were fully aware that they did not "belong," they nevertheless found themselves caught up in and fighting the process of depersonalization. Some examples: a graduate student in psychology asked his wife to bring his textbooks to the hospital so he could "catch up on his homework"— this despite the elaborate precautions taken to conceal his professional association. The same student, who had trained for quite some time to get into the hospital, and who had looked forward to the experience, "remembered" some drag races that he had wanted to see on the weekend and insisted that he be discharged by that time. Another pseudopatient attempted a romance with a nurse. Subsequently, he informed the staff that he was applying for admission to graduate school in psychology and was very likely to be admitted, since a graduate professor was one of his regular hospital visitors. The same person began to engage in psychotherapy with other patients— all of this as a way of becoming a person in an impersonal environment.

The Sources of Depersonalization

What are the origins of depersonalization? I have already mentioned two. First are attitudes held by all of us toward the mentally ill—including those who treat them—attitudes characterized by fear, distrust, and horrible expectations on the one had, and benevolent intentions on the other. Our ambivalence leads, in this instance as in others, to avoidance.

Second, and not entirely separate, the hierarchical structure of the psychiatric hospital facilitates depersonalization. Those who are at the top have least to do with patients, and their behavior inspires the rest of the staff. Average daily contact with psychiatrists, psychologists, residents, and physicians combined ranged from 3.9 to 25.1 minutes, with an overall mean of 6.8 (six pseudopatients over a total of 129 days of hospitalization). Included in this average are time spent in the admissions interview, ward meetings in the presence of a senior staff member, group and individual psychotherapy contacts, case presentation conferences, and discharge meetings. Clearly, patients do not spend much time in interpersonal contact with doctoral staff. And doctoral staff serve as models for nurses and attendants.

There are probably other sources. Psychiatric installations are presently in serious financial straits. Staff shortages are pervasive, staff time at a premium. Something has to give, and that something is patient contact. Yet, while financial stresses are realities, too much can be made of them. I have the impression that the psychological forces that result in depersonalization are much stronger than the fiscal ones and that the addition of more staff would not correspondingly improve patient care in this regard. The incidence of staff meetings and the enormous amount of record keeping on patients, for example, have not been as substantially reduced as has patient contact. Priorities exist, even during hard times. Patient contact is not a significant priority in the traditional psychiatric hospital, and fiscal pressures do not account for this. Avoidance and depersonalization may.

Heavy reliance upon psychotropic medication tacitly contributes to depersonalization by convincing staff that treatment is indeed being conducted and that further patient contact may not be necessary. Even here, however, caution needs to be exercised in understanding the role of psychotropic drugs. If patients were powerful rather than powerless, if they were viewed as interesting individuals rather than diagnostic entities, if they were socially significant rather than social lepers, if their anguish truly and wholly compelled our sympathies and concerns, would we not *seek* contact with them, despite the availability of medications? Perhaps for the pleasure of it all?

The Consequences of Labeling and Depersonalization

Whenever the ratio of what is known to what needs to be known approaches zero, we tend to invent "knowledge" and assume that we understand more than we actually do. We seem unable to acknowledge that we simply don't know. The needs for diagnosis and remediation of behavioral and emotional problems are enormous. But rather than acknowledge that we are just embarking on understanding, we continue to label patients "schizophrenic," "manic-depressive," and "insane," as if in those words we had captured the essence of understanding. The facts of the matter are that we have known for a long time that diagnoses are often not useful or reliable, but we have nevertheless continued to use them. We now know that we cannot distinguish insanity from sanity. It is depressing to consider how that information will be used.

Not merely depressing, but frightening. How many people, one wonders, are sane but not recognized as such in our psychiatric institutions? How many have been needlessly stripped of their privileges of citizenship, from the right to vote and drive to that of handling their own accounts? How many have feigned insanity in order to avoid the criminal consequences of their behavior, and, conversely, how many would rather stand trial than live interminably in a psychiatric hospital—but are wrongly thought to be mentally ill? How many have been stigmatized by well-intentioned, but nevertheless erroneous, diagnoses? On the last point, recall again that a "type 2 error" in psychiatric diagnosis does not have the same consequences it does in medical diagnosis. A diagnosis of cancer that has been found to be in error is cause for celebration. But psychiatric diagnoses are rarely found to be in error. The label sticks, a mark of inadequacy forever.

Finally, how many patients might be "sane" outside the psychiatric hospital but seem insane in it—not because craziness resides in them, as it were, but because they are responding to a bizarre setting, one that may be unique to institutions which harbor nether people? Goffman (4) calls the process of socialization to such institutions "mortification"—an apt metaphor that includes the processes of depersonalization that have been described here. And while it is impossible to know whether the pseudopatients' responses to these processes are characteristic of all inmates—they were, after all, not real patients—it is difficult to believe that these processes of socialization to a psychiatric hospital provide useful attitudes or habits of response for living in the "real world."

Summary and Conclusions

It is clear that we cannot distinguish the sane from the insane in psychiatric hospitals. The hospital itself imposes a special environment in which the meanings of behavior can easily be misunderstood. The consequences to patients hospitalized in such an environment—the powerlessness, depersonalization, segregation, mortification, and self-labeling—seem undoubtedly counter-therapeutic.

I do not, even now, understand this problem well engough to perceive solutions. But two matters seem to have some promise. The first concerns the proliferation of community mental health facilities, of crisis intervention centers, of the human potential movement, and of behavior therapies that, for all of their own problems, tend to avoid psychiatric labels, to focus on specific problems and behaviors, and to retain the individual in a relatively nonpejorative environment. Clearly, to the extent that we refrain from sending the distressed to insane places, our impressions of them are less likely to be distorted. (The risk of distorted perceptions, it seems to me, is always present, since we are much more sensitive to an individual's behaviors and verbalizations than we are to the subtle contextual stimuli that often promote them. At issue here is a matter of magnitude. And, as I have shown, the magnitude of distortion is exceedingly high in the extreme context that is a psychiatric hospital.)

The second matter that might prove promising speaks to the need to increase the sensitivity of mental health workers and researchers to the Catch-22 position of psychiatric patients. Simply reading materials in this area will be of help to some such workers and researchers. For others, directly experiencing the impact of psychiatric hospitalization will be of enormous use. Clearly, further research into the social psychology of such total institutions will both facilitate treatment and deepen understanding.

I and the other pseudopatients in the psychiatric setting had distinctly negative reactions. We do not pretend to describe the subjective experiences of true patients. Theirs may be different from ours, particularly with the passage of time and the necessary process of adaptation to one's environment. But we can and do speak to the relatively more objective indices of treatment within the hospital. It could be a mistake, and a very unfortunate one, to consider that what happened to us derived from malice or stupidity on the part of the staff. Quite the contrary, our overwhelming impression of them was of people who really cared, who were committed, and who were uncommonly intelligent. Where they failed, as they sometimes did painfully, it would be more accurate to attribute those failures to the environment in which they, too, found themselves than to personal callousness. Their perceptions and behavior were controlled by the situation, rather than being motivated by a malicious disposition. In a more benign environment, one that was less attached to global diagnosis, their behaviors and judgments might have been more benign and effective.

I thank W. Mischel, E. Orne, and M. S. Rosenhan for comments on an earlier draft of this manuscript.

Individual Resources and Mental Hospitalization: A Comparison and Evaluation of the Societal Reaction and Psychiatric Perspectives

11

WALTER R. GOVE
PATRICK HOWELL

According to the psychiatric perspective, persons enter mental hospitals because they have a serious psychiatric disorder. Furthermore, as most psychiatrists posit a developmental model of mental illness, they view prompt intervention as highly desirable because it will prevent the disturbance from becoming more severe and more difficult to treat (e.g., Milt, 1969, 81; Myers and Roberts, 1959, 216). Most psychiatrists have not paid attention to the process by which a person enters treatment. However, implicit in their perspective, as in the medical model generally, is the view that social and economic resources will help one get treatment. In particular they presume that such resources will facilitate the correct indentification of the disorder and promote prompt and effective action aimed at obtaining the appropriate psychiatric care. This means that persons with resources will be more likely to get treatment and to get it more quickly than those without resources. Furthermore, on the basis of the above premise and its developmental model of mental illness, the psychiatric perspective suggests that the disorder of

This paper was presented at the meeting of the American Sociological Association in August 1972. The research for this paper was supported in part by Public Health Service Grant 5-R1-MH00898 and in part by the Vanderbilt University Research Council. We would like to thank Antonina Gove and Terry Fain for their comments on an earlier draft.

persons with resources will, at the time of hospitalization, be less severe than the disorder of persons without resources.

Adherents of societal reaction or labeling theory view mental illness in general, and mental hospitalization in particular, from a very different perspective. They contend that whether or not one occupies a deviant role, such as that of the mentally ill, is primarily a function of the acts of others and they attach little importance to any initial acts of deviance, viewing such acts as having little intrinsic significance and, at most, only marginal implication for the psychic structure of the individual (Lemert, 1967,17; also see Becker, 1963; Erikson, 1962, 1966; Kitsuse, 1962; Goffman, 1961; Scheff, 1966; Schur, 1969, 1971; also see Laing, 1960, 1967; Szasz, 1961, 1970; Sarbin, 1972; Rosenhan, 1973). According to this perspective, the greater the individual's social and economic resources, the greater the likelihood that he will be able to deal successfully with others and the less the likelihood that he will be channeled into a deviant role. With regard to mental illness, this means that persons with resources will be more likely to avoid psychiatric treatment, particularly in a mental hospital, and that if they are hospitalized, they will have been able to delay their hospitalization. Among other things, this suggests that hospitalized persons with resources would, on the average, have a more serious disorder than those without resources; for those with resources could prevent their hospitalization unless they were seriously disturbed, whereas those without resources will be hospitalized even if they are not seriously disturbed.

In this paper we will look at the role social and economic resources play in mental hospitalization, comparing the societal reaction and the psychiatric perspectives. This topic has recently been investigated by Linsky (1970) and Rushing (1971), who view their results as supporting the societal reaction explanation. However, as we will suggest below, their results are open to an alternative interpretation. Since probably all but the most extreme societal reaction theorists recognize that there frequently is at least some behavioral pathology (e.g., see Schur, 1971, 15–16) and all but the most naive psychiatrists acknowledge that there are sometimes coercive aspects to mental hospitalization, we will assume both phenomena exist. Thus, the issue we are concerned with is not whether there are any data supporting a particular perspective, but instead which perspective best explains what typically happens.

In evaluating these perspectives, we will look at two basic resources (1) social class, with an emphasis on economic position,[1] and (2) social supports,

---

1. One reviewer of our paper suggested that, in addition to social class, we should consider race. According to the societal reaction perspective, blacks, who have less power than whites in our society, should be more readily channeled into the role of the mentally ill even after class variables are controlled for. Psychiatric theory, however, does not predict the reverse of the relationship; so when we consider race, we are not offered a clear choice between the two perspectives. Fisher's (1969) review of the evidence on race differences leads him to conclude that even without controlling for economic factors the evidence, taken in toto, does not indicate blacks have higher rates of psychiatric hospitalization than whites. Furthermore, the one year for which there is national data by race on admissions to mental hospitals indicates blacks have lower rates than whites (Malzberg, 1940, 225). In short, the available data on race differences in psychiatric hospitalization do not support the societal reaction perspective.

with an emphasis on marital status. We will attempt to discern how these resources relate to the hospitalization process and to the nature and severity of the patient's disorder at the time he enters treatment.

Our evaluation will be based on a review of the literature and on data obtained from 258 patients admitted to Northern State Hospital in the State of Washington between December, 1962, and June, 1964. These patients comprise all the psychiatric patients who entered a state hospital from a specific county during the 18-month period, and an analysis of their characteristics suggests that they are typical of state hospital admissions. At the time of the study, the county did not have an alternative inpatient facility nor an outpatient clinic; however, most of the residents were close to an adjoining county where they had access to such facilities. The patients studied were admitted to a demonstration or pilot program, a description and evaluation of which is presented in Gove and Lubach (1969). Most of the data used in this paper were systematically obtained at the time of admission. The initial purpose for obtaining data was to ascertain how effective the program was in treating different categories of patients, and these records were kept completely separate from the patients' official hospital record. Since the pilot program was set up as a research project and since the staff had a strong commitment to research and devoted considerable care to gathering data, the quality of the data is probably better than that obtained in most studies conducted in state mental hospitals. Because these data deal only with state hospital admissions, the nature of the sample works against the psychiatric perspective and in favor of the societal reaction perspective. This is because high-resource persons have more alternatives available, such as outpatient care and private mental hospitals, which could both delay a state hospital admission and screen patients with a mild disorder. In short, we would argue that for high-resource persons, admission to a state mental hospital is apt to be the last step in the search for psychiatric help; whereas for the low-resource persons, it is apt to be the first step. This position is supported by the fact that among the patients we studied the high-resource persons were much more likely than the low-resource persons to have sought help from relevant professionals and agencies prior to their hospitalization.

In this paper we will not distinguish between voluntary and committed patients for several reasons. First, according to the psychiatric perspective such a distinction is relatively unimportant. The type of admission is viewed primarily as a consequence of the severity and the nature of the illness and is believed to have little effect on the patient or his subsequent progress (e.g., see Klots, 1962, 57). Second, most of the studies we draw on do not make a distinction between voluntary and committed patients. Third, as far as we can determine, the societal reaction theorists have made no attempt to explain voluntary admissions aside from an occasional comment that such patients may have been pressured into hospitalization. Furthermore, as we understand the societal reaction perspective, it provides two contradictory views of voluntary as compared to committed patients. On the one hand, societal reaction theorists view both the commitment proceedings and the legal disabilities associated with involuntary hospitalization as factors that play a major role in channeling the committed patient into a stabilized deviant role. On the other hand, the societal reaction framework suggests at least two reasons for viewing voluntary patients as being further into an established deviant role than committed patients. First, such patients have already defined themselves as deviant (i.e., mentally ill), something the committed patients have not done; and, in fact, it is this self-definition that the societal reaction theorists focus on as an important possible consequence of the commitment process. Second, one must deal with the question of why a person would voluntarily stigmatize himself by going to a mental hospital, and it can be plausibly argued that voluntary patients do so because they are seriously disturbed; whereas, persons who are committed have been unwilling to stigmatize themselves because they are not seriously disturbed.

By not distinguishing between voluntary and committed patients, we do not wish to imply that the distinction is not important, but only that it is unclear how such a distinction should be treated. We would note that for the data presented below, the patterns of voluntary and committed patients are very similar, as are the patterns of both first admissions and readmissions. Linsky (1970) and Rushing (1971) have used the involuntary/voluntary ratio in their analysis of the societal reaction perspective. They found that the size of the ratio had an inverse relationship to class and marital status, which they take as supporting the societal reaction perspective. However, since the psychiatric perspective suggests that persons with few resources are less likely than persons with many resources to view hospitalization favorably (see below) and more likely to be seriously disturbed when hospitalized, it follows that low-resource persons are more likely to enter the hospital as committed patients. Thus, Linsky's (1970) and Rushing's (1971) results are also consistent with the psychiatric perspective.[2]

The Role of Socioeconomic Resources

According to societal reaction theorists, people with economic and educational resources have more power and are in a better position to mobilize medical and legal assistance to fight hospitalization. Furthermore, persons in the middle and

---

2. If we assume that a category of persons with a high involuntary/voluntary ratio tends to have a severe disorder, as the psychiatric perspective suggests, and that categories of persons with a low ratio tend to have many resources, as the Rushing (1971) and Linsky (1970) data indicate, then some apparent ambiguities in Rushing's paper can be explained. For example, he assumes (1) that the fewer a person's resources, the more likely he is to be involuntarily confined and (2) that persons with disrupted marriages have more resources than persons who have never married; but he finds that while the disrupted category has a small ratio, they have a higher rate of involuntary hospitalization than single persons. By focusing on the involuntary/voluntary ratio and ignoring the rate, Rushing takes the data as supporting his position on resources and hospitalization. However, it seems more plausible to us that persons with disrupted marriages have a higher rate of disturbance than either married or never-married persons, a view supported by most data (e.g., Gove, 1972), but that persons with disrupted marriages are more likely to enter treatment early and voluntarily than never-married persons because they have more resources.

upper classes can generally deal more effectively with lawyers, judges, the police, and psychiatrists than persons in the lower class, and therefore they presumably can present a more coherent and convincing defense (e.g., see Miller and Schwartz, 1966, 29). In contrast, the psychiatric perspective suggests that educational and economic resources help the emotionally disturbed individual get the proper psychiatric treatment. In short, a solid economic position would enable the individual to see the appropriate mental health professionals, and the intellectual sophistication of the individual and those close to him would assist them in coming to view the problem in psychiatric terms and in communicating the problem to relevant others.[3] Thus, among the upper classes, hospitalization is more likely to be initiated by the patient and those close to him than it is in the lower classes. To a large degree the psychiatric perspective holds that the reasons for the pattern of delay among the lower class in seeking medical treatment for physical problems[4] also apply to their delay in seeking psychiatric treatment.

Attitudes, Knowledge, and Verbal Skills.

Social classes differ in their attitude toward and knowledge of mental illness and psychiatric treatment. The lower class sees only a narrow range of aggressive, antisocial behavior as suggesting a need for psychiatric treatment; whereas, persons in the middle and upper class perceive a much wider range of psychopathological behavior as indicating a need for psychiatric care (e.g., Dohrenwend and Chin Shong, 1967). Similarly, members of the lower class have a much less clear understanding of psychiatric theory and psychiatric treatment (Hollingshead and Redlich, 1958, especially p. 36; also Myers and Roberts, 1958; Myers and Bean, 1968). Furthermore, members of the lower class have much more negative attitudes toward mental illness and psychiatric treatment (e.g., Jaco, 1957; Myers and Roberts, 1958, 202–05; Williams, 1957; Manis et al., 1963; Jones and Kahn, 1964); and there is fairly solid evidence that members of the lower class are much more concerned with and inhibited by the stigma of mental hospitalization (e.g., Myers and Bean, 1968, 193). This clearly suggests that an emotionally disturbed individual from the lower class and his family are less likely than members of the upper class to seek psychiatric treatment.

The results of the community survey by Gurin et al. (1960) bear on this expectation. This study, like most community surveys (Dohrenwend and Dohrenwend, 1969), found that persons in the lower class manifest more psychiatric symptoms than persons in the upper classes. As one would expect, the manifes-

---

3. Regarding the importance of communication, Freeman and Simmons (1959, 346–7) speculate that "By virtue of the middle-class emphasis upon and practice of the interpersonal manipulation, these families can more readily mobilize and exploit the outside community so as to facilitate the return of the patient to the hospital. Moreover, the pronounced verbal ability of middle-class persons is useful in effecting the rehospitalization of a family member in the face of the frequent reluctance of hospital personnel to readmit the former patient."

4. For evidence of the lower-class tendency to delay seeking care for physical problems see Anderson and Feldman (1956), Anderson (1963), Koos (1954), Myers and Roberts (1958, 202–12); such delay is probably one of the reasons the lower class have a higher mortality rate (e.g., Antonovsky 1972).

tation of symptoms had a strong positive relationship to the respondent's perception that he had needed professional psychiatric help. From these relationships one might assume that persons in the lower class would be more likely than persons in the upper class to see themselves as having needed psychiatric help. However, using education as an indicator of class, they found that persons in the upper class are much more likely than persons in the lower class to perceive themselves as having been in need of professional help.[5] Furthermore, education and income have a strong positive relationship to the actual use of professional help among persons who perceive that they had needed help. In short, these results indicate that persons from the upper class are more likely to get professional help despite the fact that members of the lower class manifest more symptoms of mental illness. Note also that a favorable attitude toward psychiatric treatment and being knowledgeable about psychiatric theory are positively related to rehospitalization (Raphael et al., 1966).

At least indirect support for the proposition that verbal skills and other middle-class attributes facilitate admission to psychiatric treatment is provided by Sabagh's et al. (1969) study of the factors affecting the hospitalization of the mentally retarded. They found that "patients whose families have a higher socioeconomic status tend to be hospitalized earlier and at a significantly higher rate than patients who come from a lower socioeconomic milieu" (Sabagh et al., 1966, 121). They indicate that the rapid hospitalization of the upper classes is largely due to (1) their greater skill in presenting family problems, (2) the fact that they tend to "accept the label of retardation which in turn enhances their ability to communicate with the hospital staff about their problem," and (3) the staff's perception that the upper classes have a greater claim on their services than the lower class[6] (Sabagh et al., 1966, 126–27; also see Eyman, 1966).

Delay In Treatment

Let us now examine the relationship between resources and delay in seeking treatment, tolerance (or acceptance) of psychopathologic behavior in the community and the patient's route to the hospital. A basic theme of the classic work by Hollingshead and Redlich (1958) is that members of the lower class are less likely than members of the upper class to identify disturbed behavior as mental illness, that they are more apt to delay in seeking treatment, and that when treatment is finally initiated it is frequently due to the acts of members of the general community because the patient and his immediate family either did not act, or acted inappropriately. Myers and Roberts (1958) made a detailed analysis of differences in the onset of illness and paths to treatment of a sample of middle-class and lower-class patients. Among schizophrenics they found that in the lower class "patients were obviously psychotic for over three years before psy-

---

5. This is an excellent illustration of the fact, noted by Costner and Leik (1964), that deduction based on the sign rule will frequently be incorrect.

6. We would note that in the same hospital a few years later the effect of class on admission, although still present, had been greatly reduced due to improved regulations (Sabagh et al., 1972).

Table 11-1   Characteristics of Patients and Duration between Onset of
Symptoms and Hospitalization by Income (in percentages)

Duration	Income		Gamma	p
	0-3,999	4,000+		
Record present patient as never psychiatrically "normal."	47.6 (105)	37.6 (141)	−.20	<.2
First symptoms of episode precipitating hospitalization occurred more than one year before hospitalization.	56.6 (99)	38.2 (136)	−.36	<.01
Persons diagnosed as psychotic whose psychotic episode lasted more than one month before hospitalization.	52.9 (68)	42.4 (85)	−.21	<.2

chiatric referral"; whereas among the middle class, "families recognized the patient's classic psychiatric symptoms when they appeared and called a physician" and a psychiatric referral was made in less than a month (Myers and Roberts, 1958, 285). Similar class differences were found among neurotic patients, although the differences were not as marked (e.g., Myers and Roberts, 1958, 283). These results are supported by a study of rehospitalization by Angrist et al. (1968, 97), which found that well-educated patients were more likely to be early returnees; whereas less-educated patients were more likely to be late returnees. Furthermore, Freeman, and Simmons (1959) suggest, from an analysis of the performance of ex-patients and their families' expectation, that middle-class families are less willing to tolerate deviant behavior than lower-class families and are therefore more likely to rehospitalize a former patient.[7]

Turning to our data we will look at the relationship between family income and (a) the duration between onset of symptoms and hospitalization and (b) the patient's route to the hospital. Unfortunately there were no data on the income of seven patients. To determine the time period between the first serious manifestation of symptoms and hospitalization, the patient's chart was carefully read. From these readings three things were recorded. First, whether the psychiatrist described the patient as having always appeared psychiatrically abnormal. Second, the duration between the onset of the first symptoms of the particular episode which precipitated hospitalization and the time of hospitalization. Third, the duration between the first manifestation of psychotic symptoms in the episode that precipitated hospitalization and the time of hospitalization among patients diagnosed as psychotic. As Table 11-1 shows, these data indicated that low income[8] tends to be associated with both a life history of abnormality and a longer duration between the manifestation of symptoms and hospitalization; how-

7. In their original analysis they focused on the instrumental performance of the ex-patients but in their subsequent work (Freeman and Simmons, 1963) they found that the key factor in rehospitalization was disturbed behavior and that expectations for instrumental behavior played only a secondary role.

8. We have dichotomized the patients' family income because there were too few patients in the upper income brackets to warrant a more refined analysis.

ever, two of these relationships only border on statistical significance. Although the direction of these relationships is consistent with previous research, the strength of the relationship between duration of symptoms and hospitalization is not as strong as Myers and Roberts' work (1958, 285) would suggest. The difference may be that we focused on the symptoms of the particular episode that precipitated hospitalization, whereas other investigators appear to have focused on the first sign of disturbed symptoms.

Persons Involved in the Hospitalization Progress

At the time of hospitalization the admitting psychiatrist recorded the persons responsible for the patient's admission. We have categorized these agents according to whether they were (a) laymen or (b) medical professionals or community officials. Within these two categories, we classified the agents according to how close they were to the patient. Accordingly, among the laymen we labeled the patient and his spouse as very close and other relatives (primarily children, parents, and siblings) and other unrelated individuals as somewhat more distant. Similarly we classified the family physician and psychiatrist as being close to the patient and the police and community agencies as being more distant.[9]

The data are presented in Table 11–2 They show that persons close to the patient are more likely to help initiate hospitalization for high-income persons;[10] whereas, more "distant" agents are more apt to initiate hospitalization for low-income patients. This pattern is similar to that presented by Hollingshead and Redlich (1958, 186–87). The data are thus consistent with the psychiatric perspective, which suggests that persons in the upper classes are more likely than persons in the lower classes to enter a mental hospital on their own initiative and the initiative of those close to them, and that such persons are more likely to be guided by professional advice in deciding to enter a mental hospital.

Type and Severity of Symptoms

The literature on the relationship between class and symptomatology consistently indicates that patients from the lower class typically have a more serious disorder, tending to be more disorganized and violent, whereas the symptoms of middle- and upper-class patients tend to reflect intrapsychic concerns. For example, Myers and Bean (1968, 90–91) in their study of hospitalized patients found that "anxiety, depression, obsessions, compulsions and phobias" were much

---

9. We would note that when a family physician or psychiatrist was involved in initiating hospitalization, the patient and/or his spouse were also almost invariably active agents, which suggests that the patient had gone to such persons for help and they had recommended hospitalization. A subsequent study (Gove 1968) at the same hospital found this to be the case. In contrast, when community agencies and/or the police had been active agents, typically neither the patient nor the spouse had played an active role in initiating hospitalization.

10. One of the reasons one's spouse is more likely to have initiated hospitalization among the high-income than the low-income patients is that more high-income patients are married. However, even when we look only at persons who are married, a fairly strong relationship remains (gamma = .44, p<.01).

Table 11-2   Agents Who Helped Initiate Hospitalization by Income (in percentages)

	Income		Gamma	p
	0-3,999	4,000+		
A. Relationship to Patient of Persons in the Community.				
1. Close				
Patient	48.1	65.3	.34	<.01
Spouse	27.9	69.4	.71	<.001
2. Distant				
"Other" relatives	49.0	22.9	−.53	<.001
"Other" unrelated individuals	19.2	7.6	−.48	<.01
B. Relationship to Patient of Professionals and Community Officials				
1. Close				
Family M.D.	38.5	42.4	.08	>.2
Psychiatrist	8.7	20.8	.47	<.01
2. Distant				
Community agency	12.5	3.5	−.60	<.001
Police	19.2	9.7	−.38	<.02
Total number of cases	104	144		

more frequent in the upper classes than the lower class, while "memory or orientation disturbances, disorganized thought processes, delusions and hallucinations, aggressive verbal behavior, and aggressive physical behavior" were more common in the lower class. Myers and Roberts (1958, 285-87) found a similar pattern, even after diagnosis was controlled for, and the pattern is clearly suggested in the cases presented by Hollingshead and Redlich (1958, 172-76). Turner et al. (1969, 294), in a study of schizophrenics drawn from a psychiatric case register found, for the total sample, that the schizophrenics from the lower class tended to have a more serious pathology than the schizophrenics from the upper classes. Similarly, Shader et al. (1971, 598) found that lower-class patients of a mental health center manifested many more symptoms, as indicated by the Langner scale, than upper-class patients. Myers and Bean (1968, 147) and Myers and Roberts (1958, 219) suggest that one of the reasons lower-class patients tend to have a more serious disorder is their tendency to delay treatment, and Myers and Roberts (1958, 219) indicate that the lack of delay is probably the reason their middle-class schizophrenics responded more favorably to shock therapy than their lower-class schizophrenics.

Let us turn to the symptoms of the patients in the present study. At the time of admission, the psychiatrists noted (a) whether the patient was clearly distressed (as manifested by such symptoms as dysphoria, worry and agitation), and if so, the severity of the distress, (b) whether the patient was clearly disorganized (as manifested by such symptoms as hallucinations, delusions, psychomotor retardation, flight of ideas, and gross confusion), and if so, the severity of the disorganization, and (c) whether the patient had committed serious disruptive acts just prior to hospitalization[11] (with disruptive acts being defined as overt acts that create obvious problems for others and as being something other than non-performance of duties and inwardly focused acts such as suicidal behavior). These ratings were part of some research the psychiatrists were conducting and considerable care was taken in making them.[12] A subsequent analysis of disruptive acts indicated that they could be categorized into one of two types, (a) those that were grossly inappropriate and were based on the patient's disorganization (such as a patient who stopped traffic by walking naked down the middle of the street because "God" told her to) and (b) acts that involved threatened or actual violent behavior or some other criminal act (see Gove, 1968).

Table 11–3 Patient Symptoms, by Income (in percentages)

Income	Not Significantly Present	Mild	Moderate	Severe	Present	n	Gamma
			Distress				
0-3,999	24.5	25.5	34.0	16.0		106	.14
4,000+	18.6	14.5	57.2	9.7		145	p<.2
			Disorganization				
0-3,999	27.4	17.0	34.9	20.8		106	−.28
4,000+	45.5	16.6	23.4	14.5		145	p<.01
			Disruptive Acts				
0-3,999	41.5				58.5	106	−.47
4,000+	66.2				33.8	145	p<.001

These ratings, by income, are presented in Table 11–3. As noted above, other studies show middle-class patients are more likely to show intrapsychic concerns and these data show a slight positive relationship between income and distress. Community surveys find the opposite relationship, namely that symptoms associated with distress are more common in the lower class (Dohrenwend and Dohrenwend, 1969; Phillips, 1966; Haese and Miele, 1967; Clancy, 1971; Miele and Haese, 1969; Phillips and Clancy, 1970). These conflicting patterns suggest that distress is not a middle-class symptom but that persons in the middle class, when they are acutely distressed, are more likely to seek treatment that are persons from the lower class. In contrast, the presence and severity of disorganization is negatively correlated with income as is the occurrence of disruptive acts.

---

11. The psychiatrists simply reported the presence or absence of disruptive acts and did not rate their severity.

12. A subsequent study suggested that these ratings could be made quite reliably by psychiatrists. Support for the validity of the ratings is indicated by a high degree of correspondence between these ratings and the patient's subsequent reports of what his symptoms were at the time of hospitalization (Gove, 1968).

Table 11–4 Type and Severity of Symptoms by Income (in percentages)

Severity	Almost Nil	Mild	Moderate		Severe	n	Gamma*
Type of Symptom	"No Symptom"	Distress	Disorganized but not disruptive	Disruptive but not disorganized	Disorganized and disruptive		
Income							
0-3,999	1.9	12.3	27.4	13.2	45.3	106	.44
4,000+	.7	32.4	33.1	11.7	22.1	145	p<.001

*In computing gamma, the two "moderate" categories were combined.

In Table 11–4 we have combined these ratings into a scale with a range in severity of psychiatric symptoms from (1) almost nil ("no symptoms") to (2) mild ("distressed only"), (3) moderate (a) "disorganized but not disruptive" or (b) "disruptive but not disorganized," (4) severe (both "disorganized and disruptive"). Severity, as we are using the term, reflects the degree the symptoms impair the person's ability to function effectively in society and does not necessarily reflect the symptoms' amenability to treatment. In making this scale, we defined a person as distressed only if his distress was moderate or severe; whereas, for disorganization and disruption, we used the presence or absence of the symptom. In terms of the types of symptoms noted in the table, persons who have "no symptom" do not meet any of the above criteria,[13] persons who are "distressed" have this symptom but are not disorganized and have not been disruptive, while persons in the other three categories may or may not be distressed. When the two moderate categories are combined, we feel that this scale, on the basis of face validity, provides an ordinal measure of severity. Furthermore, if we ignore the category of "disruptive only," the scale relates to a progressive model of mental illness; for it appears very likely that severe distress may, over time, lead to disorganization, which, if it persists, may in turn lead to disruptive acts (e.g., Gove, 1968, 1970c). Using this scale, we find that severity of disorder is negatively related to income.[14]

In summary, the data on social class indicate that compared to the upper classes, the lower classes have a negative attitude toward psychiatric treatment

---

13. It is possible that persons with "no symptoms"— as we have defined them—could have committed acts that might appear to warrant hospitalization. For example, a person who attempted suicide but was neither disorganized nor moderately or seriously distressed when he entered the hospital would be classified as having "no symptoms."

14. Using a more stringent cutting point for disorganization does not significantly change the results. One reviewer has suggested that we use the following scale: 1) no symptoms; 2) one symptom (either distressed, disorganized, or disruptive); 3) two symptoms and 4) three symptoms. We are reluctant to do so because the literature on both physiological indicators of distress (Schwartz, 1966; Sachar et al., 1963, 1967; Rey et al., 1961) and verbal reports of distress (Leighton and Cline, 1971; also see Dohrenwend and Crandall, 1970) indicate that a well-developed delusional system protects persons from experiencing acute distress. Our data also reflect this pattern. If we simply use the presence (mild, moderate or severe) of a symptom on such a scale, gamma = .40; but if we use only moderate or severe distress, gamma drops to .31 because the disorganized disruptives, who typically are delusional, often did not manifest a high degree of distress.

and delay in seeking psychiatric care. When they do get treatment, it is often due to acts of individuals relatively "distant" from the patient and their disorder will be relatively severe. In short, the evidence supports the psychiatric perspective with regard to the role class-related resources play in the hospitalization process. We will now turn to social resources, paying particular attention to marital status.

The Role of Social Resources (Marital Status)

As with class-related variables, the societal reaction theorists argue that the greater the individual's social or family resources, the greater the likelihood that he will be able to avoid being hospitalized, particularly in a state mental hospital (e.g., Rushing, 1971 and Linsky, 1970). Such theorists assume that interested family members will be able to pressure and manipulate the medical and legal profession to prevent hospitalization. Furthermore, a family willing to help the patient provides an alternative placement.

In contrast, the psychiatric perspective suggests that family resources would play an important role in getting a disturbed person into treatment, and that a family's action, by producing a prompt entry, would prevent the development of a severe disorder. For example, they would argue that the disturbance of a person living with his family would be noticed more quickly simply because of his close proximity with others. Furthermore, they would suggest that a person is more likely to assume the responsibility for seeing that someone get the necessary psychiatric care if close family ties are involved. In addition, it has been suggested (e.g., Hammer, 1963–64) that if one is very dependent on the behavior of another individual, as are most married persons, one will be more likely to take action if that person stops performing his tasks than if one is not dependent.

Initiation of Hospitalization

Recently the American Bar Association published what is almost undoubtedly the largest study to date of the procedures used in hospitalization and discharge of the mentally ill (Rock et al., 1968). In general, they conclude that in most cases of hospitalization the patient's disturbance is uncontestable and improper commitment is rare. An underlying thesis of the study is that family members play a central role in the commitment process and that persons without family resources are less likely to get committed than those with family resources. A major reason for this difference is that the sanctions against a negligent commitment petition rarely prevent family members from acting but do prevent other individuals and community officials (Rock et al., 1968, 86). For example, in Chicago, admission requires that a petition be presented. However, Rock et al., (1968, 89) found that

> almost without exception the (police) officer will refuse to be the petitioner. If a member of the individual's family has accompanied the police officer, or one can be summoned, he will be urged to file the petition. But if the search for a petitioner is unsuccessful, the mentally ill person will be refused admission.

Similarly they found that most social agencies avoided getting involved in the hospitalization process (e.g., Rock et al., 1968, 110). As Rock et al. (1968, 178–79) state, the inflexibility of the admission procedures and the unwillingness of officials to act in the absence of relatives "is perhaps more easily illustrated than described"; and they present a case they had observed of a man who entered the admission room of a mental health clinic. The man said he "wanted to be admitted." When it evolved that he had a letter from his physician recommending hospitalization but had no relative who could sign for him, he was told "no one is admitted without someone to sign for him."[15]

In short, the bulk of the American Bar Association study appears to support the psychiatric perspective. However, there is some evidence that the processes pointed to by the societal reaction theorists are also in operation. For example, Rock et al. (1968,112) found that if a person's relatives refused to sign a petition for him, he was even less likely to be hospitalized than a person with no relatives.[16]

Turning to the issue of the patient's path to the hospital, the literature consistently indicates that persons who occupy a critical position in the family, generally as indicated by marriage, are more likely to be hospitalized and are hospitalized more quickly than persons not in such a role. For example, Hammer (1963–64, 247) in a study of hospitalized patients found that of 19 persons having critical positions in the family, 17 were hospitalized within a year of the first manifestation of symptoms; whereas of the 36 persons who occupied noncritical positions, only 4 were hospitalized within the year following the first manifestation of symptoms. Similar, if less dramatic differences, were found by Linn (1961, 98). Studies of rehospitalization also consistently suggest that the possession of family resources is positively related to rehospitalization and to the speed with which it occurs (Brown et al., 1963; Freeman and Simmons, 1958, 1963, 94, 97; Angrist et al., 1968, 97; Myers and Bean, 1968, 45).

We have divided our patients into three marital categories, those who are married, those whose marriages have been disrupted (the divorced, separated, and widowed), and those who have never married. We would argue, as does Rushing (1971), that the married have the most social resources and the single the fewest, with those in the disrupted category falling in between. Table 11-5 presents the relationship between marital status and the duration of symptoms for the patients in the present study. The data show a strong negative relationship between marital status and a lifelong history of psychiatric abnormality. Fur-

---

15. If commitment proceedings are more frequently and easily initiated when family members are involved, the prospective patient of family-initiated petitions would tend to be less disturbed than prospective patients of non-family-initiated petitions. This would explain the finding that the courts are more likely to reject family-initiated petitions than non-family-initiated petitions (Haney and Michielutte, 1968:239).

16. In our view these processes as described by Rock et al. (1968) appear to be quite secondary. However, we would note that Rushing (1971) has cited Rock et al. and Wade (1966)—which in a slightly revised form comprises chapter 6 in Rock—in several places as supporting the societal reaction perspective; and it is apparent that Rushing feels the Bar study is more supportive of that perspective than we do. We would recommend that the reader look at Rock et al. and judge for himself.

thermore, there is a fairly strong negative relationship between marital status and the duration of psychotic symptoms, but there is no relationship between marital status and the time the first symptoms of the episode precipitating hospitalization appeared. Thus these data provide general although not uniform support for the psychiatric perspective.

Table 11–5   Characteristics of Patients and the Duration between the Onset of Symptoms and Hospitalization by Marital Status (in percentages)

Duration	Marital Status Single		Disrupted		Married		Gamma	p
Record presents patient as never psychiatrically "normal."	71.4	(35)	51.0	(49)	32.5	(169)	−.50	<.001
First symptoms of episode precipitating hospitalization occurred more than one year before hospitalization.	34.4	(47)	55.3	(47)	44.8	(163)	.01	>.2
Persons diagnoses as psychotic whose psychotic episode lasted more than one month before hospitalization.	71.4	(31)	48.4	(31)	41.2	(102)	−.34	<.02

Table 11–6   Agents Who Helped Initiate Hospitalization by Marital Status (in percentages)

	Marital Status			Gamma	p
	Single	Disrupted	Married		
A. Relationship to patient of persons in the community.					
1. Close					
Patient	44.1	41.7	65.1	.38	.001
Spouse	—	5.3	73.8	—	—
2. Distant					
"Other" relatives	67.6	54.2	21.5	−.65	.001
"Other" unrelated individuals	17.6	25.0	7.6	−.45	.001
B. Relationship to patient of professionals and community officials.					
1. Close					
Family M.D.	20.6	27.1	48.8	.47	.001
Psychiatrist	14.7	10.4	16.9	.15	.2
2. Distant					
Community agency	5.9	14.6	5.2	−.28	.2
Police	32.4	18.8	9.3	−.50	.001
Total number of cases	34.0	48.0	172.0		

Table 11-6 presents the relationship between marital status and the agents who played a role in initiating hospitalization. As the psychiatric perspective suggests, there is a positive relationship between marital status and hospitalization being initiated by someone close to the patient.

Table 11-7 Patient Symptoms, by Marital Status (in percentages)

Marital Status	Not Significantly Present	Mild	Moderate	Severe	Present	n	Gamma
		Distress					
Single	28.6	34.3	31.4	5.7		35	
Disrupted	29.2	27.1	27.2	14.6		48	.31
Married	17.2	14.4	55.2	13.2		174	p<.001
		Disorganization					
Single	25.7	22.9	31.4	20.0		35	
Disrupted	30.6	14.3	30.6	24.5		49	−.21
Married	42.5	16.7	26.4	14.4		174	p<.02
		Disruptive Acts					
Single	25.7				74.3	35	.50
Disrupted	44.9				55.1	49	p<.001
Married	64.4				35.6	174	

Type and Severity of Symptoms

An analysis of the symptoms of the patients in the present study shows a pattern similar to that associated with economic resources, with marital status being positively related to distress and negatively related to disorganization and disruptive acts (see Table 11-7). As before we combined these ratings in a manner which provides a measure of the severity of the patient's disorder. Our data, as Table 11-8 reveals, show a strong negative relationship between marital status and severity of disorder. These results closely parallel those of Turner et al. (1970), who found a strong negative relationship between marital status (married, pre-

Table 11-8 Type and Severity of Symptoms by Marital Status (in percentages)

Severity	Almost Nil	Mild	Moderate		Severe	n	Gamma*
Type of Symptom	"No Symptom"	Distress	Disorganized but not disruptive	Disruptive but not disorganized	Disorganized and disruptive		
Marital Status							
Single	0.0	8.6	17.1	17.1	57.1	35	.42
Disrupted	2.0	18.4	24.5	10.2	44.9	49	p<.001
Married	1.1	28.2	35.1	12.6	23.0	174	

* In computing gamma, the two "moderate" categories were combined.

viously married, single) and severity of pathology among schizophrenic patients (gamma = .47, p < .001 − gamma).

Conclusion

The literature and our data tend to support the psychiatric perspective regarding the role social resources play in hospitalization. This information closely parallels the information on class-related resources.

In our analysis we treated income and marital status as separate independent variables; however, in our data, they are strongly interrelated (gamma = .74, p<.001). We have therefore tried to determine whether marital status and income have effects that are independent of each other, or whether the apparent effect of one of these variables is due to its close relationship with the other. A systematic analysis shows that when one of the independent variables is used as a control, the relationship between the other independent variable and various dependent variables tends to diminish, but not to disappear. As an illustration, we have presented in Table 11−9 the relationship between marital status and the severity of symptoms controlling for income. In sum, our analysis suggests that, although the effects of marital status and income are confounded, both types of resources are important with both tending to facilitate the mental hospitalization of disturbed individuals.

Table 11−9 Type and Severity of Symptoms by Marital Status Controlling for Income (in percentages)

Severity	Almost Nil	Mild	Moderate		Severe	n	Gamma*
Type of Symptom	"No Symptom"	Distress	Disorganized but not disruptive	Disruptive but not disorganized	Disorganized and disruptive		
			Low Income				
Marital Status							
Single	0.0	4.0	16.0	16.0	64.0	25	.34
Disrupted	2.8	16.7	25.0	5.6	50.0	36	p<.01
Married	2.2	13.3	35.6	17.8	31.1	45	
			High Income				
Marital Status							
Single	0.0	22.2	22.2	22.2	33.3	9	.20
Disrupted	0.0	30.0	20.0	20.0	30.0	10	p<.02
Married	0.8	33.3	34.9	10.3	20.6	126	

* In computing gamma, the two "moderate" categories were combined.

In conclusion, the resources of the individual generally appear to facilitate entrance into psychiatric treatment, including mental hospitals. Thus the available data provide support for the psychiatric perspective,[17] a finding consistent with other research (Gove, 1970a, 1970b; Gove and Fain, 1973). In reaching this conclusion, we would emphasize that we are not implying that the processes pointed to by the societal reaction perspective do not exist, but only that in most cases they are overshadowed by the processes associated with the psychiatric model. Among other things, our conclusion indicates that, when severity of disorder is controlled for, married persons and persons from the upper classes are more likely to receive psychiatric treatment, including hospitalization, than persons who are either unmarried or from the lower class. This means that when official statistics are used to investigate the relationship between these social attributes and mental illness, the data will underestimate the rates of the lower class relative to the upper classes and the rates of the single as compared to the married.

References

Anderson, O. The utilization of health services. In H. E. Freeman, S. Levine, & L. G. Reeder (Eds.) Handbook of medical sociology. Englewood Cliffs, N.J.: Prentice-Hall, 1963, pp. 349–67.

Anderson, O., & Feldman, J. Family medical costs and voluntary health insurance: A nationwide survey. New York: McGraw-Hill, 1956.

Angrist, S., Lefton, M., Dinitz, S., & Pasamanick, B. Women after treatment: A study of former mental patients and their normal neighbors. New York: Appleton-Century-Crofts, 1968.

Antonovsky, A. Social class, life expectancy and overall mortality. In E. G. Jaco (Ed.) Patients, physicians and illness. New York: Collier-Macmillan, 1972, pp. 5–30.

Becker, H. Outsiders. New York: Free Press, 1963.

Brown, G. W., Monck, E. M., Carstairs, G. M., & King, J. K. Influence of family life on the course of schizophrenic illness. British Journal of Preventive and Social Medicine 16 (January) 1962: 55–66.

Costner, H., & Leik, R. Deductions from axiomatic theory. American Sociological Review 29 (December) 1964: 819–35.

Clancy, K. Systematic bias in field studies of mental illness. Ph.D. dissertation, New York University.

Dohrenwend, B., & Chin-Shong, E. Social status and attitudes toward psychological disorder: The problem of tolerence of deviance. American Sociological Review 32 (June) 1967: 417–33.

Dohrenwend, B., & Crandell, D. Psychiatric symptoms in community clinics and mental hospital groups. American Journal of Psychiatry 126 (May) 1970: 1116–21.

Dohrenwend, B., & Dohrenwend, B. Social status and psychological disorder. New York: Wiley, 1969.

---

17. One of our reviewers suggested that our results might be spurious, being a consequence of age and/or sex differences in the various patient categories. We have explored this possibility with all the relationships by computing partial gammas using age and sex as controls. The values of the partial gammas are virtually identical to those obtained at the zero order level. We can thus rule out the possibility that age and sex are important confounding variables.

Erikson, K. *Wayward puritans.* New York: Wiley, 1966.

Erikson, K. Notes on the sociology of deviance. *Social Problems 9* (Spring) 1962: 307–14.

Eyman, R., Dingman, H. F., & Sabagh, G. Association of characteristics of retarded patients and their families with speed of institutionalization. *American Journal of Deficiency 71* (July) 1966: 93–99.

Fisher, J. Negroes and whites and rates of mental illness: Reconsideration of a myth. *Psychiatry 32* (November) 1969: 428–46.

Freeman, H. E., & Simmons, O. Mental patients in the community: Family settings and performance levels. *American Sociological Review 23* (April) 1958: 147–54.

Freeman, H. E., & Simmons, O. Social class and past hospital performance levels. *American Sociological Review 24* (June) 1959: 345–51.

Freeman, H. E., & Simmons, O. *The mental patient comes home.* New York: Wiley, 1963.

Goffman, E. *Asylums: Essays on the social situation of mental patients and other inmates.* Garden City, N.Y.: Doubleday, 1961.

Gove, W. R. A theory of mental illness: An analysis of the relationship between symptoms, personality traits and social situations. Unpublished dissertation, University of Washington, 1968.

Gove, W. R. Societal reaction as an explanation of mental illness: An Evaluation. *American Sociological Review 35* (October) 1970 *a*: 873–84.

Gove, W. R. Who is hospitalized: A critical review of some sociological studies of mental illness. *Journal of Health and Social Behavior* (December) 1970*b*: 294–303.

Gove, W. R. Sleep deprivation: A cause of psychotic disorganization. *American Journal of Sociology 75* (March) 1970*c*: 782–99.

Gove, W. R. The relationship between sex roles, marital roles, and mental illness. *Social Forces* (November) 1972: 34–44.

Gove, W. R., & Fain, T. The stigma of mental hospitalization: An attempt to evaluate its consequences. *Archives of General Psychiatry 28* (April) 1973: 494–500.

Gove, W. R., & Luback, J. An intensive treatment program for psychiatric in-patients: A description and evaluation. *Journal of Health and Social Behavior 10* (September) 1969: 226–36.

Gurin, G., Veroff, J., & McEachern, A. *Americans view their mental health.* New York: Basic Books, 1960.

Haese, P., & Miele, R. The relative effectiveness of two models for the scoring of the Mid-town psychological disorder index. *Community Mental Health Journal 3* (Winter) 1967: 335–42.

Hammer, M. Influence of small social networks or factors on mental hospital admission. *Human Organization 22* (Winter) 1963–4: 243–51.

Haney, C., Michielutte, A., & Michielutte, R. Selective factors operating in the adjudication of incompetency. *Journal of Health and Social Behavior 9* (September) 1968: 233–42.

Hollingshead, A., & Redlich, F. *Social class and mental illness.* New York: Wiley, 1958.

Jaco, E. G. Attitudes toward and incidence of mental disorder: A research note. *The Southwest Social Science Quarterly 38* (June) 1957: 27–38.

Jones, N. F., & Kahn, M. W. Patient attitudes as related to social class and other variables concerned with hospitalization. *Journal of Consulting Psychology 28 (151)* 1964: 403–08.

Kitsuse, J. Societal reaction to deviant behavior: Problems of theory and method. *Social Problems 9* (Winter) 1962: 247–56.

Klots, A. *Mental illness and due process: A report and recommendation on admission to mental hospitals under New York law.* Ithaca, N.Y.: Cornell University Press, 1962.

Koos, E. L. *The health of Regionville.* New York: Columbia University Press, 1954.

Laing, R. D. *The divided self: An existential study in sanity and madness.* London: Penguin, 1960.

Laing, R. D. *The politics of experience.* New York: Ballantine, 1967.

Leighton, D., & Cline, N. *Use of a stress scale with mental patients.* Mimeograph, 1971.

Lemert, E. *Human deviance, social problems and social control.* Englewood Cliffs, N.J.: Prentice-Hall, 1967.

Linn, E. Agents, timing, and events leading to mental hospitalization. *Human Organization 20* (Summer) 1961: 92–98.

Linsky, A. Who shall be excluded: The influence of personal attributes in community reaction to the mentally ill. *Social Psychiatry 5* (July) 1970: 166–71.

Malzberg, B. Social and biological aspects of mental disease. New York State, Department of Mental Hygiene, 1940.

Manis, M., Houts, P., & Blake, J. Beliefs about mental illness as a function of psychiatric status and psychiatric hospitalization. *Journal of Abnormal and Social Psychology 67 (131)* 1963: 226–33.

Miele, R., & Haese, P. Social status, status incongruence and symptoms of stress. *Journal of Health and Social Behavior 10* (September) 1969: 237–44.

Miller, D., & Schwartz, M. County lunacy commission hearings: Some observations of commitments to a state mental hospital. *Social Problems 14* (Summer) 1966: 26–36.

Milt, H. *Basic handbook on mental illness.* Maplewood, N.J.: Scientific Aids Publications, 1969.

Myers, J., & Bean, L. *A decade later: A follow-up of social class and mental illness.* New York: Wiley, 1968.

Phillips, D. The 'true prevalence' of mental illness in a New England state community. *Community Mental Health Journal 2* (Spring) 1966: 35–40.

Phillips, D., & Clancy, K. Response biases in field studies of mental illness. *American Sociological Review 35* (June) 1970: 503–15.

Raphael, E., Howard, K., & Vernon, D. Social process and readmission to the mental hospital. *Social Problems 13* (Spring) 1966: 436–41.

Rey, J., Wilcox, D., Gibbons, J., Tart, H., & Lewis, D. Serial biochemical and endocrine investigations in recurrent mental illness. *Journal of Psychosomatic Research 5* (September-October) 1961: 155–69.

Rock, R., Jacobson, M., & Janopaul, R. *Hospitalization and discharge of the mentally ill.* Chicago: University of Chicago Press, 1968.

Rosenhan, D. L. On being sane in insane places. *Science, 179* (January) 1973: 250–58.

Rushing, W. Individual resources: Societal reactions and hospital commitment. *American Journal of Sociology 77* (November) 1971: 511–26.

Sabagh, G., Eyman, R., & Cogburn, D. The speed of hospitalization: A study of a preadmission waiting list cohort in a hospital for the retarded. *Social Problems 14* (Fall) 1966: 119–28.

Sabagh, G., Lei, T., & Eyman, R. The speed of hospitalization revisited: A replication of a study of a preadmission waiting list cohort in a hospital for the retarded. *Social Problems 19* (Winter) 1972: 373–82.

Sachar, E., MacKenzie, J., Binstock, & Meek, J. Corticosteroid response to psychotherapy of depression—I: Evaluations during confrontation of loss. *Archives of General Psychiatry 16* (April) 1967: 461–70.

Sachar, E., Mason, J., Kolmer, H., & Artiss, K. Psychoendocrine aspects of acute schizophrenic reaction. *Psychosomatic Medicine 25 (161)* 1963: 510–37.

Sarbin, T. R. Stimulus/response: Schizophrenia is a myth, born of metaphor, meaningless. *Psychology Today 6* (June) 1972: 18–27.

Schur, E. *Labeling deviant behavior: Its sociological implications.* New York: Harper & Row, 1971.

Schur, E. Reactions to deviance: A critical assessment. *American Journal of Sociology 75* (November) 1975: 309–22.

Schwartz, M., Mandell, A., Green, R., & Ferman, R. Mood, motility, and 17-hydrocorticoid excretion: A polyvariable case study. *British Journal of Psychiatry 112* (February) 1966: 149–56.

Shader, R., Ebert, M., & Harmatz, J. Lnagner's psychiatric impairment scale: A short screening device. *American Journal of Psychiatry 128* (November) 1971: 596–601.

Sheff, T. J. Being mentally ill. Chicago: Aldine, 1966.

Szasz, T. *The myth of mental illness: Foundations of a theory of personal conduct.* New York: Hoeber-Harper, 1961.

Szasz, T. *The manufacture of madness: A comparative study of the Inquisition and the mental health movement.* New York: Harper & Row, 1970.

Turner, R. J., Raymond, J., Zabo, L., & Diamond, J. Field survey methods in psychiatry: The effects of sampling strategy upon findings in the research on schizophrenia. *Journal of Health and Social Behavior 10* (December) 1969: 289–97.

Turner, R. J., Dopkeen, L., Labreche, G. Mental status and schizophrenia: A study of incidence and outcome. *Journal of Abnormal Psychology 76* (August) 1970: 110–16.

Wade, A. Social agency participation in hospitalization for mental illness. *Social Service Review 40* (January) 1966: 27–43.

Williams, W. Class differences in the attitudes of psychiatric patients. *Social Problems 4* (December) 1957: 240–44.

Time for a Change: From Micro- to Macro-Sociological Concepts in Disability Research

12

HERBERT BYNDER
PETER KONG-MING NEW

With the recent publication of a major work in sociology (Safilios-Rothschild, 1970) on the "state of the arts in the sociology and social psychology of disability and rehabilitation," sociologists are again taking a second look at their own research in this area and assessing its worth. This volume essentially asks, in much the same manner as an earlier compendium (Sussman, 1966), whether after all these years of research by sociologists we are making any worthwhile contributions to the field of disability and rehabilitation. Put another way, the question could be broken into two segments: First, what sociological notions have been used to tackle the various problems that are present in disability? Second, have sociologists been able to "solve" any of these problems?

Possibly, more important, have sociologists been asking the right questions? In recent years, one group of sociologists (Haber and Smith, 1971; Krause, 1973; Sussman, 1973) seem to feel that we are falling far short of the goal. While it is impossible to review all of the recent publications, the purpose of this paper is to examine to what extent sociologists have utilized various concepts to analyze some crucial issues in disability. The argument that we put forward for consideration is that sociologists seem to be mired in a number of limited concepts (even though they claim and indeed are working within broader frameworks) and this prevents them from viewing and making statements regarding the broader con-

This paper was presented at the American Psychological Association meetings (Division 22), Montreal, P.Q., Canada, August 27, 1973.

From *Journal of Health and Social Behavior 17* (March 1976): 45–52. Copyright 1976, American Sociological Association. Reprinted with permission.

sequences of disabilities, including the antecedent conditions which bring about disability.

In order to discover for the preparation of this paper what sociologists themselves feel are some of the shortcomings in the present use of concepts, we sent a two-page questionaire to approximately 100 sociologists and psychologists who are engaged in research in disability. Questions were asked in four areas: (1) What sociological concepts are most frequently used? (2) What concepts are most neglected? (3) What policy issues in disability should be explored, and (4) What support do you receive from your colleagues administration in disability research? In addition, we asked our colleagues to list one study that they feel best represents their work, and if they had any reprints of that study, to enclose it. Thirty-five responded and about 20 mailed us reprints. Considering that approximately 25 of those on the basic Sociology ASA Disability Section list are psychologists or are working mainly in psychological areas, the response rate is not discouraging. For those who responded, many wrote long and thoughtful answers. Although some may consider reporting on what a few said is not worth a paper, we nevertheless feel that their views are extremely important in our consideration of the shifts that are need to take place for investigators who are using sociological concepts to study disability. Some of these shifts are already beginning to emerge in the sociological literature.

In addition to the questionnaires and reprints, we were fortunate to receive copies of papers given at a disability conference held in Chicago, under the auspices of the Rehabilitation Institute of Chicago, "Socialization in the Disability Process," March 5–6, 1973. The above materials were supplemented by our review of other recent articles related to disability.

The purpose of this paper is not to present an inventory of research findings that have contributed to the body of work in the sociology of disability culled from the above mentioned materials. Four major works have already reviewed this literature (Safilios-Rothschild, 1970; Litman, 1972; Haber and Smith, 1971; and Nagi, 1969). Nor are we merely interested in listing useful and neglected concepts and ideas in disability research. Rather, the purpose of this paper is to illustrate the shortcomings of much of the current conceptual frameworks used in this research and to indicate both the need and the direction of the type of conceptual change that we feel will result in more significant research in the sociology of disability and in its practical applications. In the following pages we will use the framework of the questionnaire to organize our discussion, supplemented by other published and nonpublished materials, to illustrate the type of conceptual change needed and already beginning to be found in the writings of some sociologists in the area of disability.

Useful Concepts

When respondents were asked to name some of the sociological concepts that are most useful in research on disability, just about every conceivable general sociology concept was given: role theory, sick role, career, stigma, cultural beliefs, values, norms, definitions of the situations, and many others. The reprints sent to us, as well as the other articles we have reviewed, reflect the wide choice of concepts utilized in their research (e.g., Bolton and Sommer, 1970; Croog et al., 1972; Hyman, 1972; Litman, 1962; Ludwig and Adams, 1968; Ludwig and Gibson, 1969; Maddox et al., 1968; Richardson, 1969; Tittle, 1972; and Williams, 1971). In addition, epidemiological studies also have been done within the social psychological framework (e.g., Graham, 1972; Graham and Reeder, 1972; Wan, 1971, 1972, 1973; and Wan and Tarver, 1972). After reviewing some of the papers, it became evident that certain favorite concepts emerged: sick role and deviance or deviance-avowal/disavowal. Full obeisances are always paid to Goffman (stigma, labeling) and to Parsons, Freidson, and a few others. There can be no argument that Goffman and others indeed were pioneers in introducing the concepts of deviance and stigma to sociologists. However, we wonder if the followers are now relying on those few concepts a little too much as crutches to explain disability. Thus, whenever findings are reported, and not much more can be made of their significances, we immediately turn to Goffman and others to write a few more paragraphs.

The limitations of many of these so-called useful concepts are illustrated in an article by Haber and Smith (1971,95):

> disability behavior, or impairment, or disfigurement may be accompanied by stigma. . . Stigmatization does not imply nor does it require deviance. . . . Any perceived disparity of status or capacity may produce stigmatization. The acceptance of disability and the extension of role maintenance mechanisms do not restore the incapacitated individual to full use of his resources nor to full access to the social and economic advantages of capacity. The denigration of minority groups, the disabled, and other socially disadvantaged persons may be accounted for by the perceived limitations in their social capacities, rather than by violations of valued norms. It is also possible that there are no exemptions for incapacity in such areas as aesthetic norms.

Some of the papers we reviewed show that even though investigators are dealing with standard sociological concepts, they have analyzed them in macrosociological terms. For instance, Goldiamond (1973) analyzed his own illness within the structural framework of the rehabilitation hospital. Cogswell (1973) begins her discussion of family structural constraints by using frameworks from two novels dealing with family dynamics. Birenbaum (1970) discusses the effects of stigma within the family group. Haber (1970) suggests the devaluation of capacities of older men within the societal structure.

In general, most of the studies are reported within the medical framework: How can physicians and rehabilitation workers benefit by the findings and understand the sociological concepts that are at work to help or hinder the rehabilitation process? Useful concepts such as sick role and deviance fit into the medical model because it helps explain to the rehabilitation personnel why a person's rehabilitation is progressing or is being hindered. Sick role and deviance are among those sociological concepts easily grasped by the rehabilitation workers. Sociologists, eager to please, find acceptance, and demonstrate relevance for their discipline, are only too eager to utilize these concepts in study after study.

What we can imply from these studies is that sociologists in rehabilitation settings see themselves as therapists who aid the physician and other rehabilitation workers in making the proper "sociological diagnosis." What must be questioned, unfortunately, is the utility behind this approach. Is there really any evidence that they have contributed to the sociological enterprise, and as "therapists" how helpful have their analyses been to the practical details of the rehabilitation process? Haber and Smith (1971,95) indicate that, at the least, the usefulness of these concepts is limited, perhaps even inappropriate:

> We have . . . attempted to examine sick role and deviant behavior as alternative models or approaches to the concept of disability. The sick role directs attention away from the crucial element of legitimation of incapacity and introduces normative constraints which appear neither necessary nor appropriate to chronic disease and prolonged incapacity. By relating disability to the structure of existing normative relationships and the development of contingency norms, the adaptive response process avoids many of the conceptual problems raised by the sick role.

Concepts Neglected

When the question is asked of what concepts are neglected, two interesting themes emerge. First, sociologists take a 180-degree turn. Instead of supplying the usual cookbook list of sociological concepts, they now deal with the broader issues of the causes of disability and its consequences. What we find emerging in the answers to these questions is the need for structural analysis of macrosociological concepts. Consider, for instance, the following responses:

> There seems to have been little attention given to the socioeconomic factors on the disability process, particularly on the relationship between social and economic resources and outcome of the disability conditions. We need to know the relative effect of social factors in explaining the variances between those with disability conditions and those who become handicapped by the conditions. The deviance approach is too limited (J. Ivan Williams).

> All concepts implying a developmental, historical perspective on conceptions about disability and programmatic practices. The history of disability is critical to understanding the contemporary situation and this has been completely ignored (R.A. Scott).

> *Personal:* control orientation (internal vs. external locals of control and its relation to disability outcomes).

> *Interpersonal:* mechanisms of resource utilization-interpersonal support and resources utilized, e.g., informal-solo; informal-group (family and self-help groups); formal-agency.

Societal structural:(a) stages of family and personal life cycles; (b) socio-legal constructs in policy sciences and their relation to structural features (program systems) and distribution of needs in the population (Richard T. Smith).

In reviewing some of the reprints that respondents sent to us, the following may be cited as an example of a concern for the broader issues:

The power of social control agencies to sanction lies, to a large extent, in their ability to confer or deny legitimacy to behavior. Three stages may be identified in the process of normalizing incapacity:

1. Recognition of a change in behavior as a role—relevant failure of performance;
2. Attribution of responsibility for incapacity to a condition or impairment beyond the control of the individual;
3. Legitimation of the performance failure by an appropriate agent of social control (Haber and Smith, 1971, 90–91).

What they and others (especially Scott, 1970) are saying is that concepts in micro-sociology are limiting and perhaps misleading and even deluding sociologists into thinking that they can help solve the problems of the disabled. It is quite possible that not only the disabled, but even the rehabilitation workers, do not benefit by knowing about the deviance and stigmatization of the disabled. Instead, if we knew more about the conditions and constraints in society relevant to the disabled, to the professional, and to the rehabilitation process itself, the impact may be greater on the successful rehabilitation of the disabled. Unfortunately, the questionnaire indicates that most of the respondents do not consider macro-sociological analysis a neglected area.

Policy

In one of the questions asked of the respondents, we attempted to learn of the type of disability research sociologists feel should be undertaken in relation to policy issues. One major issue that emerged related to the impact of social structure on disability. Examples from two respondents illustrate this point:

The issues are political-structural. They have to do with the means by which definitions and consequences of control are derived and applied, e.g., Cloward's and Ryan's work on regulating the poor and blaming the victim (Peter Manning).

Research which places contemporary policy into its proper historical perspective. I rate this first because, as in sex, all of the basic possibilities were worked out long ago. Yet, today we treat discussions of our approaches to disabilities, as if they are new (R.A. Scott).

On this score, we point to Scott (1970) as one of the few in disability who was willing to ask some difficult and embarrassing questions regarding the social organization of the blind. He shows quite convincingly that once blind persons fall into the clutches of any blind organization, they will become more dependent rather than less dependent. Success of the blind organizations hinges on the fact that the blind are willing to follow the dictates of the blind organizations. Thus, if sociologists continue to study success and failure patterns of the disabled, based on the organization's criteria, nothing more can be gained in the way of understanding the system. One needs to ask first whether organization is perpetuating dependency or fostering myths about their good work (Stanton, 1971). One may even need to raise the question whether these organizations should be around. The few disabled who are able to escape the grasp of these organizations may be the fortunate ones.

A few of the respondents dealt with problems of measuring social disability. According to these respondents, without adequate measurement, policy questions cannot be answered. We recognize that studies dealing with policies are difficult to mount and even more difficult to evaluate (Caro, 1971; Rossi and Williams, 1972). What is so significant is that questions of measurement were raised only in respect to policy issues and that in asking about useful as well as neglected concepts in disability, no mention was made about methodological problems.

A number of respondents suggested that the entire economic structure of disability needs to be examined more fully. They have raised the question of cost-benefit to policy issues. Although research on costs tend to be within the province of other disciplines, the economic consequences to the disabled are certainly within the scope of sociological analysis. Because of the lack of concern by sociologists, this type of analysis has been taken over by economists with a different human perspective. We feel that sociological cost-benefit analysis would undoubtedly point out alternative approaches to the consequences in disability (Haber, 1964).

The politics of disability is another policy issue raised by some of the respondents. Krause (1973) has been discussing the implication of politics on disability for years: yet his voice was not heard and seldom understood. Even with the ferment of citizen participation and grass-roots decision, and involvement of community residents in rehabilitation settings, most sociologists have tended to neglect these important areas. However, now the establishment are joining this lone voice (Sussman, 1972; Safilios-Rothschild, 1973; Smith, 1973).

The significance of the study of the politics of disability by sociologists can be illustrated by analyzing the consequences of federal cuts in rehabilitation monies. When federal funding slackens, then it does not matter whether Mr. Brown or Mrs. Jones are "deviant" or not, they are not going to be treated. The more limited sociopsychological concepts in sociology cannot compete adequately with the more macro-structural concepts that occur on policy levels.

Support

To the extent that the policy issues are concerned with research having practical applications, it is no wonder that many of the respondents feel that their own sociological colleagues are not giving sufficient support to their work in the disability area. What we find here is a common experience of sociologists working in health settings. The bulk of sociologists do not see the relevance of research in disability, because they still disdain those who enter into the "applied" field. The respondents feel that their medical rehabilitation colleagues are the ones who find some of their findings more interesting. We would have thought that by now, sociologists would have eschewed the pure vs. applied quarrel; yet, this is not the case, as one of our respondents so clearly stated:

> Most reprint requests for a theoretical paper in *Social Forces* several years ago came from doctors. I still get them, along with favorable comments. This has surprised me. Sociologists have ignored my work, though I see it referred to in other disciplines (Clarice Stoll).

Basically, sociologists in disability research fall into three categories: those who are doing research only in disability, those who do other types of research as well, and those whose secondary interest is in disability. When one couples this with the fact that some sociologists are in university/disability or rehabilitation settings and those who are in university/nondisability settings, plus a small group who are in purely disability settings, the types of support varies. It is those who are in strictly rehabilitation settings and who must have their support from nonsociologists who are making key decisions regarding the types of research that are seen as legitimate. The fortunate few who have become "autonomous," that is, they can obtain the funds and do the research they would like, state that they have excellent support, but the "hired hands" have to seek the support from their sociological or nonsociological colleagues. The latter mention that at best their support is neutral, but they are seeing some shifts to positive support. Of course, a great part of their support depends on the types of research they are doing. In the next section, we deal more concretely with the research questions that are being raised.

Policy, Social Control, and Deviance

As we have stated earlier, most of the research by sociologists falls into socio-psychological micro-analyses. Yet, rehabilitation and disability must be viewed in the larger framework of systems, institutions and their policies. In a recent polemical but thoughtful statement, Krause (1973, 20–21) illustrates precisely this point:

> The theme of "who benefits" comes constantly into focus. Those who have

interests defend them by manipulating the definition process, by avoiding responsibilities for the conditions which produce disability, by fighting the disabled for compensation, and by either diverting money away from service programs or using them in a parasitic manner for organizational aggrandizement and simple profit making. The overall social system within which this takes place is the corporate-state capitalism within a nation with a withered political process and a co-opted Executive branch working for the groups that have ... produced the conditions (of inequity). To talk about minor reforms of this system is to be impossibly naive ... As to whether another form of political-economic system could handle this area better, the answer is both obvious and irrelevant. Of course it could and does ... But that means political-economic change either by revolution or a long evolutionary political struggle.

One of the shortcomings of sociologists working in the area of disability is their tendency to accept the medical model as the legitimate framework upon which to build their research. As a result, it is not uncommon for sociologists to accept the rehabilitation counselor's definition of successful rehabilitation, and proceed to confirm the latter's results. In effect, they are not questioning the obvious, and are abdicating one of the sociologists' main roles, i.e., the examination of latent structures and functions and their consequences.

Above and beyond this, there is very little attempt on the part of sociologists to undertake policy research or policy analysis. We hasten to add that we view policy research and analysis as different from making policy pronouncements. As we have stated earlier, when funds are no longer present, it does not matter much whether a disabled person has "deviant" characteristics. He is not going to be treated. It is imperative that sociologists undertake more macro-research so that they would understand what are the rules and norms that govern funding, for instance. Then when funding does become available, sociologists can have better ideas of how and where funds could be applied.

Of course, policy research does not necessarily mean that all sociologists need to look at the federal policies only. There are other policy issues that are equally germane, at the local agency or hospital levels, for example. For instance, what are the forces that create disproportionate numbers of mental retardates in certain segments of our population? We recognize that mental retardation at least in part is the result of genetic and other physiological factors. However, there are undoubtedly certain conditions relating to the organization and implementation of retardation policy that help foster more retardation in certain groups. These ought to be investigated.

At the social control level, so many more questions of the types that Scott (1970) and Haber and Smith (1971) have been posing need to be answered in all sectors of disability and rehabilitation settings. Roth and Eddy (1967) have also generated a series of questions regarding the rehabilitation hospital. What are the social control mechanisms that are present? What happens to patients who are compliant to the system and others who balk at the system? Who gets the "goodies"? Haug and Sussman (1969), among others, have cautioned us that consumers are not sitting quietly anymore. In essence, they have all echoed what Krause (1968 and 1973) has been saying for some years: Possibly, the politics of disability management have been allowed to operate and function without anyone challenging their governing principles.

Conclusion

Throughout the history of the involvement of sociology within medical disciplines, sociological literature has discussed time and time again the question of acceptance or nonacceptance. Because of the different patterns of training of physicians and sociologists, one practical and interventionist and the other theoretical and academic, almost all the work that has been done by sociologists since World War II has met only limited acceptance. It is not an uncommon theme in the medical sociology section of the ASA to hear this question of acceptance and role identity still being discussed.

The sociologist, often the low man on the totem pole, has frequently attempted to gain acceptance by modeling his own role after that of the therapist. By this we mean that his research too often has been directed to creating, developing, and expanding sociological concepts that have explanatory power—not so much in terms of sociological concepts and theories, but more in line with providing physicians with practical answers as to why the patient does not get better even though all medical knowledge and technology indicate that the patient *should* be well or rehabilitated or back on the job.

We think that this has been particularly evident in the area of the sociology of disability where an overabundance of terms such as sick role and deviance have been used loosely to explain the behavior of patients that do not fit the medical norm. In a sense, then, whether the sociologist in these settings realize it or not, they are contributing a sociological diagnosis to the other diagnoses made by other members of the rehabilitation team. The question that we raise is whether these diagnoses make any difference whatsoever on the outcome of the disability process.

This is not to say that all sociologists working in these settings and utilizing these concepts see their role as the sociologist-therapist. Most probably do not. However, to state the case differently, what we can point out is that by using terms such as sick role and deviance, attitudes, beliefs, and interpersonal relations, the sociologist has been working in an area that we can call micro-sociological analysis and is basically social psychology rather than sociology. It is our conclusion and it seems to be documented both by answers to the second question (i.e., what are the neglected concepts in disability research?) and by a few of the recent articles in papers in sociology of disability (e.g., Krause, 1973; Safilios-Rothschild, 1973; Sussman, 1973) that a more meaningful approach to the sociology of disability lies in the macro-sociological structural analysis of various institutions and how they impinge directly or indirectly on the disabled, their families, and the professionals who work in the rehabilitation field.

References

Birenbaum, A. On managing a courtesy stigma. *Journal of Health and Social Behavior 11* 1970: 196–207.

Bolton, B. & Sommer, P. Mode of address and patient satisfaction in rehabilitation: An experimental study. *Journal of Health and Social Behavior 11* 1970: 215–19.

Care, F. G. (Ed.) *Readings in evaluation research.* New York: Russell Sage, 1971.

Cogswell, B. Family response to disability. *Paper presented at a Conference on Socialization in the Disability Process.* March 5–6, Chicago.

Croog, S. H., Lipson, A., & Levine, S. Help patterns in severe illness: The roles of kin network, nonfamily resources, and institutions. *Journal of Marriage and the Family 34* 1972: 32–41.

Goldiamond, I. Coping and adaptive behavior of the disabled. *Paper presented at a Conference on Socialization in the Disability Process.* March 5–6, Chicago.

Graham, S. Cancer, culture, and social structure. In E. G. Jaco (Ed.) *Patients, physicians, and illness.* New York: Free Press, 1972, pp. 31–39.

Graham, S. & Reeder, L. G. Social factors in the chronic illnesses. In H. E. Freeman, S. Levine, and L. G. Reeder (Eds.) *Handbook of medical sociology.* Englewood Cliffs, N.J.: Prentice-Hall, 1972, pp. 63–107.

Haber, L. D., Some problems of research in disability. In G. Gordon (Ed.) *Proceedings of Conference on Medical Sociology and Disease Control.* Chicago: University of Chicago, Graduate School of Business, 1964, pp. 19–25.

Haber, L. D. Age and capacity of evaluation. *Journal of Health and Social Behavior 11* 1970: 167–83.

Haber, L. D. & Smith, R. T. Disability and deviance: Normative adaptations of role behavior. *American Sociological Review 36* 1971: 87–97.

Haug, M. R. & Sussman, M. B. Professional autonomy and the revolt of the client. *Social Problems 17* 1969: 153–61.

Hyman, M. D. Sociopsychological obstacles to L-Dopa therapy that may limit effectiveness in Parkinsonism. *Journal of the American Geriatrics Society 20* 1972: 200–08.

Krause, E. A. Functions of a bureaucratic ideology: Citizen participation. *Social Problems 16* 1968: 129–43.

Krause, E. A. The political sociology of rehabilitation. *Paper presented at the Conference on Socialization in the Disability process.* March 5–6. Chicago.

Litman, T. J. The influences of self conception and life orientation factors in the rehabilitation of the orthopedically disabled. *Journal of Health and Human Behavior 3* 1962: 249–57.

Litman, T. J. Physical rehabilitation: A social-psychological approach. In E. G. Jaco (Ed.) *Patients, physicians, and illness.* New York: Free Press, 1972, pp. 186–203.

Ludwig, E. G. & Adams, S. D. Patient cooperation in a rehabilitation center: Assumptions of the client role. *Journal of Health and Social Behavior 9* 1968: 328–35.

Ludwig, E. G. & Gibson, G. Self perception of sickness and the seeking of medical care. *Journal of Health and Social Behavior 10* 1969: 125–33.

Maddox, G. L., Back, K. W., & Liederman, V. R. Overweight as social deviance and disability. *Journal of Health and Social Behavior 9* 1968: 287–98.

Nage, S. Z. *Disability and rehabilitation.* Columbus: Ohio State University Press, 1969.

Reeder, L. G. The patient-client as a consumer: Some observations on the changing professional-client relationship. *Journal of Health and Social Behavior 13* 1972: 406–12.

Richardson, S. A. The effect of physical disability of the socialization of a child. In D. A. Goslin (Ed.) *Handbook of Socialization, Theory, and Research.* Chicago: Rand McNally, 1969, pp. 1047–64.

Rossi, P. & Williams, W. (Eds.) *Evaluating social programs: Theory, practice, and politics.* New York: New York University Press, 1972.

Roth, J. A. & Eddy, E. M. *Rehabilitation for the unwanted.* New York: Atherton, 1967.

Safilios-Rothschild, C. *Sociology and social psychology of disability and rehabilitation.* New York: Random House, 1970.

Safilios-Rothschild, C. The disabled persons' self-definitions and implications for rehabilitation. *Paper presented at the Conference on Socialization in the Disablity Process.* March 5–6, Chicago.

Scott, R. *The making of the blind.* New York: Russell Sage, 1970.

Smith, R. T. Health and rehabilitation manpower strategy: New careers and the role of the indigenous paraprofessional. *Social Science and Medicine 7* 1973: 281–90.

Stanton, E. *The clients come last.* San Francisco: Sage, 1971.

Sussman, M. B. (Ed.) *Sociology and rehabilitation.* Washington, D.C.: American Sociological Association, 1966.

Sussman, M. B. A policy perspective on the United States rehabilitation system. *Journal of Health and Social Behavior 13* 1972: 152–61.

Sussman, M. B. The disabled and the rehabilitation system. *Paper presented at the Conference on Socialization in the Disability Process.* March 5–6, Chicago.

Tittle, C. R. Institutional living and rehabilitation. *Journal of Health and Social Behavior 13* 1972: 263–75.

Wan, T. H. Status stress and morbidity: A sociological investigation of selected categories of work-limiting chronic conditions. *Journal of Chronic Diseases 24* 1971: 453–68.

Wan, T. H. Social differentials in selected work-limiting chronic conditions. *Journal of Chronic Diseases 25* 1972: 365–74.

Wan, T. H. Effects of social epidemiological factors on the severity for the white and nonwhite disabled. *Paper presented at the American Sociological Association meetings.* August 1973, New York.

Wan, T. H. & Tarver, J. D. Socioeconomic status, migration and morbidity. *Social Biology 19* 1972: 51–59.

Williams, J. I. Disease as deviance. *Social Science and Medicine 5* 1971: 219–26.

Deviants as Active Participants in the Labeling Process: The Visibly Handicapped

TERESA E. LEVITIN

> What is a handicap in social terms? It is an imputation of difference from others; more particularly, imputation of an *undesirable* difference. By definition, then a person said to be handicapped is so defined because he deviates from what he himself or others believe to be normal or appropriate.
>
> (Freidson, 1965,72)

Much of the literature of the last 15 years on social deviance has been written from a labeling perspective (Becker, 1963; Cicourel, 1968; Erikson, 1962; Gibbs, 1966; Kitsuse, 1962, 1972; Kitsuse and Cicourel, 1963; Lemert, 1951; Scheff, 1966; Schur, 1965). This perspective emphasizes the process by which actors become defined and treated as deviant. Since social norms are seen as problematic and no behavior is assumed to be inherently deviant, definitions of deviance vary with the actors who are observing and defining the activities. Indeed, the unique contribution of this perspective has been to assume that reactions to behavior, rather than any behavior itself, identify and define that which is deviant.

The conceptualization of deviance as a process by which members of a group, community, or society (1) interpret certain behaviors as deviant, (2) label persons who so behave as a certain kind of deviant, and (3) accord them the treatment considered appropriate to such deviants has clarified the active role of conventional and conforming actors (Kitsuse, 1962). However, the role of the deviant in this process has often been understated or ignored entirely: those engaged in the deviant behavior tend to be presented as passive or reactive,

From *Social Problems,* Volume 24 (April) 1975:548–57. Copyright 1975, The Society for the Study of Social Problems. Reprinted with permission.

rather than as active agents in the labeling process. (See Filstead, 1972; or Rubington and Weinberg, 1968 for comprehensive collections of readings.)[1] Thus, when a leading exponent of the labeling perspective critically assesses it, he only suggests that "the self-conceptions of the deviating individual should be considered a crucial dependent variable, to which we should pay more attention than to the deviating behavior itself" (Schur, 1969,311). Might not the self-conceptions of the deviating individual also be considered a crucial *independent* variable?

The purpose here is to demonstrate that, indeed, those labeled deviant because of a physical handicap often take an active part in the labeling process; they initiate self-definitions; they insist that others define them in preferred ways, and the strategies they choose to negotiate and settle labeling issues vary with the social context in which such labeling occurs.[2]

Unstructured interviews with adults who had recently become physically handicapped through accident or illness were conducted over a several month period in the physical therapy waiting room of a large hospital. All respondents were outpatients who regularly came to the hospital for physical therapy; their handicaps ranged from the evident (loss of a limb) to the publicly invisible (mastectomy), from the permanent (paralysis) to the more temporary (whiplash). This paper focuses on those with evident or visible handicaps only. Since the author was undergoing physical therapy, problems in gaining cooperation were minimal.[3]

Physical Handicaps as a Type of Deviance

The label "deviant" and the associated devaluation of an actor thus labeled are applicable to the physically handicapped. In a society that values physical health and attractiveness, the handicapped are less than fully acceptable. From a labeling perspective what is problematic is not whether a handicap will, in general, be defined as a type of deviance, but, rather, how specific attempts to apply that deviant label and role are initiated either by the disabled or by the normal and are negotiated in interaction.

The terms physical handicap and disability are often interchangeably used (Meyers, 1965; Wright, 1960). In this study, both terms will refer to someone who perceives himself/herself and is perceived by others as unable to meet the demands or expectations of a particular situation because of some physical

---

1. Exceptions to this tendency may be found in the work of Davis, Goffman, Lorber, Matza, Sykes and Matza, and Williams and Weinberg.

2. As Turner has suggested, deviant labels refer to roles, not isolated acts. The label "heroin addicts," for example, has an elaborate set of roles ranging from, for many, thief to, for some, musician, associated with it. The label is a summary statement about a number of expected behaviors or roles, and will be used as such in this paper. See R. Turner, Deviance avowal as neutralization of commitment. *American Sociological Review 19* 1972: 308–21.

3. This paper does not deal with the profound pain—both psychological and physical—many respondents experienced and described. Of concern here is the more social fate of the handicapped.

impairment—i.e., an anatomical and/or a physiological abnormality. This definition is consonant with a labeling perspective: the concept handicapped has meaning only within a social context, when the expectations and demands of others are taken into account. The bound feet of a Chinese noblewoman were a physical impairment that prevented her from walking easily, but she was not, by this definition, physically handicapped.[4]

Many different ways of classifying physical handicaps have been utilized (Barker et al., 1953; Dembo, Leviton, and Wright, 1956; Freidson, 1965; Goffman, 1963; Lorber, 1967). Since a deviant role cannot be attributed until the act or state that violates social expectations is perceived, how evident the handicap is to others is a crucial classificatory dimension.[5]

Physiological impairments are not always immediately evident. Although hemophiliacs cannot participate in contact sports, they can carefully structure their social lives so that these impairments do not become widely known social facts. Other types of deviance may also be selectively hidden: no one at work may know that an employee is a homosexual, although it is known to friends. In short, those to whom the deviancy is evident may represent only a small segment of the deviant's social world. One limitation of the labeling perspective is that too little attention has been given to those arenas of life and to those subgroups where labeling as deviant does not occur because the deviant states or behaviors are not evident. In the case of the physically handicapped interviewed for this paper, however, the stigma was evident to friends, family, medical personnel, and the deviants themselves. For some, the permanently disabled, the impairment was irrevocable, in that prior social roles would never be filled as before. For others, the most temporarily disabled, there would be an eventual return to prior role expectations and obligations.

Two Different Types of Social Situations and Interaction Goals

Both the permanently and the more temporarily physically handicapped share a common concern. They do not want their deviance to become the keystone for definitions of themselves. They do not want others to believe and to act as

---

4. A physically handicapped person is not conceptually identical to a person with a physical handicap. The former phrase connotes an actor who cannot meet *any* expectations or demands (a most unlikely circumstance), while the latter suggests an actor with any number of characteristics, one of which is a physical handicap. The shorter phrase is easier to use and therefore will be employed here; but it is important to remember that even severe impairments, depending on the situation, may not be handicaps.

5. The labeling perspective has been criticized (see J. Gibbs, Conceptions of deviant behavior: The old and the new. *Pacific Sociological Review 9* 1966: 9–14 and J. Lorber, Deviance as performance: The case of illness. *Social Problems 14* 1967: 131–39) for the concept of "secret deviants" (see H. S. Becker, *Outsiders: Studies in the sociology of deviance.* New York: Free Press, 1963). Those who deviance has not been discovered. This conceptualization is a logical contradiction. Becker subsequently used the term "potentially deviant" to describe those engaged in activities likely to be defined as deviant by others (see H. S. Becker, Labeling theory reconsidered. *Preecedings of the British Sociological Association,* 1971).

though the deviant part of self is the entire self, obscuring other more positive, socially valued aspects of that self, no matter how evident or permanent the handicap may be. Yet, as a psychologist describing the physically handicapped notes, there is a tendency for judgments of "inferiority on one scale to spread to total inferiority of the person" (Wright 1960,8). Similarly, a sociologist points out that "when deviant roles are compared with other roles, the most striking difference lies in the extent to which the role is identified with the *person* rather than the *actor* (Turner 1972,312). Or in the more poignant words of an amputee: "I'm not just 'that person without legs;' I'm a whole person. I didn't lose my whole personality when I lost my legs; I just lost my legs." Goffman (1963,132–133) has noted that "the painfulness, then, of sudden stigmatization can come not from the individual's confusion about his identity, but from his knowing too well what he has become."

What one becomes is determined not only by others but also by the self. Denial that any change has occurred is folly; the handicap is too evident for persistent claims that one has not changed to be believed by anyone. Given the ineluctable imputation of some deviant identity and role, the challenge to the disabled is to establish a social identity that is more favorable than the identity of a totally devalued person and to obtain the most positive social statuses or outcomes possible. However, the temporarily and the permanently disabled differ in the kind of definition and elaboration they insist be given to their evident handicap. The definition of self that the temporarily handicapped actively promote is one that states "this deviance will *not always* be me." In contrast, the definition of self actively presented by the permanently handicapped is one that states "this deviance is *not all* of me."

Two different types of situations in which deviants asserted their preferred social labels and roles in interaction with normals were observed: sociable encounters and encounters with agents of social control, physical therapists.

Sociable encounters are those face-to-face contacts vividly described by Goffman (1959) in which actors who are relatively unknown to each other project definitions of themselves, and in which a "working consensus" about those definitions of self and the situation may or may not emerge. Davis (1961) has described face-to-face encounters that are somewhat but not too prolonged, friendly but not intimate, ritualized but not completely predictable as sociable encounters. P.T.A. meetings, business lunches, classrooms, professional conventions, parties, weddings, and airplane lounges are a few settings where sociable interaction occurs. The opportunities for informal, sociable contact between the physically handicapped and the normal are legion.

A second, and more limited, class of situations in which deviant and normal interact occurs because of the deviance itself. Since the purpose of these encounters is to treat or to reform or to punish the deviant, often regardless of the deviant's wishes, the normals can be seen as agents of social control. Different types of agents, often represented by different occupations, are involved in the detection, evaluation, and response to different types of deviance (Stoll 1968). Doctors, vocational therapists, nurses, social workers, and physical therapists are all agents of social control routinely encountered by the physically handicapped. Both as members of a larger society that values physical health and attractiveness and as professionals in a particular occupational role, such agents try to return the deviant as much as possible to former, valued social roles.

Sociable Encounters with the Permanently and the Temporarily Disabled

The social consequences of a physical handicap have been described in detail by Davis (1961), Goffman (1963), and Wright (1960). All agree that sociable encounters between the disabled and the normal are strained, inhibited, and uncomfortable for both parties because of uncertainty about how, if at all, the stigma ought to be acknowledged.

Davis (1961) postulates the mechanism of deviance disavowal as a way the handicapped can manage strained interaction with normals. If successful, this process permits the normal and the deviant to engage in open and spontaneous sociable interaction, for the obvious disability is recognized rather than denied, but not made central or disruptive to the encounter.

Davis's examples are primarily drawn from those who were visibly disabled by polio; and his concept of deviance disavowal is central to understanding how the permanently disabled handle social encounters. The more temporarily disabled, however, behave differently. Their visible stigma sets the stage for the same sort of strained and superficial interaction the permanently disabled face. Paradoxically, the temporarily handicapped tend to manage this interaction tension and project the definition of self they want accepted by *avowing* their deviance. Since their disability is evident but the prognosis is not, the temporarily handicapped are active, often aggressive, in making certain they are not given a label and role that has social consequences far more serious than those of a temporary stigma. It is not simply a matter of disavowing the label "permanently handicapped," but, rather, of trying to see that the normal has no opportunity even to contemplate such a label.

Even within a moment or two of meeting someone in a sociable encounter, the temporarily handicapped may avow their deviance. They may describe their accident or injury in great detail, provide unsolicited facts about their therapy, and note their prognosis.

Both politeness and curiosity usually keep the normal from trying to stop these avowal revelations. Thus, the deviant is able to continue to draw attention to his or her handicap, and it remains a central theme until the normal indicates acceptance of the identity the deviant is presenting and acknowledges the temporariness of the disability. A statement such as "Well, I'm glad you'll be OK again soon" is evidence that the desired message has been conveyed. Once the normal indicates belief in the temporariness of the evident physical handicap, the breaking through stage analogous to that in the deviance disavowal process has occurred.

The final stage of Davis's disavowal process, that of establishing a normalized relationship, also occurs in the avowal process; but the content of the normalized definition of self is different. Those who have successfully *disavowed* their deviance have communicated a definition of self that says this handicap is only a *small part* of who I am. Those who have successfully avowed their deviance have communicated a definition of self that says this handicap is only a *temporary part* of who I am.

There are many ways the evidently handicapped provide information about preferred definitions. The permanently disabled begin to use props to introduce an unblemished aspect of self. A book, a political button, a religious symbol are newly acquired cues to their other, more socially valued labels and roles. One patient said "I bring along my knitting. Someone's bound to ask what I'm making or I'll say 'I'm knitting a scarf' or whatever and then I'll talk about all my other hobbies too." In contrast, the temporarily handicapped begin to use props to call attention to their stigma. One patient painted "Houdini" on his wheelchair, a clever way of setting the stage for his explanation that it would soon disappear.

Several of the permanently disabled noted that they were now much more apt to ask normals about their interests and activities than before they were handicapped. Such probing sometimes seemed motivated less by a genuine interest in that other's life than by the deviant's own desire to find shared concerns that would say, in effect: since I can do a lot of the things you do, I am obviously more than this stigma.

Several of the temporarily disabled noted that they were now much more apt to ask normals about their past illnesses and injuries than before they were handicapped. Reminding normals either of their own temporary deviance or that of their friends and family would permit the handicapped to say, in effect: like you or others you have known, I am only temporarily handicapped. One respondent was shocked at discovering himself insisting on a discussion of such events at a formal dinner.

Deviants other than the physically handicapped also find that their deviant aspects or roles often become the central social facts used in defining and evaluating them. Someone labeled an alcoholic may find that many other accomplishments are evaluated with the preface, "for an alcoholic" or "despite his (her) alcoholism," even though these accomplishments might have been exactly the same if the person were not an alcoholic. An outstanding, positively evaluated quality may also be taken as the focal point for labeling and evaluating the entire person. The very beautiful and the very brilliant may be heard to lament the fact that no one attends to their "true selves." In terms of social evaluation the beauty is very different from the beast, but in terms of how those social labels dehumanize each, they are, indeed, similar.

In sum, it is usually the case that spontaneous and comfortable sociable interaction between normal and deviant will not occur unless and until labeling issues have been settled in ways palatable to the handicapped, unless and until the permanently handicapped have successfully disavowed and the temporarily handicapped have successfully avowed the meaning and content of their deviant label and role.

Encounters with Agents of Social Control

In contrast, a handicap is not a potential threat to interaction in physical therapy; rather, it is the reason for that encounter. Physical therapy, therefore, provides another type of social setting in which the handicapped actively shape the content and centrality of a deviant label and role.

In physical therapy situations, just as in sociable encounters, the handicapped do not want to be defined and evaluated only in terms of their deviance. Yet, both the avowal and disavowal strategies of sociable encounters are inappropriate to and incongruent with the demands and expectations of therapy: therapists need information about how their patients are responding to treatment; they expect patients to be willing to describe themselves fully in terms of their disabilities and to cooperate in making those disabilities the continuing focus of the encounter; the handicapped need the skillful ministrations of their therapists and must provide the information about their disabilities that is needed for the exercise of those therapeutic skills. Given both the inevitable symbiotic relationship and the different goals for the interaction, interesting patterns of accommodation between physical therapists and their temporarily and permanently disabled patients evolve.

Those defined as permanently handicapped by themselves and their therapists try to present a definition of self like the definition presented in sociable interactions, one that says this handicap is *not all* of who I am. To accomplish this interaction goal in therapy, the permanently disabled find ways of introducing information about untainted parts of themselves.

Those defined as temporarily handicapped by themselves and their therapists try to present a definition of self like the definition presented in sociable interaction, one that says this handicap will *not always* be who I am. To emphasize the temporary nature of that deviance, they often act as though they have already recovered. They try to change the encounter to one of interaction between two normals by encouraging their therapists to behave in a self-disclosing and nonprofessional manner, by altercasting them into the role of friend (Weinstein and Deutschberger, 1963, 1964).

In effect, the permanently handicapped communicate that they will be "good patients" for their therapists only if they also can be "whole human beings" to them. A few were quite explicit about their demands: one said that if he were treated like a piece of damaged meat, he would be goat's (i.e. tough) meat. Since the therapists themselves tend to speak in very general terms about dealing with patients in warm and compassionate ways and about treating the person, not just the disability, there is usually a receptivity or willingness to relate to patients as multifaceted people. But it is the permanently disabled themselves who tend to initiate the introduction of and to provide the content for these other nontainted or normal roles. The mechanisms are very similar to those used by the permanently handicapped in sociable situations: props begin to be used, conversations are initiated, and topics are doggedly pursued until recognition and legitimation from the therapist of these valued identities and roles are forthcoming.

Some patients arrange to have their family and friends pick them up, not in the hospital waiting room, but right in the physical therapy area itself, even though the waiting room is the designated area. Patients will engage their therapists and friends or family in conversation, often prolonging the encounter until the therapist has indicated adequate interest in and agreement with the patient's activities with family and friends. One patient brought in her photo album to show her therapist. Later that week, another patient brought in her album to share with her therapist, and others soon followed suit. Another patient brought in samples of products he merchandized, but he made his sales pitch only to his therapist, not to other patients or therapists who were also potential customers.

Occasionally the demands to be labeled as more valuable than one's presence in therapy might suggest were blatantly manipulative: a patient changed her therapist's tepid interest in hearing about her (the patient's) son's wedding by saying something about her previous therapist not being interested and not being a very good therapist either. The duration of that therapy session was devoted to a discussion of the wedding, and of examples of what a good mother the patient both was and continued to be, despite her permanent handicap.

It is with the temporarily handicapped, however, that serious problems in negotiating an identity acceptable to both therapist and patient are apt to occur, for the temporarily handicapped tend to insist on definitions unacceptable to the therapist. To emphasize that they will soon be well, and in anticipation of that time, they try to altercast the therapist into the role of friend, almost suggesting that they have already recovered, and are only in therapy because they enjoy sociable visits with their therapists. One patient even said that since he would not need to practice his exercises much longer, he would practice being a friend.

In order to induce their therapists to step out of their professional roles and disclose personal aspects of themselves, the temporarily handicapped may ask personal questions, inquiring about their therapists' families, asking how other patients are progressing, or generally presuming the kind of easy intimacy that occurs between people who are personally involved with each other. The therapists strongly resist these attempts at intimacy, believing that they cannot do their work properly if they become too involved with their patients. They insist that their patients must face their handicaps and deal with them realistically, however temporary those handicaps might be, and that therapy is the place where patients, however many other valued labels and roles they may have, are, ultimately, patients, not intimates. Thus, altercasting attempts are usually squelched: patients who invite their therapists to parties or to dinner find that their therapists neither accept these invitations nor ask them to their own homes. One respondent was "gravely wounded" when she found that she had not been invited to a shower her therapist had given for another therapist because, as she insisted, they should be "good friends." A patient who was told that the staff coffee room was off limits to him was perplexed, chagrined, and felt rejected.

Clearly there is more room for negotiation between patient and therapist than the formal structure of the hospital, norms, or roles suggest. Since the therapist's own successful performance depends, to some extent, on the cooperation of the patient, patients are able to negotiate from a position of some strength. Participation in therapy is voluntary, and the patient can, as a last resort, terminate contact with a therapist who is not adequately sympathetic. Indeed several patients mentioned that there had been a therapist so cold and unsympathetic to their needs that patients refused to deal with her. Her tenure at the hospital was brief.

It is primarily in the early stages of physical therapy that patients are most active in trying to define themselves in relation to their therapists. When the therapy is of long duration, the *modus vivendi* established usually seems to be the cordial but distant relationship preferred by the therapists, who are more experienced and more skilled than their patients in structuring the encounter in preferred ways. Since many of the temporarily handicapped need only a short period of therapy, tension and conflict rather than stable patterns of interaction and accommodation are more often observed.

Summary

The evidently disabled adults interviewed in this study recognized the devalued statuses their recent illness or injury had brought them, but they vigorously and systematically tried to influence the content of their deviant label and role in ways most favorable to themselves. A major social problem for the handicapped is that normals tend to organize their perceptions and evaluations around the disability and to ignore the handicapped's many valued aspects and identities. These handicapped actively resisted such a social fate, but their preferred definitions and strategies varied with the duration of the disability (temporary or more permanent) and the type of encounter (sociable encounters and encounters with agents of social control).

Trying to negotiate a preferred definition of self is limited neither to the handicapped nor to other types of deviants, though examples of their behaviors are the basis of this paper. To the contrary, the active bargaining for preferred definitions, the attempts to negotiate a situation to one's own advantage, the subtle, and not so subtle, processes through which people agree to become who they are to each other are among the most basic elements of social life (see for example, Carson, 1969; Emerson, 1969; Garfinkel, 1967; Goffman, 1959, 1963; McCall and Simmons, 1966; Shibutani, 1970). It is, however, instructive to examine how those apt to be labeled deviant initiate and direct these processes. In some sense, they have the most to lose. To be labeled as a particular kind of deviant may mean to incur a number of adverse consequences, such as punishment or isolation. Therefore, deviants in encounters with normals may be more active than normals encountering normals in trying to legitimate preferred definitions.

The physically handicapped, as one class of deviants, are particularly interesting. Since there is general agreement about the devalued status of a handicap, attention can be focused on the active ways in which such deviants assert themselves, even within the rather narrow range of choices or identities and roles that their handicap has left them. Attention to the active participation of the disabled in the labeling process provides a needed addition to the labeling perspective.

References

Barker, R., Wright, B., Myerson, L., & Gonick, M. *Adjustment to physical handicap and illness: A survey of the social psychology of physique and disability.* New York: Social Science Research, 1953.

Becker, H. S. *Outsiders: Studies in the sociology of deviance.* New York: Free Press, 1963.

Becker, H. S. Labeling theory reconsidered. *Preceedings of the British Sociological Association,* 1971.

Carson, R. C. *Interaction concepts of personality.* Chicago: Aldine, 1969.

Cicourel, A. *The social organization of juvenile justice.* New York: Wiley, 1968.

Davis, F. Deviance disavowal: The management of strained interaction by the visibly handicapped. *Social Problems 9* 1961: 120–32.

Dembo, T., Leviton, G., & Wright, B. Adjustment for misfortune—a problem of social-psychological rehabilitation. *Artificial Limbs 3* 1956: 4–62.

Emerson, J. Negotiating the serious import of humor. *Sociometry 32* 1969: 169–81.

Erikson, K. Notes on the sociology of deviance. *Social Problems 9* 1962: 307–14.

Eilstead, W. (Ed.) *An introduction to deviance.* Chicago: Markham, 1972.

Freidson, E. Disability as social deviance. In S. Sussman (Ed.) *Sociology and rehabilitation,* Washington, D.C.: American Sociological Association, 1965.

Garfinkle, H. *Studies in ethnomethodology.* Englewood Cliffs, N.J.: Prentice-Hall, 1967.

Gibbs, J. Conceptions of deviant behavior: The old and the new. *Pacific Sociological Review 9* 1966: 9–14.

Goffman, E. *The presentation of self in everyday life.* New York: Doubleday Anchor Books, 1959.

Goffman, E. *Stigma.* Englewood Cliffs, N.J.: Prentice-Hall, 1963.

Kitsuse, J. I. Societal reaction to deviant behavior: Problems of theory and method. *Social Problems 9* 1962: 247–56.

Kitsuse, J. I. Deviance, deviant behavior, and deviants: Some conceptual problems. In W. Filstead (Ed.) *An introduction to deviance.* Chicago: Markham, 1972.

Kitsuse, J. I., & Cicourel, A. A note on the uses of official statistics. *Social Problems 12* 1963: 131–39.

Lemert, E. *Social pathology.* New York: McGraw-Hill, 1951.

Lorber, J. Deviance as performance: The case of illness. *Social Problems 14* 1967: 302–10.

McCall, G. J., & Simmons, J. L. *Identities and interactions.* New York: Free Press, 1966.

Matza, D. *Becoming deviant.* Englewood Cliffs, N.J.: Prentice-Hall, 1969.

Meyers, J. Consequences and prognoses of disability. In M. Sussman (Ed.) *Sociology and rehabilitation.* Washington, D.C.: American Sociological Association, 1965.

Rubington, E., & Weinberg, M. (Eds.) *Deviance–The interactionist perspective.* New York: Macmillan, 1968.

Scheff, T. *Being mentally ill.* Chicago: Aldine, 1966.

Schur, E. *Crimes without victims.* Englewood Cliffs, N.J.: Prentice-Hall, 1965.

Schur, E. Reactions to deviance: A critical assessment. *American Journal of Sociology 75* 1969: 309–22.

Shibutani, T. *Human nature and collective behavior.* Englewood Cliffs, N.J.: Prentice-Hall, 1970.

Stoll, C. Images of man and social control. *Social Forces 47* 1968: 119–27.

Sykes, G., & Matza, D. Techniques of neutralization. *American Sociological Review 22* 1957: 664–70.

Turner, R. Deviance avowal as neutralization of commitment. *Social Problems 19* 1972: 308–21.

Weinstein, E., & Deutschberger, P. Some dimensions of altercasting. *Sociometry 26* 1963: 454–66.

Weinstein, E., & Deutschberger, P. Tasks, bargains, and identities in social interaction. *Social Forces 42* 1964: 451–55.

Williams, C., & Weinberg, M. Being discovered: A study of homosexuals in the military. *Social Problems 18* 1970: 217–27.

Wright, B. *Physical disability—A psychological approach.* New York: Harper & Brothers, 1960.

Pathways to the Doctor—From Person to Patient

14

IRVING KENNETH ZOLA

The problem on which we wish to dwell is one about which we think we know a great deal but that, in reality, we know so little—how and why an individual seeks professional medical aid. The immediate and obvious answer is that a person goes to a doctor when he is sick. Yet, this term "sick" is much clearer to those who use it, namely the health practitioners and the researchers, than it is to those upon whom we apply it—the patients. Two examples may illustrate this point. Listen carefully to the words of a respondent in Koos's study of the Health of Regionville as she wrestled with a definition of this concept.

> "I wish I really knew what you meant about being sick. Sometimes I felt so bad I could curl up and die, but had to go on because the kids had to be taken care of and besides, we didn't have the money to spend for the doctor. How could I be sick? How do you know when you're sick, anyway? Some people can go to bed most anytime with anything, but most of us can't be sick, even when we need to be."[1]

Even when there is agreement as to what constitutes "sickness," there may be a difference of opinion as to what constitutes appropriate action, as in the following incident:

The data collection for the first study on which this paper is based was supported by the Departments of Medicine and Psychiatry of the Massachusetts General Hospital. All subsequent data collection as well as the final writing and analysis was supported by the National Institute of General Medical Sciences, Grant No. 11367. For her many substantive and editorial suggestions I wish to thank Dr. Leonora K. Zola.

From *Social Science and Medicine*, 7 1973: 667–89. © 1973, Pergamon Press, Ltd. Reprinted with permission.

1. Earl L. Koos, *The health of Regionville*. New York: Columbia University Press, 1954.

A rather elderly woman arrived at the Medical Clinic of the Massachusetts General Hospital three days after an appointment. A somewhat exasperated nurse turned to her and said, "Mrs. Smith, your appointment was three days ago. Why weren't you here then?" To this Mrs. Smith responded, "How could I? Then I was sick."

Examples such as these are not unusual occurrences. And yet they cause little change in some basic working assumptions of the purveyors of medical care as well as the myriad investigators who are studying its delivery. It is to three of these assumptions we now turn: (1) the importance and frequency of episodes of illness in an individual's life; (2) the representativeness of those episodes of illness which come to professional attention; and (3) the process by which an individual decides that a series of bodily discomforts he labels symptoms become worthy of professional attention. Together these assumptions create an interesting if misleading picture of illness. Rarely do we try to understand how or why a patient goes to the doctor, for the decision itself is thought to be an obvious one. We postulate a time when the patient is asymptomatic or unaware that he has symptoms, then suddenly some clear objective symptoms appear, then perhaps he goes through a period of self-treatment and when either this treatment is unsuccessful or the symptoms in some way become too difficult to take, he decides to go to some health practitioner (usually, we hope, a physician).

The first assumption, thus, deals with the idea that individuals at most times during their life are really asymptomatic. The extensive data pouring in from periodic health examination has gradually begun to question this notion. For examinations of even supposedly healthy people, from business executives to union members to college professors, consistently reveal that at the time of their annual checkup, there was scarcely an individual who did not possess some symptom, some clinical entity worthy of treatment.[2] More general surveys have yielded similar findings.[3] Such data begins to give us a rather uncomfortable sense in which we may to some degree be sick every day of our lives. If we should even think of such a picture, however, the easiest way to dismiss this notion is that the majority of these everyday conditions are so minor as to be unworthy of medical treatment. This leads to our second assumption; namely, the degree of representativeness, both as to seriousness and frequency, of those episodes which do get to a doctor. Here too we are presented with puzzling facts. For if we look at investigations of either serious physical or mental disorder, there seem to be at least one, and in many cases several, people out of treatment for every person in treatment.[4] If, on the other hand, we look at a doctor's practice, we find that the

2. General summaries: Wistar J. Meigs, Occupational medicine. New England Journal of Medicine 264 (861) 1961; Gordon S. Siegel, Periodic health examinations–Abstracts from the literature. Public Health Service Publication No. 1010, Washington, D.C.: GPO, 1963.

3. See for example: Commission on Chronic Illness, Chronic illness in a large city. Cambridge: Harvard University Press, 1957; Innes H. Pearse and Lucy H. Crocker, The Peckham experiment. London: Allen & Unwin, 1954; Biologists in search of material. Interim Reports of the Work of the Pioneer Health Center, London: Faber and Faber, 1938.

4. Commission on Chronic Illness, Chronic illness in a large city. Cambridge: Harvard University Press, 1957; Innes H. Pearse and Lucy H. Crocker, The Peckham experiment. London: Allen & Unwin, 1954.

vast bulk is concerned with quite minor disorders.[5] Furthermore, if we use symptom-check lists or health calendars, we find that for these selfsame minor disorders, there is little that distinguishes them medically from those that are ignored, tolerated, or self-medicated.[6]

With these confusions in mind, we can now turn to the third assumption. On the basis that symptoms were perceived to be an infrequent and thus somewhat dramatic event in one's life, the general assumption was that in the face of such symptoms a rational individual, after an appropriate amount of caution, would seek aid. When he does not or delays overlong, we begin to question his rationality. The innumerable studies of delay in cancer bear witness.

If we examine these studies we find that the reason for delay is a list of faults—the patient has no time, no money, no one to care for children or take over other duties; is guilty, ashamed, fearful, anxious, embarrassed, or emotionally disturbed; dislikes physicians, nurses, hospitals, or needles; has had bad medical, familial or personal experiences; or is of lower education, socioeconomic status, or an ethnic or racial minority.[7] As the researchers might put it, there is something about these people or in their backgrounds which has disturbed their rationality, for otherwise, they would "naturally" seek aid. And yet there is a curious methodological fact about these studies for all these investigations were done on *patients*, people who *had* ultimately decided to go to a physician. What happened? Were they no longer fearful? Did they get free time, more money, outside help? Did they resolve their guilt, shame, anxiety, distrust? No, this does not seem to have been the case. If anything the investigators seem to allude to the fact that the patients finally could not stand it any longer. Yet given the abundant data on the ability to tolerate pain[8] and a wide variety of other conditions, this notion of "not being able to stand it" simply does not ring true clinically.

We can now restate a more realistic empirical picture of illness episodes. Virtually every day of our lives we are subject to a vast array of bodily discomforts. Only an infinitesimal amount of these get to a physician. Neither the mere presence nor the obviousness of symptoms, neither their medical seriousness nor

5. Y. T. Clute, *The general practitioner*. Toronto: University of Toronto Press, 1963, as well as many of the articles cited in John D. Stoeckle, Irving K. Zola, and Gerald E. Davidson; The quantity and significance of psychological distress in medical patients. *Journal of Chronic Disability 17 (959)* 1964.

6. Unpublished data of the author and also John Kosa, et al., Crisis and family life: A re-examination of concepts. *The Wisconsin Sociologist 4 (11)* 1965; John Kosa, Joel Alpert, and Robert J. Haggerty, On the reliability of family health information. *Social Science and Medicine 1 (165)* 1967; Joel Alpert, John Kosa, and Robert J. Haggerty, A month of illness and health care among low-income families. *Public Health Report 82 (705)* 1967.

7. Barbara Blackwell, The literature of delay in seeking medical care for chronic illnesses. *Health Education Monographs 16* 1963, 3-32; Bernard Kutner, Henry B. Makover, and Abraham Oppenheim, Delay in the diagnosis and treatment of cancer. *Journal of Chronic Disability 7 (95)* 1958; Bernard Kutner and Gerald Gordon, Seeking aid for cancer. *Journal of Health and Human Behavior 2 (171)* 1961.

8. William P. Chapman and Chester M. Jones, Variations in cutaneous and visceral pain sensitivity in normal subjects. *Journal of Clinical Investigation 23 (81)* 1944; James D. Hardy, Harold G. Wolff, and Helen Goodell, *Pain Sensations and Reactions*. Baltimore: Williams & Wilkins, 1952; Ronald Melzack, The perception of pain. *Scientific American 204 (41)* 1961; Harry S. Olin and Thomas P. Hackett, The denial of chest pain in 32 patients with acute myocardial infection. *Journal of the American Medical Association 190 (977)* 1964.

objective discomfort seems to differentiate those episodes which do and do not get professional treatment. In short, what then does convert a person to a patient? This then became a significant question and the search for an answer began.

At this point we had only the hunch that "something critical" must ordinarily happen to make an individual seek help. Given the voluminous literature on delay in seeking medical aid for almost every conceivable disorder and treatment, we might well say that the statistical norm for any population is to delay (perhaps infinitely for many). The implementing of this hunch is owed primarily to the intersection of two disciplines—anthropology and psychiatry. The first question to be faced was how and where to study this "something." Both prospective and retrospective studies were rejected. The former because as Professor H. M. Murphy noted there is often an enormous discrepancy between the declared intention and the actual act. The retrospective approach was rejected for two reasons—the almost notoriously poor recall that individuals have for past medical experiences and the distortions in recall introduced by the extensive "memory manipulation" which occurs as a result of the medical interview. Our resolution to this dilemma was a way of studying the patient when he was *in the process* of seeking medical aid. This process was somewhat artificially created by (1) interviewing patients while they waited to see their physician; (2) confining our sample to new patients to the Outpatient Clinics of the Massachusetts General Hospital who were seeking aid for their particular problem for the first time. Thus, we had a group of people who were definitely committed to seeing a doctor (i.e. waiting) but who had not yet been subject to the biases and distortions that might occur through the medical interview (though some patients had been referred, we included only those on whom no definitive diagnosis had been made). This then was where we decided to study our problem.

In what to look for we were influenced by certain trends in general psychiatry away from defining mental illness solely in terms of symptoms possessed by a single isolated individual and instead conceptualizing it as a more general kind of disturbance in interpersonal behavior and social living. (The resemblance that this bears to early classical notions of health and illness is quite striking. For then illness was conceived to be the disturbance between ego and his environment and not the physical symptom which happens to show up in ego.)[9] On the empirical level we were influenced by the work of Clausen and his colleagues at the National Institute of Mental Health on the first admission to the hospital for male schizophrenics. Most striking about their material was the lack of any increase in the objective seriousness of the patient's disorder as a factor in this hospitalization. If anything, there was a kind of normalization in his family, an accommodation to the patient's symptoms. The hospitalization occurred not when the patient

---

9. Iago Galdston, Salerno and the atom. In Iago Galdston (Ed.) *Medicine in a Changing Society.* New York: International Universities Press, 1956.

10. John A. Clausen and Marian Yarrow Radke, The impact of mental illness on the family. *Journal of Social Issues 11 (1)* 1955.

became sicker, but when the accommodation of the family, of the surrounding social context, broke down.[10] A translation of these findings could be made to physical illness. For, given all the data on delay, it seemed very likely that people have their symptoms for a long peroid of time before ever seeking medical aid. Thus one could hypothesize that there is an accommodation both physical, personal, and social to the symptoms and it is when this accommodation breaks down that the person seeks, or is forced to seek, medical aid. Thus the "illness" for which one seeks help may only in part be a physical relief from symptoms. The research question on the decision to seek medical aid thus turned from the traditional focus on "why the delay" to the more general issue of "why come *now*." This way of asking this question is in itself not new. Physicians have often done it, but interestingly enough, they have asked it not in regard to general physical illness but rather when they can find nothing wrong. It is *then* that they feel that the patient may want or have been prompted to seek help for other than physical reasons.

The final issue which is essential to understanding the study concerns the nature of the sample. Here in particular there was an intersection of anthropology and psychiatry. Time and again anthropologists had called attention to the problem of designating certain behaviors as abnormal in one cultural situation but would be considered quite normal and even ignored in another. Usually, when they explained this phenomenon they did so in terms of value-orientations; namely that there was something about the fit or lack of fit of the particular problem (symptom or sign), into a larger cultural pattern which helped explain why it was or was not abnormal.[11] Why could not the same process be operating in regard to physical symptoms? Perhaps many of the unexplained epidemiological differences between groups may also be due to the fact that in one group the particular physical sign is considered normal and in the second group not. For given the enormous tolerance we have for many physical conditions, given that our morbidity statistics are based primarily on treated disorders, many of these differences may reflect differences in attention and not differences in prevalence or incidence. While anthropologists have reported their findings mostly in comparisons of nonliterate groups with a more "modern" society, we decided to translate their idea of a culture into a contemporary format. We thus speculated that ethnic groups, particularly in an area such as Boston, Massachusetts, might well function as cultural reference groups and thus be an urban transmitter and perpetuator of value-orientations. The specific ethnic groups we studied were determined by a demographic study at the Massachusetts General Hospital from which we were able to determine the three most populous ethnic groups, Italian, Irish Catholic, and Anglo-Saxon Protestant.

To summarize the methodological introduction, in our first study, the sample consisted of patients completely new to the outpatient clinics who were seeking medical aid for the first time for this particular problem, who were between the

---

11. Marvin K. Opler, *Psychiatry and Human Values*. Springfield: Charles C. Thomas, 1956; Marvin K. Opler (Ed.), *Culture and mental health*. New York: Macmillan, 1959.

ages of 18 and 50, able to converse in English, of either Anglo-Saxon Protestant, Irish Catholic or Italian Catholic background. The data collection took place at the three clinics to which these groups were most frequently sent—the Eye Clinic, the Ear, Nose and Throat Clinic, and the Medical Clinic, which were, incidentally three of the largest clinics in the hospital. The interviewing took place during the waiting time before they saw their physicians with the general focus of the questioning being: Why did you seek medical aid now? In addition to many such open-ended questions, we had other information derived from the medical record, demographic interviews, attitude scales, and check lists. We also had each examining physician fill out a medical rating sheet on each patient. In all we saw over 200 patients, fairly evenly divided between male and female.[12]

We first examined the presenting complaints of the patients to see if there were differing conceptions of what is symptomatic.[13] Our first finding dealt with the location of their troubles. The Irish tended to place the locus of symptoms in the eye, the ear, the nose or the throat—a sense organ—while the Italians showed no particular clustering. The same result obtained when we asked what was the most important part of the body. Here too the Irish tended to place their symptoms in the eyes, ears, nose and throat with the Italians not favoring any specific location. We noted, however, that this was not merely a reflection of epidemiological differences; for Italians who did have eye, ear, nose and throat problems did not necessarily locate their chief complaint in either the eye, ear, nose or throat. We thus began to wonder if this focusing was telling us something other than a specific location. And so we turned our attention to more qualitative aspects of symptoms, such as the presence of pain. Here we noted that the Italians much more often felt that pain constituted a major part of their problem, whereas the Irish felt equally strong that it did not. However, we had our first clue that "something else" was going on. The Irish did not merely say they had no pain, but rather utilized a kind of denial with such statements as, "No, I wouldn't call it a pain, rather a discomfort"; or "No, a slight headache, but nothing that lasts." Further analysis of our data then led us to create a typology in which we tried to grasp the essence of a patient's complaint. One type seemed to reflect a

---

12. All differences reported here are statistically significant. Given that there are no tabular presentations in this essay, it may be helpful to remember that for the most part we are not stating that all or necessarily a majority of a particular group acted in the way depicted, but that at very least the response was significantly more peculiar to this group than to any other. Moreover, all the reported differences were sustained even when the diagnosed disorder for which they sought aid was held constant. For details on some of the statistical procedures as well as some of the methodological controls, see Irving K. Zola, Culture and symptoms—an analysis of patients' presenting complaints. *American Sociological Review 31 (615)* 1966.

13. The findings re symptoms are primarily a contrast between the Irish and the Italians. This is done because (1) there is a sense in which ethnicity in Boston is a much more *real* phenomenon to the Irish and the Italians than to our Anglo-Saxon Protestant, (2) these two groups are more purely *ethnic* and constitute a fairer comparison being of similar generation, education, and socioeconomic status, and (3) the differences are frankly much more dramatic and clearly drawn. If you wish to picture where the Anglo-Saxons might be in these comparisons, think of them as midway between the Irish and Italian responses, if anything, a little closer to the Irish. Some further discussion of this issue is found both in Irving K. Zola, Culture and symptoms—an analysis of patients' presenting complaints. *American Sociological Review 31 (615)* 1966; and Irving K. Zola, Illness behavior in the working class. In Arthur B. Shostak and William Gomberg (Eds.) *Blue Collar World.* Englewood Cliffs, N.J.: Prentice-Hall, 1964.

rather specific organic dysfunctioning (difficulty in seeing, inappropriate functioning, discharge, movement, etc.) while the second type represented a more global malfunctioning (aches and pains, appearance, energy level, etc.). Looked at in this way, we found that significantly more Irish seemed to describe their problem in terms of a rather specific dysfunction whereas the Italians described their complaints in a more diffuse way. Thus, the Irish seemed to convey a concern with something specific, something that has gone wrong, or been impaired; whereas the Italian was concerned with or conveyed a more global malfunctioning emphasizing the more diffuse nature of their complaints.

We now had differentiated two ways of communicating about one's bodily complaints—a kind of restricting versus generalizing tendency and we thus sought evidence to either refute or substantiate it. Two "tests" suggested themselves. The first consisted of three sets of tabulations: (1) the total number of symptoms a patient had; (2) the total number of different types of malfunctions from which he suffered (the typology mentioned above actually consisted of nine codifiable categories); and (3) the total number of different parts of the body in which a patient located complaints. Each we regarded as a measure of "generalizing" one's complaints. As we predicted, the Italians had significantly more complaints of greater variety, and in more places, than did the Irish. Our second "test" consisted of several questions dealing with the effect of their symptoms on their interpersonal behavior. Here we reasoned that the Irish would be much more likely to restrict the effect of their symptoms to physical fuunctioning. And so it was, with the Italians claiming that the symptoms interfered with their general mode of living and the Irish just as vehemently denying any such interference. Here again, the Irish presented a "no with a difference" in such statements as "No, there may have been times that I become uncomfortable physically and afraid to show it socially. If I felt that way I even tried to be a little more sociable."

Perhaps the best way to convey how differently these two groups communicated their symptoms is by a composite picture. The two series of responses were given by an Italian and an Irish patient of similar age and sex, with a disorder of approximately the same duration and seriousness and with the same primary and, if present, secondary diagnosis.

The crux of the study is, however, the decision to see a doctor. One of our basic claims was that the decision to seek medical aid was based on a break in the accommodation to the symptoms, that in the vast majority of situations, an individual did not seek aid at his physically sickest point. We do not mean by this that symptoms were unimportant. What we mean is that they function as a sort of constant and that when the decision to seek medical aid was made the physical symptoms alone were not sufficient to prompt this seeking. Typical of the amount of debilitation people can tolerate as well as the considerable seriousness and still the decision to seek medical attention made on extraphysical grounds is the case of Mary O'Rourke.

Mary O'Rourke is 49, married and is a licensed practical nurse. Her symptom was a simple one, "The sight is no good in this eye . . . can't see print at all, no matter how big." This she claimed was due to being hit on the side of the head by a baseball four months ago, but she just couldn't get around to a doctor before this. Why did she decide now, did her vision become worse? "Well ... about a month ago I was taking care of his (a client's) mother ... he mentioned that my eyelid was drooping ... it was the first time he ever did ... if he hadn't pointed it out I wouldn't have gone then." "Why did you pay attention to his advice?" "Well it takes away from my appearance ... bad enough to feel this way without having to look that way ... the same day I told my husband to call." (Diagnosis: Chorioretinitis O.S.—permanent partial blindness) "lesion present much longer than present symptoms." Incidentally, no "drooping" was noticeable to either the interviewer or the examining physician.

Table 14-1

Diagnosis	Question of interviewer	Irish patient	Italian patient
1. Presbyopia and Hyperopia	What seems to be the trouble?	I can't see to thread a needle or read a paper.	I have a constant headache and my eyes seem to get all red and burny.
	Anything else?	No, I can't recall any.	No, just that it lasts all day long and I even wake up with it sometimes.
2. Myopia	What seems to be the trouble?	I can't see across the street.	My eyes seem very burny, especially the right eye. . . . Two or three months ago I woke up with my eye swollen. I bathed it and it did go away but there was still the burny sensation.
	Anything else?	I had been experiencing headaches but it may be that I'm in early menopause.	Yes, there always seems to be a red spot beneath this eye. . . .
	Anything else?	No.	Well, my eyes feel very heavy . . . at night they bother me most.

These cases have been chosen precisely because they are relatively minor disorders. So straightforward are they that one should expect very little difference between patients who are their "owners." And yet not only does the Italian patient consistently present more troubles than the Irish but while the Irish patient focused on a specific malfunctioning as the main concern, the Italian did not even mention this aspect of the problem but focused on more "painful" and diffuse qualities of his condition.

Case after case could be presented to make this point but even more striking is that there is a "method underlying this madness." In our data we were able to discern several distinct nonphysiological patterns of triggers to the decision to seek medical aid. We have called them as follows: (1) the occurrence of an interpersonal crisis; (2) the *perceived* interference with social or personal relations; (3) sanctioning; (4) the *perceived* interference with vocational or physical activity; and (5) a kind of temporalizing of symptomatology. Moreover, these five patterns were clustered in such a way that we could characterize each ethnic group in our sample as favoring particular decision-making patterns in the seeking of medical aid.

The first two patterns, the presence of an interpersonal crisis and the perceived interference with social or personal relations, were more frequent among the Italians. The former, that of a crisis, does not mean that the symptoms have led to a crisis or even vice versa, but that the crisis called attention to the symptoms, causing the patient to dwell on them and finally to do something about them. Two examples will illustrate this.

> Jennie Bella was 40, single, and had a hearing difficulty for many years. She said that the symptoms have not gotten worse nor do they bother her a great deal (Diagnosis: Nonsupporative Otitis Media) and, furthermore, she admitted being petrified of doctors. "I don't like to come . . . I don't like doctors. I never did . . . I have to be unconscious to go. . . ." She can nevertheless not pinpoint any reason for coming at this time other than a general feeling that it should be taken care of. But when she was questioned about her family's concern, she blurted out, "I'm very nervous with my mother, up to this year I've been quiet, a stay-at-home . . . Now I've decided to go out and have some fun. My mother is very strict and very religious. She doesn't like the idea of my going out with a lot of men. She don't think I should go out with one for awhile and then stop. She says I'm not a nice girl, that I shouldn't go with a man unless I plan to marry . . . she doesn't like my keeping late hours or coming home late. She always suspects the worst of me. . . . This year it's just been miserable . . . I can't talk to her . . . she makes me very upset and it's been getting worse. . . . The other day . . . last week we (in lowered tones) had *the* argument." Miss Bella called for an appointment the next morning.

> Carol Conte was a 45-year-old, single, bookkeeper. For a number of years she had been both the sole support and nurse for her mother. Within the past year, her mother died and shortly thereafter her relatives began insisting that she move in with them, quit her job, work in their variety store and nurse their mother. With Carol's vacation approaching, they have stepped up their efforts to persuade her to at least try this arrangement. Although she has long had a number of minor aches and pains, her chief complaint was a small cyst on her eyelid (Diagnosis: Fibroma). She related her fear that it *might* be growing or could lead to something more serious and thus she felt she had better look into it now (the second day of her vacation) "before it was too late." "Too late" for what was revealed only in a somewhat mumbled response to the question of what she expected or would like the doctor to do. From a list of possible outcomes to her examination, she responded, "Maybe a hospital (ization). . . . Rest would be all right . . . (and then in a barely audible tone, in fact turning her head away as if she were speaking to no one at all) just so they (the family) would stop bothering me." Responding to her physical concern, the examining physician acceded to her request for the removal of the fibroma, referred her

for surgery and thus removed her from the situation for the duration of her vacation.

In such cases, it appeared that regardless of the reality and seriousness of the symptoms, they provide but the rationale for an escape, the calling-card or ticket to a potential source of help—the doctor.

The second pattern—the perceived interference with social or personal relations—is illustrated by the following two Italian patients.

John Pell is 18 and in his senior year of high school. For almost a year he's had headaches over his left eye and pain in and around his right, artificial, eye. The symptoms seem to be most prominent in the early evening. He claimed, however, little general difficulty or interference until he was asked whether the symptoms affected how he got along. To this he replied, "That's what worries me . . . I like to go out and meet people and now I've been avoiding people." Since he has had this problem for a year, he was probed as to why it bothered him more at this particular time. "The last few days of school it bothered me so that I tried to avoid everybody [this incidentally was his characteristic pattern *whenever* his eyes bothered him]: and I want to go out with . . . and my Senior Prom coming up, and I get the pains at 7 or 7:30 how can I stay out . . . then I saw the nurse." To be specific, he was walking down the school corridor and saw the announcement of the upcoming Prom. He noticed the starting time of 8 P.M. and went immediately to the school nurse who in turn referred him to the Massachusetts Eye and Ear Infirmary.

Harry Gallo is 41, married, and a "trainee" at a car dealers. "For a very long time my trouble is I can't drink . . . tea, coffee, booze . . . eat ice cream, fried foods. What happens is I get pains if I do have it." (Diagnosis: peptic ulcer). He becomes very dramatic when talking about how the symptoms affected him. "It shot my social life all to pieces . . . we all want to socialize . . . and it's a tough thing. I want to go with people, but I can't. Wherever we go they want to eat or there's food and I get hungry . . . and if I eat there, I get sick." Of course, he has gone off his "diet" and has gotten sick. Most of the time he watches himself and drinks Malox. He saw a doctor once two years ago and has been considering going again but, "I kept putting it off . . . because I got lazy . . . there were so many things. I've just been starting a new job and I didn't want to start taking off and not working, but this last attack was *too much!*" He then told how day after day the "boys at work" have been urging him to stop off with them for a few quick ones. He knew he shouldn't but he so wanted to fit in and so "it was with the boys and the other salesmen . . . I drank beer . . . I knew I was going to have more than one . . . and . . . *it* happened on the way home. . . " Storming into his home, he asked his wife to make an appointment at the hospital, stating almost exasperatingly, "if you can't drink beer with friends, what the hell. . . "

In these cases, the symptoms were relatively chronic. At the time of the decision there may have been an acute episode, but this was not the first such time the symptoms had reached such a "state"; rather it was the perception of them on this occasion as interfering with the social and interpersonal relations that was the trigger or final straw.

The third pattern, sanctioning, was the overwhelming favorite of the Irish. It is, however, not as well illustrated by dramatic examples, for it consists simply of one individual taking the primary responsibility for the decision to seek aid for someone else. For many weeks it looked as if one were seeing the submissive half of a dominant-submissive relationship. But within a period of six months, a husband and wife appeared at the clinics and each one assumed the role of sanctioning for the other.

Mr. and Mrs. O'Brien were both suffering from Myopia, both claimed difficulty in seeing, both had had their trouble for some period of time. The wife described her visit as follows: "Oh, as far as the symptoms were concerned, I'd be apt to let it go, but not my husband. He worries a lot, he wants things to be just so. Finally when my brother was better he (the husband) said to me: "Your worries about your brother are over so why can't you take care of your eyes now?" And so she did. Her husband, coming in several months later, followed the same pattern. He also considered himself somewhat resistant to being doctored. "I'm not in the habit of talking about aches and pains. My wife perhaps would say, 'Go to the doctor,' but me, I'd like to see if things will work themselves out." How did he get here? It turns out that he was on vacation and he'd been meaning to take care of it, "Well I tend to let things go but not my wife, so on the first day of my vacation my wife said, 'Why don't you come, why don't you take care of it now?' So I did."

Thus in these cases both claimed a resistance to seeing a doctor, both claimed the other is more likely to take care of such problems, and yet both served as the pushing force to the other. Interestingly enough, the dramatic aspect of such cases was not shown in those who followed the general pattern which was often fairly straightforward, but in those cases which did not. Two examples illustrate this. One was a woman with a thyroid condition, swelling on the side of the neck, who when asked why she came at this time blurted out almost in a shout, "Why did I come now? I've been walking around the house like this for several weeks now and nobody said anything so I *had to come myself*." Or the almost plaintive complaint of a veteran, kind of grumbling when asked why he came now, begrudging the fact that he had to make a decision himself with the statement, "Hmm, in the Navy they just take you to the doctor, you don't have to go yourself." It is not that these people are in any sense stoic, for it seemed that they were quite verbal and open about complaining but just that they did not want to take the responsibility on themselves.

There is a secondary pattern of the Irish, which turns out to be also the major pattern of the Anglo-Saxon group.[14] It was almost straight out of the Protestant ethic; namely a perceived interference with work or physical functioning. The word "perceived" is to be emphasized because the nature of the circumstances

---

14. As we have argued elsewhere—Irving K. Zola, Illness behavior in the working class. In Arthur B. Shostak and William Gomberg (Eds.) *Blue Collar World.* Englewood Cliffs, N.J.: Prentice-Hall, 1964—this and the following pattern are also characteristic of more middle-class and more highly educated groups.

range from a single woman, 35-years-old, who for the first time noted that the material which she was typing appeared blurred and thus felt that she had better take care of it, to a man with multiple sclerosis who despite falling down and losing his balance in many places, did nothing about it until he fell at work. Then he perceived that it might have some effect on his work and his ability to continue. The secondary Anglo-Saxon pattern is worh commenting on, for at first glance it appears to be one of the most rational modes of decision making. It is one that most readers of this paper may well have used, namely the setting of external time criteria. "If it isn't better in three days, or one week, or seven hours, or six months, then I'll take care of it." A variant on this theme involves the setting of a different kind of temporal standard—the recurrence of the phenomenon. A 19-year-old college sophomore reported the following:

> Well, it was this way. I went into this classroom and sat in the back of the room and when the professor started to write on the blackboard I noticed that the words were somewhat blurry. But I didn't think too much about it. A couple of weeks later, when I went back into the same classroom, I noted that it was blurry again. Well, once was bad, but twice that was too much.

Now given that his diagnosis was myopia and that it was unconnected with any other disease, we know medically that his myopia did not vary from one circumstance to another. This imposition of "a first time, second time that's too much" was of his doing and unrelated to any medical or physical reality.

By now the role that symptoms played in the decision to seek medical aid should be clearer. For our patients the symptoms were "really" there, but their perception differed considerably. There *is* a sense in which they sought help because they could not stand it any longer. But what they could not stand was more likely to be a situation or a perceived implication of a symptom rather than any worsening of the symptom per se.

I now would like to note some of the implications of this work. When speaking of implications, I ask your indulgence, for I refer not merely to what leads in a direct line from the data but some of the different thoughts and directions in which it leads me. What for example are the consequences for our very conception of etiology—conceptions based on assumptions about the representativeness of whom and what we study. We have claimed in this paper that the reason people get into medical treatment may well be related to some select social-psychological circumstances. If this is true, it makes all the more meaningful our earlier point about many unexplained epidemiological differences, for they may be due more to the differential occurrence of these social-psychological factors, factors of selectivity and attention which get people and their episodes into medical statistics rather than to any true difference in the prevalence and incidence of a particular problem or disorder.[15] Our findings may also have implications for what one studies, particularly to the importance of stress in the etiology of so many

---

15. David Mechanic and Edmund H. Volkart, Illness behavior and medical diagnosis. *Journal of Health and Human Behavior 1 (86)* 1960.

complaints and disorders. For it may well be that the stress noted in these people's lives, at least that which they were able to verbalize, is the stress which brought them into the hospital or into seeking treatment (as was one of our main triggers) and not really a factor in the etiology or the exacerbation of the disorder.

Our work also has implications for treatment. So often we hear the terms "unmotivated, unreachable, and resistant" applied to difficult cases. Yet we fail to realize that these terms may equally apply to us, the caretakers and health professionals, who may not understand what the patient is saying or, if we do, do not want to hear it. An example of this was seen in the way physicians in this study handled those patients for whose problem no organic basis could be found.[16] For despite the fact that there were no objective differences in the prevalence of emotional problems between our ethnic groups, the Italians were consistently diagnosed as having some psychological difficulty such as tension headaches, functional problems, personality disorder, etc., whereas the Irish and Anglo-Saxon were consistently given what one might call a neutral diagnosis: something that was either a Latinized term for their symptoms or simply the words "nothing found on tests" or "nothing wrong." Our explanation is somewhat as follows; namely that this situation is one of the most difficult for a physician and one in which he nevertheless feels he should make a differential diagnosis. Faced with this dilemma he focused inordinately on *how* the Italians presented themselves—somewhat voluble, with many more symptoms, and somewhat dramatic social circumstances surrounding their decision to seek help. This labeling of the Italians is particularly interesting since, as we mentioned above, the Irish and Anglo-Saxons had similar psychological and social problems but presented them in a much more emotionally neutral and bland manner. There are no doubt other factors operating, such as the greater social distance between the Italians and the medical staff, but that would constitute another paper.

One final remark as to treatment: again and again we found that where the physician paid little attention to the specific trigger which forced or which the individual used as an excuse to seek medical aid, there was the greatest likelihood of that patient eventually breaking off treatment. Another way of putting this is that without attention to this phenomenon the physician would have no opportunity to practice his healing art. Moreover, this problem of triggers brooked no speciality nor particular type of disorder. So that being a specialist and only seeing certain kinds of problems did not exempt the physician from having to deal with this issue.

Such data alone supports those who urge more training in social and psychological sophistication for *any* physician who has contact with patients. With chronic illness making up the bulk of today's health problems it is obvious that the physicians cannot treat the etiological agent of disease and that the effect of specific therapies is rather limited. Nevertheless the physician may more intelligently intervene in the patient's efforts to cope with his disorder if he has the knowledge and

---

16. Detailed in Irving K. Zola, Problems of communication, diagnosis and patient care: The interplay of patient, physician and clinic organization. *Journal of Medical Education 38 (829)* 1963.

awareness of the patient's views of health and sickness, his expectations, and his reasons for seeking help.

This report has several different goals. To the social scientist we have tried to convey the somewhat amazing persistence of certain cultural characteristics which we in our cultural blindness have felt should have died and disappeared. The reason for their survival is that such behaviors may well be general modes of handling anxiety, sort of culturally prescribed defense mechanisms and probably transmitted from generation to generation in the way that much learning takes place, almost on an unconscious level. If this be true, then they constitute a group of behaviors which are much less likely to be changed as one wishes or attempts to become more American. Hopefully, the present research has also demonstrated the fruitfulness of an approach which does not take the definition of abnormality for granted. Despite its limitations our data seems sufficiently striking to invite further reason for re-examining our traditional and often rigid conceptions of health and illness, or normality and abnormality, of conformity and deviance. As we have contended in the early pages of this essay, symptoms or physical aberrations are so widespread that perhaps relatively few, and a biased selection at best, come to the attention of official treatment agencies. We have thus tried to present evidence showing that the very labeling and definition of a bodily state as a symptom as well as the decision to do something about it is in itself part of a social process. If there is a selection and definitional process, then focusing solely on reasons for deviation (the study of etiology) and the reasons for not seeking treatment (the study of delay) and ignoring what constitutes a deviation in the eyes of an individual and his reasons for action may obscure important aspects of our understanding and eventually our philosophy of the treatment ad control of illness.

Finally, this is not meant to be an essay on the importance of sociological factors in disease, but rather the presentation of an approach to the study of health and illness. Rather than being a narrow and limited concept, health and illness are on the contrary empirically quite elastic. In short, it is not merely that health and illness have sociological aspects, for they have many aspects, but really that there is a sense in which health and illness *are* social phenomena. The implication of this perspective has perhaps been much better put by the Leightons (though quoted out of context):

> From this broad perspective there is no point in asking whether over the span of his adult life a particular individual should or should not be considered a medical case—everyone is a medical case. The significant question becomes how severe a case, what kind of case.[17]

I myself would add—how does one become a case and, since of the many eligible, so few are chosen, what does it mean to be a case. In an era where every

---

17. Dorothea C. Leighton, et al., *The Character of Danger.* New York: Basic Books, 1963, 135–36.

day produces new medical discoveries, such questions are all too easily ignored. The cure for all men's ills seems right over the next hill. Yet as Dubos has cogently reminded us,[18] this vision is only a mirage and the sooner we realize it the better.

Note

Papers on this work which have already appeared are: John D. Stoeckle, Irving K. Zola, and Gerald E. Davidson, On going to see the doctor, the contributions of the patient to the decision to seek medical aid: A selective review. *Journal of Chronic Disability 16 (975)* 1963; John D. Stoeckle, Irving K. Zola, and Gerald E. Davidson, The quantity and significance of psychological distress in medical patients—Some preliminary observations about the decision to seek medical aid. *Journal of Chronic Disability 17 (959)* 1964; John D. Stoeckle and Irving K. Zola, After everyone can pay for medical care—Some perspectives on future treatment and practice. *Medical Care 2 (36)* 1964; Irving K. Zola, Socio-cultural factors in the seeking of medical aid—A progress report. *Transcultural Psychiatric Research 14 (62)* 1963; Irving K. Zola, Problems of communication, diagnosis, and patient care: The interplay of patient, physician, and clinic organization. *Journal of Medical Education 38 (829)* 1963; Irving K. Zola, Illness behaviour in the working class. In Arthur B. Shostak and William Gomberg (Eds.) *Blue Collar World* Englewood Cliffs, N.J.: Prentice-Hall, 1964; John D. Stoeckle and Irving K. Zola, Views, problems and potentialities of the clinic. *Medicine 43 (413)* 1964; Irving K. Zola, Motivation—A social scientist's perspective on the problem of unmotivated clients. *Education for Social Work with Unmotivated Clients–Proceedings of an Institute,* Brandeis University Papers in Social Welfare, No. 9, pp. 139–60; Irving K. Zola, Problems for research—Some effects of assumptions underlying socio-medical investigations. In *Proceedings of the Conference on Medical Sociology and Disease Control,* Gerald E. Gordon (Ed.) National Tuberculosis Association, 1966, pp. 9–17; Irving K. Zola, Culture and symptoms—An analysis of patients' presenting complaints. *American Sociological Review 31 (615)* 1966.

---

18. Rene Dubos, *Mirage of Health.* Garden City, N.Y.: Anchor, 1961; Rene Dubos, *Man Adapting.* New Haven: Yale University Press, 1965.

Physician-Patient Communication and Patient Conformity with Medical Advice   15

BONNIE L. SVARSTAD

Although many studies have tried to determine why patients do not follow medical advice, they have led to so many inconsistent findings that a more meaningful conceptual framework must be developed. This chapter reviews methods already tried and suggests an alternative approach to the study of patient conformity with medical advice. Previous approaches have placed too much emphasis on the patient and too little on the processes by which physicians transmit their expectations and attempt to motivate their patients. If it is true that patients lack high levels of knowledge and motivation, we sorely need to understand better how reasonable conformity with medical advice can be achieved.

The Individualistic Models

The most common approach to the study of nonconformity is to identify the "cooperative" and "uncooperative" patients and to search for the variables that differentiate them. The assumption is that the nonconforming patient has unique characteristics. This assumption and therefore the adequacy of various individualistic models can be questioned on several grounds.

This study was conducted under the auspices of a neighborhood health center funded by the Office of Economic Opportunity. To preserve the anonymity of the participating physicians and patients, I do not name the health center.

From *The Growth of Bureaucratic Medicine* by David Mechanic, pp. 220–38. Copyright © 1976 by John Wiley & Sons, Inc. Reprinted with permission of John Wiley & Sons.

First, the findings have been inconsistent. Researchers who have compared patients' abilities and personality traits have reported inconsistent results regarding the role of each of the following factors in adhering to medical advice: intelligence,[1-2] anxiety,[3-4] defensiveness,[5] internalization,[6] authoritarianism,[7-8] Rorschach scores,[9-10] MMPI scores,[11-12] and psychopathy.[13] Those who have used the Barron Ego Strength Scale,[14] the Stroop Color Word Test,[15] a scale measuring use of conversion defenses,[16] and a scale measuring dependent-sub-

1. S. P. Rosenzweig & R. Folman, Patient and therapist variables affecting premature termination in group psychotherapy. *Psychotherapy: Theory, Research and Practice 11* 1974: 76–79.

2. E. A. Rubinstein & M. Lorr, A comparison of terminators and remainers in outpatient psychotherapy. *Journal of Clinical Psychology 12* 1956: 345–49.

3. J. D. Frank, et al. Why patients leave psychotherapy. *Archives of Neurology and Psychiatry 77* 1957: 283–99.

4. G. A. Hellmuth, et al. Psychological factors in cardiac patients: Distortion of clinical recommendations. *Archives of Environmental Health 12* 1966: 771–75.

5. G. A. Hellmuth, et al. Psychological factors in cardiac patients: Distortion of clinical recommendations. *Archives of Environmental Health 12* 1966: 771–75.

6. G. A. Hellmuth, et al. Psychological factors in cardiac patients: Distortion of clinical recommendations. *Archives of Environmental Health 12* 1966: 771–75.

7. E. A. Rubinstein & M. Lorr, A comparison of terminators and remainers in outpatient psychotherapy. *Journal of Clinical Psychology 12* 1956: 345–49.

8. M. S. Davis, Physiologic, psychological and demographic factors in patient compliance with doctors' orders. *Medical Care 6* 1968a: 115.

9. F. Auld, Jr., & L. D. Eron, The use of Rorschach scores to predict whether patients will continue psychotherapy. *Journal of Consulting Psychology 17* 1953: 104–09.

10. R. G. Gibby, et al. Validation of Rorschach criteria for predicting duration of therapy. *Journal of Consulting Psychology 18* 1954: 185–91.

11. G. Calden, et al. The use of the MMPI in predicting irregular discharge among tuberculosis patients. *Journal of Clinical Psychology 11* 1955: 374–77.

12. M. E. Rorabaugh & C. Guthrie, The personality characteristics of tuberculosis patients who leave the tuberculosis hospital against medical advice. *American Review of Tuberculosis 67* 1953: 432–39.

13. G. Calden, et al. The use of the MMPI in predicting irregular discharge among tuberculosis patients. *Journal of Clinical Psychology 11* 1955: 374–77.

14. S. P. Rosenzweig & R. Folman, Patient and therapist variable affecting premature termination in group therapy. *Psychotherapy: Theory, Research and Practice 11* 1974: 76–79.

15. S. P. Rosenzweig & R. Folman, Patient and therapist variables affecting premature termination in group therapy. *Psychotherapy: Theory, Research and Practice 11* 1974: 76–79.

16. G. A. Hellmuth, et al. Psychological factors in cardiac patients: Distortion of clinical recommendations. *Archives of Environmental Health 12* 1966: 771–75.

17. M. S. Davis, Physiologic, psychological and demographic factors in patient compliance with doctors' orders. *Medical Care 6* 1968a: 115

18. W. M. Dixon, et al., Outpatient P.A.S. therapy. *Lancet 273* 1957: 871–73.

19. L. Gordis, et al. Why patients don't follow medical advice: A study of children on long term antistreptococcal prophylaxis. *Journal of Pediatrics 75* 1969: 957–68.

20. T. Moulding, et al. Supervision of outpatient drug therapy with the medication monitor. *Annals of Internal Medicine 73* 1970: 559–64.

21. L. Gordis, et al. Why patients don't follow medical advice: A study of children on long term antistreptococcal prophylaxis. *Journal of Pediatrics 75* 1969: 957–68.

22. T. Moulding, et al. Supervision of outpatient drug therapy with the medication monitor. *Annals of Internal Medicine 73* 1970: 559–64.

23. V. Francis, et al. Gaps in doctor-patient communication: Patients' response to medical advice. *New England Journal of Medicine 280* 1969: 535–40.

missiveness[17] have reported results that were not significant. Investigators who have compared demographic characteristics have not been much more successful. There have been contradictory findings regarding the following sociocultural characteristics: sex,[18-20] age,[21-23] income,[24-27] occupation,[28-29] education,[30-33] race,[34-36] number of siblings,[37-38] family structure,[39-40] and family stability.[41-42] Similarly, little predictability is achieved when various attitudinal orientations have been examined: future orientation,[43] ethnocentrism,[44] anomie,[45-46] attitudes

24. L. Gordis, et al. Why patients don't follow medical advice: A study of children on long term antistreptococcal prophylaxis. *Journal of Pediatrics 75* 1969: 957–68.

25. T. Moulding, et al. Supervision of outpatient drug therapy with the medication monitor. *Annals of Internal Medicine 73* 1970: 559–64.

26. D. K. Fink, et al. The management specialist in effective pediatric ambulatory care. *American Journal of Public Health 59* 1969a: 527.

27. R. Elling, et al. Patient participation in a pediatric program. *Journal of Health and Human Behavior 1* 1960: 183–91.

28. L. Gordis, et al. Why patients don't follow medical advice: A study of children on long term antistreptococcal prophylaxis. *Journal of Pediatrics 75* 1969: 957–68.

29. L. J. Moran, et al. Some determinants of successful and unsuccessful adaptations to hospital treatment of tuberculosis. *Journal of Consulting Psychology 20* 1956: 125–31.

30. T. Moulding, et al. Supervision of outpatient drug therapy with the medication monitor. *Annals of Internal Medicine 73* 1970: 559–64.

31. V. Francis, et al. Gaps in doctor-patient communication: Patients' response to medical advice. *New England Journal of Medicine 280* 1969: 535–40.

32. D. K. Fink, et al. The management specialist in effective pediatric ambulatory care. *American Journal of Public Health 59* 1969a: 527.

33. M. S. Davis & R. Eichorn, Compliance with medical regimes: A panel study. *Journal of Health and Human Behavior 4* 1963: 240–49.

34. V. Francis, et al. Gaps in doctor-patient communication: Patients' response to medical advice. *New England Journal of Medicine 280* 1969: 535–40.

35. R. Elling, et al. Patient participation in a pediatric program. *Journal of Health and Human Behavior 1* 1960: 183–91.

36. N. W. Shelton & P. J. Sparer, Recidivism: The basic problem of self-discharge among hospitalized tuberculosis patients. In P. J. Sparer (Ed.) *Personality, Stress and Tuberculosis.* New York: International Universities Press, 1956, pp. 477–89.

37. L. Gordis, et al. Why patients don't follow medical advice: A study of children on long term antistreptococcal prophylaxis. *Journal of Pediatrics 75* 1969: 957–68.

38. V. Francis, et al. Gaps in doctor-patient communication: Patients' response to medical advice. *New England Journal of Medicine 280* 1969: 535–40.

39. D. K. Fink, et al. The management specialist in effective pediatric ambulatory care. *American Journal of Public Health 59* 1969a: 527.

40. L. Gordis, et al. Why patients don't follow medical advice: A study of children on long term antistreptococcal prophylaxis. *Journal of Pediatrics 75* 1969: 957–68.

41. L. Gordis, et al. Why patients don't follow medical advice: A study of children on long term antistreptococcal prophylaxis. *Journal of Pediatrics 75* 1969: 957–68.

42. R. Elling, et al. Patient participation in a pediatric program. *Journal of Health and Human Behavior 1* 1960: 183–91.

43. L. Gordis, et al. Why patients don't follow medical advice: A study of children on long term antistreptococcal prophylaxis. *Journal of Pediatrics 75* 1969: 957–68.

44. L. Gordis, et al. Why patients don't follow medical advice: A study of children on long term antistreptococcal prophylaxis. *Journal of Pediatrics 75* 1969: 957–68.

45. L. Gordis, et al. Why patients don't follow medical advice: A study of children on long term antistreptococcal prophylaxis. *Journal of Pediatrics 75* 1969: 957–68.

46. M. S. Davis, Physiologic, psychological and demographic factors in patient compliance with doctors' orders. *Medical Care 6* 1968a: 115.

toward science,[47] and attitudes toward illness-dependency.[48]

Second, there is evidence that patients do not behave consistently across situations. For example, it is known that patient behavior varies from one time to another[49] and that patient behavior varies by the type of advice,[50-52] the number of physician instructions,[53-54] and the degree of medical supervision.[55] These data suggest that focusing on the *process* by which nonconformity is prevented and reduced may be more productive than concentrating on individual characteristics.

The Health Belief Model

Another approach to the study of nonconformity is to explore patients' beliefs about their illness and the advised actions.[56-59] Generally speaking, the "health belief model" postulates that patients' behavior is a function of the amount of threat perceived by patients and patients' perception of the value or attractiveness of the advised actions. Like the individualistic models, the health belief model places primary emphasis on patients and their motivations, predispositions, or level of "psychological readiness."

Although there is empirical support for the idea that behavior is associated with people's beliefs about their illnesses and treatments, the health belief model is limited. First, it tends to neglect the possibility that nonconformity can be unintentional. Patients may be motivated but, for various reasons, may not recall and understand what they are supposed to do. We know, for example, that patients do not recall many of the physicians' statements,[60] that they are often unaware of

47. M. S. Davis, Physiologic, psychological and demographic factors in patient compliance with doctors' orders. *Medical Care 6* 1968a: 115.

48. M. S. Davis, Physiologic, psychological and demographic factors in patient compliance with doctors' orders. *Medical Care 6* 1968a: 115.

49. M. S. Davis & R. Eichorn, Compliance with medical regimes: A panel study. *Journal of Health and Human Behavior 4* 1963: 240–49.

50. M. S. Davis & R. Eichorn, Compliance with medical regimes: A panel study. *Journal of Health and Human Behavior 4* 1963: 240–49.

51. D. Fink, et al. Effective patient care in the pediatric ambulatory setting: A study of the acute care clinic. *Journal of Pediatrics 43* 1969b: 927–35.

52. N. Berkowitz, et al. Patient follow-through in the outpatient department. *Nursing Research 12* 1963: 16–22.

53. V. Francis, et al. Gaps in doctor-patient communication: Patients' response to medical advice. *New England Journal of Medicine 280* 1969: 535–40.

54. C. Latiolais & C. Berry, Misuse of prescription medicine by outpatients. *Drug Intelligence and Clinical Pharmacy 3* 1963: 270–77.

55. D. S. Irwin, et al. Phenothiazine intake and staff attitudes. *American Journal of Psychiatry 127* 1971: 1631–35.

56. I. Rosenstock, What research in motivation suggests for public health. *American Journal of Public Health 50* 1960: 295–302.

57. S. Kasl & S. Cobb, Health behavior, illness behavior and sick role behavior: I. *Archives of Environmental Health 12* 1966a: 246–66.

58. S. Kasl & S. Cobb, Health behavior, illness behavior and sick role behavior: II. *Archives of Environmental Health 12* 1966b: 531–41.

59. M. Becker, et al. Predicting mothers' compliance with medical regimens. *Journal of Pediatrics 81* 1972: 843–54.

60. P. Ley & M. S. Spelman, *Communicating with the patient.* London: The Trinity Press, 1967.

the fact that they have been misusing medications,[61] and that they have difficulty understanding other complex regimens.[62] Further, the model does not clearly specify the determinants of patient motivation. Proponents of the model hypothesize that various social agents (e.g., doctor, family, boss, friends) affect patients' motivation, but they do not specify how such social influence occurs or why it might fail.[63]

The Interaction Models

Although many social scientists and health professionals have written about the importance of physician-patient interaction, few empirical studies have probed the relationship between physician-patient interaction and patient conformity with medical advice.

Utilizing Bales's Interaction Process Analysis and factor analytic techniques, Milton Davis examined the structure and process of physician-patient communication in a general medical clinic.[64-65] When he examined the relationship between patient compliance and certain types of physician-patient activities that occurred during the patients' subsequent visits, some significant findings were obtained.[66] Patients were more apt to comply if the physician had given suggestions and information and if the patients had asked for the physician's suggestions and opinions, expressed agreement, and expressed tension release. Noncompliance was more apt to occur if patients gave their own opinions or showed tension and if the physician engaged in certain activities (i.e., passive acceptance of the patient's active participation, asking for information without giving feedback, and expressing disagreement).

In a similarly designed study, Barbara Korsch and her associates examined the relationship between pediatrician-parent communication and the parents' subsequent conformity with advice.[67-70] Although these investigators also used a

61. C. Latiolais & C. Berry, Misuse of prescription medicine by outpatients. *Drug Intelligence and Clinical Pharmacy 3* 1969: 270–77.

62. V. Francis, et al. Gaps in doctor-patient communication: Patients' response to medical advice. *New England Journal of Medicine 280* 1969: 535–40.

63. S. Kasl & S. Cobb, Health behavior, illness behavior and sick role behavior: I. *Archives of Environmental Health 12* 1966a: 246–66.

64. M. S. Davis, Variation in patients' compliance with doctors' advice: An empirical analysis of patterns of communication. *American Journal of Public Health 58* 1968b: 274–88.

65. M. S. Davis, Variation in patients' compliance with doctors' advice: Medical practice and doctor-patient interaction. *Psychiatry in Medicine 2* 1971: 31–54.

66. M. S. Davis, Variations in patients' compliance with doctors' orders: Medical practice and doctor-patient interaction. *Psychiatry in Medicine 2* 1971: 31–54.

67. V. Francis, et al. Gaps in doctor-patient communication: Patients' response to medical advice. *New England Journal of Medicine 280* 1969: 535–40.

68. B. Korsch, et al. Gaps in doctor-patient communication: Doctor-patient interaction and patient satisfaction. *Pediatrics 42* 1968: 855–71.

69. B. Korsch & V. Negrete, Doctor-patient communication: *Scientific American 227* 1972: 66–74.

70. B. Freeman, et al. Gaps in doctor-patient communication: Doctor-patient interaction analysis. *Pediatric Research 5* 1971: 298–311.

conceptual model based on Bales's system of classifying interaction, their results were not consistent with those of Davis. Instead, they found that physician friendliness and antagonism were significantly related to the parents' subsequent behavior.[71] Davis concluded that the passive patient was more compliant;[72] Korsch and her colleagues concluded that the active parent was more compliant.[73] The latter also concluded that parent expression of agreement or tension made no difference in parents' later behavior.[74] Although Davis suggested that compliance was higher when patients asked for suggestions and opinions, Korsch and her colleagues reported that the parents' level of questioning made no difference. Contrary to Davis's conclusions,[75] they found that the permissiveness of the pediatrician made no difference.[76] One of the few consistent findings was that noncompliance was higher when physicians asked for information without giving any feedback.

It is difficult to account for these contradictions. They might partially be explained by the different populations studied, but I suspect that the Bales system for analyzing interaction is simply inadequate for the purposes being discussed. As others have noted, the 12 categories in Bales's system are too broad to be meaningful. For example, the extent to which the physician gives instruction or suggestion can be measured, but the content, clarity, or salience of the suggestions or instructions cannot be explored. The extent to which the physician expresses positive or negative affect can be measured, but the other ways in which the physician might try to motivate the patient (e.g., discussing the rationale for a given prescription) cannot be isolated. The latter communication would be included in broad categories such as "giving orientation" or "giving opinions."

In short, a more meaningful conceptual model for studying physician-patient communication as it relates to patient conformity is needed.

The Research Project

The data on which this report is based were collected as part of an exploratory study that was conducted in a neighborhood health center located in an urban ghetto. Unlike other studies that have focused on patient failure to conform with medical advice, we began by asking, "Why do physicians sometimes fail to achieve the patients' conformity with medication advice?" The design of our

71. B. Freeman, et al. Gaps in doctor-patient communication: Doctor-patient interaction analysis. *Pediatric Research 5* 1971: 298–311.

72. M. S. Davis, Variation in patients' compliance with doctors' orders: Medical practice and doctor-patient interaction. *Psychiatry in Medicine 2* 1971: 31–54.

73. B. Korsch & V. Negrete, Doctor-patient communication. *Scientific American 227* 1972: 66–74.

74. B. Freeman, et al. Gaps in doctor-patient communication: Doctor-patient interaction analysis. *Pediatric Research 5* 1971: 298–311.

75. M. S. Davis, Variations in patients' compliance with doctors' advice: An empirical analysis of patterns of communication. *American Journal of Public Health 58* 1968b: 274–88.

76. B. Freeman, et al. Gaps in doctor-patient communication: Doctor-patient interaction analysis. *Pediatric Research 5* 1971: 298–311.

study, which began in 1969, included systematic observation of physician-patient interaction, review of medical records and pharmacy files, follow-up interviews with the patients about a week after their clinic visits, and validation of the patients' reported behavior by means of a "bottle check." I observed 8 fulltime physicians and was able to obtain a complete series of data on 153 adult patients, most of whom were black and Puerto Rican. Of this group, 131 patients were expected to follow medication advice. The sample included new and old patients, walk-in patients, patients with appointments, and patients with or without language difficulties. The patients were being treated for a variety of acute and chronic conditions. The most common diagnosis was essential hypertension.

All of the participating physicians were fully trained. Two physicians were board certified internists; four were board eligible internists; and two were general practitioners. The health center was funded by the Office of Economic Opportunity and was designed to provide high quality, comprehensive, and continuous health care. Many independent observers considered the center one of the most successful in the country.

The Instruction Process

My project began with some of the same unwarranted assumptions that have characterized previous research. I assumed that the physicians' expectations regarding medication use would be, for the most part, simple and unambiguous and that the patients—after receiving verbal advice and printed instructions on their medication containers—would know what the physicians expected them to do. The pilot study led me to question these assumptions. First, patients did not always leave the clinic with an accurate perception of what the physicians expected them to do. As illustrated in the following excerpt, the physicians sometimes had to clarify earlier instructions during the follow-up visits:

> *Doctor:* Have you been taking the medicine for the gout?
> *Patient:* No, I stopped that after the pains went away.
> *Doctor:* You shouldn't have done that. I wanted you to continue taking it as that medicine prevents gout attacks.
> *Patient:* *(in a tone of surprise)* Oh, I didn't know that! You didn't tell me that last time.

Second, I also had difficulty when I tried to identify what the physicians expected. Even though I had observed the clinic visit, reviewed the record, and examined carbon copies of the prescription forms, I was often confused. Before interviewing the patients, I often had to seek clarification from the physicians, pharmacists, and the *Physicians' Desk Reference* (a reference book that provides information about pharmaceutical products).

These experiences indicated that it might be fruitful to begin by examining the nature and outcome of physician instruction. The physician-patient encounter was viewed as a situation in which the patient must learn a very specific patient role or set of expectations about (1) which drugs should be taken, (2) how long each drug should be taken, (3) the dosage schedules that should be followed, and (4) how regularly the drugs should be taken. The working hypotheses were:

1. The patient cannot conform with the physician's expectations without having an accurate perception of the physician's expectations.
2. The patient's perception of the physician's expectations will be more accurate if (a) the physician transmits the expectations in an explicit manner; (b) the physician provides a written record of the expectations (e.g., medication label); (c) the medication label is consistent with what the physician requested; and (d) the physician informs the patient about the name and/or purpose of the drug.

The Nature of Physician Instruction

Examining the physicians' verbal instructions and the instructions attached to the patients' medication containers led to some interesting findings. First, it was evident that the physicians frequently did not discuss their expectations in an explicit manner. Of the 347 drugs prescribed or proscribed, 60 were never discussed during the observed visits. The physicians gave explicit, verbal advice about how long to take the drug in only 10 percent of the 347 drug cases. How regularly the drug should be used was made explicit in about 17 percent of the cases. In addition, several physicians discussed certain dosage schedules ambiguously. For example, when discussing antibiotics, several physicians gave the dosage schedule in hourly terms (e.g., "Take two capsules every six hours") without specifying how many should be taken during a 24-hour period. Apparently, the physicians assumed that their patients would be able to infer how long their drugs should be taken, how regularly they should be used, and what certain types of dosage schedules mean.

Second, patients did not always receive printed instructions or written reminders of what the physician expected regarding medication use. When the patient received no written instructions, it was usually because the physicians assumed that the patient still had a supply of the medication at home. But sometimes the physicians changed the previously prescribed dosage schedule and gave the patient no written record of the schedule now in effect. When the patient did receive a container of medication on the day of the visit (239 of 347 drugs), we examined the attached instructions. How long the drug should be taken was noted on only 10 medication containers. Of the 97 drugs dispensed for symptomatic relief, only 42 were dispensed with labels that noted that the drug should be taken "as necessary" or "as needed." As one physician later explained, "I don't always write that, but that's what I *mean*."

A third communication problem was discovered when we compared the medication labels (the labels that are typed and attached by the pharmacist) with the physicians' prescription request forms (the forms that indicate how the physician wants the medication to be labeled). Of the 179 drugs for which both types of data were available, we found an inconsistency in 20 percent of the cases. In those cases where the physician wanted the label to include a statement about the symptom or condition being treated, the pharmacist sometimes omitted or incorrectly specified the symptom or condition. In other cases, the pharmacist did not translate the instructions into Spanish, as requested by the physician. Sometimes the containers were dispensed without the individualized labels that would have instructed the patient to take larger amounts on a more frequent basis than indicated on commercial labels (e.g., antacids for patients with peptic ulcers).

Fourth, an examination of the verbal and written instructions showed that in 29 percent of the cases the physicians gave no information about the purpose and/or names of the drug. Several physicians were more apt to give this type of information; others typically referred to the drugs by their form, color, and/or size (e.g., "Continue taking the little white tablets"). I suspected that the latter type of instruction would be less effective, because patients often have several drugs that fit the same physical description. I also suspected that if the patient learned why the physician was giving the drug, the patient might be more able to infer what the physician expected regarding its use.

After preliminary analysis, a Physician Instruction Index was developed. This composite index was used to score the verbal and written instructions received by each patient. Verbal instructions were scored as follows: how long to take the drug (+1), how regularly to take the drug (+1), the dosage schedule (+1), and the purposes or name of the drug (+1). When written instructions were provided, the following scores were added: how long to take the drug (+2), how regularly to take the drug (+2), the dosage schedule (+2), and the purpose of the drug (+2). If the labeled instructions were not consistent with the physician's prescription request form, then a score of −2 was given. The composite instruction score could range from +12 to −2.

The 131 patients studied were classified into two groups: patients receiving high instruction (a composite instruction score of +4 or more) or low instruction (a composite score of less than +4). Forty-eight patients received high instruction; 83 patients received low instruction.

The Outcomes of Physician Instruction

When we asked patients which drugs the physicians wanted them to take and how each drug was supposed to be taken, we found many misconceptions. Of the 131 patients, 68 patients made at least one error when describing what the physician expected. The patients did not recall 6 percent of the 347 drugs. They overestimated or underestimated how long 8 percent of the drugs were supposed to be taken. They had an inaccurate perception of the dosage schedule in 11 percent of the cases. They overestimated or underestimated how regularly they were supposed to take the drug in 17 percent of the cases. In addition, patients misunderstood the purpose of 23 percent of the drugs. For example, patients who had been given medication for hypertension sometimes thought that the drugs were for relief of asthma symptoms, palpitations, low back pain, and other problems.

Consistent with the working hypothesis, the patients who had a completely accurate perception of what the physician expected ($n = 63$) were more apt to conform with the physician's expectations; 60 percent of these patients conformed with the physician's treatment plan. Of the patients who made at least one error when describing what the physician expected ($n = 68$), 17 percent conformed. More importantly, there was a positive association between the amount of physician instruction, the accuracy of the patient's perceptions, and the rate of behavioral conformity. The patients who had received high instruction were more likely to have an accurate perception of the treatment plan than were the patients who had received low instruction (62 percent and 40 percent, respectively). Under the condition of high instruction, 52 percent of the patients conformed. Of the patients who had received low instruction, 29 percent conformed.

Modifying Conditions

Although many conditions might facilitate or inhibit the effectiveness of physician instruction, at least two sets of conditions should be considered. First are those affecting patient's attention, comprehension, and retention of the physician's "message." Patients' ability to learn was more limited when they were not familiar with the physician's language, be that English or medical terminology. For example, the terms "antibiotic" and "decongestant" may have different meanings or no meaning to patients who have difficulty with English or a low level of education. The patients sometimes referred to both kinds of medication as "cold pills," which were believed to serve the same purpose—the relief of cold symptoms. If any difference was attributed, it was that the antibiotic was a "stronger cold pill" which could relieve symptoms more quickly and effectively and which was given for a "bad cold." The patients' abilities to comprehend and retain information were also affected by how many drugs they had been given and whether they had prior experience with the drugs.

The second set of conditions relates to patients' willingness to ask for clarification or to make explicit statements that indicate their confusion or uncertainty about what the physician expects. These types of feedback seem to facilitate the instruction process by alerting the physician to the patient's particular need for additional instruction, interpretation, or clarification. Patients who provided such feedback received more instruction from the physician. The following excerpt illustrates how the patient can foster explicitness on the part of the physician:

Patient: Do I have to keep taking the medicine I got from Dr. —— last month?
Doctor: (looks in chart) You mean the medicine for the gas?
Patient: Yes.
Doctor: Are you still taking that?
Patient: Well, yes. I thought I was supposed to.
Doctor: No, you can stop that. You only have to take that when you have gas.

Unfortunately, few patients (n = 27) provided feedback, and even then only limited feedback. As a result, it is difficult to say how our findings might have been affected if the patients had been more actively involved during the instruction process.

The Process of Motivating the Patient

It has been suggested that patients' attitudes about taking medication might be affected by physician's attitudes about the medication,[77-78] but we know very little about the nature and outcome of physicians' efforts to motivate their patients. Physicians and patients often disagree with one another,[79] but it is not clear how physicians try to resolve these conflicts. It is useful to consider what social psychologists have suggested about the nature of social influence processes.[80-83] Physicians can be said to have at least three types of power that can be exerted in an effort to gain patients' motivation and behavioral conformity: (1) interpersonal power (i.e., appealing to patients' desire for social approval); (2) expert power (i.e., appealing to reason by justifying medication use); and (3) legitimate power or the power of medical authority (i.e., appealing to the norm that patients "should" or "ought to" comply with their physician's orders). In addition, physicians might be more apt to influence their patients if they emphasize what they expect.

With this in mind, I proceeded to the second phase of the inductive study. The physician-patient encounter was viewed as a situation in which the physician can motivate a patient by using a variety of influence strategies or appeals. We began with the following working hypotheses:

1. Patients will be more likely to conform if they have a high evaluation of the treatment plan.
2. Patients' evaluation of and conformity with the treatment plan will be higher if the physician makes a greater effort to motivate patients.

77. D. S. Irwin, et al. Phenothiazine intake and staff attitudes. *American Journal of Psychiatry 127* 1971: 1631–35.

78. E. Reynolds, et al. Psychological and clinical investigation of the treatment of anxious outpatients with three barbituates and a placebo. *British Journal of Psychiatry 111* 1965: 84–95.

79. M. S. Davis, Variations in patients' compliance with doctors' advice: An empirical analysis of patterns of communication. *American Journal Public Health 58* 1968b: 274–88.

80. J. R. P. French, Jr. & B. Raven, The bases of social power. In D. Cartright (Ed.) *Studies in Social Power.* Ann Arbor: University of Michigan Press, 1959.

81. B. Collins & B. Raven, Group structure: Attraction, coalitions, communcation, and power. In G. Lindzey & E. Aronson (Eds.) The *Handbook of Social Psychology*. Reading, Mass.: Addison-Wesley, 1969, pp. 102–204.

82. H. Kelman, Compliance, identification, and internalization: Three processes of attitude change. *Journal of Conflict Resolution 2* 1958: 51–60.

83. P. Blau, *Exchange and power in social life.* New York: Wiley, 1967.

Friendliness, Justification, Authority, and Emphasis

The first strategy the physician might use is to express friendliness and receptivity toward the patient. Presumably, this is an appeal to the patient's desire for social approval, or an effort to get the patient to like the physician so that the patient will be more receptive to the physician's advice. This strategy involves greeting the patient in a courteous manner, showing interest in the patient's questions and remarks, expressing positive affect toward the patient, and extending a courteous farewell. A content analysis of transcripts showed that this was the most commonly used influence strategy; the physicians were friendly and receptive toward 42 percent of the patients. Patient conformity was somewhat higher in those cases where the physician had been friendly, but the strategy by itself was not very effective. Further analysis indicated that friendliness was more effective if the patient also received high instruction. When there was both high instruction and friendliness, 78 percent of the patients conformed. Under high instruction and low friendliness, 42 percent conformed with the physician's treatment plan.

The second type of influence strategy is what can be called "justification"—an appeal to the patient's reason. Although the physicians in this clinic rarely gave the patients detailed explanations of the nature of their illness or of the long-term benefits that might be gained by using the prescribed medications, there was evidence that the physicians tried to justify why they were advising the use of drugs. In other words, they sometimes reported on the current status of the patient's condition before giving instructions, mentioned that the drug was important, or mentioned some other reason for taking the medication as advised. For example, one physician justified his advice by telling the patient, "Your second blood pressure (measurement) is still high so I would like to change the blood pressure medicine."

The strategy of high justification was evident in 40 percent of the cases and was one of the more effective influence strategies. Under the condition of high justification, 55 percent of the patients conformed with medical advice. Patients who received low justification conformed in only 27 percent of the cases.

To determine whether the physicians exerted their medical authority, we did a content analysis of the language they used when advising the patient about medication. Physicians were regarded as having exerted their authority if they gave instructions in a demanding or authoritative manner (e.g., "You *must* take three pills a day") or if they appealed to the norm that patients have an obligation to comply with medical orders (e.g., "You should take the medicine every day"). To our surprise, the physicians exerted their authority with only 18 percent of the patients. As in the case of physician friendliness, the strategy of exerting medical authority—by itself—was not highly effective. However, when the amount of physician instruction was controlled, the difference was more evident. When there was high instruction and high authority, 71 percent of the patients conformed with the treatment plan. Under the condition of high instruction and low authority, 51 percent of the patients conformed.

The fourth influence strategy—emphasis on what was expected—involved making two or more statements about the need to refill and continue taking the prescribed medications. Although it was not used often—there was emphasis in 12 percent of the cases—this strategy seemed effective. When physicians placed emphasis on their expectations, 65 percent of the patients subsequently conformed with advice. In comparison, low emphasis was associated with 34 percent conformity.

Monitoring Patients' Use of Previously Prescribed Drugs

One of the most notable differences among the eight physicians was that some engaged in more extensive monitoring (or follow-up) of how their patients had taken previously prescribed medications. These doctors asked the patients whether they had taken each drug, how many tablets they were taking a day, how much medication was left in the container, and other probing questions. Other physicians asked global questions without asking for details (e.g., "Are you taking your medicines?"). Some physicians did not ask any questions and seemed to assume, sometimes mistakenly, that the patient had been conforming with advice.

Extensive monitoring or follow-up seemed to be important in several respects. First, patients who were advised to follow instructions regarding previously prescribed drugs ($n = 81$) may have made certain assumptions, depending on whether the physician questioned them about their behavior. If the physician did not always question them and did not ask probing questions, they may have assumed that the physician did not attach much importance to the drug or their use of it.

Second, high monitoring seemed to be an integral aspect of the physician's efforts to maintain effective control over the patient and to resolve any conflicts between them. More specifically, monitoring was a means of eliciting more accurate feedback about which patients had a low evaluation of the previously prescribed treatment and which patients were not conforming with previous advice. It was anticipated that when physicians received such feedback they would make a greater effort to motivate patients and, as a result, would be more successful in achieving the desired pattern of behavior.

In general, these anticipations were confirmed. When physicians engaged in high monitoring ($n = 31$), 52 percent of the patients subsequently conformed with advice. Under low monitoring ($n = 50$), only 26 percent of the patients conformed. Several important findings emerged on the dynamics of the monitoring. First, physicians who engaged in more extensive follow-up received more *accurate* feedback from the patients; their patients were more apt to express their complaints and to admit that they had not been conforming with previous advice.[84] When physicians did not engage in extensive follow-up or monitoring,

---

84. Pharmacy files, medical records, and patient interview data indicated that at least 40 patients had not been following advice *before* the observed clinic visit. Thus, we could determine which patients admitted or concealed the fact that they had not been conforming with previous advice.

patients were less apt to express complaints about their medication and more apt to conceal the fact that they were not taking the medication as prescribed at the previous visit. Second, we found that the physicians made a greater effort to motivate the patient when patients admitted nonconformity and/or complained that the medicine was not necessary, did not seem to help, or caused side effects. Under these circumstances, physicians were more apt to express friendliness, provide justification, exert authority, emphasize what was expected, or engage in other influence tactics (e.g., reassure the patient about side effects or suggest ways in which the patient could cope with the negative features of the drug).

Physicians occasionally tolerated or ignored patient deviation from previous advice and, in some instances, changed the treatment plan (i.e., lowered the dosage, gave a different drug, or temporarily stopped all treatment). In addition to the strictly medical reasons for changing a treatment plan, several additional explanations might account for such physician adaptations. Some physicians may believe that it is not essential or desirable to take the previously prescribed dosage or to take certain drugs (such as tranquilizers) on a regular basis. As one of the physicians explained:

> I rarely start a patient on a tranquilizer. If someone else has given it to them and they (patients) request it again, I am more likely to give it. But I feel funny starting it myself, and I refill it only if the patient brings it up again. Otherwise, I just wait until they mention it . . . I don't care if they take it.

Such an adaptation may also be a strategy for maintaining the patients' commitment to at least some degree of long-term treatment and follow-up care, particularly where the patient is being treated for a chronic disease such as essential hypertension. Some physicians weigh the benefits and risks of *demanding* that patients follow the "ideal" treatment plan and decide that there are too many risks involved in pursuing a particular issue.

A Note on the Limitations of Medical Authority

Some evidence in this study suggests that physicians risk losing their power to influence patients if they frequently demand that patients follow "ideal" treatment plans and if they do not respond to patient's complaints about such plans. Two of the eight physicians frequently gave their instructions in a demanding or authoritative manner and frequently did not respond to patients' complaints about their medications. Their patients were more likely to conceal their nonconformity when the physician questioned them and were also less likely to conform even when the physician attempted to motivate them. On the basis of in-depth case analysis, it appeared that ignoring patients' complaints and demanding compliance eventually led to a breakdown in physician-patient communication, errors in clinical judgment, and patient mistrust of the physician's claims and appeals for conformity.

When physicians ignore patients' complaints and demand compliance, patients are faced with a dilemma. On the one hand, they may be afraid to take the medicine as prescribed. On the other, they may be reluctant to terminate their association with the clinic, believing that they need some type of treatment and follow-up for a chronic condition. Rather than follow the physician's plan of treatment, patients then decide to "test" the validity of an alternate plan—their own plan of treatment. For example, a patient may try taking less than the prescribed dosage or number of drugs. Since the patient may consider the physician intolerant and unresponsive, the patient will probably conceal his or her nonconformity on return visits to the physician. In effect, the physician begins to receive inaccurate information from the patient. In some cases, the physician may assume that the patient's condition improved or remained under control because the patient was taking the medicine as prescribed. By telling the patient that his or her condition is improved, the physician unwittingly confirms the patient's belief that it may not be necessary to take as much medicine as the physician claimed. This leads the patient to begin doubting the credibility and/or legitimacy of the physician's claims and appeals.

Consider the cases of Ms. A and Ms. B. According to Ms. A, her medication for hypertension did not help. When asked why, she told the interviewer:

sometimes I don't take the medicine and the pressure goes down by itself. And when I go back to the doctor, he would say, "Yeah, it has come down good." And I haven't even taken any medicine for quite awhile.

Next, consider the case of Ms. B, a patient who had been seeing one of the two physicians who frequently demanded that his patients follow advice and who frequently ignored complaints. Ms. B had hypertension and had not been following medication advice for about six months before the observed physician-patient visit. She was supposed to be taking three medications: (1) "water pills" (hydrochlorothiazide), (2) "kidney pills" (hydralazine), and (3) "artery pills" (guanethidine). However, before the observed visit, she had been only taking the "water pills," some of the "kidney pills," and none of the "artery pills." The medical record indicated that the physician was probably unaware of her nonconformity until the observed visit, despite the fact that the patient had made several other visits to the clinic. The following is an excerpt of the observed physician-patient interaction. The discussion about hypertension was initiated by the patient, who seemed surprised that her blood pressure had gone up on the day of the visit.

Patient: Why did my pressure go up?
Doctor: I don't know.
Patient: Maybe she (assistant) didn't take it right?
Doctor: (*laughs*) Yes. You've done very well. The least it could do is go down. You taking the water pills?
Patient: Yes.
Doctor: How many?
Patient: Morning and evening.
Doctor: That's two a day?

Patient: Yes.
Doctor: The artery pill?
Patient: Which one is it?
Doctor: For the blood vessels.
Patient: The blue one?
Doctor: No, that's the kidney pill. Are you taking the kidney pill?
Patient: Yes.
Doctor: How many?
Patient: *(responds slowly)* Twice a day—or four times a day.
Doctor: Maybe it is up because you're not taking enough. You should take it at least three times a day, sometimes four.
Patient: I take two instead of four. It never went up *before* when I didn't take it four times! *(said very assertively)*
Doctor: *(laughs)* Caught you now! *(reads chart)* 150 over 98. It's up a little.
Patient: Maybe I'm nervous. Comin' to the clinic and waiting makes me nervous.
Doctor: Take them a little more—right on the nose, the kidney pills. At least three a day, preferably four a day. Do you need any more?
Patient: No. It was like I was drunk. I stopped taking so many.
Doctor: Oh, that was it, huh. (Physician dropped the subject. There was no further discussion about this condition, the medications, or the patient's complaint that the medicine made her feel "drunk.")

Although the physician expressed friendliness, exerted authority, and justified medication use by reporting on the patient's condition, this patient did not modify her behavior after the observed visit. She continued to take less than prescribed. To the patient, it appeared quite logical to challenge the physician's claim that she should take the medicine as prescribed.

Although the physician takes certain risks when exerting authority, this influence strategy may be effective, particularly if it is used sparingly and if the physician does not, at the same time, ignore the patient's point of view. The more successful physicians are probably those who realize that their authority is limited.

The Physician's Total Effort To Motivate the Patient

Since physicians sometimes used a combination of influence strategies, it seemed useful to consider whether the *total* effort to motivate the patient was associated with the patient's subsequent evaluation of the treatment plan and behavioral conformity. A composite index was developed and used to score the physician's total efforts to influence the patient. The items were (1) friendliness, (2) justification, (3) exertion of authority, (4) emphasis, (5) monitoring, (6) responding to complaints, and (7) responding to admissions of nonconformity. The 131 patients studied were classified into groups where the physician made a high effort to motivate the patient ($n = 20$), a moderate effort ($n = 71$), and a low effort ($n = 40$).

There was a positive association between the physician's total effort to motivate and the patient's subsequent evaluation of the treatment plan. In the high effort group, 50 percent of the patients had a high evaluation of the treatment plan. They tended to believe that their medications were efficacious and important, that the drugs were not causing side effects or harm, and that they would suffer various negative consequences if they stopped the medications (e.g., risk of having a stroke or heart attack). In the moderate and low effort groups, patients were less apt to have a high evaluation of their drugs (19 percent and 11 percent, respectively). The relationship between physician effort and patient's subsequent behavior was even more considerable. Under the conditions of high, moderate, and low effort to motivate, the rates of behavioral conformity were 80 percent, 41 percent, and 13 percent, respectively. The relationship between physician effort to motivate and patient behavior was even more evident when the amount of physician instruction was taken into account. Under high instruction, patient conformity ranged from 100 percent (high effort) to 11 percent (low effort). In contrast, patient conformity ranged from 60 percent (high effort) to 13 percent (low effort) under the condition of low physician instruction.

Recapitulation

I do not pretend to have developed a refined theory of physician-patient communication as it relates to patient conformity with medication advice. But the approach described in this paper suggests a meaningful way of conceptualizing the problem. Two major dimensions of physician communication have been identified: (1) the physician's effort to instruct the patient and (2) the physician's effort to motivate the patient. Complementary dimensions of the patient's attitudes and behavior have also been noted: (1) the patient's perception of what the physician expects, (2) the patient's evaluation of the treatment plan, and (3) the patient's behavioral conformity. At least two major dimensions of patient communication must be recognized by physicians: (1) patient feedback, which indicates the patient's need for clarification, instruction, or interpretation, and (2) patient complaints about the treatment plan and information about whether previous advice has been followed. Other conditions that might facilitate or inhibit the processes by which physicians instruct and influence their patients are those that limit the patient's ability to learn the instructions and those that lead the patient to mistrust the physician's claims and appeals.

The Negotiated Diagnosis and Treatment of Occlusal Problems

16

GARY L. ALBRECHT

While there is recognition that dental health status is dependent on a host of genetic, environmental, nutritional, cultural, and familial factors [1–3], a careful examination of dental practice reveals that the success of modern dentistry is strongly influenced by the social interaction between dentists and patients. Effective repair and preventive maintenance of the gums, teeth, and mouth can only occur in a population when appropriate restoration and prevention techniques have been made available to an entire public. This process implies that effective treatment techniques are readily accessible to the user population at a low cost and that individuals are knowledgeable in their use. However, this transfer of technology and knowledge is not sufficient to produce optimal dental health in a population. The individuals must make regular use of the accessible technology to maintain and restore dental function and cosmetics. There are numerous examples of accessible technology that remains relatively useless because inappropriate means are often employed to achieve the articulated goals of dental health. At this moment, for example, there are many well-educated people who daily brush their teeth but suffer from gingivitis because they were not properly instructed to brush and were not encouraged to use dental floss. While considerable advances in dental technology have made high levels of dental function and cosmetics possible, the satisfactory implementation of this technology has not occurred. Indeed, incidence and prevalence statistics [4–7] suggest that large discrepancies exist between dental technology and utilization.

From *Social Science and Medicine, 11* 1977 277– 83. © 1977, Pergamon Press, Ltd. Reprinted with permission.

This gap between technology and utilization points to difficulties in the dentist-patient interaction process. In order to produce higher levels of dental health more must be known about dentist-patient interactions. This knowledge can enable the dentist to educate and treat the patient more effectively. The diagnosis and treatment of occlusal problems provides an excellent context within which to study dentist-patient interactions because the restorative problems and cosmetic problems seen by the orthodontist and the oral surgeon characterize many aspects of modern dental practice. While there is much talk of preventive dental care, most of dentistry today is concerned with restoration. Orthodontists and oral surgeons are confronted with acute problems requiring immediate intervention and chronic conditions that necessitate an entire rehabilitation program. For these reasons, this paper examines the social interactions between the orthodontist and oral surgeon and the individual with the occlusal problem.

While others have indicated the importance of dentist-patient interactions in dental practice [8–10], a considerable bias exists in the research literature. The social interaction between the dentist and the patient usually is not conceptualized or studied as a reciprocal process. Linn, in a review of research literature on dentist-patient relationships, points out that most of the literature is on children and that "research about the dentist-patient relationship has been mainly concerned with variations in the behavior, feelings, and attitudes of *patients*. The dentist appears only insofar as he may be advised about the management of patients. His personality and social expectancies are not included among the variables of the relationship. Perhaps his exclusion fits the realities of the relationship. At least from the present writer's observations in dental operatories, it would seem that the dentist's psychological and social individuality is hidden behind his professional manner." [18] Linn then proceeds to review the literature on dentist-patient interactions, emphasizing the patient and measurement aspects of the relationship. However, a careful examination of the relationship between dentist and patient requires that equal attention be given to each if the dynamics of the reciprocal social interaction are to be understood.

There is substantial evidence to demonstrate that social interaction is a reciprocal process [11–13], that individuals in the classical dependent role often socialize the traditional agent of socialization [14, 15], and that adults are continually being socialized as well as socializing others [16]. Children socialize parents and teachers, prisoners socialize guards and wardens, and clients socialize professionals [17]. To strike a balance in the dental literature on dentist-patient interactions, this discussion will attend to the social and cultural influences that affect the provider of services to the individual with an occlusal problem. To understand the interactions between providers of services and the individual with the problem, there is need to consider the individual's problem and the type of people that diagnose and treat those problems. The emphasis throughout this paper will be on the dynamic, reciprocal interaction process that occurs between the dentist and the patient with an occlusal problem.

The Occlusion Problem

Malocclusion is both an overt and latent problem of major dimensions that can be treated by orthodontists and oral surgeons. A review of the dental research literature on prevalence of conditions requiring treatment in England and the United States shows that up to 90 percent of the population may need dental treatment of one kind or another [4, 18, 19]. Yet in two different areas in England where 90 percent of the population needed dental treatment, only 60 percent thought that they required dental treatment [4]. In a large national study conducted in the United States, 83 percent of the respondents reported that "their dental needs for the coming year were 'not much' or 'none.' " [7] Thus there is an obvious disparity between the high actual need and the low or moderate perceived need for dental treatment. Similar patterns hold true for malocclusion. Estimates of occlusal problems among young children range from 10 [20] to 45 percent [21]. In a study of senior high school students, Ast, Carlos and Cons [22] conclude that up to 95 percent of that population may experience some form of malocclusion. In a summary of 15 research studies, Massler and Frankel [23] state that the reported prevalence of malocclusion in the 14–22 age group varied from 30 to 100 percent. Yet the evidence indicates that not all of these individuals with occlusal problems perceive the need and seek or receive proper dental treatment [4, 6, 24]. Linn [18] reports that 22 percent of the respondents in a national study of the United States were reported by the interviewers to have visibly missing teeth and another 15 percent were reported to have discolored teeth. In this study, visibility of dental problems was not a sufficient reason to perceive a need and seek dental care. This pattern was modified by the variables of education, race, and age in the predicted directions.

The discrepancies in the ranges of the reported prevalence rates for malocclusion underline the measurement problems in the field. Whereas Christensen and Coughlin [25] argue that the majority of dental practice in the United States is concerned with restoration, others assert that a considerable portion of dentistry focuses on cosmetics [26–29]. The difficulty in distinguishing between restorative and cosmetic needs is a problem of measurement. It is diffcult to decide: (1) when a malocclusion ceases to be a functional problem and becomes an issue of cosmetics; (2) the level of severity of the problem; and (3) whether severity should be defined in terms of both physical function and cosmetics.

Malocclusion is one of the most difficult oral conditions to measure because there are no clear criteria of what constitutes the *mal*occlusion [30]. For this reason, the author prefers the phrase occlusal problems to the term malocclusion. There are physical, social, and cultural components to the definition and measurement of malocclusion. The determination of a malocclusion is a value judgment based on anatomical deviations, social ideals, and cultural values. On the physical level occlusal function might include the physical equipment necessary for eating and speaking. On the social level occlusal function might include the verbal and nonverbal cues requisite for presentation of one's self and interpersonal attraction. Measurement problems persist because the same parts of the head and the face are used for bodily functioning and social communication. On the cultural level occlusal function is dependent on cultural values such as aesthetics and body image. For example, an overbite in the United States may be judged to need correction, while in Japan it may be cosmetically desirable. In discussing the need and demand for orthodontic treatment, Jenny [31] shows that there is wide cultural variation in the conception of what is an aesthetically pleasing dentofacial appearance. African and South American tribespeople file upper anterior teeth to a point, inlay decorative stones and gold in their incisors and canines, and insert large disks in their lips to meet cultural values of physical attractiveness. In the United States even children respond to sociocultural norms by preferring straight, even teeth to crooked teeth [32, 33]. For these reasons, malocclusion cannot be defined by an orthodontic clinician or dental scientist alone.

Malocclusion also has objective and subjective components. The dental professional, the individual, the significant others, and the larger society may well define and interpret the situation quite differently and therefore have different and even conflicting expectations. Therefore, because of measurement problems and differential interpretation, malocclusion is often ambiguously defined by the major parties who must join in a social interaction process over time to define, meet, and solve the perceived problem. This perceived ambiguity is the basis for negotiated diagnosis and treatment of the occlusal problem. The negotiation occurs between the major parties in the social interaction: the dentist, the individual, the significant others, and representatives of the larger society. The final negotiated definition of malocclusion is important because it affects the individual's self-image, the expectations of others, the treatment received, and payment for treatment.

Occlusal problems are found in all social and cultural groups. However, the providers of dental services are not representative of all social and cultural groups but tend to belong to very restricted sections of society. A brief look at the providers on dental services will give some insight into their particular position in the diagnosis and treatment negotiation process.

The Professionals Trained to Meet the Occlusal Problem

Although over 95 percent of the population experiences dental decay and almost every adult is affected during the adult years by periodontal disease, there is but 1 dentist for every 2½ physicians [34]. Over 70 percent of the dentists in the United States are self-employed and practice without partners [35].

Unlike medical practice, the dentist's work is only rarely seen by any other person trained in a health field. It is also interesting to note that while there is a high value placed on professional specialization in American society [36], less than 10 percent of the dentists in the United States are specialists. Of the 123,349 dentists in the United States, 11,142 are specialists. Of these, 4566 are orthodontists and 2714 are oral surgeons [37]. Among the dental specialists, oral surgeons and orthodontists rank number two and three behind endodontists in average income [37] and seem to have the most prestige [37, 38]. They also tend to live and practice in urban areas [34, 39].

While women comprise 50 percent or more of the dentists in Greece, South America, Norway, Poland, Finland, and Russia, they account for only 1.2 percent of the American dentists [40]. They definitely constitute a minority group within the profession that reports little manifest but considerable subtle and covert discrimination against females [41]. There has been a disproportionate rise in the percentage of women entering dental school during the last two years so there will be a gradual increase in women in the profession in the years ahead. Blacks are also underrepresented in the dental profession

In 1969 there were only 356 blacks in American dental schools and 90 percent of these attended Howard and Meharry [42]. The impact of these statistics is realized when it is pointed out that although there is one dentist for every 2000 people in the total American population, there is only one black dentist for every 12,500 blacks in the population. There are almost no other racial minority groups represented in the group of dental professionals. There are even proportionately fewer minority dentists represented among the oral surgery and orthodontics specialities. Thus the characteristics of the dental professionals are in marked contrast to the populations that need care and are served. The professional dentists in the United States and particularly the oral surgeons and orthodontists are white, upwardly mobile, male sons of middle-and upper-middle-class parents who tend to practice alone in urban areas on a fee for service basis [43, 44]. These facts have considerable repercussions for the practice of dentistry and the negotiations of diagnosis and treatment that occur in the social interaction process between dentist, individual, significant others, and representatives of the larger society because they help to establish the position from which the dentist will bargain.

Dentist-Consumer Interactions:
The Negotiation Process

The perception and identification of a dental problem is complex. An examination of Table 16–1 suggests that an individual may or may not have an occlusal problem as determined by objective criteria [26].

In addition, an objectively identified occlusal problem may or may not be perceived by self and others. There are even instances in which occlusal problems are perceived by self and others but there is no objective evidence to substantiate the existence of the problem. For effective diagnosis and treatment to occur, the individual with the perceived and/or real occlusal problem and the dental professional must arrive at a consensus. This consensus is reached through a reciprocal social interaction process often characterized by bargaining and negotiation. Each party has his own interests, costs he is willing to pay, and anticipated rewards. The exchange between the individual and the dentist most often results in a compromise acceptable to each. A careful examination of this bargaining and negotiation process permits a better understanding of modern dental care.

Table 16-1   Identification and Perception of Occlusal Problems

	Determination of occlusal problem by objective criteria	
Perception of Occlusal Problems by Self and Others	**Occlusal Problem**	**No Occlusal Problem**
	Perceived by self Perceived by others	Perceived by self Perceived by others
	Perceived by self Not perceived by others	Perceived by self Not perceived by others
	Not perceived by self Perceived by others	Not perceived by self Perceived by others
	Not perceived by self Not perceived by others	Not perceived by self Not perceived by others

The traditional model of dental care has assumed that the patient seeks out the dentist and presents his symptoms. The dentist, then, is expected to examine the patient, produce a clear diagnosis, and prescribe treatment. The patient, in turn, is expected to accept the diagnosis without question and to faithfully undertake and complete the prescribed treatment. The dentist is typically in control of the interaction. He works on a passive, supine patient who frequently cannot even respond while undergoing examination and treatment. Underlying these expectations in the dentist-patient interaction are the assumptions that individuals with "serious" dental problems will come to the dentist for help, that there are clearly defined physical causes that have produced the symptoms, that the doctor knows best, that the patient will agree with the dentist's diagnosis and treatment prescription, and that the patient will carry out the treatment without questioning the authority of the dentist. These expectations persist even in light of evidence which indicates that patients react much more favorably to low authoritarian dentists than they do to high authoritarian dentists [45].

While many people assume that patients conform to the doctor's orders, 37 percent of the patients in a study by Davis were noncompliant [46]. Noncompliance occurred when the patient took the active role in the relationship and/or refused to execute the doctor's orders. The social interaction between the doctor and the patient is very important to the effectiveness of the treatment and the satisfaction of the doctor and the patient. Patient compliance with the doctor's orders and the satisfaction of doctor and patient are dependent on accurate communication and good rapport [47, 48]. These data emphasize the importance of doctor-patient negotiation. Successful negotiation is based on a reciprocal relationship, good rapport, open communication, clear understanding of the issues, and goal consensus. Therefore, it is to the benefit of both the dentist and the patient to negotiate diagnosis and treatment, but in order to negotiate well, both the issues and the process must be clearly understood.

The interactional relationship and type of consensus between the dentist and the patient certainly affect treatment outcome. The primary goal of the dentist and the patient is likely to be optimal dental health for the patient, but the interpretation and operationalization of this goal belie the apparent goal consensus. The dentist may be interested in preventing caries and periodontal disease, performing the restorative work necessary to save the patient's teeth, bringing existing periodontal disease under control, solving occlusal problems, earning a high professional income, having the prestige and lifestyle of a "doctor," owning a burgeoning private dental practice to secure the future, and achieving peer recognition. The patient may on the other hand be interested in alleviating pain, improving craniofacial appearance, and utilizing trained specialists at a low cost. The dentist's and patient's significant others and the representatives of the larger society such as insurance companies, legislators, accreditation boards, boards of health, and consumer protection groups may have other expectations of optimal dental health for the patient. Thus, the perception and interpretation of optimal dental health for the patient might be quite different depending upon one's perspective.

Just as there are considerable differences in the judgment of what constitutes optimal dental health for the patient, interested individuals and organizations also bring different expectations about specific aspects of diagnosis and treatment with them to the interactional setting. The dentist, consumer, significant others, and representatives of the larger society exhibit expectations, norms, and performance characteristics that typify their own socialization experiences, social reference groups, and cultural settings. These social and cultural influences upon the dentist and the patient produce divergent definitions of the situation. Lindegard et al. [49] report the prevalence of malocclusion among 5000 Danish school children to approximately 75 percent of the population. Yet the parents' demand for orthodontic treatment was well below this level. In a study of 305 dental hygiene and dental assistant students in the Boston area, Hilgenrath [5] found a noticeable difference between self-perceived and objectively determined orthodontic conditions. More than 36 percent of those students judged as needing orthodontic treatment reported that they were satisfied with their tooth alignment. In this study, lower-class subjects were less likely than upper-class subjects to have received treatment when it was needed. These data are particularly interesting because they describe diagnostic and utilization patterns among paraprofessional dental students who should be sensitized to dental care. These data also underscore the fact that social and cultural factors influence the social interaction between dentist and patient.

Occlusal problems can be conceptualized as a type of deviance. The individual with the malformed face, mouth, or head is judged to be deviant and therefore in need of treatment. But as we have just observed, the perception and interpretation of deviance is dependent upon the individual's own viewpoint and culture. Freidson [50] distinguishes between the professional and the lay construction of illness which are often conflicting perspectives. Is deviance something "objective" and an absolute or is it a product of the participants of a society? Most dental researchers undertake a professional construction of malocclusal deviance based on "objective and absolute" criteria. Malocclusion is measured in terms of dentofacial deviation [26]. The severity of malocclusion is determined by the amount and number of dentofacial anomalies [51] and is measured in terms of overjet, labiolingual spread, anterior spacing, arch length and width, lingual crossbite, buccal crossbite, number of missing teeth, and upper median diastema [52]. However, nowhere in these discussions is there mention of social and cultural definitions or determinants of occlusal deviance.

Because of the difficult measurement problems and lack of consideration of the social and cultural factors that influence the diagnosis and treatment of malocclusions, there is considerable ambiguity about the definition and treatment of the problem. What constitutes the normal and the deviant mouth? How are the functional and cosmetic aspects of craniofacial malformations distinguished? Who defines the problem, identifies the level of severity, and prescribes an acceptable treatment? Contrary to the traditional dental model, I argue that the dentist and the patient do negotiate a diagnosis and treatment in terms of their own social construction of the problem. This is the only fashion in which divergent and ambiguous expectations can be clarified and treatment goals contracted. However, this negotiation process is not well understood.

The dentist and patient first have to determine the nature and extent of the problem before they agree to a mutually acceptable treatment program. At the outset it should be noted that American dentists are a relatively homogeneous group of white males from lower-middle and middle-class backgrounds while the user population spans race, sex, education, social class, and geographic and cultural groupings. This disparity is compounded by the fact that the dentist sees the patient in his office and rarely ever sees a patient in a home or on the patient's terms. In fact, waiting in a "sterile" waiting room with strangers and being entirely at the mercy of the dentist are all circumstances that reinforce the dependency relationship of the patient on the dentist [53]. The dentist possesses the expertise and the time to alleviate the patient's problem. On the other hand, the patient is a consumer who can control the behavior of the dentist through the use of money and manipulation of prestige. The relationship between dentist and consumer is symbiotic. Neither party will achieve their goals without the cooperation of the other party.

The negotiation between dentist and patient is a mutual education that takes differentially perceived costs and rewards into account. The consumer often comes to the dentist because he is frightened by his perceived symptoms, he is in pain, or he desires some cosmetic changes [54, 55]. The dentist takes the visit as an occasion to assess the dental needs of the patient. He attempts to communicate these needs to the patient. The patient-consumer may or may not perceive the same needs. If the consumer does perceive the need, he may not want the work done and he may not be able to pay for it. The dentist is trained to look toward the future while the patient is usually interested only in solving the immediate problem. The mutual education continues. What needs to be done? Is it necessary? How much will it cost? When do I have to have it done? When can I pay for the work? bill? Do third party payers encourage some dental treatments and not others? The consumer needs to have some dental work done and therefore must rely on a dentist. However, he does not have to rely on *this* dentist. The consumer can do some comparative shopping to find the professional whom he likes, believes, and can afford. The dentist knows this so he is caught in a calculus of maximizing his rewards and minimizing his losses. He desires to help the patient with both the perceived and unperceived problems, increase his practice, and generate an acceptable cash flow and income [56]. It is not to his benefit to lose patients [57].

A basic problem of the negotiation process, then, is the definition of actual need versus perceived need. Yet, even after the issue of distinguishing between real and perceived occlusal problems has been met, the problem of defining the severity of the occlusal problem remains. How much of the work of oral surgeons and orthodontists is aimed at improving function and how much is designed to make individuals cosmetically attractive? For example, Freidson [50] reviews literature documenting what seems to be unwarranted and unnecessary surgery. Denenberg [58] warns the consumer that much of the surgery performed in the United States is not needed to save lives or preserve function. In fact, he suggests a medical variation of Parkinson's law: patient admissions for surgery increase to fully utilize surgeon's time and fill operating suites. In a context where dental manpower is not sufficient to meet the demand, do orthodontists and oral surgeons perform work that is neither warranted nor necessary? In fact, is cosmetic work performed while functional problems go untreated because the paying customer gets the service?

The relationship between the cosmetic and functional aspects of occlusal problems can be explored in Table 16–2.

While dentists and the public are taught to be concerned primarily with the physical function of the mouth, physical appearance is very important for social functioning. Physical attractiveness cannot be disregarded when there is substantial evidence to indicate that high value is placed on physical appearance in American society. Therefore, consumers of dental services have demanded treatment to improve both appearances and physical function. Sound free market economics dictates that suppliers of services will meet the market demand if it is profitable. Cosmetic dental care is profitable so there are many orthodontists and oral surgeons performing these services. While some would argue that highly trained dentists in short supply ought not to waste their time dealing with cosmetic problems when there are many untreated persons with malocclusions in the community, others contend that cosmetic treatment is necessary and important to improve the social functioning of individuals in a society where there is a high value placed on physical attractiveness. Regardless of one's values, there is a consumer demand for cosmetic treatment and the dental profession has responded to this market. Thus, the type of diagnosis and treatment is negotiated between the consumer with his perceived needs and the dentist with his perceived needs. This negotiation of diagnosis and treatment has cosmetic and functional components.

In examining the matrix in Table 16–2, one could hypothesize that highly dysfunctional, highly visible occlusal problems are easier to negotiate than low visible, high dysfunction and high visible, low dysfunction occlusal problems. Zahn has pointed out that individuals usually identify and adapt better to highly visible disabilities than they do to those that are less obvious. The marginal case is difficult to classify and negotiate. One could further hypothesize that few individuals with low dysfunction, low visible occlusal problems would seek dental help. However, in fact, these hypotheses might not be supported when put to the test.

Table 16–2 Typology of Occlusal Problems Seen by Dentists

| | | Degree of physical dysfunction | |
		High	Low
Degree of Visibility	High	High High	Low High
	Low	High Low	Low Low

The person with a highly visible, highly dysfunctional occlusal problem may find it difficult to negotiate diagnosis and treatment because his problem is beyond the technology, skill, and competence of the majority of dentists. This person would probably be referred to a specialized university or research oriented clinic. Perhaps not much can be done with the severely impaired so there may be little to negotiate. People who have a highly dysfunctional and highly visible occlusal problem usually are of the lower and working classes [5, 31]. The middle and upper classes have fewer of these problems, usually prevent these problems from occurring and, when they do arise, deal with them early in the disease process. The middle and upper classes have more money and insurance coverage to pay for treatment and are socialized to care for their teeth. Therefore there is a high demand for dental care aimed at low to moderate cosmetic and functional occlusal problems. There is a wide based technology to deal with these problems and a large consumer group who desires these services and have the means to pay.

The negotiation of diagnosis and treatment of occlusal problems is, then, greatly influenced by the available technology, consumer demand, and ability to pay. It should be noted that dental services and fees, like legal services and fees, are not as closely regulated as fees for and quality of medical service. This is due in part to the lack of comprehensive dental insurance plans. Therefore, the dentist and the patient-consumer have a broad range in which to negotiate diagnosis, service and fee.

The matrices in Tables 16–1 and 16–2 are useful because they allow the generation of many testable empirical hypotheses based on a model of negotiation. The model serves as a basis for research and the results of hypothesis testing have immediate implications for dental practice.

Conclusion

The negotiation of the diagnosis and treatment of occlusal problems is important because the effectiveness of the treatment and the satisfaction of the patient and the dentist depend on it. Quality of dental care is judged by change in oral health status before, during and after treatment and by consumer satisfaction. Negotiation does have a direct effect on quality of dental care.

There is evidence that differential perceptions, norms and expectations, age, race, sex, education, visibility of the problem, dysfunction related to the problem, situational contexts, cultural values, social class, income, ability to pay, perception of fear and pain, and insurance benefits contribute to the outcome of the negotiation of diagnosis and treatment between the dentist and the consumer [27, 62–64]. Just as diagnosis and treatment are negotiated, the evaluation of quality of care and treatment outcome is also a complex negotiated process involving the patient's function, appearance, fear, pain, and cost of treatment as perceived by the dentist, consumer, significant others, and societal representatives. Research is needed to better define this negotiation process and to assess the effects of the negotiation on the quality of dental care. A fruitful approach to the study of this negotiation process would consist of systematic, in-depth, prospective analyses of dental-patient interactions over time.

References
1. Lilienthal, B., Amerena, L., & Gregory, C. An epidemiological study of chronic periodontal disease. *Archives of Oral Biology 10 (553)* 1965.
2. Cheraskin, E. & Ringsdorf, W. Familial enzymic patterns: II. Lactic dehydrogenase in the dentist and his wife. *Nutrition Reports International 1 (125)* 1970.
3. Chung, C., Runck, D., Niswander, J., Bilben, S., & Dan M. Genetic and epidemiological studies of oral characteristics in Hawaii's schoolchildren: I. Caries and periodontal disease. *Journal of Dental Research 49 (1374)* 1970
4. Dulman, J., Richards, N., Slack, G., & Willcocks, A. *Demand and need for dental care.* London: Oxford University Press, 1968.
5. Hilgenrath, S. *Social and psychological factors related to malocclusion and the seeking of orthodontic treatment.* Boston: Harvard University Thesis, 1970.
6. Andersen, R., Greely, R., Kravits, J., & Anderson, O. *Health Service use. National trends and variations 1953–71.* DHEW Publication (HSM) 73–3004, 1972, p. 20.
7. Newman, J., & Anderson, O. *Patterns of dental service utilization in the United States: A nationwide social survey.* Center for Health Administration Studies, University of Chicago, Chicago, 1972.

8. Howitt, J., & Stricker, G. *Child patient responses to different dental procedures. Journal of the American Dental Association 70 (70)* 1965.
9. Martin, R. *An exploratory investion of the dentist-patient relation.* Dental Health Education and Research Foundation. Sydney: University of Sydney, 1965.
10. Croxton, W. Child behavior and dental experience. *Journal of Dentistry for Children 34 (212)* 1967.
11. Bell, R., A reinterpretation of the direction of effects in studies of socialization. *Psychological Review 75 (81)* 1968.
12. Bell, R., Stimulus control of parent or caretaker behavior by offspring. *Developmental Psychology 4 (63)* 1971.
13. Albrecht, G. The alcoholism process: A social learning viewpoint. In P. Bourne (Ed.) *Alcoholism: Progress in research and treatment.* New York: Academic Press, 1973.
14. Gerwirtz, J. Mechanisms of social learning: Some roles of stimulation and behavior in early human development. In D. Goslin (Ed.) *Handbook of socialization theory and research.* Chicago: Rand McNally, 1969.
15. Gray, F., Graubard, P., & Rosenberg, H. Little brother is changing you. *Psychology Today 7 (42)* 1974.
16. Brim, O. & Wheeler, S. *Socialization after childhood.* New York: Wiley, 1966.
17. Katz, E. & Danet, B. Petitions and persuasive appeals: A study of official-client relations. In E. Katz & B. Danet (Eds.) *Bureaucracy and the public.* New York: Basic Books, 1973.
18. Linn, E. Social meaning of dental appearance. *Journal of Health and Human Behavior 7 (289)* 1966.
19. DeGeyndt, W. Health behavior and health needs of urban Indians in Minneapolis. *Health Services Report 88 (360)* 1973.
20. Messner, C., Gafafer, W., & Cady, F. Dental survey of school children ages 6–14 years made in 1933–34 in 26 states. *Public Health Bulletin,* No. 226, Washington, D.C.
21. Fulton, J. The public health aspects of orthodontics. *Bulletin of the American Association of Public Health and Dentistry 12 (10)* 1952.
22. Ast, D., Carlos, J., & Cons, N. The prevalence and characteristics of malocclusion among senior high school students in upstate New York. *American Journal of Orthodontics 51 (437)* 1965.
23. Massler, M., & Frankel, J. Prevalence of malocclusion in children aged 14–18 years. *American Journal of Orthodontics 37 (751)* 1961.
24. Scarrott, D. Attitudes to dentists. *British Journal of Dentistry 127 (583)* 1969.
25. Christensen, G., & Coughlin, J. Restorative dentistry in the seventies. *Journal of Dental Education 37 (23)* 1973.
26. Salzmann, J. Malocclusion severity assessment. *American Journal of Orthodontics 53 (109)* 1967.
27. Tulley, W. Attitudes to orthodontics. *Schweiz Monatsschrift für Zahnheilkunde 80 (622)* 1970.
28. Dummett, C. Consumer-provider conflict in health service recommendations. *Health Service Reports 88 (795)* 1973.
29. Weiss, J. Body image in orthodontics. *Journal of the New Jersey Dental Association 45 (14)* 1973.

30. Cohen, L. & Jago, J. Toward the formulation of sociodental indicators. *International Journal of Health Service 6 (681)* 1976.
31. Jenny, J. A social perspective on need and demand for orthodontic treatment. *International Dental Journal 25 (248)* 1975.
32. Cohen, L., & Horowitz, H. Occlusal relations in children born and reared in an optimally fluoridated community. III. Sociophysical findings. *Angle Orthodontist 40 (159)* 1970.
33. Richardson, S. Age and sex differences in values toward physical handicaps. *Journal of Health and Social Behavior 11 (207)* 1970.
34. Young, W., & Smith, L. The nature and organization of dental practice. In H. Freeman, S. Levine, & L. G. Reeder (Eds.) *Handbook of medical sociology.* Englewood Cliffs, N.J.: Prentice-Hall, 1972.
35. Bureau of Economic Research and Statistics, Growth in population and number of dentists to 1985. *Journal of the American Dental Association 87 (901)* 1973.
36. Miller, S. Prescriptions for leadership: Training for the medical elite. Chicago: Aldine, 1970.
37. Bureau of Economic Research and Statistics, *Distribution of dentists in the United States by state, region, district, and county.* Chicago: American Dental Association, 1974.
38. O'Shea, R., & Cohen, L. Social sciences and dentistry. *Journal of Public Health and Dentistry. 28 (135)* 1968.
39. Durban, E., D.D.S. M.D. . . . what's the hang-up? *Dental Economics 63 (42)* 1973.
40. Bureau of Economic Research and Statistics, *Distribution of orthodontists by state, city, and federal dental service 1973.* Chicago: American Dental Association, 1973.
41. Campbell, J. Women dentists—an untapped resource. *Journal of the American College of Dentists 37 (265)* 1970.
42. Austin, G., Maher, M., & Lomonaco, C. Women in dentistry and medicine: Attitudinal study of educational experience. *Journal of Dental Education 38 (11)* 1973.
43. Henry, J. Bridging the gap. *Journal of the American College of Dentists 37 (249)* 1970.
44. Fusillo, A., & Metz, A.S. Social science research on the dental student. In N. D. Richards & L. Cohen (Eds.) *Social sciences and dentistry: A critical bibliography.* The Hague: Federation Dentaire Internationale, 1971.
45. Bureau of Economic Research and Statistics, *The 1971 survey of dental practice.* Chicago: American Dental Association, 1973.
46. Hirsch, B., Levin, B., & Tiber, N. Effects of dentist authoritarianism on patient evaluation of dentures. *Journal of Prosthetic Dentistry 30 (745)* 1973.
47. Davis, M. Variation in patients' compliance with doctors' orders: Medical practice and doctor-patient interaction. *Psychiatry in Medicine 2 (31)* 1971.
48. Davis, M. Attitudinal and behavioral aspects of the doctor-patient relationship as expressed and exhibited by medical students and their mentors. *Journal of Medical Education 43 (337)* 1968.
49. Korsch, B., & Negrete, V. Doctor-patient communication. *Scientific American 230 (66)* 1972.
50. Lindegard, B., Lindegard, L., Carlson, M., & Larson, S. Need and demand for orthodontic treatment. *Tandlaegebladet 75 (1198)* 1971.

51. Friedson, E. *Profession of medicine.* New York: Dodd-Mead, 1970.
52. Baume, L., & Marechaux, S. Uniform methods for the epidemiologic assessment of malocclusion. *American Journal of Orthodontics 66 (121)* 1974.
53. Freer, T. Selection of predictor variables in assessing the severity of malocclusion. *American Journal of Orthodontics 64 (155)* 1973.
54. Schwartz, B. Waiting, exchange and power: The distribution of time in social systems. *American Journal of Sociology 79 (841)* 1974.
55. Burns, M., Psychological aspects of orthodontics. In W. Cinotti, G. Arthur, & H. Springob (Eds.) *Applied psychology in dentistry.* St. Louis: Mosby, 1972.
56. Kleinknecht, R., Klepac, R., & Alexander, L. Origins and characteristics of fear of dentistry. *Journal of the American Dental Association 86 (842)* 1973.
57. Waldman, H. B. Usual and customary: Philosophy and fees. *Annals of Dentistry 31 (36)* 1972.
58. Huntington, J. Distant early warning system for your practice. *Dental Management 13 (52)* 1973.
59. Denenberg, H. *Shopper's guide to surgery.* Harrisburg, Pa.: State of Pennsylvania, 1973.
60. Berscheid, E., Walster, E., & Bonrnstedt, G. The happy American body: A Survey report. *Psychology Today 7 (119)* 1973.
61. Zahn, M. Incapacity, impotence and invisible impairment: Their effects upon interpersonal relations. *Journal of Health and Social Behavior 14 (115)* 1973.
62. Kisch, A., & Reader, L. Client evaluation of physician performance. *Journal of Health and Social Behavior 10 (51)* 1969.
63. Silverman, M. Orthodontics and body image. *Pennsylvania Dental Journal 38 (10)* 1971.
64. Jones, R., Dentists' views on reimbursement arrangements under prepayment and insurance plans. *Journal of the American Dental Association 84 (125)* 1972.
65. Bell, D. Prosthodontic failures related to improper patient education and lack of patient acceptance. *Dental Clinic North America 16 (109)* 1972.

Some Contingencies of the Moral Evaluation and Control of Clientele: The Case of the Hospital Emergency Service

17

JULIUS A. ROTH

The moral evaluation of patients by staff members has been explored in detail in the case of "mental illness" (Scheff, 1966, Chap. 5; Strauss et al., 1964, Chaps. 8 and 12; Belknap, 1956; Scheff, 1964; Goffman, 1961, 125–70, 321–86; Hollingshead and Redlich, 1958; Szasz, 1960). The assumption is made by some (especially Thomas Szasz) that mental illness is a special case which readily allows moral judgments to be made because there are no technical criteria to be applied and because psychiatric concepts in their historical development have been a pseudoscientific replacement of moral judgments. Charles Perrow (1965) stresses lack of technology as a factor which forces psychiatric practitioners to fall back on commonsense concepts of humanitarianism which open the way to moral evaluations of the clientele.

I contend that the diagnosis and treatment of mental illness and the "care" of mental patients are not unique in incorporating moral judgments of the clientele, but are only obvious examples of a more general phenomenon which exists no matter what the historical development or the present state of the technology. Glaser and Strauss (1964) put forward such a notion when they demonstrated

The study on which this paper is based was supported by National Institutes of Health grants HM-00437 and HM-00517, Division of Hospital and Medical Facilities. Dorothy J. Douglass, currently at the University of Connecticut Health Center, worked with me and made major contributions to this study.

how the "social worth" of a dying patient affects the nursing care he will receive. I would add that moral evaluation also has a direct effect on a physician's diagnosis and treatment recommendations. This is obvious in extreme cases, such as when a monarch or the president of the United States is attended by teams of highly qualified diagnosticians to insure a detailed and accurate diagnosis and has outstanding specialists flown to his bedside to carry out the treatment. I will discuss some aspects of this same process as it applies on a day-to-day basis in a routine hospital operation involving more "ordinary" patients.

The data are taken from observation of six hospital emergency services in two parts of the country—one northeastern location and one West Coast location. My coworkers and I spend several periods of time (spread over two or three months in each case) in the emergency department of each of the hospitals. In one hospital we worked as intake clerks over a period of three months. At other times we observed areas in the emergency unit without initiating any interaction with patients, visitors, or personnel. At other points we followed patients through the emergency service from their first appearance to discharge or inpatient admission, interviewing patient and staff during the process. During these periods of observation, notes were also kept on relevant conversations with staff members.

The hospital emergency service is a setting where a minimum of information is available about the character of each patient and a long-term relationship with the patient is usually not contemplated. Even under these conditions, judgments about a patient's moral fitness and the appropriateness of his visit to an emergency service are constantly made, and staff action concerning the patient—including diagnosis, treatment, and disposition of the case—are, in part, affected by these judgments.

The Deserving and the Undeserving

The evaluation of patients and visitors by emergency-ward staff may be conveniently thought of in two categories: (1) the application by the staff of concepts of social worth common in the larger society and, (2) staff members' concepts of their appropriate work role. In this section I will take up the first of these.

There is a popular myth (generated in part by some sociological writing) that persons engaged in providing professional services, especially medical care, do not permit the commonly accepted concepts of social worth in our culture to affect their relationship to the clientele. An on-the-spot description of *any* service profession—medicine, education, law, social welfare, etc.—should disabuse us of this notion. There is no evidence that professional training succeeds in creating a universalistic moral neutrality (Becker et al., 1961, 323–27). On the contrary, we are on much safer ground to assume that those engaged in dispensing professional services (or any other services) will apply the evaluations of social worth common to their culture and will modify their services with respect to those evaluations *unless discouraged from doing so by the organizational arrangements under which they work.* Some such organizational arrangements do exist on emergency wards. The rapid turnover and impersonality of the operation is in itself a protection for many patients who might be devalued if more were known about them. In public hospitals, at least, there is a rule that *all* patients presenting themselves at the registration desk must be seen by a doctor, and clerks and nurses know that violation of this rule, if discovered, can get them into serious trouble. (Despite this, patients are occasionally refused registration, usually because they are morally repugnant to the clerk.) Such arrangements restrict the behavior of the staff only to a limited extent, however. There remains a great deal of room for expressing one's valuation of the patient in the details of processing and treatment.

One common concept of social worth held by emergency-ward personnel is that the young are more valuable than the old. This is exemplified most dramatically in the marked differences in efforts to resuscitate young and old patients (Glaser and Strauss, 1964; Sudnow, 1967, 100–109). "Welfare cases" who are sponging off the taxpayer—especially if they represent the product of an immoral life (such as a woman with illegitimate children to support)—do not deserve the best care. Persons of higher status in the larger society are likely to be accorded more respectful treatment in the emergency ward just as they often are in other service or customer relationships, and conversely those of lower status are treated with less consideration. (The fact that higher-status persons are more likely to make an effective complaint or even file lawsuits may be an additional reason for such differential treatment.)

Of course, staff members vary in the manner and degree to which they apply these cultural concepts of social worth in determining the quality of their service to the clientele. The point is that they are in a position to alter the nature of their service in terms of such differentiation, and all of them—porters, clerks, nursing personnel, physicians—do so to some extent. Despite some variations, we did in fact find widespread agreement on the negative evaluation of some categories of patients—evaluations which directly affected the treatment provided. Those who are the first to process a patient play a crucial role in moral categorization because staff members at later stages of the processing are inclined to accept earlier categories without question unless they detect clear-cut evidence to the contrary. Thus, registration clerks can often determine how long a person will have to wait and what kind of treatment area he is sent to, and, occasionally, can even prevent a person from seeing a doctor at all. Some patients have been morally categorized by policemen or ambulance crewmen before they even arrive at the hospital—categorization which affects the priority and kind of service given.

In the public urban hospital emergency service, the clientele is heavily skewed toward the lower end of the socioeconomic scale, and nonwhite and non-Anglo ethnic groups are greatly overrepresented. Also, many patients are in the position of supplicating the staff for help, sometimes for a condition for which the patient can be held responsible. With such a population, the staff can readily maintain a stance of moral superiority. They see the bulk of the patients as people undeserving of the services available to them. Staff members maintain that they need not tolerate any abuse or disobedience from patients or visitors. Patients and visitors may be issued orders which they are expected to obey. The staff can, and sometimes does, shout down patients and visitors and threaten them with ejection from the premises. The staff demands protection against possible attack and also against the possibility of lawsuits, which are invariably classified as unjustified. There is no need to be polite to the clientele and, in fact, some clerks frequently engage patients and visitors in arguments. The staff also feels justified in refusing service to those who complain or resist treatment or refuse to follow procedures or make trouble in any other way. From time to time the clients are referred to as "garbage," "scum," "liars," "deadbeats," people who "come out from under the rocks," by doctors, nurses, aides, clerks, and even housekeepers who sweep the floor. When we spent the first several days of a new medical year with a new group of interns on one emergency service, we found that an important part of the orientation was directed toward telling the interns that the patients were not to be trusted and did not have to be treated politely. At another public hospital, new registration clerks were told during their first few days of work that they would have to learn not to accept the word of patients but to treat everything they say with suspicion.

Despite the general negative conception of the clientele, differentiations are made between patients on the basis of clues which they present. Since this is typically a fleeting relationship where the staff member has little or no background information about the patient, evaluations must usually be made quickly on the basis of readily perceivable clues. Race, age, mode of dress, language and accents and word usage, and the manner in which the client addresses and responds to staff members are all immediate clues on which staff base their initial evaluations. A little questioning brings out other information which may be used for or against a patient: financial status, type of employment, insurance protection, use of private-practice doctors, nature of medical complaint, legitimacy of children, marital status, previous use of hospital services. In the case of unconscious or seriously ill or injured patients, a search of the wallet or handbag often provides informative clues about social worth.

Some characteristics consistently turn staff against patients and affect the quality of care given. Dirty, smelly patients cause considerable comment among the staff, and efforts are made to isolate them or get rid of them. Those dressed as hippies or women with scanty clothing (unless there is a "good excuse," e.g., a woman drowned while swimming) are frowned upon and are more likely to be kept waiting and to be rushed through when they are attended to. We observed hints that certain ethnic groups are discriminated against, but this is difficult to detect nowadays because everyone is extremely sensitive to the possibility of accusations of racial discrimination. If a woman with a child is tabbed a "welfare case" (from her dress, speech, and manner, or in the explicit form of a welfare card which she presents), the clerk is likely to ask, "Is there a father in the house?" while better-dressed, better-spoken women with children are questioned more discreetly.

Attributes and Categories: A Reciprocal Relationship

On one level, it is true to say that the staff's moral evaluation of a patient influences the kind of treatment he gets in the emergency room. But this kind of causal explanation obscures important aspects of the network of interrelationships involved. On another, the definition of devalued or favored categories and the attributes of the patient reinforce each other in a reciprocal manner.

Take, for example, patients who are labeled as drunks. They are more consistently treated as undeserving than any other category of patient. They are frequently handled as if they were baggage when they are brought in by police; those with lacerations are often roughly treated by physicians; they are usually treated only for drunkenness and obvious surgical repair without being examined for other pathology; no one believes their stories; their statements are ridiculed; they are treated in an abusive or jocular manner; they are ignored for long periods of time; in one hospital they are placed in a room separate from most other patients. Emergency-ward personnel frequently comment on how they hate to take care of drunks.

Thus, it might seem that the staff is applying a simple moral syllogism: drunks do not deserve to be cared for, this patient is a drunk, therefore, he does not deserve good treatment. *But* how do we know that he is drunk? By the way he is treated. Police take him directly to the drunk room. If we ask why the police define him as drunk, they may answer that they smell alcohol on his breath. But not all people with alcohol on their breath are picked up by the police and taken to a hospital emergency room. The explanation must come in terms of some part of the patient's background—he was in a lower-class neighborhood, his style of dress was dirty and sloppy, he was unattended by any friend or family member, and so on. When he comes to the emergency room *he has already been defined as a drunk.* There is no reason for the emergency-room personnel to challenge this definition—it is routine procedure and it usually proves correct insofar as they know. There is nothing to do for drunks except to give them routine medications and let them sleep it off. To avoid upsetting the rest of the emergency room, there is a room set aside for them. The police have a standard procedure of taking drunks to that room, and the clerks place them there if they come in on their own and are defined as drunk on the basis, not only of their breath odor (and occasionally there is no breath odor in someone defined as drunk), but in terms of their dress, manner, and absence of protectors. The physicians, having more pressing matters, tend to leave the drunks until last. Of course, they may miss some pathology which could cause unconsciousness or confusion because they believe the standard procedure proves correct in the great majority of cases.

They really do not know *how* often it does not prove correct since they do not check up closely enough to uncover other forms of pathology in most cases, and the low social status of the patients and the fact that they are seldom accompanied by anyone who will protect them means that complaints about inadequate examination will be rare. There *are* occasional challenges by doctors—"How do you know he's drunk?"—but in most cases the busy schedule of the house officer leaves little time for such luxuries as a careful examination of patients who have already been defined as drunks by others. Once the drunk label has been accepted by the emergency room staff, a more careful examination is not likely to be made unless some particularly arresting new information appears (for example, the patient has convulsions, a relative appears to tell them that he has diabetes, an examination of his wallet shows him to be a solid citizen), and the more subtle pathologies are not likely to be discovered.

Thus, it is just as true to say that the *label* of "drunk" is accepted by hospital personnel because of the way the patient is treated as it is to say that he is treated in a certain way because he is drunk. Occasional cases show how persons with alcohol on their breath will not be treated as drunks. When an obviously middle-class man (obvious in terms of his dress, speech, and demands for service) was brought in after an automobile accident, he was not put in the drunk room, although he had a definite alcohol odor, but was given relatively quick treatment in one of the other examining rooms and addressed throughout in a polite manner.

Most drunks are men. A common negative evaluation for women is PID (pelvic inflammatory disease). This is not just a medical diagnostic category, but, by implication, a moral judgment. There are many women with difficult-to-diagnose abdominal pains and fever. If they are Negro, young, unmarried, lower class in appearance and speech, and have no one along to champion their cause, doctors frequently make the assumption that they have before them the end results of a dissolute sex life, unwanted pregnancy and perhaps venereal disease, illegal abortion, and consequent infection of the reproductive organs. The label PID is then attached and the patient relegated to a group less deserving of prompt and considerate treatment. This is *not* the same thing as saying a diagnosis of PID leads to rejection by medical personnel.

We observed one patient who had been defined as a troublemaker because of his abusive language and his insistence that he be released immediately. When he began to behave in a strange manner (random thrashing about), the police were promptly called to control him and they threatened him with arrest. A patient who was not defined as a troublemaker and exhibited like behavior prompted an effort on the part of the staff to provide a medical explanation for his actions. Here again, we see that the category into which the patient has been placed may have more effect on determining the decisions of medical personnel than does his immediate behavior.

Thus, it is not simply a matter of finding which "objective" pathological states medical personnel like or dislike dealing with. The very definition of these pathological states depends in part on how the patient is categorized in moral terms by the screening and treatment personnel.

The Legitimate and the Illegitimate

The second type of evaluation is that related to the staff members' concept of their appropriate work roles (Strauss et al., 1964, Chap. 13). Every worker has a notion of what demands are appropriate to his position. When demands fall outside that boundary, he feels that the claim is illegitimate. What he does about it depends on a number of factors, including his alternatives, his power to control the behavior of others, and his power to select his clientele (more on this later).

The interns and residents who usually man the larger urban emergency services like to think of this assignment as a part of their training which will give them a kind of experience different from the outpatient department or inpatient wards. Here they hope to get some practice in resuscitation, in treating traumatic injuries, in diagnosing and treating medical emergencies. When patients who are no different from those they have seen *ad nauseam* in the outpatient department present themselves at the emergency ward, the doctors in training believe that their services are being misused. Also, once on the emergency ward, the patient is expected to be "cooperative" so that the doctor is not blocked in his effort to carry out his tasks. Nurses, clerks, and others play "little doctor" and to this extent share the concepts of the boundaries of legitimacy of the doctors. But, in addition to the broadly shared perspective, each work specialty has its own notions of appropriate patient attributes and behavior based on their own work demands. Thus, clerks expect patients to cooperate in getting forms filled out. Patients with a "good reason," unconsciousness, for example, are excused from cooperating with clerical procedures, but other patients who are unable to give requested information or who protest against certain questions bring upon themselves condemnation by the clerks who believe that a person who subverts their efforts to complete their tasks has no business on the emergency ward.

A universal complaint among those who operate emergency services is that hospital emergency rooms are "abused" by the public—or rather by a portion of the public. This is particularly the case in the city and county hospitals and voluntary hospitals with training programs subsidized by public funds which handle the bulk of emergency cases in urban areas. The great majority of cases are thought of as too minor or lacking in urgency to warrant a visit to the emergency room. They are "outpatient cases" (OPD cases), that is, patients who could wait until the outpatient department is open, or if they can afford private care, they could wait until a physician is holding his regular office hours. Patients should not use the emergency room just because it gives quicker service than the outpatient department or because the hours are more convenient (since it is open all the time). Pediatricians complain about their day filled with "sore throats and snotty noses." Medical interns and residents complain about all the people presenting long-standing or chronic diseases which, though sometimes serious, do not belong in the emergency room. In every hospital—both public and private—where we made observations or conducted interviews, we repeatedly heard the same kinds of "atrocity stories": a patient with a sore throat of two-weeks' duration comes in at 3:00 A.M. on Sunday and expects immediate treatment from an intern whom he has got out of bed (or such variations as an itch of 75-days' duration, a congenital defect in a one-year-old child—always coming in at an extremely inconvenient hour).

Directors of emergency services recognize that some of their preoccupation with cases which are not "true emergencies" is not simply a matter of "abuse" by patients, but the result of tasks imposed upon them by other agencies—for example, giving routine antibiotic injections on weekends, caring for abandoned children, giving routine blood transfusions, receiving inpatient admissions, giving gamma globulin, providing venereal disease follow-up, examining jail prisoners, arranging nursing-home dispositions for the aged. But the blame for most of their difficulty is placed upon the self-referred patient who, according to the emergency-room staff, does not make appropriate use of their service.

The OPD case typically gets hurried, routine processing with little effort at a careful diagnostic work-up or sophisticated treatment unless he happens to strike the doctor as an interesting case (in which case he is no longer classified as an OPD case). Thus, pediatric residents move rapidly through their mass of sore throats and snotty noses with a quick look in ears and throat with the otolaryngoscope, a swab wiped in the throat to be sent to the laboratory, and if the child does not have a high fever (the nurse has already taken his temperature), the parent is told to check on the laboratory results the next day, the emergency-ward form is marked "URI" (upper respiratory infection), and the next child moves up on the treadmill. If a patient or a visitor has given anyone trouble, his care is likely to deteriorate below the routine level. Often, doctors define their task in OPD cases as simply a stopgap until the patient gets to OPD on a subsequent day, and therefore a careful work-up is not considered necessary.

Medical cases are more often considered illegitimate than surgical cases. In our public hospital tabulations, the diagnostic categories highest in the illegitimate category were gynecology, genitourinary, dental, and "other medical." The lowest in proportion of illegitimate cases were pediatrics (another bit of evidence that children are more acceptable patients than adults), beatings and stabbings, industrial injuries, auto accidents, other accidents, and "other surgical." Much of the surgical work is suturing lacerations and making other repairs. Although these are not necessarily serious in terms of danger to life (very few were), such injuries were seen by the staff as needing prompt attention (certainly within 24 hours) to reduce the risk of infection and to avoid scarring or other deformity.

It is not surprising that in surgical cases the attributes and behavior of the patients are of lesser consequence than in medical cases. The ease with which the condition can be defined and the routine nature of the treatment (treating minor lacerations becomes so routine that anyone thinks he can do it—medical students, aides, volunteers) means that the characteristics and behavior of the patient can be largely ignored unless he becomes extremely disruptive. (Even violence can be restrained and the treatment continued without much trouble.) Certain other things are handled with routine efficiency—high fevers in children, asthma, overdose, maternity cases. It is significant that standard rules can be and have been laid down in such cases so that everyone—clerks, nurses, doctors (and patients once they have gone through the experience)—knows just how to proceed. In such cases, the issue of legitimacy seldom arises.

We find no similar routines with set rules in the case of complaints of abdominal pains, delusions, muscle spasms, depression, or digestive upset. Here the process of diagnosis is much more subtle and complex, the question of urgency much more debatable and uncertain. The way is left open for all emergency-ward staff members involved to make a judgment about whether the case is appropriate to and deserving of their service. Unless the patient is a "regular," no one on the emergency service is likely to have background information on the patient, and the staff will have to rely entirely on clues garnered from his mode of arrival, his appearance, his behavior, the kind of people who accompany him, and so on. The interpretation of these clues then becomes crucial to further treatment and, to the casual observer, may appear to be the *cause* of such treatment.

It is also not surprising that "psychiatric cases" are usually considered illegitimate. Interns and residents do not (unless they are planning to go into psychiatry) find such cases useful for practicing their diagnostic and treatment skills,[1] and therefore regard such patients as an unwelcome intrusion. But what constitutes a psychiatric case is not based on unvarying criteria. An effort is usually made to place a patient in a more explicit medical category. For example, a wrist slashing is a surgical case requiring suturing. An adult who takes an overdose of sleeping pills is a medical case requiring lavage and perhaps antidotes. Only when a patient is troublesome—violent, threatening suicide, disturbing other patients—is the doctor forced to define him as a psychiatric case about whom a further decision must be made. (In some clinics, psychiatrists are attempting to broaden the definition by making interns and residents aware of more subtle cues for justifying a psychiatric referral and providing them with a consulting service to deal with such cases. However, they must provide a prompt response when called upon, or their service will soon go unused.)

It is no accident either that in the private hospitals (especially those without medical school or public clinic affiliation) the legitimacy of a patient depends largely on his relationship to the private medical system. A standard opening question to the incoming patient in such hospitals is, "Who is your doctor?" A patient is automatically legitimate if referred by a physician on the hospital staff

---

1. The authors of *Boys in White* (Becker, et al. *Boys in White: Student Culture in Medical School.* Chicago: University of Chicago Press, 1961, pp. 327–38) make the same point. A "crock" is a patient from whom the student cannot learn anything because there is no definable physical pathology which can be tracked down and treated.

(or the physician's nurse, receptionist, or answering service). If he has not been referred, but gives the name of a staff doctor whom the nurse can reach and who agrees to handle the case, the patient is also legitimate. However, if he does not give a staff doctor's name, he falls under suspicion. The hospital services, including the emergency room, are designed primarily to serve the private physicians on the staff. A patient who does not fit into this scheme threatens to upset the works. It is the receptionist's or receiving nurse's job to try to establish the proper relationship by determining whether the case warrants the service of the contract physician or the doctor on emergency call, and if so, to see to it that the patient gets into the hands of an attending staff doctor for follow-up treatment if necessary. Any patient whose circumstances make this process difficult or impossible becomes illegitimate. This accounts for the bitter denunciation of the "welfare cases"[2] and the effort to deny admission to people without medical insurance or other readily tappable funds. (Most physicians on the hospital staff do not want such people as patients, and feel they have been tricked if a colleague talks them into accepting them as patients; neither does the hospital administration want them as inpatients.) Also, such hospitals have no routine mechanism for dealing with welfare cases, as have the public hospitals which can either give free treatment or refer the patient to a social worker on the premises. Such patients are commonly dealt with by transferring them to a public clinic or hospital if their condition permits.

The negative evaluation of patients is strongest when they combine an undeserving character with illegitimate demands. Thus, a patient presenting a minor medical complaint at an inconvenient hour is more vigorously condemned if he is a welfare case than if he is a "respectable citizen." On the other hand, a "real emergency" can overcome moral repugnance. Thus, when a presumed criminal suffering a severe abdominal bullet wound inflicted by police was brought into one emergency ward, the staff quickly mobilized in a vigorous effort to prevent death because this is the kind of case the staff sees as justifying the existence of their unit. The same patient brought in with a minor injury would almost certainly have been treated as a moral outcast. Even in the case of "real emergencies," however, moral evaluation is not absent. Although the police prisoner with the bullet would received prompt, expert attention, the effort was treated simply as a technical matter—an opportunity to display one's skill in keeping a severely traumatized person alive. When the same emergency ward received a prominent local citizen who had been stabbed by thugs while he was trying to protect his wife, the staff again provided a crash effort to save his life, but in this case they were obviously greatly upset by their failure, not simply a failure of technical skills but the loss of a worthy person who was the victim of a vicious act. One may speculate whether this difference in staff evaluations of the two victims may have

---

2. "Welfare cases" include not only those who present welfare cards, but all who are suspected of trying to work the system to get free or low-priced care.

resulted in an extra effort in the case of the respected citizen despite the appearance of a similar effort in the two cases.

Staff Estimates of "Legitimate" Demands

As is common in relationships between a work group and its clientele, the members of the work group tend to exaggerate their difficulties with the clients when they generalize about them. In conversations, we would typically hear estimates of 70 percent to 90 percent as the proportion of patients who were using the emergency service inappropriately. Yet, when we actually followed cases through the clinic, we found the majority were being treated as if they were legitimate. In one voluntary hospital with an intern and residency training program, we classified all cases we followed during our time on the emergency room as legitimate or illegitimate whenever we had any evidence of subjective definition by staff members, either by what they said about the patient or the manner in which they treated the patient. Among those cases suitable for classification, 42 were treated as legitimate, 15 as illegitimate, and in 24 cases there was insufficient evidence to make a classification. Thus, the illegitimate proportion was about 20 percent to 25 percent depending on whether one used as a base the total of definite legitimate and illegitimate cases or also included the unknowns. In a very active public hospital emergency room we did not use direct observation of each case, but rather developed a conception of what kind of diagnostic categories were usually considered legitimate or illegitimate by the clinic staff and then classified the total census for two days according to diagnostic categories. By this method, 23 percent of 938 patients were classified as illegitimate. This constitutes a minimum figure because diagnostic category was not the only basis for an evaluation, and some other patients were almost certainly regarded as illegitimate by the staff. But it *does* suggest that only a minority were regarded as illegitimate.

The numbers of specific undesirable or inappropriate categories of patients were also consistently exaggerated. Thus, while in the public hospital the interns complained about all the drunks among the men and all the reproductive organ infections among women ("The choice between the male and the female service is really a choice between alcoholics and PIDs," according to one intern), drunks made up only 6 percent of the total emergency-room population and the gynecology patients 2 percent. Venereal disease was also considered a common type of case by clerks, nurses, and doctors, but in fact made up only about one percent of the total E.R. census. Psychiatric cases were referred to as a constant trouble, but, in fact, made up only a little over 2 percent of the total. Some doctors believed infections and long-standing illnesses were common among the E.R. population and used this as evidence of neglect of health by the lower classes. Here again, however, the actual numbers were low—these two categories made up a little more than 3 percent of the total census. In two small private hospitals, the staffs were particularly bitter toward "welfare cases" whom they regarded as a constant nuisance. However, we often spent an entire shift (eight hours) in the emergency rooms of these hospitals without seeing a single patient so classified.

Workers justify the rewards received for their labors in part by the burdens which they must endure on the job. One of the burdens of service occupations is a clientele which makes life hard for the workers. Thus, the workers tend to select for public presentation those aspects of the clientele which cause them difficulty. Teachers' talk deals disproportionately with disruptive and incompetent students, policemen's talk with dangerous criminals and difficult civilians, janitors' talk with inconsiderate tenants. A case-by-case analysis of client contacts is likely to demonstrate in each instance that the examples discussed by the staff are not representative of their total clientele.

Control of Inappropriate Demands for Service

When members of a service occupation or service organization are faced with undesirable or illegitimate clients, what can they do? One possible procedure is to select clients they like and avoid those they do not like. The selecting may be done in categorical terms, as when universities admit undergraduate students who meet given grade and test standards. Or it may be done on the basis of detailed information about specific individuals, as when a graduate department selects particular students on the basis of academic record, recommendations from colleagues, and personal information about the student. Of course, such selection is not made on a unidimensional basis and the selecting agent must often decide what weight to give conflicting factors. (Thus, a medical specialist may be willing to take on a patient who is morally repugnant because the patient has a medical condition the specialist is anxious to observe, study, or experiment with.) But there is an assumption that the more highly individualized the selection and the more detailed the information on which it is based, the more likely one is to obtain a desirable clientele. Along with this process goes the notion of "selection errors." Thus, when a patient is classed as a good risk for a physical rehabilitation program, he may later be classed as a selection error if doctors uncover some pathology which contraindicates exercise, or if the patient proves so uncooperative that physical therapists are unable to conduct any training, or if he requires so much nursing care that ward personnel claim that he "doesn't belong" on a rehabilitation unit (Roth and Eddy, 1967, 57–61).

Selectivity is a relative matter. A well-known law firm specializing in a given field can accept only those clients who demands fit readily into the firm's desired scheme of work organization and who are able to pay well for the service given. The solo criminal lawyer in a marginal practice may, for financial reasons, take on almost every case he can get, even though he may despise the majority of his clients and wish he did not have to deal with them (Smigel, 1964; Wood, 1967). A common occupational or organizational aspiration is to reach a position where one can be highly selective of one's clientele. In fact, such power of selection is a common basis for rating schools, law firms, hospitals, and practitioners of all sorts.[3]

If one cannot be selective in a positive sense, one may still be selective in a negative sense by avoiding some potentially undesirable clients. Hotels, restaurants, and places of entertainment may specifically exclude certain categories of persons as guests, or more generally reserve the right to refuse service to anyone they choose. Cab drivers will sometimes avoid a presumed "bad fare" by pretending another engagement or just not seeing him. Cab driving, incidentally, is a good example of a line of work where judgments about clients must often be made in a split second on the basis of immediate superficial clues—clues based not only on the behavior and appearance of the client himself, but also on such surrounding factors as the area, destination, and time of day (Davis, 1959; Henslin, 1968, 138–58). Ambulance crewmen sometimes manage to avoid a "bad load," perhaps making a decision before going to the scene on the basis of the call source or neighborhood, or perhaps refusing to carry an undesirable patient if they can find a "good excuse" (Douglas, 1969, 234–78).

Medical personnel and organizations vary greatly in their capacity to select clients. Special units in teaching hospitals and specialized outpatient clinics often are able to restrict their patients to those they have individually screened and selected. The more run-of-the-mill hospital ward or clinic is less selective, but still has a screening process to keep out certain categories of patients. Of all medical care units, public hospital emergency wards probably exercise the least selectivity of all. Not only are they open to the public at all times with signs pointing the way, but the rule that everyone demanding care must be seen provides no legal "out" for the staff when faced with inappropriate or repugnant patients (although persons accompanying patients can be, and often are, prevented from entering the treatment areas and are isolated or ejected if troublesome). In addition, the emergency ward serves a residual function for the rest of the hospital and often for other parts of the medical-care system. Any case which does not fit into some other program is sent to the emergency ward. When other clinics and offices close for the day or the weekend, their patients who cannot wait for the next open hours are directed to the emergency service. It is precisely this unselective influx of anyone and everyone bringing a wide spectrum of medical and social defects · that elicits the bitter complaints of emergency-service personnel. Of course, they are not completely without selective power. They occasionally violate the rules and refuse to accept a patient. And even after registration, some patients can be

---

3. I am glossing over some of the intraorganizational complexities of the process. Often different categories of organizational personnel vary greatly in their participation in the selection of the clientele. Thus, on a hospital rehabilitation unit, the doctors may select the patients, but the nurses must take care of patients they have no direct part in selecting. Nurses can influence future selection only by complaining to the doctors that they have "too many" of certain kinds of difficult patients or by trying to convince the doctors to transfer inappropriate patients. These attempts at influencing choice often fail because doctors and nurses have somewhat different criteria about what an appropriate patient is (J. A. Roth & E. M. Eddy, *Rehabilitation for the unwanted*. New York: Atherton, 1967).

so discouraged in the early stages of processing that they leave. Proprietary hospitals transfer some patients to public hospitals. But compared with other parts of the medical-care system, the emergency-service personnel, especially in public hospitals, have very limited power of selection and must resign themselves to dealing with many people that they believe should not be there and that in many cases they have a strong aversion to.

What recourse does a service occupation or organization have when its members have little or no control over the selection of its clients? If you cannot pick the clients you like, perhaps you can transform those you *do* get somewhat closer to the image of a desirable client. This is particularly likely to occur if it is a long-term or repeated relationship so that the worker can reap the benefit of the "training" he gives the client. We tentatively put forth this proposition: *The amount of trouble one is willing to go to to train his clientele depends on how much power of selection he has. The easier it is for one to avoid or get rid of poor clients (that is, those clients whose behavior or attributes conflict with one's conception of his proper work role), the less interested one is in putting time and energy into training clients to conform more closely to one's ideal. And, of course, the converse.*

Janitors have to endure a clientele (that is, tenants) they have no hand in selecting. Nor can a janitor get rid of bad tenants (unless he buys the building and evicts them, as happens on rare occasions). Ray Gold (1964, 1–50) describes how janitors try to turn "bad tenants" into more tolerable ones by teaching them not to make inappropriate demands. Tenants must be taught not to call at certain hours, not to expect the janitor to make certain repairs, not to expect him to remove certain kinds of garbage, to expect cleaning services only on given days and in given areas, to expect heat only at certain times, and so on. Each occasion on which the janitor is able to make his point that a given demand is inappropriate contributes to making those demands from the same tenant less likely in the future and increases the janitor's control over his work load and work pacing. One finds much the same long-term effort on the part of mental hospital staffs who indoctrinate inmates on the behavior and demands associated with "good patients"—who will be rewarded with privileges and discharge—and behavior associated with "bad patients"—who will be denied these rewards (Stanton and Schwartz, 1954, 280–89; Belknap, 1956, Chaps. 9 and 10). Prisons and schools are other examples of such long-term teaching of clients.[4]

The form that "client training" takes depends in part on the time perspective of the trainers. Emergency ward personnel do not have the long-time perspective of the mental hospital staff, teachers, or janitors. Despite the fact that the majority of patients have been to the same emergency ward previously and will probably be back again at some future time, the staff, with rare exceptions, treats each case as an episode which will be completed when the patient is discharged.

---

4. Of course, my brief presentation greatly oversimplifies the process. For example, much of the teaching is done by the clients rather than directly by the staff. But, ultimately, the sanctions are derived from staff efforts to control work demands and to express their moral evaluation of the clients.

Therefore, they seldom make a direct effort to affect the patient's future use of their services. They are, however, interested in directing the immediate behavior of clients so that it will fit into their concept of proper priorities (in terms of their evaluation of the clients) and the proper conduct of an emergency service, including the work demands made upon them. Since they do not conceive of having time for gradual socialization of the clients, they rely heavily on demands for immediate compliance. Thus, patients demanding attention, if not deemed by staff to be urgent cases or particularly deserving, will be told to wait their turn and may even be threatened with refusal of treatment if they are persistent. Visitors are promptly ordered to a waiting room and are reminded of where they belong if they wander into a restricted area. Patients are expected to respond promptly when called, answer questions put to them by the staff, prepare for examination when asked, and cooperate with the examination as directed without wasting the staff's time. Failure to comply promptly may bring a warning that they will be left waiting or even refused further care if they do not cooperate, and the more negative the staff evaluation of the patient, the more likely he is to be threatened.[5]

Nursing staff in proprietary hospitals dealing with the private patients of attending physicians do not have as authoritative a position vis-á-vis their clients as public hospital staff have; therefore, the demands for prompt compliance with staff directions must be used sparingly. In such a case more surreptitious forms of control are used. The most common device is keeping the patient waiting at some step or steps in his processing or treatment. Since the patient usually has no way of checking the validity of the reason given for the wait, this is a relatively safe way that a nurse can control the demands made on her and also serves as a way of "getting even" with those who make inappropriate demands or whom she regards as undeserving for some other reason.

In general, we might expect that: *The longer the time perspective of the trainers, the more the training will take the form of efforts toward progressive socialization in the desired direction; the shorter the time perspective of the trainers, the more the training will take the form of overt coercion ("giving orders") if the trainers have sufficient power over the clients, and efforts at surreptitious but immediate control if they lack such power.*

Conclusion

When a person presents himself at an emergency department (or is brought there by others), he inevitably sets off a process by which his worthiness and legitimacy are weighed and become a factor in his treatment. It is doubtful that

---

5. Readers who are mainly interested in what happens on an emergency ward should not be misled into thinking that it is a scene of continuous orders and threats being shouted at patients and visitors. Most directives are matter-of-fact, and most clients comply promptly with directions most of the time. But when the staff's directive power is challenged, even inadvertently, the common response is a demand for immediate compliance. This situation arises frequently enough so that on a busy unit an observer can see instances almost every hour.

one can obtain any service of consequence anywhere without going through this process. The evidence from widely varying services indicates that the servers do not dispense their service in a uniform manner to everyone who presents himself, but make judgments about the worthiness of the person and the appropriateness of his demands and take these judgments into account when performing the service. In large and complex service organizations, the judgments made at one point in the system often shape the judgments at another.

The structure of a service organization will affect the manner and degree to which the servers can vary their service in terms of their moral evaluation of the client. This study has not explored this issue in detail. A useful future research direction would be the investigation of how a system of service may be structured to control the discretion of the servers as to whom they must serve and how they must serve them. This paper offered some suggestions concerning the means of controlling the inappropriate demands of a clientele. The examples I used to illustrate the relationships of power of selection and the nature of training of clients are few and limited in scope. An effort should be made to determine whether these formulations (or modifications thereof) apply in a wider variety of occupational settings.

References

Becker, H. S., Geer, B., Hughes, E. C., & Strauss, A. *Boys in white.* Chicago: University of Chicago Press, 1961.

Belknap, I. *Human problems of a state mental hospital.* New York: McGraw-Hill, 1956.

Davis, F. The cab driver and his fare. *American Journal of Sociology 65* 1959: 158–65.

Douglas, D. J. Occupational and therapeutic contingencies of ambulance services in metropolitan areas. Ph.D. dissertation, University of California, 1969.

Glaser, B., & Strauss, A. The social loss of dying patients. *American Journal of Nursing 64* 1964: 119–21.

Goffman, I. *Asylums.* New York: Doubleday, 1961.

Gold, R. L. In the basement—The apartment building janitor. In P. L. Berger (Ed.) *The human shape of work.* New York: Macmillan, 1964.

Henslin, J. Trust and the cab driver. In M. Truzzi (Ed.) *Sociology and everyday life.* Englewood Cliffs, N.J.: Prentice–Hall, 1968.

Hollingshead, A. B., & Redlich, F. C. *Social class and mental illness.* New York: Wiley, 1958.

Perrow, C. Hospitals, technology, structure, and goals. In J. G. March (Ed.) *Handbook of organizations.* Chicago: Rand McNally, 1965.

Roth, J. A., & Eddy, E. M. *Rehabilitation for the unwanted.* New York: Atherton, 1967.

Scheff, T. J. The societal reaction to deviance: Ascriptive elements in the psychiatric screening of mental patients in a midwestern state. *Social Problems 11* 1964: 401–13.

Scheff, T. J. *Being mentally ill.* Chicago: Aldine, 1966.

Smigle, E. *Wall street lawyers.* New York: Free Press, 1964.

Stanton, A., & Schwartz, M. *The mental hospital.* New York: Basic Books, 1954.

Strauss, A., Schatzman, R. B., Ehrlich, D., & Sabshin, M. *Psychiatric ideologies and institutions.* New York: Free Press, 1964.

Sudnow, D. *Passing on.* Englewood Cliffs, N.J.: Prentice-Hall, 1967.

Szasz, T. The myth of mental illness. *American Psychologist 15* 1960: 113–18.

Wood, A. L. *Criminal lawyer.* New Haven, Conn.: College and Universities Press, 1967.

PART IV

Medical Personnel: Conflicting Perspectives

Society's response to illness is evident through the organization and delivery of health care and the personnel who provide it. This section of readings examines conflicting perspectives within and among various health personnel. While doctors, nurses, orderlies, pharmacists, psychiatrists, and others are all involved in providing health care, their roles may conflict with one another. Even within each profession or group of health personnel, there often are differing views of how that profession's or group's tasks should be carried out.

Freidson presents an overview of the differing perspectives of the patient, the aide, the nurse, and the doctor within a hospital. Daniels shows how psychiatry involves conflicting functions—advisory and coercive—which are differentially emphasized depending on whether the setting is private practice or an institution. Scheff analyzes two competing perspectives on decision rules and their consequences for diagnosis. Navarro demonstrates that in health occupations, as in other occupations, women hold less powerful jobs. He argues that the division of labor between men and women in the family also appears within the health sector.

Conflicting Perspectives in the Hospital

18

ELIOT FREIDSON

We usually assume that those who are administratively responsible for an organization possess the resources to make that organization pursue the officially approved goals set for it—that is, that actual behavior in the organization will be in accord with the official view of what the organization *should* be doing. But frequently it is not. The classic study of a state mental hospital by Ivan Belknap[1] showed how an institution supposedly devoted to curing illness was instead devoted to maintaining a cruel custodial order among inmates, without making significant attempts at therapy. Furthermore, even when an official goal is more or less pursued, it is pursued in the context of interaction between the conflicting perspectives of the participants. A surgical ward, or a lying-in hospital, may be run like a tight ship by the surgical captains, but not without the friction created by the resistance of patients who may want more deference, personal service, and emotional support.[2] To understand what actually goes on in the ward, therefore, one must understand the perspectives of the participants, how they conflict with each other, and what resources each has available to allow him to assert his perspectives over the others. We may mention four perspectives here — that of the patient, of the nonprofessional aide, of the professional nurse, and of the physician in charge.

From *The Profession of Medicine,* by Eliot Freidson: pp. 121–27, Copyright © 1970 by Harper & Row, Publishers, Inc. By permission of the publisher.

1. Ivan Belknap, *Human problems of a state mental hospital* New York: McGraw-Hill, 1956.

2. Note Cartwright's finding that British maternity patients more than others are critical of the care they receive in hospital—apparently because they are often left alone during labor. Medically, maternity patients are not in so critical condition as to be believed to "need" the company of nurse or physician Ann Cartwright, *Human relations and hospital care.* London: Routledge and Kegan Paul, 1964, pp. 177–88.

The Patient

A great deal has been written about the personal anxiety attached to being ill and about the consequent irrational character of much of the patient's behavior on the ward. The staff is less involved in the illness than is the patient. Furthermore, as a layman the patient is also less capable of arriving at the proper diagnosis of his complaint than those who take care of him and is less likely to be able to evaluate his treatment. Finally, the individual patient is concerned with his own fortunes. In contrast, the staff is concerned with the fortunes of all patients, balancing off the relative need of one patient against the need of another, in the context of the limited time and energy available. While patients may certainly vary as individuals in the degree to which they are marked by such characteristics, those characteristics distinguish patients as a group from the staff as a group.

By the nature of the situation the perspective of the patient is in conflict with that of the staff, and some of the staff effort will be devoted to controlling behavior that disrupts the ward routine. Depending on its mandate and ideology, the staff may seek to control such conflict by physical means (mechanical, electrical, chemical, or whatever), by efforts at rational explanation, pedagogy, and training, and by the techniques of psychotherapy. However, all members of the staff are not able to use all techniques of control if only by virtue of the division of labor that limits each level of the staff to use of techniques appropriate to its "level of skill" or occupational jurisdiction. Furthermore, the resources of the patient himself can impose constraints on staff behavior.

From the accumulation of studies of interaction on the ward, a number of patient attributes seem to have important bearing on what techniques of control can be exercised by staff members seeking to order their work.[3] The grossest attribute is physical incapacity: an unconscious patient obviously poses fewer problems to the staff than a conscious one; a weak and bedridden patient fewer than an ambulatory. Another critical attribute is the patient's sociolegal identity: if he is a public charge by virtue of his "welfare" status, or a prisoner by virtue of legal commitment (in the case of drug addiction, tuberculosis, or psychosis), or something less than a responsible human being by virtue of being labeled psychotic, senile, retarded, or otherwise deficient in the qualities that grant one the right to be taken seriously, then he will have difficulty asserting his perspective in interaction on the ward. Also may be mentioned his socioeconomic resources: if he has the money (or, in socialist countries, the political importance) to gain special care — a private-duty nurse or a hospital with a low patient-staff ratio, for example — and if he has the active support of healthy, knowledgeable, and influential friends or relatives outside the institution, he is a special problem of management. Finally, it is probable that organized and persistent problems of patient management are most likely to occur when patients are able to be in regular

---

3. Perhaps the most important work bearing on the patient's perspective on and resistance to staff procedures is that of Julius A. Roth, *Information and the Control of Treatment in Tuberculosis Hospitals*. In E. Friedson, op cit., pp. 293–318; and Julius A. Roth, *Timetables*. Indianapolis: Bobbs-Merrill, 1963.

social interaction with each other, when they will all have the same general class of ailment about which they can exchange information, and when they share a relatively long-term, chronic prognosis. Under such circumstances they are likely to form their own little society which, whether it involves "living in the cracks" or "colonizing", nonetheless becomes a source of social strength which staff must take into account.[4]

Aides, Orderlies, Attendants

Empirically, many differences may be expected among patients on wards due both to variation in patient values and knowledge and to variation in the social resources which allow the patients to assert their own perspective. Such variation exists to a much lesser degree among the staff whose function it is to get done the necessary housekeeping jobs of the ward—at least so far as values and knowledge go. It seems no accident that attendants in mental hospitals, who are lower class in the United States and the United Kingdom, and lower-class but *not* middle-class mental patients, both have a high "custodial" orientation to the management of mental illness.[5] These poorly paid, essentially untrained workers, whose job it is to handle the dirty work of the wards, cannot be expected to hold, much less to exercise, the complex conceptions of treatment espoused by professionals. However, this is not to say that they have *no* conception of treatment. Their sin is in having a lay conception that is not shared by some influential professionals. As the "Custodial Mental Illness Ideology Scale" implies, their conception of mental illness is that it is so abnormal, hopeless, irrational, and dangerous as to surpass human understanding and to require close surveillance and control in hospitals. This conception is quite similar to that described by the Cummings among the citizens of a Canadian community.[6] Nonetheless, as Strauss and his associates have pointed out, the view does not imply merely punitive reactions on the part of aides: their lay orientation to the management of the mentally ill contains within it specific modes of "training" and otherwise helping patients.[7]

By definition as nonprofessional workers, then, aides, orderlies, and attendants have nonprofessional perspectives on their work. This, however, is not a

4. The tuberculosis patients studied by Roth were of this character, which is perhaps what made them such effective antagonists. For a very useful general discussion of the organized contingencies bearing on the degree to which patients could learn from each other how to manage the ward setting (by resistance or cooperation), see Stanton Wheeler, The Structure of Formally Organized Socialization Settings. In O. G. Brim, Jr., and Stanton Wheeler, *Socialization after Childhood, Two Essays.* New York: Wiley, 1966, pp. 53–115.

5. See D. C. Gilbert and D. J. Levinson, Role performance, ideology and personality in mental hospital aids. In M. Greenblatt, et al. (Eds.) *The Patient and the Mental Hospital.* Glencoe, Ill.: Free Press, 1957, pp. 197–208; and G. M. Carstairs and A. Heron, The Social Environment of Mental Hospital Patients: A Measure of Staff Attitudes. In M. Greenblatt and D. J. Levinson, pp. 218–230. For patients, see E. Gallagher and D. J. Levinson, *Patienthood.* Boston: Houghton-Mifflin, 1965.

6. E. Cumming and J. Cumming, *Closed ranks, an experiment in mental health education.* Cambridge, Mass.: Harvard University Press, 1957.

7. A. Strauss, et al. *Psychiatric ideologies and institutions.* New York: Free Press, 1964, pp. 54–57. See also the excellent discussion in Richard R. Salisbury, *Structures of Custodial Care.* Berkeley: University of California Press, 1962, pp. 37–40.

terribly important practical issue for interaction on the ward unless the aide is in a position to impose his perspective on others in the ward. By virtue of being involved in work on the ward day and night, he is in a position to exercise some leverage over the patient, both by physical restraint, and by the age-old evasive tactics of the underdog everywhere — "not hearing," "forgetting," and otherwise evading the demands of the more powerful. This certainly gives him a position of some influence on any ward. What apparently consolidates and strengthens the aide's position in the state mental hospital, however, is the effective absence from the ward of other workers, combined with circumstances that effectively neutralize patient demands. It seems no accident that these "first-line" workers are powerful precisely in those settings where the patients are stripped of their identity as responsible, adult human beings, and where there is no extensive and continuous participation by professional workers in some regular, effective thera-peutic process on or off the wards. The aide's role has been powerful enough to warrant extended attention only in those institutions so underfinanced as to sup-port at best a skeleton staff of professional workers, and in those institutions filled with patients with ailments for which there is no straightforward therapy with any immediate and definite results. In the former case, there are insufficient profes-sional staff to allow effective supervision and control of aides: they must rely on what the aide reports to them. In the latter, there is insufficient foundation of observable, unambiguous results (such as frequently follows medical or surgical treatment) to persuade attendants that there are professional techniques whose outcomes surpass lay common sense.

The Nurse

The professional qualities of the nurse are, particularly in the hospital, contingent on her relation to the physician.[8] She is the agent of the supervising physician in carrying out treatment and patient care. In this sense, she represents the profes-sional perspective on the ward. However, insofar as she represents the day-to-day administration of the ward, she is also concerned with patients as a batch — something that, in the United States, at least, the physician is less con-cerned with. She must, therefore, balance individual physicians' orders for the care of individual patients against the independent demands of the patients as such and against the need to manage an aggregate of cases in an administra-tively acceptable way. It is because, unlike the aide, the nurse serves as an adjunct of both medical and administrative authority, that she seems to be the intense focus of conflicting perspectives. Unlike the aide, the nurse is imputed professional identity, and so she is likely to be engaged in a considerably more complex system of bargaining. In bargaining with physicians, one of her prime resources lies in her first-hand knowledge and professional evaluation of what

---

8. There is a huge literature on the nurse and her role conflicts some of which has already been cited in Chapter 3. For a recent excellent statement see Hans O. Mauksch, The Nurse; Coordinator of Patient Care. In James K. Skipper, Jr., and Robert C. Leonard (Eds.) *Social Interaction and Patient Care.* Philadelphia: Lippincott, 1965, pp. 251–65. And see the extensive discussion in Duff and Hollingshead.

goes on in the ward through her continued presence—a strategic advantage no doubt lost in such hospitals as those in the Soviet Union, where physicians are also present in enough number on a full-time basis to make a difference. In bargaining with patients, her prime strength lies in her access to the physician, both in knowing his inside information and in being able to discuss cases with him. Thus, while she may serve as a troubled focus of conflicting perspectives, she also may very well hold the balance of power in determining the outcome of bargaining among patient and staff.

The Physician

As I have already noted, in an active treatment setting the physician largely determines what therapeutic efforts are made and, if he does not make all such efforts himself, he orders and supervises the efforts of others. Aside from preventing interaction in the ward from damaging his relation with those patients for whom he is responsible, his problem is to obtain conformity with his orders by the other staff. But while it is relatively easy to have orders followed to the letter, the spirit is more difficult. When the lay common sense of aides, orderlies, or attendants is contradicted by the physician's philosophy of treatment, there is trouble. And when the physician's philosophy of treatment threatens the routine order of the ward, his approach is even less likely to be followed. The nurse may be involved in these difficulties when her training leads her to hold a "professional" philosophy of treatment that is at variance with that of the physician. Should such conflict in philosophy exist, a considerably more delicate process of manipulation and bargaining must occur for the physician to get his way, as Strauss and his associates have shown.

When all is said and done, however, it is the physician's expertise that is his ultimate resource in his interaction with others. As the final arbiter of practice in the medical division of labor, sustained by prestige and legal mandate, he has an "authority" that is independent of administrative authority as such.[9] The "authority" of his knowledge, judgment, and responsibility being ultimately exercised in the division of labor, it follows that a "hierarchy" of expertise exists independently of the administrative hierarchy in the hospital, the physician ordering and supervising those below his superior level of skill. This leads to hierarchical behavior even in those settings where the philosophy of treatment involves attempts to set up "democratic" or "therapeutic communities" which, while nonhierarchical in intent, turn out to be hierarchical in practice. There is no court of appeal from superior training, knowledge, and judgment; technical decisions are not made by vote.

---

9. See my discussion of the authoritarian implications of expertise in Eliot Freidson, *Professional Dominance*. New York: Atherton.

Advisory and Coercive Functions   19
in Psychiatry

ARLENE KAPLAN DANIELS

In recent years sociologists have questioned the adequacy of assuming that professions consist of homogeneous groups of practitioners. Bucher and Strauss (1961) have shown that even within the specialties of one profession, medicine, it is possible to discover various types of internal segmentalization. Groups of physicians emerge along specialized lines and develop their own perspectives, along with highly specialized forms of practice and relationships with clients and colleagues. This phenomenon may continue until practitioners in different segments of a specialty share little more than a common professional title.

This development of specialties and subspecialties occurs totally within the domain of medicine. The emergence of new forms of practice proceeds along lines acceptable to the profession and is ultimately validated within the profession. There is no accountability to outside agencies or publics. To be sure, the major rhetorical stance of the emerging specialty and the profession as a whole is that the increase in expertise represented by specialization is in the interests of better service to the public. The fact remains that the profession remains solely in control — its autonomy intact — in making such judgments.

While it is valuable to trace these internal differences within a profession, analysis of the process should go beyond the profession's definitions. Such analysis should also examine those elements in professional work which to *not* change during the process of differentiation. One such commonality ignored by analyses supplied by the profession of medicine is a direct consequence of the increasing specialization of the field: namely, that as the profession's claims to

From *Sociology of Work and Occupations, 2 (1)* 1975, pp. 55–78. Reprinted by permission of the publisher, Sage Publications, Inc.

expertise have gained ground, the power of the profession vis-à-vis the client has increased. The assumption that specialization will lead to higher quality service does not include consideration of how the role of expert can encroach on the rights of the individual. In this paper I examine the issue of professional power in the specialty of psychiatry, a specialty which has developed a number of subspecialities.

Generally, the psychiatric expert may have primarily advisory (indirect) or coercive (direct) power in relation to a client. And the setting where the professional practices may encourage overt or covert control over a client. But it is important to remember that the presence of professional power, whether expert-advisory or expert-coercive, always implies some element of control in the professional-client relationship. I will consider the issue of how the expert function in psychiatry (to advise and to help clients solve problems) becomes especially permeated with controlling functions—and coercive powers—as psychiatrists adapt their specialty to institutional settings. At the same time, I wish to emphasize that these powers exist in private practice. It is only their concentration in the institutional setting which permits us to see how fateful they may be in the lives of patients and to examine their general significance.

If we focus on the issue of how power is accorded to practitioners in psychiatry, we raise questions not traditionally asked. How, for example, do practitioners' relations with clients change when they move from a private to an institutional setting? How is their work affected by accepting clients predominantly from one social class or another? In short, what differences can we find in the practice of therapy, or in the formulation of diagnoses, prognoses, and dispositions, which can be attributed to the exigencies of work in that setting? In order to answer such questions we must focus on the place of work to distinguish between such settings as private office, clinic, or total instituion. We need to consider what structural opportunities each offers the practitioner to control his patient. While pure types do not exist, certain contexts clearly contain more coercive potential than others. Total institutions for example, offer many opportunities (or requirements) to control, if for no other reason than they contain more involuntary patients. Psychiatrists' roles are shaped, then, according to the requirements of the setting, the options it makes available to them, and the constraints it puts upon them.

The type of analysis presented in this paper shows how varying conditions of practice affect the array of possible relationships that psychiatrists may have with their patients. Such variations are important because they suggest the serious consequences to patients which may result from facing a psychiatrist in one relationship rather than another.

How Historical Developments Serve to Confuse the Advice-Control Functions

One function around which psychiatry has developed has been the social control of deviants. The conditions of practice for psychiatrists filling this function usually vary markedly from those of other practitioners more concerned with a different function—offering therapy to the individual. These two functions—to control societal deviants and to advise individuals about their mental health—indicate the extremes of the two concerns around which the legitimation of the practice of psychiatry has emerged. In summarizing two major concerns which have influenced the development of a therapeutic approach to mental illness, we might call one the attempt to help or serve the individual, and the other the necessity to protect society. Expression of concern for the welfare of the mentally ill person has developed rather recently in the history of Western civilization (Perrow, 1965). In accordance with our concern for individualism or individual rights to self-expression, treatment of the mentally ill has emphasized therapy. Yet concern for the preservation of social order and the necessity for constraints against disruptive influences has also continued. The two functions have become elaborated in Western society. The "madhouse" and then the state hospital have been the institutionalized setting for control (Rosen, 1969); the therapist's office and the analyst's couch have provided the context for advice (Frank, 1963).

In this country, the tradition of madhouse doctors and superintendents has been represented by such figures as Benjamin Rush, who formulated methods and principles of management and psychiatric care in both custodial-type hospitals and in military hospitals, and Adolph Meyer, who introduced reforms and argued for humane treatment of inmates in mental hospitals (Bromberg, 1959, 87–90, 162–64). It is also from organizational (hospital) psychiatry that the great diagnosticians and formulators of the psychiatric nosology emerge (Bromberg, 1959, 182–83).

Diagnoses take on a significance in psychiatric institutions which they do not have in private practice. Private psychiatrists treat patients on an individualistic basis where concern for the therapeutic interaction and its results outweighs interest in the diagnostic label. But diagnosis has an importance in hospital psychiatry similar to the place of diagnosis in the more general practice of medicine. In the development of institutional psychiatry, expectations and predictions of the course of disease and the consequences of mental illness enabled hospital personnel to plan courses of treatment and to formulate reports indicating how patients were progressing. These classifications also became important and useful in the justification of changes in treatment and the termination of hospitalization (Miller, 1970). And they are useful in protecting the psychiatrist from later charges that he mismanaged the case as well. Thus, psychiatrists in bureaucratic institutions may be conservative in decisions that permit patients with certain types of history indicating violence or aberration to leave the hospital (Maisel, 1970). In their fear of reprisal or criticism by high-ranking public officials, such psychiatrists reveal the extent to which professionals with a control mandate are themselves controlled. The records they maintain about patients may also be records which can be used to evaluate the psychiatrist's performance. (See Garfinkel, 1967, 186–207 for discussion of records in psychiatric clinics; also Erikson and Gilbertson, 1969, 389–414.) And the risks inherent in facing evaluations are part of the exigencies of institutional practice; those who treat the mentally ill are also expected to take custodial responsibilities and to uphold the established values of society. Such requirements place the direct client's welfare in a subordinate rule, for meeting them sometimes goes against a patient's interests.[1] Only those practitioners who follow the tradition begun by Freud and his followers, in work with voluntary, middle-class patients, can focus entirely upon the therapeutic goals—as accepted by the patient.

Concentration upon the expert's advisory functions in psychiatry can only occur under rather special circumstances. This approach requires relatively capable, self-sufficient, and well-off patients.[2] The rationale for concentrating on such individuals was supplied by Freud and his followers. They turned from the focus on severe disorders (the psychoses) to less severe problems that hamper but do not obstruct ordinary functioning in the society. New concepts about "ideal" standards of social performance developed along with this perspective. The neurotic often functions tolerably well—but he or she wishes to reach higher or better levels. And so distinctions between mere existence and a creative life are increasingly important. Advisory functions may be viewed in this light as creative and prestigious, for the psychiatrist works with people who are creative and prestigious. These practitioners also do the most "dramatic" work in psychiatry. The analyst or other therapist in a private office is the representative most likely to come into public view as he or she helps the patient wrestle with personal problems. Novels and drama in film or on television are more often about these practitioners than they are about Captain Newman, M.D. And even when military psychiatrists are represented, as in the foregoing example, the public more often sees them in their advisory rather than their coercive functions.

Thus a commonly held view of psychiatry focuses on these practitioners who work toward goals of self-awareness, personal growth, and disappearance of neurotic symptoms in private, vis-à-vis therapy. And from these general public expectations, it follows that the major functions of this specialty are perceived as advisory. Such expectations not only influence laypersons, they also are reflected in the aspirations and self-images of professional recruits and young practitioners. Smith (1958) points out that aspirants to professional fields are often attracted by the myths of a field embodied in the person of heroic early figures. In psychiatry it is such figures as Freud and his followers—the psychoanalysts in private practice—who are important figures to the young psychiatrists and residents. They are not attracted or inspired by the superintendents of hospitals who formulated much of the nosology—such figures as Kraepelin and Breuer (Coser, forthcoming).

---

1. Of course, protecting the society is a function intermingled with the idea of protecting the sick as well. Reformers have been criticized for sending sick people out into the world to fend for themselves (see Caplan 1969).

2. This situation changes drastically if the psychiatrist makes the decision (or feels he "has to" make the decision) to hospitalize the patient. The advisory model will no longer be suitable when such circumstances arise. See Greenley (1972) for a good analysis of the dilemma of the psychiatrist when this eventuality arises.

Actually, more psychiatrists in this country spend most of their time in some institutionalized setting rather than in private practice.[3] One reason for this distribution is that they are in highest demand for evaluating and processing certain types of people in institutions. Since psychiatry has been given the mandate to "protect" society from the insane (and the unmanageable), control over (and management of) those in such categories has developed as a special function in the field. Thus, how much power comes with the professional mandate to use special expertise becomes a critical issue when the mandate is expanded to mean the protection of society against an individual.

Using the ideological perspective of psychiatry, advisory and coercive functions can be disentangled from the more general picture of service to society which the psychiatric specialty presents. In this view, psychiatry might easily be subdivided into settings where responsibilities are primarily coercive, settings where these functions are mixed, and settings where they are primarily advisory. By mixed I mean settings which contain a great array of opportunities for either advice or coercion. Which element of practice predominates may vary quite widely by context and case within any one of these mixed settings.

Styles of Control in Coercive Settings

The control of patients for their own and society's protection has traditionally been connected with the custodial functions involved in managing insane or psychotic patients by explicit restraint. Even to this day, control of patients can entail solitary confinement, physical restraints, locked wards, involuntary commitment procedures, or threats of commitment. Furthermore, control of patients also involves therapies which may be construed as restraint (or even punishment) and which may be used (or threatened) as a means to subdue unwilling or unruly patients. Perhaps the clearest examples of such ambiguous therapies are the use of electroshock treatments, heavy and repeated doses of drugs with unpleasant and possibly dangerous side effects, and withdrawal of privileges in the hospital (as grounds privileges, passes to return home on visits). Finally, control may involve indirect activities designed to control or modify patient behavior shown in the attitudes of staff and the arrangement and management of the patient's living environment. Patients may be treated as stigmatized or unworthy, or as nonpersons. Their dependence on the staff for small courtesies and favors (cigarettes, matches, opportunities to use personal possessions) makes them vulnerable to

---

3. Whiting (1969) indicates that only psychoanalysts spend more than half of their practicing hours in private, as opposed to other forms of organizational practice. In 1967, according to an APA survey, there were 1,297 psychoanalysts spending 81.5 percent of their time in private practice. Compared with the total population of psychiatrists—around 21,476—this is a small number. The remainder vary from a few hours—7.4 percent of their time is spent in private practice for the 60 correctional psychiatrists in the sample—to almost half of their time—46.1 percent of their hours are spent in private practice for the 2,555 adult psychiatrists in the sample.

personnel who can gratify or withhold in these matters and who can do so in the name of treatment (see Goffman, 1961, 321–86; Rosenhahn, 1973).

The importance of control is also reflected in the allocation of psychiatrists' responsibilities in hospital practice. Psychiatrists are typically responsible for one or more wards (depending on the type of hospital). Psychiatrists in private hospitals usually manage fewer patients (generally around 5 to 25) than in state and federal hospitals (anywhere from 50 to more than 100). University affiliated hospitals have a complex structure of clinicians and ward administrators operating with attendant parapsychiatric personnel (social workers, occupational and rehabilitation therapists, psychologists, as well as attendants, nurses, and other physicians; see Strauss et al., 1964). State and federal hospitals are less likely to distinguish between ward and clinical psychiatrists though they usually also have additional professionals and semiprofessionals on the psychiatric team. In both types of hospital, however, psychiatrists fill the higher administrative positions and are formally responsible for the course of treatment and the discharge of patients.

Occasionally the power of professionals to control the lives of others is checked when patients can summon legal aid. Some findings (Wenger and Fletcher, 1969) suggest that patients represented by a lawyer avoid involuntary hospitalization more often than those that are not. However, this opportunity for legal counsel is not within the grasp of many patients—lawyers are expensive.

The setting of most control is represented by prison psychiatry. Professionals in this setting serve a quite special clientele. Prison psychiatrists see a captive population under circumstances and regulations rather stringently ordered by the prison administration (Powelson and Bendix, 1951; Morgan, 1974). Under these circumstances, both the definition and the treatment of mental illness are quite different from any understandings other psychiatrists hold. Control in the prison setting exists because psychiatrists must act as an agent of prison authorities. Accordingly, whether or not psychiatrists define patients as mentally ill has fateful consequences for prisoners: identification as mentally ill might exonerate them or at least provide them with special treatment to which they are not otherwise entitled.

The prison psychiatrist is, like the military psychiatrist, an agent of the institution and not of the patient in adversary situations where institution and patient are at odds (Daniels, 1969). Sometimes the institution requires psychiatric certification (something like a blessing on an otherwise dubious act) in order to justify a really drastic decision against the personal interest of one of its members. Psychiatrists certify that they have found no mental illness in the examined which might prevent the institutional authorities from taking action. In such cases a psychiatric evaluation may help send persons to their death—as when they are judged sane enough for capital punishment or "normal" enough to return to combat (Daniels, 1970). Under the circumstances it is not surprising that patients often do not "trust" the psychiatrists.

The most important (and fateful) decisions that psychiatrists may be found in various organizational contexts, where psychiatrists decide whether people are sick or well enough to face punishment, receive special dispensation, or are to be denied opportunities. By their judgments or their contribution to some process of judging, psychiatrists add their sanction to the moral and legal actions taken by others in the society. Many heavy responsibilities are allocated to psychiatrists in these contexts. Often psychiatrists act as consultants to organizations, or as advisers to some third party rather than to the patient. One setting for psychiatric power was provided by the Peace Corps, where decisions made by psychiatrists affected an applicant's chance to enter. Psychiatrists were active from the inception of the Peace Corps in the process of evaluating candidates (Duhl et al., 1964). Persons requiring security clearances in military and other federal employment are generally evaluated by psychiatrists as part of the requirement (Daniels, 1969).

Decisions about who should get the use of the kidney machine or the opportunity for an organ transplant often include a psychiatrist's evaluation of the ability of one or another candidate to endure attendant problems. Similarly, psychiatrists may contribute to the decision to permit or to deny the opportunity of donating a kidney on the basis of their assessment of a potential donor's motivation (Fox, 1970). The opportunity to have transsexual operations may depend upon psychiatric evaluation of underlying "sexual" traits (Garfinkel, 1967, 116–85). Prior to the 1972 Supreme Court decision striking down state's rights in the matter, some states required a woman desiring an abortion to have psychiatric evaluation asserting this action indispensable to her mental health (Beck et al. 1969). Most hospital review committees consider one ground for sterilization mental instability. Psychiatric evaluation may be used either with or against the wishes of a woman to be sterilized (Lader, 1972). Psychiatric judgment is often required about the ability of an accused to stand trial, or of one convicted to receive sentence (Guttmacher and Weihofen, 1952, 206–207; Powelson and Bendix, 1951). Assessment of eligibility for special educational facilities may often require psychiatric evaluation (Szasz, 1967). This list of extremely varied and, in some cases, gravely serious decisions in which the psychiatrist may play a major role suggests what the powers of these practitioners may be.

Mixed Settings

Some organizational settings and some settings that mix organizational and private practice—as in many forms of community psychiatry—may offer the psychiatrist a mixed responsibility. The expectations of the service that psychiatrists will offer in special clinic settings within organizations or within the general community are not always overtly coercive. One of the major ideological tenets of the community psychiatry movement is to prevent new recruits from entering the controlling agencies. Community psychiatry programs attempt to break the cycle— as that of the revolving door in drunk courts where alcoholics are jailed over and over again reported by Rubington (1966) and Wiseman (1970), or that of the pattern of readmissions for the mentally ill reported by Miller (1965). While no substantial record of success has yet been accumulated by community psychiatry programs, the professionals in them sometimes do interject themselves between the potential recruit (about to be a patient, criminal, or incompetent) and the usual agencies which might accept him (hospitals, jails, homes for the disabled). In this context, professionals use their power for the patient rather than for a third party. Yet many latent tendencies in community psychiatry programs to seek an attractive clientele are at war with these efforts (Rein, 1965, 21–22). For example, recent studies of alcoholism programs in community psychiatry (Wiseman, 1970, 239–68) indicate that middle-class patients still in the "social drinker" definition and still fairly well integrated in the community are preferred to lower-class and skid-row drunks who are clearly labeled alcoholics. The less desirable patients are referred to the more controlling agencies (state hospitals) or ultimately fall into the hands of the most controlling agencies (drunk courts and jails; see Rubington, 1965). These clients also have few alternative resources—no family, friends, or home—and society has no further alternatives on which the psychiatrist can draw for assistance in treating such clients. But in addition, it can be argued the preferred clients allow the practitioners in community psychiatry to focus upon their professional notions of valued activities. The preferred patients are not so badly off that they must be directly controlled; they are also more likely to respond to advice and indirect pressures than might persons from a different value system and social class.

The context for the practice of community psychiatry is highly variable. A focus on professional ideology about the emergence of subspecialties might lead one to see this context as comprising a special area and requiring some special expertise. But if we focus on the potential for control over patients, we find a much more heterogeneous situation than the notion of a subspecialty suggests. Depending on the characteristics of the niche in which they practice, community psychiatrists have much more latitude to choose whether to advise or explicitly control. For example, psychiatrists in "hip" clinics where street people are welcomed may, if they wish, encounter and deal tolerantly with a variety of persons and social problems not so easily condoned in more traditional psychiatric settings.

The foregoing suggests the important difference between the most controlling contexts for psychiatric practice and those which are less so. In the most controlling settings, prison and military regulations permit the psychiatrist very little leeway for making judgments and instituting programs of therapy or advice. But in community psychiatry settings, treatment of such clients as adolescent runaways, drug users, and homosexuals may proceed under local policies which can allow considerable discretion to the psychiatrist. Community psychiatrists also see a wider variety of patients (in terms of age, sex, seriousness of symptomatology, and legal problems), and they have more opportunity to exercise the control involved in professional discretion about how long to treat and what therapeutic measures to use than can ever be available to prison psychiatrists, whose patients come from a prison population. But community psychiatrists and their patients need not be locked within such an inexorable system. Often patients do come voluntarily—or else they can withdraw from the contact if they find it without value. There are fewer situations in which psychiatrists are likely to be required by the institution to use their expertise to accomplish purposes directly against the patient's wishes.[4]

Mixed therapy (or advice) and evaluation (or control) functions are also often found in the duties of psychiatrists in clinics attached to teaching hospitals, private hospitals, universities, and colleges. Sometimes psychiatrists make judgments and affect administrative decisions about student (or other) careers. But in these settings, psychiatrists may also sidestep controlling activity (Halleck, 1971; Kahne and Schwartz, 1975). For example, when they realize that they have a patient with potentially serious enough problems to require some sort of report to university authority, they may suggest that the patient not reveal information in that setting but go to a private psychiatrist instead.[5] In this way the clinic psychiatrist may absolve himself of the responsibility by referral to another. The tendency of referral patterns is to send the potentially unmanageable client further into the advisory rather than the coercive channels of psychiatry (see Schwartz, forthcoming). Such alternatives, of course, depend on the client's "suitability" for therapy. Whatever the alternatives available, they suggest how different mechanisms or structures of opportunity for both patient *and* psychiatrist may operate in different social contexts to influence the treatment of patients (Coser, 1967).

But in this context of community psychiatry, as in the aforementioned contexts, public expectations of the psychiatric performance are unclear. Psychiatrists operate under the general mandate of the medical profession; they possess the license which accompanies this mandate: to advise, consult, and heal the sick who wish to be helped. The dominant expectation of psychiatrists is that they give therapy in an advisory context. At the same time, psychiatrists also possess, at least in the organizational and consultation settings discussed, an explicit mandate to control. In prisons, some treatments that psychiatrists may approve on therapeutic grounds may be seen as punishment, or even torture, by the inmates or their advocates (Opton, 1973). Under these circumstances, it is not just the public; psychiatrists also may be confused about which directive dominates. They often argue they are *not* making harmful or fateful decisions, but only offering medical treatment or adding neutral data to the decision-making process.

The actual control aspects of the psychiatrist's work in these settings may be left in an ambiguous and unclarified state, permitting focus on the more prestigious and personally rewarding image of the profession contained in the private practice model. In order to maintain this picture of work—and to receive the mon-

---

4. Alternatively, one could say that a patient in a mental health clinic can better afford to be wary because he has more resources at his command, while the prisoner may simply have to take "the best there is." In this view, being "wary" depends not only on perception of the psychiatrist's role restriction, but also depends on perception of alternatives in the system—other potential "helpers" who might be enlisted to aid the patient (personal communication, Rose Laub Coser 1972).

5. Here the practitioner adopts a strategy sometimes used by psychiatrists in much more coercive — or total — institutions, such as the army. Officers and any other sensitively placed personnel may be referred to civilian psychiatrists to avoid a "record" which might hurt their career (Daniels 1972, 159).

etary rewards that accompany advisory functions — psychiatrists in controlling settings often "moonlight." They see private patients after hours—some are not overscrupulous about separating this activity from the times and places associated with their salaried position. Therapy rather than custody or control offers the ideal picture of functions of the psychiatrist, wherever his location or his responsibility.

Through all these means, the control of unwilling or hostile clients, the kind of unpleasant or "dirty work" (Hughes, 1962) that professionals do not like to do in any society, is deemphasized. As Hughes points out, "good people" do not like to do the scut-work of society. Nevertheless this work must be done and by "proper" authorities. While psychiatrists may agree that they are the proper authorities to take final responsibility for restraining mental patients, such aspects of work are delegated or deemphasized as much as possible. Psychiatrists, in organizational settings, are thus inclined to minimize the actual amount of control they have over their patients, or in consultive settings they minimize the part their evaluation plays in some fateful decision for their clients.

Styles of Control in Advisory Settings

While the community psychiatry situation may contain fewer requirements for the psychiatrist to exercise explicit control over patients than the situation in military or prison psychiatry, both of these types of psychiatry differ greatly from what one finds when entering the world of the traditional psychoanalyst or other psychiatrists in private practice. By necessity, patients will need less control here than patients do in these other worlds. Private patients are more likely to come voluntarily. For one thing, therapy, and especially analysis, is a costly undertaking. The surroundings, the acceptance by patients of the therapists' definitions of how the patient is to behave, the length of treatment—all reinforce the belief that patients are strongly motivated and that they come willingly to the psychiatrist for advice or help. Within this context, practitioners may have no awareness that they use *any* system of controls. Here, as in the medical model generally, the more subtle forms of control exerted over patients by practioners become apparent only after sophisticated consumers begin pointing them out.[6]

The fact that psychiatrists do not see elements of control in their practice is not surprising. Such an idea goes against the ideal picture of psychiatry as consultation and facilitation rather than direction or command. The usual view of the therapeutic context in private practice ignores or minimizes such possibilities in perceiving the setting as primarily advisory. Therapists in the private practice tradition operate in a fee-for-service setting very closely modeled on the ideal of medical practice. In this perspective, patients voluntarily seek out the therapist,

---

6. Seaman (1972) provides a good overview of the controls exercised over female patients by male doctors in general medical care. See also Frankfort (1973), who discusses these controls and those exercised over female patients in the psychiatric setting as well.

and the relationship may be terminated by either party at will. Since the generally accepted form of treatment requires an hour (technically, 45–50 minutes) for therapy at least once a week (and as often as five days a week), the psychiatrist does not have many patients. He sees the same patients over a longer period of time than is usually the case in the organizational context, where the turnover may be relatively rapid. In private practice a relatively close relationship can develop. So it is the psychiatrist who is warned against being controlled (through countertransference to the patient) rather than the opposite.

Once the relationship between doctor and patient is established, the main emphasis in the transaction is not on diagnosis and evaluation (as it often is in organizational settings) but on treatment. However, what the actual content of treatment will include varies quite widely and is thus part of the matter which patients may choose to negotiate as they search for treatment. When mutually agreeable to therapist and patient, this treatment may include modalities from the organizational setting: i.e., patients may enter hospitals and receive shock and drugs and inpatient services. But such therapies are always supposed to be voluntarily initiated. Furthermore, treatment is, ideally, private and confidential in private practice. As long as the complications attendant on hospitalization do not arise, no outside parties or agencies are involved, and so the psychiatrist has no responsibilities to them. Thus, he has little reason to see himself as making controlling or fateful decisions for the patient.

Yet, the opportunity for fateful decisions, where psychiatric judgments affect the future course of one's life, do occur in this setting. The same structure which permits a psychiatrist to make fateful decisions also permits the possibility of exploitation. Greenley (1972) has argued that psychiatrists sometimes change their diagnosis and evaluation of a patient in response to pressures from his family. Relatives and other agents of the patient may come to speak for him and collude with the psychiatrist to control the patient under certain circumstances (Goffman, 1969). Even where this collusion does not arise, many tactics and strategems of control by the therapist over the patient are actually present in this setting. Psychiatrists may "lead" patients into deciding that they are or are not ready to marry, enter graduate school, or leave home. However, despite the awesome powers patients may attribute to their psychiatrist, these tactics are generally implicit or indirect rather than overtly restraining (Haley, 1963; Ross, 1963). Unfortunately, systematic data are not available on the extent to which psychiatrists may actively intervene in the lives of their patients. However, case studies (Chesler, 1972) and impressionistic accounts (Adler, 1967) indicate that psychiatrists and other group therapists do sometimes use their authority and the powers imputed to them to exploit patients sexually and exercise "undue influence" in the course of treatment. And the existence of power is always signaled by its abuse.

The possibilities suggest that the ability to influence fateful decisions through the exercise of professional authority—and the subtle communication of it possible in the intense, private, interpersonal relationship developed through psychotherapy—are as important to consider as the overt or coercive powers available to practitioners in many institutional settings. Yet it is difficult to assign blame to any psychiatrist for unscrupulous intervention in the lives of patients; there are not clear standards of professional performance (Daniels, forthcoming). Generally speaking, there are no specific behavioral indicators of successful treatment outcome, though the psychiatric patient is expected to take an active role in reaching it. The professional controls in this setting have to be indirect rather than direct to preserve this expectation. Since practitioners are not accustomed to perceiving indirect influence as a form of control, they have no reason to question the extent of their own intervention in this process.

Conclusion and Discussion

The underlying mandates for both control and advice that pervade psychiatric practice in differing settings have been suggested to direct attention to the coercive elements present in a profession traditionally and ideologically labeled as a service profession. Contexts where coercion may be an inevitable part of treatment are likely to elicit quite different behavior from practitioners than will contexts where advisory relationships predominate. The major point of this paper is to suggest that an understanding of control functions exercised by professionals in the most coercive settings of practice leads us to see how pervasive coercive elements are throughout this specialty.

Most generally, we need to know what "structure of opportunities" face client and professional in the various contexts wherein they meet. Does the public defender give the same service to his client that the criminal lawyer gives? Some evidence suggests that he does not. There are patterned differences arising from the structure of expectations that the public defender has of his client, his knowledge of and ranking of alternatives available to manage the case, and the consequent evaluation of experience in each case that he will bring with him to the next one (Sudnow, 1965). This comparison between the public defender and the criminal lawyer bears some striking similarities to that of psychiatrists serving in institutions compared to private practitioners.

The professional responds to his definition of the situation in which he practices; his understanding of how service can be most appropriately delivered is likely to be very important. Naturally this picture is modified when clients are powerful or vocal enough to insist on a different definition. There are obviously some restrictions on the power of the professional in addition to those placed there by the power of his client (Daniels, 1973; Kahn-Hut, 1971; Rueschemeyer, 1972). Clients increasingly resist being told what is good for them by experts. In effect, they want to share in the definition of their problem. One indication of this strain is what has been called the revolt of the client (Haug and Sussman, 1969). Doctors, lawyers, clergymen, social workers, and others raise protests against the traditional organization of work in the professions. Too narrow a study of the professions in their own most traditional terms may not help us understand these problems or predict these changes.

In sum, we are likely to learn more about professions if we follow Hughes's advice (1971) or the advice of Friedson (1970a, 1970b) not to accept professional ideology as unquestioned fact when it can be examined in the light of evidence. In this case we have critically considered that aspect of the ideology which suggests that professions (or at the very least, their specialities) are mainly service occupations (which primarily advise or help) and should be studied as such. Perhaps we ought to study the special contexts within which professions are practiced in order to see how true this aspect of the ideology may be. One conceptual scheme for this study—that of examining advisory and coercive functions—has been suggested in this paper. Comparable advice-control problems—and strategies for managing them—should be discernible *across* professions. Once we discover patterns of coercion in some aspect of professional practice, how do we explain their acceptance by clients? What institutions or social agents support professionals when they exert powers over clients? Do professionals who become accustomed to explicit coercion over clients develop similar strategies and approaches to their work? Do psychiatrists who make their careers in areas like military or prison psychiatry approach their clients in ways similar to psychoanalysts? Or are they more like probation officers or other agents within the institutions of criminal justice? If we attend only to the professional ideologies—the representations presented by professional spokesmen—these questions would never arise. For the ideal characteristics presented by these spokesmen do not dwell sufficiently on the practical exigencies of everyday performance in the field.

One question implicit in the foregoing is not about the differences within professional practice which can be ascribed to the performance of primarily advisory or coercive functions. Rather the issue may be that in the actual performance of day-to-day service, professionals slip from settings where they possess overt, coercive powers to those where covert controls are important—never understanding the nature of their use of either form of control over clients in their daily practice. Thus one sociological opportunity, not suggested by professional ideology and outside the awareness of professionals themselves, is to uncover this area for investigation. An even more important responsibility of sociologists may be to add their efforts to the amassing of evidence through which social policies develop. In this way, eventually, the powers of professionals will be understood more clearly and, accordingly, fall under a system of controls so that rights and freedoms of patients are fully protected.

References

Alder, R. The thursday group. New Yorker (April 5) 1967: 55–146.

Beck, M. B., Newman, S. H., & Lewit, S. Abortion: A national public and mental health problem — past, present, and proposed research. *American Journal of Public Health 59* 1969: 2131 – 43.

Bromberg, W. *The mind of man. A history of psychotherapy and psychoanalysis.* New York: Harper & Row, 1959.

Bucher, R. & Strauss, A. Professions in process *American Journal of Sociology* *65* 1961: 325–34.

Caplan, R. B. *Psychiatry and the community in nineteenth century America.* New York: Basic Books, 1969.

Chesler, P. *Women and madness.* New York: Doubleday, 1962.

Coser, R. L., *Training in ambiguity: Socialization and social structure in a mental hospital.*

Coser, R. L., *Training in ambiguity: Socialization and social structure in a mental hospital.*

Coser, R. L. Evasiveness as a response to structural ambivalence. *Social Science and Medicine 1* 1967: 203–18.

Daniels, A. K. Does the umbrella of medicine protect the patient as well as the psychiatrist? *Psychiatry Digest* (forthcoming).

Daniels, A. K. How free should the professions be? In E. Freidson (Ed.) *Professions and their prospects.* Beverly Hills, Calif.: Sage, 1973

Daniels, A. K. A sub-specialty within a professional specialty: Military psychiatry. In E. Friedson and J. Lorber (Eds.) *Medical men and their work,* pp. 145–62. New York: Atherton, 1972.

Daniels, A. K. Normal mental illness and understandable excuses. *American Behavioral Scientist 14* 1970: 167–84.

Daniels, A. K. The captive professional: Bureaucratic limitation in the practice of military psychiatry. *Journal of Health and Social Behavior 10* 1969: 225–65.

Duhl, L. J., Leopold, R. I., & English, J. T. A mental health program for the Peace Corps. *Human Organization 23* 1964: 131–36.

Erikson, K. T. & Gilbertson, D. E., Case records in the mental hospital. In S. Wheeler (Ed.) *On record.* New York: Russel Sage, 1969.

Fox, R. C. A sociological perspective on organ transplantation and hemodialysis. *Annals New York Academy of Sciences 169* 1970: 406–28.

Frank, J. *Persuasion and healing.* New York: Schocken, 1963.

Frankfort, E. *Vaginal politics.* New York: Quadrangle, 1973.

Friedson, E. *Profession of medicine.* New York: Dodd, Mead, 1970a.

Friedson, E. *Professional dominance.* New York: Atherton, 1970b.

Garfinkel, H. *Studies in ethnomethodology.* Englewood Cliffs, N.J.: Prentice-Hall, 1967.

Goffman, E. Insanity of place. *Psychiatry 32* 1969: 357–88.

Goffman, E. The medical model and mental hospitalization: Some notes on the vicissitudes of the tinkering trades. In E. Goffman, *Asylums: Essays on the social situation of mental patients and other inmates.* Garden City, N.Y.: Doubleday, 1961.

Greenley, J. R. Alternative views of the psychiatrist's role. *Social Problems 20* 1977: 252–62.

Guttmacher, M. S. & Weihofen, H. *Psychiatry and the law.* New York: Norton, 1952.

Haley, J. *Strategies of psychotherapy.* New York: Grune & Stratton, 1963.

Halleck, S. L. *The Politics of therapy.* New York: Science House, 1971.

Haug, M. & Sussman, M. Professional autonomy and the revolt of the client. *Social Problems 17* 1969: 153–61.

Hughes, E. C. *The sociological eye.* Chicago: Aldine, 1971.

Hughes E. C Good people and dirty work. *Social Problems 10 (1)* 1962: 3–11.

Kahne, M. F. & Schwartz, C. G. The college as a psychiatric workplace: a sociological perspective. *Psychiatry* 1975.

Kahn-Hut, R. Psychiatric perspectives on powerlessness. Prepared for the meeting of the Society for the Study of Social Problems. Denver, Colorado, 1971.

Lader, L. *Foolproof birth control, male and female sterilization.* Boston: Beacon, 1972.

Maisel, R. Decision making in a commitment court. *Psychiatry 33* 1970: 352–61.

Miller, D. Records of madness. Prepared for the meeting of the Society for the Study of Social Problems, Washington, D.C., 1970.

Miller, D. *Worlds that Fail: Part I and II.* Research Monographs 6 and 7, California Department of Mental Hygiene, 1965.

Morgan, T. Entombed. *New York Times Magazine* (February 17) 1974: 14–26.

Opton, E. M., Jr. Coercive psychological and psychiatric treatment as a rationalization for official violence. Prepared for the meeting of the American Psychological Assocation, Montreal, Canada, 1973.

Perrow, C. Hospitals: Technology structure and goals, In J. G. March (Ed.) *Handbook of organizations* pp. 910–97. Chicago: Rand McNally, 1965.

Powelson, H. & Bendix, R. Psychiatry in prison. *Psychiatry 14* 1951: 73–86.

Rein, M. The strange case of public dependency. *Trans-Action 2* 1965: 16–23.

Rosen, G. *Madness in society.* New York: Harper & Row, 1969.

Rosenhahn, D. L. *On being sane in insane places.* Andover, Mass.: Warner Modular Publications, 1973.

Ross, L. *Vertical and horizontal.* New York: Simon & Schuster, 1963.

Rubington, E. The 'revolving door' game. *Crime and Delinquency* 1966: 332–38.

Rubington, E. The alcoholic and the jail. *Federal Probation 24* 1965: 30–33.

Rueschemeyer, D. Doctors and Lawyers: A comment on the theory of the professions. In E. Freidson and J. Lorber (Eds.) *Medical men and their work,* pp. 5–19. New York: Atherton, 1972.

Schwartz, C. G. Definitions of reality: the emergence of the social meaning of using a college clinic. Ph.D. dissertation. Brandeis University

Seaman, B. *Free and female.* Greenwich, Conn.: Fawcett, 1972.

Smith, H. Contingencies of professional differentiation. *American Journal of Sociology 63* 1958: 410–14.

Stanton, A. II. & Schwartz, M. S. The mental hospital. New York: Basic Books, 1954.

Strauss, A., Schatzman, L., Bucher, R., Ehrlich, D., & Sabshin, M. Psychiatric ideologies and institutions. New York: Free Press, 1964.

Sudnow, D. Normal crimes: sociological features of the penal code in a public defender's office. *Social Problems 12* 1965: 255–76.

Szasz, T. S. The psychiatrist as a double-agent. *Trans-Action 4* 1967: 16–25.

Wenger, D. E. & Fletcher, R. The effect of legal counsel on admissions to a state mental hospital: a confrontation of professions. *Journal of Health and Social Behavior 10* 1969: 66–73.

Wheeler, S. *On record.* New York: Russell Sage, 1969.

Whiting, J. F. Psychiatric services, systems analysis and manpower utilization. Washington, D.C.: American Psychiatric Association, 1969.

Wiseman, J. P. *Stations of the lost: The treatment of skid row alcoholics.* Englewood Cliffs, N.J.: Prentice-Hall, 1970.

Decision Rules, Types of Error, and Their Consequences in Medical Diagnosis

20

THOMAS J. SCHEFF

Members of professions such as law and medicine frequently are confronted with uncertainty in the course of their routine duties. In these circumstances, informal norms have developed for handling uncertainty so that paralyzing hesitation is avoided. These norms are based upon assumptions that some types of error are more to be avoided than others; assumptions so basic that they are usually taken for granted, are seldom discussed, and are therefore slow to change.

The purpose of this paper is to describe one important norm for handling uncertainty in medical diagnosis, that judging a sick person well is more to be avoided than judging a well person sick, and to suggest some of the consequences of the application of this norm in medical practice. Apparently this norm, like many important cultural norms, "goes without saying" in the subculture of the medical profession; in form, however, it resembles any decision rule for guiding behavior under conditions of uncertainty. In the discussion that follows, decision rules in law, statistics, and medicine are compared, in order to indicate the types of error that are thought to be the more important to avoid and the assumptions underlying this preference. On the basis of recent findings of the widespread distribution of elements of disease and deviance in normal populations, the assump-

This paper was written with the financial support of the Graduate Research Committee of the University of Wisconsin. Colleagues too numerous to list here made useful suggestions. David Mechanic was particularly helpful. An earlier version was presented at the Conference on Mathematical Models in the Behavioral and Social Sciences, sponsored by the Western Management Sciences Institute, University of California at Los Angeles, Cambria, California, November 3-5, 1961.

From *Behavioral Science 8 (2)* (1963). Reprinted with permission of James G. Miller, M.D., Ph.D., Editor.

tion of a uniform relationship between disease signs and impairment is criticized. Finally, it is suggested that to the extent that physicians are guided by this medical decision rule, they too often place patients in the "sick role" who could otherwise have continued in their normal pursuits.

Decision Rules

To the extent that physicians and the public are biased toward treatment, the "creation" of illness, i.e., the production of unnecessary impairment, may go hand in hand with the prevention and treatment of disease in modern medicine. The magnitude of the bias toward treatment in any single case may be quite small, since there are probably other medical decision rules ("When in doubt, delay your decision") which counteract the rule discussed here. Even a small bias, however, if it is relatively constant throughout Western society, can have effects of large magnitude. Since this argument is based largely on fragmentary evidence, it is intended merely to stimulate further discussion and research, rather than to demonstrate the validity of a point of view. The discussion will begin with the consideration of a decision rule in law.

In criminal trials in England and the United States, there is an explicit rule for arriving at decisions in the face of uncertainty: "A man is innocent until proven guilty." The meaning of this rule is made clear by the English common-law definition of the phrase "proven guilty," which according to tradition is that the judge or jury must find the evidence of guilt compelling *beyond a reasonable doubt*. The basic legal rule for arriving at a decision in the face of uncertainty may be briefly stated: "When in doubt, acquit." That is, the jury or judge must not be equally wary of erroneously convicting or acquitting: the error that is most important to avoid is to erroneously convict. This concept is expressed in the maxim, "Better a thousand guilty men go free, than one innocent man be convicted."

The reasons underlying this rule seem clear. It is assumed that in most cases, a conviction will do irreversible harm to an individual by damaging his reputation in the eyes of his fellows. The individual is seen as weak and defenseless, relative to society, and therefore in no position to sustain the consequences of an erroneous decision. An erroneous acquittal, on the other hand, damages society. If an individual who has actually committed a crime is not punished, he may commit the crime again, or more important, the deterrent effect of punishment for the violation of this crime may be diminished for others. Although these are serious outcomes they are generally thought not to be as serious as the consequences of erroneous conviction for the innocent individual, since society is able to sustain an indefinite number of such errors without serious consequences. For these and perhaps other reasons, the decision rule to assume innocence exerts a powerful influence on legal proceedings.

Type 1 and Type 2 Errors
Deciding on guilt or innocence is a special case of a problem to which statisti-

314 Thomas J. Scheff

cians have given considerable attention, the testing of hypotheses. Since most scientific work is done with samples, statisticians have developed techniques to guard against results which are due to chance sampling fluctuations. The problem, however, is that one might reject a finding as due to sampling fluctuations which was actually correct. There are, therefore, two kinds of errors: rejecting a hypothesis which is true, and accepting one which is false. Usually the hypothesis is stated so that the former error (rejecting a hypothesis which is true) is the error that is thought to be the more important to avoid. This type of error is called an "error of the first kind," or a Type 1 error. The latter error (accepting a hypothesis which is false) is the less important error to avoid, and is called an "error of the second kind," or a Type 2 error (Neyman, 1950, 265–66).

To guard against chance fluctuations in sampling, statisticians test the probability that findings could have arisen by chance. At some predetermined probability (called the alpha level), usually .05 or less, the possibility that the findings arose by chance is rejected. This level means that there are five chances in a hundred that one will reject a hypothesis which is true. Although these five chances indicate a real risk of error, it is not common to set the level much lower (say .001) because this raises the probability of making an error of the second kind.

A similar dilemma faces the judge or jury in deciding whether to convict or acquit in the face of uncertainty. Particularly in the adversary system of law, where professional attorneys seek to advance their arguments and refute those of their opponents, there is often considerable uncertainty even as to the facts of the case, let alone intangibles like intent. The maxim, "Better a thousand guilty men should go free, than one innocent man be convicted," would mean, if taken literally rather than as a rhetorical flourish, that the alpha level for legal decisions is set quite low.

Although the legal decision rule is not expressed in as precise a form as a statistical decision rule, it represents a very similar procedure for dealing with uncertainty. There is one respect, however, in which it is quite different. Statistical decision procedures are recognized by those who use them as mere conveniences, which can be varied according to the circumstances. The legal decision rule, in contrast, is an inflexible and binding moral rule, which carries with it the force of long sanction and tradition. The assumption of innocence is a part of the social institution of law in Western society; it is explicitly stated in legal codes and is accepted as legitimate by jurists and usually by the general populace, with only occasional grumbling, e.g., a criminal is seen as "getting off" because of "legal technicalities."

Decision Rules in Medicine

Although the analogous rule for decisions in medicine is not as explicitly stated as the rule in law and probably is considerably less rigid, it would seem that there is such a rule in medicine which is as imperative in its operation as its analogue in law. Do physicians and the general public consider that rejecting the hypothesis of illness when it is true, or accepting it when it is false, is the error that is most important to avoid? It seems fairly clear that the rule in medicine may be stated as: "When in doubt, continue to suspect illness." That is, for a physician to dismiss a patient when he is acutally ill is a Type 1 error, and to retain a patient when he is not ill is a Type 2 error.

Most physicians learn early in their training that it is far more culpable to dismiss a sick patient than to retain a well one. This rule is so pervasive and fundamental that it goes unstated in textbooks on diagnosis. It is occasionally mentioned explicitly in other contexts, however. Neyman, for example, in his discussion of X-ray screening for tuberculosis, states:

> [If the patient is actually well, but the hypothesis that he is sick is accepted a Type 2 error] then the patient will suffer some unjustified anxiety and, perhaps, will be put to some unnecessary expense until further studies of his health will establish that any alarm about the state of his chest in unfounded. Also, the unjustified precautions ordered by the clinic may somewhat affect its reputation. On the other hand, should the hypothesis [of sickness] be true and yet the accepted hypothesis be [that he is well, a Type 1 error], then the patient will be in danger of losing the precious opportunity of treating the incipient disease in its beginning stages when the cure is not so difficult. Furthermore, the oversight by the clinic's specialist of the dangerous condition would affect the clinic's reputation even more than the unnecessary alarm. From this point of view, it appears that the error of rejecting the hypothesis [of sickness] when it is true is *far more important* to avoid than the error of accepting the hypothesis [of illness] when it is false (1950, 270, italics added).

Although this particular discussion pertains to tuberculosis, it is pertinent to many other diseases also. From casual conversations with physicians, the impression one gains is that this moral lesson is deeply ingrained in the physician's personal code.

It is not only physicians who feel this way, however. This rule is grounded both in legal proceedings and in popular sentiment. Although there is some sentiment against Type 2 errors (unnecessary surgery, for instance), it has nothing like the force and urgency of the sentiment against Type 1 errors. A physician who dismisses a patient who subsequently dies of a disease that should have been detected is not only subject to legal action for negligence and possible loss of license for incompetence, but also to moral condemnation from his colleagues and from his own conscience for his delinquency. Nothing remotely resembling this amount of moral and legal suasion is brought to bear for committing a Type 2 error. Indeed, this error is sometimes seen as sound clinical practice, indicating a healthily conservative approach to medicine.

The discussion to this point suggests that physicians follow a decision rule which may be stated, "When in doubt, diagnose illness." If physicians are actually influenced by this rule, then studies of the validity of diagnosis should demonstrate the operation of the rule. That is, we should expect that objective studies of diagnostic errors should show that Type 1 and Type 2 errors do not occur with equal frequency, but in fact, that Type 2 errors far outnumber Type 1 errors. Unfortunately for our purposes, however, there are apparently only a few studies which provide the type of data which would adequately test the hypothesis. Although studies of the reliability of diagnosis abound (Garland, 1959), showing that physicians disagree with each other in their diagnoses of the same patients, these studies do not report the validity of diagnosis, or the types of error which are made, with the following exceptions.

We can infer that Type 2 errors outnumber Type 1 errors from Bakwin's study of physicians' judgments regarding the advisability of tonsillectomy for 1,000 school children. "Of these, some 611 had had their tonsils removed. The remaining 389 were then examined by other physicians, and 174 were selected for tonsillectomy. This left 215 children whose tonsils were apparently normal. Another group of doctors was put to work examining these 215 children, and 99 of them were adjudged in need of tonsillectomy. Still another group of doctors was then employed to examine the remaining children, and nearly one-half were recommended for operation" (Bakwin, 1945, 693). Almost half of each group of children were judged to be in need of the operation. Even assuming that a small proportion of children needing tonsillectomy were missed in each examination (Type 1 error), the number of Type 2 errors in this study far exceeded the number of Type 1 Errors.

In the field of roentgenology, studies of diagnostic error are apparently more highly developed than in other areas of medicine. Garland (1959, 31) summarizes these findings, reporting that in a study of 14,867 films for tuberculosis signs, there were 1,216 positive readings which turned out to be clinically negative (Type 2 error) and only 24 negative readings which turned out to be clinically active (Type 1 error)! This ratio is apparently a fairly typical finding in roentgenographic studies. Since physicians are well aware of the provisional nature of radiological findings, this great discrepancy between the frequency of the types of error in film screening is not too alarming. On the other hand, it does provide objective evidence of the operation of the decision rule "Better safe than sorry."

Basic Assumptions

The logic of this decision rule rests on two assumptions:

1. Disease is usually a determinate, inevitably unfolding process, which, if undetected and untreated, will grow to a point where it endangers the life or limb of the individual, and in the case of contagious diseases, the lives of others. This is not to say, of course, that physicians think of all diseases as determinate: witness the concept of the "benign" condition. The point here is that the imagery of disease which the physician uses in attempting to reach a decision, his working hypothesis, is *usually* based on the deterministic model of disease.
2. Medical diagnosis of illness, unlike legal judgment, is not an irreversible act which does untold damage to the status and reputation of the

patient. A physician may search for illness for an indefinitely long time, causing inconvenience for the patient, perhaps, but in the typical case doing the patient no irradicable harm. Obviously, again, physicians do not *always* make this assumption. A physician who suspects epilepsy in a truck driver knows full well that his patient will probably never drive a truck again if the diagnosis is made, and the physician will go to great lengths to avoid a Type 2 error in this situation. Similarly, if a physician suspects that a particular patient has hypochondriacal trends, the physician will lean in the direction of a Type 1 error in a situation of uncertainty. These and other similar situations are exceptions, however. The physician's *usual* working assumption is that medical observation and diagnosis, in itself, is neutral and innocuous, relative to the dangers resulting from disease.[1]

In the light of these two assumptions, therefore, it is seen as far better for the physician to chance a Type 2 error than a Type 1 error. These two assumptions will be examined and criticized in the remainder of the paper. The assumption that Type 2 errors are relatively harmless will be considered first.

In recent discussions it is increasingly recognized that in one area of medicine, psychiatry, the assumption that medical diagnosis can cause no irreversible harm to the patient's status is dubious. Psychiatric treatment, in many segments of the population and for many occupations, raises a question about the person's social status. It could be argued that in making a medical diagnosis the psychiatrist comes very close to making a legal decision, with its ensuing consequences for the person's reputation. One might argue that the Type 2 error in psychiatry, of judging a well person sick, is at least as much to be avoided as the Type 1 error, of judging the sick person well. Yet the psychiatrist's moral orientation, since he is first and foremost a physician, is guided by the medical, rather than the legal, decision rule.[2] The psychiatrist continues to be more willing to err on the conservative side, to diagnose as ill when the person is healthy, even though it is no longer clear that this error is any more desirable than its opposite.[3]

There is a more fundamental question about this decision rule, however, which concerns both physical illness and mental disorder. This question primarily concerns the first assumption, that disease is a determinate process. It also implicates the second assumption, that medical treatment does not have irreversible effects.

---

1. Even though this assumption is widely held, it has been vigorously criticized within the medical profession. See, for example, Darley (1959). For a witty criticism of both assumptions, see Ratner (1962).

2. Many authorities believe that psychiatrists seldom turn away a patient without finding an illness. See, for example, the statement about large mental hospitals in Brown (1961, fn. p. 60), and Mechanic (1962). For a study demonstrating the presumption of illness in psychiatric examinations, see Scheff (1963).

3. "The sociologist must point out that whenever a psychiatrist makes the clinical diagnosis of an existing need for treatment, society makes the social diagnoses of a changed status for one of its members." (Erickson 1957, p. 123).

In recent years physicians and social scientists have reported finding disease signs and deviant behavior prevalent in normal, noninstitutionalized populations. It has been shown, for instance, that deviant acts, some of a serious nature, are widely admitted by persons in random samples of normal populations (Wallerstein and Wyle, 1947; Porterfield, 1946; Kinsey, Pomeroy, and Martin, 1948). There is some evidence which suggests that grossly deviant, "psychotic" behavior has at least temporarily existed in relatively large proportions of a normal population (Clausen and Yarrow, 1955; Plunket and Gordon, 1961). Finally, there is a growing body of evidence that many signs of physical disease are distributed quite widely in normal populations. A recent survey of simple high blood pressure indicated that the prevalence ranged from 11.4 to 37.2 percent in the various subgroups studied (Rautahargu, Karvonen, and Keys, 1961; cf. Stokes and Dawber, 1959; Dunn and Etter, 1962).

It can be argued that physical defects and "psychiatric" deviancy exist in an uncrystallized form in large segments of the population. Lemert (1951, 75) calls this type of behavior, which is often transitory, *primary deviation.* Balint (1957, 18), in his discussion of the doctor-patient relationship, speaks of similar behavior as the "unorganized phase of illness." Balint seems to take for granted, however, that patients will eventually "settle down" to an "organized" illness. Yet it is possible that other outcomes may occur. A person in this stage might change jobs or wives instead, or merely continue in the primary deviation stage indefinitely without getting better or worse.

This discussion suggests that in order to know the probability that a person with a disease sign would become incapacitated because of the development of disease, investigations quite unlike existing studies would need to be conducted. These would be longitudinal studies of outcomes in persons having signs of disease in a random sample of a normal population, in which no attempt was made to arrest the disease. It is true that there are a number of longitudinal studies in which the effects of treatment are compared with the effects of nontreatment. These studies, however, have always been conducted with clinical groups, rather than with persons with disease signs who were located in field studies.[4] Even clinical trials appear to offer many difficulties, both from the ethical and scientific points of view (Hill 1960). These difficulties would be increased many times in controlled field trials, as would the problems which concern the amount of time and money necessary. Without such studies, nevertheless, the meaning of many common disease signs remains somewhat equivocal.

Given the relatively small amount of knowledge about the distributions and natural outcome of many diseases, it is possible that our conceptions of the danger of disease are exaggerated. For example, until the late 1940s histoplasmosis was thought to be a rare tropical disease, with a uniform fatal outcome.

---

4. The Framingham study is an exception to this statement. Even in this study, however, experimental procedures (random assignment to treatment and nontreatment groups) were not used (Dawber, Moore, & Mann 1957, p. 5).

Recently, however, it was discovered that it is widely prevalent, and with fatal outcome or impairment extremely rare (Schwartz and Baum, 1957). It is conceivable that other diseases, such as some types of heart disease and mental disorder, may prove to be similar in character. Although no actuarial studies have been made which would yield the true probabilities of impairment, physicians usually set the Type 1 level quite high, because they believe that the probability of impairment from making a Type 2 error is quite low. Let us now examine that assumption.

The "Sick Role"

If, as has been argued here, much illness goes unattended without serious consequences, the assumption that medical diagnosis has no irreversible effects on the patient seems questionable. "The patient's attitude to his illness is usually considerably changed during and by, the series of physical examinations. These changes, which may profoundly influence the course of a chronic illness, are not taken seriously by the medical profession and, though occasionally mentioned, they have never been the subject of a proper scientific investigation" (Balint, 1957, 43).

There are grounds for believing that persons who avail themselves of professional services are under considerable strain and tension (if the problem could have been easily solved, they would probably have used more informal means of handling it). Social-psychological principles indicate that persons under strain are highly suggestible, particularly to suggestions from a prestigeful source, such as a physician.

It can be argued that the Type 2 error involves the danger of having a person enter the "sick role" (Parsons 1950) in circumstances where no serious result would ensue if the illness were unattended. Perhaps the combination of a physician determined to find disease *signs,* if they are to be found, and the suggestible patient, searching for subjective *symptoms* among the many amorphous and usually unattended bodily impulses, is often sufficient to unearth a disease which changes the patient's status from that of well to sick, and may also have effects on his familial and occupational status. (In Lemert's terms [1951], the illness would be *secondary deviation* after the person has entered the sick role.)

There is a considerable body of evidence in the medical literature concerning the process in which the physician unnecessarily causes the patient to enter the sick role. Thus, in a discussion of "iatrogenic" (physician-induced) heart disease, this point is made:

> The physician, by calling attention to a murmur or some cardiovascular abnormality, even though functionally insignificant, may precipitate [symptoms of heart disease]. The experience of the work classification units of cardiac-in-industry programs, where patients with cardiovascular disease are evaluated as to work capacity, gives impressive evidence regarding the high incidence of such functional manifestations in persons with the diagnosis of cardiac lesion (Warren and Wolter, 1954, 78).

Although there is a tendency in medicine to dismiss this process as due to quirks of particular patients, e.g., as malingering, hypochondriasis, or as "merely functional disease" (that is, functional for the patient), causation probably lies not in the patient, but in medical procedures. Most people, perhaps, if they actually have the disease signs and are told by an authority, the physician, that they are ill, will obligingly come up with appropriate symptoms. A case history will illustrate this process. Under the heading "It may be well to let sleeping dogs lie," a physician recounts the following case:

> Here is a woman, aged 40 years, who is admitted with symptoms of conges- tive cardiac failure, valvular disease, mitral stenosis, and auricular fibrillation. She tells us that she did not know that there was anything wrong with her heart and that she had had no symptoms up to five years ago when her chest was X-rayed in the course of a mass radiography examination for tuberculosis. She was not suspected and this was only done in the course of routine at the factory. Her lungs were pronounced clear but she was told that she had an enlarged heart and was advised to go to a hospital for investiga- tion and treatment. From that time she began to suffer from symptoms— breathlessness on exertion—and has been in the hospital four or five times since. Now she is here with congestive heart failure. She cannot understand why, from the time that her enlarged heart was discovered, she began to get symptoms (Gardiner-Hill, 1958, 158).

What makes this kind of "role-taking" extremely important is that it can occur even when the diagnostic label is kept from the patient. By the way he is handled, the patient can usually infer the nature of the diagnosis, since in his uncertainty and anxiety he is extremely sensitive to subtleties in the physician's behavior. An interesting example of this process is found in reports on treatment of battle fatigue. Speaking of psychiatric patients in the Sicilian campaign during World War II, a psychiatrist notes:

> Although patients were received at this hospital within 24 to 48 hours after their breakdown, a disappointing number, approximately 15 percent, were salvaged for combat duty . . . any therapy, including usual interview methods that sought to uncover basic emotional conflicts or attempted to relate cur- rent behavior and symptoms with past personality patterns, seemingly pro- vided patients with logical reasons for their combat failure. The insights obtained by even such mild depth therapy readily convinced the patient and often his therapist that the limit of combat endurance had been reached as proved by vulnerable personality traits. Patients were obligingly cooperative in supplying details of their neurotic childhood, previous emotional difficul- ties, lack of aggressiveness, and other dependency traits . . . (Glass, 1953, 288; cf. Kardiner and Spiegel, 1947, Chaps. 3,4).

Glass goes on to say that removal of the soldier from his unit for treatment of any kind usually resulted in long-term neurosis. In contrast, if the soldier was given only superficial psychiatric attention and *kept with his unit*, chronic impair- ment was usually avoided. The implication is that removal from the military unit and psychiatric treatment symbolizes to the soldier, behaviorally rather than with verbal labels, the "fact" that he is a mental case.

The traditional way of interpreting these reactions of the soldiers, and perhaps the civilian cases, is in terms of malingering or feigning illness. The process of taking roles, however, as it is conceived of here, is not completely or even largely voluntary. (For a sophisticated discussion of role-playing, see Goffman 1959, 17–22). Vaguely defined impulses become "real" to the participants when they are organized under any one of a number of more or less interchangeable social roles. It can be argued that when a person is in a confused and suggestible state, when he organizes his feelings and behavior by using the sick role, and when his choice of roles is validated by a physician and/or others, that he is "hooked," and will proceed on a career of chronic illness.[5]

Implications for Research

The hypothesis suggested by the preceding discussion is that physicians and the public typically overvalue medical treatment relative to nontreatment as a course of action in the face of uncertainty, and that this overvaluation results in the creation as well as the prevention of impairment. This hypothesis, since it is based on scattered observations, is put forward only to point out several areas where systematic research is needed.

From the point of view of assessing the effectiveness of medical practice, this hypothesis is probably too general to be used directly. Needed for such a task are hypotheses concerning the conditions under which error is likely to occur, the type of error that is likely, and the consequences of each type of error. Significant dimensions of the amount and type of error and its consequences would appear to be characteristics of the disease, the physician, the patient, and the organizational setting in which diagnosis takes place. Thus for diseases such as pneumonia which produce almost certain impairment unless attended, and for which a quick and highly effective cure is available, the hypothesis is probably largely irrelevant. On the other hand, the hypothesis may be of considerable importance for diseases which have a less certain outcome, and for which existing treatments are protracted and of uncertain value. Mental disorders and some types of heart disease are cases in point.

The working philosophy of the physician is probably relevant to the predominant type of errors made. Physicians who generally favor active intervention probably make more Type 2 errors than physicians who view their treatments only as assistance for natural bodily reactions to disease. The physician's perception of the personality of the patient may also be relevant: Type 2 errors are

---

5. Some of the findings of the Purdue Farm Cardiac Project support the position taken in this paper. It was found, for example, that "iatrogenics" took more health precautions than "hidden cardiacs," suggesting that entry into the sick role can cause more social incapacity than the actual disease does (Eichorn and Andersen 1962, 11–15).

less likely if the physician defines the patient as a "crock," a person overly sensitive to discomfort, rather than as a person who ignores or denies disease.

Finally, the organizational setting is relevant to the extent that it influences the relationship between the doctor and the patient. In some contexts, as in medical practice in organizations such as the military or industrial setting, the physician is not as likely to feel personal responsibility for the patient as he would in others, such as private practice. This may be due in part to the conditions of financial remuneration, and perhaps equally important, the sheer volume of patients dependent on the doctor's time. Cultural or class differences may also affect the amount of social distance between doctor and patient, and therefore the amount of responsibility which the doctor feels for the patient. Whatever the sources, the more the physician feels personally responsible for the patient, the more likely he is to make a Type 2 error.

To the extent that future research can indicate the conditions which influence the amount, type, and consequences of error, such research can make direct contributions to medical practice. Three types of research seem necessary. First, in order to establish the true risks of impairment associated with common disease signs, controlled field trials of treated and untreated outcomes in a normal population would be needed. Second, perhaps in conjunction with these field trials, experimental studies of the effect of suggestion of illness by physicians and others would be necessary to determine the risks of unnecessary entry into the sick role.

Finally, studies of a mathematical nature seem to be called for. Suppose that physicians were provided with the results of the studies suggested above. How could these findings be introduced into medical practice as a corrective to cultural and professional biases in decision-making procedures? One promising approach is the strategy of evaluating the relative utility of alternative courses of action, based upon decision theory or game theory.[6]

Ledley and Lusted (1959) reviewed a number of mathematical techniques which might be applicable to medical decision making, one of these techniques being the use of the "expected value" equation, which is derived from game theory. Although their discussion pertains to the relative value of two treatment procedures, it is also relevant, with only slight changes in wording, to determining the expected values of treatment relative to nontreatment. The expected values of two treatments, they say, may be calculated from a simple expression involving only two kinds of terms: the probability that the diagnosis is correct, and the absolute value of the treatment (at its simplest, the absolute value is the rate of cure for persons known to have the disease).

The "expected value" of a treatment is:

$$E_t = p_s \nu_s^s + (1 - p_s)\nu_h^s$$

(The superscript refers to the way the patient is treated, the subscript refers to his

6. For an introductory text, see Chernoff and Moses (1959).

actual condition, s signifies sick, h healthy.) That is, the expected value of a treatment is the probability that the patient has the disease, multiplied by the value of the treatment for patients who actually have the disease, plus the probability that the patient does not have the disease (1-p), multiplied by the value (or "cost") of the treatment for patients who do not have the disease.

Similarly, the expected value of nontreatment is:

$$E_n = p_s \nu_s{}^h + (1 + p_s)\nu_h{}^h$$

That is, the expected value of nontreatment is the probability that the patient has the disease multiplied by the value (or "cost") of treating a person as healthy who is actually sick, plus the probability that the patient does not have the disease, multiplied by the value of not treating a healthy person.

The best course of action is indicated by comparing the magnitude of E_t and E_n. If E_t is larger, treatment is indicated. If E_n is larger, nontreatment is indicated. Evaluating these equations involves estimating the probability of correct diagnosis and constructing a payoff matrix for the values of $\nu_s{}^s$ (proportion of patients who actually had the disease who were cured by the treatment), $\nu_h{}^s$ (the cost of treating a healthy person as sick: inconvenience, working days lost, surgical risks, unnecessary entry into sick role), $\nu_s{}^h$ (cost of treating a sick person as well: a question involving the proportions of persons who spontaneously recover, and the seriousness of results when the disease goes unchecked), and finally, $\nu_h{}^h$ (the value of not treating a healthy person: medical expenses saved, working days, etc.).

To illustrate the use of the equation, Ledley and Lusted assign *arbitrary* absolute values in a case, because, as they say, "The decision of value problems frequently involves intangibles such as moral and ethical standards which must, in the last analysis, be left to the physician's judgment" (1959, 8). One might argue, however, that it is better to develop a technique for systematically determining the absolute values of treatment and nontreatment, crude though the technique might be, than to leave the problem to the perhaps refined, but nevertheless obscure, judgment processes of the physician. Particularly in a matter of comparing the value of treatment and nontreatment, the problem is to avoid biases in the physician's judgment due to the kind of moral orientation discussed above.

It is possible, moreover, that the difficulty met by Ledley and Lusted is not that the factors to be evaluated are "intangibles," but that they are expressed in seemingly incommensurate units. How does one weigh the risk of death against the monetary cost of treatment? How does one weigh the risk of physical or social disability against the risk of death? Although these are difficult questions to answer, the idea of leaving them to the physician's judgment is probably not conducive to an understanding of the problem.

Following the lead of the economists in their studies of utility, it may be feasible to reduce the various factors to be weighed to a common unit. How could the benefits, costs, and risks of alternative acts in medical practice be expressed in monetary units? One solution might be to use payment rates in disability and life insurance, which offer a comparative evaluation of the "cost" of death, and permanent and temporary disability of various degrees. Although this approach does not include everything which physicians weigh in reaching decisions (pain and suffering cannot be weighed in this framework), it does include many of the major factors. It therefore would provide the opportunity of constructing a fairly realistic payoff matrix of absolute values, which would then allow for the determination of the relative value of treatment and nontreatment using the expected value equation.[7]

Gathering data for the payoff matrix might make it possible to explore an otherwise almost inaccessible problem: the sometimes subtle conflicts of interest between the physician and the patient. Although it is fairly clear that medical intervention was unnecessary in particular cases, and that it was probably done for financial gain (Trussel, Ehrlich, and Morehead, 1962), the evaluation of the influence of remuneration on diagnosis and treatment is probably in most cases a fairly intricate matter, requiring precise techniques of investigation. If the payoff were calculated in terms of values to the patient *and* values to the physician, such problems could be introduced into the matrix. The following statements by psychiatrists were taken from Hollingshead and Redlich's study of social class and mental disorder:

> Seeing him every morning was a chore; I had to put him on my back and carry him for an hour. He had to get attention in large doses, and this was hard to do. The patient was not interesting or attractive; I had to repeat, repeat, repeat. She was a poor unhappy, miserable woman—we were worlds apart (1958, 344).

This study strongly suggests that psychiatric diagnosis and treatment are influenced by the payoff for the psychiatrist as well as for the patient. In any type of medical decision, the use of the expected value equation might show the extent of the conflict of interest between physician and patient, and thereby shed light on the complex process of medical decision making.

References
Bakwin, H. Pseudocia pediatricia. *New England Journal of Medicine, 232* 1945: 691–697.

Balint, M. *The doctor, his patient, and the illness.* New York: International Universities Press, 1957.

Brown, Esther L. *Newer dimensions of patient care,* New York: Sage, 1961.

Chernoff, H., & Moses, L. E. *Elementary decision theory.* New York: Wiley, 1959.

Clausen, J. A., & Yarrow, M. R. Paths to the mental hospital. *Journal of Social Issues. 11* 1955, 25–32.

---

7. It is possible that more sophisticated techniques may be applicable to the problem of constructing medical payoff matrices (Churchmann, Ackoff, & Arnoff 1957, Ch. 6 & 11). The possibility of applying these techniques to the present problem was suggested to the author by James G. March.

Churchman, C. W., Ackoff, R. L., & Arnoff, E. L. *Introduction to operations research.* New York: Wiley, 1957.

Darley, W. What is the next step in preventive medicine? *Association of Teachers Preventive Medicine Newsletter, 6* 1959.

Dawber, T. R., Moore, F. E., & Mann, G. V. Coronary heart disease in the Framingham study. *American Journal of Public Health 47* (Part 2) 1957: 4–24.

Dunn, J. P., & Etter, L. E. Inadequacy of the medical history in the diagnosis of duodenal ulcer. *New England Journal of Medicine 266* 1962: 68–72.

Eichorn, R. L., & Anderson, R. M. Changes in personal adjustment to perceived and medically established heart disease: a panel study. Paper presented at American Sociological Association Meeting, Washington, D.C., 1962.

Erickson, K. T. Patient role and social uncertainty — a dilemma of the mentally ill. *Psychiatry 20* 1957: 263–274.

Gardiner-Hill, H. *Clinical involvements.* London: Butterworth, 1958.

Garland, L. H. Studies of the accuracy of diagnostic procedures. *American Journal of Roentgenology, Radium Therapy, Nuclear Medicine, 82* 1959: 25–38.

Glass, A. J. Psychotherapy in the combat zone. *Symposium on stress.* Washington, D.C.: Army Medical Service Graduate School, 1953.

Goffman, E. *The presentation of self in everyday life.* Garden City, N.Y.: Doubleday Anchor, 1959.

Hill, A. B. (Ed.). *Controlled clinical trails.* Springfield, Ill.: Charles C. Thomas, 1960.

Hollingshead, A. B., & Redlich, F. C. *Social class and mental illness.* New York: Wiley, 1958.

Kardiner, A., & Spiegel, H. *War stress and neurotic illness.* New York: Hoeber, 1947.

Kinsey, A. C., Pomeroy, W. B., & Martin, C. E. *Sexual behavior in the human male.* Philadelphia: W. B. Saunders, 1948.

Ledley, R. S., & Lusted, L. B. Reasoning foundations of medical diagnosis. *Science 130* 1959: 9–21.

Lemert, E. M. *Social pathology.* New York: McGraw-Hill, 1951.

Mechanic, D. Some factors in identifying and defining mental illness. *Ment. Hygiene 46* 1962: 66–74.

Neyman, J. *First course in statistics and probability.* New York: Holt, Rinehart, 1950.

Parsons, T. Illness and the role of the physician. *American Journal of Orthopsychiatry 21* 1950: 452–460.

Plunkett, R. J., & Gordon, J. E. *Epidemiology and mental illness.* New York: Basic Books, 1961.

Porterfield, A. L. *Youth in trouble.* Fort Worth, Tex.: Leo Potishman Foundation, 1946.

Rautahargu, P. M., Karvonen, M. J., & Keys, A. The frequency of arteriosclerotic and hypertensive heart disease in ostensibly healthy working, populations in Finland. *Journal of Chronicle Diseases 13* 1961, 426–439.

Ratner, H. Medicine. *Interviews on the American character.* Santa Barbara: Center for the Study of Democratic Institutions, 1962.

Scheff, T. J. The presumption of illness in psychiatric screening. *Paper presented at Midwest Sociological Society Convention,* Milwaukee, 1963.

Schwartz, J., & Baum, G. L. The history of histoplasmosis. *New England Journal of Medicine 256,* 1957: 253–258.

Stokes, J., & Dawber, T. R. The "silent coronary": the frequency and clinical characteristics of unrecognized myocardial infarction in the Framingham study. *Annals of Internal Medicine, 50* 1959: 1359–1369.

The quantity, quality and costs of medical and hospital care secured by a sample of teamster families in the New York area. New York: Columbia Univ. School of Public Health and Administrative Medicine, 1962.

Wallerstein, J. S., & Wyle, C. J. Our law-abiding law-breakers. *Probation 25* 1947: 107–112.

Warren, J. V., & Wolter, Janet. Symptoms and diseases induced by the physician. *Gen. Practitioner 9* 1954: 77–84.

Women in Health Care 21

VICENTE NAVARRO

In the growing bibliography on sexism in the United States, a large number of references have documented the nature and extent of sexism in the health sector, with primary focus on the problems faced by professional women.[1] However, the condition not only of some women—the professionals—but that of all women as producers of services in the health sector requires analysis. The objectives of this article, then, are to describe the situation of women as producers in the health labor force within the context of the overall labor force in the United States, to give my own interpretations of some of the factors that cause that situation, and to describe both a strategy for change, ·and the leverage points within that strategy.

The Health Labor Force

First to be considered is the structure of the United States labor force in general, and secondly, that of the health sector in particular. Figure 21-1 shows the sex,

From the Department of Health Care Organization, School of Hygiene and Public Health, The Johns Hopkins University, Baltimore, M.D., 21205.

This paper is based on testimony presented before the Hearings on Women and Health Care of the Governor's Commission on the Status of Women, Commonwealth of Pennsylvania, June 27, 1974.

Supported in part by Grants 5T01 HS00012 from the Bureau of Health Services Research and 5 DO4 AH00076 from the Bureau of Health Manpower Education. Health Resources Administration. Department of Health, Education, and Welfare and a grant from the Commonwealth Fund, New York.

Reprinted with permission from the *New England Journal of Medicine 202* 1975: 398 – 402.

1. Among the most comprehensive bibliographies on this topic is that contained in the resource booklet prepared as a supplement to Report of a Workshop entitled "Women in Medicine: Action Planning for the 1970s," held by the Center for Women in Medicine in Philadelphia, March 14–15, 1974.

class, and income distribution according to the eight occupational categories described below.[2]

1. *Corporate owners and managers* include both stock owners and managers of the large corporations who, by virtue of ownership or control or both, command the most important sectors of economic life. They are predominantly male and are the main components of what Galbraith [6] and O'Connor [7] call the corporate class.

2. *Professionals and technical experts,* again predominantly male, comprise among others, physicians, lawyers, and academicians. The main feature that they share is that their work is intellectual, as opposed to manual, and usually requires professsional training.

3. *Business-middle-class executives* include executives of small and middle-size enterprises, ranging from businesses employing a few workers, to owners and managers of family-size enterprises of every kind. They are predominantly male and are the owners and controllers of what Galbraith [6] calls the market sector, and O'Connor [7] the competitive sector of the economy.

Groups 2 and 3 constitute the majority of the upper-middle class.

4. *Self-employed shopkeepers, craftsmen, and artisans,* predominantly male, represent the sector of the labor force that is declining most rapidly in the majority of western industrialized societies.

5. *Clerical and sales workers,* predominantly female, constitute the majority of white-collar workers, the sector of the labor force that is growing most rapidly.

Groups 4 and 5 constitute the majority of the lower-middle class. Worth underlining is the fact that the lower-middle class is closely related to the working class in terms of income, status, and lifestyle. For example, most women clerical and sales workers are married, and about half are married to working-class men. [8]

6. *Blue-collar or manual workers,* predominantly male, constitute a percentage of the labor force that has been fairly constant since 1950.

7. *Service workers,* predominantly female, constitute, with the blue-collar workers, the majority of the working class.

8. *Farm workers,* predominantly male, make up the other group within the working class.

The sex, occupational, and class structure can also be examined in terms of

---

2. In my categorization of classes and the strata within classes, I have followed Miliband[1] very closely. It is recognized that this categorization is far from complete, comprehensive, or all inclusive. Still, it is here used as an entry point to an understanding of the composition of the labor force in the health sector and of the distribution of economic and political power both outside and within the health sector.

Figure 21–1   Occupational and Social Class Distribution in the United States in 1970.

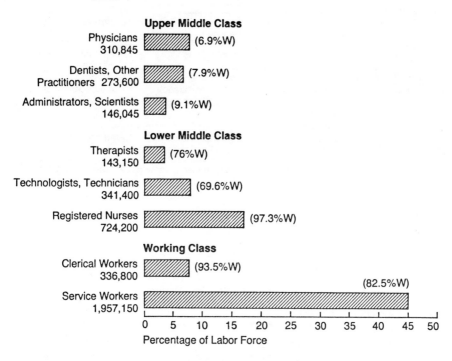

Based on Bonnell and Reich (2), *Current Population Reports,* 1970 (3), Giddens (4), and Anderson (5).

the three sectors of the United States economy: the monopolistic sector, the state sector, and the competitive sector.

The monopolistic sector (primarily manufacturing, insurance, and banking) employs approximately one-third of the labor force, which is predominantly male, is relatively unionized, and receives high wages and salaries, as compared to wages in the other sectors. The labor force in the *competitive sector* (primarily trade and services) also employs approximately one-third of the labor force and tends to be predominantly female, nonunionized, and low salaried. The other third of the labor force is employed by the *state or public sector,* which can be subdivided into service and contractual subsectors. The *service subsector,* which runs, funds, and is administered by the state sector (e.g., public-health services), employs one-sixth of the labor foce, with a slight predominance of females and low unionization. The other subsector within the state sector is the *contractual subsector,* which funds and contracts with the monopolistic sector for the provision of goods and services (e.g., the defense industry). [6,7] Table 21–1 summarizes the characteristics of production and of the labor force of each sector.

Within this tripartite structure of the economy, the health labor force has the characteristics of the competitive sector (i.e., is predominantly female, poorly paid and poorly organized, and unionized). Indeed, the occupational and sex composi-

Table 21-1   Production and Labor-Force Characteristics of Each Sector of the
United States Economy

	Monopolistic State Contractual	Service	Competitive
Characteristics of Production	–primarily manufacturing –economic concentration –vertical and horizontal integration (conglomerates) –national and international	–primarily service –economic deconcentration –vertical and sectorial –federal, state, local	–primarily trade and service –economic deconcentration –vertical and sectorial –regional, local
Characteristics of Labor Force	–predominantly male –nonwhites under represented –unionized –salaries: relatively high	–predominantly female –nonwhites proportionally represented –nonunionized –salaries: medium	–predominantly female –nonwhites overrepresented –nonunionized –salaries: low

Based on Galbraith and O'Connor [6,7].

tion of the health labor force, as shown in Figure 21–2, parallels that of the labor force in the competitive sector.

This figure indicates that the health professionals, belonging to the upper-middle class of the previous categorization, are predominantly male. Incidentally, only one other country in the Western developed world, Spain, has a lower percentage of women among the professional health labor force.

Below the health professionals is the group referred to as the paramedicals, including, among others, nurses, physical and occupational therapists, and social workers, which is predominantly female and which represents the lower-middle class in the health sector. Below this group is the majority of the labor force in the health sector, the service workers, predominantly female, who represent the working class within the health sector.

It is interesting, in this analysis of the health labor force, that the income differentials among these groups have increased very dramatically over time. From 1949 to 1970, the growth in the approximate annual net median income has been from $17,000 to $44,000 for general surgeons, $12,000 to $42,000 for internists, $12,000 to $37,000 for general practitioners, [12] and $6,000 to $27,000 for dentists. [13-14] For the same period, however, the approximate annual gross median income has grown from $2,400 to $5,800 for paramedicals, and from $1,300 to $3,500 for service workers. [11, 15]

This analysis demonstrates that within the labor force in the health sector, women constitute the majority of all producers, a majority concentrated in the lower-middle-class and working-class echelons of the labor force. It is for this reason that sex and class are clearly intertwined for most, though not all, women in the health sector. The analysis of the whys of the situations of women in the

Figure 21–2   Persons Employed in the Health Labor Force in 1970 According to Sex

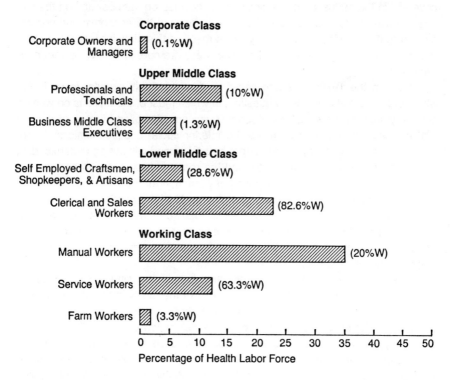

Based on *Health Resources Statistics,* 1971 (9), Pennell and Renshaw (10), and United States Bureau of the Census (11).

health sector is clearly related to the analysis of the class composition of the health sector.

The Whys of Sex Discrimination in the Health Sector

What factors account for the sex and class structure of the health labor force? Indeed, why, within a class society such as the United States, are working women found primarily among the lower-middle and working classes? Let me state here that I disagree with the majority of social analysts who have sought answers to these questions by focusing only on women and by framing their analysis in terms of the "women question" and the "women's problem." I disagree not only with the analysis but also the terminology. Indeed, the so-called women's problem is the problem of men and society. Thus, to understand the situation of women in the health sector the distribution of political and economic power in the world of men must be studied. Actually, what is happening in the analysis of the socalled women's question in the 1970s is very similar to the study and analysis of poverty and the poor in the 1960s. When poverty was "discovered" in the 1960s, many studies were conducted on the poor and on the culture of poverty. Very few studies, however, examined the economic and political system that determined that poverty. As a result of this singular focus, the strategies for improving the lot of the poor were framed in terms of the poor themselves.

Now, in the 1970s, one can see a replication of this singular focus in the study of the so-called women's question, in which most of the focus is on women and very little on the social and economic system controlled by men of defined class backgrounds that determines the inferior social and economic status of working women. Just as poverty cannot be understood without an understanding of wealth, the distribution of wealth, and the reasons for the wealth and income differentials in this country, the situation of women in the health sector cannot be understood without an understanding of the world of men and the distribution of social, economic, and political power within that world. To understand the situation of women, then, one must analyze not women as such, but the entire socioeconomic and political system that generates, creates, and perpetuates the situation of women.

Among the socioeconomic factors that explain the situation of women, I would single out the social and economic role of the family in society as being a main determinant of the division of labor in the economy, including the division of labor within the health sector. Indeed, in the distribution of responsibilities within the family, the main function of the husband is to be an active member of the labor force and the agent of production. The wife has the responsibility for maintaining (taking care) and reproducing the family. Within this distribution of responsibility, the employer pays for the work of one, but actually gets the work of two. If employers paid for the housewife's work, there would be considerable economic costs that are now completely avoided, and the savings of which to the employer are not even taken into account. Instead, the only compensation for this work is what is usually referred to as the "emotional rewards" that the wife derives in working and caring for her family. This "emotional rewards philosophy," with the concomitant division of labor within the family, however, benefits primarily the employers in society, again, who pay for the work of one and get the work of two.

Another socioeconomic factor that explains the division of labor within the family is the economic usefulness for the economic system of having a reserve army of workers (i.e., the women who work at home whose value to the economy as workers outside the home depends on the need for labor within the economy). Therefore, it is in periods of labor shortage that women are encouraged to move into the labor force, but when there is large unemployment, as there is now, the political and economic structure does not encourage, but hinders the entry and involvement of women in the labor force. No doubt, the lack of receptivity of the Nixon and Ford Administrations towards the creation of day-care centers in this country can be explained, in large degree, by the fear of further increasing the unemployment situation in the United States.

These two socioeconomic factors, among others, explain the social and economic usefulness of the present division of labor within the family, with the "woman's" work being primarily at home. Moreover, this very division of labor and the values that support it are continually reinforced and perpetuated by all the systems of communication and education in this country that sustain the conventional social virtues—the virtues that, as Galbraith[16] writes, are the ones supported by the powerful in society. One of those virtues is the merit ascribed to the woman who is a good homemaker. To do something else would be "neglecting her home and family, i.e., her real work. She ceases to be a woman of acknowledged virtue."

This role division within the family also appears in the health sector, with the predominantly upper-class, white, male physicians being, according to the conventional wisdom, the unquestioned leaders of the health team, the nurses and paraprofessionals, predominantly female, the dependents and appendages to the physicians, and the auxiliary and ancillary personnel, predominantly females, and working class by definition. Actually, this set of relations was seen in just this way by none other than Florence Nightingale, who perceived the characteristics of the nurse as providing wifely support to the physician, motherly devotion to the patient, and firm but kind discipline to the attendants and auxiliaries.[17] And an example of how the media reinforce these role definitions and the values that support them is the most popular television program in the United States dealing with health care, "Marcus Welby," which has been identified by Congresswoman Chisholm as the "great lie in TV on medical care" — i.e., all M.D.s, who are men and upper class, are thoughtful and compassionate, with the nurses being presented as nice, sweet females who are appendages to the physician.[18]

Given these social and economic needs of the system, it is quite logical that women tend to be the majority of workers in a sector whose main function within the economy is to provide care to and maintenance of the population, and that, within that sector, women tend to perform the conditional and dependent jobs.

This situation, briefly described above, is found not only in the social and economic spheres of society, but also in the political ones, owing to the patterns of control and dominance over the decision-making process of institutions both outside and within the health sector.

This fact can be seen by a glance at the sex and class composition of the boards of trustees of institutions in the health sector. Actually, within the health institutions there are the reproductive institutions, such as the foundations and medical teaching institutions, that serve to reproduce the human resources in the health sector, and the delivery institutions — e.g., the acute hospitals—that provide the services. Of the delivery institutions, the acute hospital sector is the most important one in terms of consumption of resources. For both types of institutions, Figure 21–3 shows the class and sex composition of the labor force within and outside the health sector in the United States, and of the board of trustees of the top ten foundations in the medical sector in this country and of a representative sample of private and state medical schools, and of acute hospitals.

One can see in Figure 21–3 the very low representation of both women and

Figure 21-3 Estimated Social Class Composition of the United States Labor Force and of the Boards of Trustees of Reproductive and Delivery Institutions in the Health Sector

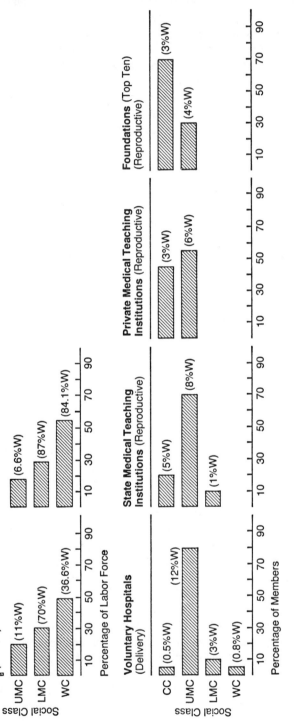

Based on Pfeffer (19), Hartnett (20), and Navarro (unpublished data).

the lower-middle and working classes, the majority of the United States population, in the decision-making bodies of health institutions. The majority of producers both in the health sector and in the rest of society (who in the health sector are women) are practically nonexistent in the corridors of power in the health sector. A similar situation appears in the different agencies of government in the health sector, in which corporate leaders and the professional and business upper-middle class, most of them males, predominate in the federal, state, and local branches of government.

The Strategy for Change

From this analysis of the class and sex structure of the labor force in the health sector, it should be quite clear that it is highly unlikely that profound and meaningful changes will take place that would benefit the majority of women in the health sector unless the patterns of control of that sector change, with a change in the sex and class composition and the system of governance of the agencies in the health sector and its institutions.

Indeed, a condition for the liberation of the majority of women in the health labor force is the implementation of institutional democracy in the health sector, in which the health institutions are controlled by those who work in it and by those who are served by it. And I would postulate that unless the composition of the decision-making bodies in the health sector changes substantially to reflect better the sex and class composition of the producers and consumers of the health sector, no real changes will take place to benefit the majority of women in the health sector. And since the majority of the labor force — the working class and lower-middle class—are women, the struggle for control of the sector by the producers should go side by side and should be the same as the struggle for control of the health sector by women.

I shall emphasize, however, that the inclusion of women in the corridors of power of institutions will be a necessary but not sufficient condition to improve the situation of the majority of women in the health sector. Thus, I believe that the appearance of women in positions of power in the health sector will serve to improve the positions of women in the health sector in general, only to the extent that these women are representative of and accountable to the workers in the sector as a whole, the majority of whom are lower-middle-class and working-class women. I emphasize this point because it has been my experience that when the boards of trustees of health institutions expand to include, besides the city fathers, also the city mothers, the situations of the majority of the citizens, the city orphans, do not necessarily improve. Moreover, experience indicates that class loyalties are far stronger than sex loyalties. And in terms of socioeconomic behavior, the female physician is far closer to and supportive of the male physician than of the cleaning women in the hospital. Indeed, other oppressed groups in this country, such as the blacks, are finding out that the broadening of opportu-

nity for the black upper-middle class has not resulted in betterment of the situation of the majority of the blacks in this country, the oppression of whose daily
lives continues undiminished. My own experience in the health sector suggests
that the much needed improvement and correction of unfair policies affecting
upper-middle-class women in the health sector does not imply and is not necessarily followed by the betterment and more urgent need of betterment of the lives
of the majority of women in the health sector, the lower-middle class and working
class. Indeed, the betterment of a few does not imply, nor does it result in, the
betterment of the many.

The betterment of the many will be related to the degree that the many are
represented in the sources and corridors of power, now controlled by the few. It is
because of this fact that the demand for the rights of women in the health sector
is intrinsically related to the demand for a more democratic, representative, and
accountable system that is current today. It is in terms of this understanding that
the struggle for women's liberation also implies the struggle for the liberation of
everyone.

References

1. Miliband, R. *The state in capitalist society: An analysis of the western systems of power.* London: Weidenfeld and Nicolson, 1969, pp 23–48.
2. Bonnell, V. Reich, M. *Workers and the American economy: Data on the labor force.* Boston: New England Free Press, 1973.
3. Consumer Income: Income Growth Rates in 1939 to 1968 for Persons by Occupation and Industry Groups, for the United States (Current Population Reports, Series P60, No. 69). Washington, DC: Government Printing Office, 1970.
4. Giddens, A. *The class structure of the advanced societies.* London: Hutchinson University Library, 1973.
5. Anderson, C. H. *The political economy of social class.* Englewood Cliffs, N.J.: Prentice-Hall, 1974.
6. Galbraith, J. K. *Economics and the public purpose.* Boston: Houghton Mifflin, 1973.
7. O'Connor, J. *The fiscal crisis of the state.* New York: St. Martin's Press, 1973.
8. Levison, A. The working class majority. *The New Yorker* (September 2) 1974, 36.
9. National Center for Health Statistics. *Health resources statistics: Health manpower and health facilities,* 1971 (DHEW Publication [HSM] 72–1509). Washington, DC: Government Printing Office, 1972.
10. Pennel M. Y., Renshaw, J. E. *Distribution of women physicians, 1970. Journal of the American Medical Women's Association, 27* 1972: 197–203.
11. United States Bureau of the Census. *Census of population: 1970: Subject reports: Final report PC(2)–7A, occupational characteristics.* Washington, DC, Government Printing Office, 1973, pp 476–503, Table 24.
12. The Survey of Physicians. Oradell, New Jersey, *Medical Economics* 1972.
13. Dentists' incomes surveyed by Commerce Department. *Journal of the American Dental Association 45* 1952: 248.

14. 1971 survey of dental practice III. Income of dentists by type of practice, personnel employed, and other factors. *Journal of the American Dental Association 84* 1972: 636–39.

15. United States Bureau of the Census. U.S. Census of Population: 1950. Vol 2, Characteristics of the Population, Part 1, Summary, Chapter C. Washington, DC, Government Printing Office, 1953, pp 1–279–1–282. Table 129.

16. Galbraith, J. K. *Economics and the public purpose.* Boston: Houghton-Mifflin, 1973, p. 32.

17. Ehrenreich, B. & English, D. *Witches, midwives, and nurses; A history of women healers.* Old Westbury, N. Y.: The Feminist Press, 1973, pp 34–5.

18. Rintels, D.W. Will Marcus Welby always make you well? *New York Times,* March 12, 1972.

19. Pfeffer, J. Size, composition and function of hospital boards of directors: a study of organization-environment linkage. *Administrative Science Quarterly 18* 1973: 349–64.

20. Hartnett, R. T. College and university trustees: their backgrounds, roles, and educational attitudes. In S. Currie (Ed.), Crisis in American institutions. Boston: Little, Brown, 1973, pp 359–72.

PART V

Organization and Delivery of Health Care

Much controversy surrounds the issue of how medicine should be organized, delivered, and financed. The traditional, solo, free-for-service practice is being replaced by new forms of medical practice: group practice, prepayment health care organizations, and other arrangements. Longest's and Freidson's selections provide an overview of the traditional organization of health care in America and some of the recent changes it has undergone. Their research indicates that the future of the American health care delivery system is nebulous.

Concern is also voiced over whether existing programs deliver health services as intended. Davis analyzes the Medicare program for the aged and finds that benefits are unevenly distributed according to income, race, and geographical location.

Health care is the result of competing values and interests. The politics of health care therefore are important in the organization and delivery of health services. Roth argues that for their own good patients need to have greater control over what is done to them during their hospital stay. Rubsamen discusses the increase in malpractice suits, which he attributes to increased consumer expectations in the medical community's ability to provide care. He concludes that trial by jury may not be the most satisfactory way of settling the complex issues involved in such suits. Finally Navarro argues that the organization of health care in the United States is determined by the distribution and control of economic and political power in the country.

The U.S. Health Care System   22

BEAUFORT B. LONGEST, JR.

Introduction

This chapter is a description of the U.S. health care system. The scope of the subject is broad and the system is very dynamic. Although every attempt is made to exclude judgments and criticisms, the mere description is a demanding task. Thus, the description is partial at best and only reflects the view seen from the author's vantage point.

As a beginning point, three definitions are necessary. First, *health* has been defined by the World Health Organization as a state of "complete physical, mental, and social well-being and not merely the absence of disease." From this lofty ideal, the World Health Organization has tried to give meaning to the term "health" by setting as a goal, "the attainment by all citizens of the world by the year 2000 of a level of health that will permit them to lead a socially and economically productive life." Health or health status in a human being is a function of many factors including the basic biological characteristics and processes that comprise human biology (some diseases are inherited); the conditions external to the body (some diseases are caused by or exacerbated by environmental conditions); and the behavior patterns that constitute lifestyle (some diseases result from the pattern or style of life). This definition of health describes an ideal state—one which is impossible to measure; yet, it represents a target that permits a definition of a second important term.

Dictionaries generally define service as "an act of helpful activity." Thus *health services,* in their simplest terms, are acts of helpful activity specifically intended to maintain or improve health. Health services can be divided into three

Adapted from Beaufort B. Longest, Jr., *Management Practices for the Health Professional* published by Reston Publishing Company.

Figure 22–1   Determinants of Health Status.

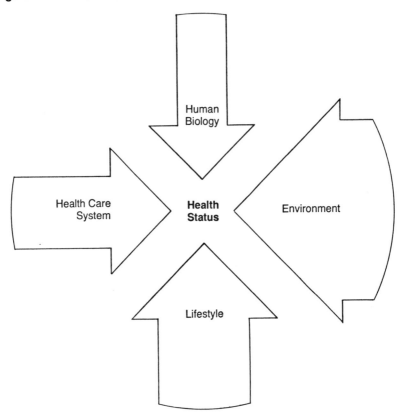

Source: This figure is similar to one developed by Henrik L. Blum, *Planning for Health; Development and Application of Social Change Theory,* New York; Human Sciences Press, 1973, p. 3. Reprinted with permission.

basic types: public health services which are activities that must be conducted on a community basis such as communicable disease control and the collection and analysis of health statistics; environmental health services, which often overlap with public health services, and include such activities as insect and rodent control and air pollution control; and personal health services which are activities directed at individuals and include promotion of health, prevention of illness, diagnosis and treatment (sometimes leading to a cure), and rehabilitation. Helpful activities as diverse as the delicate corneal transplant performed on a 60-year-old woman, the drainage of a swamp in Louisiana during mosquito season, the counseling of an obese member of an HMO, and the separation of smokers and nonsmokers on a commercial airliner are all health services.

Building on these definitions, it is possible to define the *health care system* as the resources (money, people, physical plant, and technology) and the organizational configurations necessary to transform these resources into health ser-

Figure 22-2   Federal Health Expenditures by Health Determinant (estimated)

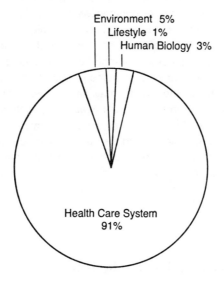

vices. It is the "acts of helpful activity specifically intended to maintain or improve health" that form the ultimate purpose of the health care system and the accessibility, quality, appropriateness, and efficiency of these health services should constitute the basis of fair and rational judgments about the health care system.

It is important to note that the health care system and the services it provides are only one of a set of factors that impact on health status. Figure 22-1 represents, through the relative size of the arrows, assumptions about the relative importance of these determinants of health status. Thus, when a man with a family history of (genetic tendency toward) cancer, who smokes heavily, lives in a polluted urban environment, and sees a physician long after symptoms emerge dies of lung cancer that is not a fair and rational basis upon which to judge the health care system inadequate. The death of an infant whose mother could not get good pre-natal care (accessibility), the unnecessary surgery performed by a less than fully qualified surgeon (appropriateness and quality), and the patient who pays a grossly inflated price for a diagnostic procedure because the machine necessary to conduct the procedure is owned by a hospital in a town where too many such machines exist (efficiency) are fairer and more rational bases upon which to judge the health care system inadequate.

Ironically, expenditures on health services, especially at the federal level, are not at all consistent with the view of the determinants of health status represented in Figure 22-1. Figure 22-2 depicts a rough estimate of the distribution of federal health expenditures by these determinants.[1] This paradox between determinants of health and expenditures for health is not likely to change dramatically

---

1. Michael S. Koleda, Carol Burke, & Jane S. Willems, *The Federal health dollar: 1969-1976.* Washington, D.C.: Center for Health Policy Studies, National Planning Association, 1977, 62-67.

in the years immediately ahead. The historical causes of the paradox are far too complex to explore in detail here. Yet, it serves to put the discussion of the health care system in the U. S. in proper perspective: the health care system absorbs the vast majority of dollars spent to impact on health status, but it is increasingly seen to be very limited in terms of future positive impact on the status of health of the U. S. population. This is not to say that the health care system is not important to health status. It is after all the source of intervention when illness or disease occurs even though their roots may lie in environmental, biological or behavioral determinants. In this sense, the health care system can be viewed as a line of defense against the awful toll of untreated environmentally, biologically and/or behaviorally caused illness and disease. It is largely because preventive measures in the areas of environmental, biological and behavioral determinants have been neither sufficient nor effective that the health care system is so vital to maintaining, to say nothing of improving, the health status of the U. S. population. With this perspective as background, attention can be turned to a description of the health care system.

The Dynamics of the Health Care System

The resources—money, people, physical plant, and technology—and the organizational configurations necessary to transform them into health services are described in the sections which follow. Also, consideration will be given to the problems confronting the system as it attempts to provide services that are simultaneously of high quality, appropriate, efficiently produced, and accessible to all who need them. As a precursor to these considerations, however, it is important to recognize the dynamic nature of the U. S. health care system. The dynamics are nowhere more explicit than in numbers of dollars spent. In 1978, total health expenditures climbed toward the $200 billion level (some expect it to be $250 billion and 9 percent of GNP in a few short years).[2] This is up from $118.5 billion in 1975 and only $60.6 billion in 1969. These dramatic increases reflect several things including inflation and increased utilization but also growth and change in the system.

The changes in the health care system reflect social change, different priorities, new technology, more regulation of the system, changes in disease trends, new delivery methods, and new approaches to paying for health care. All of these factors contribute to the dynamic state of the U. S. health care system. For example, there have been significant increases in drug addiction, particularly alcoholism, and venereal disease in recent years. Increasingly, these problems are viewed as health problems rather than social or criminal problems with the concomitant increased expectation that the health care system should provide solu-

---

2. Congressional Budget Office, *Budget options for fiscal 1977: A report to the Senate and House committees on the budget.* Washington, D.C.: U.S. Government Printing Office, March 15, 1977. See pages 49 -50 and 151-67.

tions. The president of one of the nation's leading health care organizations has summarized the impact of new technology by pointing out that "one of the significant results of advances in medical technology has been greater specialization of facilities, equipment, and personnel. This specialization has led to a decline in the number of general or primary care practitioners, has increased fragmentation of the delivery of care, and has produced a greater need for coordination of the various components of the delivery process."[3] When the effects of similar factors are considered, the dynamic nature of the health care system begins to come into focus.

Resources in the Health Care System

The U. S. health care system, ultimately devoted to the provision of health services, requires an enormous quantity and variety of resources. Resources are defined here, simply, as the basic building blocks of the system: money, people, physical plant, and technology.

Money   As already noted, the health care system requires a total expenditure approaching $200 billion. Table 22–1 shows the national health expenditures, including percent of GNP, and sources of funds for personal health care expenditures for selected years. It is important to look at the rate of increase in the growth of government expenditures. This has resulted largely from the massive infusion of federal dollars into the health care system since the mid-1960s when the Medicare and Medicaid programs were introduced. It is also important to realize that the bulk of federal health dollars, about 83 percent, pays for the provision of health care services, about 7 percent goes for research, about 4 percent for manpower training, about 3 percent for facilities construction, and only about 1 percent to improve the organization and delivery of health care services.

Table 22–1   National Health Expenditures and Sources of Payment for Personal Health Care, Selected Years

			Sources of Payment for Personal Health Care (Rounded Percent)[a]			
Fiscal Year	Total National Health Expenditures (billions)	Percent of GNP	Direct Payment	Private Health Insurance	Government	Philanthropists and others
1950	$ 12.0	4.5	68	9	20	3
1955	17.3	4.5	59	15	23	3
1960	25.9	5.2	55	21	22	2
1965	38.9	5.9	52	25	21	2

3. James A. Campbell & Richard DuFour, Organization of hospital resources. In American Hospital Association, *Hospitals in the 1980s*. Chicago: American Hospital Association, 1977, p. 9.

Table 22-1 (Continued)

	Total National Health Expenditures (billions)	Percent of GNP	Sources of Payment for Personal Health Care (Rounded Percent)[a]			
Fiscal Year			Direct Payment	Private Health Insurance	Government	Philanthropists and others
1970	69.2	7.2	40	24	34	2
1975	122.2	8.4	34	25	40	1
1976	139.3	8.6	33	26	40	1
1977	163.0	8.8	—	—	—	—
1980[b]	226.4	9.0	—	—	—	—

Source: This data is from *Health, United States, 1976–1977, Chartbook*. Washington, D.C.: U. S. Department of Health, Education, and Welfare, 1977.
a. Personal health care includes hospitalization, physicians' and dentists' services, drugs, and other services and supplies provided to individuals. In 1976, personal health care expenditures were $120.4 billion out of total national health expenditures of $139.3 billion.
b. These figures represent DHEW estimates.

Personal health care services are paid for in a variety of ways, as shown in Table 22-1, including: (1) Direct or "out-of-pocket" payment in which an individual pays for his care directly from his own funds; (2) Private insurance in which an individual or someone on his behalf, such as an employer, enters into a contractual arrangement with an insurer who agrees to pay for a specified set of services under specified conditions in return for premium payments; or a prepayment is made to a provider such as a health maintenance organization or an organization such as Blue Cross who then contracts with providers to provide services to subscribers; (3) Government programs, principally Medicare, in which the federal government pays for health care services provided to social security recipients over age 65 and Medicaid in which federal funds are combined with state funds in participating states to pay for health care services received by welfare recipients and other people, defined by state law, to be medically indigent. Payments under both Medicare and Medicaid are made to providers of service on behalf of program beneficiaries; (4) Although the relative amount is decreasing, some care is paid for through charitable contributions, endowment funds, or revenue generated by providers from other sources of income such as hospital parking lots. All but the first of these mechanisms of payment are termed "third-party payments" because the providers of health care services receive payment from a source other than directly from the individual who has received the care. Direct, out-of-pocket payment now accounts for only about one-third of total expenditures for personal health care services. The complex flow of funds for the payment for health care services in the U. S. is shown in Figure 22-3.

People Another basic building block of the health care system is manpower. The Department of Labor lists more than 225 categories of workers who are

Figure 22-3   Flow of Funds for Payment of Health Care Services in the United States.

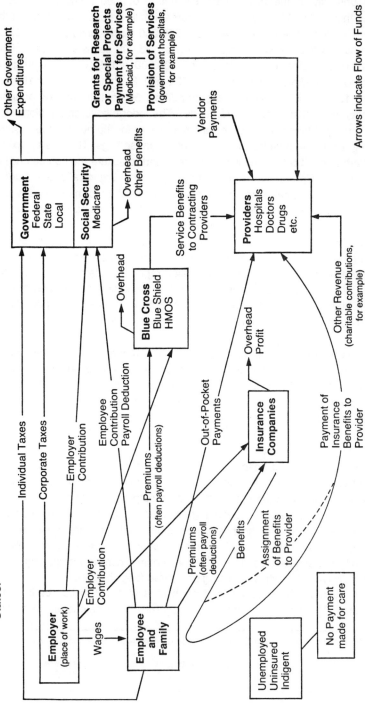

Source: Florence A. Wilson and Duncan Neuheuser, *Health Services in the United States*, Cambridge, Mass.: Ballinger, 1974, p. 91. Reprinted with permission.

employed primarily in the health care system. (Rounded numbers are used throughout this section.) There are more than 4.4 million people who work in the health care system. There are now about 350,000 active physicians, 900,000 registered nurses and 500,000 practical nurses, 125,000 dentists, 145,000 pharmacists, 80,000 medical technologists, and 100,000 radiologic technologists at work in the U. S. health care system. By 1980 the U. S. should have, per 100,000 population, 197 physicians, 485 registered nurses, 56 dentists, and 64 pharmacists to meet the nation's health care needs.[4] The federal government alone now spends about $1.5 billion annually to train manpower for the health care system. The training occurs in a wide variety of educational settings. There is an extensive program of certification and licensure designed to assure the competency of health manpower. Certification is granted by a variety of organizations and/or the states to people who meet certain requirements established for many health care occupations. Certification does not exclude others from working in that occupation. Licensure is a good deal stronger in that it is a recognition of competence granted by the states. Without a license, pharmacists, physicians, professional nurses, dentists, and optometrists among other health professionals cannot practice their profession. Licensure and certification represent attempts to assure the availability of health manpower resources with acceptable levels of preparation. In addition, these programs tend to restrict the supply of health manpower and, thus, drive up the cost of this critical resource of the health care system.

Physical Plant   Another building block of the health care system is the nation's investment in the "bricks and mortar" of physical facilities required to meet health care needs. (Rounded numbers are used throughout this section). The investment in hospital physical plants alone now totals more than $50 billion. New investment in construction of health care and medical research facilities is now about $4.5 billion annually. The federal government spent $1.1 billion for health facilities construction in 1976.[5]

There are over 7,000 hospitals in the U. S. health care system with more than 1.4 million beds. On any given day, about 1.1 million people are patients in the nation's hospitals and more than 263 million outpatient visits occur annually.[6] Table 22-2 shows trends in utilization, personnel, and finances for selected years going back to 1946 in U. S. hospitals. It is important to recognize that there is substantial variation in U. S. hospitals in terms of size, scope of service, ownership and other characteristics. This variation requires care in interpreting statistics, especially when hospitals are being compared to each other.

There are now about 23,000 nursing homes with 1.2 million beds in the United States. The federal government recognizes three categories of nursing

---

4. DHEW, *Health in the United States: A chartbook.* Washington, D.C.: DHEW Publication No. HRA-76-1233, 1976.

5. Michael S. Koleda, Carol Burke, & Jane S. Willems, *The Federal health dollar: 1969-1976.* Washington, D.C.: Center for Health Policy Studies, National Planning Association, 1977, p. 38.

6. American Hospital Association, *Guide to the health care field.* Chicago: American Medical Association, 1978, p. 7.

Table 22-2 U.S. Hospital Statistics, 1946–1977

Year	Hospitals	Beds (000)	Admissions (000)	Average Daily Census (000)	Occupancy (%)	Outpatient Visits (000)	Number of Personnel (000)	Expenses Payroll (000)	Expenses Total (000)	Assets Plant (000,000)	Assets Total (000,000)
1946	6,125	1,436	15,675	1,142	79.5		830	$1,103	$1,963	$5,639	$7,791
1950	6,788	1,456	18,483	1,253	86.0		1,058	2,191	3,651	9,833	11,986
1955	6,956	1,604	21,073	1,363	85.0		1,301	3,582	5,594	14,743	17,714
1960	6,876	1,658	25,027	1,402	84.6		1,598	5,588	8,421	19,993	24,502
1965	7,123	1,704	28,812	1,403	82.3	125,793	1,952	8,551	12,948	20,824	26,336
1966	7,160	1,679	29,151	1,398	83.3	142,201	2,106	9,286	14,198	21,813	27,922
1967	7,172	1,671	29,361	1,380	82.6	148,229	2,203	10,461	16,395	23,113	31,019
1968	7,137	1,663	29,766	1,378	82.9	156,139	2,309	11,997	19,061	25,061	33,547
1969	7,144	1,650	30,729	1,346	81.6	163,248	2,426	13,803	22,103	26,575	36,159
1970	7,123	1,616	31,759	1,298	80.3	181,370	2,537	15,706	25,556	28,175	38,625
1971	7,097	1,556	32,664	1,237	79.5	199,725	2,589	17,635	28,812	31,048	43,157
1972	7,061	1,550	33,265	1,209	78.0	219,182	2,671	19,530	32,667	33,914	47,369
1973	7,123	1,535	34,352	1,189	77.5	233,555	2,769	21,330	36,290	36,971	51,706
1974	7,174	1,513	35,506	1,167	77.2	250,481	2,919	23,821	41,406	40,696	57,302
1975	7,156	1,466	36,157	1,125	76.7	254,844	3,023	27,135	48,706	44,608	64,029
1976	7,082	1,434	36,776	1,090	76.0	270,951	3,108	30,173	56,655	49,786	72,219
1977	7,099	1,407	37,060	1,066	75.8	263,775	3,213	33,742	63,630		

Source: Guide to the Health Care Field. Chicago: American Hospital Association, 1977, p. 7.

homes based on the type of service they provide: skilled nursing facilities (SNF) which provide continuous nursing service on a 24-hour basis, intermediate care facilities (ICF), and residential facilities called rest homes. More than $9 billion is spent on nursing home care annually and about $110 million is spent annually on the construction of new nursing home facilities.

Another major category of physical plant resources in the health care system is represented by the facilities necessary for the office practices of the nation's physicians. A great deal of personal medical care is rendered in physicians' offices. More than 90 percent of active physicians are engaged in the direct care of patients as their primary activity. Of these, approximately 68 percent are engaged in office-based practice and 32 percent are in hospital-based practice.[7] While the majority of office based physicians are in solo practice (independent practice by a physician usually with his own facilities and equipment) there are now about 8,500 group practices (three or more physicians formally organized to provide medical care, consultation, diagnosis, and/or treatment, through the joint use of equipment and personnel, and with income from medical practice distributed in accordance with methods previously determined by members of the group). These groups, involving some 67,000 physicians, may be organized as general practice, single specialty or multi-specialty groups.[8] The physical facilities necessary to support physicians in office practices represent a substantial investment in physical plant.

While all of the physical plant resources of the health care systems are too numerous to even mention here, some of its other components include about 13,000 ambulance services and 2,800 medical laboratories independent of those in physician's offices and hospitals. In addition there are about 9,000 commercial dental laboratories, and about 90 percent of the nation's active dentists are in private office practices.

Technology The technological base of modern medicine is truly remarkable and must be viewed as one of the building blocks of the health care system. It has made organ transplants and microscopic surgery possible; many diseases have been eradicated and treatment for others has been improved greatly; and early diagnosis for many diseases has been made possible through technological advances. These advances have had a marked impact on the health care system: diseases are treated that once were not even diagnosed, societal expectations of the health care system have risen (often unrealistically) as technology has advanced, and the costs of health care have risen dramatically as expensive new technology has been adopted in the system. The paradox of technological advance is that as people benefit from it (live longer) they are then in a position to need and utilize other health services; the net effect is to drive up total health care expenditures. This phenomenon becomes important, even critical, when it

7. American Medical Association, Profile of medical practice. Chicago: American Medical Association, 1978, p. 145.

8. American Medical Association, Profile of medical practice. Chicago: American Medical Association, 1976, p. 9.

occurs in a context of limited dollars for health care expenditures. The result is complex and frustrating. As one observer has said, "if someone told me ten years ago that now that we have a way to arrest death from kidney disease that ... we'd be fighting over how to pay for it, I wouldn't have believed it."[9] Yet, this is precisely the problem that technology presents the health care system today. It is likely now that as new technology is developed its adoption will be carefully weighed in terms of its relative cost against projected benefits—a new *modus operandi* for the health care system.

It is clear that the health care system is structured from building blocks that include vast sums of money, many different kinds of people with specialized training, an impressive investment in physical plant, and technology that is growing at an expanding rate. In the next section, we turn our attention to some of the organizations which these resources have been used to build and maintain and which, in turn, convert these resources into health services.

Organizations in the Health Care System

The most visible part of the health care system is the organizations within it. There are thousands of organizations and they give form and substance to the system. The variety of these organizations defies easy categorization. Figure 22–4, however, can serve as a starting point for their description. The shortcomings of such a categorization become apparent quickly when one considers for example that Blue Cross plans, which are primarily providers of a basic resource

Figure 22-4.   Organizations in the Health Care System.

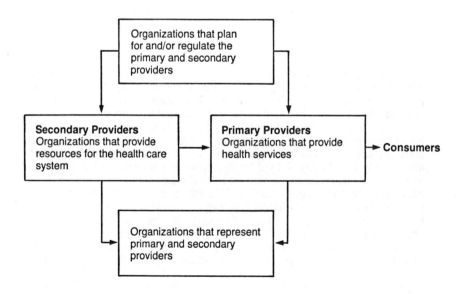

---

9. Belding Scribner, Personal interview described in R. Fox and J. P. Swazey, *The courage to fail.* Chicago: University of Chicago Press, 1974, p. 329.

(payment for services rendered to its subscribers), sometimes *require* hospitals that receive payment from them to prove the need for expansion of services and Blue Cross plans typically have representatives on areawide planning boards. These activities could qualify them as a planning and regulating organization. Or consider the case of a hospital, whose primary purpose is the provision of health care services, but that also operates a school of nursing; or the medical school that operates a hospital. It is not always easy to categorize organizations in the health care system.

Organizations that Provide Health Services

This category of primary providers includes the following kinds of organizations: hospitals, nursing homes, physician's offices, health maintenance organizations, home care programs, clinics, and local health departments among others. Their distinguishing characteristic is that they provide the location for the delivery of health care services directly to consumers whether the purpose of those services is curative, preventative, or rehabilitative. Three of these primary provider organizations are described in some detail below.

Hospitals are perhaps the most complex organizations in the health care system. They come in many types and sizes but a useful prototype is the general hospital defined as an organization "with an organized medical staff; with permanent facilities that include inpatient beds; and with medical services, including physician services and continuous nursing services, to provide diagnosis and treatment for patients who have a variety of medical conditions, both surgical and nonsurgical."[10] A general hospital will usually be organized along the lines shown in Figure 22–5, although the reader should be cautioned that hospitals will almost invariably differ in details of their organization. The functions of the general hospital have been described as follows:

> First, there are diagnostic and treatment services to inpatients. Within this broad function are many subdivisions of medical, surgical, obstetrical, pediatric, and other special forms of care. Psychiatric service and rehabilitation may be included. Involved in all of these inpatient services are various modalities, including nursing, dietetics, pharmaceutical skills, laboratory and X-ray services, and varying refinements of diagnosis and therapy. Second, there are services to outpatients, with an equally wide range of specialties and technical modalities. A third hospital function concerns professional and technical education, for many classes of health personnel must work in hospitals and thereby receive training. A fourth function is medical research, since the accumulation of patients in hospitals provides the basis for scientific investigation into the causes, diagnosis, and treatment of diseases. A fifth function concerns prevention of diseases or health promotion in the surrounding population; there are many ways that hospitals, as centers for technical skill, can offer services to people before they are sick or can protect

10. American Hospital Association, *Classification of health care institutions.* Chicago: American Hospital Association, 1974, p. 8.

Figure 22-5   Hosptial Organizations Structure.

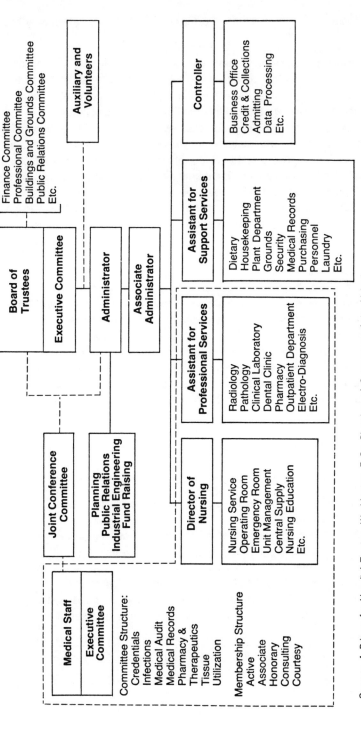

Source: A Primer for Hospital Trustee, Washington, D.C.: Chamber of Commerce of the United States, 1974. p. 31. Reprinted with permission.

patients from the hazards of disease beyond that for which they have come to the hospital.[11]

The emphasis given to these various functions will vary from hospital to hospital, depending largely upon the basic objectives and goals of the particular hospital. For example, the large medical center may emphasize education and research to a much greater extent than the small general hospital.

The hospital is a very complex social system with substantial conflicts among the participants—patients, physicians, trustees, administrative staff, and other personnel. The diversity of the organization creates major problems. The governing board has the legal authority over, and responsibility for, the organization. The medical staff possesses the technical knowledge to make decisions regarding patient care and treatment. The administrative staff is responsible for day-to-day functioning of the hospital. These three elements, sometimes referred to as the organizational triad, share the same basic objectives. However, each element of the triad must interpret the means for meeting these objectives in terms of its own values and personalities which are not identical. This makes the hospital one of the most complex institutions in American society.

Since the enactment of the Social Security Act of 1935, which made public assistance funds available for the needy aged, the nursing home industry has flourished in the United States. Several other factors have exacerbated the need for institutional care for the aged. Among them, and perhaps most important, are the increased percentage of older people (65+) in the population and changes in the family structure. The skilled nursing care institution has been defined as "An establishment that provides, through an organized medical staff, a medical director, or a medical advisor, and permanent facilities that include inpatient beds, medical services, continuous nursing services, and health-related services—diagnosis and treatment for patients who are not in an acute phase of illness but who primarily require skilled nursing care on an inpatient basis."[12]

The nursing home serves several basic health care functions. Among them:

1. To provide continuing care for those recovering from surgical or medical disorders.
2. To assist patients in reaching optimal physical and emotional health.
3. To provide for the total needs of patients—physical, emotional, and spiritual.
4. To assist the aging toward an active participation in life.
5. To provide for rehabilitative services when the need exists.
6. To work cooperatively with other community and social agencies.[13]

---

11. Milton I. Roemer, & J. W. Friedman, *Doctors in hospitals.* Baltimore: Johns Hopkins, 1971, pp. 1-2.

12. American Hospital Association, *Classification of health care institutions.* Chicago: American Hospital Association, 1974, p. 10.

13. Florence L. McQuillan, *Fundamentals of nursing home administration,* 2nd ed. Philadelphia: W. B. Saunders, 1974, p. 3.

The typical organization pattern of the nursing home is very similar to that given for the hospital, the main difference being that the nursing home offers a much narrower range of services. A second major difference is a less complex medical staff organization in the nursing home where medical staff are not as involved in day-to-day patient care. A typical nursing home organization is shown in Figure 22–6. The reader is cautioned that, as with hospitals, there are many alternative patterns of organization.

While the hospital and the nursing home represent two of the most important traditional health service provider organizations, there are new types of organizations that fit this category. Few subjects have aroused more interest or generated more discussion in the health care community during the past few years than the concept of health maintenance organizations—or, as they are more commonly called, "HMOs."

The following description of an HMO was presented at the 1971 Annual Conference on State Comprehensive Health Planning Agencies by Beverlee A. Myers, Assistant Administrator for Resource Development, Health Services and Mental Health Administration, U.S. Department of Health, Education and Welfare.

Basically, an HMO is a four-way arrangement between—

1. An organized health care delivery system, which includes health manpower and facilities capable of providing or at least arranging for all the health services a population might require.
2. An enrolled population, consisting of individuals and groups of individuals who contract with the delivery system for provision of a range of health services which the system assumes responsibility to make available.
3. A financial plan which incorporates underwriting the costs of the agreed-upon set of services on a prenegotiated and prepaid per-person or per-family basis.
4. A managing organization which assures legal, fiscal, public, and professional accountability.

All four of these elements must be present in an HMO, and all must play an active role. Any one element may assume the corporate focal point for organizing and managing an HMO. For example, physician groups, medical societies, or hospitals may initiate HMO development; or consumers may sponsor them; or insurance companies or industrial or management corporations may take the initiative to organize the other three elements into an HMO.

Organizations that Provide Resources for the Health Care System

This category of secondary providers includes educational institutions, financing mechanisms, and drug and equipment suppliers among others. Their distinguishing characteristic is that they provide resources needed for the direct provision of health services.

Figure 22–6 Nursing Home Organization.

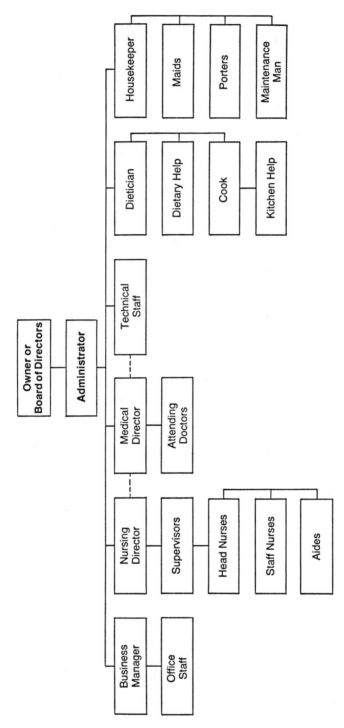

Physicians, still the key manpower in the health care system, are trained in the nation's 116 medical schools or they are trained in foreign medical schools. Foreign medical graduates (FMGs) now represent about 20 percent of the total active physicians in this country. While there is considerable variation among U. S. medical schools in terms of curriculum, they generally provide four years of post-baccalaureate training consisting of two years of pre-clinical or basic sciences work and two years of clinical courses and practical experience. The present mold for medical education was largely cast in the 1910 document written by Abraham Flexner, *Medical Education in the United States and Canada, A Report to the Carnegie Foundation for the Advancement of Teaching* which criticized (well deserved) extant medical schools and led to major improvements. Following medical school, almost all physicians enter a hospital-based internship year and most follow this with further specialty training in a residency program that lasts from two to five years depending on the particular specialty. The physician who wishes, after specialty training, can apply to be certified in that specialty by a specialty board. After meeting the requirements which generally include completion of an approved internship and residency, written and oral examination, and varying years of experience, the physician becomes a board certified specialist. This certification is in addition to licensure which is granted by each state and which requires graduation from an approved medical school and passing an examination as set forth in each state's Medical Practice Act. Many states have reciprocity agreements with other states through which a physician may move his license from one state to another. The arduous path through a medical education serves not only to impart necessary knowledge but also to instill a distinctive group identity and, for many physicians, a rather homogenous set of values.

Professional nurses, usually called registered nurses (RNs), are trained in three different types of organizational settings: baccalaureate programs which are four or five year university based programs leading to a bachelor of science degree, associate degree programs which are two year programs usually based in junior or community colleges, and diploma programs which usually provide three years of training past high-school and are based in hospital operated schools of nursing. Following completion of one of these approved programs, the nurse can become a registered nurse by passing a state licensure examination. There are also master's degree programs which provide nurses with advanced training in education, administration or such clinical nursing specialties as public health, medical-surgical nursing, mental health, maternal and child health, and cardiovascular nursing. Other specialty training includes nurse anesthetists, nurse midwives, and pediatric and family nurse practitioners. A pediatric nurse practitioner, for example, is a registered nurse who has received additional training permitting an expanded role in the care of children.

Space does not permit a description of the tremendous variety of educational organizations that supply health manpower. The mere listing (in small print) of the various schools from blood banking technology to speech pathology requires more than thirty pages in the 1978 *Guide to the Health Care Field*.[14] The medical schools and the nursing schools are perhaps the dominant examples, but all of the educational organizations make an impact on the health care system.

A second important category of organizations that provide resources for the health care system are those that pay for care. As noted earlier, except for "out-of-pocket" payments by individuals, health care in the United States is largely paid for through third parties. The current maze of third parties has been created fairly recently—since the Great Depression—and has grown largely in response to the rising cost of health care and the concurrent financial risk that individuals run if they make no provision through insurance or prepayment for protection against their potential health care costs. More than half the third party payments now come from two sources: Blue Cross Plans and the federal government (principally Medicare and Medicaid).

The Blue Cross organization began as a prepayment plan for hospital expenses for school teachers in Dallas, Texas in 1929. The original plan provided 21 days of hospitalization for a prepayment of 50 cents a month.[15] Today, there are about 70 Blue Cross organizations covering almost 84 million subscribers. Blue Shield organizations provide for prepayment of physician fees in a similar manner. There are now about 86 million people covered by 70 Blue Shield organizations (or "Plans" as they are typically called). The Blue Cross plans are linked together as members of the Blue Cross Association.[16] [17]

One of the most important dates in history, in terms of understanding the U.S. health care system, is July 1, 1966. On that date the federal government initiated two programs that had their basis in the 1965 amendments to the Social Security Act. These amendments (Title XVIII—Health Insurance for the Aged and Title XIX—Grants to the States for Medical Assistance Programs), more commonly known as Medicare and Medicaid, were the culmination of many years of national debate. Although substantial changes have been made in the Medicare and Medicaid programs in the intervening years, they were at their inception and still are insurance mechanisms to help pay for the health care of the elderly and the poor. Together, these programs account for more than 30 percent of the revenues that flow into the nation's hospitals. In 1976, federal expenditures for Medicare topped $17.4 billion and their share of Medicaid expenditures was almost $8.2 billion.[18] Medicare is made up of two parts: Part A which is compulsory insurance for hospital care and related services for the U. S. population over age

14. American Hospital Association, *Guide to the health care field*. Chicago: American Hospital Association, 1978, pp. C-32 to C-66.

15. Blue Cross Association, *Blue Cross fact book, 1977*. Chicago: Blue Cross Association, 1977, p. 2.

16. Blue Cross Association, *Blue Cross fact book, 1977*. Chicago: Blue Cross Association, 1977, pp. 2, 12.

17. A comprehensive review of Blue Cross Organizations can be found in Howard J. Berman & Lewis E. Weeks, *The financial management of hospitals*, 3rd ed. Ann Arbor, Mich.: Health Administration Press, 1976. See chapter 6 entitled "Blue Cross."

18. Michael S. Koleda, Carol Burke, & Jane S. Willems, *The federal health dollar: 1969-1976*. Washington, D.C.: Center for Health Policy Studies, National Planning Association, 1977, pp. 18-19.

65 and Part B which is voluntary supplementary insurance to partially cover the costs of physician and surgeon fees, clinic visits, diagnostic and laboratory tests and home health visits. Part A is financed through Social Security payroll taxes and Part B is financed from premium payments by enrollees and matching general federal revenues.

Medicaid is a program through which the federal government provides a subsidy to the states, 50–85 percent of the total cost depending on per capita income in the state, to help participating states provide health insurance to its poor and near poor population. Each state administers its own Medicaid program under certain federal requirements. Certain basic services must be provided including: inpatient and outpatient hospital care, laboratory and X-ray services, skilled nursing services, home health care, physician services, and family planning services.

The private, or commercial as they are often called, insurance companies represent another component of the third party payers. There are several hundred private insurance companies in the U.S. including some major ones like Prudential, Equitable, Aetna, Metropolitan, and Connecticut General. These companies, through their policies, provide "protection by written contract against the hazards (in whole or in part) of the happenings of specified fortuitous events."[19] Although private insurance companies were initially reluctant to enter the health insurance market, the market created by the large industrial unions that grew up during World War II provided a suffecent stimulus for their entry and by carefully experience rating the various groups they serve they have been successful.

A third category of resource providing organizations to be described briefly here are those found in the pharmaceutical and medical supply industries. Currently, the national expenditures for drugs are more than $11 billion. This represents both prescription drugs (also called ethical drugs) which are sold by prescription written by a physician only and non-prescription drugs (also called over-the-counter drugs) which are sold directly to the public and for which no prescription is necessary. The pharmaceutical manufacturers direct their advertising of prescription drugs to physicians and to a lesser extent to pharmacists and of non-prescription drugs to the general public. The organizations supplying prescription drugs spend a great deal of money advertising and promoting their products to physicians. Roughly, the amounts represent one out of four dollars made on the wholesale prices of their products and almost four times the amount they spend on research and development.[20] The research and development costs are themselves quite large due to the complexity of the search for new, effective drugs and the nature of the process of obtaining approval from the Food and Drug Administration before the new drug can be placed on the market. Even with high marketing and R & D costs, the pharmaceutical industry has consistently earned high profits. During the period 1960–1970, the average rate of

19. Health Insurance Institute, *Source book of health insurance data*. New York: Health Insurance Institute.

20. J. L. Goddard, The medical business. *Scientific American* (September) 1973: 161-66.

return of U. S. industrial business was 11 percent; the pharmaceutical industry averaged 18 percent during this period.[21] The pharmaceutical manufacturers who make and sell prescription drugs are represented by the Pharmaceutical Manufacturers Association. Some of the larger members include: Abbott, Baxter, Bristol Meyers, Johnson and Johnson, Eli Lilly, Miles Laboratories, Pfizer, Squibb, and Upjohn.

The organizations that manufacture and distribute medical supplies are as diverse as their products which range from cottonballs to computerized axial tomography (CAT) scanners costing about $400,000 each and capable of producing remarkably informative "pictures" of the inside of the human body. There are more than 1,100 medical supply organizations in the United States ranging from very large firms such as American Hospital Supply Corporation to relatively small firms such as Cordis Corporation specializing in a few products. Although there is proposed legislation to alter the situation, there is no agency with responsibility for approving the safety or efficacy of their products before they are marketed. During the 1960–1970 period, firms in this industry had an average rate of return very close to the 11 percent rate for all U. S. industrial business.

While space has not permitted a comprehensive view of all the organizations, the reader can see that a diverse and diffuse set of organizations provide the resources necessary to sustain the U. S. health care system.

Organizations That Plan for and/or Regulate the Primary and Secondary Providers

It is important to note that the title of this subsection does *not* include "the health care system." This choice of title was made to drive home the point that no one, to date, plans for or regulates the health care system. Instead, planning and regulating occurs for many components of the system, but not the system as a whole. This fact is, if nothing more, consistent with the pluralism that characterizes the system itself. While there is a good deal of internal, self-regulation and self-planning in health care organizations—for example, hospitals can regulate their own performance through organizational policies and procedures—we shall look mainly at external regulation and planning; that is, those organizations that are separate from but that regulate the primary and secondary providers or plan for the provision of health services.

Regulation of health care providers has historically been on a voluntary basis. The voluntary regulatory process does not carry the mandate of law. The best example of voluntary regulation, among many possible choices, is the Joint Commission on Accreditation of Hospitals (JCAH) which can trace its origin to a 1915 program of the American College of Surgeons and whose board now includes representation from the American Medical Association, American Hospital Association, American College of Surgeons, American College of Physicians, and more recently the American Association of Homes of the Aging and the American Nursing Home Association. The JCAH, through established standards,

21. G. Nelson, Drug advertising. *Trial Magazine* (July-August) 1973: 53-54.

accredits hospitals and nursing homes who voluntarily seek such accreditation and thus guide and direct (regulate) much of the operation of these providers. The mission of the JCAH, as stated by its former president, is to determine "how health services shall be provided that makes them the best possible quality."[22]

The voluntary regulation of organizations that train health manpower is extensive. The following partial list of education programs and the agencies that accredit them and thus regulate their activities to a large extent, illustrates this:[23]

Educational Program	Accreditating Agency
Cytotechnology	Council on Medical Education of the American Medical Association (AMA) and The American Society of Clinical Pathologists
Dentistry	Commission on Accreditation of the American Dental Association
Dietetics	American Dietetic Association
Hospital Administration	Accrediting Commission on Education for Health Administration
Medical Records	Council on Medical Education of the AMA and the Committee on Education and Registration of the American Medical Record Association
Medical Technology	Council on Medical Education of the AMA and the American Society for Medical Technology
Medicine	Council on Medical Education of the AMA and the Association of American Medical Colleges
Professional Nursing	State government agencies and the National League for Nursing
Pharmacy	American Council on Pharmaceutical Education
Physical Therapy	Council on Medical Education of the AMA and the American Physical Therapy Association
Radiologic Technology	Council on Medical Education of the AMA, American College of Radiology, and the American Society of Radiologic Technologists

Although the level of voluntary regulation in the health care system has been and continues to be high, governmental involvement in planning for and regulating the quality, cost, availability, and delivery of health care services in the U. S. has increased dramatically in recent years, especially since the enactment of the Medicare and Medicaid programs in the mid-1960s. It must be noted, however, that their involvement has been piece-meal, often with one attempt counter-productive to others, and generally unsuccessful. With the enactment, in 1974, of the

22. John Porterfield, What is the J.C.A.H.? Hospital Management (August) 1971: 17.
23. See Guide to the Health Care Field. Chicago: American Hospital Association, 1978, pp. C-33 to C-66 for a complete listing.

National Health Planning and Resources Development Act (PL 93–641) and its subsequent implementation, this is beginning to change. This legislation created Health Systems Agencies (HSAs) which will be responsible for health planning at the local level. Their responsibilities include forecasting demand and developing area-wide plans for services and facilities. In addition, PL 93–641 calls for the establishment of State Health Planning and Development Agencies (SHPDAs) who will develop state health plans. The single strongest element in PL 93–641 is the requirement that all states enact certificate-of-need (CON) legislation that meets federal standards. This feature will permit tighter control (regulation) of capital expenditures for many existing health care providers and will restrict the addition of new capacity in places where it is not needed. The long-term impact of PL 93–641 on the health care system will essentially be a subordination of the goals and plans of individual provider organizations to those of the larger health care system. Proposals by providers will have to be based on more thorough needs analysis and cost justification. Planning by the individual provider organization will have to relate to the specific plans developed for its area by the local HSA.

An earlier example, also with substantial continuing impact, of governmental regulatory activity is the Professional Standards Review Organizations (PSROs) mandated by the Social Security Amendments of 1972 (PL 92–603). PSROs are local panels of practicing physicians organized to review the health care services provided to Medicare and Medicaid patients. The purposes of PSRO review are to assure that health services provided under the Medicare and Medicaid Programs are of high quality and provided in a cost effective manner.

The overall federal involvement in the health care system is largely centered in the massive (proposed 1979 budget of $181.3 billion) Department of Health, Education and Welfare (DHEW). Established in 1953, DHEW has undergone several major reorganizations. The most recent, and still underway, began in early 1977. Figure 22–7 represents a highly abbreviated view of DHEW as it is currently structured.

State government (and those aspects delegated to counties, cities and towns) involvement in the health care system is made through a very complex and ever changing variety of organizations and agencies that vary from one state to another. Some of this involvement is lodged in a department of public health but ranges from assurance of water quality to education of physicians in state supported medical schools. State governments are heavily involved in planning for and regulating the health care system. Their involvement in planning under PL 93–641 which mandates State Health Planning and Development Agencies is extensive and all but one state now have certificate-of-need legislation through which they control the investment in various components of the health care system. The regulatory involvement by the states includes licensing of many categories of health care workers and provider organizations, and the establishment and enforcement of insurance laws and health and safety codes. A final, and potentially very important, example of state regulatory involvement is rate review already enacted in a number of states and being seriously considered in others.

Figure 22–7 Department of Health, Education, and Welfare. (abbreviated)

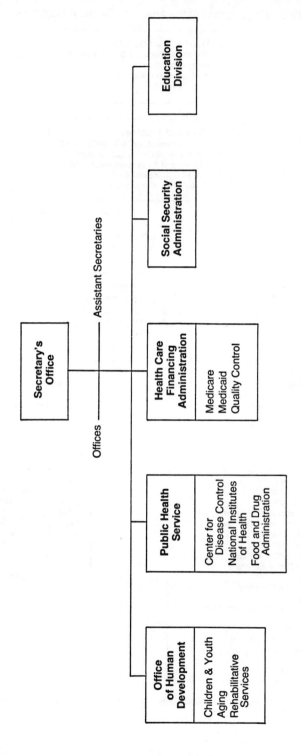

Figure 22–8   Organization of the American Dental Association.

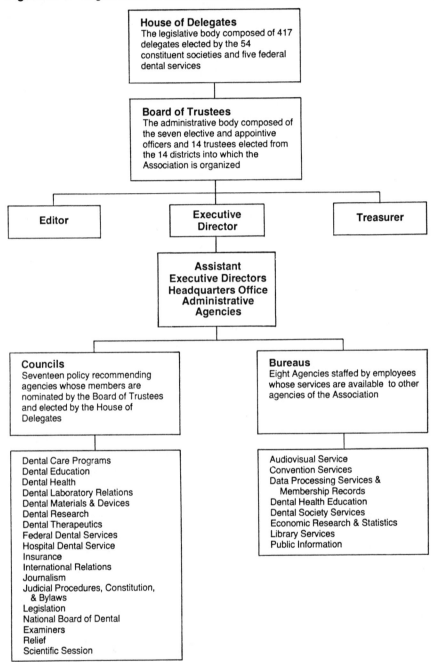

Source: *The American Dental Association: Its Structure and Function,* Chicago: American Dental Association, 1975, p. 9.

Under these programs the rates charged by providers for health services rendered are subject to review and approval by rate review agenices.

Two facts should be clear from this abbreviated description of organizations that regulate health care providers: (1) there is a tremendous amount of regulation of the system—it has been argued that the health care system is one of the most highly regulated components of the U. S. economy; and (2) there is a dramatic shift toward more governmental (especially federal) regulation of the health care system.

Organizations That Represent the Primary and Secondary Providers

The providers of health services, whether groups of individual professionals such as physicians, dentists, nurses, and the many other categories of manpower, or the provider organizations such as hospitals and nursing homes are almost invariably represented by an association whose main purpose is to represent the interest of its constituency. In addition to national associations, such as the American Medical Association and the American Hospital Association, there are usually state associations such as the Illinois Hospital Association and the Kentucky Medical Association and local organizations that represent the interests of members such as the Prince George's County (Maryland) Medical Society and the Chicago Hospital Council.

As an example of one association, the American Dental Association[24] can be described as "the national voluntary organization for the dental profession in the United States" with the informal objective "to encourage the improvement of the health of the public, to promote the art and science of dentistry and to represent the interests of the dental profession and the public which it serves." The ADA has more than 124,000 members, all of whom also belong to a state society and one of the more than 480 county or city dental societies. The House of Delegates of the ADA, composed of representatives from the constituent state societies, is the "supreme authoritative body of the Association and possesses its legislative powers." It determines policy, approves the annual budget, and elects members of the Board of Trustees of the Association among other functions. The Board of Trustees holds the administrative authority of the Association and "has the power to conduct all business activities of the Association, to establish rules and regulations to govern Association procedures, to direct production and distribution of the Association's publications and to supervise financial affairs . . . appoints the appointive officers . . . prepares the annual budget . . . (and has the power to) establish *ad interim* policy when the House of Delegates is not in session, provided such policies are later presented for review to the Delegates." Figure 22–8 is an organizational chart of the ADA.

---

24. Material adapted from *The American Dental Association: Its structure and function.* Chicago: American Dental Association, 1975.

Consumers

Perhaps the largest, and least organized, component of the health care system are those people who consume its services. Potentially at least, the ultimate consumers of health care services include everyone in the United States. In reality, not all consumers have equal access to health care services nor do they utilize services in the same way. The experiences with the health care system and the opinions about it are almost as diverse as the U. S. population itself. The results of a recent survey of nearly 8,000 people bear this out:[25]

–A greater percentage of rural Southern blacks can identify a regular source of health care than can urban blacks.

–Rural farm dwellers are less likely than city residents to see a physician.

–Among all ethnic groups, low-income Spanish-heritage persons are least likely to see a physician.

–Blacks spend more time in physicians' waiting rooms than do whites.

–Members of disadvantaged minorities see physicians less often than do the affluent, but once they start receiving health care, they're apt to seek it more often than the well-to-do.

–City residents use specialists more frequently than other groups do.

–Farmers and rural residents make the greatest use of family and general practitioners.

–More than six of every ten people can get an appointment to see a physician within two days but 8 percent of the population has to wait more than two weeks.

–Older people are more satisfied with treatment received.

–People living in the South are least satisfied.

–People with higher incomes and more education are the most satisfied.

–Blacks are less satisfied than whites.

–People who see one physician regularly are more satisfied than those who see a number of physicians.

–Of all groups, rural Southern blacks are least satisfied.

–People of Spanish-heritage living in the Southwest are less satisfied than are other whites.

On the whole, consumers are remarkably satisfied with the *quality* of health care they receive—88 percent of all Americans express satisfaction with it.[26] Yet, demand for a larger voice in the decision-making processes that exist in the health care system (a phenomenon termed consumerism) has never been

---

25. Results are from a survey conducted in 1975-76 by National Opinion Research Center at the University of Chicago as reported in *American Medical News* (January 23) 1978: 12.

26. Results are from a survey conducted in 1975-76 by National Opinion Research Center at the University of Chicago as reported in *American Medical News* (January 23) 1978: 12.

stronger than today. Traditionally the consumer role has been passive. As one authority has noted, "it is very difficult to say that consumers as yet have had anything but the most intentionally devised passive role in our health care system. It is difficult to argue that consumers of health services have, to any significant degree, been involved in the health field in any more than a window dressing role."[27]

Perhaps the most obvious reason for the paucity of active participation in the health care system by consumers, except of course as consumers, is the difficulty any individual faces in relating to large complex systems. (What impact does an individual citizen have on the steel industry for example?) However, it is likely that the consumer's voice will be heard more clearly in the health care system in the years ahead. The National Health Planning and Development Act of 1974, which created HSAs, mandated that the governing body of each HSA be made up of a majority (up to 60 percent) of consumers who are residents of the area served with the other members being providers who are also residents of the area. Although this mechanism gives the consumer a forum, the critical problems of their knowledgeability and their relative persuasive strength remain to be fully tested. What is no longer seriously questioned is that the consumer, who directly or indirectly pays for the services provided by the health care system, is no longer willing to leave the decision-making power in the health care system entirely in the hands of the other components of the system.

Problems Confronting the Health Care Systems

To conclude, the health care system faces a dizzing array of problems. The more complex of these problems are not transitory nor will they be solved soon or easily. Full enumeration of the set of problems is not possible, for the set developed by one individual or group will differ, frequently in content and almost always in priority, from those developed by someone else. There are even those, although their number has diminished to a naive few, who claim there are no serious problems. The general public, at a time when most (88 percent) are personally satisfied with their own health care, feel overwhelmingly (61 percent) that "there is a health care crisis" in the United States today.[28]

One of the most encouraging signs that the health care system can resolve many of its problems, and perhaps the single greatest strength of the system, is that central components of the system spend considerable energy in identification of its own problems. For example, one of the most comprehensive examinations of problems confronting the health care system today has come from a symposium of leading experts convened by the American Hospital Association

---

27. Robert McGarrah in Dale Shields (ed.) The time for responsibility and accountability in the Health field: Public expectations in today's economic climate. Report of the 1975 National Health Forum, Lake Buena Vista, Florida, March 17-19, 1975: 75.

28. Results are from a survey conducted in 1975-76 by National Opinion Research Center at the University of Chicago as reported in *American Medical News* (January 23) 1978: 12.

with support from the National Center for Health Services Research. A recent book reporting the deliberations of this symposium and summarizing its results sets forth the following set of questions (problems) that face the U. S. health care system:[29]

- *Cost*   How should society establish means for determining limits on the quantity of resources to be expended on health care services?
- *Entitlement*   How should society establish a guaranteed minimum set of health care services available for all citizens?
- *Technology*   How should society establish methods for evaluating the development and use of new medical technologies?
- *Decision-Making*   How should society achieve better decision-making capability by individuals who are not providers of health care services in matters concerning the appropriate allocation, distribution, and use of these services?
- *Structure*   How should society exert substantial pressures for the reorganization and restructuring of the health care, education, financing, and delivery system to make it more efficient, effective, or economical?

The premier position of cost concerns reflects the staggering level of total health care expenditures and the steep increases in those expenditures in recent years. Total health care expenditures are doubling every five years now and with a base approaching $200 billion the consequences of this are of great importance. These facts have led to another example of the health care system's self-evaluation. In 1976, the Board of Trustees of the American Medical Association established an independent Commission on the Cost of Medical Care and mandated it to provide a comprehensive overview of health care costs and possible approaches to solutions. Their report examines the myriad reasons for these escalating costs and offers many constructive suggestions for mitigating the problem.[30]

In the U. S., health care is viewed by many people as a basic right of every citizen. Yet, what that right entitles citizens to has not been specified. If the right to health care is to be given meaning beyond a proclamation then entitlement must be clarified. This may well occur in the context of a national health insurance program—one of the most controversial topics in the health care system. Under such a program the government, by paying part or all of the premiums, would develop an insurance program which might provide coverage to all Americans. Such a mechanism could assure that each citizen's health care services would be paid for. Although there has been interest for the past 60 years, the

---

29. Donald F. Phillips, The public policy issues facing hospitals in the 1980s. *In* American Hospital Association, *Hospitals in the 1980s*. Chicago: American Hospital Association, 1977.

30. National Commission on the Cost of Medical Care, *Commission recommendations, task force reports, research agenda, Volume 1*. Chicago: American Medical Association, 1978.

needed consensus for a national (some call it universal) health insurance program is only now gelling. Many people believe that some form of national health insurance will be enacted by 1980 and will be in place by the mid-1980s. The form of such a program is open to debate. The rate of increase in expenditures for health care services has caused the policy makers to hesitate about committing the government to the level of expenditure that would be needed to support a truly universal health insurance program.

The paradox of introducing costly new technology into a system where cost constraint is a primary objective presents not only difficult economic problems but ethical ones as well. On what basis will society decide issues such as permitting the heroic and incredibly costly maintenance of signs of life in some patients by advanced technology when there are pockets of people in America who cannot get the most rudimentary medical care for their malnourished children?

Finally, the problems of including the consumer in the decision-making process within the health care system in a meaningful and productive way and of finding more effective organizational configurations to provide health services can best be described as agenda items for further research! This set of problems serves to demonstrate the complexity, breadth, and interrelatedness of problems facing the health care system. They will, in all likelihood, be solved in the years ahead because they are such important problems; but as solutions emerge we can be sure that other, equally thorny and important problems, will move to center stage. That is the price of society's effort to achieve a goal so important and so illusive as "complete physical, mental, and social well-being."

Everyday Work Settings of the Professional   23

ELIOT FREIDSON

Empirical Types of Practice Organization

Everyday medicine is practiced in privacy. In the other established professions, work goes on in the publicity of the court, the church, and the lecture hall as often as in the office. The work of the doctor is characteristically conducted in the closed consulting room or the bedroom. Furthermore, the physician usually renders personal services to individuals rather than to congregations or classes. Perhaps because of these characteristics medicine is more likely than other established professions to be seen as a simple practitioner-client relationship than as an organization. But it is much more than merely a relationship: medicine is practiced in an organized framework which influences the behavior of both doctors and patients. Indeed, at present in the United States, the framework of practice seems to be moving toward more elaborate forms which may be expected to change the nature of the doctor-patient relationship.

The typical mode of medical practice in the United States is "solo practice." This involves a man working by himself in an office which he secures and equips with his own capital, with patients who have freely chosen him as their personal physician and for whom he assumes responsibility. Stereotypically he lacks any formal connection with colleagues.

But the phrase "solo practice" is as often used in an ideological as in a descriptive mode. It is, as Evang noted, a sacred cow in the medical profession of more than one country.[1] The ideological connotation has interesting analytical implications. One of the central themes is independence—the notion of "professional autonomy" — in which a man can do as he pleases. In order for autonomy to exist, the practitioner must work alone and must have no long-term obligation to his clients; he must be able to sever the relationship to his client at any time, and vice versa; a fee-for-service rather than a contractual financial arrangement is likely to encourage autonomous practice.

A truly autonomous fee-for-service solo arrangement is inherently unstable, however: it is eventually bound to fall under the control of either patients or colleagues. In a system of free competition the physician may neither count on the loyalty of his patient (with whom he has no contract) nor on that of his colleagues (with whom he has no ties and who are competing with him). Since his colleagues are competitors, he is not likely to solicit their advice or trade information, and he certainly will not refer his patients to them. Under these circumstances, he is quite isolated from his colleagues and relatively free of their control but at the same time he is very vulnerable to control by his clients. To keep them, he must give them what they want—whether tranquilizers, antibiotics, or hysterectomies— or someone else will. Obviously, conscientious practice under these conditions is difficult and frustrating. It is hardly accurate to describe it as "autonomy."

Simple restriction of competition by banding together against the tyranny of client choice leads to the alternative tyranny of colleague choice. Realistically, "total autonomy" can result only under very special circumstances. It is plausible to think that when the supply of physicians is sufficiently restricted to fail to meet demand, control by the client may be avoided. If, in addition to a scarcity of physicians and other potential competitors, no large capital is required for initiating a practice and no consultations or extra consulting room institutions like hospitals are necessary for its pursuit, control by colleagues can be avoided and "total autonomy" approached.

In the United States today, the supply of physicians in many areas is such that client control can be avoided; but increasingly, colleague control cannot. Dependence on colleagues in one way or another is the rule today in the United States because consultations, hospitals, and capital equipment are essential to modern practice. In short, present practice is not solo: it embraces a large variety of organized relationships, most of which currently emphasize colleague rather than client controls.

How do cooperative arrangements develop? Let us start with an ostensibly "solo" fee-for-service practice in a situation like that of the United States, where the supply of physicians is at least moderately restricted. Under such circumstances practice is only partially secure because the continual entrance of younger men into a system which does not include predictable retirement of the

---

1. Karl Evang, *Health service. Society and medicine.* London: Oxford University Press, 1960.

older practitioner always presents some threat of competition. In answer to the threat, one keeps his patients to himself, but to do this involves a deadly grind of perpetual availability for service. In order to take an evening or weekend off, or a vacation, or in order to be sick, one's practice must be "covered" by colleagues who can be relied on to avoid "stealing" patients. A cooperative arrangement is necessary.

The need for such organization becomes even more pressing when specialization is involved. Patients who must see more than one physician in the normal course of obtaining medical care might become attracted to any one of them and not go back to the man who made the referral. The danger of losing patients by referring them to a young internist seems to have led at least some general practitioners to avoid referring patients at all. In one study of Negro doctors, it was found that some refer patients to white rather than Negro consultants operating under the assumption that whites do not want to keep Negro patients and so will refer them back.[2] Effort to prevent referrals is patently unsatisfactory, however, since the conscientious practitioner on one occasion or another knows that his patient needs help he cannot give himself. He can send some, but not all, patients to a clinic or an outpatient department whose staffs presumably will not "steal" them. A rather natural and conventional solution is to work out a fairly definite reciprocal arrangement: the general practitioner habitually refers his patients to a limited number of specialists who may be trusted to act "ethically" by eventually returning his patients to him, and who, in turn, will refer patients needing general services to him.

The time has passed in the United States when the general practitioner was in a strong enough position to be the key "feeder" to a network of specialists. As the patient has developed more sophistication and the number of accessible specialists has increased, the patient circumvents the general practitioner and seeks out his own specialists. Indeed, the general practitioner's place is being taken by the internist and the pediatrician, and nonprofessional referrals are the major source of patients in urban settings for the average ophthalmologist, otorhinolaryngologist and orthopedist, if not also for the obstetrician-gynecologist, allergist, and dermatologist. Since there has ceased to be a single key "feeder" in the division of labor, there is danger of considerable confusion and irregularity in the disposition of the patient. Fairly well integrated arrangements among physicians become important not only as a way of gaining and regulating access to patients but also as a way of establishing among physicians regular channels of communication for information about the patient and his illness. The "colleague network" described by Hall may be used as the prototype of such an informal but well-integrated arrangement in American solo practice.[3] Indeed, one may suspect that this network is a strategic mode of regulating recruitment and access to work in all occupations in which objective criteria are not readily available to assess per-

---

2. Cf. Dietrich Reitzes, *Negroes and Medicine*. Cambridge: Harvard University Press, 1958.
3. Oswald Hall, The informal organization of the medical profession. *Canadian Journal of Economics and Political Science* 12 1946: 30 – 41.

formance. Certainly the colleague network is very important in the academic and legal worlds.

Hall provides a lucid description of the colleague network:

> Insofar as the doctors of a given community are established and possess relatively loyal clientele, they form a system. This system can effectively exclude the intruding newcomer. On the one hand they have control of the hospital system through occupying the dominant posts therein. On the other they tend to develop, in the course of time, through association, a sort of informal organization. Rights to position, status, power become recognized and upheld; mechanisms of legitimate succession and patterns of recruitment become established.
>
> The provision of medical facilities in a given community, insofar as a system or an order has been established, depends heavily on such an organization. As a matter of fact, the two matters discussed above, i.e., institutions and clienteles, are intimately related to the working of the informal organization. The allocation of positions in the institutions, the pace at which one receives promotions, the extent to which one has patients referred to him, all hinge on the workings of the informal organization. . . .
>
> Sponsorship is not necessarily a one-sided process. It permits the newcomer to share in the established system of practicing medicine, but it also imposes responsibilities upon him. It obligates him to fulfill the minor positions in the institutional system. Where he needs expert advice or assistance it obligates him to turn to his sponsor. And if he is designated as successor to an established member of the profession he necessarily takes over the duties and obligations involved there. Hence the protege is essential to the continued functioning of the established inner fraternity of the profession.[4]

The kind of network Hall describes is more likely to exist in localities where there is a variety of hospitals and other medical institutions ordered hierarchically, with limited access by physicians. It is much less likely to be so definite and articulated in small cities where hospitals are virtually open community institutions. And even in large cities, the municipal and proprietary institutions at the bottom of the prestige hierarchy provide fairly free access to physicians irrespective of their location in colleague networks.[5] For this reason we can assume that the sociometric studies of Coleman, Katz, and Menzel portray the looser, more common form of colleague network in the United States.[6]

Because it is entirely informal, the colleague network represents the most elementary type of cooperative practice. But it has sufficient weakness to make it uncomfortably vulnerable to collapse. Under the solo system of practice, patients and hospitals are not always completely monopolized. Often the colleague network cannot completely control the treatment environment and so may lack the reliable patronage necessary to gain the cooperation of hungry young men.

4. Oswald Hall, The informal organization of the medical profession. *Canadian Journal of Economics and Political Science 12* 1946: 30 – 41.

5. Cf. David Solomon, Ethnic and class differences among hospitals as contingencies in medical careers. *American Journal of Sociology 66* 1961: 463 – 471.

6. James Coleman, Elihu Katz, and Herbert Menzel, *Medical innovation: A diffusion study.* Indianapolis: Bobbs-Merrill, 1966.

Furthermore, the good faith among peers upon which an informal system depends may break down in petty jealousies and antipathies. The large solo practice in the United States has developed some formal techniques of protecting itself. The successful physician may, as Hall suggested, send his overflow to a young physician in whom he takes an interest,[7] but he may and often does avoid sending out any cases at all by hiring the younger man to handle the routine cases and the grueling house and emergency calls. This lightens his burden while it reduces the danger of permanently losing patients. The employer-physician's position is particularly strong when the man he hires is not fully qualified to practice on his own (as is the case with some English medical assistants) or when it is very expensive or otherwise difficult to set up a practice (as is the case where practices must be bought or where competition is severe).

When the junior is in a position to break away and be a competitor, however, the hiring physician is very vulnerable, for each young man he introduces to his patients may take some of those patients with him when he leaves. One way to prevent that is by means of a legal document whereby the younger man agrees not to set up an independent practice in the same community when he does leave. Another way, which by no means rules out the first, is to take the young man into partnership.

The most common type of formal cooperative arrangement among peers is not the partnership, however, but what might be called the *association*—an arrangement whereby physicians share the expense of maintaining such common facilities as offices, equipment, assisting personnel, and the like, while they have their own patients. In addition, it is possible for physicians to "cover" each other by seeing each other's patients during vacations and other absences. In one form or another, this rudimentary type of formal cooperation is very widespread in the United States, particularly in city "professional buildings" with elaborate suites and in "medical arts centers" owned by the resident physicians.

From the association it is a short though by no means simple step to the *small legal partnership* in which profits from fees as well as overhead expenses are shared. The division of pooled fees is likely to be a constant bone of contention, however, since the practices of the partners, though overlapping, are not identical. This is particularly the case when specialties are involved, for one specialist may feel he brings in more money than the other and that he accordingly deserves a larger proportion of the profits. Nonetheless, if those problems can be overcome, the partnership is more reliable and more calculable than simpler forms of cooperation. In the colleague network doctors can arrange trustworthy coverage for each other so as to be able to enjoy leisure hours in spite of unpredictable patient demand. In the simple association this virtue is carried over, but the sharing of overhead costs reduces the ordinary expenses of practice per person and makes it possible to have more laboratory and diagnostic equipment. The partnership adds to these virtues its increased long-term financial security.

---

7. Oswald Hall, Types of medical careers. *American Journal of Sociology 55* 1949: 243 – 253.

Where practitioners of different ages are involved, the younger man may treat more patients at a time in his career when he could not expect many. In turn, the older man may have a higher income at a time in his career when patients would be retiring him or when he himself would be forced by his decreasing energy to relinquish patients. Moreover, where more than one specialty is involved, each can function as a referring agent to the other, with mutual advantage: the dubious ethics of fee splitting, often functional in informal cooperative forms, becomes regularized in the partnership without raising an ethical problem. It constitutes some protection against the competition of practitioners outside the cooperative arrangement and also creates a situation where communication among practitioners about the patient is facilitated.

One requirement common to all forms of cooperation is access to a fairly large number of patients. Cooperative practice is comparatively large scale in character and involves the ordering of expenses, referrals, consultations, and — in the case of partnerships—profits into a system which meets the demands of a larger number of people than one man alone can handle. The more formal the arrangement, the more systematized and rational it becomes. At a certain point in the expansion of scale, however, a qualitative change in the form of cooperative practice occurs. "Group practice" is very often used to designate a form of association that goes beyond the scope connoted by the two-man partnership, but definitions have not been very helpful in delineating such difference. The value of the term, like the value of the term "solo practice," is limited by its ideological overtones. Rather than emphasizing autonomy and independence, the term emphasizes "groupness" and interdependence. But if "medical group practice is a formal association of three or more physicians providing services in more than one medical field or specialty, with income from medical practice pooled and redistributed to the members according to some prearranged plan," as one definition would have it,[8] it is hard to see how it need differ from the partnership except as such partnership does not involve more than one specialty. The difference between a two- and a three-man partnership does not seem sociologically significant, nor does the difference between a two-man partnership and a three-man "group." Since 57 percent of the medical groups surveyed by Pomrinse and Goldstein had only three to five full-time physicians, obviously a large proportion of what are called "medical groups" are on the surface insignificantly different from partnerships.[9]

If numbers are to be used to define group practice, Jordan's[10] suggestion of the minimum number of five full-time physicians seems reasonable. Five full-time physicians, not all of them giving day-to-day routine medical care, can serve an ordinary population of anywhere from five to twenty thousand, depending on the

8. This is the definition in S. David Pomrinse and Marcus S. Goldstein, Group practice in the U.S., *Group Practice 9* 1960: 845 – 859.

9. S. David Pomrinse and Marcus S. Goldstein, Group practice in the U.S., *Group Practice 9* 1960: 845 – 859.

10. Edwin P. Jordan. (Ed.), *The physician and group practice.* Chicago: Year Book, 1958.

proportion of general practitioners, internists, and pediatricians, the financial arrangements with patients, and the general style of practice. As the number of patients and doctors increases further, it seems likely that, modified somewhat by the strength of the doctor's bargaining position, some of the technical characteristics of bureaucracy will emerge: hierarchical organization, extensive division of labor, systematic rules and procedures, and the like. In a logically ideal sense, this may be seen as a bureaucratic practice.

Medical Performance in Office Practice

Thus far I have sketched a number of forms of medical practice and some of their functional characteristics. The variety may be seen to distribute itself between two logically but not numerically important extremes. At one end there is a rarity, true solo practice. Empirically, it is unstable, merging into more common, loose forms of informal cooperation with colleagues. The colleague network represents a tighter but still informal type of cooperative practice. The "association" represents a simple variety of formal cooperation, while the small partnership and then the group practice are tighter and more complex forms. Finally, there is the tightest and most formal variety of practice, which may be called organizational or bureaucratic. But in order to make use of *empirical* materials dealing with practice, we must divide all these work settings into two types to be able to parallel the common sense distinction between solo and group practice. The former category includes true solo and all types of informally cooperative practice. The latter includes, from the "association" on, all types of formally cooperative practice. By means of this distinction, we can ask how the form of work setting is related to professional performance.

Since the foremost claim of a profession is to special expertise, it follows that the first question to ask about various forms of professional practice concerns technical performance, or the quality of service provided. It is, unfortunately, the question about which there is least information. The opinion is fairly widespread that a physician cannot practice the best possible medicine without easy access to modern diagnostic and therapeutic facilities. Thus, it is reasonable to assume that the solo practitioner who lacks access to such facilities is least likely to do the best for his patient. Formal cooperative arrangements, whether simple or complex, are more likely to provide the capital to buy an extensive amount of equipment.

Furthermore, the isolation of the practicing physician from his colleagues is believed to be a significant element in the quality of care. It is presently believed that a physician must continually keep abreast of advances in scientific knowledge, relying less on the questionable but ubiquitous "education" of drug manufacturers and their representatives, and more upon the "education" provided by colleagues and scientific publications. As we have seen, solo practice as such cannot readily be classified as more or less isolated, for a considerable degree of

to stay outside the scheme if he wishes. Hence, a physician in any
d scheme of practice can always find some way to work outside, even if
personal risk or sacrifice.

ay be noted furthermore that job satisfaction is inevitably a function of the
lternatives that exist at any particular time and of the symbolic and mate-
ards of these alternatives. In medicine in the United States today, for
, the symbolically valued work setting is the successful, fee-for-service,
cialty practice. The general practitioner may genuinely enjoy the proces-
minor cases (called "garbage" by specialists), the laying-on of hands, and
ial calls at humble homes—the human rather than the scientific side of
e. But in depressed moments he may realize that he is not a social or
onal success because he is not a specialist with limited practice and
nt clients. Thus, environment must be considered a partial influence on
tion, both in the way it defines any form of practice and in the way if offers
ive possibilities.

matter what the tyranny of the patient, the solo work setting has the qual-
otentially complete autonomy. The physician working in the privacy of his
nsulting room can examine, prescribe, diagnose, and treat as he sees fit.
is no one to soften patient pressure to honor lay prejudices, of course, and
practice is insecure it is likely that the doctor will feel obliged to do what he
not really want to do, but theoretically, the solo physician may dismiss his
s rather than give in to them. Autonomy perhaps more extensive than in
her profession thus exists, at least *in potentia,* in solo practice. This is what
tressed by medical students in response to survey questions on why they
reject salaried positions in organizations. In contrast to this apparently
ing side of solo entrepreneurial practice are a number of potential handi-
isolation from one's colleagues and their information and support, the
ssity to be preoccupied daily with the financial basis of practice, the lean-
of early and late stages of the career, and the difficulty of controlling and
arizing work hours. These are the very things which are said to be solved by
practice. Indeed, medical students who preferred salaried positions
sed opportunities to work in close association with colleagues, to obtain a
ar income, and to work regular hours.[26]

On the whole, one should expect that a doctor-owned, fee-for-service part-
hip or group practice would provide most of the gratifications and fewest of
eficiencies of the two extremes of solo and bureaucratic practice. It seems
low the greatest amount of room for self-determination without in turn sacri-
g the major virtues of cooperative practice. It is a very popular form in the
west and Southwest of the United States. The Cahalan survey of medical stu-
ts reported that of those who preferred a nonsalaried form of practice, only 26
cent preferred solo to group practice, partnership, or some other form of for-
y cooperative practice.[27] Since more freshmen than seniors preferred solo

26. Cahalan *et al.,* op. cit.
27. *Ibid.*

informal but nonetheless real and important interaction can take place among
loose networks of practitioners. Much of it, as Peterson observed, is bound to be
about fishing, bridge, and golf [11] but some is certainly about medicine.[12] Nonetheless, the fact that isolation in solo practice is *possible* marks it off from "group
practice," whether a small partnership or a large-scale medical group. In this
sense, group more than solo practice seems to encourage a higher quality of
care. Indeed, Peterson reported a slight tendency for those in group practice to
give a higher quality of care than those working alone,[13] though Clute apparently
did not find such a tendency.[14]

In addition, care by a variety of specialists is held to be necessary these
days. While solo practice does not preclude the use of specialists, group practice
facilitates frequent consultation and exchange of professional information. Where
a number of physicians of varied specialties work together within the same organization, it is not only easier to refer patients, but also to communicate and coordinate information about them. Coleman, Katz, and Menzel have demonstrated
the importance of colleague relations to one facet of care—prescribing drugs.[15]
Thus, it is to be expected that in group practice the fragmentation of care following upon specialization can be compensated for and that so-called comprehensive care is more likely to ensue.

Finally, there is the element of supervision, the quality of which Seeman and
Evans have shown to influence medical performance.[16] The most reputable medcal institutions—for example, medical school clinics and teaching hospitals—are
characterized by doctors working in close association with each other and with
some systematic supervision of work by chiefs of services, staff committees
reviewing the treatment of patients who died, the tissue removed by surgery, and
the like. Except in a purely educational context, where it is ideologically acceptable, the nature of supervision in such medical bureaucracies has received little
attention, but it is indubitable that at least some formal administrative supervision
almost always exists. Furthermore, the cultivation of a medical records system
and the continuous accumulation of information in records is in itself supervisory,
for while the records may not be subject to routine inspection, they may always
be examined if some doubt arises about a physician's work. If, as Peterson
assumes, systematic and complete records are an important element of competent medical care, bureaucratic practices, which are far more likely to encourage
record keeping, can to this extent provide a higher quality of care.

In theory, then, formal and cooperative rather than informal and individual

11. Peterson, op. cit., p. 83.
12. James Coleman, Elihu Katz, and Herbert Menzel, *Medical innovation: A diffusion study.* Indianapolis: Bobbs-Merrill, 1966, p. 110. Coleman found that when one shared his office, he adopted a
new drug more quickly than one who works alone.
13. Peterson, op. cit.
14. Clue, op. cit., p. 318.
15. James Coleman, Elihu Katz, and Herbert Menzel, *Medical innovation: A diffusion study.* Indianapolis: Bobbs-Merrill, 1966, p. 110.
16. Seeman and Evans, op. cit.

practice arrangements are more likely to provide good medical care. However, there are only scattered bits of evidence to support this theory. A negative reflection on the system of solo practice predominant in the United States might be noted in the finding that somewhat less than half of all surgical in-hospital procedures performed in the nation during 1957–58 were by men formally certified to practice surgery,[17] but this is not direct evidence that the quality of care in group practice is higher. Comparative studies are necessary.

One of the rare comparative studies in this area was made by the Health Insurance Plan of Greater New York, in which the hospitalization and perinatal mortality of a population served by medical groups under contract with the insurance plan compared favorably with that of the New York City population.[18] That study, however, was concerned with an additional element in the arrangement of medical care—the prepaid service contract. It is believed that when people can be insured so that no financial barrier stands between them and medical care, they will not hesitate to use services and so can obtain the care they need early in the course of illness, thus preventing complications. Consequently, a comprehensive prepaid service contract is believed to be — of itself — conducive to better medical care. With insurance and organizational variables undifferentiated, the influence of either on quality of care is difficult to establish.

The same difficulty holds when the mode of compensating the physician is undifferentiated from organization. A study by Densen and his associates compared the hospital utilization of members of a single union who were under two different medical insurance plans—one involving medical group practice compensated on a per capita basis, and the other solo fee-for-service practice. Hospital utilization in the former proved to be lower, even though the comprehensiveness of insurance was much the same.[19] But it is difficult to tell whether the lower utilization resulted from group practice as such or from the fact that the group plan provided no additional compensation to the group physician for in-hospital surgery.[20] Clearly, present evidence is inadequate.[21]

Whether or not people are deeply involved emotionally with their doctors, they must in any case be sufficiently happy with the care they receive to make use of their doctors. Patient satisfaction assumes additional importance when medicine becomes a political issue. In a number of national sample surveys in the United States, most people have expressed general satisfaction with medical services which typically are organized on only a loosely cooperative, fee-for-service basis, and the solo general practitioner is part of the national folklore. In

17. Health Information Foundation, Physicians who perform surgery, *Progress in Health Services* 10 1961.

18. S. Shapiro, L. Weiner, and P. M. Densen, Comparison of prematurity and perinatal mortality in general population and in population of prepaid group practice, *American Journal of Public Health 48* 1958: 170–187.

19. P. M. Densen, et al., Prepaid medical care and hospital utilization in a dual choice situation, *American Journal of Public Health 50* 1960: 1710–1726.

20. For some evidence bearing on this see Robin F. Badgley and Samuel Wolfe, *Doctors' strike: Medical care and conflict in Saskatchewan.* New York: Atherton Press, 1967, pp. 115–118.

21. For a recent review of the evidence bearing on these difficult questions, see Avedis Donabedian, A review of some experiences with prepaid group practice, *Bureau of Public Health Economics, Research Series,* No. 12. Ann Arbor: The University of Michigan School of Public Health, 1965.

spite of this, fairly large proportions of the population. They complain that doctors keep them waiting on nights and weekends, and do not give enough report the largest proportions of dissatisfaction,[22] wł that people are less likely to complain about their ow in general.[23]

This material, however, like the data on in-hos practice only insofar as it is the most common and m United States. Again, comparative studies provide Anderson and Sheatsley compared two groups of so insured patients, one being served by solo physicians ance organization on a fee-for-service basis, the othe groups, paid on a per capita basis.[24] The finding was t program elicited more patient satisfaction than did the Patients of the latter were prone to complain of lack o cient explanation of their condition by the doctor, waitin getting house calls. In Freidson's study, where patient ence with these two types of practice, there was also a sense of "personal interest" was more likely to be obtair practice than in capitation group practice. But there was cal care of a technically higher quality could be obt group.[25] In both studies, however, solo fee-for-service capitation group practice, and no way is provided to cont and compare forms of practice as such. Plainly, the mat tion is equivocal, but none contradicts the idea that emot part of the patient seems more likely to be gained from position to be more immediately responsive to (and dep than are group physicians who have obligations to a work

Physician satisfaction, too, may be more influenced work than by the arrangement of payment. In assessing ever, we must first recognize that it is much easier for t lance" than for the professor or the minister, since both congregations rather than an assortment of successive in can count on the fairly strong motivation provided by illness that even in an environment where the state sets the te average practitioner—as in England and the Soviet Union—

22. E. L. Koos, Metropolis—What city people think of their medical serv *Public Health 45* 1955: 1551–1557.

23. Ben Gaffin Associates, *What Americans think of the medical profe* Association brochure, n.d.

24. Odin W. Anderson and Paul B. Sheatsley, Comprehensive medical mation Foundation Research Series, No. 9, 1959.

25. Eliot Freidson, *Patients' views of medical practice.* New York: Russell See also the review of Weinerman, Patients' perceptions, op. cit., and of Avedi: of some experiences with prepaid group practice, *Bureau of Public Health Econ* No. 12. Ann Arbor: The University of Michigan School of Public Health, 1965.

practice, we can assume that interest in cooperative forms increases as the medical students come closer to being a physician. However, the Cahalan study notes that those students expressing a preference for group practice were less likely to expect that their preferences would be realized than were those preferring the solo form. Testimony to the realism of their expectation is provided by Weiskotten's finding that 64 percent of those in the class of 1950 engaged in private practice were practicing alone.[28]

Analytical Types of Practice Organization

Thus far, we have discussed medical work settings as a variable *quantity* of professional cooperation and organization, from the isolated solo practitioner to the member of an elaborate medical bureaucracy. However, this simplistic mode of analysis does not pick out some of the important analytical qualities of practice, particularly those bearing directly on the differential performance of physicians in practice. For example, as has already been noted, the solo practitioner is not generally considered to give as good technical care as the man in group practice but is generally considered to have better interpersonal relations with his patients. And on another level, the specialist is reputed to give better technical care than the general practitioner, though he is considered to be more cold and impersonal. And finally, different specialists—for example, obstetricians as opposed to pathologists—are reputed to have different "personalities" and certain significantly different practices.

How can we explain such differences? We can explain them by assuming that people select themselves—that they know enough about practices in advance, and can assess themselves precisely enough to select their practices to fit their capacities. Certainly self-selection is one element to be taken into account, but to use it as the prime explanation is to put faith into a miraculously precise prescience and self-knowledge that surpasses reason. We can, alternately, assume that some individuals, after experiencing one kind of practice, try another, and perhaps even another. It is certainly true that there is some degree of trial and error in medical practice. Some move from general to specialty practice, others from solo to group practice, or vice versa. But the personal and economic cost of such movement, particularly from one *specialty* to another, is so great that this kind of self-selection simply cannot be very common.

Quite another kind of explanation lies in the press of the situation on the individual after he has landed in a position—on the influence of the setting of work on transforming the individual who has become committed to adjusting to it, on the consequences of being in a situation in which persistent and powerful demands cause the individual to behave in a certain way regardless of his personal qualities. The structural contingencies of practice that would seem to have

28. Weiskotten, op cit.

the greatest significance for the profession are those that influence the maintenance, raising, or lowering of the standards of ethical and technical performance.
These are established and assessed by members of the profession as such and
may be labeled "colleague" standards. Many such standards are by no means
universally agreed upon by all members of the profession, but we can distinguish
them grossly by contrasting them with lay standards. We may take it as axiomatic
that the patient has a different perspective on health services than does the physician and that on occasion he will almost certainly ask for medication or procedures which colleagues would not approve. Opposing laymen and colleagues to
each other, then, we may distinguish practices by *the degree to which they are
amenable to lay or colleague control.*

On this basis we can distinguish two logically extreme types of practice for
purposes of analysis.[29] On one extreme is a work setting that is wholly dependent
for its economic continuance on lay evaluations—client-dependent practice.
When he first feels ill, the patient feels he is competent to judge whether he is
actually ill and what general class of illness it is. On this basis he treats himself.
Failure of this and other informal modes of treatment leads him to a physician.
This physician, it should be clear, is chosen on the basis of lay conceptions of
what is needed, not by professional criteria. In order to be chosen—in order to
stay in practice—he must offer services of a sort that laymen themselves feel
they need: he must give antibiotics for colds, vitamin injections for being "run
down," and sedatives or tranquilizers for "nerves." And to be chosen again and
survive, he must be prepared to provide services that honor the client's prejudices sufficiently to make him feel that what he thinks bothers him is being
treated properly. Furthermore, if it is wholly dependent on client choice, this type
of work setting is unlikely to be either very observable to or dependent upon colleagues. Its professional standards are therefore likely to be comparatively low.
At the other extreme may be seen a colleague-dependent practice that does not
in and by itself attract its own clientele but that instead serves the needs of other
colleagues or professional organizations that do attract such clientele. It is
dependent for its clientele on colleagues rather than laymen: colleagues transmit
clients to it. In this sense, in order to survive, it must honor the prejudices of colleagues more than those of clients. Here, obviously, we should expect that the
degree to which it honors professional standards will be relatively great.

The logical extreme of client-dependent practice does not seem fully applicable to any professional work setting, if only because the license of a professional practitioner ultimately depends upon the approval of his colleagues. The
quack, however, seems most usefully defined as a practitioner who fits this
extreme, having no obligations to or identity with an organized set of colleagues.
Close to this extreme in the United States is the independent solo neighborhood
or village general practitioner, with at best loose cooperative ties to colleagues
and local medical institutions. Also close to this extreme are specialists who must

---

29. This criterion was first suggested in my Client control and medical practice, *American Journal
of Sociology 65* 1960: 374 – 382.

attract a clientele directly and who do not need to make everyday use of hospitals—for example, in urban areas in particular, some internists and pediatricians, as well as some ophthalmologists and gynecologists. At the other logical extreme of colleague-dependent practice, empirical cases are easier to find. Such medical specialties as pathology, anesthesiology, and radiology are almost completely dependent upon colleague referrals and have little significant need for such client-oriented techniques as bedside manners. Somewhat less pure, but moved toward that extreme nonetheless, are practices to be found in hospitals, clinics, and other professional bureaucracies. Here, while the client very often does exercise choice, organizational requirements minimize his influence. By and large, practice is dependent upon organizational auspices and equipment. And while practitioners within the organization may be chosen by clients, the practitioner's visibility and vulnerability to his colleagues in the organization should lead him to minimize his responsiveness to clients.

This classification of medical practice provides a foundation for understanding some of the mechanisms involved in creating observed differences in performance among physicians in one setting rather than another. If the physicians are as individuals unusually conscientious and ethical, we are in a position to understand what practice settings can make them uncomfortable if not significantly change their performance. If the physicians are individuals who are only ordinarily conscientious and ethical, we can understand why, in one setting, they fail to apply the standards taught them in school, and why, in another, they are more likely to maintain such standards. And, given physicians who are equally "cynical" upon graduating from medical school, we can predict the degree of "cynicism" they maintain when they disperse into practices that pose distinctly different structural pressures on them.[30]

---

30. Gray, op. cit.

Equal Treatment and Unequal Benefits: The Medicare Program

24

KAREN DAVIS

Medicare is a uniform, federal program providing medical care benefits to all elderly persons covered by the Social Security retirement program. Even though the same set of benefits is available to all covered persons regardless of income, race, or geographical location, wide differences exist in the use of services and receipt of payments on the basis of each of these factors. Higher-income elderly persons are more likely to visit physicians and to see physicians charging higher prices than are lower-income elderly persons. Elderly blacks, either because of current or past discriminatory practices, receive medical care less often than elderly whites. Elderly persons in areas with a limited availability of medical manpower receive a less than proportionate share of Medicare benefits.

These outcomes are at variance with one of the basic aims of the Medicare program (see Somers and Somers, 1967; Corning, 1969; Marmor, 1973). It was originally hoped that the removal of financial barriers would enable all elderly persons to receive medical care services largely on the basis of medical need. Yet, many elderly population groups with poor health receive only limited Medicare payments.

This variation in distribution of benefits raises several important questions. The first concern is the magnitude and nature of variations in benefits. How large are the differentials, and do they reflect primarily differences in utilization of medical services or in prices charged for medical care? Second, given that the program favors whites, higher-income persons, and persons residing outside of the South, how should the program be financed? Third, what measures can be taken

From *Milbank Memorial Fund Quarterly*, 53 (4) 1975: 449–88. Copyright 1975, Milbank Memorial Fund Quarterly. Reprinted with permission.

to redress any inappropriate patterns of medical care utilization? Finally, is experience with the Medicare program instructive for the design of future medical care financing plans affecting all age groups?

This paper addresses these questions by first reviewing the provisions and overall experience of the Medicare program; examining the evidence on distribution of benefits by income, race, and geographical location; and finally concluding with recommendations for changes both in the Medicare program and in medical care financing and delivery programs affecting all age groups.

Medicare Benefits

The Medicare program provides a basic hospital insurance plan for all persons 65 and over covered by the Social Security retirement program and pays half the cost of a voluntary supplementary medical insurance plan (SMI) covering physicians' services and certain other benefits. By July 1971, 20.7 million persons were entitled to hospital insurance, and 20.0 million of these (96 percent) had enrolled for SMI (U.S. Department of Health, Education, and Welfare, 1971, 40).

Under the basic hospital insurance plan, the elderly receive a broad range of hospital and post-hospital services subject to certain deductible and coinsurance provisions.[1] For a given benefit period, beneficiaries must pay a deductible for hospital care set at approximately the cost of one day of hospital care, currently $84. No further charges to the patient are made for covered services for hospital stays of less than 60 days (patients may, however, face charges for noncovered services such as private rooms, private duty nurses, televisions, telephone, and physician services provided in the hospital). Between the 61st and 90th days, beneficiaries must pay $21 per day; for the next 60 days they must pay $42 a day, after which hospital insurance ceases.[2]

In order to encourage early discharge from hospitals, the Medicare program also covers certain types of post-hospital care, such as extended-care facility services. Extended-care services are intended for patients who have been hospitalized for treatment of a medical condition and who, while no longer requiring the full range of hospital services, still need full-time, skilled nursing care in an institutional setting.[3] Benefits are payable for persons who have had at least three consecutive days of hospital care and who are admitted to an extended-care facility within 14 days from the date of hospital discharge. Beneficiaries are required to

---

1. A deductible is the amount to be paid by the patient before insurance benefits begin. A coinsurance rate is the percentage of the medical bill paid by the patient himself. These patient charges are sometimes referred to as out-of-pocket costs or as cost-sharing.

2. Under current law, the last 60 days of coverage constitute a "lifetime reserve." After that is used, no coverage is provided after the first 90 days. The first 90 days of hospital coverage, however, are renewed whenever the patient has been out of a hospital or nursing home for 60 days. The deductible and coinsurance payments then begin anew under a new benefit period.

3. An extended care facility is an institution, or a distinct part of an institution, which is primarily engaged in providing skilled nursing care or rehabilitation services and which has in effect a transfer agreement with one or more hospitals.

pay $10.50 per day for the 21st through the 100th day in an extended-care facility, at which point benefits terminate.

In order to be eligible for participation in the Medicare program, institutions must be in substantial compliance with conditions of participation established by the Secretary of Health, Education, and Welfare, and must also agree to provide services on a nondiscriminatory basis in accordance with Title VI of the Civil Rights Act of 1964.

The supplementary medical insurance program provides coverage of physicians' services, outpatient hospital services, additional home health services, other medical services and supplies, and outpatient physical therapy services furnished by qualified providers. Individuals 65 years of age and over may enroll in the program regardless of whether they are eligible for social security retirement benefits. Monthly premiums paid by the individual are matched by the federal government out of general revenues.

Beneficiaries pay the first $60 of supplementary medical insurance services incurred during the year.[4] After the deductible is met, the SMI program pays for 80 percent of the allowed charges for covered physician services and other medical services. If the physician will not accept assignment of insurance benefits, the patient is required to pay all charges in excess of the allowable charge as well as 20 percent of the allowable charge.

The 1965 amendments to the Social Security Act, which authorized Medicare, provided for purchase of SMI coverage for aged public assistance recipients by states. Subsequent amendments in 1967 permitted states to purchase SMI coverage for all elderly persons eligible for Medicaid (whether receiving cash assistance or medically indigent). State election of these provisions is referred to as "buying into" the SMI program, and recipients under such an agreement are called "buy-ins." Under a buy-in agreement, a state is responsible for the payment of the beneficiary's premium and share of SMI medical expenses—the deductible and coinsurance charges. By the end of 1970, 46 states and the District of Columbia had such agreements, covering two million persons (U.S. Department of Health, Education, and Welfare, 1971, 23).

The Medicare program now represents a major item in the federal budget. Expenditures have nearly quadrupled from $3.3 billion in fiscal year 1967 to an estimated $12 billion in 1974. A portion of this tremendous growth is attributable to an increase in number of persons eligible for the program (from 19.1 million initially to 22.9 million in 1974). Some of the increase represents greater utilization of medical care services per enrolled person. The major portion of the increase, however, is attributable to increases in the costs of medical care (e.g., the consumer price index for hospital daily service charges increased 74 percent from 1967 to 1972). As a consequence of rising prices, the elderly now pay more for medical care than before the Medicare program started. Private payments for personal health care averaged $293 per elderly person in fiscal year 1966 and

---

4. Expenses incurred in the last three months of the previous year may be applied toward the current year's deductible.

$404 per capita in fiscal year 1972, including $67 in Medicare premiums (Cooper and Worthington, 1973, 14).

Since this program represents a major governmental expenditure, it is important that the distributional impact of the program be thoroughly explored. How are Medicare payments distributed on the basis of income, race, and location? How does utilization of medical care services under the program vary by these characteristics, and how much of the variation in payments is traceable to differences in prices for medical care faced by different population groups? The following sections turn to these questions, and consider in turn the distribution of payments by income, race, and location.

The Role of Income in Medical Care Utilization and Medicare Payments

One objective of the Medicare program was elimination of financial barriers discouraging the elderly from seeking "necessary" medical care. Removal of important financial barriers could not be expected to result in equal utilization of medical care services by all elderly persons, since the elderly vary with respect to health status and medical condition. It should, however, have increased the utilization of medical care services by the poor relative to higher-income elderly persons, since charges for medical care (before Medicare) could have been expected to pose the strongest deterrent to the poor in seeking necessary medical care. In the absence of financial barriers to care, in fact, medical care utilization might be inversely related to income since the poor typically are in poorer health than higher-income persons.

Several factors, however, may offset such an inverse relationship. First, the Medicare program does not completely eliminate all out-of-pocket costs for medical care, nor does it vary cost-sharing provisions in accordance with income. Both the basic hospital insurance plan and, to a greater extent, the supplementary medical insurance plan require some fixed deductible and coinsurance payments on the part of the elderly. A $60 deductible and 20 percent coinsurance rate for physicians' services is more of a deterrent to use of medical services for a person with $3,000 income than for one with $15,000 income. Higher-income persons are also more likely to be able to purchase supplementary private insurance, picking up all or part of out-of-pocket costs. For those poor "bought into" Medicare coverage by state Medicaid programs, the deductible and coinsurance amounts are paid by the Medicaid program—rather than levied directly on the individual. This combination of supplementary public and private insurance, as well as direct income effects, predicts that utilization will be lowest for low-income persons not covered by the state Medicaid "buy-in" programs, and somewhat greater for higher-income individuals, elderly persons with private insurance, and elderly persons covered by Medicaid.

In addition to the importance of Medicare cost-sharing provisions in determining utilization of services by elderly persons of different income classes, variations in the availability of medical resources may reinforce the tendency for high-income persons to obtain care more readily. In areas with limited, scarce medical manpower and facilities, those elderly persons with relatively minor ailments may have to yield to younger persons with more urgent medical problems. In addition, the time, search, and transportation costs required to obtain medical care, which tend to be systematically related to the availability of medical resources, can pose important barriers to the receipt of medical care for elderly persons even in the absence of substantial out-of-pocket medical costs. Since physicians tend to be more densely located in high-income areas, persons in such areas can expect to incur much lower nonmedical costs in seeking and obtaining medical care.

The costs of medical care may also vary systematically with income. Physicians in high-income areas may be able to charge higher prices for any type of service; and a greater abundance of specialist physicians may lead to a more expensive mix of available services in high-income areas. Similarly, hospitals in high-income — high-wage areas may have higher costs than hospitals located in poor communities. If hospitals respond to high income and extensive insurance coverage in the surrounding community by providing higher quality or at least a more expensive style of care, hospital costs will be concomitantly higher in such areas. All of these availability factors would lead to greater utilization, higher quality, and higher costs of medical care services for higher-income elderly persons.

Education may play an independent role in influencing decisions to seek medical care and the type and amount of care obtained. Since education and income tend to be related, relatively greater benefits for higher-income persons may be a reflection, at least in part, of educational factors. Education may affect use of medical services in a variety of ways. More educated persons may be more aware of the Medicare program and the benefits it provides, and hence submit claims for benefits for which they are eligible to a greater degree than less educated persons. This effect may be reduced over time, as publicity about the program makes the program more familiar to all members of society. More educated persons, in addition to being relatively more informed about the Medicare program, may also be more knowledgeable about the benefits of medical care, more perceptive about symptoms requiring medical attention, and more inclined to seek out specialized care for specific types of medical problems.

Some patterns of medical care utilization among the elderly may be traceable to habit persistence, with persons neglecting to seek medical care over a long period of time for financial or other reasons, continuing to do so even with adequate financing. Again, this effect might be reduced over time as more elderly persons have longer experience with the Medicare program.

Finally, it should be noted that attitudes of physicians and other medical care providers may also affect patterns of medical care utilization. To the extent that physicians prefer to treat patients from a similar socioeconomic class, physicians may either consciously or unconsciously discourage lower-income persons from obtaining care. Signs in the office indicating that the physician does not accept Medicaid patients are a blatant manifestation of discrimination among patients, but more subtle tactics may be equally effective.

In summary, even with a uniform financing program which removes most major financial barriers to the receipt of medical care services, substantial variations in utilization of services and distribution of payments may occur on the basis of income. Low-income persons without private insurance or without coverage under a supplementary Medicaid program may find the cost-sharing provisions of Medicare prohibitive. The nonmedical costs of seeking medical care—the time, search, and transportation costs—faced by the poor may further discourage use. Higher prices in high-income areas may lead to a disproportionate share of payments to high-income elderly persons. The interrelated effects of income and education — or the persistence of habitual neglect of health — may reinforce the tendency for the poor to fail to obtain adequate care.

The following sections first present data on the extent of inter-income class variation in benefits and then attempt to isolate the underlying factors giving rise to this variation.

Medicare Benefits by Income

Wide differences do exist in the level of payment for medical care services under the Medicare program by income class.

Table 24–1 presents data on three components of Medicare reimbursements for persons covered by the voluntary supplementary medical insurance plan in 1968: (1) the percentage of all persons enrolled who receive services in excess of the deductible ($50 in 1968); (2) the number of reimbursable services received by persons exceeding the deductible (reimbursable services are counted only after the deductible is exceeded); and (3) the average Medicare payment per reimbursable service.

As shown in the table, marked disparities in the distribution of medical payments by income occur in the SMI program. Medicare reimbursements for medical services per person with family income above $15,000 was $160 in 1968, compared with $79 for persons with incomes below $5,000 — or more than *twice* as much for the highest income group as for the lowest. This wide difference in benefits reflects in large part the higher level of reimbursement per service received by high-income persons, but there are also significant differences by income class in percentage of eligible persons exceeding the deductible.

As expected, higher-income elderly persons see physicians charging higher prices. Average Medicare reimbursement per service is $10.40 for persons with family incomes above $15,000 compared with $6.06 for persons with incomes below $2,000. Part of the difference could reflect higher quality care received by higher-income persons or more expensive types of services—such as specialist physician care or in-hospital physician care. While the Medicare survey does not

Table 24–1   Medicare Reimbursements for Covered Services under the Supplementary Medical Insurance Program and Persons Served, by Income, 1968

	Medicare reimbursement per person enrolled	Persons receiving reimbursable services per 1000 Medicare enrollees	Number of reimbursable services per person receiving reimbursable services	Medicare reimbursement per reimbursable services
Total	$ 88.60	460.1	26.6	$ 7.27
Under $5,000	78.77	431.7	26.0	7.02
Under $2,000	76.32	438.2	28.7	6.06
$ 2,000–4,999	80.95	425.9	23.4	8.11
$ 5,000–9,999	103.87	475.0	26.6	8.21
$10,000–14,999	115.10	527.2	27.5	7.95
$15,000 and over	160.30	552.3	27.9	10.40
Ratio, over $15,000 income to under $5,000 income	2.04	1.28	1.07	1.48

Source: U.S. Department of Health, Education, and Welfare, Social Security Administration, Office of Research and Statistics, calculated from unpublished tabulations from the 1968 Current Medicare Survey.

provide information on the type of physician rendering Medicare services, the Health Interview Survey conducted by the National Center for Health Statistics does indicate the type of physician and place of visit for physician visits of non-hospitalized patients. As shown below, higher-income elderly persons are more likely to see internists, while lower-income persons receive a greater proportion of their medical care from general practitioners.

While type of physician may explain part of the variation in average reimbursement by income class, higher charges for medical services in high-income areas may also account for some of the variation. The Medicare program follows the practice of setting allowable charges in relation to the prevailing level of usual and customary charges in the area. Thus physicians practicing in a low-income, low-prevailing charge area, will be compensated for services provided Medicare patients at a lower rate than physicians choosing to practice in higher-income areas. This method of setting allowable charges perpetuates incentives for physicians to avoid practicing in lower-income communities—rather than posing positive incentives for changes in the distribution of medical manpower.

While price variations in medical care services raise important issues with respect to appropriate methods of reimbursing physicians and deriving revenue, variations in the use of medical services by income class are also a source of concern. Fifty-five percent of Medicare enrollees with family incomes above $15,000 use medical services in excess of the deductible ($50 in 1968) and hence receive some Medicare reimbursement, compared with only 43 percent of enrollees with family incomes below $5,000. The number of services received for those persons exceeding the deductible does not vary markedly by income class. However, since fewer poor persons exceed the deductible, it might be expected that the medical condition of those who do is relatively more serious, and hence would require even more physician visits than persons with higher income. The deductible provision of Medicare, and perhaps the coinsurance payment on medical service in excess of the deductible, appears to be a major deterrent to the poor in seeking medical care.[5]

Unfortunately, only limited data are available directly from the Medicare program on the distribution of hospital benefits by income class. The 1969 Current Medicare Survey, however, does provide some information on SMI benefits for persons with hospital stays. As shown in Table 24–2, 32 percent of public medical assistance recipients are hospitalized during the year, compared with only 16 percent of lower-income persons not covered by Medicaid or private insurance. No marked differences exist between the percentage of higher-income persons without complementary private insurance coverage who are hospitalized (17 percent) and lower-income persons not covered by either Medicaid or private insurance (16 percent). Persons with private insurance coverage have somewhat higher rates of hospitalization (21 percent).

Table 24–2   Percentage Distribution of Ambulatory Physician Visits, by Family Income, 1969

	By Type of Physician		
	General Practitioner	Internist	Other Specialists
All persons age 65 and over:	71%	10%	19%
Under $5,000 income	75,	7	18
Aid[a]	85	5	10
No aid	74	8	18
$ 5,000–9,999	70	10	20
10,000–14,999	60	14	26
15,000 and over	65	17	18

Source: Calculated from 1969 Health Interview Survey tapes supplied by U.S. Department of Health, Education, and Welfare, National Center for Health Statistics.
[a]Aid includes all persons receiving welfare assistance.

In spite of the fact that higher-income persons do not tend to be hospitalized with greater frequency than lower-income persons, nonhospital Medicare payments are substantially higher for higher-income persons ($541 per person with hospital stay compared with $405 for lower-income persons). This difference

---

5. A similar conclusion was reached in a study by Peel and Scharff (1973). They used 1969 data and grouped Medicare beneficiaries by: public medical assistance recipients, persons with out-of-hospital insurance coverage, and others divided into higher and lower income on the basis of family size and income.

occurs primarily because higher-income persons receive a greater number of SMI services. This might reflect a greater tendency for higher-income elderly persons to have several specialist physicians, for their physicians to make more frequent visits during hospitalization, or for higher-income persons to make more visits to physicians for pre- and post-hospital care. Since hospital based physicians—such as anesthesiologists, radiologists, and pathologists—are reimbursed under the SMI plan rather than the basic hospitalization plan, the greater number of SMI services received by higher-income persons could also reflect more ancillary hospital services. Differences in the rate of surgery may also partially account for the tendency for higher-income persons to receive more SMI services.

Explanations of Inter-Income Class Variation in Medicare Benefits

While the preceding section has attempted to summarize the magnitude and nature of inter-income class variations in Medicare benefits, it has not provided any thorough explanation of the causes of such variations. Higher-income persons could receive more medical services and higher payments for any number of reasons—they can afford the cost-sharing amounts imposed on the patient more readily than the poor; they are more likely to purchase complementary private insurance; they are likely to live in areas with more available medical resources and higher medical prices; they are more highly educated and are more likely to seek out higher quality and specialized care; they have established past habits of seeking medical care for a wide variety of conditions; and, not unimportantly, physicians may have preference for treating patients of a similar socioeconomic background and hence encourage more visits from higher-income persons.

Several studies have been conducted which examine a number of important factors simultaneously. Feldstein (1971) has analyzed state data on Medicare benefits and looked at the effect of state per capita income and other factors on: (1) whether or not an elderly person enrolled in the basic hospital insurance plan will also voluntarily purchase the supplementary medical insurance coverage; (2) hospital and extended care facility admissions; and (3) average benefits of both the basic hospital plan and SMI. Feldstein did not find any significant income effects. His study, however, is not ideally suited for an explanation of inter-income class variation in Medicare benefits. Variations in benefits among income classes within a state are obscured by working with state averages. In addition, it was not possible in the interstate analysis to hold constant for health status. Thus, systematic relationships among income and health may obscure the effect of income. Finally, average income of all persons within a state may not be an accurate proxy for spending power of the elderly in the state.

Koropecky and Huang (1973) have investigated SMI benefits with 1969 Current Medicare Survey data using a multivariate regression model. Their study used 30 different variables representing various combinations of income, prices, and patient payments; income enters in 11 different forms in the same equation. Thus, it is not surprising that no single variable indicates much effect of income.

Table 24-3 Supplementary Medical Insurance Charges for Persons with Hospital Stays, by Income and Insurance Coverage, 1969

	Charges per person enrolled with hospital stays	Persons with hospital stays per 1000 enrollees	Number of services per person with hospital stay	Charges per service
Total	$452.40	220.1	35.59	$12.71
Public medical assistance	500.84	313.9	42.41	11.81
Lower income[a]	405.07	159.7	29.34	13.81
Higher income[a]	541.06	171.7	37.01	14.62
Complementary out-of-hospital insurance coverage	422.44	207.3	35.63	11.85
Ratio, higher income to lower income	1.34	1.08	1.26	1.06

Source: U.S. Department of Health, Education, and Welfare, Social Security Administration, Office of Research and Statistics, calculated from unpublished tabulations from the 1969 Current Medicare Survey.

[a]The dividing point between higher and lower income is $4,000 for a one-person family, $7,500 for a two-person family, $10,000 for a three-person family, and $15,000 for a family with 4 or more persons. See Peel and Scharff (1973) for a description of classification on the basis of income and insurance.

Note: The author wishes to thank Peel and Scharff for making these unpublished tabulations available.

A summary tale indicates that average physician visits increase from 3.6 per person for a family with $1,000 income to 4.7 for persons with family incomes of $5,000. It would appear, therefore, that the total effect of income is quite important. These results must be treated as quite tentative, however, because of methodological and data-handling procedures.

Econometric Estimation of the Elderly's Use of Medical Services, Health Interview Survey

It is possible to shed additional light on some of the unresolved questions about the effect of income on Medicare benefits by analyzing the use of medical services by the elderly as contained in the Health Interview Survey conducted by the National Center for Health Statistics. This household interview survey, conducted annually on about 130,000 individuals (of which about 12,000 are age 65 or over) is an excellent source of data on utilization of physician and hospital services, health status, money income, welfare status, and demographic characteristics. Tapes of the 1969 survey have been supplied, making possible a detailed econometric analysis of utilization patterns of the elderly. The major limitation of the 1969 survey is the absence of any data on medical expenditures or private insurance coverage. It is not possible, therefore, to analyze interincome class differences in average prices for medical services, or to examine the effect of net out-of-pocket costs on utilization of services.

Table 24–3 presents estimates of the effect of income on physician visits by the elderly, derived from regressions reported in Table 24–4. The results presented are adjusted for health status of the elderly as well as other factors such as race, geographical location, and availability of health providers (see Table 24–4 for a complete list of variables).

Once physician visits are standardized for health condition, physician visits are seen to increase uniformly with income (excluding from consideration those persons on welfare). Among elderly persons with average health, the lowest users of physicians services are persons with incomes below $5,000, who average 6.1 visits annually; compared with 9.5 visits for elderly persons with family incomes above $15,000. Elderly persons receiving public assistance see physicians much more frequently than other low-income elderly and slightly more frequently than elderly persons in the $5,000 to $15,000 income range. Calculation of these utilization rates assumes that elderly people in each income class have the same average education, availability of medical care, and geographic distribution. Thus, this adjustment for other factors affecting utilization removes any differences in utilization among income classes that could be traced to these other determinants of utilization which may be associated with income.

Table 24–4   Average Physician Visits for the Elderly, by Health Status and Family Income, Adjusted for other Determinants

	Health status[a]		
	Good	Average	Poor
Family income:			
Under $5,000			
No aid[b]	2.78	5.64	10.47
Aid	3.86	7.52	13.42
$ 5,000 – 9,999	3.14	6.60	11.70
$10,000 –14,999	3.75	7.27	12.98
$15,000 and over	5.35	9.53	16.98

Source: Calculated from Table 4 and tabulations from the 1969 HIS.
[a]Good health status is defined as without any chronic conditions, limitation of activity, or restricted activity days. Average and poor health are defined as at the mean and twice the mean level, respectively, of the three morbidity indicators used.
[b]Aid indicates public assistant recipients.

In summary the regression results indicate that substantial differences in use of physician services by the elderly exist on the basis of income, and that these differences are not attributable solely to factors associated with higher incomes such as greater availability of physicians in high-income areas or higher levels of education. One major explanation which may account for these persistent differences is, of course, the deterrent effect of the cost-sharing provisions of Medicare physician coverage for persons with low incomes.

Table 24–5   Tobit Regression Analysis of Medical Care Utilization by Persons Age 65 and Over, 1969[a]

	Physician visits	Hospital episodes	Hospital days
Constant	−2.072	−3.107	−63.22
	(4.81)[b]	(6.55)	(7.48)
Chronic conditions	0.317	0.151	2.23
	(14.02)	(6.90)	(5.71)
Limited in activity	0.304	0.603	12.00
	(3.95)	(8.17)	(9.11)
Age	−0.018	0.008	0.16
	(3.45)	(1.57)	(1.79)
Restricted activity days	0.120	0.115	2.02
	(16.82)	(17.24)	(17.11)
Income $5,000–10,000	0.145	0.253	3.72
	(1.73)	(3.20)	(2.64)
Income $10,000–15,000	0.309	0.392	3.99
	(2.30)	(3.08)	(1.74)
Income $15,000+	0.721	0.492	7.94
	(5.02)	(3.45)	(3.13)
Public assistance recipient	0.370	−0.044	−0.82
	(2.69)	(0.32)	(0.34)
Family size	−0.063	0.015	0.43
	(2.05)	(0.55)	(0.86)
Female	0.144	−0.064	−1.30
	(2.17)	(1.02)	(1.17)
Individual education, 9 years and over	0.181	−0.025	−0.14
	(2.67)	(0.39)	(0.12)
Working	−0.066	−0.304	−6.02
	(0.67)	(3.10)	(3.42)
Black–South	−0.491	−0.670	−10.03
	(2.93)	(4.17)	(3.52)
Black–Nonsouth	−0.122	−0.055	1.64
	(0.67)	(0.32)	(0.54)
Physicians	0.257	−0.422	−6.41
	(2.26)	(3.76)	(3.23)
Hospital beds	—	0.079	2.50
		(1.18)	(2.10)
Non SMSA–South	−0.015	−0.159	−3.82
	(0.11)	(1.24)	(1.67)
Non SMSA–Nonsouth	0.180	−0.137	−3.44
	(1.59)	(1.24)	(1.75)
Chi-square	904	813	790

[a]Tobit analysis is the appropriate regression technique when the dependent variable has many zero values. See Tobin (1.58).
[b]t-statistics in parentheses.

Table 24–5 presents a similar analysis derived from regression estimates of days of hospital care by the elderly. Again, comparing elderly persons with comparable health status indicates that hospital episodes and hospital days increase directly with higher family income. No significant differences are observed, however, between public assistance recipients and other low-income elderly persons.

In summary, persons with incomes above $15,000 receive significantly more hospital care than lower-income persons with similar health condition, and this differential is not accounted for by a greater abundance of hospital facilities in higher-income areas or by higher levels of education.

Summary

Medicare benefits are distributed quite unequally among income classes. In spite of the better health condition of higher-income elderly persons, they receive more medical services and a more expensive mix of services. Furthermore, these differences are not attributable solely to certain advantages which most higher-income persons in the United States possess—such as more education or living in areas with a greater concentration of specialized medical resources. Instead, available evidence suggests that the structure of the Medicare program through its reliance on uniform cost-sharing provisions for all elderly persons may be largely responsible for the greater use of medical services by higher-income persons. Major findings include the following:

- Under the voluntary supplementary medical insurance part of Medicare which covers physician and other medical services, elderly persons with income above $15,000 receive twice the payments received by persons with incomes below $5,000.
- The average reimbursement per physician visit for higher-income persons is 50 percent higher than for lower-income persons. This difference in average price level is not purely a monetary difference, but reflects at least in part the tendency of higher-income persons to receive higher quality and more specialized services. While 75 percent of physician visits for lower-income persons are to general practitioners, only 65 percent of physician visits of higher-income persons are to such physicians.
- Adjusting for the poorer health status of the elderly poor, higher-income persons visit physicians almost 60 percent more frequently than lower-income persons with similar health conditions.
- Those poor persons covered by both Medicare and Medicaid receive substantially more medical services than other poor persons not covered by Medicaid.
- Elderly persons with incomes above $15,000 receive 45 percent more days of hospital care than lower-income persons with similar health conditions.

Race and Access to Medical Care

From its initiation, the Medicare program took the position that services were to be made available to all elderly persons on a nondiscriminatory basis. In order to qualify for eligibility in the program, hospitals were required to desegregate facilities for all patients—not just elderly patients. This provision was rigorously enforced with on-site examination to certify integration not just for the hospital as a whole but by assignment to semi-private rooms as well (Ball 1973). Although some hospitals, particularly in the South, initially elected not to serve Medicare patients, within a few years of operation of the program nearly all hospitals in the U.S. had indicated a willingness to meet Medicare certification requirements.

Evidence indicates that substantial reductions in racial disparities in the use of hospital care for all age groups occurred with the introduction of Medicare. As shown in Table 24–6, the rate of hospitalization of whites was 30 percent higher than that for blacks in 1961 and 1962. This situation had changed little by 1966, the year in which Medicare was initiated. But by 1968, the rate of white hospitalization was only 17 percent higher than that of blacks. While disparities between the races were greatest for elderly persons in the early 1960s, these had also been reduced substantially by 1968. These simple comparisons make no adjustment for health status. Since blacks tend to have more serious health problems than their white counterparts, equality in the rate of utilization of hospital services does not imply equal treatment for persons of equivalent health condition. The trends over the 1960s, however, are indicative of the possible impact of the Medicare program in reducing discriminatory barriers to hospitalization for all age groups.

Table 24–6   Average Hospital Utilization for the Elderly by Health Status and Family Income, Adjusted for Other Determinants

| Family income | Health Status[a] | | |
	Good	Average	Poor
		Hospital episodes	
Under $5,000	.114	.210	.362
$ 5,000 – 9,999	.140	.250	.427
10,000 –14,999	.159	.285	.472
15,000 and over	.177	.312	.512
		Hospital days	
Under $5,000	2.31	4.21	7.21
$ 5,000 –9,999	2.78	4.93	8.16
10,000 –14,999	2.85	5.02	8.29
15,000 and over	3.52	6.06	9.77

[a]See Table 24 –5 for definitions of health status levels.

While the Medicare program has had notable achievements in the area of access to hospital care for minority persons, the program has been less successful in assuring equality in treatment for other types of medical services, particularly physicians' services and nursing home services. The following sections first explore the extent of inequality of Medicare benefits by race, noting important regional variations in utilization patterns by race, and then investigate the underlying causes for these inequalities.

Medicare Services by Race

As shown in Table 24–7, Medicare reimbursements per person enrolled average $273 for whites, compared with only $195 for blacks and other races—or 40 percent higher average benefit levels for whites than for others. Disparities on the basis of race vary considerably by type of medical service. Inpatient hospital service differentials are fairly low. In the case of physicians' services, however, whites receive more than 60 percent higher payments than blacks. In part, this reflects the greater tendency for blacks to receive medical services in hospital outpatient departments, but even including hospital outpatient services, whites average 53 percent more benefits under the supplementary medical insurance plan than blacks. The most blatant inequality in distribution of benefits occurs for skilled nursing home services, with whites receiving more than double the extended-care facility benefits received by blacks.

Table 24–7   Persons Hospitalized per 1000 Population, by Race and Age, Selected Years

	White	Black and other races	Ratio, white to other
All ages			
1961–62	95	73	1.301
1966	103	81	1.272
1968	97	83	1.169
Under age 15			
1961–62	52	36	1.444
1966	58	43	1.349
1968	46	39	1.180
Age 15 to 44			
1961–62	125	114	1.097
1966	125	120	1.042
1968	113	116	.974
Age 45 to 64			
1961–62	98	68	1.441
1966	112	83	1.349
1968	102	90	1.133
Age 65 and over			
1961–62	114	78	1.462
1966	134	88	1.522
1968	158	126	1.254

Source: U.S. Department of Health, Education, and Welfare, National Center for Health Statistics, *Persons Hospitalized by Number of Hospital Episodes and Days in a Year, July 1960 – June 1962; July 1965 – June 1966; 1968,* Series 10, nos. 20, 50, and 64.

In all cases, differences in Medicare reimbursements between races are almost totally a reflection of differences in proportion of persons exceeding the Medicare deductible—rather than in other factors. As shown in Table 24–8, only 30 percent of blacks enrolled in the Medicare program receive any reimbursable services compared with 41 percent of whites. Thirty-nine percent of whites, but only 28 percent of blacks, receive reimbursement for physicians' services.

Table 24 – 8   Medicare Reimbursement per Person Enrolled, by Type of Service and Race, 1968

	White	Black and other races	Ratio, white to other
All Medicare services	$272.63	$194.68	1.400
Hospital and post-hospital services	194.10	146.59	1.324
Inpatient hospital services	175.00	136.98	1.278
Extended care facility services	17.03	7.84	2.172
Supplementary medical insurance services	82.70	54.20	1.526
Physicians' services	78.76	48.44	1.626
Hospital outpatient services	2.79	4.53	.616

Source: U.S. Department of Health, Education, and Welfare, Social Security Administration, Office of Research and Statistics, *Medicare: Health Insurance to the Aged, 1968, Section 1: Summary, Utilization and Reimbursement by Person, 1973.*

The only type of service for which the average Medicare reimbursement per service is substantially higher for whites than for blacks is private physicians' services, with average reimbursement per person served approximately 15 percent higher for whites than for blacks. This could reflect differences in number of services per person, differences in types of services, or differences in the average price charge per service. Although data are not available directly from the Medicare program on these components, the Health Interview Survey indicates that elderly blacks receive a greater proportion of their physician care from general practitioners than do elderly whites.[6] Part of the difference in average reimbursement levels, therefore, is undoubtedly attributable to less specialized medical care received by blacks.

It is not possible on the basis of aggregative data such as those published by the Medicare program to determine whether the quality of care received by blacks is comparable to that received by whites. The greater tendency of elderly blacks to receive medical care from hospital outpatient departments, however, strongly suggests that blacks receive more fragmented, impersonal care than whites who have greater access to private physicians.[7] The mere fact that blacks must turn to hospital outpatient departments for care to a greater extent than whites is itself a reflection of the failure of the Medicare program to provide equal treatment for all elderly persons.

---

6. Eighty-one percent of elderly black physician visits are to general practitioners, compared with only 70 percent of elderly white physician visits (calculated from the 1969 Health Interview Survey tapes).

7. Fifteen percent black elderly physician visits take place in hospital outpatient or emergency departments compared with 5 percent of white visits for medical care (calculated from 1969 Health Interview Survey tapes).

Regional data on Medicare reimbursements by race indicate some striking patterns. As shown in Table 24–9, the only region in which hospital benefits are substantially greater for whites than for blacks is the South—where Medicare reimbursement per person enrolled is 54 percent higher for whites than for blacks. Whites receive more physicians' benefits than blacks in every region, but in the South whites receive almost double the physicians' services received by blacks. Similarly, the disparity in extended-care facility services is widest in the South, with whites receiving two and one-half times the benefits received by blacks.

Table 24–9   Persons Served and Medicare Reimbursements per Person Served, by Type of Service and Race, 1968

	White	Blacks and other races	Ratio, white to other
	Persons served per 10000 enrollees		
All Medicare services	407.1	301.7	1.349
Hospital and post-hospital services	203.1	161.7	1.287
Inpatient hospital services	201.3	153.8	1.309
Extended care facility services	20.9	9.4	2.223
Supplementary medical insurance services	402.7	304.0	1.325
Physician services	394.9	279.4	1.413
Hospital outpatient services	71.6	89.9	.796
	Reimbursement per person served		
All Medicare services	$669.70	$645.19	1.038
Hospital and post-hospital services	932.75	906.72	1.029
Inpatient hospital services	869.47	890.36	.977
Extended care facility services	816.60	836.53	.974
Supplementary medical insurance services	205.34	178.27	1.152
Physicians' services	199.44	173.37	1.150
Hospital outpatient services	39.02	50.43	.774

Source: U.S. Department of Health, Education, and Welfare, Social Security Administration, Office of Research and Statistics, *Medicare: Health Insurance for the Aged, 1968, Section I: Summary, Utilization and Reimbursement by Person, 1973.*

The latest available data are for 1968. It is possible that some improvement in this pattern has been made in more recent years. However, since these patterns are found persistent well after the implementation of extensive civil rights legislation, there is genuine cause for alarm that the safeguards providing for nondiscriminatory practices in the Medicare program have not been sufficient to guarantee equal access to medical care for blacks and other minorities.

While discrimination is the most obvious explanation of differences among races in the use of medical services, other causes may contribute to the low utilization of blacks. Elderly blacks are poorer, have less education, are more concentrated in the South, and are sicker than elderly whites. Sorting out "pure" racial differences requires adjusting utilization patterns for these other possible sources of racial variation.

Data from the 1969 Health Survey make it possible to separate some of the independent effects of race on utilization of medical services (refer to Table 24–4). Holding constant for health status, income, welfare status, education, availability of physicians, and age and sex composition of the elderly population, low-income elderly blacks in the South have half as many physician visits as comparable whites. Differences by race, however, are not significant outside the South. No systematic differences in utilization of hospital services occur by race for the nation as a whole.

Summary

The Medicare program has contributed to the reduction of discriminatory barriers to medical care for all persons through its insistence that hospitals provide services on a nondiscriminatory basis as a prerequisite for participation in the Medicare program. In spite of the notable achievements in the area of access to hospital care for minority persons, however, the program has been less successful in assuring equality in treatment for other types of medical services, particularly physicians' services and nursing home services. The difficulties faced by elderly blacks in receiving equal access to these services is particularly regrettable in view of their poorer health status and limited supporting services in the home. The major findings regarding race and access to medical care under the Medicare program are the following:

- In 1968, whites received 30 percent more payments for inpatient hospital care per person enrolled than elderly blacks, 60 percent more payments for physicians' services, and more than twice the payments for extended-care facility services.
- In the South, disparities in benefits between races are even wider; whites received 55 percent more inpatient hospital care, 95 percent more payments for physicians' services, and more than two and one-half times the payments for extended-care services received by elderly blacks enrolled in Medicare.
- In 1969, 96 percent of elderly whites enrolled under the Medicare basic hospital insurance plan were also covered under the supplementary medical insurance plan, compared with 90 percent of elderly blacks. The disparities in physician payments per elderly person, therefore, are even wider than indicated by average payments per enrollee.
- Most of the difference in average reimbursement is a consequence of difference in proportion of enrollees served by the program—rather than in the average price of services.

–The lower utilization of medical services by blacks in the South is not attributable to their lower average incomes or poorer education. Even holding constant for these and other determinants of utilization such as health status, blacks in the South receive fewer physicians' services.

Geographical Variation in Medicare Benefits

Despite the national uniformity of the Medicare program, substantial variations in benefits occur according to geographical location. Elderly persons residing in the South and the North Central region receive far lower benefits than elderly persons in the Northeast and the West. As shown in Table 24–10, elderly persons in the West receive 32 percent more payments for inpatient hospital care than elderly persons residing in the South; 43 percent more physicians' benefits, and two and one-half times the payments for extended care facility services.

Table 24–10   Medicare Reimbursement per Enrollee for Selected Services, by Region and Race, 1968

	White	Black and other	Ratio, white to other
Inpatient hospital services			
All areas	$175.00	$136.98	1.278
Northeast	186.75	216.28	.863
North central	178.27	194.45	.917
South	156.99	101.87	1.541
West	197.71	181.34	1.090
Physicians' services			
All areas	$ 78.76	$ 48.44	1.626
Northeast	84.05	64.22	1.309
North central	64.44	51.85	1.243
South	76.80	39.37	1.951
West	102.86	80.17	1.283
Extended care facility services			
All areas	$ 17.03	$ 7.84	2.172
Northeast	18.28	8.81	2.075
North central	13.37	10.96	1.220
South	13.01	5.23	2.488
West	30.37	18.98	1.600

Source: Unpublished tabulations from the 1968 Medicare Summary based on bills for reimbursed services for a 5 percent sample of the enrolled population, Office of Research and Statistics, Social Security Administration, U.S. Department of Health, Education, and Welfare.

Different policy issues are raised by variations in the costs of medical care and in the use of medical services. Variation in the costs of medical care raises issues about the appropriate method of financing the program and the appropriate method of reimbursing providers of care. For example, under the SMI plan, the elderly pay a premium covering one-half the cost of the program. With a uniform premium assessment for all persons, persons in low medical cost areas pay not only the expected cost of their medical services but also a portion of the expected cost of services for elderly persons in high medical cost areas. Higher medical cost areas also tend to be higher-income areas. Therefore, the premium method of financing derives revenue neither on the basis of expected benefits nor on the basis of ability to pay, but instead transfers funds from elderly persons whose incomes tend to be lower to those whose incomes tend to be higher.

Somewhat paradoxically, medical care costs are also higher in areas with a greater availability of medical resources. Medicare follows the practice of reimbursing hospitals and physicians on the basis of prevailing costs and charges. Physicians practicing in scarcity areas and charging low prices, therefore, will continue to receive low levels of reimbursement for Medicare patients. Even though coverage under Medicare may stimulate demand by the elderly for additional medical services, the method of reimbursing physicians is not one which will serve to attract additional physicians to these areas.

Geographical variation in use of medical services under Medicare raises quite different kinds of questions. How much of the variation is a reflection of differences in health status, availability of medical resources, and various demographic determinants of medical care utilization? Are some elderly persons receiving inadequate or insufficient medical care? Are some elderly persons taking scarce medical resources away from younger age groups for medical problems that are not as severe?

The following sections first decompose variations in average benefits by use of services and by cost of services and then return to an examination of evidence bearing on these questions.

Persons Using Medicare Services

As shown in Table 24–11, hospitalization rates of the elderly are not particularly sensitive to geographical region. Persons living in the West, however, are much more likely to receive Medicare physician or extended care benefits than are persons in the South.

Several explanations of this regional pattern are possible. First, persons may be healthier in some regions than in others. Second, medical resources may be more abundant in some areas than others. In areas with many physicians, the time and travel costs involved in obtaining care may be lower, thus inducing more elderly persons to obtain medical care. In such areas, it may not be necessary for physicians to ration scarce physician time among elderly and nonelderly patients, so that with adequate financing more elderly persons obtain care. Or it may be that with an abundance of physicians, physicians encourage greater utilization greater requests for repeat visits.

The health status explanation, while perhaps accounting for some variation, does not adequately explain regional use patterns. As shown below, restricted activity days, bed disability days, and presence of limiting chronic conditions are more prevalent among the elderly in the South than in the West. However, elderly

Table 24-11   Medicare Reimbursement per Person Enrolled, Selected
Services, by Geographical Region, 1968

	All services	Inpatient hospital services	Physician services	Extended care facility services
United States	$266.56	$172.04	$ 76.42	$16.56
Northeast	293.55	187.99	83.13	18.27
North central	257.85	178.94	63.73	13.37
South	231.24	148.29	71.10	12.04
West	332.80	195.44	101.88	30.17
Ratio, West to South	1.44	1.32	1.43	2.51

Source: U.S. Department of Health, Education, and Welfare, Social Security Administration, Office of Research and Statistics, *Medicare, 1968: Section 1, Summary, 1973.*

persons in the North Central region are somewhat healthier than persons in other regions—so that part of the relatively low use of services by persons in the North Central region may be a consequence of their better health.

Availability of resources, however, appears to be a major contributor to variations in use of services. Both the South and the North Central regions have few patient-care physicians per capita (1.01 patient-care physicians per 1000 persons in the South and 1.09 in the North Central region). The Northeast and the West have much higher concentrations of physicians (1.59 in the Northeast and 1.43 in the West). Regional patterns in use of physician services, therefore, are quite consistent with regional patterns in numbers of physicians per capita.

Similarly, the regional pattern in utilization of extended-care facility services mirrors the availability of beds in those facilities. Extended-care facility beds are most widely available in the West (3.2 beds per 100 Medicare enrollees), and the proportion of hospitalized patients transferred to such facilities is correspondingly highest in the West. The South and the North Central region lag behind, both in the availability of extended care facility beds and in the proportion of Medicare enrollees receiving such services.

Interestingly, the one medical service for which utilization rates do not vary markedly by geographical region—inpatient hospital care—is also the service with the least geographical variation in availability. Twenty-one percent of Medicare enrollees in the South are hospitalized each year compared with 20 percent in the West. Hospital beds per capita, however, are also virtually the same in those two regions (3.74 beds per 1000 persons in the South and 3.72 beds per 1000 persons in the West).

Cost of Medical Services

Just as the regional variation in persons using Medicare services is largely a reflection of the availability of medical resources, regional variation in the average amounts reimbursed by Medicare to persons using services corresponds closely to the pattern of medical prices throughout the country. Average reimbursements are highest in the Northeast and West—areas that also have the highest levels of hospital costs and physician charges.

Regional variation in average reimbursements to persons receiving services, however, is not as substantial as the regional variation in persons receiving services. As shown in Table 24–12, persons using Medicare services in the West receive reimbursements only 15 percent above that received by the elderly in the South. Differences in reimbursement levels are most marked for hospital care— with reimbursement averaging $960 in the West and only $700 in the South.

Table 24–12   Persons Served under Medicare per 1000 Enrollees, Selected Services, by Geographical Region, 1968

	All services	Inpatient hospital services	Physician services	Extended care facility services
United States	397.8	197.1	385.6	20.3
Northeast	417.1	179.3	397.0	20.0
North central	383.6	208.5	358.0	16.8
South	388.7	214.1	368.6	17.1
West	490.6	202.9	476.4	36.0
Ratio, West to South	1.26	.95	1.29	2.11

Source: U.S. Department of Health, Education, and Welfare, Social Security Administration, Office of Research and Statistics, *Medicare, 1968: Section 1, Summary, 1973.*

Nearly all the variation in average reimbursements is accounted for a variation in prices of medical care—rather than in regional differences in the mix of services received. For example, hospital costs per day of hospital care are 40 percent higher in the West than in the South—accounting for nearly all of the difference in average hospital reimbursement levels between those regions. It is quite possible that the quality of hospital care, scope of services, or level of amenities are highest in the high cost regions. If so the elderly in high-cost regions in some sense receive "more" hospital care than elderly persons in other regions. However, even if this is the case, it does not appear that the regional variation in quality or style of hospital care received by the elderly is markedly different from that for younger age groups.

Similarly, it appears that regional variations in Medicare reimbursement for physician services per person served are largely a consequence of regional variation in physician charges—rather than a systematic difference in the mix of types of physician services (e.g., greater use of specialist physician services in the Northeast). Average reimbursement levels of physician services are lowest in the North Central region and highest in the West—but the average Medicare charge for an office visit to a general practitioner also ranges from a low of $7.50 in the North Central region to a high of $9.80 in the West (calculated from Medi-

Table 24–13   Health Status of the Elderly by Geographical Region, 1968–1969

	Restricted activity days per elderly person per year	Bed disability days per elderly person per year	Percentage of elderly persons with some limitation due to chronic conditions
United States	34.3	13.7	42.4
Northeast	31.3	13.1	39.4
North Central	30.9	11.4	39.6
South	38.8	16.6	49.5
West	37.3	13.6	38.9

Source: U.S. Department of Health, Education, and Welfare, National Center for Health Statistics, Age Patterns in Medical Care, Illness, and Disability, U.S. 1968–69 Series 10, no. 70, Tables 20 and 26.

care data on mean physician charges by specialty and by state and number of Medicare enrollees by state). Again, these price differences—even within a single specialty such as general practitioner services—may reflect some quality differences among regions.

Urban-rural Differences

Similar variations in Medicare benefits occur between rural and urban areas. As shown in Table 24–13, Medicare monthly reimbursement per person enrolled ranges from $30 in metropolitan counties with central cities compared with $21 in nonmetropolitan areas—or 40 percent higher in the central city county. Medicare monthly reimbursement for physician services per person enrolled are 56 percent higher in counties with central cities than in nonmetropolitan counties.

As in the regional variations, these variations are a reflection of the distribution of medical resources, the cost of health services in rural and urban areas, and Medicare reimbursement policies which reimburse urban physicians at a

Table 24–14   Reimbursement per Person Served, Selected Services by Geographical Region, 1968

	All services	Inpatient hospital services	Physician services	Extended care facility services
United States	$670.08	$ 872.75	$198.18	$817.05
Northeast	703.75	1,048.36	209.37	911.55
North Central	672.13	858.16	178.01	798.04
South	594.88	692.71	192.91	701.84
West	678.36	963.13	213.83	838.69
Ratio, West to South	1.140	1.390	1.108	1.195

Source: U.S. Department of Health, Education, and Welfare, Social Security Administration, Office of Research and Statistics, Medicare 1968: Section 1, Summary, 1973.

higher rate than rural physicians. Some rural areas are beginning to overcome the scarcity of physicians by establishing rural health centers staffed by nurse practitioners and physician assistants, with part-time physician services from larger, more distant communities. Medicare, however, does not reimburse for these services; nor does it certify these primary health centers as providers eligible for direct reimbursement. Thus, the Medicare program through its reimbursement policies is an obstacle to improved rural health care by freezing in place payment patterns based on the current system which in turn is biased in favor of urban areas.

Summary

Geographical variation in Medicare benefits raises somewhat different issues than those raised by differences on the basis of income or race. Some geographical variation in utilization of medical services by the elderly is undoubtedly desirable since medical resources are not uniformly distributed. Were the elderly's use of medical services not sensitive to available supply of hospitals or physicians, younger age groups in scarce resource areas could face even greater difficulty in obtaining adequate medical care. Major findings of an examination of regional differences in Medicare benefits are as follows:

-Medicare benefits are highest in the Northeast and the West, and lowest in the North Central region and the South. Elderly persons in the West receive 32 percent more payments for inpatient hospital care than elderly persons residing in the South: 43 percent more physicians' benefits; and two and one-half times the payments of extended care facility services.
-Most of the regional variation in hospital benefits occurs because of regional differences in hospital costs per patient day for all persons.
-About two-thirds of the difference in Medicare physician benefits between the West and the South is attributable to differences in number of persons receiving any services, with the remaining one-third attributable to physician charge levels in the two regions.
-Nearly all of the regional variation in nursing home benefits is accounted for by variations in the percentage of Medicare enrollees receiving such services—which in turn is largely determined by the availability of nursing home and hospital beds.

There are two major policy issues raised by the geographical variation in the distribution of Medicare benefits. First, since half of the funding for the physician portion of Medicare is derived from premiums set at uniform levels for all elderly persons, the program effectively transfers funds from elderly persons in the South and North Central regions to pay for medical care of elderly persons in the Northeast and West. Persons in the South and North Central region, therefore, are doubly disadvantaged both because they receive fewer services as a consequence of the relative scarcity of medical resources, and because they must subsidize the services received by persons in other areas. Alternative methods of dealing with this inequity are (1) elimination of the premium; (2) variation of the premium with geographical differences in expected benefits; or (3) perhaps even disproportionately lower premiums for elderly persons in shortage areas to compensate for the inconveniences generated by the scarcity of resources (perhaps greater reliance on home-care services from family members, longer waiting times for medical care, foregoing medical attention for minor, but perhaps painful, medical conditions).

Table 24–15   Medicare Average Monthly Reimbursement per Person Enrolled in Metropolitan and Nonmetropolitan Counties, by Region, January-December 1969

	Metropolitan Counties			Ratio, Central City Counties to Nonmetropolitan Counties
	With Central City	Without Central City	Nonmetropolitan Counties	
	Medicare monthly reimbursement per person enrolled			
United States	$29.85	$27.12	$21.16	1.41
Northeast	31.52	28.73	23.14	1.36
North Central	28.65	25.52	21.61	1.33
South	25.60	23.33	19.44	1.32
West	33.82	31.59	23.91	1.41
	Medicare monthly reimbursement for physician services per person enrolled			
United States	$ 8.53	$ 7.40	$ 5.48	1.56
Northeast	8.70	8.04	5.93	1.47
North Central	6.80	6.07	4.98	1.37
South	8.23	6.56	5.33	1.54
West	10.79	9.79	7.08	1.52

Source: Eugene C. Carter, "Health insurance for the aged: amounts reimbursed by state," U.S. Department of Health, Education, and Welfare, Social Security Administration, Office of Research and Statistics, H1–32, October 19, 1971.

The other major policy question raised by the geographical variation in Medicare benefits concerns the manner in which providers are reimbursed for services. Medicare follows the policy of reimbursing physicians on the basis of prevailing charges. Since areas in which physicians have been able to charge relatively higher prices for medical services in the past have attracted a disproportionate share of the nation's physicians, the Medicare program reinforces the poor geographical distribution of physicians by rewarding physicians for practicing in areas of relative physician abundance. Establishment of a uniform standard of physician reimbursement would eliminate these negative incentives for physician location, and, to the extent that the costs of medical practice are higher in areas of relative physician abundance, might even pose a positive incentive for physicians to locate in underserved areas.

Conclusions and Recommendations for Change

The distribution of benefits under the Medicare program, which has been in operation for eight years and now spends almost $15 billion annually on medical care services for the elderly, has somewhat surprisingly not been subjected to a thorough, in-depth examination. As a consequence, few fundamental changes in the program have been incorporated since its initiation. Such a gap in our knowledge is unfortunate not only because inequities have been permitted to persist for so long but also because experience with this program has not been scrutinized for its relevance to future financing plans such as national health insurance. This study has been conducted both so that the Medicare program—which has without question been an important force in improving the medical care of the elderly and in reducing the financial burden of medical care expenditures of many elderly persons—may be improved, and so that appropriate lessons may be drawn from the Medicare experience and applied to the design of national health insurance.

The major conclusion of the study is that a uniform medical care financing plan has not been sufficient to guarantee equal access to medical care for all elderly persons. Those elderly population groups with the poorest health are the lowest utilizers of medical care services under the program—the poor, blacks, and residents of the South. Furthermore, differences on the basis of income, race, and location are of sizeable magnitude. Elderly persons with incomes above $15,000 receive twice the payments for physician services as those received by persons with family incomes below $5,000. Whites receive 30 percent more payments for inpatient hospital care per person enrolled than elderly blacks, 60 percent more payments for physicians' services, and more than twice the payments for extended-care facility services. In the South, disparities in benefits between races are even wider. The Medicare program has also not resulted in a uniform standard of care in all geographical areas. Medicare benefits are almost 40 percent higher in the West than in the South.

Differences in Medicare benefits on the basis of income are not solely attributable to certain advantages which most higher-income persons possess, such as more education or living in areas with a greater concentration of specialized medical resources. Instead, available evidence suggests that the structure of the Medicare program, through its reliance on uniform cost-sharing provisions for all elderly persons, is largely responsible for the greater use of medical services by higher-income persons. Similarly, the lower utilization of medical services by elderly blacks is not attributable to their lower average incomes or poorer education.

Geographical variations in Medicare benefits are largely a reflection of regional patterns of availability of medical resources and costs of medical care.

Greater uniformity in use of medical services across geographical regions, there-fore, can not be achieved without remedying the underlying maldistribution of medical resources. The program, however, could help provide some incentives for a better geographical distribution of medical resources—particularly physi-cians—by redesigning the system of provider reimbursement. Furthermore, inequality of benefits on the basis of geographical location, as well as on the basis of income and race, call for a change in the uniform-premium method of financing the physician portion of Medicare.

Recommended Changes in the Medicare Program

Several changes in the Medicare program are required to reduce the inequities revealed by the current distribution of benefits. Four areas which seem particu-larly in need of reexamination are (1) the cost-sharing structure of Medicare, (2) efforts to improve access of minorities to medical care, (3) the sources of financ-ing for Medicare, and (4) the method of physician reimbursement.

Cost-Sharing   An examination of the use of services by elderly persons in dif-ferent income classes indicates that the deductible and coinsurance provisions of the physician portion of Medicare pose significant deterrents to use of medical services by many poor persons. For those poor persons "bought into" Medicare by state Medicaid plans—and hence exempt from cost-sharing requirements—use of medical services is commensurate with health needs and with utilization of middle-income persons. For poor persons not covered by Medicaid "buy-in" arrangements, use of medical services lags substantially behind that of higher-income persons with similar health conditions.

In addition to deterring access to adequate medical care for low-income elderly persons, the cost-sharing provisions can add significantly to the financial burden of many poor persons. Currently, as a result of the Medicare cost-sharing provisions, premiums for physician coverage, and noncovered services (such as drugs), the elderly now pay out-of-pocket, on average, more than $400 per per-son annually. Therefore, an elderly couple with only average medical expenses could expect to pay at least $800 for medical care. Such an expenditure repre-sents a fairly significant fraction of income for a couple with family income below $8,000.

For couples with unusually heavy medical bills, out-of-pocket costs can go much higher. Under the physician portion of Medicare, the patient is responsible for the first $60 of medical bills and 20 percent of all bills above that amount (plus any excess of the actual charge over the allowable charge if the physician does not accept assignment). Therefore, a patient with physician bills of $5,000 could expect to pay over $1,000 for physician services alone. Similarly, because of the limitations on hospitalization, an elderly person with a hospital stay of 150 days is required to pay over $3,000 toward the hospital bill (which can be substantially higher than $3,000 if he or she has already used part of the 60-day lifetime reserve).

In order to assure that lower-income elderly persons receive adequate access to medical care and that all elderly persons are protected from undue financial burdens, the following changes in the cost-sharing provisions of Medicare are recommended:

- –The deductible and coinsurance requirements of supplementary medical insurance should be graduated with income. All elderly persons below the poverty level should be exempted from deductible and coinsurance amounts. Deductible and coinsurance amounts should be gradually increased with income, reaching current levels only at an income level of approximately $7,000 or $8,000 for a two-person family. Some further increases in cost-sharing amounts might be appropriate for relatively higher income persons, such as above $12,000 or $15,000.
- –Similar changes in the cost-sharing provisions of the basic hospitalization plan should be made—with somewhat more substantial charges for higher income persons.
- –A ceiling should be placed on the cost-sharing amounts required of the elderly. This should be reasonable in relation to income (such as requiring that out-of-pocket payments by the elderly not exceed 10 percent of income) and should take account of the elderly's financial responsibility for noncovered services. To provide adequate protection against excessive financial obligations, some expansion in the scope of covered services is also called for—particularly coverage of all medically necessary hospitalization (rather than the restriction to 90 days for any one stay in a benefit period, plus a lifetime reserve of 60 days) and perhaps prescription drugs.

Access of Minorities to Medical Care   Much of the lower utilization of medical services by elderly minorities is undoubtedly a consequence of deep-seated discriminatory practices some of which will take time to correct. Solutions to this more basic underlying problem lie outside the scope of the Medicare program.

However, even within the Medicare program, certain enforcement practices should be strengthened to improve the access of minorities to medical care. The following areas seem particularly appropriate for more intensive enforcement:

- –Since disparities by race in use of extended care facility services are particularly severe, much stricter inspection and enforcement of nondiscriminatory provisions is called for.
- –Hospitals should be required to prove nondiscriminatory practices not only in the admission of patients, but also in the granting of staff privileges to physicians.
- –Physicians discriminating among patients on the basis of race should be ineligible for federal funds.
- –Informational efforts to advise minority elderly persons of their benefits and rights to medical care along with procedures for filing complaints of discriminatory treatment should be promoted.
- –Since the South remains the only major area where disparities in use of

hospital care by race are particularly marked, enforcement efforts should be concentrated more heavily in the South.

Sources of Medicare Financing   The method of financing the supplementary medical insurance plan half by a premium and half from general revenues is particularly in need of change. Because of the wide variation in benefits on the basis of income, race, and geographical location in premium bears little relation to the benefits which the individual can expect to receive. Furthermore, the premium requirement and the voluntary nature of the plan has the effect of excluding from Medicare benefits a dispropriate number of the poor and minorities.

Financing for the basic hospitalization plan comes from the payroll tax. As other studies have extensively documented (Pechman et al., 1968; Brittain, 1972), this method of financing medical expenses of the elderly falls disproportionately on low-income workers. Because of the rapid growth in Medicare expenditures since its initiation, the payroll tax has been steadily increased, and now represents a much larger share of all tax revenues. Reliance upon the payroll tax as a method of financing has also led to the exclusion of a few elderly persons from Medicare benefits on the grounds that they are ineligible for social security retirement benefits.

Recommended changes in the methods of financing Medicare include:

–Elimination of the premium for supplementary medical insurance plan.
–Coverage of all elderly persons, regardless of eligibility for social security retirement benefits, under both parts of Medicare.
–Reform in the structure of the payroll tax to reduce its burden on lower-income workers, or replacement of payroll tax funds with general revenues as a source of financing the basic hospitalization plan.

Reimbursement Policies   The method of reimbursing physicians on the basis of customary charges prevailing in the area rewards physicians for practicing in high-income areas—areas in which physicians are relatively abundant. This method of reimbursement reinforces existing geographical maldistribution of medical resources, and poses little positive incentive for an increase in the supply of services to underserved areas.

Furthermore, permitting physicians to charge patients more than the allowable charge has undercut any effort to maintain reasonable restraints on physician charges. Reducing allowable charges has the effect of saving the Medicare program, but does so simply by shifting those costs onto the elderly population.

For many rural areas, however, few physicians are available to provide services. Increasingly, rural communities are organizing to sponsor primary health centers, using the services of nurse practitioners and physician assistants. Backup physician support is obtained from larger communities to serve as referrals for more difficult cases and to monitor the quality of care. Medicare currently does not pay for such services, nor does it recognize the health centers as providers of care.

Three major changes in reimbursement policies should be considered:

–Move toward establishment of a nationally uniform reimbursement schedule for physician services, beginning with uniform fee schedules within each state. This would remove the negative incentives created by the present system and would act as a positive incentive toward redistribution, inasmuch as the costs of medical practice tend to be lower in underserved areas.

–Stipulate that physicians may not collect from the elderly any charge in excess of the Medicare allowable charge.

–Provide for the coverage of nurse practitioner services rendered in primary health centers meeting certain standards, and establish a separate reimbursement policy for such centers.

Implications for National Health Insurance

Experience with the Medicare program can also provide useful lessons for the design of national health insurance, particularly for the financing of medical care services for the nonelderly. While the major concern generated by the Medicare program is the impact of financing plans on costs of medical care, the distributional consequences of Medicare also have important implications for the design of national health insurance. There are three major lessons which may be derived from the very unequal distribution of benefits—even under a financing plan in which all persons are nominally eligible for equal benefits.

First, uniform cost-sharing provisions discriminate against lower-income persons in access to medical care. As a consequence, a disproportionate share of payments and medical services go to higher-income persons. The magnitude of this problem for the Medicare program is limited by the fact that few elderly persons have substantial incomes. Thus, even though elderly persons with incomes above $15,000 receive twice the physician payments received by persons with family incomes below $5,000, less than 10 percent of elderly persons are in the higher-income class, so the absolute amount of redistribution is not extensive. For the population as a whole, inequality in benefits of that dimension could cause fairly substantial redistributions in the share of goods and services received by persons of different income classes.

While uniform cost-sharing provisions can be quite inequitable, the absence of any cost-sharing is not only unlikely totally to eliminate such inequities but also to add to inflationary pressures on the cost of medical care. See Davis (1973) for a discussion of the relationship between third-party payments and medical care inflation. One way in which inequities in access to medical care on the basis of income can be reduced, and a greater proportion of funds channeled to those persons most in need both of medical services and in assistance in paying for those services, is a system of cost-sharing provisions systematically related to income. Such a plan might require no cost-sharing for persons below the poverty line, with gradual increases in cost-sharing amounts as income rises. A ceiling placed on the patient's financial responsibility for medical expenses, which is reasonable in relation to income, would ensure that such expenses did not form an undue financial burden on patients (see Fried et al., 1973, 120–126, for a discussion of several income-related, national health insurance plans).

The second major implication of the pattern of benefits under Medicare concerns the problems of minorities in achieving access to medical care. Rigorous enforcement of nondiscriminatory practices on the part of all providers of medical services must be an essential part of any financing plan. In addition, however, it is obvious that financing medical services and enforcement of nondiscriminatory provisions alone is inadequate to counter the persistence of discriminatory patterns. Instead, supplementation of national health insurance with specific supply programs designed to increase access of minorities to medical care is clearly called for. Expanded medical school scholarships for persons willing to practice in minority neighborhoods, subsidies to neighborhood health centers serving disadvantaged persons, and paramedical training programs designed to increase the supply of supporting medical personnel in minority neighborhoods are all promising approaches to reducing disparities in access to care.

The third implication of the distribution of Medicare benefits is the need for programs to improve the geographical distribution of medical care resources. If greater equality in access to medical care is to be achieved, special programs to increase resources in underserved areas—or to reduce the transportation costs for persons in shortage areas seeking care in more distant areas—must be undertaken. One step in this direction would be expansion of Medicare coverage to nurse-practitioner services, and inclusion of primary health centers as providers of health services.

References

Ball, R. M. Unpublished talk before the Health Staff Seminar, Washington, D.C., 1973.

Brittain, J. A. *The payroll tax for social security*. Washington, D.C.: The Brookings Institute, 1972.

Cooper, B. S., & Worthington, N. L. Age differences in medical care spending fiscal year 1972. *Social Security Bulletin 36 (5)* 1973: 14.

Corning, P. A, *The evolution of medicare*. DHEW (SSA) Office of Research and Statistics Research Report No. 29, Washington, D.C.: U.S. Government Printing Office, 1969.

Davis, K. Lessons of medicare and medicare and medicaid for national health insurance. Hearings before the subcommittee on Public Health and Environment Committee on Interstate and Foreign Commerce, U.S. Congress (December 12) 1973.

Feldstein, M. S. An econometric model of the medicare system. *Quarterly Journal of Economics 85 (1)* 1971: 1–20.

Feldstein, M. S. The quality of hospital services: An analysis of geographic variation and intertemporal change. In M. Perlman (Ed.) *Economics of Health and medical care*. New York: Halsted, 1974.

Fried, E. R., Rivlin, A. N., Schultze, C. L., & Teeters, N. H. *Setting national priorities: The 1974 budget.* Washington, D.C.: The Brookings Institute, 1973.

Koropecky, O. & Huang, L. *The effects of the medicare method of reimbursement on beneficiaries' utilization.* Volume II, Part II of the contract report submitted by Robert R. Nathan Associates to the Social Security. Administration, 1973.

Marmor, T. *The politics of medicare.* Chicago: Aldine, 1973.

Pechman, J. A., Aaron, H. J., & Taussig, M. K. *Social Security.* Washington, D.C.: The Brookings Institute, 1968.

Peel, E., & Scharff, J. The impact of cost-sharing on use ambulating services under medicare, current medicare survey, 1969. *Social Security Bulletin 36 (10)* 1973.

Somers, H. M., & Somers, A. R. *Medicare and the hospitals: Issues and prospects.* Washington, D.C.: The Brookings Institute, 1967.

U.S. Department of Health, Education, and Welfare, *Fifth annual report on medicare for fiscal year 1971,* 1971.

Tobin, J. Estimation of relationships for limited dependent variables. *Econometrica 26 (1)* 1958: 24 – 36.

The Necessity and Control of Hospitalization   25

JULIUS A. ROTH

Justifying Hospitalization

Institutions for the resident care of the sick have a very long history. In Europe
they appear to have been in existence throughout most of the Middle Ages as
one of the functions of the established churches. It is not my intention to provide
a history of hospitals. I have a point to make, and I am going to give just enough
historical background to make that point.[1]

In writings about the early-nineteenth-century hospital, these institutions are
sometimes referred to as pest-houses. They were scarcely medical instititions in
the sense that we think of them today. They were charity institutions, usually
operated by religious groups to care for the poor and unwanted who also happened to be sick. They were depressing and frightening places for the patients.
The rate of hospital-acquired infections was extremely high. The mortality rate
was high. The professional medical care was limited, sometimes nonexistent.

In the latter part of nineteenth-century England and the United States, the
hospital began to be used by prominent physicians and surgeons as a convenient place to treat certain kinds of cases. This was especially true of the developing specialties. This introduced a middle-class clientele who desired private
accommodations, and led to the improvement of hospitals both as medical treat-

From *Social Science and Medicine 6* 1972. © 1972, Pergamon Press, Ltd. Reprinted with
permission.

1. For a brief history of European and American hospitals, see George Rosen, The hospital: Historical sociology of a community institution. In Eliot Freidson (Ed.) *The Hospital in Modern Society*. Glencoe, Ill.: Free Press, 1963. For a more detailed history of British hospitals, see Brian Abel-Smith, *The
hospitals in England and Wales 1800–1948*. Cambridge, Mass.: Harvard University Press, 1964.

ment institutions and as a place where the more prosperous patient could find a level of comfort somewhat above that of the workhouse.

This trend continued in the Western world into the twentieth century, with the various aspects interacting with one another to steadily increase the use of hospitals for a wider and wider range of medical diagnosis, treatment, and convalescence. As the domestic aspects of hospitals improved and the death rate decreased, acceptance of hospitalization by the higher socioeconomic segments of the population (the ones most likely to engage physicians' services) increased. The more the specialists used the hospital, the more convenient they found it and the more they insisted that patients be hospitalized to receive "proper care." The greater the use by specialists, the more the hospitals had to be geared to supply the facilities (equipment and assistant personnel) for specialists' practices.

By the time we get well into the twentieth century, hospitals had come to be thought of as the center of "scientific medicine." This was the place most doctors preferred to put patients for any illness which was at all serious, or which required the use of expensive equipment or the assistance of other medical personnel, and sometimes even for routine diagnostic work-ups. Many members of the public considered the hospital the place to be if one were "really sick." Medical schools organized almost their entire clinical training around hospital cases. In England, and to a large extent in other British Commonwealth nations, most specialist practices became almost entirely hospital practices. The urban general practitioner became a second-class doctor largely because he had limited access to hospital beds. The National Insurance Scheme in England and later the National Health Service tended to promote this dichotomy.

In the United States, home calls had virtually ceased by mid-century. If a matter could not be taken care of in a doctor's office, the patient belonged in a hospital. The kinds of hospital appointments a doctor had was an important determinant of the kind of practice he could acquire. Almost everyone who wrote about hospitals declared how much better they were than at an earlier time and how fortunate our population was to have access to such good medical care.

This trend might be expected to continue. Hospitals could expand their services to include still more medical care, even the relatively minor aspects, especially for diagnostic purposes. Medical practitioners could eliminate home calls—already almost accomplished in the United States—and relegate more of their office practice to the hospital—already largely the case for specialists under the British system. Regional medical centers could be developed for in-patient treatment of all complex or difficult diagnostic and treatment problems of a wide geographical area. There has been some movement toward this latter plan in both England and the United States, although at this point it is very incomplete. The general attitude to such a move toward greater use of hospital in-patient services would be: If you are really sick, you belong in the hospital. This philosophy is already applied to certain populations who are removed from their usual family relationships; for example, the military, resident students.

But this trend has not continued unabated. In fact, in some areas it has been reversed. Around the middle of the twentieth century, doubt about such complete dependence on hospitals for medical care began to develop. More and more criticisms were made of certain aspects of hospital care.

One category of criticism is based mainly on the studies and critical commentary of medical and public health specialists and medical care investigators. Another category is based largely on the work of social scientists. And another is based mainly on the analyses of economists. Let me summarize briefly the three types of criticisms of hospital care.

Hospitals are Dangerous Places

Brian Abel-Smith in his book on British hospitals quotes Florence Nightingale as writing "the very first requirement in a hospital [is] that it should do the sick no harm" [2, p. 1]. Abel-Smith says the early British hospitals failed to meet this requirement. Many observations of present-day hospitals in the United States, Australia, and elsewhere suggest that they too do not meet this requirement.

True, hospitals are much less dangerous than the old pest-house. The mortality rate is far lower (although we still have a few special institutions where most patients die). This lower mortality rate is one of the things speech-makers have in mind when they tell us how far hospital care has improved over the last century. But still, regardless of how great the improvement over the pest-house may be, hospitals can still be regarded as dangerous compared to some ideal, but potentially obtainable, standard.

Let us take, for example, the issue of hospital-acquired infections. In one U.S. study of five university medical centers, the post-surgical infection rate was close to 10 percent. A survey of a pediatric unit showed that 6.5 percent of the patients acquired infections following admission, in most cases traced to a hospital source. Such hospital-acquired infections tend to be more resistant to treatment than those acquired at home. Various common hospital procedures, such as injections, urethral catherization, and cut-downs are associated with significant infection rates.[2]

A number of epidemics in hospital nurseries have been reported in recent years. Hospital cross-infections continue to be a serious problem despite the special facilities in hospitals to control pathogenic organisms and personnel trained in aseptic and antiseptic techniques.

Other studies have looked into errors made by hospital personnel. Perhaps the most carefully researched is the area of medication errors by nurses. It has been estimated that 15 percent of all medication orders in United States general hospitals are not given or are given incorrectly.

A disguised observation in one hospital revealed a number of medication errors which, if projected, indicated a yearly estimate of 51,000 errors in that hospital alone [4]. Of these, there were

---

2. A comprehensive, though somewhat floridly written, compilation of the dangers of hospital treatment is provided by Martin L. Gross, *The doctors*. New York: Dell, 1966, chap. 5. Infections are discussed on pp. 179–92.

37 percent omissions
18 percent given, but not ordered
13 percent underdoses
8 percent overdoses
10 percent extra doses
10 percent incorrect time
4 percent wrong form of medication.

Projected to all of the U.S., this would be about 100 million a year or

four for each acute hospital patient
one out of every six medications orders
more than one a day for the average patient.

In the disguised study, the best nurse made an error in filling 1 out of 13 medication orders; the poorest 1 out of 3.

In a recent conference in Perth, a pharmacist reported British surveys in which, in one case, "it was found that 20 percent of drugs prescribed to patients were wrongly administered," and in another hospital the error was said to be 25 percent. These figures are close enough to the U.S. findings to suggest a common pattern in the difficulty of controlling the administration of doctors' medication orders in hospitals. Even though the great majority of these errors do no serious harm, the threat to the patient's health from a proportion of mistakes on such a grand scale is obviously substantial.[3]

Nursing errors, other than those involving medications, have not been examined as carefully, but my own observations in hospitals convince me that nonmedication procedures probably have an even higher rate of error. For example, doctors' orders for turning comatose or partially paralyzed patients at regular intervals are ignored or forgotten more often than they are carried out. Changes of dressings are often forgotten or done so improperly that the protective effect of the dressing is impaired. Instances of neglect to change oxygen bottles or intravenous infusions are common. Vital signs, intake-output measures, and other records are frequently forgotten. Patients sometimes fall from beds because bed rails or other restraints have been neglected.[4] And so on. In fact, almost every hospital patient whose care requires a series of nursing procedures or errands

3. Several other studies—e.g., Miriam A. Safren and Alphonse Chapanis, A critical incident study of hospital medication errors, *Hospitals* 34 1960: 32–34, 57–66, and B. C. Hoddicott, et al., Drug reactions and errors in administration on a medical ward. *Canadian Medical Association Journal* 97 1967: 1001–06, report error rates which are very much smaller, a fraction of one percent. All such studies rely on nurses to report their errors. Kenneth N. Barker and Warren E. McConnell (How to detect medical errors. *Modern Hospital* 99 1962: 95–106) showed that such self-report reveals only a tiny proportion of the errors committed, a result which anyone familiar with the literature on the sociology of occupations could have predicted.

4. For a catalog of hospital "accidents" see Martin L. Gross, *The doctors.* New York: Dell, 1966, and Henry M. Parrish and Thomas P. Weil, Patient accidents occurring in hospitals: Epidemiological study of 614 accidents. *New York State Journal of Medicine* 58 1958: 838–46, although the studies cited obviously suffer from gross underreporting.

carried out by auxiliary personnel is likely to have a portion of them not performed or incorrectly performed. The more medically sophisticated patient (and sometimes this simply means someone who has been through the same thing before) will often realize what is happening and become quite frustrated by the apparent impossibility of obtaining the service he thinks he should be getting.

But it is not only in nursing procedures where mistakes are made. Doctors, technicians, and other hospital staff provide their share as well. Failure to call upon consultants when needed is common [3, p. 259]. Injury during diagnostic procedures, or surgery to the wrong patient or to the wrong part of a patient are fairly common errors in hospitals. And add to this list: sponges, instruments, and other foreign bodies left inside patients; induced labor when there is no medical indication for it; unnecessary, careless, or incompetent surgery on a very large scale—almost half of the total surgery cases according to the Trussel study in New York City [3, pp. 229–233, 245–249; 8]. And there is the "laboratory error," probably just as ubiquitous in American hospitals as the medication error and sometimes leading to diagnostic inferences which are seriously mistaken. Anesthetists contribute their many errors of judgment and technique and insufficient post-surgical follow-up—causes for an estimated 10,000–30,000 deaths in the United States according to one study [3, pp. 192–202]. Another common source of error are the blood transfusion accidents—mislabeling, misidentification of patients, blood mismatch, and contamination [3, pp. 205–208].

The rationale which is sometimes given for hospitalization is that it will make prompt medical attention available if needed by the patient. This is perhaps the most absurd argument of all. There is probably *no* place where it is more difficult for a patient to gain access to a doctor when he wants one than on a hospital inpatient service. Rather than being able to call a doctor on the telephone or to take himself off to a hospital casualty department, he is placed in a position where he must filter his request through a nursing staff which has been taught that doctors should not be disturbed except in the most urgent circumstances—and their conception of urgency often differs radically from that of the patient. As a result, a patient is usually unable to get attention for a significant symptom or to obtain relief from discomfort as quickly as he could if he were at home. Hospital inpatient services, far more even than telephone answering services and receptionist barriers, are designed to keep the patient from seeing the doctor when he needs one.

Most Patients Find Hospitals Very Unpleasant, Entirely Aside from the Effects of Their Illness or the Diagnostic and Treatment Procedures

This proposition first became evident to students of hospital life in the case of mental hospitals where it was found that most patients not only reacted bitterly against hospitalization—particularly during the early part of their stay—but that much of their symptomatology came to be ascribed, by critics of mental hospitals, to the effects of hospitalization itself rather than to the mental disorder from which the patient was supposedly suffering. Even in recent years many medical people on the staff of mental hospitals have begun to say that their institutions are destructive to the psyche and that we should avoid placing people in them if possible, or get them out as quickly as we can if they *must* be hospitalized. The state of California is now engaged in a massive depopulation-of-mental-hospitals program, partly as a result of this kind of criticism.[5]

We might argue—and some people have argued—that the mental hospital is a special case. Naturally their inmates will not like it because most of them have been put there against their will, and besides, their illness would make any social situation difficult for them. This argument does not hold up. We find that the things which disturb mental hospital patients about their institution are only slight exaggerations of the things that disturb most people about all kinds of hospitals.

In the hospital, one's plan of life is totally disrupted, not so much by one's illness or treatment, but by the organization of routines designed for the convenience of other people who are not interested in one's overall welfare, but only in very limited aspects of it—and *that* very inefficiently. Many of the staff demands have no conceivable rationale to the patients—they are not even able to offer a rationale when directly asked, in many cases. Yet the patient cannot successfully defy the staff unless he abandons his treatment and leaves the hospital. And the various parts of the medical-care structure are so intimately related that his doctor is likely to refuse to treat him outside the hospital if he leaves the hospital against advice. The general hospital is so organized that even the physically able ambulatory patient cannot take care of his own needs. At the same time, he is often frustrated by his lack of success in trying to get hospital personnel to take care of those needs for him.

I have seldom found a person who was a patient who was not glad to get out of hospital, both among my own acquaintances and among those I have talked to in the course of my hospital studies. This includes both acute and chronic disease institutions. Those who say they do not want to get out are almost always those who have literally nowhere to go—who have been abandoned by their family and friends, who have no funds, and who are physically or otherwise unable to lead a viable existence by themselves, or whose life on the outside was of exceptionally poor quality. I am afraid that the psychiatric literature has given a misleading picture of patients' desires to stay in the hospital. When I was carrying out my study of tuberculosis hospitals, I repeatedly came across papers by psychiatrists describing patients who resisted being discharged after their tuberculosis was under control. Yet, in my own stay in tuberculosis hospitals, I rarely met a patient who was not extremely anxious to get out and, in fact, over half of them, according to a variety of studies, left the hospital (prematurely) against medical advice. On those rare occasions where I did observe a patient who did not want to leave, he was considered by the staff to be a very strange creature, and consequently *was referred to a psychiatrist.* I gradually came to realize why most

---

5. A good summary of this view of the mental hospital is the Dilemma of Mental Hospital Commitments in California: A Background Document, California Legislature, Assembly Interim Committee on Ways and Means, 1967.

psychiatric articles about tuberculosis patients dealt with patients who did not want to leave the hospital.

Ironically, it tends to be the sickest and most dependent patients who most dislike the hospital and are most anxious to leave, although they are precisely the ones who are most unlikely to be able to leave. Those who feel well and are permitted considerable freedom of movement, perhaps even leaving the hospital for periods of time, are more likely to find the hospital tolerable for a time. Most *doctors* intensely dislike hospital patients even though they are treated incomparably better by the staff than is the ordinary patient.

Although dangerousness and unpleasantness have been dealt with as separate topics, it should be noted that in practice, there is considerable overlap between the two. Some of the things which make a hospital dangerous are the same things that make it unpleasant. Just as the patients' medications and other treatments are often forgotten, so urinals and bed pans are forgotten repeatedly. Just as the control of the patient's treatment is taken out of his hands and information about his treatment hidden from him (thus losing an important means of control of error), so his time and manner of waking, going to bed, eating, and other activities are imposed on him and he is discouraged from participating in the ordering of his daily pattern of life, offered no rationale for the demands made upon him, and punished if he does not conform.

Hospital Treatment Is An Extremely Costly Way to Treat Most Ailments

This statement is not always true. In underdeveloped countries, collecting the sick in one place is often the cheapest way to provide medical diagnosis and treatment. But as industrial development proceeds, a common pattern is for the costs of institutional operations to rise faster than other costs and a gap appears between treating a person in hospital and treating him outside, for many types of illness and diagnostic procedures—a gap unfavorable to hospital treatment. This has reached its greatest extent in the United States, but other Western countries are moving in the same direction. In any area or country where hospital costs are rising, the difference between cost of care in a hospital and care at home becomes an ever-more-pressing issue.

Why spend in the neighborhood of $50–$100 a day for room and board and general nursing care to keep a person in hospital, when by living at home he might, for a fraction of that cost:

Be visited by a nurse to give an injection or other treatment
Be brought into a clinic for a test or treatment procedure
Be visited by a doctor for an examination and advice
Be provided with nursing care by his family under the advice of a doctor

Of course, if a hospital is already in operation, the unit cost of adding more patients is relatively small. It is when the hospitals of a given region are being used to capacity and construction of new hospitals is being considered that the cost factor becomes a major issue. And such a strain on hospital facilities is what we have almost everywhere in the English-speaking world at the present time. Before appropriating funds for expansion, government administrators and legislators ask: Is there some other (less expensive) way to deal with these needs? Although the California depopulation scheme for mental hospitals is based on an ideological argument, the thing that got it started was the state government's reluctance to go to the expense of replacing condemned buildings in some of their older mental hospitals.

I consider the cost argument the least compelling of all the arguments for limiting hospital care, but it must be given serious attention because it has great impact on those responsible for the public treasury. An ideological argument may not move them, especially when it is obvious that the subject is controversial and any action will alienate *some* constituents. But show the officials that you can save them money without suffering a deterioration in the end product and you may well win their support.

If we take the position that hospital inpatient services are not necessarily the best places to carry out diagnostic procedures or to treat and care for the sick, we may approach the issue of hospitalization along a different line. Instead of justifying *not* going to hospital or leaving hospital once one is in, we might, rather, insist that hospitalization be justified in each case and that every additional day's stay be justified anew. *And there should be no type of procedure or illness exempt from requiring such justification.* Surely, you may say, some things such as major surgery, cannot be considered outside hospital. But when the King of Greece needed major surgery, he had it done in his palace. Surgical equipment and the surgical team were moved to the palace instead of the king moving to the hospital. But, you say, most people do not have the social power or the financial resources of a king. Quite true. You have just provided a justification for performing major surgery in a hospital in the great majority of cases, under the social conditions currently present in our Western society. It is such a process of justification which we should force ourselves to go through repeatedly. We will then find that in many cases we can do things outside of the hospital that we have routinely done on an inpatient service. The need for justification will stimulate our imaginations to find methods which do not require hospitalization. (Comparisons with other places can be helpful here.) It will also make us alert to changes in technology, social demands, and social conditions which will permit procedures which are now most effectively done in hospital to be done just as effectively on the outside. The day may well come when major surgical procedures can be performed on most people, safely and efficiently, in an outpatient clinic or in the patient's home, but we may miss the change in conditions if we fall into the rut of thinking that "of course, major surgery can be done only in hospital." It is here that the king of Greece did us a service. His decision demonstrated that major surgery in hospital is not an absolute rule, but merely a matter of social and economic convenience. (I will admit that the moral of my story is somewhat tarnished by the fact that the king died several weeks after his surgery.)

Once one is sensitized to the notion of convenience as a major factor in hospitalization, many examples can be found. Thus, in the United States, the pattern of insurance coverage affects the rates of hospitalization for given categories of ailments. In Australia, people in country areas are hospitalized much more often than those in cities. Why? Because there are fewer outpatient facilities provided in the country and it is more difficult for patients and doctors to travel to and fro. Residents of Melbourne are hospitalized less often than residents of Sydney. Why? Because Victoria has 20 percent fewer beds per 1000 population and therefore urban Victorian hospitals have long waiting lists and many people (and their doctors) tire of the wait and find other ways to handle their health problems.[6]

If we are going to try to get people out of hospital inpatient services as much as possible, we must consider alternatives. For the most part, this is not a matter of thinking up completely new approaches. This trend has already begun. We can, however, make it a matter of principle and planning rather than accident and drift.

Let me comment on some of the more obvious alternatives:

Medical Care in the Home

In this day and age when home visits by doctors have been on the wane for years and have almost completely disappeared in large parts of the United States, recommending more medical care in the home may seem like an absurdity. Yet the advantages of home care to many patients, and even for some medical personnel, seems obvious, and a number of United States medical centers have been launching home-care programs in recent years. These programs are still on a small scale and are usually called experimental, but they may portend a major alternative to inpatient medical care in the future. Many patients in hospitals do not need professional medical attendance the greatest part of the time. Care by family members plus occasional visits by medical personnel may serve as well or better. "Medical personnel" does not necessarily mean doctors. Visiting nurses are already doing a job and could do a bigger one. If we could break away from the notion that nursing is primarily a hospital function (and this, after all, has been the case for only about half a century), we might be willing to train for, and offer desirable careers for, community nursing, which would attract a much larger number of nurses (or doctors' assistants, for other nondoctor medical aides) into community health care. It is absurd to say that it cannot be done because there are not enough nurses or other medical professions available. If the conditions are made sufficiently attractive, there will be enough, and if we are sufficiently convinced that this is a useful program, we will make job conditions more attractive, and we will create new occupational categories (such as the phy-

---

6. Statistical data on hospitalization in Australia can be found in J. S. Deeble and R. B. Scotton, Health care under voluntary insurance, Technical Paper No. 1, University of Melbourne, Institute of Applied Economic Research, 1968.

sicians' assistants program now being launched in the United States) to fill the need.

Home care programs in the United States are being used for some of the following types of care:

Patients needing injections once or twice a day or once or twice a week (or other similarly brief treatments)

Partially disabled patients who can do much for themselves or with family assistance, but need periodic checkups (perhaps by social workers, physical therapists, nurses, as well as doctors)

Seriously chronically ill (perhaps terminal) patients whose families prefer to have them at home, but who need periodic examinations and/or treatment

A thorough survey of home-care programs would no doubt reveal other categories of patients receiving this service.

If we apply the need for justification of hospitalization, we should be suspicious of the reason that the patient is unable to take care of himself and is unable to come to the outpatient department. In many of these cases, home care can be arranged once a home-care organization *has been established.*

Efforts at establishing home-care services and providing for the expansion of these services in the future are already being made in some parts of Australia. A hospital being constructed in Perth, for example, has included in its plans a home-care building which will constitute a center out of which medical, nursing, social service, and domestic care services will carry out direct patient care in the community, on a major scale. Canberra too is making a deliberate effort to include substantial home-care programs in the planning of health facilities for its expanding suburbs. The Royal Newcastle Hospital operates a large and comprehensive home-care program for its geriatric population. It is my impression that such services are on a more comprehensive scale in Australia than in the United States.

Outpatient Clinics

Outpatient clinics are usually part of a hospital, but may be physically removed as independent community clinics. Such clinics must have diagnostic facilities and many of the treatment facilities of a complete general hospital. The outpatient department is, of course, already in large-scale operation throughout much of the world. But these clinics could take on even more of the medical diagnosis and treatment if we were to ask, in each case, whether the task could be carried out just as well on an outpatient basis as on an inpatient service. We could encourage the use of outpatient clinics by better staffing and better and more complete equipment. Outpatient clinics are now often the step-child of the inpatient services. They should be made a central service of general and specialized practices and in the training of medical students, residents, nursing students, and other personnel-in-training. After all, this is where most people are treated for most ailments—the greatest variety of medical conditions.

An important advantage of the outpatient clinic is that it gives the patient and his family more control over their health regimen and over their relationship to medical personnel, and leaves them free to control their lives except during that relatively short period in the clinic. In most cases, too, this form of medical care is far less costly than the inpatient service.

Transport Services

Some patients, although able to get on at home for the most part, must have access to equipment or scarce personnel which can be found only in a hospital. If they are unable to get to the hospital or clinic by themselves or with help of family members or friends, this is commonly considered a reason for hospitalization as inpatients. But this need not follow. Public transport of ambulatory and bedridden patients can be arranged. This in fact, is now done on a large scale in urban areas in New South Wales. In Sydney, during the day on weekdays, the major task of the Central District Transport Ambulance Service is taking people from home to hospital clinics (occasionally to doctors' surgeries) and back home again. This may be a one-shot service: the doctor wants a bedridden patient to have a diagnostic procedure carried out in hospital, and he calls the ambulance service and arranges to have the patient delivered to hospital and then home again. Or it may be a repeated service: the doctor wants his patient to have physical therapy in the hospital rehabilitation center five days a week; each day an ambulance delivers the patient to hospital and later returns him home, often using a buslike vehicle carrying a number of patients at once. Ambulance and hospital administrators in Sydney are now working on plans to make the whole process more efficient so that it can be used on an even greater scale. There are similar transport services in most Australian cities.

Many areas are not equipped for mass transport of patients. No part of the United States has an ambulance organization comparable to that of New South Wales. But if we are convinced of the desirability of such an arrangement, both for its economy and for the satisfaction of the patient, it certainly can be organized almost anywhere.

Patients coming long distances who cannot return home after each procedure (for example, patients from New South Wales country towns coming to Sydney hospitals) need not necessarily be hospitalized. If they do not need the full panoply of acute hospital services, there is no reason for them to occupy an acute hospital bed other than the lack of other accommodation. "Other accommodation" could be hotel-type arrangements near the hospital from which the patient could attend hospital outpatient clinics as needed. A few major American clinics, for example the Mayo Clinic, already have such an arrangement. It deserves consideration elsewhere.

Casualty Department

Outpatient departments, as they are commonly organized, have some disadvantages for certain kinds of people and certain kinds of cases. They are often run on an appointment-only basis with the appointments having to be made days or even weeks in advance. They are usually organized entirely into specialty services, especially under British tradition. This means that the patient's ailment must already have been classified and a referral made.

This form of organization leaves out the patient who desires more prompt attention or who is making his first contact. It does no good to say that he should see a private doctor—for a variety of reasons, including unavailability of doctors and their expense, patients often do not wish to do this or cannot do it. Besides, if the environment of a hospital or a clinical center is so important to good medical practice as medical publicists claim, why the strong insistence on having the patient consult an isolated practitioner who must often send the patient to hospital anyway for tests or X-rays or specialist consultation.

Casualty departments in Australia and emergency wards in the United States have been filling this need to some extent. The fact that their clientele is rapidly increasing in numbers shows the utility such service has to the public. Medical personnel working in casualty departments, or those administering such a service, almost always complain about how this service is being misused (or "abused" as they say in the United States) by the public. It might be more helpful if we recognize that this 24-hour unscheduled clinic is performing a vital community service and try to improve its function, rather than complaining of the interference with the accident center by people with nonurgent problems who should go to their general practitioner.

All these suggestions for facilities other than inpatient services leave a greater degree of control in the hands of the patient or his agent. The value assumption here is that medical care personnel and organizations should serve people rather than rule their lives. If it is believed that people are not following appropriate practices for healthful living, an effort can be made to persuade them to change rather than coercing them to change temporarily while they are under the control of medical authority. In any case, people should be allowed their own choices on matters of health care as in other things, even choices that medical experts believe will lead to ill health (and remember that experts have often been mistaken in the past).

Through most of nineteenth-century England and the United States, hospitals were mainly institutions for the care of the sick poor, "whose home conditions were deficient in the accommodation their distress needed" [1, p.24]. The wards were crowded, hygienic conditions were poor, and the nursing was primitive. In 1877, W. Gill Wylie, a prominent English physician, asserted that hospital care did more harm than good by removing the "healthful stimulus of necessity" that was essential to recovery. In his opinion, hospitalization should be limited "to those who have no homes and to those who cannot be assisted at their homes" [1, p. 26].

Although hospital care in advanced industrial countries has undoubtedly improved enormously over the last century, the deficiencies of hospitals are still such that we should consider applying Dr. Wylie's principle today, perhaps modifying "home" to include outpatient clinics, 24-hour clinics, day hospitals, and similar agencies.

In view of the response I received when I set forth my views in lectures to medical audiences, let me make clear what I have *not* said.

I have not said that hospital inpatient services should close down or that large categories of patients now commonly treated on an inpatient basis should be systematically eliminated from the hospital. I can think of many types of medical services in which, under present conditions of social organization and the state of medical art, I would prefer to have performed in hospital myself. What I *am* saying is that the place for performing a given type of medical care is a matter of convenience and therefore as the social organization and the state of medical art changes, considerations of convenience also change and our conceptions of what may best be performed in hospital and what may best be performed elsewhere will change. We will not keep abreast of changes that have occurred, or changes which we may want to bring about, unless we make a point of justifying hospitalization at every step.

For example, for observation of a serious medical condition, one might argue:

1. It should be done in hospital because it is the best place for carrying out medical diagnosis and treatment.

Or one might argue:

2. There would be undue strain upon highly trained medical personnel in scarce supply if they were required to visit patients' homes for such a purpose.

Does it make any difference which argument we use? In either case, the patient ends up in hospital. Are such differences in rationale mere academic quibbling? I contend that there is a crucial difference between such arguments. The first is an overgeneralized homily, demonstrably incorrect in some cases. The second argument is an effort at justification of hospitalization for certain kinds of medical (and social) categories of patients. The first assumes a constant condition. The second assumes the possibility of change. It identifies what changes in conditions may change our views on the necessity of hospitalization. Even more important, it points out changes we would need to make hospitalization less necessary, for example: increase trained personnel through more training programs and by making professional careers more attractive; reorganizing the tasks involved so that less trained persons (perhaps the patient or his family) can do some part of it themselves. It is this process of justification—a process which reveals the underlying conditions of social convenience and points to possible changes—which I am recommending, not a flat rejection of hospitalization.

Organization of Hospital Care and The Welfare of Patients

Although I believe we may substantially reduce the use of hospital inpatient services to everybody's benefit, such services obviously cannot be dispensed with entirely. We should, therefore, strive to improve the welfare of those patients who must utilize this service.

A variety of suggestions have been made to this end. Suggestions to protect the patients from danger have included such things as:

Triple counts of surgical sponges and the use of radio-opaque sponges
Double check by nurses of all medication orders before dispensing
Lower beds which can be raised for bed-making or for nursing procedures
Crucial laboratory tests repeated by a second technician
More information given to patient or his agent at every step of the process so that he will be more able to judge whether an error is being made
Positive identification of all patients before *any* procedure is carried out
Consultation on all serious steps, such as all surgery
Increase of numbers of resident doctors for more effective emergency coverage
Periodic inspection of equipment and personnel as potential sources of infection.

Suggestions to make the hospital stay more comfortable and endurable for the patient have included such suggestions as:

Longer visiting hours
Allowing the patient to dress up his room to his own taste
Listening to complaints and encouraging complaints
Adjusting work hours of the ward staff to the normal sleep and waking hours of most people so that patients will not be awakened unnecessarily
More palatable meals
More auxiliary staff to take care of errands and domestic chores of the patients
Allowing patients to follow their own habits (for example, staying up late reading) so long as they do not disturb other patients

These suggestions are useful and, if instituted (and, of course, they have all been instituted somewhere), would no doubt make the hospital a somewhat safer and more tolerable place.

However, I believe there are some general principles, which include and greatly extend this list of proposals, which would modify the nature of the control of hospital treatment and the control of patients' behavior, so as to make hospital care more of a service to patients, reduce the dangerousness of hospitals, make hospitals a more tolerable place to stay, and perhaps even make them somewhat less costly in the long run.

One such principle is: *Make hospital procedures as independent of human intervention as possible.* For example, when we replaced the oxygen tank with a wall outlet, we did not simply eliminate the labor and inconvenience of moving heavy tanks through corridors and assure ourselves of an oxygen supply by each bed at all times. More importantly, perhaps, we eliminated the need for someone to be ever alert to change the tank before it was empty—a task which was often forgotten and presumably still is where tanks are used. We did away with the fear of many patients dependent on an oxygen supply that they would be forgotten at a crucial time, a fear which caused some patients to avoid going to sleep until their oxygen tank was changed. If we could devise a mechanism which would automatically change a drip from one bottle to another or perhaps set up an alarm when the level in one bottle fell below a certain level—an alarm which could be shut off only by replacing the near-empty bottle with a full one—we would remove another source of error and of fear.

Automatic procedures are still in a primitive state of development in hospitals and I see no chance of substantial extension of this approach in the foreseeable future. Some people have suggested a kind of human automation by using checklists similar to those used by commercial airline crews. But even in something as obviously critical as the control of a commercial airliner, the crews often fudge on some of the checklist items (the subject of intense controversy in the United States a few years ago). I see no reason to expect more faithful compliance in hospitals. But the automatic procedure approach should nevertheless be kept in mind; it almost certainly can be greatly extended.

A second principle which I want to discuss in much more detail is the following: *Place as much of the control of the treatment and hospital care as possible directly into the hands of the patient or his agent.*

Before describing how this principle might be applied to patient care in hospitals, let me provide some information and ideas from social science literature which led me to formulate this principle.

In the typical factory, the members of work groups develop informal norms concerning levels of effort and production and do not go beyond those norms (referred to in some sociological studies as "restriction of output"). Deviations from engineering specifications and job rules are common and many defective items are produced. Some of these items are detected and eliminated with an inspection system (with considerable waste), but inspectors too are hired hands whose devotion to duty is far from complete. Thus many defective products reach the consumer, as we all know from experience. We pay for waste and inefficiency through higher prices and higher maintenance costs. Both the reduction of restriction of output and the detection of defective products has been improved in some industries by automatic devices which replace human decision making and direct on-the-job controls to a considerable extent. However, in most industrial production, automatic controls are still absent or limited. Since there is usually no ultimate consumer exerting a direct influence on the producers in factories, this potentially powerful source of control is lacking and we must reconcile ourselves to a production system which is relatively inefficient and wasteful and whose products have a high rate of defects. Note too that, in those instances where the functioning of a product is considered crucial, we do not rely on the usual production controls. The vehicles and mechanisms which carry the astronauts are not only made to order and checked repeatedly by a number of interested parties other than the producers, but the ultimate consumers (the astronauts) themselves have a major part in the final checking.

To take another example with a more clear cut clientele—government agencies which deal directly with the public. The constant complaints we hear about such agencies makes it abundantly clear that the individual employees are usually not concerned with the welfare of the individual client. Rather they are concerned with applying a set of rules which will keep their work demands within bounds and will keep them out of trouble with their superiors. There are several ways in which this typical pattern can be (and sometimes has been) modified. One is a form of automatic decision making—a client fitting into a given objective category is entitled to certain benefits, and discretionary power is taken out of the hands of the public servant (e.g., everyone charged with a felony will be provided with an attorney at public expense; if this rule is not observed, any conviction obtained will be void). Another way to modify the control of the public agency is to give the client more bargaining power, e.g., giving the public direct access to information available to the public servants; providing ready avenues of complaint to an authoritative body which is not part of the organization complained against (such as a civilian review board as a check on the actions of the police); or have the clientele organized to bargain directly with the agency (as welfare clients have done in some American cities).

To take an example which includes a professional group—teaching. Of course, in teaching we cannot so neatly define errors as we can in some aspects of medicine and nursing or in factory production. It is much harder to tell what "good teaching" is or when a teacher has made a mistake. However, teaching as a profession has been under massive and continuous criticism for its deficiencies in recent decades. There have been numerous efforts at reform at all levels of education. It is significant that when new programs are developed that are regarded as an improvement over the usual school situation, they have one thing in common: they involve the student more directly in his own learning. The details vary greatly. Sometimes it is a matter focusing on the students' current interests. Sometimes students are brought into the curriculum planning and the conduct of the class sessions. Sometimes students are provided with learning tools—both mechanical and conceptual—and given time and facilities to work on their own. Such participatory learning not only proves to be a more effective pedagogical approach by appropriate measuring instruments (the participating learners are not always ahead in the short run, especially on measurements emphasizing rote memorization, but almost always better in the long run and in generalizing information and concepts), but the students enjoy much more freedom in constructing their own patterns of activity and suffer less oppression from authority than in the more orthodox school situation. The conscientious teacher also benefits from the more detailed and more continuous feedback he gets from the students—he has less doubt about what is being accomplished because they are willing to let him know.

Let me take one more example closer to home: the mental hospital. Here we have another institution which has been severely criticized. As in the case of the school, criteria for the evaluation of success and failure are imprecise and controversial. Yet there is growing agreement that the traditional state mental hospital does not provide effective therapy for the vast majority of its inmates, and in fact, more often results in symptomatic deterioration. It has also become clear that from the beginning of the commitment process through the minute control of the inmates' daily life, the patient's civil liberties are violated on a massive scale. Reform efforts in mental hospitals show a striking resemblance to those in schools—the clients must participate directly in the process of change. From the early experiments with group therapy to comprehensive programs of patient government and therapeutic communities, the trend has been to place more control in the hands of the patients all the way from running the day-to-day hospital activities to making decisions on leaves, discharges, and even medications. It is becoming more and more accepted that a lasting rehabilitation will not occur unless the patient is an active part of the process. Involvement of patients also reduces the changes of careless errors by staff and minimizes the dangers to the civil liberties of the inmates, since the patients themselves are placed in the position of guarding their own welfare.

The hospital as an institution is no better and no worse than comparable social organizations and the people who work in hospitals no better or worse than those who do analogous work in other institutions. It is reasonable to assume that the motives and actions of hospital staff will be similar to those of persons who find themselves in comparable roles elsewhere. Empirical observations in hospitals confirm this expectation. Thus, it should be useful to compare hospitals with other organizations which have been studied by social scientists to see what general principles of explaining behaviour and bringing about change might be applied.

Looked at in this way, the typical hospital has a work force with a complex delegation of tasks and authority and a weak sense of personal responsibility for the individual client. The hospital structure largely cuts off the clientele from most aspects of decision making, discourages questioning by the patient and his agents, limits the flow of information to the patient, and diminishes his control over his own actions and the actions of those who are serving him. It is clear from our knowledge of work performed in complex organizations that such conditions make the risk of error, and failure to respond to the demands of the patient, much greater than would be the case if a given medical professional or domestic servant were directly serving a given patient. The risk of medication errors by nurses working in a patient's home is not as great as it is in hospital and this is so even if the nurse has many patients and must make her rounds through the day. The chance of an error in a routine pathology test which the doctor carries out in his own back room is not as great as the risk of error when he sends the specimen to a laboratory with a vast production-line system of processing. And if we say we cannot afford the personnel for such piecework, we might consider whether much of this work cannot be done automatically or by people with lesser credentials, often including the patient and his family and friends. Such a shift of responsibility is not only likely to reduce errors, but will increase the patient's satisfaction by making it possible for him to control the manner in which his treatment is carried out to a much greater degree.

I might add that, although the bulk of my observations have been in U.S. hospitals, and the medical and social science studies I have relied on are also mostly American ones, I have no reason to believe that the internal operation of hospitals is different in any important way in other Western countries so far as patient care is concerned. The experience I had with hospitals in Australia was strikingly similar to that in the United States. This is not surprising since the division of labor and authority and the nature of control over patients and their families is much the same in the two countries.

If you want to improve the service to hospital patients, there is one thing you should *not* waste your time on—EXHORTATION. You never change people's ways of working by urging them to do better. Factory workers do not increase production because somebody tells them it is good for the country, or good for humanity, or even good for themselves. Public servants do not respond positively to patriotic speeches. You do not produce better teachers by exhorting them to love their pupils, or better mental hospital staff by urging them to treat patients more humanely. If you want to bring about a change in the way in which the activity of an organization is conducted, you have to change the structure of the organization. It is my contention, based not only on my observations in hospitals, but also on comparisons with evidence from the organization of work in other kinds of institutions, that essential changes in the organizational structure of hospitals to improve the service to the clientele, are those changes which would place greater control in the hands of patients and/or the personal agents of patients.

Let me give some examples of what this might mean in practice.

If a patient visits a doctor's surgery with a complaint and the doctor decides to prescribe a given medication and the patient agrees to take the medication:

The doctor provides the patient with a prescription.
The patient obtains the medicine from a chemist.
The patient takes the medicine at prescribed times and in prescribed dosage.

The patient is being trusted with the treatment. Why not do the same thing in the hospital?

Doctor and patient agree on the medication and the doctor writes a prescription and gives it to the patient.
The patient (if ambulatory) goes to the hospital dispensary and obtains the medicine (if not ambulatory, one of his visitors or a hospital messenger can get the medicine).
The patient keeps the medication in his bedside cabinet and takes it when prescribed.

You might say that patients may not take the medicine, or take the incorrect dosage under such circumstances. This is quite true. But is the patient likely to make as many errors as the nursing staff? As sociologists like to say, this is an empirical question. We can experiment and find out. My expectation is that in most cases the patient would make far fewer errors. It is his welfare which is at stake and if he is convinced that the medicine may be helpful, he is unlikely to forget or get it wrong. The fact that he has only prescribed medicine available limits his errors to incorrect dosage or failure to take the medicine. He is cut off from the error of giving the wrong medicine, which is not uncommon in the case of nurses who have access to a varied supply.

Suppose the treatment requires a skill that the patient does not possess—for example, a prescription for injectable medication. Actually some patients can be trained to give such medications to themselves—this is done with some diabetics—and it might be better if they were trained to do this in many cases. If cautioned about the appropriate locations to avoid nerve damage and aspiration to avoid blood vessels, they are likely to be more careful in giving the injection than a nurse or a doctor. But, if the patient requires skilled assistance, he can still largely control the situation:

The doctor gives the prescription.
The patient obtains the prescribed medication in individual dosages and keeps it in his possession.
When the time comes to take the medication, he signals for a nurse and requests it.

Note that in this case the nurse still has some control. She can refuse to give the injection and call the doctor to settle the matter. But the nurse is placed in a position where she must justify her refusal—for example, that the doctor has made a mistake in dosage or that the patient's condition has changed since the medication was ordered—and contact the doctor to find out what to do. It cannot simply be forgotten or the patient put off without explanation as commonly occurs now.

Let us take the case of a mother taking care of a young child who is ill at home. The doctor relies on her to take rectal temperatures and report signs of illness. He orders enemas to be given by the mother. He prescribes a diet which the mother prepares. The doctor often does this over a telephone if he is familiar with the patient and the mother.

But suppose the child is hospitalized for surgery. He is told to come in on the previous day. Why? Because regular temperatures must be taken by the nursing staff. An enema must be given in the early morning before surgery. Nurses must make sure that the child does not ingest anything for some hours before surgery. Why does the mother suddenly become incompetent when the child is hospitalized? Of course, she may make an error in taking his temperature, she may forget the enema or do it incompletely, she may give the child something to eat or drink after midnight. But so may the nurses. Which one is most likely to make an error? Again, this is an empirical question. My guess is that the modern educated mother would make fewer errors. Also, if she is with the child at all times, she can check on the activities of the hospital staff and keep *them* from making mistakes.

If a patient is ambulatory (and even some who are not ambulatory), some treatments and even some diagnostic procedures can be carried out by the patient without the need of any professional personnel:

> He can be left with a thermometer and record his own temperature.
> If accurate weight is required every day, he can be shown the scales and provided with a record form.
> If he needs to soak his finger in hot water, he can be provided with a basin and directed to the hot water supply.
> He can take care of the most notoriously inaccurate of all hospital procedures—the intake-output record.
> And so on.

Many of these things are already commonly done in chronic disease hospitals. My impression is that the proportion of staff errors in such hospitals are far lower than in the acute disease hospital. Of course, there are a number of reasons for this, including the fact that the nursing care routines tend to be far simpler and more routinized. However, I believe that the fact that much of it is left in the hands of the patients is one important reason for fewer errors.

It is my contention that many such procedures would be carried out more accurately by an alert patient than by the nursing or medical staff, though for some tasks the patient would need some instruction. Some things may require some special skill, but here again, the same approach may be applied as I described in the example of giving injections. The doctor can, for example, provide the patient with a written order for having his dressing changed and he will then be in a better position to see that it is changed at the appropriate times and with the appropriate frequency.

There is no need to restrict a patient to bed if his physical condition does not call for this. He should be able to keep his clothes and move about, including leaving the hospital entirely during periods when he is not due for a diagnostic or treatment procedure. He should be no more restricted in his movements than he is at home except when the welfare of other patients necessitate it—for example, if he is in a room with other patients, he may be limited in his movements or in reading at night, sometimes even during the day, because others are resting. He should be able to get his own water, take care of his own toilet needs, and do other domestic chores that he is capable of carrying out. He should go to a central dining room to eat, rather than being served at his bed. (This may also help to improve the palatability of the meals which are a source of complaint of patients in virtually every hospital I have ever seen or heard about.) One might also experiment with catering services which could run dining rooms on hospital grounds to serve patients (and others) who wish to eat there (with the hospital reducing its charges to allow for this). Again, we should have no fear of the patient getting an incorrect diet through such an arrangement, because, if he has been properly instructed and is convinced that a certain diet will promote his health, he is just as likely to stay within its bounds than if he relies on dietary workers and nursing staff to control his diet for him.

With a shift of emphasis from staff control to patient control, patients and their families would have to re-educate and be urged to take a more active part in their care. They should, for example, be specifically instructed to demand that staff members properly identify them (name, type of illness, doctor's name) before permitting any diagnostic or treatment procedures to be carried out to avoid the many errors of carrying out a procedure on the wrong patient. They should also be urged to question hospital staff members closely concerning any medicine or procedure which has not been explained to them in advance.

Up to this point, I have been assuming a patient who is alert and rational and physically able to do much for himself, preferably ambulatory. Of course, many patients in acute disease hospitals are unconscious, weak or nauseated, in great pain, or otherwise disabled. Some are senile; some are young children with insufficient knowledge to care for themselves; some are adults of very limited intelligence or education; others are so fearful of authority that they are afraid to assert themselves for their own welfare. How are these to be cared for?

A number of times earlier I spoke of the patient "or his agent." More generally, we might speak simply of the patient's agent, recognizing that often the patient may be his own agent. Otherwise, someone may act on his behalf. Preferably this will be a close member of his family. But it may also be a friend or someone hired by the patient or the family to look after his interests, though the last is perhaps a less satisfactory solution.

If someone else is acting as his agent, this person would have the prescriptions filled, give the patient the medicine at the correct times, call on nursing or other technical care when needed, fulfill the less-skilled nursing needs such as getting water, washbasins, taking temperatures, preparing and serving food and drink, keeping bedside records, watching the oxygen tank and I.V. infusion equipment, raising and lowering the bed, getting the bedpan, and so on. Hospitals should provide for the comfort of people who stay with the patient with comfortable chairs and sufficient space, cots if necessary. This is already done at times in the case of young children, but should also be the case with any patient who must in part or whole be treated as relatively helpless. In some cases, it may not be important for someone to stay all the time, but simply to make frequent visits to take care of certain needs and to check on the patient's care. Also, the form that the responsibliity will take will typically vary in the course of an acute illness or surgical recovery. Thus, at first the patient may be completely dependent on his agent who stays with him all the time. (In practice, members of the family or friends would relieve one another at this task.) As his condition improves, he can act as his own agent to a greater extent and others may reduce their care and supervision to occasional visits each day. Eventually, the patient can be his own agent, although if we follow the principle of not hospitalizing people any longer than is necessary, most patients will not remain in this category long.

Of course, there are patients who have no friends or family ties whatever. It is precisely such patients, especially the aged, who tend to fill our chronic disease hospitals and nursing homes, often to spend the rest of their life. Perhaps we should explore the possibility of some kind of ombudsman position in hospitals to look after the interests of such people, especially if they are very sick, or old, or poorly educated. Social workers sometimes fulfill this role to a limited extent, but the fact that social workers are part of the hospital staff who must maintain more-or-less good relationships with other members of the staff limits their ability to promote the patients' interests, protect him from mistakes, and provide for his needs as *he* sees them.

One of the most important changes needed on hospital inpatient services is to give the hospital patient direct access to his doctors. There is no reason why a person who is hospitalized should not have at least the same access to his doctors as he has when he is at home. There has been much criticism of the difficulty that people have getting a doctor when they need one, especially on nights and weekends. But at home, most people who are persistent and are willing to go through receptionists and telephone answering services, use emergency service locums, or go to hospital casualty services, can get to see a doctor within two to three hours in the great majority of cases. Once in hospital, however, this often becomes impossible. Doctors frequently delay responding to a patient's request for as much as ten to twelve hours or even a full day or more, if indeed the request is passed on to the doctor at all. Patients are placed in the position of calling for their doctor through nurses who are dedicated to keeping patients from getting into contact with doctors, and doctors often punish nurses who have not learned this lesson. The resident medical officer (if any) is completely inaccessible except through a nurse—the patient or his agent simply does not know how to reach the house doctor unless he just happens to come along (and even then he may deny responsiblity for the case). If the patient has a private doctor, he can telephone him if a phone is available, but this is regarded by nurses and doctors as a serious breach of etiquette which will be punished, not only with a scolding, but often by reducing a patient's medical and nursing services.

Doctors—like all other workers—like to control their work load and their work schedule. One way to do this is to restrict access by patients. But why should the hospital patient be *more* restricted than the patient at home? The patient or his agent should be encouraged to call his doctor directly rather than through the nurse when he thinks he needs the doctor. He is in a better position to give information to the doctor than is the nurse (who often has not been well informed about what the patient's needs are) and thus obtain more useful advice. If the doctor needs information from the nurse, he can always call her.

This means, in practice, that all patients or their agents should be provided with easy access to a telephone *at all hours.* The patient should know how to call his own doctor or a replacement emergency service. The locums for private doctors should be allowed to visit patients in hospital even if they are not on the hospital staff—they are working for the patient, *not* for the hospital. The patient should also be provided with the internal telephone extension of the resident house doctor. The doctor may not want to see the patient, but as least he will know that the patient has requested him and know what the request is about. If the patient asks the nurse, the message often is not even communicated to the resident doctor. If the patient is able to get about, he should also be permitted to leave his ward and visit the hospital casualty department if he thinks he needs urgent care. If the patient is not able to get about and if the person looking after him has difficulty getting a doctor to come to his bedside when needed, he should be permitted to place the patient in a wheelchair or stretcher and take him to the hospital's casualty department.

A crucial aspect of control is access to information. The better informed the patient (or his agent), the more competent he will be to participate in the treatment and to guard against error. He should be informed about how hospitals operate and how doctors and nurses and other hospital personnel carry out their duties and what mistakes they may make. Perhaps a brief simplified form of a book like Gross's *The Doctors* [3] would make enlightening reading. He should be well informed about his own case—the nature and purpose of diagnostic procedures, the medications prescribed and their anticipated effects and potential dangers, the reason for transfusions, and the importance of requiring proper identification when specimens are drawn or blood transfused. He should be urged not to permit anyone to carry out a procedure which has not been satisfactorily explained to him. He should be permitted to examine his chart, especially with an eye to correcting errors in his history and in certain aspects of his treatment. And so on. (Read "patient's agent" in those cases where the patient is incompetent for any reason.)

Some of the foregoing suggestions may appear horrifying to many members of the hospital staff who may regard it as impossible to operate a hospital on such a basis. However, what constitutes the proper conduct of a hospital (or anything else) is largely a matter of what we are accustomed to and the customs on hospital operation, as in other things, vary from place to place and time to time. There is no reason to believe that people working in the modern acute hospital cannot become accustomed to a mode of operation different from what we typically have at the pressent time. We already have some limited models of variations in degree of patient control. Several of these are described by anthropologists who have made observations in other lands, although their descriptions are unfortunately very skimpy.

Ernestine Friedl [11], states that hospitals in rural Greece leave much of the care of patients to family members. Some family members stay with the patient, give nursing care, prepare meals, carry out the instructions of the doctor. The doctor consults with them when he makes his visits. This is not to argue that the rural Greek hospital is an ideal to copy. I know nothing of their cross-infection rate, for example, and it may be much higher than what we are accustomed to. This is simply intended to show that active participation and control by the patient and his family can exist in hospital care without making the work of doctors and nurses impossible. Such family care is the pattern expected by the rural Greek hospital staff. They would think that the patient was abandoned by his family if no one stayed with him. It does not constitute an extra burden on the nursing staff and, in fact, relieves them of some of the duties they would otherwise have to carry out. Presence of relatives assures the patient that someone is watching out for his interests, while the doctor finds the relatives useful as witnesses that he has done his job—for example, that the baby was delivered by him and not by a ghost, as sometimes happens in the United States.

William Caudill made observations in Japanese hospitals during the early 1950s [12, 363–373]. He found it common practice for women (often with little nursing training) to be hired to care for single patients on a full- time basis in a hospital. This *tsukesoi* took almost total responsiblity for the patient's care, living in his room and being on call at all times to serve his needs. She could call upon other members of the hospital staff when certain specialized skills were needed. The *tsukesoi* come from a tradition of dedicated personal service, rather than professional nursing or technical service. As Japanese hospitals, especially in the large urban centers, strive to imitate prestigious western models, the *tsukesoi* is gradually being eliminated. Caudill wonders whether the hospital patient may not find himself more poorly served than he has been in the past.

In Papua, New Guinea, hospitals, members of the family (called "guardians" by the Europeans who run the hospitals) accompany and take care of native patients—feed them, perform domestic duties, carry out simple nursing tasks. The European staff have long recognized that the hospitals could not function without the aid of the guardians and it would be difficult to induce many natives to remain in hospital without family members present. However, in the larger urban centers such as Port Moresby, the European medical staff is becoming concerned about turning their institutions into more presentable western models and the guardians are becoming regarded as a nuisance which must gradually be disposed of. Whether the natives have been sufficiently westernized to accept impersonal controls and separation from their families remains to be seen. Whether or not such a change represents an "improvement" of care is, I contend, a matter of viewpoint and of value orientation.

Then there is the example of our own chronic disease hospitals which I have referred to before. These rely heavily on the patient to take care of his own needs, especially when the patient is alert and physically capable of self-care. In tuberculosis hospitals, I found it a common practice for:

Patients to provide for almost all of their own bodily needs

Patients to carry out many nursing tasks for the less-able patient

Patients check their own medications and tell the nurse when she has made a mistake

Patients remind doctors and nurses of their schedule of diagnostic and treatment procedures

Patients determine much of their own physical activity, when they should have passes, and when they should be considered for discharge

It seems to me that what we need in our hospitals is a concept of extraterritorial rights. The patient and his family should be able to transfer to hospital the rights and privileges and the control of their lives which they exercise in their home. The fact that he requires specialized facilities because of illness is no justification for depriving a person and his family of many of their liberties and protections. Clearly, there must be *some* modification of the concept of complete extraterritorial rights in most of our present-day hospitals because of the competing needs of different patients. An ambulatory patient with a room of his own could most readily keep his rights intact; the bedridden patient in a ward with many others would have to modify those rights in substantial ways to avoid interfering with the treatment and the needs of his fellow patients (but this is no different from the problems of communal living elsewhere, for example, college dormitories). However, if we accept extraterritorial rights as desirable, we can change our patterns of organization and control of hospitals (and the laws governing hospital authority and responsibility) to bring us closer to this goal. We can also design future hospitals and modify present structures to facilitate this goal.

Let me briefly sum up what I see as the potential advantages of giving greater control to the hospital patient or his agent.

Make Hospitals Less Dangerous

Many hospital procedures require relatively little skill, but do require some care, attention to detail, watchfulness, concern about getting a task done on time. This is likely to be done better by someone with a special concern for the welfare of the patient than by one who is simply an employee with many other persons making demands upon him. Those most concerned with the welfare of the patient are the patient himself, members of his family, friends, and possibly someone hired just to take care of him. Even when special skills are required that the patient or his agent cannot provide (and with a little training we can get them to do much more), they can still control much of the initiation of activities by the staff and obtain the services of the doctor when needed. The patient, or those caring for him, should be in a position to demand more information before procedures are carried out or decisions made and so be in a better position to protect the patient's welfare and to avoid the mistakes of the staff.

Making the hospital less dangerous is not the only reason for giving patients greater control over their own care, so the whole control issue does not stand or fall on the question of relative danger. But this *is* an important issue. It is an empirical matter and can be studied. When such changes are introduced (and, of course, they already exist in some hospitals), they should be studied to see what difference it makes for differing populations under differing circumstances.

Make the Hospital Stay More Tolerable

Giving the patient more control over his own actions and what is done to him means that his pattern of living is less upset, he is better able to do for himself what *he* thinks is right rather than having other people's values imposed on him. His welfare, after all, is a matter for his own decision and that of people who are close to him. Experts can give him advice and make recommendations, *but cannot tell him what is good for him.* Yet this latter is what is commonly attempted in hospitals.

The patient should be able to fill his own needs, either through his own actions or those of his agent who stays with him. One of the most frustrating parts of hospital experience is the inability to get many of one's comforts attended to—matters which are rarely life-threatening, but which often mean the difference between a tolerable and intolerable stay in the hospital. Exhorting ward personnel to be more attentive to patients' needs has proved to be a waste of effort. The only way to get these tasks carried out with any consistency is to turn them over to the patient (if he is physically able) or to those who are vitally interested in his welfare if he is not physically able.

Make Medical Care Less Costly

If patients and their agents take over much of the control of hospital care, there will be less need for close attention from hospital personnel and thus fewer staff will be necessary. In the United States, chronic disease hospitals are operated at a far lower cost per patient than the acute disease hospitals. There are a number of reasons for this, but certainly one of them is that patients take care of many of the tasks which are largely in the hands of staff in acute hospitals. Although a precise copy of chronic hospitals is not possible, there are many aspects of care which can better be left to the patient in acute hospitals and thus reduce the pressure for constant increase in staff.

My effort in this paper has been to conceive of the hospital not as a physical repository of patients undergoing treatment under the control of experts who make all the decisions, but rather to see it as a cluster of services available to the public on the advice of medical authorities—services which may be drawn upon by patients when needed without relinquishing their civil liberties or relinquishing control over decisions which affect them.

Medical Malpractice   26

DAVID S. RUBSAMEN

In 1972, according to a federal commission studying medical malpractice, the cost to the average patient of malpractice insurance charges passed on to him by physicians and hospitals was from 20 to 50 cents of every $10 he paid to a physician and about 52 cents for every day he spent in a hospital. It has been estimated that by 1980, if the present trend continues, the charges will have increased tenfold. The figures dramatize what is widely known as "the medical malpractice crisis," which paradoxically arises from the great progress of medical science over the past three decades and the resulting public expectation that medicine should have a cure for every ill. Now errors of omission are brought into court as well as errors of commission, and juries tend to make big awards. My experience as a consultant on the medical aspects of litigation has led me to the conclusion that the solution of the malpractice crisis requires two things: (1) better control by the medical profession of the quality of medical practice and (2) a rational system of compensating negligently injured patients.

Until quite recently a complete recovery from an illness was rarely a certainty, and the physician's management was seldom questioned after an unsatisfactory outcome. For example, a failure to diagnose appendicitis, followed by perforation and death from peritonitis, was regarded as one of life's hazards. The timely detection of cancer was the exception rather than the rule for many years after the development of surgical techniques that made it possible to cure a malignancy discovered early.

Even the best care in those times was frequently ineffective. Parents who raised children before the discovery of antibiotics can recall the feeling of helplessness evoked by a diagnosis of pneumonia or infection of the middle ear. It was not until about 1945 that medicine recognized the role of an imbalance of electrolytes in the fatal outcome of a variety of acute disease states. Such techniques as electronic monitoring, easily available studies of blood gases, and the rapid determination of serum electrolytes—all indispensable in the effective treatment of many severe illnesses today—are developments of the period since World War II. It is only a slight exaggeration to say that the era of scientific medicine began about 30 years ago.

Improved medical technology disclosed previously unsuspected pathophysiological changes in serious illness and trauma. Therapies were developed to deal with many such changes. As a result the prognosis for a large number of sick people improved sharply. The proportion of patients of whom physicians had to conclude that "there's nothing we can do here" decreased dramatically; most of them entered an arena of challenging medical problems where good results could reasonably be expected. (This prospect was much less likely for the chronically ill patient, for whom prevention was and still is the only real solution.)

Naturally the expectations of patients have matched the progress of medical science. More important, in terms of malpractice litigation, is a similar shift in attitude among physicians. This fact leads, subtly but inevitably, to the crucial issue of how medical negligence is defined.

The simplest statement of the issue is that the physician owes it to his patient to be careful. If, as a result of the physician's carelessness, the patient suffers injury, then liability exists. Like most legal formulations, however, this one is simple in theory but complex in practice. It requires closer examination.

Both carelessness and injury must be established; neither is sufficient alone. An example is provided by the case of a 55-year-old housewife in California who consulted her family physician in July, 1970, for treatment of cough and chronic fatigue. She saw him 23 times over the next six months, but her complaints continued and she lost 60 pounds. Finally, in January, 1971, the physician ordered a chest X ray, which revealed a bilateral pulmonary malignancy. The patient died a few weeks later.

Her husband sued. Three medical witnesses testified that, considering the patient's symptoms, a chest X ray was required by at least the fall of 1970. On the other hand, the attorney for the defendant physician presented two medical witnesses who testified that the cancer was multifocal in origin and therefore inoperable from the beginning. The defense made no attempt to justify the doctor's delay in accomplishing the diagnosis. The jury accepted the testimony of the defense on the origin of the illness and returned a verdict in favor of the doctor.

Sometimes a physician's carelessness may be egregious, and yet no injury results. Years ago a well-trained obstetrician was called to the hospital late at night to perform an emergency Caesarean section. He was moderately intoxicated, and his initial incision was accomplished with a sweep of the scalpel that cut down through the wall of the uterus and even through the amniotic membrane. The infant lay exposed for extraction, and there was not a scratch on him. The physician's reckless action, let alone the fact that he was operating under the influence of alcohol, clearly identified his carelessness. There was no injury, however, and so, although the physician might have been disciplined by his county medical society or expelled from the staff of the hospital, neither the mother nor the child had a basis for a negligence suit.

Although these questions of causation (that is, the connection between carelessness and injury) are not infrequent in malpractice litigation, most of the time the central issue concerns the definition of carelessness. Many physicians believe only the most obvious errors of commission should be called to account, and many contend too that errors of omission—the "honest mistakes of judgment"—should not provide grounds for a lawsuit. There is, however, no logical reason why an error of judgment should be any less subject to a malpractice action than an overt blunder. The test remains the same: Did the physician meet his legal duty to the patient to be careful? The discussion can become abstruse at this point, turning on such matters as what the standard of care in medical practice should be and how it would be elucidated in an enlightened system. In the real world of a jury trial, however, the issue is simple: the physician has violated the standard of due care when the jury, having considered all the evidence and the judge's instructions, votes against him.

What, then, is the basis for a jury's judgment? In most cases testimony from at least one physician appearing as a witness for the patient provides the critical evidence. Sometimes the patient's attorney will obtain the necessary testimony by skillful questioning of the defending physician, and in some states the law allows the jury to infer negligence from certain types of medical accident. Ordinarily, however, the jury hears one physician or more testify for the patient and one physician or more testify for the doctor defendant and then decides what standard of care should be applied in the case and whether the doctor violated it. Thus medical testimony is usually vital to the patient's cause.

What legal principle makes the medical witness necessary? Medical malpractice litigation involves scientific facts. The common law has long recognized that juries cannot resolve conflicting points of view on scientific matters without hearing expert witnesses.

The development of medical malpractice litigation in the U.S. has paralleled the increasing availability of expert medical witnesses. In other words, it has depended on the willingness of at least some physicians to testify against other physicians. Thirty years ago physicians were so reluctant to testify against one another that the phrase "conspiracy of silence" had real meaning. In some states the same situation prevails today, but a majority of the states have experienced a growth in malpractice litigation as expert witnesses have become available to plaintiffs. In the states leading this trend (notably California, New York, Florida, Illinois, Pennsylvania, and New Jersey) there has also been an extraordinary escalation in the size of awards.

California's experience, involving both physicians and hospitals, is illustrative. In 1969 the state had only 3 cases in which a verdict or an out-of-court settlement of a malpractice action amounted to $300,000 or more. The number rose

Table 26–1

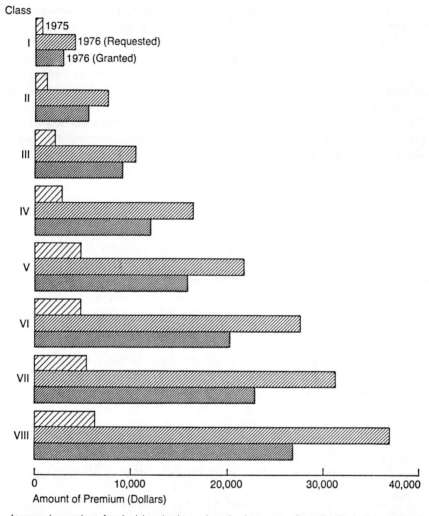

Increase in premiums for physicians buying malpractice insurance reflects the rise in the number of malpractice lawsuits and in the size of the awards made to successful plaintiffs. The chart shows the premiums paid by various classes of physicians in southern California in 1975, the level of premiums sought for 1976 by the insurance company and the amounts granted by the state's insurance commissioner. The premiums are for coverage of $1 million in a single case and an aggregate of $3 million for two or more cases in one year. The class numbers refer to different types of practice; the highest premiums (Class VIII) apply to physicians who do specialized surgery or specialize in obstetrics and gynecology. Although the data are limited to southern California, they are indicative of what has been happening elsewhere.

steadily to about 34 in 1974. By 1975 the attitude of jurors had apparently been influenced by the publicity about California's malpractice crisis, and the figure dropped to 24. The state's first case resulting in an award of $1 million or more was in 1967; since then there have been 22 more, 14 of them after January, 1974.

What determines the accessibility of medical witnesses for patients who become plaintiffs? The absolute requirement is an expansion, usually by judicial fiat, of the traditional "locality rule." Under this rule the only expert witnesses who can testify in a malpractice action are physicians practicing in the defendant physician's community. The rule reflects a situation of more than 50 years ago, when schools of thought on medical practice were often geographically insular. Given the professional and social contacts among physicians in a community, the rule effectively suppresses malpractice litigation. Most states have abandoned the rule as the courts have come to the view that medical schools and the professional literature are national in scope. Discarding the locality rule, however, does not automatically open the door to malpractice litigation. Something else must happen.

Again California is illustrative. Although the state's supreme court eliminated the locality rule in 1952, it was another eight years or so before medical witnesses for plaintiffs began appearing more than rarely, and their appearance was not common in malpractice actions throughout the state until about 1969. The availability of these witnesses has brought about a striking change in the type of malpractice case litigated in California. The shift occurred between 1968 and 1972. The pattern of change is bound to appear in any state where medical witnesses for plaintiffs in malpractice actions become freely available.

I have alluded to the fact that negligent medical injury can be divided into two categories: errors of commission and errors of omission. The first category includes the slip of the surgeon's scalpel, the inadvertent administration of an injurious drug, the application of a cast so tightly that circulatory impairment results, and so on. The amount of injury resulting from errors of commission is quite limited; taking all negligent medical injuries together (not just the cases that are litigated), only a small percentage are caused by errors of commission.

Errors of omission can be characterized as mistakes in judgment. If the physician had given this drug instead of that one, if his therapeutic intervention had been better timed, if his diagnostic acumen had been a bit sharper, then the unsatisfactory outcome could have been avoided.

In the majority of states malpractice litigation involves mainly errors of commission. Unless a judgmental error is gross it will not be the subject of a lawsuit. The reason is that physicians in those states still share the belief that "honest mistakes" should not be litigated. In the half-dozen or so states where this attitude no longer exists, however, the incidence of successful malpractice actions has risen sharply. The reason is that the number of unsatisfactory outcomes that might be regarded as the consequence of judgmental errors is large, provided that a high enough standard of care is applied.

Two cases in California are illustrative. Both of them entailed complex medical facts of the kind that are common when alleged errors of judgment are litigated. The first case arose in December, 1968, when a college student suffered a dislocation of his right knee while playing touch football. The popliteal artery (the major artery, lying just behind the knee, that carries blood to the lower leg and the foot) was severed by the injury. The broken ends of the artery constricted, thus preventing bleeding and the formation of a local hematoma, which would have signaled the catastrophic event.

The patient was seen soon after his injury at the emergency room of the college hospital. The physician on duty could not identify the pulsations normally found in the two branches of the popliteal artery that supply blood to the foot, and he called for an orthopedic consultation. The orthopedist saw the patient shortly thereafter and noted on the patient's chart a "probable" injury to the popliteal artery, but he concluded that there was most likely just a spasm of the artery, since he thought he could detect faint pulsations in the arteries of the foot. A general surgeon was also consulted. He wrote that the arterial pulsations were "extremely weak on the right," but he agreed with the orthopedist that the popliteal artery was probably only in spasm. "I think we can safely observe without arteriogram or exploration," he wrote.

Table 26–2

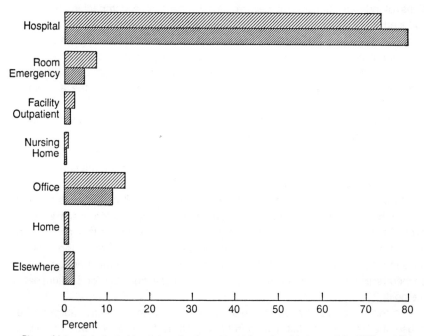

Percent

Place of injury is indicated for malpractice insurance claims closed between July, 1975, and February, 1976, covering a total of 9,471 claim reports received by the National Association of Insurance Commissioners. The lighter bars refer to the number of incidents occurring in each place and the darker bars indicate the amount of indemnity paid on the basis of those incidents. Hospitals accounted for 80 percent of incidents and 84 percent of indemnity.

These examinations were made during the first two hours after the patient was injured. There was then a delay of about 18 hours before an arteriogram was performed. It demonstrated the obstruction of flow through the popliteal artery. The patient's leg had to be removed.

When the case was tried in October, 1971, the attorney for the plaintiff concentrated on the early medical decisions and called them substandard. He presented the testimony of a well-qualified vascular surgeon who practiced in a community 400 miles away. This expert witness concentrated on two themes in telling the jury what standard of care should be applied. First, since the popliteal artery is the main source of blood to the lower leg and the foot, an obstruction of its flow for more than about six hours creates a substantial risk of gangrene, and the risk increases with time. Second, an arteriogram and/or a surgical exploration of the area behind the knee are fairly simple procedures, and they make possible a definite diagnosis. Therefore since the defendants suspected an arterial injury but could not be certain about an obstruction, their failure to perform an arteriogram or a surgical exploration in the period shortly after the injury violated the standard of due care.

The expert medical testimony for the defense stressed the judgmental aspect of the case and the fact that the physicians who saw the patient were well-qualified specialists. It was noted that the patient did not present the typical signs of arterial interruption: severe pain in the foot accompanied by a pronounced drop in the temperature of the skin and by blanching of the skin. The judge gave the jury the usual instructions, pointing out that the mere fact of an error is not a basis for liability on the part of the physician and that the plaintiff must show that the error was a product of carelessness, that is, of substandard care. The jury nonetheless returned a verdict for the plaintiff in the amount of $475,000.

Did the jury apply too high a standard of care? Many surgeons with whom I have discussed the case feel that it did not. Yet five years earlier the case almost certainly would not have been brought to trial because the plaintiff's attorney would not have been able to find an expert witness to comment adversely on the errors of omission.

What is the limit on errors in judgment? Conceivably it could be as large as the number of untoward medical occurrences. Such a conclusion assumes, however, that juries might eventually adopt a rule of prescience for the medical profession, which would be absurd. Nevertheless, the complexity of the medical facts in most cases of judgmental error means that juries will often not be able to deliberate intelligently about them. The second case from California illuminates the point.

In the fall of 1973 a 33-year-old woman consulted a general surgeon because she had recently felt a lump in her right breast. The lesion was somewhat tender and the skin over it showed redness. The doctor concluded that the patient had a localized infection. He put her on antibiotic therapy and told her to return in two weeks.

According to the doctor, on the second visit the inflammation appeared to have subsided. He told the patient to discontinue the antibiotic, observe the effect, and return in a month. Two weeks later she telephoned to say that the lesion had flared up. The doctor told her to go back on the antibiotic and to keep the appointment she had been given.

On the third visit she reported that the inflammation had subsided until the day before and then had flared up again. The doctor told her to continue the antibiotic for two weeks and said that if it had not subsided by then, he would perform a biopsy. He was concerned about the possibility that the lesion might be an inflammatory carcinoma, an extremely rare but highly malignant breast cancer.

This time the antibiotic was ineffective, and the patient returned in 11 days. A biopsy the following day revealed an inflammatory carcinoma. The lesion measured 7.5 centimeters in diameter; on the initial examination it had been about a third that size. The pathologist who studied the tissue saw evidence of an associated bacterial infection, thus explaining the patient's initial response to antibiotic therapy.

Now the woman was treated by the removal of her adrenal glands, followed by radiotherapy and chemotherapy. (Mastectomy was not done, since it does not improve the prognosis in inflammatory carcinoma.) When the case was tried, early in 1974, there was no evidence of cancer, but all the treating physicians agreed that this response to the intensive therapy must be viewed as temporary and that the patient's prognosis for an extended remission was poor.

At the trial the patient contended that the antibiotic therapy had never been significantly effective. The medical witness who testified on the patient's behalf said the lesion should have been biopsied within two weeks after the first examination. The defending physician testified that he had told the patient from the beginning that the diagnosis was either an infection or a malignancy. He said the question of cancer was of concern to him, but he was reluctant to perform a biopsy since cutting into infected tissue virtually guaranteed a bad scar.

Three expert witnesses for the defendant testified that the delay of some six weeks in doing a biopsy was well within the normal standard of care. They emphasized that the treatment would have been identical even if the cancer had been identified on the patient's first visit to the physician. The plaintiff's expert witness agreed with this point but asserted that a six-week delay in treatment could make a difference in the patient's response to treatment, even though success in this context was regarded as affecting the length of her life rather than the possibility of a cure.

The jury returned a verdict of $200,000 in favor of the patient. Most observers of the trial thought the verdict was a compromise, since an award two or three times larger would have been expected for a woman of the patient's age if the jury had been convinced that the physician had been negligent. The defense filed a motion for a new trial, but the day before the judge was to rule on the motion the case was settled for $100,000.

These two cases show that medical negligence is not to be equated with what is normally regarded as bad practice. From a strictly legal point of view the young man who lost a leg was a victim of negligent treatment because the plaintiff's expert said so and the jury accepted his testimony. From a medical point of view it is not unreasonable to say that the jury was right, but it is also apparent

Table 26-3

Type of Injury

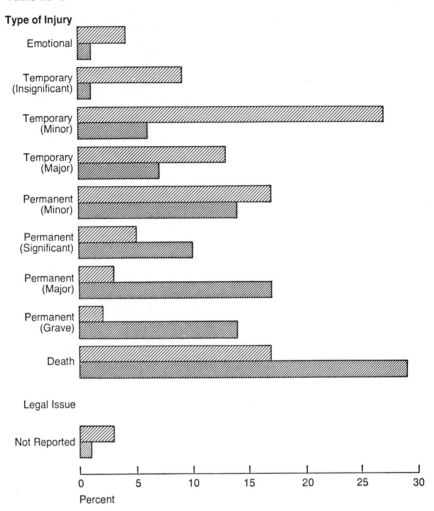

Type of injury is indicated for the malpractice insurance claims represented by the illustration on the opposite page. The lighter bars show the percent of the malpractice incidents represented by each type of injury; darker bars, the percent of indemnity paid in each category. "Legal issue" ordinarily is whether the physician obtained the informed consent of the patient.

that the jurors were applying a relatively high standard of care to the conduct of the defendants.

As for the second case, it is difficult to believe the judge would not have ordered a new trial on the ground that the jury's verdict was unreasonable. The verdict emphasizes the capriciousness of juries in cases of medical malpractice and demonstrates why many authorities in medical law argue for specialty courts, where experienced judges would sit without juries. An alternative is a private system of arbitration for malpractice cases. Nevertheless, most defense attorneys prefer the jury system. The reason is that in the rural areas of all states and even in a number of metropolitan areas juries generally favor physicians. Therefore it is the quite obvious error of commission that characterizes the great majority of adverse malpractice verdicts.

Perhaps the most interesting aspect of medical malpractice litigation is the manner in which standards of medical care can be set by juries. For example, in 1973 a jury in California returned a verdict of $1.5 million against an anesthesiologist. The plaintiff was a woman who had suffered a cardiac arrest at the conclusion of a brief elective operation. She was left with moderately severe brain damage. During the trial her attorney presented medical testimony in support of two arguments. First, there were certain oversights in the management of the anesthesia that led to the cardiac arrest. Second, even with the arrest the patient would not have suffered significant brain damage if the anesthesiologist had been monitoring her pulse constantly, so that the arrest would have been detected the moment it occurred and resuscitative measures could have been started immediately. Interviews with jurors after the trial revealed that this second argument was central to their decision.

Does due care require an anesthesiologist to monitor the pulse continuously as a matter of routine? The defendant and three other witnesses said that this was not the standard practice in the local community in a simple case such as this one. Their standard was to take the pulse for 15 seconds every two minutes. The anesthesiologist who testified for the plaintiff asserted that the standard of due care requires constant monitoring of the pulse in every case.

Shortly after the trial I asked several anesthesiologists in teaching centers in California if constant monitoring of the pulse during all anesthesia really was the due-care standard in California. Each replied that he adhered to this standard himself and regarded it as being the preferred practice, but most of them doubted that it was widely enough observed to constitute the standard of practice among anesthesiologists generally. It does constitute the standard now, however, particularly since verdicts in three of four subsequent cases in California involving the same issue have gone against the anesthesiologists.

Against this background the origins of the malpractice crisis, which began about two years ago, are readily seen. The immediate cause was the sudden and drastic increase in the rates for malpractice insurance in most states. Malpractice insurance has become much more difficult to get in recent years; some 22 commercial carriers offered it five years ago, whereas perhaps seven offer it today. Resistance among physicians to higher premiums can lead the only company left in a state to withdraw, thereby compounding the crisis. This has already happened in Maryland and is a possibility in several other states.

One would suppose that the high level of premiums (as much as five times higher than they were in 1974) would cause the commercial companies to hurry back into the market. The main reason they do not is that they cannot be sure of making a profit. More than half of the states have statutes of limitation that allow suits for negligent medical injury to be brought for as long as three years after the discovery of the injury (not the date when the injury occurred). The malpractice

Table 26-4

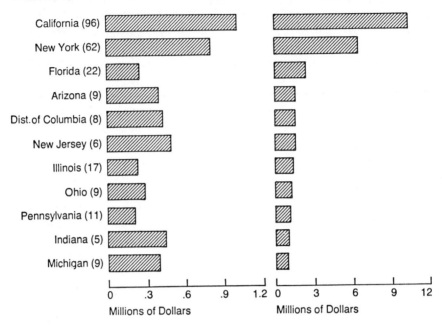

Amount of payment for medical malpractice is listed for the 11 jurisdictions in the U.S. where the largest amounts were paid between July, 1975, and February, 1976, according to data provided to the National Association of Insurance Commissioners. Associated with the name of each area is a number in parentheses giving the number of claims of $50,000 or more paid by insurance companies on behalf of defendants in malpractice actions. The bars at the left represent the largest payment made in each jurisdiction and the bars at the right show the full amounts paid. On a national basis 611 claims involved payments of $50,000 or more; they represented only 3 percent of the total number of claims but accounted for 63 percent of the total indemnity paid for all the claims included in this survey.

actuary will therefore not have a good idea of his losses within 12 months after a policy is issued. Indeed, it will be at least three years before he will know of even half of the suits attributable to a given policy year.

This extended "tail" of liability has two important consequences. First, the adequacy of the malpractice premiums charged for a given year cannot be judged for three or four years. Second, the length of the tail is uncertain. How many of the negligent medical injuries that occurred in 1975 will have been reported by 1978 or 1982? What will the effect of currency inflation have been by then? Will juries be more willing to decide complex cases against physicians and to award large amounts of money to injured patients?

In some areas physicians have responded to the problems of high premiums and limited availability of malpractice insurance by forming their own insurance companies. Such carriers have two advantages: as new companies they do not suffer from an overhang of losses from previous years, and they can take full advantage of cost-containment legislation that may have been adopted recently in their state. Existing commercial companies are likely to find that this legislation will not be retroactive.

A number of states have recently enacted legislation directed at the malpractice crisis. The new laws accomplish such things as clarifying judicial rules, providing for stricter statutes of limitation, and creating mandatory review boards to examine malpractice cases before they go to trail in order to discourage frivolous suits. It is likely that most of these reforms will be largely ineffective in reducing malpractice awards.

A few effective cost-containment laws have been enacted. They reflect two general approaches, exemplified by the statutes of Indiana and California. Indiana's law limits the liability of the "healthcare provider" to $100,000. In addition a compensation fund was created by a charge of up to 10 percent of the malpractice premiums paid by physicians and hospitals; the patient can receive compensation from the fund for as much as $400,000. Florida, Louisiana, Oregon, Wisconsin, Idaho, Pennsylvania, and Illinois have followed this general approach. Unless a fund has no ceiling or a high one, however, the statute is vulnerable to the challenge that it is unconstitutional; a challenge of this kind has already been successful in the Illinois Supreme Court.

California's legislation contains four important reforms. When the patient receives a verdict or a settlement that exceeds $50,000 for the payment of future damages, the money will be paid periodically in amounts ordered by the judge, thus avoiding prolonged payments for damages that may become moot, as when a patient dies sooner than had been expected. Collateral benefits arising out of the patient's injury are disclosed to the jury under California's new law, the idea being that juries will make lower awards when it is known that a patient is receiving money from health or disability insurance, Social Security payments, and the like. Where suits are settled out of court, as more than 80 percent are, the benefits will reduce settlements dollar for dollar. California also has limited to $250,000 the amount the plaintiff can recover for noneconomic losses such as pain and suffering and loss of bodily function. Finally, the state has adopted a sliding scale of contingent fees for the plaintiff's attorney.

Among physicians in the states where the malpractice crisis has been the most severe there is substantial pressure for taking malpractice claims out of the jury system. I have already mentioned the specialty court. Other possibilities are arbitration, which retains the negligence rule, and a "no-fault" arrangement under which the concept of malpractice would be abolished and a patient who had been injured would be compensated regardless of the culpability of the physician.

The cost of the no-fault approach could be enormous. It should also be kept in mind that a more objective method of determining negligent medical injury (such as arbitration, where textbook evidence can be substituted for the testimony of a medical expert) would greatly increase the number of awards granted to patients in the states that now have a low incidence of malpractice claims. Hence it would be inadvisable to introduce such a reform without effective cost-containment legislation.

Ultimately the losses on malpractice insurance should stabilize at an affordable level, given fair determination of issues of liability, reasonable apportionment of damages, effective cost-containment legislation, and the establishment of

Table 26–5

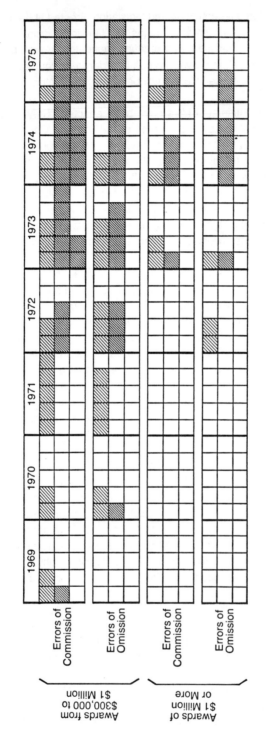

Rise in awards in malpractice actions in California is charted. The chart covers awards of $300,000 or more made as a result of jury verdicts (*lighter*) or settlements reached out of court (*darker*) and also shows whether the injury on which the malpractice award was based resulted from an error of commission by the defendant physician or hospital or was an error of omission, that is, of judgment.

insurance companies owned by physicians. A vital proviso would be for such companies to apply carefully considered underwriting restrictions, aimed at making certain that an insured physician assumes only those medical tasks he can do well. It can be argued that such a system would amount to a form of licensing through insurance rather than by state law. Such limitations are rational, however, in the light of the growing complexity of modern medicine. Moreover, if physicians own the insurance companies, the problem of fairness in applying the limitations should be minimal.

Table 26–6

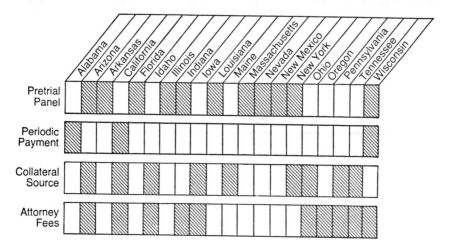

Recent legislation directed at the medical malpractice crisis is summarized. The chart reflects laws that were passed or became effective between January 1, 1975, and March 15, 1976, but does not include all the laws. Laws affecting attorneys' fees limit the amount a lawyer can charge as a fee in a malpractice case. Collateral source laws require disclosure to the jury of payments the defendant will receive from sources other than his lawsuit; the aim is to reduce correspondingly the size of the award made by the jury. Periodic-payment laws apply to future damages and seek to eliminate the windfall that results when a plaintiff receives a lump sum award but then dies shortly afterward. Pretrial panels review malpractice claims with the aim of discouraging frivolous malpractice lawsuits.

A number of physicians believe restrictions of this kind will have little value, since it is generally the "good" doctor who is sued; the less adequate practitioner, who is likely to have a stable practice in a small community, will escape lawsuits regardless of his mistakes. Although this generalization overlooks the numerous jury verdicts and out-of-court settlements against substandard physicians, it contains an element of truth. The best physicians are likely to be in charge of the most difficult cases and so may be the target of a number of claims. Most such claims will not result in the payment of an indemnity although even the best physician can be guilty of a "slip" that is equated with negligence by expert testimony. It will be the job of a rational system for determining facts in malpractice cases—a system that will do away with juries—to achieve better justice for patients and physicians alike.

27

Health and the Corporate Society

VICENTE NAVARRO

In trying to understand the present composition, nature, and functions of the health sector in the United States, one is hampered by a great scarcity of literature, both in the sociological and the medical-care fields, that would explain how the forces shaping the political and economic system of the United States affect the shape and form of the health sector. In fact, health services literature reveals that C. W. Mills, N. Birnbaum, and others have found in other areas of social research: a predominance of empiricism, leading to dominance of experts on trees who neither analyze nor question the forest but accept it as given. Because I believe that the composition and distribution of health resources — the tree — can be fully understood only in the context of the distribution of economic and political power in our society — the forest — I will proceed to analyze first the current social-class and economic structures of the United States, both outside and within the health sectors, and then the ways by which these social structures successively influence and determine the finance and delivery framework of American health care.

The U.S. Class Structure

A key question in any society is: Who owns and controls the income and wealth of the society? In the United States there are a relatively small number of people on the top who own a markedly disproportionate share of personal wealth and whose income is largely derived from ownership. Many of these owners also con-

From *Social Policy* 5 (5) 1975: 41– 49. *Social Policy* is published by Social Policy Corporation, New York. Copyright 1975 by Social Policy Corporation. Reprinted with permission.

trol the uses to which their assets are put. But, increasingly, this control is vested in people who, although wealthy themselves, do not personally own more than a small part of the assets they control; they are the managers of that wealth. Both the owners and controllers of wealth constitute what can be defined as the upper or corporate class, and they command, by virtue of ownership or control, or both, the most important sectors of economic life. According to Hunt and Sherman, the most complete study of the distribution of ownership of wealth ever undertaken in the United States showed that in 1956 the wealthiest 1.6 percent of the population owned at least 80 percent of all corporate stocks (the most important type of income-producing wealth) and virtually all state and local government bonds.[1] And, although no subsequent studies have been done on individual ownership of wealth, it seems highly unlikely that this high concentration of economic wealth has changed between 1956 and the present time.[2]

At the other end of the social scale is the working class, composed primarily of industrial or blue-collar workers, the workers of the services sector, and also the agricultural wage earners, although the last form a steadily decreasing part of the labor force.[3] In 1970 these groups represented 35 percent, 12 percent, and 1.8 percent of the labor force, respectively. It is primarily from their ranks that the unemployed, the poor, and the subproletariat come.

In between the "polar" classes is the middle class, consisting of (1) the professionals—including doctors, lawyers, middle-rank executives, academicians, etc., whose main denominator is that their work is intellectual as opposed to manual and usually requires professional training; (2) the business middle class—associated with small and medium-sized enterprises, ranging from business people employing a few workers to owners of fairly sizable enterprises of every kind, and who are the owners and controllers of O'Connor's competitive sector or of Galbraith's market sector of our economy;[4] (3) the self-employed shopkeepers, crafts workers, and artisans—a declining sector of the labor force, representing less than 8 percent; and (4) the office and sales workers—the majority of white-collar workers, the group that has increased most rapidly within the labor force in the last two decades and today represents almost a quarter of the labor force of the United States and of most Western European countries.

For reasons of brevity, and accepting the simplifications that this categorization implies, I will refer to Groups 1 and 2 as the upper-middle class and Groups 3 and 4 as the lower-middle class. Table 27–1 summarizes the percentage of the labor force in each occupational category and social class and the annual median income for each category.

1. R. J. Lampman, The share of top wealth-holders in national wealth: 1922–1956. In E. K. Hunt and H. J. Sherman, Economics: An Introduction to Traditional and Radical Views. New York: Harper & Row, 1972.

2. L. Upton and N. Lyons, Basic facts: Distribution of personal income and wealth in the United States. Cambridge, Mass.: Cambridge Institute, 1972.

3. In my categorization of classes and the strata within classes, I have very closely followed R. Miliband, The State in Capitalist Society. London: Weidenfeld and Micolson, 1969, pp. 23–48.

4. J. O'Connor, The fiscal crisis of the state. New York: St. Martin's, 1973, pp. 13–15; J. K. Galbraith, Economics and the public purpose. Boston: Houghton Miflin, 1973, pp. 55–71.

The distributions of wealth and income following these class lines, with the highest possession of both at the top and the lowest at the bottom have remained remarkably constant over time. In the last retrospective study of the distribution of income, published in the 1974 annual *Economic Report of the President* and widely reported in the press, it was found that "the bottom 20 percent of all families had 5.1 percent of the nation's income in 1947 and had almost the same amount, 5.4 percent, in 1972. At the top, there was a similar absence of significant change. The richest 20 percent had 43.3 percent of the income in 1947 and 41.4 percent in 1972."[5]

Table 27–1   Occupational and Social-Class Distribution of the U.S. Labor Force

Social Class and Occupational Group	Percentage	Estimated Annual Median Income
Corporate class	1.3	$80–100,000
Upper-middle class		
Professionals and technicals	14.0	18,000
Business middle-class executives	6.0	16,000
Lower-middle class		
Self-employed shopkeepers, crafts workers, and artisans	7.0	8,500
Clerical and sales workers	23.0	6,500
Working class		
Manual workers	35.0	6,000
Service workers	12.0	4,000
Farm workers	1.8	2,600

Sources: V. Bownell and M. Reich, *Workers and the American Economy: Data on the Labor Force.* New England Free Press, 1973); *Current Population Reports, Consumer Income: Income Growth Rates in 1939 to 1968 for Persons by Occupational and Industry Groups, for the United States,* Series P60, No. 69, 1970; A. Giddens, *The Class Structure of the Advanced Societies.* New York; Hutchinson University Library, 1973.

Class Structure in the Health Sector

This class structure in our society is reflected in the composition of the different groups in the health sector, either as owners, controllers, or producers of services. Members of the upper class and, to a lesser degree, the upper-middle class (Groups one and two of the middle class) predominate in the decision-making bodies of our health institutions, i.e., the boards of trustees of foundations, teaching hospital institutions, medical schools, and hospitals. Among the producers of health services, at the top are the physicians who represent 7.3 percent of the health sector labor force. They are mainly from upper-middle-class backgrounds and their 1970 median net income of $40,000 places them in the top 5 percent of our society. The majority of persons in this group are white and male.

Very much below the upper class of the health sector are the nurses, physi-

5. New York Times (February 2) 1974: 10.

cal therapists, occupational therapists, technologists, etc., who can be defined as equivalent to the lower-middle class (Group 4) of the previous categorization. This group represents 26.5 percent of the health sector labor force and had an annual median income of approximately $6,000 in 1970. Employees in this group are primarily female and members of the lower-income group; 9 percent is black.

Below this group is the working class per se of the health sector, the auxiliary, ancillary, and service personnel, representing 54.2 percent of the health labor force, 94.1 percent of whom are women and who include an over representation of blacks (30 percent). In 1970 this group's median income was $4,000.

Thus the income distribution in the health sector parallels that of society in general. However, data collected between 1949 and 1970 show a very dramatic

Figure 27–1   Annual Rise in Median Income of Selected Personnel in U.S. Health Labor Force, 1949–70

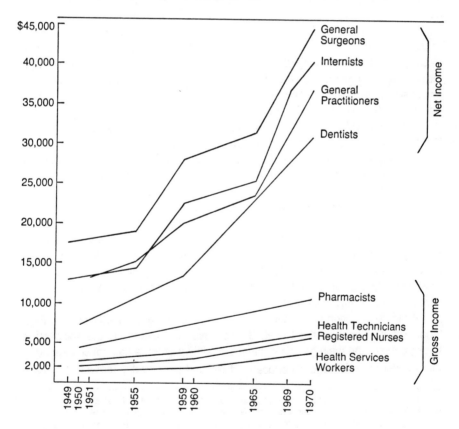

Sources: For income of physicians: "The Survey of Physicians," copyright 1972 by *Medical Economics,* Oradell, New Jersey. Figures are for self-employed physicians in solo practice, under age 65. For income of dentists: *Journal of the American Dental Association,* continuing income survey. For income of other wage groups: U.S. Bureau of the Census, 1950, 1960, and 1970.

increase in the income differentials between the top and bottom income groups of the health industry. (See Figure 27–1.)

The Determinants of Income Differentials

Much has been written about the reasons for these income differentials. Orthodox economics holds that workers' incomes depend on their productivity, i.e., "on the amount of capital available, on the one hand, and on workers' skills and education, on the other."[6] According to this interpretation, the necessary conditions for social mobility are (1) increased education, to improve the workers' position in the market for their skills and (2) equal opportunity for each worker in the competitive labor market. This view is shared by the majority of people in the black and women's movements within and outside the health sector. However, this analysis neglects property and class considerations. Actually, one of the widely accepted theoretical works on social inequality in today's United States, Rawls's *A Theory of Justice,* does not even mention the value of property as a source of social cleavage. Indeed, following the Weberian interpretation of status, Rawls and most of the exponents of what Barry calls the liberal paradigm maintain that social stratification is multidimensional, depending on a variety of factors such as education, income, occupation, religion, ethnicity, and so on.[7]

Empirical evidence, however, seems to question the main assumption of the liberal paradigm. Regarding the social mobility that is supposed to be the result of the widening of opportunities and of the free flow of labor market forces, and that is supposed to have caused the withering away of the social classes, Westergaard and others have recently shown that although there has been some mobility among the different social groups or strata within each social class, there has been practically no mobility between social classes.[8] Moreover, the primary objective of education, instead of being the transmission of skills to aid upward mobility, seems to have been the perpetuation of social roles within the predefined social classes. Indeed, Bowles and Gintis, among others, have indicated how education, labor markets, and industrial structures interact to produce distinctive social strata *within* each class.[9]

A similar situation prevails in the health sector. Simpson and Robson in England, and Kleinbach in the United States have shown that (1) the social-class background of the main groups within the health labor force has not changed during the last 25 years and (2) education fixes and perpetuates those social back-

---

6. J. B. Clark, The distribution of wealth. New York: Macmillan, 1924. *In* B. Silverman and M. Yanowitch, Radical and Liberal Perspectives on the Working Class. *Social Policy 4 (4)* 1974: 43.

7. J. Rawls, *A theory of justice.* Cambridge, Mass.: Harvard University Press, 1971; B. Barry, *The liberal theory of justice: A critical examination of the principal doctrines in "A Theory of Justice" by John Rawls.* Oxford: Clarendon Press, 1972.

8. J. H. Westergaard, Sociology: The myth of classlessness. *In* R. Blackburn (ed.) *Ideology in Social Science.* New York: Fontana, 1972, pp. 119 – 63.

9. S. Bowles and H. Gintis, IQ in the U.S. class structure. *Social Policy 3 4–5:* 65–96.

grounds and replicates social roles.[10] Indeed, Flexner's statement earlier in this century that a primary aim of medical education was to separate the gentlemen (the upper class) from the quacks (the lower class) is equally descriptive of the current situation.

Lyden, Geiger, and Peterson reported in 1968 that only 17 percent of physicians were the children of crafts workers or skilled and unskilled laborers (who represented 57 percent of the labor force), while over 31 percent were children of professionals (representing 4.9 percent of the labor force).[11] It is interesting, and not surprising, that while the underrepresentation of women and blacks among new entrants to the medical schools diminished slowly but steadily over the last decade, the underrepresentation of entrants from working-class and lower-middle-class backgrounds remained remarkably constant during the same period. Indeed, women, who represent 51 percent of the U.S. population, made up 6 percent of all medical students in 1961 and 16 percent in 1973, while Blacks, representing 12 percent of the overall U.S. population, went from 2 percent to 6 percent of all medical students during the same time period. By contrast, the percentage of medical students coming from families earning the median family income or below, representing approximately one-half of the population, has remained at 12 percent since 1920.[12]

These data indicate that there is not an automatic trend toward diminishing class differences or bringing about social-class mobility within and outside the health sector, but rather that, as Harold Laski said, "the careful selection of one's own parents" remains among the most important variables explaining one's own power, wealth, income, and opportunities.

It would seem, then, that the liberal paradigm does not sufficiently explain the composition of the labor force and its class and income structure, and that a better explanation can be postulated, i.e., the inequalities of income, wealth, and economic and political power are functionally related to the way in which the means of production and reproduction of goods, commodities, and services, and the organs of legitimization in the United States, are owned, controlled, influenced, and directed. Overall wealth and income differentials among social classes, then, do not have so much to do with the free operation of the labor market forces, but more with the patterns of ownership and control of the main means of income-producing wealth and of the organs of legitimization, i.e., communications, education, and the agencies of the state. And according to this alternate explanation, education and other means of socialization are not the means of creating upward mobility among social classes, but actually are means

---

10. M. A. Simpson, *Medical education: A critical approach.* London: Butterworths, 1972; J. Robson, The NHS company, Inc. The social consequence of the professional dominance in the National Health Service. *International Journal of Health Services 3 (3)* 1973: 413–26;

11. F. J. Lyden, H. J. Geiger, and O. Peterson, The training of good physicians. Cambridge, Mass.: Harvard University Press, 1968, cited in M. A. Simpson, *Medical Education: A Critical Approach.* London: Butterworths, 1972, p. 35.

12. All of these figures are cited in G. Kleinbach, *Social Class and Medical Education.* Department of Education, Harvard University, 1974.

of perpetuating patterns of control and ownership.

Moreover, the prevalent patterns of class control over the main means of production, reproduction, and legitimization in the U.S. social system are replicated in the health sector as well. My purpose in the discussion that follows is to show how the corporate or upper class, augmented by the upper-middle class (the professionals and business middle class of my categorization), maintain a dominant influence on two main components of the health sector: (1) the financial and health delivery institutions and (2) the health teaching institutions.[13]

Corporate-Class Involvement in the Health Sector

A main characteristic of the United States is the high concentration of economic wealth in the monopolistic sector. In 1967, a few giant corporations (958 or just 0.06 percent) held a majority of all assets ($1,070 billion or 53.2 percent), while a large number of small corporations (906,458 or 59 percent of the total) held a very small, almost minuscule portion of corporate assets ($31 billion or 1.5 percent).

This concentration of corporate economic power replicates itself in the several sectors that constitute the U.S. economy. For example, in the key sector of manufacturing, Hunt and Sherman point out that the largest 20 manufacturing firms owned a larger share of the assets than the smallest 419,000 firms combined. The financial capital sector, which includes the banks, trusts, and insurance companies, and is itself highly concentrated,[14] exerts a dominant influence in the corporate sector, primarily through lending to the corporations, which are becoming increasingly dependent on the financial institutions for their capital needs. The financial capital institutions influence corporate policies through ownership of corporate stocks and the interlocking of directorships in their boards. Summarizing the findings of the report of the Senate Committee on Government Operations, *Disclosure of Corporate Ownership,* Morton Mintz of the *Washington Post* (January 6, 1974) wrote, "Most of the nation's largest corporations appear to be dominated or controlled by eight institutions, including six banks." Through their boards, these banks have a close interlocking relationship with insurance companies such as Aetna Life, Prudential, and others. Also according to the committee report, the top four banks in the country own 10 percent of ITT stocks, 12 percent of Xerox, 22 percent of Gulf Oil, 10 percent of International Paper, 12 percent of Polaroid, and parts of many other powerful corporations. The significance of these figures can best be appreciated in light of the House Banking and

---

13. The state health agencies are a third component of the health sector. For an analysis of the class influence in those agencies, see V. Navarro, Social Policy Issues: An Explanation of the Composition, Nature, and Functions of the Present Health Sector of the United States. *Bulletin of the New York Academy of Medicine 51 (1)* 1975: 199–234.

14. The 100 largest banks (out of a total of 13,775 commercial banks) hold 45 percent of all deposits (Pattman Committee Staff Report for the Domestic Finance Subcommittee of the House Committee on Banking and Currency, *Commercial Banks and Their Trust Activities: Emerging Influence on the American Economy.* Washington, D.C.: U.S. Government Printing Office, 1968.

Currency Subcommittee's statement that 5 percent ownership of stock in a corporation is sufficient for a controlling vote in that corporation.

The top financial institutions likewise play an important role in the health industry, the second largest in the country. The flow of health insurance money through private insurance companies in 1973 was $29 billion, slightly less than half of the total insurance, health and other, sold in this country that year.[15] Over half of this money flowed through the commercial insurance companies. Among these companies, we find, again, a high concentration of financial capital, with the ten largest commercial health insurers (Aetna, Travellers, Metropolitan Life, Prudential, CNA, Equitable, Mutual of Omaha, Connecticut General, John Hancock, and Provident) controlling close to 60 percent of the entire commercial health insurance industry. Most of these are also the biggest life insurance companies, which are, with the banks, the most important controllers of financial capital in this country. Metropolitan Life and Prudential, for instance, each control $30 billion in assets, making them far larger than General Motors, Standard Oil of New Jersey, and ITT.[16] These financial entities have close links with banking, and through the banks they exercise a powerful influence over the top corporations. An example of this influence is that, out of 28 directors of Metropolitan Life, 23 sit on the boards of banking institutions, particularly of the Chase Manhattan Bank, which owns 10 percent of the stocks of American Airlines, 15 percent of CBS, 6 percent of Mobil Oil, and portions of very many other corporations.[17] The importance of this influence, defined by some, such as the Senate Subcommittee on Government Operations, as dominance over the overall economy, is reflected in the present debate on the different proposals for national health insurance: on whether to open the doors to the commercials or keep them out of the coming national health insurance scene. The great political influence and power of these financial capital institutions is attested by the fact that all the proposals, with the exception of the Kennedy-Giffiths whose main constituency was the trade unions of the monopolistic sector (AFL-CIO and UAW), have left room for, and even encouraged, the involvement of the commercials in the health sector. The administration proposal, for example, would increase the flow of money through the private insurance industry (including commercial health insurance) from $29 billion to $42 billion, with another $14 billion handled by the private carriers in their role as intermediaries in the publicly financed segment of the proposal.[18] Moreover, due to the power of the commercial insurance companies, changes were made in the Kennedy-Griffiths proposal to include a role for the insurance companies in the form of the new Kennedy-Mills proposal. A *New York Times* editorial (April 7,

---

15. J. K. Iglehart, National insurance plan tops ways and means agenda, *National Journal* 6 387 1974.

16. T. Bodenheimer, S. Cummings, and E. Harding, Capitalization on illness: the health insurance industry, *International Journal of Health Services* (in press).

17. T. Bodenheimer, S. Cummings, and E. Harding, Capitalization on illness: the health insurance industry, *International Journal of Health Services* (in press).

18. J. K. Iglehart, National insurance plan tops ways and means agenda, *National Journal* 6 387 1974.

1974) indicated that the decision of the Kennedy-Mills proposal "to retain the insurance companies' role was based on recognition of that industrh's power to kill any legislation it considers unacceptable. The bill's sponsors thus had to choose between appeasing the insurance industry and obtaining no national health insurance at all."

We can see, then, that the same financial and corporate forces that are dominant in shaping the American economy also increasingly shape the health services sector. The commercial insurance companies, however, although the largest financial power in the premium market in the health sector, are not the only one. They compete with the power of the providers, expressed in the insurance sector primarily through the Blues—Blue Cross and Blue Shield. The controllers of both the commercials and the Blues, although sharing class interests, have opposite and conflicting corporate interests. Actually, it is likely that the predominance of financial capital in the health sector, specifically of commercial insurance, could mean the weakening of the providers' control of that sector. If this should come about, we would probably see the proletarianization of the providers, with providers being mere employees of the finance corporations—the commercial insurance companies. In this respect, unionization of the medical profession would be a symptom of its proletarianization, so that the present incipient but steady trend toward unionization of the medical profession may be an indication of things to come in the health sector.

Class Control of the Health Institutions

In order to understand the patterns of control in the health sector, we have to look not only at the patterns of control in the financing of health services, but also the patterns of control and influence in the health delivery institutions. Indeed, financial capital, the money or energy that moves the system, goes through prefixed institutional channels that are owned, controlled, and/or influenced by classes and groups similar to those who have dominant influence through financing. We can group the institutions into (1) those that reproduce and legitimize the patterns of control and influence, e.g., teaching institutions and foundations such as Carnegie, Rockefeller, and others, and (2) those that deliver the services.

The teaching institutions and foundations are controlled by the financial and corporate communities and by the professionals, i.e., the corporate class and the upper-middle class (Group 1 referred to earlier). As R.M. MacIver wrote, "In the non governmental (teaching) institutions, the typical board member is associated with large-scale business, a banker, manufacturer, business executive, or prominent lawyer," to which, in the health sector, we could add a prominent physician.[19] One study showed that of the 734 trustees of 30 leading universities, half were recognized members of the professions, and half were proprietors, manag-

---

19. R. M. MacIver, *Academic freedom in our time* New York: Gordian Press, 1967, p. 78. In R. Miliband, *The State in Capitalist Society*. London: Weidenfeld and Nicolson, 1969, p. 251.

ers, bankers.[20] It is quite misleading to assume that the class and corporate role of such board members is a passive one or that their function is to rubber-stamp what the administrators and medical faculty decide. In fact, their seeming passivity is really delegated control. In an infrequently quoted part of his report, Flexner said that "the influence of the board of trustees . . . determines in the social and economic realms an atmosphere of timidity which is not without effect on critical appointments and promotions."[21] Concerning the highest decisions, theirs is the first and final voice. And their first role, as Galbraith has indicated, is to insure that "the aims of higher education . . . are to be attuned to the needs of the industrial (corporate) system" which is usually also referred to as the private enterprise system.[22] In 1961, N.M. Pusey, then president of Harvard, stated quite explicitly that "the end of all academic departments . . . is completely directed towards making the *private enterprise system* continue to work effectively and beneficially in a very difficult world."[23] Such a commitment, which is far more typical than atypical of our academic institutions and foundations, cannot be disassociated from the fact of the predominant membership of corporate and business leaders on the boards of trustees of academia and foundations. The function and purpose of this dominant influence on the boards of trustees are to perpetuate the sets of values that optimize their collective benefits as class and as corporate interests. While I do not believe that there is monopoly control in the value-generating system, I do think that the system of influence and control in that system is highly skewed in favor of the corporate and financial value system. And this dominant influence is felt not only in universities, foundations, and institutions of higher learning, but also in most of the value-generating systems from the media to all other instruments of communication.[24]

This class dominance also appears in the control of the delivery institutions. Analyzing the class composition of the voluntary community hospitals (the largest component of the health delivery institutions), one sees less predominance of the representatives of financial and corporate capital, and more of the upper-middle class, and primarily of Groups 1 and 2 defined earlier, i.e., the professionals—including physicians—and representatives of the business middle class. Even here, the working class and lower-middle classes, which constitute the majority of the U.S. population, are barely represented. For instance, not one trade union leader (even a token one), sits on any board in the hospitals in the region of Baltimore.[25] And, of course, even less represented on hospital boards are the unorganized workers. Table 27–2 summarizes the social-class distribution of the U.S. labor force and on the boards of the reproductive and delivery health institutions.

20. H. P. Beck, *Men who control our universities* London: King's Crown Press, 1947, p. 51.

21. A. Flexner, *Universities: American, English, German* New York: Oxford University Press, 1930, p. 180.

22. J. K. Galbraith, *The new industrial state* Boston: Houghton Mifflin, 1973, p. 370.

23. N. M. Pusey, *Age of the scholar: Observations on education in a troubled decade* Cambridge: Harvard University Press, 1963, p 171.

24. See J. L. Servan-Schreiber, *The power to inform: Media-The business of information* New York: McGraw-Hill, 1974.

25. P. VanGelder, Baltimore AFL-CIO leader. Personal communication.

Table 27–2   Social-Class Distribution of the U.S. Labor Force and of the Boards of Trustees of Reproductive and Delivery Institutions in the Health Sector

	Social-Class Distribution			
	Corporate Class	Upper-Middle Class	Lower-Middle Class	Working Class
U.S. labor force	1.0%	19.0%	30.0%	49.0%
Board members of				
Reproductive institutions				
Foundations (top 10)	70.0	30.0	0.0	0.0
Private medical teaching				
institutions	45.0	55.0	0.0	0.0
State medical teaching				
institutions	20.0	70.0	10.0	0.0
Board members of				
Delivery institutions				
Voluntary hospitals	3-5.0	80.0	10.0	5.0

Sources: V. Navarro, "The Control of the Health Institutions," Johns Hopkins University, Department of Health Care Organization (in progress); J. Pfeffer, Size, composition, and functions of hospital boards of directors: a study of organization-environment linkage, *Administrative Sciences Quarterly* **18** *349* 1973; R. T. Hartnett, College and university trustees: their backgrounds, roles and educational attitudes, in *Crisis in American Institutions,* ed. J. Skolnick and E. Currie Boston: Little, Brown, 1973.

A New Dialectic

From the previous analysis it should be clear that I disagree with those who perceive the present basic dialectical conflict both in the financing and in the delivery of health services to be between the consumers and the providers. While the present health sector seems to be controlled primarily by the providers and their different components (the "patricians" or academia-based medicine, the practitioners or the AMA, and the hospital organizations or AHA), they do not have an inherent control by virtue of their "unique" knowledge. In fact, the power of the medical profession is delegated power. As Freidson has indicated, "A profession attains and maintains its position by virtue of the protection and patronage of some elite segment of society which has been persuaded that there is some special value in its work."[26] But as Frankenberg has pointed out, this section or segment of the population is not so much an economic elite as a class, i.e., the corporate class described before.[27]

Thus, the great influence of the providers over the health institutions, which amounts to control of the health sector, is based on power delegated from other groups and classes, primarily the corporate class and the uppermiddle class, to which the providers belong. Their specific interests may actually be in conflict

26. E. Freidson, *Profession of medicine: A study of the sociology of applied knowledge* New York: Dodd, Mead, 1970, p. 72.

27. R. Frankenberg, Functionalism and after theory and developments in social science applied to the health field, *International Journal of Health Services* (in press)

with the power of other groups or strata within the upper-middle class and with the greater power of the corporate class. Indeed, as I have indicated elsewhere, the corporate powers of England and Sweden not only tolerated but even supported the nationalization of the health sector when the corporate interests required it, formalizing a dependency of the medical profession on those corporate and state interests.[28]

To define the main dialectical conflict in the health sector as one of providers versus consumers assumes that (1) providers have the final and most powerful control of decision making in the health sector and (2) consumers have a uniformity of interests, transcending class and other interests. Control of the health institutions, however, is primarily class control by the classes and groups described earlier, and only secondarily control by the professions. The dialectical conflicts that exist are not, then, between the providers and the consumers, but (1) between the corporate class and the providers over the financing of the health sector and (2) between the majority of the U.S. population, who belong to the working and lower-middle classes, and the controllers of the health care institutions—the corporate class and the upper-middle class, including the professionals.

In summary, then, the same economic and political forces that determine the class structure of the United States also determine the composition and nature of the U.S. health sector. This interpretation runs contrary to the most prevalent interpretation, which assumes that the shape and form of the health sector is a result of prevailing American values. But this explanation assumes that values are the cause, and not, as I postulate, a symptom of the distribution of economic and political power in the United States. In fact, that explanation avoids the question of which groups and classes have a dominant influence on the value-generating system and maintain, perpetuate, and legitimize it. According to my interpretation, they are the very same groups and classes that have a dominant influence over the systems of production, reproduction, and legitimization both within and outside the health sector.

---

28. V. Navarro, A critique of the present and proposed strategies for redistributing resources in the health sector and a discussion of alternatives. *Medical Care* 12 (9) 1974: 721–742.

PART VI
The Future of Medicine

The field of health, illness, and medicine is changing rapidly. Its future is uncertain, for what was undreamed of only years ago is now a reality. Organ transplants that once seemed a miracle are everyday occurrences and scientists are predicting that soon we will be able to regenerate new limbs. What will be next?

The advances in medicine and health care present us with new problems as well. Many people are now living to old age. Managing chronic illness, a frequent companion of age, will require new approaches that are not yet fully developed. Medical advancements are also helping us to uncover health problems that would have gone undetected in a less sophisticated age—problems such as the health hazards arising from advanced technology. Who will pay for and benefit from these new medical technologies? Can we establish an equitable health care system in which all citizens are adequately covered? As medicine becomes more sophisticated, so must our management of it.

Ethical issues are becoming increasingly important in health, illness, and medicine. Who is and who should be responsible for health and illness, for life and death: doctors, patients, patients' families, the Supreme Court? We are just beginning to address these basic questions.

As the title of this section suggests the future of health, illness, and medicine depends on our understanding of the issues we face as we head toward the 21st century. That understanding will influence the choices we make about our future.

The Future of Health and Medicine: The Issues We Face

28

PAUL C. HIGGINS

Overview

Predicting the future of health, illness, and medicine in America is a difficult, if not an impossible task. The future, though, depends on the choices we make (Fuchs, 1974). These choices can be conscious decisions made through public discussion or they can be made by default through neglect and ignorance. Either way the consequences will be real. The choices depend on the issues we consider as America moves into the last quarter of the 20th century. Our decisions will be based on our understanding of the issues and on our values. People may agree on what the issues in health, illness, and medicine are, but they may disagree about which ones are more or less important and about what should be done. Some people may even disagree about what the issues are.

In this chapter we will try to clarify some of the basic issues in health, illness, and medicine that confront America as it moves toward the 21st century. It is important to realize that the issues that are vital enough to discuss and to plan for are themselves the results of value judgments. The readings in this book have demonstrated that values are an integral part of health, illness, and medicine and they will continue to be so in the future.

America faces a wide range of issues in health, illness, and medicine: changing patterns of illnesses; rising health care costs; uneven delivery of health services; the right-to-die controversy; increased malpractice suits; organ transplantation; and many others. Some issues address our basic assumptions about health, illness, and medicine. For example, what is death and who controls its arrival? Other issues deal with repairing or improving our present system of medicine. For example, what type of national health insurance program should Congress enact, if it enacts one at all?

The issues that deal with refinements of the medical system are most likely to be dealt with in the near future. They will entail modest changes in how we live and view our lives as compared to those issues that question our basic assumptions. Yet, those basic assumptions and the manner in which we deal with them will have a profound impact on health, illness, and medicine. We shall now examine some of those basic assumptions.

Basic Assumptions

Our understanding of health, illness, and medicine and who is responsible for them are the basic issues we face. What is health or illness? Do we have a *right* to health? What is our responsibility in maintaining the quality of our lives? Should medical professionals be the guardians of our lives and deaths? These and similar questions address our basic assumptions about health, illness, and medicine.

Health

Health is an elusive concept. As was discussed previously, what people think health is and when they think they are healthy or not healthy depends partly on cultural and social factors. Health is a matter of degree. One feels more or less healthy. Yet what is health? How do we recognize a minimal level of health below which individuals are hindered in carrying out other activities? The World Health Organization states that health is a "state of complete physical, mental and, social well-being and not merely the absence of disease or infirmity." This definition is too inclusive for it attributes to health much of human happiness (Callahan, 1973).

Why should we be concerned with defining and reexamining our notion of health? The most obvious reason is that we spend more than $150 billion a year trying to attain it. Obviously, it is essential to understand what we are trying to attain. More importantly, an attempt to define health will also help us understand our priorities about our physical well-being. A sore toe concerns us less than a broken arm which in turn bothers us less than cancer. But not all comparisons are so obvious. Understanding these priorities helps us put our troubles in perspective. Our attempt to define health will also force us to examine our reasons for cherishing health. We all want to be healthy, but why? Don't we also want to be wise, attractive, athletic, and many other desirable characteristics? Can health be pursued without regard for these other desires? An examination of health will also help us understand the limitations of medicine in maintaining and restoring our health. No definition of health will be universally accepted, but discussion will be healthy.

Even if we agree on *what* health is, do we have a right to health or to health care? We cannot insure that no one will ever become ill. No one can be guaranteed health but do we have a right to guaranteed health care? If we agree that everyone has a right to health care, how will it affect our rights to a good education, decent food and housing, a meaningful job, a stimulating and aesthetically pleasing environment, and so on? However important health is, it still must compete for scarce resources with our other desires (Fuchs, 1974).

Illness

Illness also poses a complex issue. While doctors agree that certain diseases and traumas are illness, some behaviors are not so clearly defined. Is every behavior that is disapproved of to be considered an illness and therefore to be treated by the medical profession? Robert Veatch (1973) argues that deviant behavior will be seen as illness if it is viewed as nonvoluntary and organic, if the attending expert is a physician, and if the deviant behavior falls below a minimal standard of acceptability.

Historically there has been a shift in how deviant behavior has been viewed. Initially these behaviors were viewed as sinful, later as criminal, and today as sick. As the conception of deviant behavior has changed so have the agents of society who deal with it: first, religious leaders, then the police, and now doctors. For example, alcoholism is now seen as a sickness rather than a crime and alcoholics are treated by doctors rather than by the police.

Many people may agree that alcoholism and other deviant behaviors are dealt with more humanely by the medical profession than by the police. Other people might argue that this is another example of the continuing *medicalization* of life—more and more behaviors are seen as falling within the province of medicine. For example, people are rarely discouraged and are even encouraged to go to the doctor for what can only be called the "blahs." A pill for every ill is a prominent theme in America. What we must recognize, though, is that whether doctors treat alcoholics *humanely* or the police *inhumanely* arrest them, both practices control those individuals and limit their freedom. Both practices signify that the individual's condition and even the individual is undesirable. Something must be done to restore these individuals to an acceptable state. They *are* different from us.

The view that a particular behavior is an illness can be changed. Homosexuality recently has been deleted by the American Psychiatric Association from its official catalogue of mental disorders (Fox, 1977). If illnesses can be undone, then the medical profession recognizes that it is fallible. If it is fallible, should America *unthinkingly* allow it to decide upon all issues of illness? Thus we confront the issue of what is illness and who will decide it. And even if illness is one type of socially deviant behavior, perhaps we need to examine carefully what is bad about it (Callahan, 1977).

Not only must we confront our ideas about health and illness, but our understanding of life and death must be reexamined. Abortion and "test-tube" babies indicate the necessity of grappling with the meaning of life. Organ transplanta-tions and extraordinary means of keeping people alive emphasize that we must deal with death. Not only do we need to ask when life starts and ends, but also what the quality of life and death should be? Is our own humanity diminished if a malformed fetus is medically aborted which otherwise would be a gross parody of our humanity? Is time so precious and death so ugly that painfully prolonging the inevitability of death should be sought at all cost?

We are just beginning to deal with these issues. For example, a recently developed definition of brain death has gained wide acceptance in medicine and has resulted in life and death consequences. The criteria for brain death are total unawareness of externally applied stimuli, absence of breathing or spontaneous movement for at least one hour, absence of reflexes, and the absence of elec-troencephalograph readings (which indicate brain activity) during a 24-hour period (Reiser, 1977). Concern with the quality and not merely the length of life is evidenced in debates over prolonging the suffering of terminally ill patients by extraordinary means.

Responsibility

The final issue that challenges our basic assumptions is who is responsible for health, illness, and medicine. Historically, we have put our health and illness, our life and death in the hands of the medical profession. Whatever responsibility we may have had for our own bodies, most of it we have given up. With an often unrealistic hope in medicine's ability to heal, we have ignored our own ability to influence our health.

Evidence suggests that our collective decision has been shortsighted. For example, medicine affects only about 10 percent of what we commonly think of as health problems: infant mortality; days lost due to sickness; and adult mortality (Wildavsky, 1977). Major causes for increased life expectancy are a result of environmental and social factors such as improved nutrition and personal hygiene, provisions for safe water and milk supplies, and better sewage disposal. The nation's health and illness has been the medical profession's business. But thousands of premature deaths, disabilities and incapacitating illnesses could be prevented and billions of dollars could be saved each year if we exercised our collective responsibility (Knowles, 1977). Safe driving, proper exercise, adequate rest, and refraining from excessive eating, drinking, and smoking could improve the quality of our health. But these "costly and high-powered" technologies require the individual responsibility of us all to be effective.

Such collective responsibility will be difficult to achieve. Competing interests always are important in health, illness, and medicine. Disagreement among health professionals, between doctors and patients, between the government and the medical establishment are evidence of such conflicting interests.

The exercise of collective responsibility in improving the quality of health may conflict with people's desires to eat, drink, or behave as they please. For example, scientists generally agree that smoking is hazardous to health, yet millions of people continue to smoke. The tobacco industry recently opposed a national government campaign to persuade people to stop smoking. If individuals do not take responsibility for the quality of their lives, should we as a society take on the responsibility for treating and paying for self-inflicted illnesses? The issue is an old and complicated one: the good of society vs. the freedom of the individual. We live in a society that espouses health while simultaneously advertising health-inhibiting activities (e.g., smoking or drinking).

More profoundly, some people argue that *medicine* has become a hazard to our health and to the quality of our lives (Illich, 1976). As a result of mistakes by admittedly fallible practitioners and its dominance over our lives, medicine threatens our well-being; a well-being based on individual responsibility. For example, should powerful medical associations and professionals both in and outside of government decide if cancer patients may use Laetrile or should the cancer patients make that decision? When may parents discontinue medical treatment for their children? The established medical profession would argue that it is protecting us from quacks and unscientific ideas. But who is to protect us from our medical protectors?

Just as the issue of who should be responsible for our health and illness must be confronted, so also must the issue of responsibility of our lives and deaths be confronted. Public discussion rages over abortion. In 1973 the Supreme Court ruled that a woman has a right to an abortion during the first three months of pregnancy, but later held that public funds could be denied for those abortions. The Court will likely rule on this issue many more times in the future. Abortion is not the only arena in which the control of life is at stake. For example, should genetic counseling and screening be mandatory? Couples with a high risk of having a genetically deformed child, (what is high and who decides?) which would be costly to the state, could be prohibited from having that child. What are the implications of producing human life outside of the womb or of cloning? "Test-tube" babies are no longer science fiction. How far should we go in that direction and who decides? Governments have already regulated research in the recombination of genes—the creation of new forms of life by combining the genes of various micro-organisms. Increasingly, in health, illness, and medicine we face ethical and political and not merely technological issues.

Death comes to us all. But who is to be responsible for its arrival; the individual, the individual's agent (e.g., parents or spouse), or the doctor? The question is complex. There is growing sentiment that terminally ill individuals should be allowed to refuse extraordinary life-sustaining measures. But do individuals also have the right to sacrifice their lives in order to save others through organ donation? These issues are just beginning to be recognized and dealt with. The life of Karen Ann Quinlan is evidence of that. For reasons that will never be fully known, on April 15, 1975 Karen stopped breathing for at least two 15-minute periods. She sustained serious brain damage with only "vegetative" functioning remaining but was not "brain dead." She was hooked to a mechanical respirator. One year later the Supreme Court of New Jersey overturned a lower court ruling that had stated that decisions about medical care were the physician's responsibility. Karen's parents were allowed to remove her from the respirator and thereby fulfill their daughter's earlier expressed wishes (Reiser, 1977).

Right to die legislation is a further testament to the growing public concern about who is responsible for an individual's death. Right to die legislation permits individuals to request in a "living will" that their lives not be prolonged artificially in a terminal condition. Such legislation has been considered in more than half the states and was first passed in California in 1976. This concern, however, has existed for a long time, but was managed secretly between the suffering terminally ill patients and their physicians (Garland, 1976). Now it has become a public issue.

Doctoring Medicine

As we head toward the 21st century, we not only face issues that challenge our basic ideas about health, illness, and medicine, but also issues related to the improvement of our existing medical system. When the American public feels that there is a crisis in medical care they are not referring to such basic issues as who controls an individuals's death. Rather they are concerned about more mundane, but still vitally important, issues such as access to quality care and the cost of that care. Access and cost involve many health care issues that we are facing now and will continue to face in the future. We shall discuss only a few of those issues.

Changing Patterns of Illness

American medicine has made great progress in combating the health problems of the first half of the 20th century. Infectious diseases such as tuberculosis, influenza, pneumonia, and diphtheria have been managed effectively through sulfur-based drugs and later penicillin and streptomycin. The discovery of insulin in the treatment of diabetes and the creation of effective vaccines against smallpox, polio, and other infectious viruses have improved the health of many. As a result of medicine's success in preventing and treating infectious diseases and due to improved public health, better sewage disposal, and cleaner drinking water, our health problems have changed (Glazier, 1973).

Chronic illnesses such as heart disease, cancer, stroke, and diabetes are now the leading causes of death and suffering. People who would have died in infancy or childhood are now living to middle and old age only to be afflicted by chronic illnesses. Surely our hazardous environment plays a part in these illnesses and is likely to play a larger part in the future. Yet medicine has lagged behind the changes in our health problems.

Medicine has been developed to combat infectious diseases, acute illnesses, and accidents which require the advanced resources of a hospital. Yet our medical system does not now effectively serve the increasing numbers of chronically ill people in the United States. Our medical system waits for the patient to come to it. Chronically ill patients may see the doctor late in the progress of the disease. A short hospital stay may not be effective. Longer stays as well as extended care outside of the hospitals are often needed. Rather than one doctor the chronically ill may need the coordinated services of several health professionals—specialists, therapists, and nurses. Our existing medical system simply has not been designed to deal with such issues.

The chronically ill demand effective treatment for their illnesses. Unfortunately, the technology available to treat chronic illnesses are only "halfway" technologies that ease the pain of the disease whose underlying processes are not yet understood. Definitive prevention, control, or cures have not been devised for most chronic illnesses. Kidney transplantation and kidney dialysis are well known "halfway" technologies. The management of chronic illnesses can be compared to the management of polio *before* the development of the polio vaccine. Halfway technologies such as braces, warm compacts on the legs, and trips to a mineral spa were used extensively. Only with complete understanding of the disease come definitive technologies that are effective (Bennett, 1977).

Complete understanding of chronic illnesses and the accurate assessment of whether new technologies are effective in preventing, treating, or curing illnesses are difficult to achieve; more so than if the illnesses resulted from microbial diseases. For example, with the infectious diseases that were predominant in the first half of the 20th century, individual cases were similar and it was only a matter of hours or days from the onset of the illness to its full clinical appearance. Knowledge of the natural history (the course that the illness takes) could be gathered easily and technologies could be tested for effectiveness in preventing or curing the illness.

Chronic illnesses, however, pose a greater problem. They often begin (unnoticed) several decades before their clinical outcome. Recent work, though, in detecting heart disease before its symptoms appear is promising. Individual cases of any particular illness may be widely different. Therefore understanding the natural history of a chronic illness becomes difficult. Evaluating new technologies designed to treat the illness is also difficult for several reasons. Evaluation is done through comparison. For example, two groups, one which receives the technology and the other which does not may be compared. While the comparison groups may have the same illness, they may be (unknown to the researchers) at different stages in the illness. Such comparisons would make no sense. A second type of comparison involves the same chronically ill group before and after it receives the technology. In order to evaluate the technology's effectiveness, we need to know the illness' natural history, how it would progress without the technology (McDermott, 1977). The illness' natural history, though, is difficult to obtain. And we have not even mentioned ethical issues of assigning some patients to a possibly beneficial treatment and others to no treatment or possibly less beneficial treatment.

As we have seen, changing health problems, in part due to the success of medicine, have created new issues in health care. It is difficult to assess the effectiveness of technologies. The technologies are mostly halfway technologies and they are expensive and scarce. For example, renal dialysis for those with kidney failure costs about $24,000 a year. Resources, though, are limited. Yet those suffering from kidney failure and other chronic illnesses want help. How will it be decided who receives the scarce resources?

In the 1960s the Seattle Artificial Kidney Center established criteria for the allocation of kidney machines to those with renal failure. Their procedure, however, was criticized greatly. Concern about who was and who was not given dialysis led to the passage of congressional legislation that provided complete medical care coverage for those with kidney failure (Bennett, 1977). Complete coverage might be the only procedure that everyone would agree upon. Yet the problem of allocating scarce resources was not solved by that legislation.

Should not complete coverage be provided for those suffering from other chronic illnesses? Or, might the scarce resources spent on dialysis be used for the development of definitive technologies that would help future generations but not the present one? More resources could be spent on medical training, renovating hospitals, or a host of other health issues. If our resources are scarce, then how should they be allocated? Without considering fully the issues, decisions that were intended to alleviate suffering and to improve health care may have unintentional negative consequences.

The use of expensive halfway technologies for treating the chronically ill highlights this crucial issue: America's resources must be shared among health and other concerns such as education, welfare, and the arts. Unless our resources are limitless we must take upon ourselves the difficult task of setting dollar limits on what is done for health and thereby, deprive individuals of care for their health problems.

The Cost of Care

Halfway technologies for chronic illnesses also help to emphasize that the cost of health care is a concern to Americans. Health care costs exceed $150 billion a year and may approach $250 billion in the 1980s. The proportion of the GNP (the market value of all goods and services produced by the economy) devoted to health care has doubled since 1940; it is now above 8 percent (Klarman, 1977). The public is concerned about health care insurance premiums and the out-of-pocket costs for medical services. They are worried that a health crisis may mean a financial disaster. Because many medical services must be paid for out-of-pocket, those people with fewer resources receive inadequate care. Thus the concern over the costs of health care also carries with it the concern for the provision of health care—its organization and delivery.

The reasons for rapidly escalating health care costs are not understood completely. Many arguments have been advanced: aging of the population; greedy doctors; advances in expensive medical technology; rising wages for health care personnel; unnecessary provision of services; increased third-party payments for health care (either health insurance or government funding); increased malpractice suits; and our existing insurance programs.

Our present health insurance coverage, like our health care system, is based on illness patterns of the first half of the 20th century. Illnesses were often treated during a short stay in the hospital where the patient hopefully got better, though sometimes died. Expenses were high during the hospital stay but did not accumulate significantly afterwards. Private and public insurance programs therefore have emphasized short-term care in a hospital, limited coverage outside of the hospital, little assistance in long-term extended care and have provided few preventive services (Enos and Sultan, 1977). Chronic illnesses, though, often require those services that are neglected by our existing insurance programs. Further, there is little incentive for the doctor or the patient to forego hospitalization if they are covered by insurance. Furthermore, with rising malpractice suits, doctors are understandably concerned that nothing is overlooked. Therefore they protect themselves by performing additional tests which are often conducted in the hospitals.

Whatever the reasons for rising health care costs, the public wants to limit them. As Mechanic (1978) explains, medical care costs can be controlled through stringent rationing of medical care services (who gets what). They can also be controlled through a combination of strategies aimed at reducing the consumption of services, improving the efficiency of services, or changing the structure of service provision. Better prevention would be one way of reducing the consumption of services. The development of definitive technologies or the substitution of nurses for physicians in certain tasks would improve the efficiency of services. The development of self-help groups or the decreased reliance on nursing homes for the management of the elderly might improve the structure of service provision. All of these and other changes demand careful consideration.

National Health Insurance is one specific strategy that has been proposed. Several different proposals for National Health Insurance are before the Congress. It is likely that some form of National Health Insurance will be enacted by the 1980s. What form it will take is not yet clear. Several issues must be addressed in establishing National Health Insurance. Who should be covered? Should coverage be voluntary or compulsory? How should the system be managed? What should the payment procedures be? (Enos and Sultan, 1977; Saward, 1977). Each of these and other issues are difficult to face.

One plan calls for universal coverage of the American population, whereas others would exclude certain segments; for example, those who are self-employed or young adults who are not covered by their parents' plan and who have not yet worked long enough to qualify for their own coverage. All plans emphasize in-hospital and ambulatory services, but other services like dental care, nursing-home care, and maternity care are covered in differing degrees or not covered at all. In some programs the federal government would administer National Health Insurance; in others, state governments would have much of the responsibility, and in some there would be little government involvement. Payment procedures also vary among the programs; differing in their impact on employers, individuals, private insurance companies and reimbursement to health care providers (Davis, 1975). It is unlikely that National Health Insurance will cause a profound change in America's health care. It, however, signals an intense reevaluation of health, illness, and medicine in the United States and promises greater changes in the future.

National Health Insurance deals with issues of cost, but only begins to address the issue of how medicine should be organized. Historically, medicine has been practiced by individual physicians on a fee-for-service bases. That solo, fee-for-service practice has been modified gradually by group practices, prepayment plans (where individuals sign up for a health care program through their employer and pay a flat fee for all visits and services during the year), and government provision of services for the armed forces and other arrangements. The basic question is, to what degree can the health care of this nation be left up to its practioners, and to what degree should the government control health care? Clearly, we are moving toward more government involvement as witnessed by the Medicare and Medicaid programs of the 1960s. How far government's involvement will go remains to be seen.

A National health system, similar to those in Great Britain, Scandanavia, or Eastern Europe could be established. The government would provide our health care with health professionals earning some, if not all of their income through government wages. However, a national health system such as this seems unlikely in the 20th century. While the government has played an increasing role in health care in the past 25 years, there is too much opposition toward and disagreement about a national health system for it to be established in the near future. For a national health system to be established, fundamental changes in other areas of our society must occur first (Saward, 1977).

America will face many other issues in modifying its health care system. Our demand for quality care and accountability (especially as the government's participation in providing health care increases) will lead to increased concern for evaluating the effectiveness of medical personnel, not to mention the technologies they use. Medical professionals, like most people, resist evaluation and criticism by "outsiders." Our demand for quality care will also lead to greater use of computers in recording our medical histories, tracking them over time and space, and in diagnosing our illnesses. The recruitment and education of doctors, the management of mental health issues, the health hazards created by all forms of pollution, and other health care issues confront us as we move toward the 21st century.

It is important to remember that as old issues are resolved new ones will appear. The more sophisticated our medical knowledge and health technologies become, the more difficult issues in health, illness, and medicine will be. The search for the cause of the "Legionnaire's" disease in the summer of 1976 and the following months illustrates this trend. Problems that we never knew existed now require immediate attention. We must realize that decisions will *always* have to be made, that they will be based on imperfect knowledge, and that the consequences will be uncertain. No matter how advanced we become health, illness, and medicine will provide important issues to be faced.

References

Bennett, I. L., Jr. Technology as a shaping force. *Daedalus 106* 1977: 125–133.

Callahan, D. Health and society: Some ethical imperatives. *Daedalus 106* 1977: 23–33.

Callahan, D. The WHO definition of health. *The Hastings Center Studies 1* 1973: 77–88.

Davis, K. *National health insurance: Benefits, costs, and consequences.* Washington, D.C.: The Brookings Institute, 1975.

Enos, D. D., and Sultan, P. *The sociology of health care: Social, economic, and political perspectives.* New York: Praeger, 1977.

Fox, R. C. The medicalization and demedicalization of American society. *Daedalus 106* 1977: 9–22.

Fuchs, V. R. *Who shall live? Health, economics, and social choice.* New York: Basic Books, 1974.

Garland, M. Politics, legislation, and natural death. *The Hastings Center Report 6* 1976: 5–6.

Glazier, W. H. The task of medicine. *Scientific American 228* 1973: 13–17.

Illich, I. *Medical nemesis: The expropriation of health.* Toronto: Bantam Books, 1976.

Klarman, H. E. The financing of health care. *Daedalus 106* 1977: 215–234.

Knowles, J. H. The responsibility of the individual. *Daedalus 106* 1977: 57–80.

McDermott, W. Evaluating the physician and his technology. *Daedalus 106* 1977: 135–57.

Mechanic, D. Approaches to controlling the costs of medical care: Short-range and long-range alternatives. *The New England Journal of Medicine 198* 1978: 249–54.

Reiser, S. J. Therapeutic choice and moral doubt in a technological age. *Daedalus 106* 1977: 47–56.

Saward, E. W. Institutional organization, incentives, and change. *Daedalus 106* 1977: 191–202.

Veatch, R. The medical model: Its nature and problems. *The Hastings Center Studies 1* 1973: 59–76.

Wildavsky, A. Doing better and feeling worse: The political pathology of health policy. *Daedalus 106* 1977: 105–23.

Name Index

Abel-Smith, B., 417, 419
Ackerknecht, E. W., 44
Ackoff, R. L., 325, 326
Adams, J. E., 126
Adams, S. D., 208, 215
Adler, R., 308, 310
Albrecht, G. L. [ref. 13], 1–12, 144,
    260–270, 271
Alexander, L., [ref. 56], 273
Alpert, J., 46, 230
Amerena, L., [ref. 1], 260, 270
Anderson, C. H., 337
Anderson, O. W., [ref. 16] [ref. 27][ref.
    7], 19, 21, 22, 37, 190, 202,
    260, 262, 270, 380
Anderson, R. [ref. 16] [ref. 27] [ref. 5],
    19, 21, 22, 37, 260, 262, 270,
    322, 326
Angrist, S., 192, 198, 202
Antonovsky, A., 115, 125, 127, 190,
    202
Apple, D., 146
Appley, M. H., 109, 125
Arensberg, C. M., 49, 58
Arnoff, E. L., 325, 326
Asch, S. E., 173

Ash, P., 167
Ast, D., [ref. 22], 262, 271
Auld, F., Jr., 244
Austin, G., [ref. 42], 264, 272
Avnet, H. H., [ref. 15], 19, 20, 21, 28,
    37

Back, K. W., 216
Bacon, D. P., 13
Badgley, R. F., 379
Bahnson, C. B., [ref. 85] [ref. 86], 32,
    40
Bakwin, H., 317, 325
Balint, M., 319, 320, 325
Ball, R. M., 397, 415
Barber, H., 164
Barker, K. N., 420
Barker, R. G., [ref. 65], 30, 39, 219,
    226
Barker-Benfield, B., [ref. 59], 29, 34,
    39
Barrabee, E., 127
Barrabee, P., 55
Barry, A., 169

Barry, B., 461
Bartels, R., 169
Barzini, L., 58
Bateson, G., 136, 138
Baum, G. L., 320, 327
Baumann, B., 146
Baume, L., [ref. 52], 267, 273
Bean, L., 190, 193, 194, 198, 204
Beck, A. T., 167
Beck, H. P., 466
Beck, M. B., 304, 310
Becker, H. S., 2, 5, 12, 43, 168, 187,
    202, 217, 219, 226, 275, 282,
    289
Becker, M., 246
Becket, M. B., 42
Behrens, M. I., 135, 138, 140
Belknap, I., 169, 274, 287, 289, 293
Bell, D. [ref. 65], 273
Bell, R., [ref. 12], 261, 271
Bella, Jennie [case study], 236
Bendix, R., 303, 304, 312
Benedict, R., 167
Benjamin, B., 126
Bennett, I. L., Jr., 476, 477, 480
Bepler, C. R., 128
Bergen, B., 61
Berkman, P. L., [ref. 49], 27, 38
Berkowitz, N., 246
Berlin, J. E., 18
Berman, H. J., 359
Berry, C., 246, 247
Berscheid, E., [ref. 60], 273
Bigman, S. K., 42
Birenbaum, A., 208, 215
Birley, J. L. T., 133, 138
Birnbaum, N., 457
Blackwell, B., 57, 230
Blake, J., 204
Blau, P., 253
Bleuler, E., 129, 139, 168
Block, W. D., 127
Blood, M. R., 119, 125
Bloom, S. W., 146
Blum, R. H., 44
Blum, Z. D., 136, 137, 141
Bock, G., 42
Bodenheimer, T., 464

Bohr, R. H., 169
Boisen, A. T., 167
Bolton, B., 208, 215
Bonnell, V., 330, 337
Bonrnstedt, G., [ref. 60], 273
Boucher, L., [ref. 35], 21, 38
Bowles, S., 461
Bownell, V., 459
Braginsky, B. M., 168
Braginsky, D. D., 168
Brawne, Fanny [case study], 155, 156
Brim, O. G., Jr., [ref. 16], 261, 271,
    295
Brittain, J. A., 413, 415
Brody, E. B., 169
Brofenbrenner, U., 135, 139
Bromberg, W., 300, 310
Brooks, G., 126
Broverman, I. K., [ref. 5], 17, 36
Brown, E. L., 318, 325
Brown, G. W., 133, 138, 198, 202
Bruhn, J. G., 146
Bruner, J. S., 173
Bucher, R., 298, 311
Bulm, H. L., 343
Burke, C., 344, 349, 359
Burns, M., [ref. 55], 267, 273
Butler, S., 62
Bynder, H., 144, 206–214
Byron, Lord G. G. [case study], 156

Cady, F., [ref. 20], 262, 271
Calden, G., 244
Callahan, D., 9, 12, 471, 472, 480
Campbell, J., [ref. 41], 264, 272
Campbell, J. A., 346
Caplan, R., 117, 118, 119, 120, 121,
    125, 301, 311
Care, F. G., 215
Carlos, J., [ref. 22], 262, 271
Caro, F. G., 211
Caron, H. S., [ref. 85], 32, 40
Carson, R. C., 225, 226
Carstairs, G. M., 295
Carter, B. L., 44

Carter, E. C., 409
Cartwright, A., [ref. 39], 22, 38, 293
Cassell, J., [ref. 80], 32, 40
Castorp, Hans [case study],
    148–150, 158, 161, 162
Caudill, W., 169, 440
Chapanis, A., 420
Chapman, W. P., 51, 230
Cheek, F. E., [ref. 6], 17, 29, 34, 36,
    147
Cheraskin, E., [ref. 2], 260, 270
Chernoff, H., 323, 325
Chesler, P., 308, 311
Childs, B., [ref. 75] [ref. 76], 32, 40
Chin-Shong, E., 190, 202
Chisholm, S., 334
Chodoff, P., 138, 140
Christensen, G., [ref. 25], 262, 271
Chucng, C., [ref. 3], 260, 270
Churchman, C. W., 325, 326
Cicourel, A., 217, 226
Clancy, K., 195, 202, 204
Clark, J. B., 461
Clark, M., 44
Clark, T. W., 42
Cline, N., 196, 204
Clute, Y. T., 230
Cobb, S., 108, 113, 117, 125, 126,
    127, 146
Cockerham, W., C., 2, 12
Coelho, G. V., 11, 126
Cogburn, D., 205
Cogswell, B., 208, 215
Cohen, L., [ref. 30] [ref. 38], 262, 263,
    264, 272
Cole, P., [ref. 17], 19, 26, 37
Cole, S., 113, 126
Coleman, J., 374, 378
Collins, B., 253
Cons, N., [ref. 22], 262, 271
Conte, Carol [case study], 236–237
Cooper, B. S., 388, 415
Cooperstock, R., [ref. 58], 29, 34, 39
Corey, L., 13
Cornerly, P. B., 42
Corning, P. A., 385, 415
Coser, R. L., 146, 301, 306, 311
Costner, H., 191, 202

Cottrell, L. S., 134, 139
Cotzias, G., 103
Coughlin, J., [ref. 25], 262, 271
Crandall, D., 196, 202
Crocetti, G. M., 168
Crocker, L. H., 42, 229
Croog, S. H., 48, 55, 208, 215
Croxton, W., [ref. 10], 261, 271
Cumming, E., 61, 172, 295
Cumming, J., 61, 172, 295
Cummings, S., 464

Dalton, K., 46
Danet, B., [ref. 17], 261, 271
Daniels, A. K., 292, 298–310, 311
Darley, W., 318, 326
Davidson, G. E., 230, 242
Davidson, R. G., [ref. 74], 32, 40
Davis, F., 150–151, 152, 218, 220,
    221, 222, 226, 286, 289
Davis, K., 340, 385–415, 478, 480
Davis, M. S., 244, 245, 246, 247, 248,
    253, 265, 272
Dawber, T., R., 319, 326, 327
Day, B., 154
de Beauvoir, S., 45
Deeble, J. S., 425
DeGeyndt, W., [ref. 19], 262, 271
Dembo, T., 219, 226
Denenberg, H., [ref. 59], 273
Densen, P. M., 21, 37, 379
Deutsch, H., 45
Deutschberger, P., 223, 227
Dingman, H. F., 203
Dinitz, S., 202
Dittman, D. A., 13
Dixon, W. M., 244
Dodge, D. L., [ref. 81], 32, 40
Dodge, H. J., 127
Dohrenwend, B. P., [ref. 7], 17, 36,
    129, 130, 133, 134, 139, 190,
    195, 196, 202
Dohrenwend, B. S., [ref. 7], 17, 36,
    129, 130, 133, 134, 139, 190,
    195, 196, 202

Donabedian, A., 7, 13, 42, 380
Douglas, D. J., 286, 289
Douglass, D. J., 274
Draguns, J. G., 167
Dubos, R., 41, 62, 242
DuFour, R., 346
Duhl, L. J., 304, 311
Dulman, J., [ref. 4], 260, 262, 270
Dummett, C., [ref. 28], 262, 271
Dunham, H. W., 130, 139
Dunn, J., 126
Dunn, J. P., 319, 326
Dunnel, K., [ref. 39], 22, 38
Durban, E., [ref. 39], 264, 272
Durkheim, E., 2, 27, 39

Ebert, M., 205
Eddy, E. M., 213, 216, 285, 286, 289
Ehrenreich, B., [ref. 63] [ref. 64], 29,
    34, 39, 334, 338
Eichorn, R., 245, 246, 322, 326
Eilstead, W., 226
Eitinger, L., 133, 139
Elias, T., 42
Elling, R., 245
Elsom, K. O., 42
Elsom, K. A., 42
Emerson, J., 225, 226
English, D., [ref. 63], 29, 34, 39, 334,
    338
English, J. T., 311
Enos, D. D., 478, 480
Enright, J. B., 48
Enterline, P. E., [ref. 12], 19, 22, 26,
    32, 37
Epstein, F. H., 108, 126
Epstein, M. F., 13
Erhardt, C. L., [ref. 8], 18, 22, 29, 36
Erikson, K. T., 43, 146, 187, 203, 217,
    226, 300, 311, 318, 326
Eron, L. D., 244
Etter, L. E., 319, 326
Evang, K., 372
Eyman, R., 191, 203, 205

Fain, T., 186, 202, 203
Fairfield, L., [ref. 14], 19, 37
Fantl, B., 48, 55
Farina, A., 172
Faulkner, J. A., 127
Feld, S., 61
Feldman, J. J., [ref. 31], 21, 37, 48,
    190, 202
Feldstein, M. S., 393, 415
Feldstein, P. J., [ref. 38], 22, 38
Felton, J. S., 113, 126
Fidell, L., [ref. 88], 34, 40
Filstead, W. J., 218
Fink, D. K., 245, 246
Fischer, H. K., 128
Fisher, J., 187, 203
Fletcher, R., 303, 312
Flexner, A., 358, 462, 466
Folman, R., 244
Fonda, C. P., 167
Foote, N. N., 134, 139
Foster, A.,.[ref. 29], 21, 37
Foster, G., 4, 13
Fox, R., [ref. 68], 30, 39, 146, 304,
    311, 351, 472, 480
Francis, V., 244, 245, 246, 247
Frank, J. D., 244, 300, 311
Frankel, J., [ref. 23], 262, 271
Frankenberg, R., 467
Frankfort, E., 307, 311
Freeman, B., 247, 248
Freeman, H. E., 2, 13, 19, 61, 146,
    172, 190, 192, 198, 203
Freer, T. [ref. 53], 267, 273
Fried, E. R., 415
Friedan, B., 45
Friedl, E., 439
Friedman, J. W., 355
Friedman, M., 118, 120, 125, 126
Friedman, S., 13
Freidson, E., 2, 5, 13, 146, 208, 217,
    219, 226, 267, 273, 292,
    293–297, 310, 311, 340, 417,
    467
French, J. R. P., Jr., 108, 109, 111,
    117, 119, 125, 126, 253
Freud, A., 57

Freud, S., 165, 301
Fuchs, V. R., [ref. 9], 18, 22, 25, 26,
    36, 470, 472, 480
Fulton, J., [ref. 21], 262, 271
Fusillo, A., [ref. 44], 264, 272

Gafafer, W., [ref. 20], 262, 271
Gaffin, B., 380
Galbraith, J. K., 329, 330, 331, 337,
    338, 458, 466
Galdston, I., 231
Gallagher, E., 295
Gallo, Harry [case study], 237
Gardiner-Hill, H., 321, 326
Garfinkle, H., 225, 226, 300, 304, 311
Garland, L. H., 317, 326
Garland, M., 475, 480
Garmezy, N., 129, 139
Geer, B., 12
Geiger, H. J., 462
Gerwirtz, J., [ref. 14], 261, 271
Gibbons, J., 204
Gibbs, J., 217, 219, 226
Gibby, R. G., 244
Gibson, G., 208, 215
Gibson, R. M., 1, 13
Giddens, A., 337, 459
Gilbert, D. C., 295
Gilbertson, D. E., 300, 311
Gilmore, H. R., 169
Gintis, H., 461
Glaser, B., 274, 276, 289
Glaser, W. A., [ref. 67], 30, 39
Glass, A. J., 321, 326
Glazier, W. H., 7, 13, 475, 480
Goddard, J. L., 360
Goffman, E., 43, 130, 139, 168, 184,
    187, 203, 208, 218, 219, 220,
    221, 225, 226, 274, 289, 303,
    308, 311, 322, 326
Gold, R. L., 287, 289
Goldberg, E. M., 130, 139
Goldiamond, I., 208, 215
Goldman, A. R., 169

Goldstein, M. S., 376
Gomberg, W., 61
Goodell, H., 51, 230
Gordis, L., 244, 245
Gordon, G., 62, 146, 230, 242
Gordon, J. E., 319, 326
Gordon, K. K., 45
Gordon, R. E., 45
Gottesman, I. I., 131, 139
Gove, A., 186
Gove, W. R., [ref. 3] [ref. 42] [ref. 53],
    17, 22, 26, 27, 31, 32, 33, 36,
    38, 39, 130, 139, 144, 168,
    186–202, 203
Graham, S., 3, 13, 47, 48, 55, 108,
    113, 126, 208, 215
Graubard, P., [ref. 15], 261, 271
Gray, F., [ref. 15], 261, 271
Green, R., 46
Greenblatt, M., 146, 295
Greenley, J. R., 301, 308, 311
Gregory, C., [ref. 1], 260, 270
Gross, H. S., [ref. 56], 29, 34, 39
Gross, M. L., 419, 420, 439
Grossman, R. S., 60
Gunther, J., 157
Gunther, M., 45
Guralnick, L., 115, 126
Gurin, G., 61, 190, 203
Gursslin, O. R., 137, 140
Guthrie, C., 244
Guttmacher, M. S., 304, 311

Haber, L. D., 206, 207, 208, 209, 210,
    211, 213–215
Hackett, T. P., 51, 230
Haese, P., 195, 203, 204
Haggerty, R. J., 46, 230
Haley, J., 308, 311
Hall, O., 373, 374, 375
Halleck, S. L., 306, 311
Hamburg, D. A., [ref. 73], 32, 40, 126
Hammer, M., 197, 198, 203
Handlin, O., 47

Haney, C., 198, 203
Harding, E., 464
Harding, J. S., 43
Hardy, J. D., 51, 230
Hare, E. H., 131, 139
Harkins, E. B., 108, 119, 126
Harmatz, J., 205
Hartnett, R. T., 335, 338, 467
Haug, M. R., 213, 215, 309, 311
Hauser, P. M., 122, 127
Hehman, E. W., 126
Hellmuth, G. A., 244
Henry, J., [ref. 43], 264, 272
Henslin, J., 286, 289
Heron, A., 295
Hessler, R. M., 2, 13
Heston, L. L., 131, 139
Hilgenrath, S., [ref. 5], 260, 266, 269,
    270
Hill, A. B., 319, 326
Hindley, M., 57
Hinkle, L. E., Jr., [ref. 82], 32, 40, 43,
    112, 118, 119, 126
Hirsch, B., [ref. 46], 265, 272
Hoddicott, B. C., 420
Hodge, R. W., 119, 126
Hoffer, C. R., 42
Hollingshead, A. B., 2, 129, 133, 134,
    135, 139, 171, 190, 191, 193,
    194, 203, 274, 289, 296, 325,
    326
Holmes, T. H., 113, 119, 126
Horder, E., 42
Horder, J., 42
Horowitz, H., [ref. 32], 263, 272
Ho Shi-Chang, 66, 67
House, J. S., 79, 108–125, 126, 128
House, W. F., 108
Houts, P., 204
Howard, A., 132, 141
Howard, K., 204
Howell, P., 144, 186–202
Howitt, J., [ref. 8], 261, 271
Huang, L., 393, 416
Hubbard, J. P., 42
Hughes, E. C., 12, 307, 310, 311
Hughes, E. F. X., 13
Hulin, C. L., 119, 125

Hunt, E. K., 458, 463
Huntington, J., [ref. 58], 268, 273
Hyman, M., [ref. 86], 32, 40, 208, 215

Iglehart, J. K., 464
Illich, I., 5, 10, 13, 474, 480
Irwin, D. S., 246, 253

Jaco, E. G., 131, 139, 146, 190, 203
Jacobsen, L., 174
Jacobson, M., 204
Jaeckle, W. R., 48
Jago, J., [ref. 30], 262, 272
Janopaul, R., 204
Jeffers, F., 122, 127
Jenkins, C. D., 108, 109, 115, 116,
    119, 120, 126
Jenner, E., 91
Jenny, J., [ref. 31], 263, 269, 272
Johanssen, W. J., 172
Johnson, S., 164
Johnson, W., 43
Jones, C. M., 51, 230
Jones, N. F., 190, 203
Jones, R., [ref. 64], 270, 273
Jordan, E. P., 376
Joseph, J., 118, 127

Kadushin, C., 48
Kahn, M. W., 190, 203
Kahn, R. L., 121, 126
Kahne, M. F., 306, 311
Kahn-Hut, R., 309, 312
Kalimo, E., [ref. 23], 20, 37
Kaplan, B., 108
Kaplan, J., 169
Kardiner, A., 321, 326
Karvonen, M. J., 319, 326
Kasl, S. V., 117, 126, 127, 146, 246,
    247

Kassebaum, G. G., 61, 146
Katz, E., [ref. 17], 261, 271
Katz, E., 374, 378
Katz, J., 42
Keats, J. [case study], 155–157, 161
Kelman, H., 253
Kessel, N., [ref. 25], 21, 37
Kessler, I. I., [ref. 79], 32, 40
Kety, S. S., 131, 139
Keys, A., 319, 326
Kimball, S. T., 49, 58
King, R., 126
King, R., 168
King, S., 61, 146
Kinsey, A. C., 43, 319, 326
Kisch, A., [ref. 62], , 270, 273
Kittigawa, E. M., 122, 127
Kitsuse, J. I., 43, 187, 204, 217, 226
Klarman, H. E., 477, 480
Kleinbach, G., 462
Kleiner, R. J., 131, 139, 140
Kleinknecht, R., [ref. 56], 268, 273
Klepac, R., [ref. 56], 273
Klots, A., 188, 204
Kluckhohn, C., 57, 61, 146
Kluckholn, F. R., 57, 59
Knowles, J. H., 473, 480
Kohn, M. L., 79, 129–138, 139, 140
Koleda, M. S., 344, 349, 359
Koos, E. L., 44, 190, 204, 228, 380
Koropecky, O., 393, 416
Korsch, B., 247, 248, 266, 272
Kosa, J., 46, 127, 230
Kramer, B. M., 141
Kramer, H., 147
Krause, E. A., 5, 11, 13, 206, 211,
    212, 214, 215
Kreitman, N., 167
Kretschmer, E., 168
Kringlen, E., 131, 140
Krueger, D. E., [ref. 78], 32, 40, 127
Kutner, B., 57, 230

Lader, L., 304, 312
Laing, R. D., 168, 187, 204

Lampman, R. J., 458
Landy, D., 5, 13
Langer, T. S., 43
Langner, T. S., 133, 134, 140
Laski, H. 462
Latiolais, C., 246, 247
Lawrence, P. R., 119, 128
Lazarus, R. S., 109, 111, 127, 132,
    140
Lederer, H. D., 148
Ledley, R. S., 323, 324, 326
Lefton, M., 202
Lei, T., 205
Leighton, A. H., 43
Leighton, D. C., 43, 131, 140, 196,
    204, 241
Leik, R., 191, 202
Lemert, E. M., 43, 187, 204, 217, 226,
    319, 320, 326
Lemkau, P. V., 168
Lennane, K. J., [ref. 61], 29, 34, 39
Lennane, R. J., [ref. 61], 29, 34, 39
Leopold, R. I., 311
Lerner, M., [ref. 32], 21, 37, 122, 127
Levin, B., [ref. 46], 265, 272
Levin, M. L., [ref. 79], 32, 40
Levine, J., [ref. 40], 22, 38
Levine, S., 2, 13, 109, 127, 146, 215
Levinson, D. J., 146, 295
Levison, A., 337
Levitin, T. E., 144, 217–226
Leviton, G., 219, 226
Lewis, D., 204
Lewis, O., 137, 140
Lewit, S., 310
Ley, P., 246
Liebow, E., 137, 140
Liederman, V. R., 216
Likert, R., 121
Lilienfeld, A. M., [ref. 79], 32, 40
Lilienthal, B., [ref. 1], 260, 270
Lindegard, B., [ref. 50], 266, 268, 272
Lindzey, G., 61
Linn, E., 198, 204, 261, 262, 271
Linsky, A. S., 172, 187, 189, 197, 204
Linton, R., [ref. 1], 16, 33, 36
Lipson, A., 215
Lister, J., 91

Litman, T. J., 207, 208, 215
Liu Yu-cheng, 68
Lohman, J. D., 62
Lomonaco, C., [ref. 42], 264, 272
Longest, B. B., Jr., 13, 340, 342–370
Lorber, J., 218, 219, 226
Lorr, M., 244
Lubach, J., 188, 203
Ludwig, E. G., 208, 215
Lunde, D. T., [ref. 73], 32, 40
Lusted, L. B., 323, 324, 326
Lyden, F. J., 462
Lynd, H., 2
Lynd, R., 2
Lyons, N., 458

McCall, G. J., 225, 226
McConnell, W. E., 420
McDermott, W., 476, 480
MacDonald, B., 157–158, 160, 161
McEachern, A., 203
McGarrah, R., 368
McGrath, J. E., 109, 127
MacIver, R. M., 465
MacMillan, A. M., 43
McQuillan, F. L., 355
Macklin, D. B., 43
Maddox, G., 108, 208, 216
Madigan, F. C., [ref. 11], 19, 36
Maher, M., [ref. 42], 264, 272
Maisel, R., 300, 312
Makover, H. B., 230
Malcover, H. B., 57
Malinowski, B., 5, 9, 13
Malzberg, G., 187, 204
Mancuso, J. C., 177
Manis, M., 190, 204
Mann, G. E., 319, 326
Mann, H., 147
Mann, T., 148
Manning, P., 210
Mao Tse-Tung, 65, 66, 68, 74, 77
March, J. G., 325
Marechaux, S., [ref. 52], 267, 273
Marks, R., 110, 115, 127

Marmor, T., 385, 416
Martin, C. C., 43, 319, 326
Martin, R., [ref. 9], 261, 271
Martin, W. T., [ref. 81], 32, 40
Masserman, J. H., 57
Massler, M., [ref. 23], 262, 271
Matsumoto, Y. S., 121, 127
Matza, D., 218, 226, 227
Mauksch, H. O., 296
May, J. M., 4, 13
Mead, M., 45, 46
Mechanic, D., [ref. 66], 2, 4, 13, 30,
    39, 111, 112, 127, 146, 239,
    243, 313, 318, 326, 478, 480
Medearis, D., [ref. 75], 32, 40
Meigs, J. W., 42, 229
Melzack, R., 51, 230
Mensh, I. N., 173
Menzel, H., 374, 378
Messner, C., [ref. 20], 262, 271
Metz, A. S., [ref. 44], 264, 272
Meyer, A., 300
Meyers, J., 218, 226
Michael, S. T., 43, 133, 134, 140
Michaels, R. H., [ref. 77], 32, 40
Michielutte, A., 198, 203
Michielutte, R., 198, 203
Miele, R., 195, 203, 204
Mikkelson, W. M., 127
Miles, H. H. W., 118, 127
Miliband, R., 329, 337, 458
Miller, D., 190, 300, 304, 311
Miller, S., [ref. 36], 263, 272
Miller, S. M., 137, 140
Miller, W. B., 61
Mills, C. W., 457
Milt, H., 186, 204
Mintz, M., 463
Mintz, N. L., 131, 141
Mischel, W., 176, 185
Mishler, E. G., 129, 135, 136, 140
Montoye, H. J., 118, 127
Moore, F. E., 319, 326
Moran, L. J., 245
Morgan, T., 303, 312
Moriyama, I. M., [ref. 78], 32, 40, 113,
    114, 115, 127
Morrisey, J., 167

Morrison, S. L., 130, 139
Moses, L. E., 323, 325
Moss, G. E., 10, 13
Moulding, T., 244, 245
Mueller, M. S., 1, 13
Murphy, F. J., 43
Murphy, H. H., 231
Murray, H. A., 57, 61, 146
Myers, B. A., 356
Myers, J. K., 131, 140, 186, 190, 191,
    192, 193, 194, 198, 204

Naeye, R. L., [ref. 72], 32, 39
Nagi, S. Z., 207, 216
Nathanson, C. A., [ref. 2] [ref. 83], 15,
    16–36, 17, 19, 20, 32, 33, 36,
    40
Navarro, V., 5, 11, 13, 292, 328–337,
    340, 457–468
Negrete, V., 247, 248, 266, 272
Nelson, G., 361
Neuheuser, D., 348
New, P. Kong-Ming, 144, 206–214
Newell, S., 147
Newman, J., [ref. 7], 260, 262, 270
Newman, S. H., 310
Neyman, J., 315, 316, 326
Nightingale, F., 334, 419
Nunnally, J. C., 61, 177
Nye, F. I., 43
Nyman, K., [ref. 23], 20, 37

O'Brien [case study], 238
O'Connor, J., 329, 330, 331, 337, 458
Ødegaard, O., 130, 140
Ogburn, 2
Olin, H. S., 51, 230
Omran, A. R., 79, 81–93
Opler, M. K., 43, 48, 49, 55, 61, 232
Oppenheim, A., 57, 230
Opton, E. M., Jr., 306, 312
Orne, E., 185

O'Rourke, Mary [case study],
    234–235
Ortmeyer, C. E., [ref. 51], 27, 38
Osborn, R. W., [ref. 57], 29, 34, 39
O'Shea, R., [ref. 38], 264, 272
Osmond, H., 10, 13, 144, 146–166

Palmore, E. B., 108, 122, 127
Parker, S., 131, 139, 140
Parrish, H. M., 420
Parsons, A., 55, 58
Parsons, T., [ref. 68], 2, 10, 13, 30, 39,
    144, 146, 147, 208, 320, 326
Pasamanick, B., 202
Passman, M. J., [ref. 48], 26, 38
Paterson, T. T., 166
Paul, B. D., 61
Pauly, M. V., 13
Pearse, I. H., 42, 229
Pearson, H. E. S., 118, 127
Pechman, J. A., 413, 416
Peel, E., 392, 394, 416
Pell, John [case study], 237
Penfield, W., 157
Pennel, M. Y., 332, 337
Pepitone, A., 118, 127
Perrow, C., 274, 289, 300, 312
Peterson, O., 462
Pfeffer, J., 335, 338, 467
Philips, D. F., 369
Philips, D. L., [ref. 4], 17, 36, 168,
    195, 204
Philips, L., 134, 140, 167, 176
Pickering, M. R., 46
Pinsett, R. J. F. H., 42
Plummer, Norman, 43
Plunkett, R. J., 319, 326
Polgar, S., 146
Pomeroy, W. B., 43, 319, 326
Pomrinse, S. D., 376
Porterfield, A. L., 43, 319, 326
Porterfield, J., 362
Powelson, H., 303, 304, 312
Prather, J., [ref. 88], 34, 40
Preston, S. H., [ref. 13], 19, 22, 32, 33,
    37

Pugh, T. F., 131, 141
Pusey, N. M., 466

Quinlan, K. A., [case study], 474
Quinn, R. P., 126

Radke, M. Y., 231
Rahe, R. H., 113, 119, 126
Rainwater, L., 136, 140
Ramsey, G. V., 61
Raper, A. B., 44, 47
Raphael, E., 191, 204
Ratner, H., 318, 326
Rautahargu, P. M., 319, 326
Raven, B., 253
Rawls, J., 461
Reader, L., [ref. 62], 270, 273
Redlich, F. C., 129, 139, 169, 171,
    190, 191, 193, 194, 203, 274,
    289, 325, 326
Redmont, R., 43
Reeder, L. G., 2, 3, 13, 108, 109, 113,
    126, 128, 146, 208, 215, 216
Regan, T., 108
Reich, M., 330, 337, 459
Rein, M., 305, 312
Reiser, S. J., 473, 474, 480
Reitzes, D., 373
Renne, K. S., [ref. 52], 27, 38
Rennie, T. A. C., 43
Renshaw, J. E., 332, 337
Retherford, R. D., [ref. 10], 18, 19, 22,
    26, 32, 33, 36
Rey, J., 196, 204
Reynolds, E., 253
Rhyne, M. B., [ref. 83], 32, 40
Richardson, S., [ref. 33], 263, 272
Richardson, S. A., 208, 216
Ring, K., 172
Ringsdorf, W., [ref. 2], 260, 270
Rintels, D. W., 334, 338
Rivkin, M. O., [ref. 50], 27, 38

Roach, J. L., 137, 140
Roberts, B. H., 131, 140, 186, 190,
    191, 192, 193, 194
Rock, R., 197, 198, 204
Rodgers, W., 126
Rodman, H., 137, 140
Roemer, M. I., 355
Rogers, K. D., [ref. 77], 32, 40
Rogler, L. H., 133, 134, 135
Rollin, H. R., 128
Roman, P. M., 129
Rorabaugh, M. E., 244
Rosen, G., 3, 13, 300, 312, 417
Rosenbaum, C. P., 129, 135, 140
Rosenberg, C., [ref. 46], 23, 29, 34,
    38
Rosenberg, H., [ref. 15], 261, 271
Rosenfeld, L. S., 42, 49
Rosenhan, D. L., 144, 167–185, 187,
    204, 303, 312
Rosenhan, M. S., 185
Rosenman, R. H., 119, 125, 126
Rosenstock, I., 246
Rosenthal, A. J., 135, 138, 140
Rosenthal, D., 131, 141
Rosenthal, R., 174
Rosenthal, R. A., 126
Rosenzweig, S. P., 244
Ross, L., 308, 312
Rossi, P. H., 136, 137, 141, 211, 216
Roth, J. A., 144, 158, 159, 161, 213,
    216, 274–289, 294, 295, 340,
    417–442
Rubington, E., 218, 226, 304, 305,
    311
Rubinstein, E. A., 244
Rubsamen, D. S., 340, 443–456
Rueschemeyer, D., 309, 312
Rush, B., 300
Rushing, W. A., 129, 141, 187, 189,
    197, 198, 205
Russek, H. I., 118, 127

Sabagh, G., 191, 203, 205
Sachar, E., 196, 205

Safilios-Rothschild, C., 206, 207, 211, 214, 216
Safren, M. A., 420
Sainsbury, P., 167
Sales, S. M., 116, 118, 120, 128
Salisbury, R. R., 295
Saltman, S. E., 13
Salzmann, J., [ref. 26], 262, 264, 267, 271
Sandroni, R. E., 42
Sanua, V. D., 135, 141
Sarbin, T. R., 168, 177, 187, 205
Saunders, L., 61
Saunders, W. B., 43
Saward, E. W., 478, 479, 480
Scarrott, D., [ref. 24], 262, 271
Schacter, S., 46
Scharff, J., 392, 394, 416
Scheff, T. J., 2, 43, 130, 141, 168, 187, 205, 217, 227, 274, 289, 292, 313–325, 327
Schenthal, J. E., 42
Schiro, J., 48, 55
Schmitt, H. O., 167
Schneider, D. M., 57, 61, 146
Schor, S., 42
Schuham, A. I., 136, 141
Schuler, E. A., 42
Schur, E. M., 62, 168, 187, 205, 217, 218, 227
Schwartz, B., [ref. 54], 267, 273
Schwartz, C. G., 306, 311, 312
Schwartz, D. T., 131, 141
Schwartz, J., 320, 327
Schwartz, M., 190, 196, 205
Schwartz, M. S., 178, 287, 290
Scotch, N. A., [ref. 84], 32, 40, 109, 127, 129, 140
Scott, R., 132, 141
Scott, R. A., 209, 210, 211, 213, 216
Scotton, R. B., 425
Scoville, S. E., 181
Scribner, B., 351
Scrivener, J., 167
Seaman, B., 307, 312
Seashore, S., 121, 128
Seeman, W., 167
Segal, B. E., [ref. 4], 17, 36

Seipp, M., 61
Selye, H., 46, 112, 128
Servan-Schreiber, J. L., 466
Shader, R., 194, 205
Shapiro, D., 173
Shapiro, L., 379
Sheatsley, P. B., 380
Shelton, N. W., 245
Shepard, M., [ref. 25], 21, 37
Sherman, H. J., 458, 463
Shibutani, T., 225, 227
Shields, J., 131, 139, 141
Shirley, M. M., 43
Short, J. F., 43
Shostak, A. B., 61
Shuval, J. T., [ref. 22], 20, 37
Sidel, R., 15, 63–78
Sidel, V. W., 15, 63–78
Siegel, G. S., 42
Siegel, P. M., 119, 126
Siegel, S., 50
Siegler, M., 10, 13, 144, 147–166
Silver, E., 60
Silverman, M., [ref. 63], 270, 273
Simmons, J. L., 225, 226
Simmons, O. G., 172, 190, 192, 198, 203
Simpson, M. A., 462
Singer, B. S., [ref. 57], 29, 34, 39
Singer, J., 46, 48, 49, 55
Singer, M. T., 136, 141
Slater, E., 131, 141
Smigel, E., 285, 289
Smith, B., 134
Smith, H., 301, 312
Smith, K. R., 13
Smith, L., [ref. 34], 263, 264, 272
Smith, M. B., 134, 141
Smith, R. T., 206, 207, 208, 209, 210, 211, 213, 215, 216
Smith, T., 119, 128
Smith-Rosenberg, C., [ref. 46] [ref. 60], 23, 29, 34, 38, 39
Snock, J. D., 126
Solomon, D., 374
Solomon, L., 141
Solon, J., [ref. 26], 21, 37
Somers, A. R., 385, 416

Somers, H. M., 385, 416
Sommer, P., 208, 215
Sparer, P. J., 245
Spelman, M. S., 246
Spencer, G., 2
Spiegel, H., 321, 326
Spiegel, J., 57, 59
Spiegelman, M., [ref. 8], 18, 22, 29, 36
Sprenger, J., 147
Srole, L., 43
Stamler, J., [ref. 78], 32, 40, 127
Stanton, A. H., 178, 287, 290, 312
Stanton, E., 211, 216
Star, S., 61
Steinberg, T. A., 169
Stevens, R., 3, 10, 13
Stoeckle, J. D., 45, 230, 242
Stocks, P., 42
Stokes, J., 319, 327
Stoll, C., 212, 220, 227
Strauss, A. L., 2, 12, 274, 276, 280, 289, 290, 295, 298, 303, 311, 312
Strauss, R., 2, 6, 13
Stricker, G., [ref. 8], 261, 271
Strodtbeck, F. L., 57
Suchman, E. A., [ref. 30] [ref. 87], 21, 33, 37, 40, 44, 115, 128
Sudnow, D., 276, 290, 309, 312
Sultan, P., 478, 480
Summers, M., 147
Sussman, M. B., 206, 211, 213, 214, 215, 216, 309, 311
Svarstad, Bonnie L., 144, 243–259
Swazey, J. P., 351
Sykes, G., 218, 227
Syme, S. L., 108, 109, 112, 128
Szasz, T., 62, 168, 187, 205, 274, 290, 304, 312

Tagiuri, R., 173
Tart, H., 204
Terreberry, S., 119, 128
Thomas, C. C., 61

Thomas, L., 5, 13
Thomas, L., 79, 94–107
Thorpe, J., 42
Tiber, N., [ref. 46], 265, 272
Tittle, C. R., 208, 216
Tobin, J., 396, 416
Towers, J., 167
Tracy, V., 153–154
Trice, H. M., 129
Trumbull, R., 109, 125, 128
Tudor, J., [ref. 3], 17, 27, 32, 36
Tulley, W., [ref. 27], 262, 270, 271
Tupper, C. J., 42
Turner, A. N., 119
Turner, R., 218, 220, 227
Turner, R. J., 130, 132, 141, 194, 200, 205
Twaddle, A. C., 2, 13

Upton, L., 458

Vaillant, G., 154–155
Valentine, C. A., 137, 141
VanGelder, P., 466
Veatch, R. M., 10, 13, 472, 480
Verbrugge, L. M., [ref. 18], 19, 22, 23, 37
Vernon, D., 204
Veroff, J., 61, 203
Volkart, E. H., 146, 239

Wade, A., 198, 205
Wade, L., 42
Wagenfield, M. O., 132, 141
Waldfogel, S., 127
Waldman, H. B., [ref. 57], 268, 273
Walker, N. E., 136, 140
Wallace, A. F. C., 45
Wallerstein, J. S., 43, 319, 327

Walster, E., [ref. 60], 273
Wan, T. H., 208, 216
Ward, E., 155, 156
Wardwell, W. I., [ref. 85] [ref. 86], 32, 40
Warner, W. L., 49
Warren, J. V., 320, 327
Washburn, T., [ref. 75], 32, 40
Waxler, C. Z., 135, 136
Wechsler, H., 131, 141
Weeks, L. E., 359
Wegroski, H. J., 61
Weihofen, H., 304, 311
Weil, T. P., 420
Weinberg, M., 218, 226, 227
Weiner, L., 379
Weinstein, E., 223, 227
Weiss, E., 118, 128
Weiss, J., [ref. 29], 262, 271
Wenger, D. E., 303, 312
Westergaard, J. H., 461
Wexler, D. B., 181
Wheeler, S., [ref. 16], 43, 261, 271, 295, 311
White, K. L., [ref. 21], 20, 37
White, W. A., 41
Whiting, J. F., 302, 312
Whitney, L. H., 126
Whyte, W. F., 137, 141
Wilcox, D., 204
Wildavsky, A., 473, 480
Willems, J. S., 344, 349, 359
Williams, C., 218, 227
Williams, J. I., 209, 216
Williams, R. H., 146
Williams, W., 190, 205
Williams, W., 208, 211, 216
Willis, R. W. III, 127
Wilson, F. A., 348
Wilson, R. N., 146
Wiseman, J. P., 304, 312
Wishner, J., 173
Witmer, H. L., 43
Wolfe, D. M., 126
Wolfe, S., 379
Wolff, H. G., [ref. 82], 32, 40, 43, 51, 230
Wolter, J., 320, 327

Wood, A. D., [ref. 62], 29, 34, 39
Wood, A. L., 285, 290
Woodward, J. L., 61
Woolsey, T. D., 48
Worthington, N. L., 388, 415
Wright, B., 218, 219, 220, 221, 226, 227
Wyle, C. J., 43, 319, 327
Wylie, W. G., 428
Wynne, L. C., 136, 141

Yang, Hsio-hua, 69
Yarrow, M. R., 319, 325
Young, W., [ref. 34], 263, 264, 272

Zahn, M., [ref. 61], 269, 273
Zborowski, M., 48, 50, 51, 55, 60
Zigler, E., 176
Zola, I. K., 5, 13, 15, 41–62, 127, 144, 288–242
Zola, L. K., 228
Zubin, J., 167

Subject Index

abnormality, 41, 43, 62, 167. *See also* insanity
abortion, 472–74
accessibility, health care, 7, 344, 474–78
accidents and male mortality, 26
accountability, 297
acupuncture, 75, 76
acute illness, 30
acute respiratory infections, 101
advisory psychiatric settings, 306–09
age:
    and nonconformity with medical advice, 245
    and sex differences in morbidity and mortality
Age of Degenerative and Man-Made Diseases, 82, 83, 84, 85, 87, 89, 91
Age of Pestilence and Famine, 81–82, 84, 85, 86, 87, 88, 90, 91
Age of Receding Pandemics, 82, 84, 85, 86, 87, 89, 91
aged, 340, 384–415

agrarian culture, 82
aides, medical, 294–95
    concept of illness, 294–95
    social class of, 294
    tasks of, 294
Alcoholics Anonymous, 152–54
Alcoholism, 345
    differential treatment in, 278
    as medical problem, 471
    and sick role, 147–48, 153–54
ambulance services, 350
American Bar Association, 197
American Dental Association, 365
American Hospital Association, 365, 367
American Medical Association, 11, 365
American Psychiatric Association, 168, 472
American Sociological Association, 3
anomie, 245
anthropologists, medical, 4–5, 231–32
antibiotics, 82
anxiety, 168, 241

arthritis, 102
associations, doctors', 375
attendants. *See* aides
attitudes toward medicine, 105, 246,
        294, 309, 367–68
authoritarianism, 244
authority, as physician's strategy,
        254

Bales Interaction Process Analysis,
        247
barefoot doctors, Chinese, 66–67
Barron Ego Strength Scale, 244
benefits, Medicare, class variations
        in, 392–94
biosocial resonation, model of, 10
birth control:
        in China, 71–74
        in Japan, 83
Blue Cross Plans, 358
brain death, 473
Britain, medical care in, 15, 418
British General Household Survey, 18
bronchitis and male mortality, 22

cancer, 22, 98–99
cardiovascular disease, 22, 98
career stigma and disability, 208
cerebrovascular disease, 99
Ceylon, epidemiologic transition of,
        90
Chairman Mao's June 26 Directive
        (on medical care), 65
change as stress in heart disease,
        120
chemotherapy, 82
Chile, epidemiologic transition of, 90
China, 15
        delivery of medical care in,
        63–78
        health stations in, 66–68
chronically ill, 474–76

chronic disease, 30, 41–43
        in developed countries, 83, 240
        and lifestyle, 7, 475
        by sex, 22
cirrhosis of the liver, 100
class, effect on health and illness, 15,
        114–15, 122, 129–42, 186–
        205, 266, 270, 274–89, 327–
        36, 396–402, 458–61
        and emergency services,
        274–89
        and schizophrenia, 129–42
classifications of medical practice,
        370–84
class structure:
        in the health sector, 458–60
        in the U.S., 465–67
client-professional relationship, 299,
        309–10
clientele, control of in emergency
        services, 274–89
coercive psychiatric settings,
        301–06
colleague network, doctors', 374
commitment, 197
competition, role of among doctors,
        371–77
communicable diseases, 11, 63, 475
communication, patient-physician,
        243–59
congenital malformation and de-
        ficiencies, 100–01
conspiratorial model of illness, 148
consumerism, 309, 367–68, 419–25
consumers, health care, 1, 266–70,
        309, 366–67, 473
cooperative practice, doctors', 373
coping, 110, 111, 124
coronary heart disease (CHD), 98,
        108–27. *See also* stress
corporate society and health, 466–67
cost-benefit analysis, 8
cost-effectiveness, 8
costs, medical care, differences by
        sex, 21
cultural:
        background as diagnostic aid,
        61

beliefs and disability, 208
    norms, 208
    revolution (China), 65
culture of poverty, theory of, 137
culture and symptoms of illness,
    41–62

data collection, health survey, 30–31
death, 104, 473
death rates. *See* mortality
decentralized system, advantages of,
    77
decision rules, 314–15
decision rules for medical diagnosis,
    312–25
decision theory, 322–25
defense mechanisms, socially
    prescribed, 241
defenses, psychological, 110, 111,
    244
delay, study of, 228, 230, 231, 241
delivery of health care, 63–78, 334,
    353–55, 384–415, 477
demography, medical role of, 4, 79
demystification of medicine, 77
denial, handicapped, 220
dental care:
    class distinctions in, 266
    cultural component of problems
        in, 262–63
    traditional model of, 265
dental laboratories, 350
dentists, 263–64
    authoritarianism of, 265
    backgrounds of, 264, 267
    blacks, numbers of, 264
    -patient interactions, 260–70
    -patient negotiations, 264–70
    women, numbers of, 264
dentofacial appearance, cultural var-
    iation in, 263
depersonalization, 181–84
deviance, social, 217
    avowal/disavowal, 208

and disability, 212–14, 472
    occlusal problems as, 266–67
    physically handicapped as,
        218–26, 472
diabetes mellitus, 100
diagnosis, 292
    game and decision theory in,
        323–25
    medical, errors in, 313–25
    organizational setting, effects
        on, 323
    role of culture in, 61
    sick role effect on, 320–22
    sociological, in disability, 214
Diagnostic and Statistical Manual,
    168
disability, 144
    acceptance of, 208
    consequences of, 209–10
    and deviance, 212–14
    policies for, 210–14
    and social control, 212–14
discipline, effects on schizophrenics,
    135
discrimination:
    race, in Medicare, 385, 397–402
    sex, in health fields, 332–36
disease, 7, 22
    basic medical assumptions of,
        317–18
    causal chains in, 7
    communicable and infectious in
        undeveloped countries, 79,
        81–82, 85, 86, 88, 89, 90
    conception of, 41–44, 62
    as a cultural product, 5
    incidence of, 79
    man-made and degenerative in
        developed countries, 79, 82,
        83, 84, 85, 87, 89, 91
    proportion untreated or unre-
        ported, 42
    social factors in, 7, 57, 144, 241.
        See also illness
doctors, 5, 220, 240–41
    decision to see, 231–41
    work settings of, 371–84. *See
        also* physicians

drug addiction, 76–77, 345
drugs, prescribed, 182, 183, 255–59.
 See also patient conformity to
 medical advice
Duke Longitudinal Study of Aging,
 122
dysmenorrhea, cultural factors of,
 45–46

economics, medical, 3–4, 21, 186–
 93, 346–47, 457–68, 471,
 477–79
economics, personal health, 21,
 103–06, 186–202, 475,
 477–79
efficiency of health care, 344
elderly, medical services utilization
 by, 394–97
electroshock therapy, 302
emergency services. *See* hospital
 emergency services
emphasis, as physicians' strategy,
 254
emphysema, 99–100
employees, health care. *See* health
 labor force
environmental:
 health service, 343
 influences on medical practice,
 11–12
 sanitation, 82
epidemiologic transition, theory of,
 81–87
epidemiology, 4, 88
error, types of in medical diagnosis,
 172, 313–25
essential hypertension, 103
ethnic membership, 47
 effect on symptoms, 47–60
 effect on seeking medical aid,
 232–39
ethnocentrism, 245
etiology, 241
expenditures, health care, 344,
 346–47

family, 144, 333
 interaction model of illness, 148
 and nonconformity with medical
 advice, 245
 and schizophrenia, 129–38
fees, Chinese medical workers',
 69–70
fee structures, physician, 10–11
female morbidity, 19, 35. *See also*
 mortality
female troubles, differences in, 45
fertility, 84, 85, 86
financial resources, effects on treatment, 186–93, 202
friendliness, as a physician strategy,
 254

game theory, 323–25
gastrointestinal infections, 101–02
gender, effect on health of, 34–35,
 119–22
General Household Survey (GHS), 18
geographic mobility, 109
gingivitis, 260
group practice, doctors', 376–79
guilt, 151–52
gymnastic exercises as treatment, 75

Hagerstown, Maryland population
 health study, 2–3
hallucinations, 45, 168
handicapped, visibly, 217–25
health, 1, 2, 12
 basic assumptions of, 471–75
 belief model of, 246–47
 as a consumer demand, 1,
 267–70, 367–68
 definition of, 9, 342, 471, 472
 economics of, 1, 340. *See also*
 economics
 historical interpretations of, 8–9
 as a human right, 1

indices, 8, 29–30, 35–36, 41–42
institutions, class control of,
    465–67
labor force, 328–32, 347–49
maintenance organizations, 343,
    353, 356
politics of, 1, 11, 417–68
professionals, conflicting roles
    of, 292
as a social phenomenon, 241
health care, 1, 3, 4
    delivery of, 63–78, 292, 334,
        353–55, 385–415, 477
    politics of, 340, 417–79
    production of, 328–32, 342–70,
        371–84
health care system, 90, 94, 103–06,
    343–44
    description of, 342–69
    problems of, 90, 368–70
health service, 17, 342–43
    research, field of, 7–8
Health of Regionville study, 228
health sector, corporate-class in-
    volvement in, 463–65
health surveys, 29–31
healthy, definition of, 104
heart disease, 119–20, 121. See also
    coronary heart disease, stress
herbal remedies, Chinese, 75
historians, medical, 3
home, medical care in, 425–26
homosexuality, 472
hospital emergency services,
    275–89
hospitals, 349–51
    as costly, 423–25
    as dangerous, 419–23
    sex discrimination in, 334,
        353–55
    utilization by elderly, 397–98
hospitalization, 21, 23, 340
    avoidance of, 149, 158, 189, 208
    control of, 417–42
    psychiatric, 176–84, 186–201
human services, access and utiliza-
    tion models of, 6

hyperopia, 235
hypochondriacs, U.S. as a nation of,
    104

iatrogenic disease, 320–21
illness, 2, 15, 43, 62, 472
    beliefs and values in, 15, 44–47
    conflicting interests in, 144
    social psychology of, 144, 241
    stress as, 57, 112–13, 108–25
    terminal, 474. See also chronic
        disease, morbidity
impaired model of illness, 148
incidence of disease, 79
income, 82, 186–202, 245, 331–32,
    388–93, 461–63
incongruity and stress in heart dis-
    ease, 120
infant mortality, 25. See also mortality
influenza, 99–100
innovation diffusion, theories of, 6
insanity, 167–85
    labeling in, 173–76
    pseudopatients role in, 169–85
insecticides, 82
institutional democracy, 336–37
institutions, effects on therapy, 300
insurance, malpractice, 443, 452–53
in-take workers, 276
intelligence, 244
interaction models, 247–48
interdisciplinary study, 5
interest groups, effect on medical
    care, 11
interference, perceived, 236–38
intermediate care facilities (ICF), 351
internalization, 244
International Classification of Dis-
    ease, 18
International Sociological Associa-
    tion, 3
interpersonal crises and doctor
    visits, 236

Japan, epidemiologic transition in, 87–92
job pressures, 117–18
job satisfaction, effect of on heart disease, 116–17
Joint Commission of Accreditation of Hospitals (JCAH), 361–62
Journal of Health and Social Behavior, 3
Juries, medical role of in malpractice
justification, as a physician strategy, 254

kidney disease, 99

labeling, 6, 10, 144
  consequences of, 183–85
  and disability, 208, 217–25
  psychodiagnostic, 173–76, 187–89
  of symptoms, as a social process, 241
labels, psychodiagnostic, 173
labor force, health, 328–32, 347–49
labor force, U.S., structure of, 329–30
legionnaire's disease, 479
legitimacy, patient, 284–85
life expectancy, 63
lifestyle, 33–35, 79, 343
living will, 475
longevity, 121–22
lower class and schizophrenia, 137–38

macro-sociological structural analysis, 214
Magic Mountain, The, 148

Magic, Science and Religion, 9
Male mortality, 19, 11, 26, 35. *See also* mortality, morbidity, female morbidity
Males and coronary heart disease, 108–25
malingering, suspected, 150–51
Malleus Malificarum, 147
malocclusion. *See* occlusion
malpractice, 443–56
marital status, 36
  and morbidity/mortality, 26–28, 36
  and symptoms of illness, 198–202
mass movement medical approach, 76–77
medical, 11
  advice, patients conformity to, 243–59
  anthropologists, 4
  authority, limitation on, 256–58
  care, 144, 228–41
  change, as political change (China), 78
  delivery, 340. *See also* delivery of health care
  financing, 340. *See also* economics, medical economics, personal
  geography, 4
  historians, 3
  laboratories, 351
  malpractice, 443–56
  model, the, 9–10, 148
  phenomena, social interpretations of, 2, 8–10
  practice, 3, 8–10, 371–84
  profession, 10–11, 473
  school. *See* schools, medical
  services, 4
  sociologists, institutional affiliations of, 6
  sociology, 2–3, 6
  stations, Chinese, 66–68
  technology, 12. *See also* technology

Medicare, 340, 369, 385–415
  benefits, 386–88
  benefits, geographical var-
    iations of, 403–09
  class variations in, 393–94
  cost-sharing in, 411–12
  national health insurance and,
    414–15
  reimbursement policies of,
    413–14
  role of income in, 388–93
  utilization by elderly, 394–97
medicine, as a health hazard, 474
mental illness, 129–38, 167–85,
    190–91, 189–202
methodology of health surveys,
    29–31
microscopic surgery, 351
midwifery, Chinese, 66
Minnesota Multiphasic Personality
    Inventory (MMPI), 244
mobility, 6
  rates of, 131–32
moral evaluation, patient, 274–89
moral model of health, 10, 148
morbidity, 1, 15, 16–36, 44
  international sources of, 17, 18
  by sex, 17–29
  sex differences in, 18–22
morning sickness, 45
mortality, 1, 15, 16–36
  causes of, by sex, 17, 22–23
  differences in, by sex, 17, 18–22
  international data sources of, 17,
    18
  variations in by marital status,
    26–28
  See also infant mortality
moxibustion, 75–76
murder, 167
myopia, 235, 238, 239

narcotics addiction and sick role,
    the, 147–48

National Center for Health Services
    Research, 369
national health, assessment of,
    95–96
national health insurance, 4, 414–15,
    478
National Institute of Health, 3
National Institute of Mental Health, 3
negotiation process, dentist-patient,
    267–70
neuroses, 102
nonconformity, study of, 243–44
normal, 171–73. See also sanity
nurse, the, 296–97
  as agent of control, 220
  as agent of physician, 296
  in health system, 358–59
  power relationships of, 11,
    296–97
nursing home industry, 353, 355–56

occlusion, 262–70
occupational distribution, U.S.,
    329–30, 459
occupational stress, 109–21
  and longevity, 121–22
operations research, 8
orderlies. See aides
organization theory, 6
organizational setting, effects on
    diagnosis, 323
organizational structure of health
    care system, 352–68, 430–41
organ transplants, 351, 472–73
outpatient clinics, 426–27

parasitology, 4
parental role:
  in schizophrenia, 135
  in sickness, 151–52
Parkinsonism, 103

participant-observer technique, 4–5
patient, 293–94
    in conflict with medical staff, 293
    conformity to medical advice,
        243–59
    as consumer, 266–70
    control therapies, 302
    conversion from nonpatients,
        228–41
    as deserving, 275–76
    drunken, 278
    as illegitimate, 280–84
    inappropriate demands of,
        285–87, 289
    as legitimate, 280–84
    moral evaluation of, 253–59, 309
    negligently injured by doctors,
        443
    effects of physical incapacity on,
        293
    selection, 285–86
    socioeconomic resources of,
        189–202, 294
    sociolegal identity of, 294
    -staff segregation, 177
    welfare of, in hospitals, 430–41
    as undeserving, 275–76
pediatrician-parent communication,
        247–48
peptic ulcer, 101
perinatal disease, 100
periodontal disease, prevalence of,
        263
personal growth, 301
pharmaceutical and medical supply
        industries, 360–61
physical anthropology, 4
physical examinations, 21
physical facilities of health system,
        349–51
physically handicapped. See handi-
        capped
physical therapists, 11, 220, 223–25
physician, the, 297, 349
    as biased toward treatment, 314,
        322
    conflicts with staff, 297
    duties and powers of, 297

efforts to motivate patients,
        258–59
    iatrogenic heart disease and,
        320
    liability, malpractice, 445
    limitation on authority of, 256–68
    -patient communication, 243–59
    effects of specialization on, 298
    visits, elderly, 395
    urban general practitioner, 418
    work settings of, 371–84
physicians' assistants, 11
pneumonia, 99–100
policy, disability research, 210–14
polio, 150–51
political change and medical care,
        15
political scientists, 4
politics of health care, 417–68
population rate and health standards,
        82
power, abuse of by psychiatric pro-
        fessionals, 308
powerlessness, 181–82
pre-industrial societies, health in, 82
prevalence of disease, 79
preventative care, 18, 21, 69, 105,
        260–61
professional roles questioned, 298
professionalization, theories of, 6
pseudopatients, 169–85
psychedelic model of illness, 148
psychiatric diagnosis, failure of,
        172–73
psychiatric settings, control in,
        302–09
psychiatrists, 173, 178, 179, 182,
        186, 193
    advisory role of, 292, 298–310
    and anthropologists, 231
    coercive role of, 292, 298–310
    military, 310
    moral evaluation of patients by,
        274
    prison, 310
psychiatry, 298–310
    community, 305–06
    historical forces in, 299–302

psychoanalytic model, 10, 148
psychodiagnostic labels, 173
psychopathy, 244
psychosis, 102–03
pulmonary diseases, 99–100
pyelonephritis, chronic, 99

quality, control of in medical prac-
    tice, 443, 475
quality of life as a medical issue, 1,
    473

race:
    discrimination in Medicare, 385,
        397–402
    effects of on health and illness,
        15
recall, patient, 231
regulation of medical profession, 11
Rehabilitation Institute of Chicago,
    207
rehabilitation, social psychology of,
    206–15
research tecnhiques, socio- and an-
    thropological, 4–5
resident care, 417–19
resources, socioeconomic, effects on
    mental health care, 191–201
resources, health care system. See
    expenditures, labor, physical
    facilities, technology
respiratory exercises, 75
responsibility and stress, 118
right to die legislation, 475
role:
    allocation, familial, in schizo-
        phrenics, 135
    conflict as stress, 118
    -playing (-taking), 321–22
    theory and disability, 208
Rorschach Inkblot Test, 244

sanity, 167–85
schizophrenia, 129, 167, 171, 173,
    175, 176
    and class, 129, 135–38
    depersonalization in, 181–83
    and family, 129–38
    genetics of, 131–35
    labeling, effects on, 183–84
    methodological error in, 130
    minority position as cause of,
        131
    and sick role, the, 147, 154
    social isolation as cause of, 131
    stress as cause of, 131–35, 138
    use of drugs in, 182–83
    victimization of the powerless
        theory of, 130, 181
schools:
    Chinese medical, 64
    dental, 264
    medical, 3, 358, 418
    nursing, 3
    public health, 3, 8
selection, patient by staff, 285–86
self:
    -awareness, 301
    definition by handicapped, 220
    -esteem and job satisfaction,
        116–17
    pity, 157–58
sex, 16–17, 328–29
    differences in morbidity and
        mortality, 17–29
    differences in use of health serv-
        ices, 17, 18–22
    discrimination in health profes-
        sions, 332–36
    effects on health and illness, 15
    international health data on,
        16–36
    -ism in health fields, 328–37
    -ism in the U.S., 328
    role (gender) effects on illness,
        34–35, 119–22
sick role, the, 6, 10, 144
    and alcoholism, 147–48, 153–54
    blame in, 151
    conspiratorial, 149

definition of, 147
deviance from, 146–60
and disability, 208
doctor's role in, 164–66
and drug addiction, 147–48
guilt and the, 151–52
impaired, 149
medical, 149
effects of, on medical diagnosis, 320–22
moral, 149
parental role in, 150–51
psychoanalytic, 149, 154
and schizophrenia, 147, 154
self pity in, 157–58
social, 149
termination of, 164
skilled nursing facilities (SNF), 351
social context of illness, 231–32
social control:
of disability, 212–14
theories of, 6
social distance, 240, 323
social epidemiology, 7
social hierarchy, effects on schizophrenia incidence, 136–38
socialization in disability process, 207
social mobility, 109
social model of health, 10, 36, 148
social reality, schizophrenic, 136–38
Social Science and Medicine, 3
Social Security Act of 1935, 355
1965, 1967 amendments to, 387
social traditions and health
standards, 82
social workers as agents of social
control, 220
social worth, patient, 275
societal reaction theory. See labeling
society, protection of, by psychiatry, 299–302
sociological research, acceptance
by medical profession, 214
sociology in medicine, 2, 3, 6
solo, fee-for-service doctor, 371, 379, 380
specialization, 298, 346

status inconsistency, 109
stigmatization, 208–09
stratification, 6
stress, 15, 108–25, 132–33
coping and defenses in, 110, 111, 124
as general cause of disease, 112–13
and heart disease, 113–25
and longevity, 121–22
occupational, 109–23
as perceived by individual, 110–11
psychological, 15, 57
research, 109–12, 123
and schizophrenia, 131–35
social, 15
and social reality, 136–38
Stroop Color Work Test, 244
structure of opportunities, 309
structure of society, medical, 5
support, of disability researchers by
colleagues, 212
symptoms, 15, 44–47, 59–62, 190–
91, 198–99, 200–02, 230,
232–39, 241
systems analysis, 8

technological transition models, 83
technology, health care, 79, 94–107,
351–52, 476–77
assessment of changes in, 96–98
costs of, 12
tension release and patient conformity, 247
test-tube babies, 472, 474
therapist, research sociologist as, 214
therapy, institutional and individual,
300–02, 309–10
tuberculosis, 155–57, 158
Type A behavior pattern, 119–20, 125

undernutrition, 82
U.S. Health Interview Survey, 18
U.S. National Center for Health Statis-
    tics, 18
U.S. Public Health Service, 3
University of Munich Study Group on
    Health Systems Research, 8
urban-rural differences in medical
    usage, 407–08
utilization of medical care, 7, 21, 35,
    394–97, 419–23, 430, 441,
    442

venereal disease, 76–77, 345
verbal skills, 190–91
victimization of the powerless theory
    of schizophrenia, 130
visits to physicians numbers of by
    sex, 20
vulnerability, social, 136–38

wealth, distribution of in U.S., 458–59
welfare cases, discrimination in, 276
western-style medicine, Chinese, 64
women, 328–37
    dentists, percent internationally,
        264
    drugs prescribed for, 34
    in health care professions,
        328–37
    health status as index of social
        change, 84, 85
    illnesses as psychosomatic, 34
    income differentials of, 331–32
    job discrimination, 292
    liberation, 337
    as medical consumers, 21–22
    and morbidity/mortality, 16–36
    as producers in health labor
        force, 328–32
    "question," 332–33
    as reserve work force, 333–34

work overload as stress, 118
World Health Organization (WHO), 9,
    18, 342
worry, cost of, in health system,
    103–06

youth, use of emergency services by,
    276

informal but nonetheless real and important interaction can take place among loose networks of practitioners. Much of it, as Peterson observed, is bound to be about fishing, bridge, and golf [11] but some is certainly about medicine.[12] Nonetheless, the fact that isolation in solo practice is *possible* marks it off from "group practice," whether a small partnership or a large-scale medical group. In this sense, group more than solo practice seems to encourage a higher quality of care. Indeed, Peterson reported a slight tendency for those in group practice to give a higher quality of care than those working alone,[13] though Clute apparently did not find such a tendency.[14]

In addition, care by a variety of specialists is held to be necessary these days. While solo practice does not preclude the use of specialists, group practice facilitates frequent consultation and exchange of professional information. Where a number of physicians of varied specialties work together within the same organization, it is not only easier to refer patients, but also to communicate and coordinate information about them. Coleman, Katz, and Menzel have demonstrated the importance of colleague relations to one facet of care—prescribing drugs.[15] Thus, it is to be expected that in group practice the fragmentation of care following upon specialization can be compensated for and that so-called comprehensive care is more likely to ensue.

Finally, there is the element of supervision, the quality of which Seeman and Evans have shown to influence medical performance.[16] The most reputable medical institutions—for example, medical school clinics and teaching hospitals—are characterized by doctors working in close association with each other and with some systematic supervision of work by chiefs of services, staff committees reviewing the treatment of patients who died, the tissue removed by surgery, and the like. Except in a purely educational context, where it is ideologically acceptable, the nature of supervision in such medical bureaucracies has received little attention, but it is indubitable that at least some formal administrative supervision almost always exists. Furthermore, the cultivation of a medical records system and the continuous accumulation of information in records is in itself supervisory, for while the records may not be subject to routine inspection, they may always be examined if some doubt arises about a physician's work. If, as Peterson assumes, systematic and complete records are an important element of competent medical care, bureaucratic practices, which are far more likely to encourage record keeping, can to this extent provide a higher quality of care.

In theory, then, formal and cooperative rather than informal and individual

---

11. Peterson, op. cit., p. 83.

12. James Coleman, Elihu Katz, and Herbert Menzel, *Medical innovation: A diffusion study.* Indianapolis: Bobbs-Merrill, 1966, p. 110. Coleman found that when one shared his office, he adopted a new drug more quickly than one who works alone.

13. Peterson, op. cit.

14. Clue, op. cit., p. 318.

15. James Coleman, Elihu Katz, and Herbert Menzel, *Medical innovation: A diffusion study.* Indianapolis: Bobbs-Merrill, 1966, p. 110.

16. Seeman and Evans, op. cit.

practice arrangements are more likely to provide good medical care. However, there are only scattered bits of evidence to support this theory. A negative reflection on the system of solo practice predominant in the United States might be noted in the finding that somewhat less than half of all surgical in-hospital procedures performed in the nation during 1957–58 were by men formally certified to practice surgery,[17] but this is not direct evidence that the quality of care in group practice is higher. Comparative studies are necessary.

One of the rare comparative studies in this area was made by the Health Insurance Plan of Greater New York, in which the hospitalization and perinatal mortality of a population served by medical groups under contract with the insurance plan compared favorably with that of the New York City population.[18] That study, however, was concerned with an additional element in the arrangement of medical care—the prepaid service contract. It is believed that when people can be insured so that no financial barrier stands between them and medical care, they will not hesitate to use services and so can obtain the care they need early in the course of illness, thus preventing complications. Consequently, a comprehensive prepaid service contract is believed to be — of itself — conducive to better medical care. With insurance and organizational variables undifferentiated, the influence of either on quality of care is difficult to establish.

The same difficulty holds when the mode of compensating the physician is undifferentiated from organization. A study by Densen and his associates compared the hospital utilization of members of a single union who were under two different medical insurance plans—one involving medical group practice compensated on a per capita basis, and the other solo fee-for-service practice. Hospital utilization in the former proved to be lower, even though the comprehensiveness of insurance was much the same.[19] But it is difficult to tell whether the lower utilization resulted from group practice as such or from the fact that the group plan provided no additional compensation to the group physician for in-hospital surgery.[20] Clearly, present evidence is inadequate.[21]

Whether or not people are deeply involved emotionally with their doctors, they must in any case be sufficiently happy with the care they receive to make use of their doctors. Patient satisfaction assumes additional importance when medicine becomes a political issue. In a number of national sample surveys in the United States, most people have expressed general satisfaction with medical services which typically are organized on only a loosely cooperative, fee-for-service basis, and the solo general practitioner is part of the national folklore. In

---

17. Health Information Foundation, Physicians who perform surgery, *Progress in Health Services* *10* 1961.

18. S. Shapiro, L. Weiner, and P. M. Densen, Comparison of prematurity and perinatal mortality in general population and in population of prepaid group practice, *American Journal of Public Health 48* 1958: 170–187.

19. P. M. Densen, et al., Prepaid medical care and hospital utilization in a dual choice situation, *American Journal of Public Health 50* 1960: 1710–1726.

20. For some evidence bearing on this see Robin F. Badgley and Samuel Wolfe, *Doctors' strike: Medical care and conflict in Saskatchewan.* New York: Atherton Press, 1967, pp. 115–118.

21. For a recent review of the evidence bearing on these difficult questions, see Avedis Donabedian, A review of some experiences with prepaid group practice, *Bureau of Public Health Economics, Research Series,* No. 12. Ann Arbor: The University of Michigan School of Public Health, 1965.

spite of this, fairly large proportions of the population cite grounds for dissatisfaction. They complain that doctors keep them waiting too long, are difficult to reach on nights and weekends, and do not give enough time to them. Koos's studies report the largest proportions of dissatisfaction,[22] while the Gaffin study showed that people are less likely to complain about their own doctors than about doctors in general.[23]

This material, however, like the data on in-hospital surgery, bears on solo practice only insofar as it is the most common and most characteristic form in the United States. Again, comparative studies provide the most useful evidence. Anderson and Sheatsley compared two groups of socioeconomically equivalent, insured patients, one being served by solo physicians compensated by an insurance organization on a fee-for-service basis, the other by physicians in medical groups, paid on a per capita basis.[24] The finding was that the solo fee-for-service program elicited more patient satisfaction than did the capitation group practice. Patients of the latter were prone to complain of lack of personal interest, insufficient explanation of their condition by the doctor, waiting in office, and difficulty in getting house calls. In Freidson's study, where patients contrasted their experience with these two types of practice, there was also a tendency to feel that the sense of "personal interest" was more likely to be obtained in solo fee-for-service practice than in capitation group practice. But there was some feeling that medical care of a technically higher quality could be obtained from the medical group.[25] In both studies, however, solo fee-for-service practice is compared to capitation group practice, and no way is provided to control the financial variable and compare forms of practice as such. Plainly, the material on patient satisfaction is equivocal, but none contradicts the idea that emotional satisfaction on the part of the patient seems more likely to be gained from a physician who is in a position to be more immediately responsive to (and dependent on) the patient than are group physicians who have obligations to a work organization.

Physician satisfaction, too, may be more influenced by the arrangement of work than by the arrangement of payment. In assessing job satisfaction, however, we must first recognize that it is much easier for the physician to "free-lance" than for the professor or the minister, since both of the latter require congregations rather than an assortment of successive individuals, and neither can count on the fairly strong motivation provided by illness. This by itself means that even in an environment where the state sets the terms of work for the average practitioner—as in England and the Soviet Union—it is possible for the

22. E. L. Koos, Metropolis—What city people think of their medical services, *American Journal of Public Health 45* 1955: 1551–1557.

23. Ben Gaffin Associates, *What Americans think of the medical profession*, American Medical Association brochure, n.d.

24. Odin W. Anderson and Paul B. Sheatsley, Comprehensive medical insurance, *Health Information Foundation Research Series*, No. 9, 1959.

25. Eliot Freidson, *Patients' views of medical practice*. New York: Russell Sage Foundation, 1961. See also the review of Weinerman, Patients' perceptions, op. cit., and of Avedis Donabedian, A review of some experiences with prepaid group practice, *Bureau of Public Health Economics Research Series*, No. 12. Ann Arbor: The University of Michigan School of Public Health, 1965.

physician to stay outside the scheme if he wishes. Hence, a physician in any organized scheme of practice can always find some way to work outside, even if at some personal risk or sacrifice.

It may be noted furthermore that job satisfaction is inevitably a function of the career alternatives that exist at any particular time and of the symbolic and material rewards of these alternatives. In medicine in the United States today, for example, the symbolically valued work setting is the successful, fee-for-service, solo specialty practice. The general practitioner may genuinely enjoy the procession of minor cases (called "garbage" by specialists), the laying-on of hands, and the genial calls at humble homes—the human rather than the scientific side of medicine. But in depressed moments he may realize that he is not a social or professional success because he is not a specialist with limited practice and prominent clients. Thus, environment must be considered a partial influence on satisfaction, both in the way it defines any form of practice and in the way if offers alternative possibilities.

No matter what the tyranny of the patient, the solo work setting has the quality of potentially complete autonomy. The physician working in the privacy of his own consulting room can examine, prescribe, diagnose, and treat as he sees fit. There is no one to soften patient pressure to honor lay prejudices, of course, and when practice is insecure it is likely that the doctor will feel obliged to do what he does not really want to do, but theoretically, the solo physician may dismiss his patients rather than give in to them. Autonomy perhaps more extensive than in any other profession thus exists, at least *in potentia,* in solo practice. This is what was stressed by medical students in response to survey questions on why they would reject salaried positions in organizations. In contrast to this apparently gratifying side of solo entrepreneurial practice are a number of potential handicaps: isolation from one's colleagues and their information and support, the necessity to be preoccupied daily with the financial basis of practice, the leanness of early and late stages of the career, and the difficulty of controlling and regularizing work hours. These are the very things which are said to be solved by group practice. Indeed, medical students who preferred salaried positions stressed opportunities to work in close association with colleagues, to obtain a regular income, and to work regular hours.[26]

On the whole, one should expect that a doctor-owned, fee-for-service partnership or group practice would provide most of the gratifications and fewest of the deficiencies of the two extremes of solo and bureaucratic practice. It seems to allow the greatest amount of room for self-determination without in turn sacrificing the major virtues of cooperative practice. It is a very popular form in the Midwest and Southwest of the United States. The Cahalan survey of medical students reported that of those who preferred a nonsalaried form of practice, only 26 percent preferred solo to group practice, partnership, or some other form of formally cooperative practice.[27] Since more freshmen than seniors preferred solo

26. Cahalan *et al., op. cit.*
27. *Ibid.*